AF712007

The Oxford Introductions to U.S. Law

Criminal Law

The Oxford Introductions to U.S. Law

Criminal Law

GUYORA BINDER

Dennis Patterson
Series Editor
The Oxford Introductions to U.S. Law

OXFORD
UNIVERSITY PRESS

OXFORD
UNIVERSITY PRESS

Oxford University Press is a department of the University of Oxford. It furthers the University's objective of excellence in research, scholarship, and education by publishing worldwide. Oxford is a registered trademark of Oxford University Press in the UK and certain other countries.

Published in the United States of America by Oxford University Press
198 Madison Avenue, New York, NY 10016, United States of America.

Library of Congress Cataloging-in-Publication Data

Names: Binder, Guyora, author.
Title: The Oxford introductions to U.S. law. Criminal law / Guyora Binder.
Other titles: Criminal law.
Description: New York : Oxford University Press, 2016. | Series: The Oxford introductions to U.S. law | Includes bibliographical references and index.
Identifiers: LCCN 2015050545 | ISBN 9780195321203 ((pbk.) : alk. paper)
Subjects: LCSH: Criminal law—United States.
Classification: LCC KF9219 .B47 2016 | DDC 345.73—dc23 LC record available at http://lccn.loc.gov/2015050545

Note to Readers

This publication is designed to provide accurate and authoritative information in regard to the subject matter covered. It is based upon sources believed to be accurate and reliable and is intended to be current as of the time it was written. It is sold with the understanding that the publisher is not engaged in rendering legal, accounting, or other professional services. If legal advice or other expert assistance is required, the services of a competent professional person should be sought. Also, to confirm that the information has not been affected or changed by recent developments, traditional legal research techniques should be used, including checking primary sources where appropriate.

(Based on the Declaration of Principles jointly adopted by a Committee of the American Bar Association and a Committee of Publishers and Associations.)

Contents

Acknowledgments

I AM GRATEFUL first and foremost to Dennis Patterson, series editor of the Oxford Introductions to U.S. Law, who honored me with this invitation. Second, I owe a continuing debt of gratitude to my former teacher, George Fletcher, whose ideas and whose example profoundly influenced this work.

This work has also benefited from the resourceful research efforts of many talented students, including Mark Myott, Ali Mosfer, Griffin Dault, Kayla Drickel, Megan McGuiggan, and Ahmed Bilal. I am particularly grateful to the late Duane Bores Jr., whose work was harder than I ever knew.

Several colleagues improved the book by commenting on chapters. These include Bob Weisberg, Mike Seidman, Luis Chiesa, Tony O'Rourke, Jim Whitman, the late Andrew Taslitz, Ed Rubin, Gerard Lynch, and Jonathan Bush. None are responsible for my errors.

—Guyora Binder

About the Editor

DENNIS PATTERSON HOLDS the Chair in Legal Philosophy and Legal Theory at the European University Institute in Florence, Italy. He is also Board of Governors Professor of Law and Philosophy at Rutgers University School of Law, New Jersey, and Chair in Jurisprudence and International Trade at Swansea University, UK. Patterson is author of *Minds, Brains, and Law: The Conceptual Foundations of Law and Neuroscience* (with Michael S. Pardo) (Oxford University Press 2013; Paperback 2015). He is the author of *Law and Truth* (Oxford University Press 1996) and *The New Global Trading Order* (with Ari Afilalo) (2008). He is General Editor of *The Blackwell Companion to the Philosophy of Law and Legal Theory* (2010). He has published widely in commercial law, trade law, and legal philosophy.

About the Author

Guyora Binder is Distinguished Professor, Hodgson Russ Faculty Scholar, and Vice Dean for Research and Faculty Development at the State University of New York at Buffalo Law School. He was previously a law clerk to federal Judge Jack B. Weinstein, Leah Kaplan Visiting Professor of Human Rights at Stanford, and a visiting professor at the law schools of the University of Michigan, Georgetown University, and Vanderbilt University. Professor Binder authored *Treaty Conflict and Political Contradiction* (1988), and *Felony Murder* (2012), and he was a coauthor of *Criminal Law* (1996, 2000, 2004, 2008, 2012, 2016), and *Literary Criticisms of Law* (2000). His articles have appeared in the *Yale Law Journal, University of Chicago Law Review, Stanford Law Review, Texas Law Review, Michigan Law Review, Georgetown Law Journal, Boston University Law Review, Notre Dame Law Review, Cardozo Law Review, University of Toronto Law Review*, and the *Yale Journal of Law and Humanities.*

ONE

What is Criminal Law?

I. Introduction

This chapter introduces our subject by offering an analysis of criminal law as an institution of government with a distinctive combination of features. This is not the usual way to proceed. It is common to introduce criminal law by discussing moral theories of when and why we should punish. We will certainly review such theories (in Chapter 3), however they do not really explain why we have criminal law. Criminal law is one of those institutions, like markets and elections, that many societies have developed and retained, and that are now seen as basic requisites of a decent modern society. An understanding of criminal law should begin with a description of the institution, and an acknowledgment of why it is seen as a practical necessity. Our reliance on the institution is not motivated by moral philosophy. Instead, moral justifications for punishment are important in criminal law because criminal law solves problems of governance in part by mobilizing moral judgments.

Criminal law is, obviously, one type of law. Law is a social practice of organizing human behavior with two important features. First, law imposes *duties*. Thus a legal system is in force only if at least some people accept that they should obey its directives. Second, law conditions the authority of a directive on its *source*, on who issues it, and how. Most legal systems back at least some of their directives with coercive sanctions, but in a book about criminal law we need not resolve whether this is a necessary feature of all law.

Criminal law is distinctive in *forbidding* conduct and imposing *state punishment* for committing it. This type of law is closely identified with the idea of the "rule of law." Thus, when we say that law replaces a state of nature, suppresses feuding and vengeance, or gives the state a "monopoly on legitimate force," it is primarily criminal law we are talking about. Whatever the other purposes of criminal law, it asserts public control over the use of violence. Of course there are other things that we expect an effective state to do. For example, some economists tell us that protecting property rights is very important to prosperity.[1] Yet protecting property includes protecting it from robbery and theft. Moreover, these economists tell us that protecting life and personal liberty are even more important. Finally, they add that the governments have historically posed at least as much a threat to freedom and security of person and property as brigands.[2] So if we are interested in criminal law as part of the basic institutional architecture of a modern liberal state, we need to emphasize its character as *law*. Thus conceived, criminal law makes a normative appeal for allegiance from those it commands and is bound by its own rules. Chapter 2 will describe how a criminal law of this kind emerged with the growth of the American state.

This chapter develops the concept of criminal law as a legal system of public proscription and punishment that regulates violence. First, we will find that *proscription* implies disapproval, and is paradigmatically directed against conduct intentionally injuring known victims. Second, we will find that *punishment* deprives and denounces on the basis of blame for violating an authoritative proscription. Blame implies a judgment that wrongful conduct has been committed culpably. The expressive character of punishment in denouncing and blaming enables it to redress the indignity suffered by victims. The authoritative character of punishment differentiates it from revenge, and enhances its dignitary benefits. Third, we will see how *state* proscription and punishment of violence can use these dignitary benefits to motivate support for the rule of law. Finally, we will consider the importance of criminal law as we have conceived it. Insofar as criminal law helps establish a rule of law, it serves the welfare of society. Yet because criminal law serves this end by distributing the highly valued good of dignity, it is subject to political contestation. Inevitably, lawmakers will be tempted to use criminal law for purposes beyond securing a rule of law.

II. Prohibition

Criminal law is distinguishable from some other kinds of law because it proscribes conduct. Law sometimes assigns burdensome legal consequences to conduct without evaluating it. Consider an example involving contract law. A agrees to provide B with a product by a certain date for a certain price. American contract law generally provides that if A fails, he must instead provide B with the profits reasonably expected from the use of the promised

1. Daren Acemoglu & James A. Robinson, Why Nations Fail: The Origins of Power, Prosperity and Poverty 3–5 (2012).

2. *Id.*

product. Yet A is free to increase his own profits by paying such expectation damages to B, and selling the product to another purchaser at a price exceeding the sum of B's price and B's expectation damages. Under such a system, breach of contract triggers a duty to pay damages, but is not forbidden. Indeed, this regime encourages breach when doing so will allocate a good or service to its most profitable use.

By contrast to contract law, criminal law does not merely attach a consequence to offending. It profoundly disapproves offenses. In punishing offenders it denounces them personally and forces them to suffer, with no direct benefit to anyone else. In justifying the cost of all this, officials often express disdain for the crime committed, or the hope of preventing similar crimes. Moreover, criminal law authorizes the use of coercive force, sometimes deadly force, to prevent offenses. Thus criminal law does not just disapprove offenses ex post: it forbids them ex ante. Criminal guilt therefore implies not only wrongdoing, but also defiance of the law. Offending expresses a message of disrespect for law, and punishment responds by reasserting the authority of law.[3]

Criminal law's emphatic disapproval of offending implies that the penalty imposed is quite different from a price. To be sure, we sometimes say that by suffering punishment the offender "pays" for her crime, or pays a "debt" to society. Yet punishment does not cancel the offense, in the way that payment cancels a debt. To punish is to assert that the offender should not have acted as she did, and should now regret doing so, no matter how gratifying the offense may have been for her. Ideally, the offender should associate her suffering with this denunciation and feel remorse. Yet even if punishment fails to elicit subjective feelings of guilt, it humbles the offender by forcing her to confront authoritative disapprobation.

Legal theorists have tried to give a little more precision to this contrast between legal consequences that permit conduct and those that forbid it. In a famous article, Guido Calabresi and Douglas Melamed distinguish three different types of rules protecting entitlements. A liability rule imposes a duty to compensate for injury, but does not forbid injury. American tort and contract law mostly create liability entitlements. By contrast a property rule imposes a duty to avoid injuring an entitlement without the consent of the holder. Finally, an inalienability rule imposes a duty to avoid injury regardless of the consent of the owner, who may not sell a privilege to injure at any price. Both property rules and inalienability rules forbid injury. Criminal prohibitions against injury therefore may be seen as either property or inalienability rules. Criminal

3. Jean Hampton, *Correcting Harms versus Righting Wrongs: The Goal of Retribution*, 39 UCLA L. Rev. 1659, 1700–01 (1992).

protections of consent, such as prohibitions of theft and sexual assault against an adult, may be seen as property rules. Criminal injuries to which the victim may not consent, such as child molestation and homicide, may be seen as violating inalienability rules.[4]

Why should some conduct be forbidden, rather than just priced or discouraged?

There are two reasons to protect entitlements by a property rather than a liability rule, one economic and one dignitary. From an economic standpoint, transfers are likely to be more "efficient"—that is, more beneficial—if they are consensual. Calabresi and Melamed argue that intentional injuries should be forbidden by a property rule, because it should be possible to bargain with a targeted and therefore known victim and find out how much compensation they will demand before consenting to a specific injury. Careless injuries resulting from the imposition of risk on many people should merely be discouraged by a liability rule, however, because it would be too difficult for the risk imposer to bargain with all potential victims in advance. Such voluntary transactions would be too "costly" to negotiate.

Yet an additional reason for prohibiting intentional injury is that ignoring the owner's will is an insult, implying the owner counts for less than the offender. Thus there are dignitary costs to a liability rule when the victim is known and the injury is intentional. Both an efficiency analysis and an expressive analysis converge on the same point: when a known victim is injured intentionally, compensation is an inadequate response. That I know a victim implies not only that I can bargain with him at a low cost, but also that we are already in a communicative relationship. In this context, avoiding communication—for example by injuring without asking permission—is nevertheless expressive. Intentional injury of a known victim is *personal* and is understood as such.

Calabresi and Melamed's analysis raises the question why breach of contract should be protected by a liability rather than a property rule. After all, the victim is known, breach is sometimes intentional, and promissors could buy their way out of the contract. Indeed, some legal systems do typically treat contractual performance as a property entitlement, by ordering specific performance rather than the payment of damages. Yet the American legal system also has some good reasons for permitting breach in some cases. For some contracts, those involving personal service, promissors have a much greater dignitary interest in consenting to perform than promissees have in consenting to

4. Guido Calabresi & Douglas Melamed, *Property Rules, Liability Rules, and Inalienability: One View of the Cathedral*, 85 HARV. L. REV. 1089, 1092–93, 1124–27 (1972).

nonperformance. Compelling unwilling service would treat the promissor like a slave, whereas breaching a promise to serve does not degrade the promissee. The right to withhold personal service, even after promising it, is so important to dignity that we make it inalienable. Compelled service is enslavement, a crime, or a form of punishment for crime. Apart from the special case of military service, which we have taken great pains to ennoble, compulsory service is seen as degrading. So it seems that the choice of whether to protect entitlements by liability, property, or inalienability rules is driven in part by dignitary concerns.

Not all criminal offenses involve injury or risk to individuals. Some are violations of duties to cooperate in the production of public goods. Examples include evading taxation or military service, violating licensing or reporting requirements, and violating prophylactic rules such as those against possessing dangerous objects. Often these offenses involve only conduct, whether active or passive, rather than the intentional causation of a harmful result. It is often said that coercion is required to motivate cooperation in producing public goods because government cannot easily bargain with individual defectors by, for example, withholding the benefits of national defense, clean air, or safe traffic conditions. Defectors can "free ride," getting the benefit of government services without contributing. Criminalizing defection in effect gives the public—as represented by the state—a property interest in our compliance, whether in the form of taxes or services.

Criminalization supports these cooperative ventures not only by coercing compliance, but also by denouncing defection. Proscribing and punishing morally ambiguous offenses such as tax evasion or pollution associates them with violent crimes against identifiable persons. Criminal law thereby mobilizes our gratitude for the state's protection against violence, and uses it to motivate compliance with other cooperative institutions. It encourages us to identify our participation in the provision of public goods with our enjoyment of public goods, including the enforcement of our entitlements. Criminalizing defection denounces it as disloyal to the civic community that protects our persons and property. Yet this effort to trade on civic loyalty is a delicate business. When a cooperative institution is sufficiently unpopular, coercing compliance with it can backfire and erode loyalty to the rule of law. Prohibition and the Vietnam War draft are examples of unpopular policies that eroded respect for law and were accompanied by increases in violent crime. [5]

---

5. Louis Michael Seidman, *Soldiers, Martyrs and Criminals: Utilitarian Theory and the Problem of Crime Control*, 94 YALE L.J. 315, 346–48 (1984).

III. Punishment

Criminal law is also distinctive in imposing punishment. We can define punishment as affliction imposed by any institution because of blame for committing forbidden conduct.

Punishment is a use of force, inflicting deprivation or suffering on the offender regardless of his or her wishes. Punishment is unusual as a legal remedy because it inflicts injury purposefully, not just as an expected byproduct of some other aim. Paying compensation is unpleasant, but its purpose is to benefit the victim or internalize external costs. Civil confinement in a mental hospital is inconvenient, but this is a regrettable cost of protecting the patient or others from future harm. Removal from office may humiliate and impoverish, but can be aimed at preventing misconduct or maintaining institutional credibility. Neither compensation nor preventive detention are punishment, although we might choose to direct a monetary penalty to a victim, and penal incarceration of a dangerous offender might also have the benefit of preventing crime. Disbarment is not punishment if aimed only at preventing unqualified legal representation; it is punishment if aimed at inflicting suffering for wrongdoing.

Because punishment afflicts on the basis of blame it is not only a violent, but also an expressive practice. Punishment denounces an offender as responsible for a forbidden act. By thus denouncing the offender, punishment implicitly justifies the violence it imposes as deserved for wrongdoing.[6]

---

6. Other theorists who have drawn attention to criminal law's expressive function include ANTONY DUFF, ANSWERING FOR CRIME: RESPONSIBILITY AND LIABILITY IN THE CRIMINAL LAW (2007); George Fletcher *The Metamorphosis of Larceny*, 89 HARV. L. REV. 469 (1976); MICHEL FOUCAULT, DISCIPLINE AND PUNISH: THE BIRTH OF THE PRISON (Alan Sheridan ed., Vintage Books 1995) (1975); John Gardner, *The Gist of Excuses*, 1 BUFF. CRIM. L. REV. 575 (1998); DAVID GARLAND, THE CULTURE OF CONTROL: CRIME AND SOCIAL ORDER IN CONTEMPORARY SOCIETY (2001); Jean Hampton, *Correcting Harms Versus Righting Wrongs: The Goal of Retribution*, 39 UCLA L. REV. 1659 (1992); Adil Ahmad Haque, *Group Violence and Group Vengeance toward a Retributivist Theory of International Criminal Law*, 9 BUFF. CRIM. L. REV. 273 (2005); Kyron Huigens, *Virtue and Inculpation*, 108 HARV. L. REV. 1423 (1995); DOUGLAS HAY, PROPERTY, AUTHORITY AND THE CRIMINAL LAW, ALBION'S FATAL TREE: CRIME AND SOCIETY IN EIGHTEENTH-CENTURY ENGLAND 17–64 (1975); Dan Kahan, *Social Influence, Social Meaning & Deterrence*, 83 VA. L. REV. 349 (1997); WILLIAM IAN MILLER, EYE FOR AN EYE (2006); Victoria Nourse, *Passion's Progress: Modern Law Reform and the Provocation Defense*, 106 YALE L.J. 1331, 1338 (1997); SAMUEL H. PILLSBURY, JUDGING EVIL: RETHINKING THE LAW OF MURDER AND MANSLAUGHTER (1998); Paul Robinson & John Darley, *The Utility of Desert*, 91 NW. L. REV. 453 (1997); JONATHAN SIMON, GOVERNING THROUGH CRIME: HOW THE WAR ON CRIME TRANSFORMED AMERICAN DEMOCRACY AND CREATED A CULTURE OF FEAR (2007); Kenneth W. Simons, *Rethinking Mental States*, 72 B.U. L REV.463, 495–522 (1992); Jeannie Suk, *Criminal Law Comes Home*, 116 YALE L.J. 2, 5–8 (2006); JAMES Q WHITMAN, HARSH JUSTICE: CRIMINAL PUNISHMENT AND THE WIDENING DIVIDE BETWEEN AMERICA AND EUROPE (2005).

The concept of blame accounts for many of the requirements of criminal liability explored in this book. First, in punishing we denounce an offender for some particular *conduct*—not for being a bad person, or a foreigner, or for being sick. An offender must do more than harbor evil desires: she must choose to put them into effect. Nor do we punish her for being disposed or likely to violate prohibitions, or even for doing so habitually. We punish her for some specific violation.

Second, the concept of blame implies the belief that the offender knew or should have known the conduct was wrong. Perhaps the act was of a kind generally condemned among members of the community including the offender and the imposer of blame. Perhaps an authority accepted by both had previously communicated to the offender that the act was forbidden. Indeed, to blame an offender for violating a prohibition, we must be confident the offender is aware of the prohibition. Thus, in blaming an offender, criminal punishment continues a communicative process that begins with the *proscription* of offenses. If blame is imposed for defying a prohibition, that prohibition should have been *prospective* and *public*. We will examine the requirements of conduct and of the violation of a prior prohibition in Chapter 4.

In attaching blame for a particular forbidden act, punishment implies the offender acted *culpably*. Thus, the offender chose to do wrong intentionally, or knowingly, or carelessly. If a legal system acknowledges that an actor was not culpable in any of these senses, it concedes the actor was blameless. We will examine this requirement of culpability in American criminal law in Chapter 5.

Blame implies the proscribed conduct was *wrongful*. It presupposes some normative criterion for assessing conduct. To punish is to invite the question of why the proscribed conduct is blameworthy. One possible answer is simply that it is proscribed—that disobedience is blameworthy in itself. This conditions the legitimacy of punishment on the legitimacy of the proscribing authority. For example, a religious community might ascribe its laws to religious revelation and follow some—dietary or dress codes, for example—more out of loyalty to the creed than because the laws have any intrinsic moral appeal. In a modern state, citizens might accept that conduct proscribed by democratically elected officials is blameworthy simply on the view that it is fair to accept the results of majority decision. Yet because punishment does not merely redistribute cost but imposes cost without necessary or immediate benefit to anyone, it seems the sort of issue on which majorities should be constrained. If we value democratic process, we will want to be sure that majorities are not merely criminalizing the customs of minority communities or the expression of minority views. Thus, even lawmakers accepted as legitimate may have to justify their proscriptions in terms of the values that legitimate their authority.

What makes criminal offenses wrong? Early English criminal law viewed unauthorized violence as a violation of the "king's peace" and so a challenge to royal authority. The influential eighteenth-century jurist William Blackstone presented English criminal law as primarily protecting the legal interests or entitlements of the king's subjects against injury rather than protecting the authority of the king. Late eighteenth-century philosophers, including Cesare Beccaria, Imanuel Kant, and Jeremy Bentham, developed accounts of criminal law in a democratically governed state, focusing on protection of rights or the prevention of cost. In the nineteenth century John Stuart Mill offered an influential argument that preventing harm to others was the only legitimate aim of punishment by a liberal state. This book examines many criminal wrongs. Chapter 6 outlines homicide, a crime of causing injury. Chapter 7 explores two important violations of consent, rape and theft. Chapter 8 explains attempt, conspiracy and complicity.

If we impose blame for violating certain values, it follows that acting in defense of those values should at least partially absolve the offender of blame. Thus, if we blame offenders for imposing a net cost or violating rights, they should be able to object that they pursued a countervailing benefit or protected a superior right. The offender thereby acknowledges the act was proscribed, but denies it was wrongful under the circumstances. If a legal system *justifies* a proscribed act for such reasons, it does not attach blame.

A final requirement of blaming is the ascription of *responsibility*. Suppose an actor knowingly violated a proscription without justification, but could not help it. The actor was delusional, or was forced at gunpoint. Legal systems may condemn the resulting act as wrong, but *excuse* the offender from responsibility for the wrongful act. If so, they do not attach blame. Chapter 9 reviews defenses of justification and excuse.

American criminal law conditions punishment on the basic requisites of blameworthiness—proscription, conduct, culpability, wrongdoing, and responsibility—and translates these into rules of law.

Because punishment expresses blame for a previously forbidden act, it also implies a certain relationship between the offender and a punishing institution. The offender is to blame not just for a wrong, but also for disobedience. Thus punishment expresses not only blame, but also a claim to *authority*, the authority to direct behavior. To punish is to act in a role, as an agent of an institution that also imposes obligations on the person punished. Punishment enforces an institutional norm, not a personal preference or feeling.[7] The wrong

---

7. Guyora Binder, *Punishment Theory: Moral or Political?*, 5 BUFF. CRIM. L. REV. 321, 321 (2002).

it denounces is not just an injury to an individual, but is also an injury to an institutional interest. In responding to the violation of a norm punishment treats the person punished as also an agent with institutional responsibilities. Thus it implies a shared enterprise, uniting those subject to the authority of the punishing power in a moral community.

This is not true only of state punishment. Even punishment of children within a family or school setting has this structure. The family, too, is an institution. In our society, parental authority over children is not just a matter of ownership, but is a fiduciary responsibility, contingent on the parents' competence and benevolence. Thus, their authority is conditioned on their fidelity to their offices as custodians of their children's interests. Children are obliged to obey not only out of personal devotion, but also to help the parents discharge their duty of care and advance the collective interests of the family. We would recognize as abusive a parent who simply used a child as an instrument of her own gratification without regard to the child's welfare. Disobedience might understandably induce hurt feelings in a parent, but this is not by itself an adequate reason for punishment. If efforts to control a child by inflicting suffering are wholly self-regarding they cease to be punishment and become simply coercion or retaliation. Thus punishment presupposes that the punisher acts as the agent of an authority binding on the person punished, and subject to justifying principles.

Not everyone agrees that punishment requires an institutional setting. The philosopher Leo Zaibert offers as an example of unofficial punishment a spectator slapping a noisy fellow spectator at a movie theater.[8] Yet it seems to me odd to call this response punishment precisely insofar as one spectator lacks any official standing to violently enforce norms of courtesy against a fellow spectator. Even though disrupting a performance might violate custom and morality, an individual spectator lacks authority either to set or to impose punishment. The individual spectator could remind the offender of the norms of decorum and criticize violation of it. The offender could complain to the theater management and ask them to quiet or expel the disruptor. But an individual could not inflict punishment unless we add to the example by imagining a culture with a norm permitting any individual to violently chasten a noisy spectator. A norm condemning certain conduct is not enough for punishment. We also need a norm authorizing certain persons to enforce it and setting the parameters of a proper penalty.

8. Leo Zaibert, *The Ideal Victim*, 28 PACE L. REV. 885, 897–99 (2008).

Let us explore the institutional dimension of punishment by considering two more realistic examples of decentralized use of violence to enforce social norms. In each of these cases private actors assert they are punishing, precisely in order to make a contestable claim to governing authority.

One example is a society in which small groups of men physically harass young women who appear in public unaccompanied by men and who are not wearing religious symbols of modesty.[9] Here it seems clear that these men are claiming authority by virtue of gender hierarchy, to enforce a religious norm. Now their authority to inflict violence may not be universally or even widely accepted. The important point is that their behavior is only intelligible as a *claim* to such authority. This claim is legible to us because we recognize their violence as punitive in intent and because punishment implies an authorizing institution. Often an additional expressive implication of such religiously inflected gender violence is a critique of a modern secular state as illegitimate in permitting such scandalous behavior, as alienated from the true and traditional source of legitimacy.

A second example of such unofficial punishment is a mob lynching in the Jim Crow South.[10] Here again we see private parties appropriating the punitive idiom of public power in order to express several political claims. Lynching is intelligible against the historical background of slavery, a system of publicly authorized private governance. It conferred on masters the power to corporally punish and confine their slaves, and conferred on white males generally a power to join armed bands to hunt down runaways. Frontier vigilante justice is a tradition of local self-governance with roots in the colonial and revolutionary periods.[11] Thus, lynching was not just an assertion of racial hierarchy but more specifically a reassertion of the collective authority of whites to govern African Americans directly, without the intermediation of the (presumably inauthentic) state. Again, this practice of private punishment is intelligible as grisly political theater only against the background assumption that to punish is to act on behalf of an authoritative institution.

On the other hand, the choice to eschew criminal punishment and act outside the state could have had another connotation as well. Often carried out with great atrocity, lynching dehumanized African Americans and placed them

9. Lama Abu-Odeh, Feminism and Islam: Legal and Literary Perspectives ch.7 141–55 (1996); Mary Anne Franks, *Obscene Undersides: Women and Evil between the Taliban and the United States*, Hypatia, 18: 135, 139–40 (2003).

10. David Garland, Peculiar Institution: America's Death Penalty in an Age of Abolition 50 (2010).

11. Samuel Walker, Popular Justice: A History of American Criminal Justice. 11–12 (1980).

outside the moral community. Lynching implied African Americans were governed by force only, rather than by any social contract conferring legal rights and imposing obligations of compliance. Thus the practice of lynching deliberately maintained an ambiguity between authoritative public punishment and arbitrary private revenge.

The idea of punishment as institutionally authorized enforcement of norms helps us to distinguish punishment, or retribution as it is sometimes called, from revenge. Revenge lacks the claim to represent an institution toward which both punisher and punished owe a duty of obedience. Revenge can be taken against an avowed enemy toward whom one recognizes no duties. It need not be motivated by a claim of injustice. Yet revenge can also serve as a customary response to perceived wrongs. In a fragmented stateless society revenge may be the only means of redressing a grievance between members of different social groups.

How does revenge differ from punishment as a means of redress? Because revenge lacks authority, it cannot easily resolve disputes. The difficulty is that unilateral force is often seen as the prerogative of superiors in disciplining subordinates. It is an implicit claim to governing authority. Thus unrequited violence among equals is demeaning, an insult threatening the status of the victim. Some societies associate status with courage and honor. Social theorists refer to these societies as "heroic" or "timocratic." They include not only ancient warrior societies such as the Vikings, but modern criminal subcultures such as those developing among gangsters, prisoners, and some irregular military forces.[12] In such a setting, accepting violence without resistance implies either a shameful acceptance of subordinate status, or an equally shameful display of cowardice. It can render the victim vulnerable to more violence. Thus victims can face intense social pressure to avenge injuries, or even minor slights and snubs the acceptance of which might be taken as signs of weakness. Because revenge lacks the backing of a higher authority, however, it is often experienced as a fresh wrong. It demeans the original perpetrator by making a contestable claim to authority over him. The original perpetrator is then honor-bound to continue the dispute by avenging this insult. This dialectic of responsive vengeance is known as a blood feud, and it can continue indefinitely.

Unlike vengeance, punishment is ordinarily authorized by an institution to which the person punished owes allegiance. There are of course cases where one government punishes citizens of another state. Yet such cases are fraught

12. William Ian Miller, Bloodtaking and Peacemaking: Feud, Law, and Society in Saga Iceland 29–34 (1990); Jack Henry Abbott, In the Belly of the Beast: Letters from Prison 75–77 (1981).

with diplomatic danger, and their peaceful resolution may require that states enter into treaties that authorize each to act as agents of the other in enforcing shared norms of conduct. In other words, prosecution and punishment of foreign nationals is always in danger of being perceived as a provocative act of revenge. If so, punishment fails one of its central purposes, which is to settle disputes by offering an authoritative assignment of blame. Punishment removes the burden of pursuing vengeance from the victim, and precludes the punished offender from reasserting the justice of his initial offense by retaliating against the victim. If the offender accepts the authority of the punishing institution, he can only establish the justice of his position by addressing arguments to that institution. Punishment achieves *retribution* insofar as it stably restores the injured dignity of a victim by basing reprisal on an authoritative judgment of blame.

IV. State Punishment

In criminal punishment, the punishing institution is the *state*. In proscribing and punishing, the state promises to suppress the cyclic violence of the blood feud in several ways: discouraging provocative violence through denunciation and coercion, and discouraging retaliatory violence by both of these means, and also by substitution. State punishment offers an attractive substitute for vengeance, not only because it spares the avenger trouble and risk, but also because it denounces the offender with an authority the avenger cannot command. The general acceptance of this moral authority to denounce is what makes state punishment retributive, rather than merely retaliatory. By delegating their power of revenge to the state and accepting its retributive authority, private parties cooperate to achieve the public good of a *rule of law*.

Criminal law arguably makes the state—at least in theory—the sole arbiter over disputes of violence. Thus, English criminal law emerged from claims brought in the royal courts for violation of the peace decreed by the king. Criminal law still permits some violence as justified—in order to prevent or resist crime, apprehend suspects, and confine convicts. Yet these justified uses of violence are authorized by the state. Some would argue that defensive force should be seen as the exercise of a natural right. Yet early English criminal law did not treat self-defense as justified, but only as grounds permitting the purchase of a pardon. Thus even self-defense was an offense to the king's peace until and unless authorized.

Accordingly, when social theorist Max Weber defined the sovereignty of the state as its monopoly on *legitimate* force, he treated a system of criminal law as an important attribute of sovereignty.[13] Weber's identification of sovereignty with legitimate force acknowledged that no state has an effective monopoly on force—but to the extent unauthorized violence is interpreted as crime rather than rebellion, the state is accepted as sovereign. Thus by defining offenses and justificatory exceptions, criminal law classifies every act of violence as either state-authorized or illegitimate. This pervasive classificatory scheme blankets all social interaction and helps bring to mind the ruling authority of the state even when no official is nearby. If citizens accept the state's authority to legitimate or condemn conduct, they will likely feel a powerful pull to obey its dictates and defer to its officials. Even before the criminal law punishes a single offender, the very idea of crime helps to suppress violence by conditioning its social acceptability on state authorization. It seems there can be no state in the familiar sense of that term without criminal law. Thus an essential purpose of criminal law—so basic and obvious as almost to escape our notice—is to proclaim the rule of law by forbidding unauthorized violence.

It is sometimes said that criminal punishment redresses a public wrong rather than a private wrong. As we have seen, crimes of violence were traditionally seen as offenses against the king in England, and Blackstone classified crimes as public wrongs in his treatise on the common law. Today, government has a monopoly on criminal prosecution in the United States (although not in all countries). Yet this idea of crime as an offense against the public interest does not tell us very much about what conduct should be criminal, because the concept of the public interest is so contested. The content of this concept is determined politically, and so criminal law punishes public wrongs largely in the sense that the decision to criminalize conduct defines it as a matter of public interest. Because state punishment implies public disapprobation, the limitation of criminal offenses to public wrongs is arguably a logical truth, rather than a normative claim. Criminal law transforms private injuries into public wrongs by punishing them.

To be sure, criminal punishment can be levied for crimes such as treason, perjury, tax evasion, or driving without a license that injure governmental interests. Offenses involving possession of the means to commit crimes or to avoid detection are arguably aimed at protecting the government's interest in law enforcement rather than the interests of potential victims. On the other hand, these crimes are generally seen as somewhat anomalous. Offenses such as tax evasion and perjury in civil trials are often tolerated or subjected to noncriminal sanctions. Violations of licensing and record-keeping schemes are not

---

13. Max Weber, From Max Weber: Essays in Sociology 78 (1946).

always seen as properly subject to blame and moral condemnation. Possession offenses are punished with increasing severity in the American criminal justice system, and yet this pattern is deeply controversial.[14] Some argue that popular support for severe punishment of drug possession is driven by concern about violent crime committed by dealers and addicts.[15] In sum, crimes defined by injury to governmental interests are somewhat peripheral to the main purpose of criminal law.

By contrast, acts of violence against persons are seen as the core problem criminal law must address, and as clearly worthy of disapproval. Moreover, we punish violence in a way that focuses concern on actual injuries to particular victims. Thus we reserve our most severe punishment for causation of death, rather than use of weapons, or other dangerous conduct. We punish causing actual harm more severely than attempting or risking harm.

Even though punishment does not compensate the victim for physical or financial injuries, victims often feel that they have a very strong dignitary interest in punishment. If victimization damages social status, punishment operates like revenge, to repair it. In a blood-feud society, vicarious revenge shows that the victim is valued by her social group, which views the affront to the victim's dignity as an affront to the dignity of all the group's members. Criminal punishment repairs damaged social status in much the same way, with the difference that the social group recognizing the victim's dignity is the entire public. Thus, it is important to the effectiveness of punishment in redressing the victim's dignitary injury that it treats that injury as a matter of public concern.[16] This message is strengthened by public prosecution, which brings the public onto the side of the victim at an earlier stage, and absolving the victim of having to plead in court for recognition and redress.

Thus, public adoption of wrongs against individuals as wrongs against the public is crucial to the cultural work the criminal law does. This transformation of private into public wrongs gives each individual a dignitary stake in the rule of law. It allows civic identity to provide some of the social control that group identity provides in more traditional societies. State punishment is an

---

14. Markus Dubber, *Policing Possession: The War on Crime and the End of Criminal Law*, 91 J. CRIM. L. & CRIMINOLOGY 829 (2001).
15. WILLIAM J. STUNTZ, COLLAPSE OF AMERICAN CRIMINAL JUSTICE 269–70 (2011).
16. Kenworthey Bilz, *The Puzzle of Delegated Revenge*, 87 B.U. L. REV. 1059, 1062 (2007); ANTONY DUFF, ANSWERING FOR CRIME: RESPONSIBILITY AND LIABILITY IN THE CRIMINAL LAW 140–42 (2007); Adil Ahmad Haque, *Group Violence and Group Vengeance toward a Retributivist Theory of International Criminal Law*, 9 BUFF. CRIM.L. REV. 273, 280–82 (2005); Jean Hampton, *Correcting Harms versus Righting Wrongs: The Goal of Retribution*, 39 UCLA L. REV. 1659, 1666 (1992).

expression of social solidarity among citizens, treating any violation of certain interests as an expression of disrespect for a status held by all.[17]

V. Why Criminal Law Matters

Criminal law is an important instrument of policy and an important political issue. The importance of criminal law as an instrument of policy can be illuminated by comparing developed states like the United States to societies without effective criminal justice systems. First, consider ancient societies without centralized government. The Icelandic sagas—recounting ninth- and tenth-century blood feuds—portray medieval Vikings as status-conscious, quarrelsome, and bellicose. They could press their grievances before arbitral assemblies of their neighbors, but these courts had little power to enforce their judgments on unwilling disputants. Moreover, disputants risked losing face if they retreated from conflict by accepting arbitration. As their social status declined, they could become subject to ever more slights and injuries. Moreover, this loss of status could also weaken the position of their family and friends. Thus Icelanders felt intense social pressure to avenge perceived offenses in blood. Yet each act of vengeance could provoke further retaliation. Because there was no institution with the authority to resolve disputes, these feuds had no necessary end.[18]

We see similar dynamics of retaliatory violence in our own society among members of criminal subcultures who cannot use the law to resolve their disputes. The rest of us generally enjoy the benefits of an effective criminal justice system that discourages violence, and preempts and suppresses revenge when violence occurs. Thus, an effective system of criminal justice protects us twice. Not only does it secure us against the material and dignitary injuries inflicted by violence, it also removes the burden of risking our lives to restore our damaged social status through private vengeance. Instead, we can rely on the state to vindicate us by exacting public retribution. Indeed, once vengeance is forbidden, we can no longer be faulted for cowardice in failing to avenge injuries. Our civic virtue as law-abiding citizens can substitute for martial virtue as a source of dignity.

---

17. Antony Duff, Answering for Crime: Responsibility and Liability in the Criminal Law 140–41 (2007); Jean Hampton, *Correcting Harms versus Righting Wrongs: The Goal of Retribution*, 39 UCLA L. Rev. 1659, 1668–69 (1992).
18. William Ian Miller, Bloodtaking and Peacemaking: Feud, Law, and Society in Saga Iceland 180–81 (1990).

Philosophers sometimes argue that preventing vengeance is not a very good reason to punish. They see this as surrendering to the illegitimate demands of those who are willing to use violence. They reason that if victims' demands for punishment are just, we should grant them whether or not they will otherwise wreak vengeance. Yet this does not explain why deserved public punishment is any better than deserved private revenge. To be sure, a private vigilante might be less capable than an impartial court to correctly assess when revenge is deserved. But why punish the vigilante who gets it right? The answer is that the rule of law has political as well as epistemic advantages over vigilante justice. Public punishment does a better job of resolving disputes justly mostly because it does a better job of resolving disputes. We do not want victims taking private revenge even if they only give wrongdoers what they deserve, because victims should not have to face the risks of defensive and retaliatory violence or the indignity of failure.

Next consider modern societies without effective governments. In such settings crime can have very large social costs. Thus, in the first year following the overthrow of the Saddam Hussein regime in Iraq, homicides in Baghdad are said to have increased twenty-fivefold, excluding military casualties and deaths from terrorist attacks. As homicide historian Randolph Roth explains of such situations

> Some of the homicides . . . will be aimed at creating stable regimes by eliminating political rivals. But these homicides are inevitably accompanied by others that may appear to be apolitical but that correlate just as strongly with the lack of political stability. For example, some men become predatory killers, raping, robbing, and murdering as individuals or members of gangs. They may begin killing as political partisans . . . but when they find themselves on the losing side or at odds with an emerging political order, they may begin to prey on former allies and noncombatants. . . . Old neighborhood feuds are likely to turn murderous during periods of instability. When government breaks down, men kill for what appear to be purely personal reasons, avenging wrongs, settling scores, and simply getting rid of people they don't like.[19]

When civil order breaks down, the distinction between warfare and criminality becomes elusive. In any case, the resulting violence can have further destructive consequences. In postinvasion Iraq, factional conflict displaced millions

19. RANDOLPH A. ROTH, AMERICAN HOMICIDE 18–19 (2009).

of people and looting degraded infrastructure, including water, sanitation, and hospitals. Mortality rates soared, resulting in hundreds of thousands of deaths from "natural" causes. The fall of the Barre government in Somalia in the early 1990s led to warfare among five armed factions. Fighting dispersed the population and disrupted the food supply, as crops were destroyed and farmers were displaced. International relief efforts brought food, but it was stolen and traded for arms. With a monopoly on food, armed bands found it easy to recruit new members and violence spread. The resulting famine killed 300,000 people, and Somalia's gross national income declined virtually to zero.

These examples show that uncontrolled violence and theft can have profound indirect effects on life, health, and welfare. From this point of view, it seems that law can have no more important function than controlling crime. Yet if what really matters is the control of violence, law has the equally important function of controlling the state functionaries who assert the state's monopoly. Saddam Hussein's police state suppressed a good deal of crime, but also made war on its own population. And not all conduct government proscribes merits suppression. Stalin's Soviet Union imprisoned millions and executed hundreds of thousands for the "crime" of shirking forced labor.[20]

But even if we confine criminal law to the worthy task of suppressing violence, can it really make a difference? Yes and no. According to Roth

> Deterrence is essential to keeping homicide in check. When law and order break down . . . homicide rates jump to hundreds and sometimes thousands of people per 100,000 per year. By ending outright lawlessness, effective policing can drive homicide rates down to 10 or 20 per 100,000. But policing and other forms of deterrence can go only so far toward making societies nonhomicidal, and there is not much evidence that America's [comparatively high homicide rate] stems from a lack of deterrence.[21]

Ordinarily, economic analysis of law focuses on the marginal effects on utility of discrete changes in the law. Research shows that the marginal deterrent effects of increasing the severity of punishment in societies such as ours are trivial. Increasing the certainty of punishment is more effective but, as Roth points out, this is hard to do. "Forty percent of known homicides in the United States never result in an arrest. Many suspects who are caught are not convicted, so

20. Daren Acemoglu & James A. Robinson, Why Nations Fail: The Origins of Power, Prosperity and Poverty 131 (2012).

21. Randolph A. Roth, American Homicide 9 (2009).

a majority of killers, usually three-fifths or more each year, escape punishment. That pattern has prevailed since colonial times. The primary cause is not poor law enforcement but a lack of evidence. . . ."[22] It may be that punishment has declining marginal utility and that we are close to or even past the point where increases yield any benefit. Yet the small marginal effect of punishment in our society does not mean that punishment makes no difference. If we had no punishment, the increase in violence might be very substantial. A great deal of legal scholarship asks what legal rules will maximize wealth—but without an adequate degree of social peace there will be no wealth to worry about.

Of course what is at stake here is not just money, but the social conditions for the pursuit of whatever purposes make life meaningful. This idea of the priority of suppressing violence is a venerable theme in political theory. A society without criminal law may become what Hobbes called a "war of all against all."[23] Even the idealistic Kant, who generally put moral principle ahead of expedience, thought social order so important that he rejected any right to disobey an unjust law. Both philosophers were social contractarians who saw a sovereign state with an effective legal system as a prerequisite to meaningful rights and freedoms.

Of course a philosophical distinction between a state of nature and a legal state oversimplifies a more complex range of social institutions. On one hand, all human communities, however informally organized, regulate violence to some extent. All such communities defer to the strong, recognize entitlements, and resolve disputes.[24] On the other hand, no state succeeds in suppressing violence altogether. Some states exercise effective control only over a part of their territory. Criminal law authorizes some private violence, and officials charged with enforcement informally tolerate more. Finally, states themselves use violence in enforcing law and keeping order.

We should remember that modern states also suppress violence by other means than criminal law. Most states with effective criminal justice systems also have effective armed forces. Indeed, sometimes military weakness leads to lawlessness. Economically weak regimes sometimes lose control of their armies, who turn to brigandage to support themselves. Politically weak regimes

22. *Id.* at 10.

23. THOMAS HOBBES, LEVIATHAN: OR THE MATTER, FORME & POWER OF A COMMONWEALTH, ECCLESIASTICALL AND CIVILL 87 (A.R. Waller ed., Cambridge University Press 1935) (1651).

24. MEYER FORTES & E. E. EVANS-PRITCHARD, AFRICAN POLITICAL SYSTEMS 273 (1970); Marshall D. Sahlins, *The Segmentary Lineage: An Organization of Predatory Expansion*, 63(2) AMERICAN ANTHROPOLOGIST NEW SERIES, pt. 1, 322, 324–25 (1961); PIERRE CLASTRES, SOCIETY AGAINST THE STATE 14–15 (1977); Thomas Blom Hansen & Finn Stepputat, *Sovereignty Revisited*, 35 ANNUAL REV. ANTHROPOLOGY 295, 298–99 (2006).

sometimes recruit criminals to defend them against external threats or internal rivals, by implicitly offering them carte blanche to prey on the population.[25]

Yet this does not mean that military strength inevitably leads to effective criminal justice. Sometimes strong repressive states suppress violence by military rather than legal means. Dictatorships such as the Hussein and Barre regimes rely on military and security forces to keep the peace—quite effectively in the first case. Yet the impact of such regimes on public welfare may be almost as bad as civil war. Dictatorships are more likely to go to war than democracies, and international war is just as destructive as civil war or gang war. For example, Iraq's war with Iran cost Iraq hundreds of thousands of lives and hundreds of billions of dollars. Nor is military force a very efficient way to keep civil peace. Coercion is costly and inherently involves violence. The Hussein regime provoked and brutally suppressed internal resistance. Moreover, Roth argues, coercion can only reduce homicide rates to moderate amounts. It is never as effective as widespread belief in the legitimacy of government and the justice of society.

So although criminal law is not the only way states can keep the peace, it is better than relying on military force. Criminal law is not just a cumbersome system of coercion, a police state supervised by courts. As stipulated at the beginning of this chapter, edicts should only be seen as law to the extent they are accepted as a source of obligation. In mobilizing frequent voluntary compliance, an effective criminal justice system achieves social order with less violence than does a police state. Of course popular acceptance of a social order is no guarantee of its justice. Nevertheless, reliance on popularly accepted criminal law to control violence distinguishes the United States from both failed states and police states. The aspiration to mobilize popular acceptance of criminal prohibitions sets some limits to what the state can criminalize, as the ultimate abandonment of Prohibition illustrates.

In the United States, criminal law is important, not only politically and economically, but also culturally. America has more crime and much more punishment than other prosperous liberal states, and that may be just the way we want it. Criminal law is law as we love to imagine it. We may not be eager to encounter crime or criminal justice personally, but we love to watch or read about crime committed by and to someone else. Crime stories offer us the guilty thrills of vicarious transgression, followed by the satisfactions of schadenfreude and sanctimony when the villain gets his due, while we escape unharmed.

---

25. John E Mueller, The Remnants of War 17 (2004).

Our culture's interest in criminal law sometimes seems disproportionate. Since 1972, some 30 governors have won office after promising to pass death penalty laws.[26] Some observers concluded that Michael Dukakis's mishandling of the death penalty issue cost him the presidency, while Bill Clinton's unwillingness to be outflanked on the issue was crucial to his electoral success.[27] Yet Americans seem much more committed to supporting the death penalty than inflicting it. The electoral triumph of pro-death-penalty sentiment has resulted in the actual execution of only about three killers per thousand. It seems the importance of the death penalty is more expressive than instrumental.

Yet crime is also a serious problem in the United States. Compared to other developed democracies, the United States has much more violent crime, particularly in cities and in the South, and this has been true since the early twentieth century (although homicide rates have dropped by about 50 percent from their peak). Moreover, our intense interest in criminal justice and our high rates of violence are related in complex ways. To be sure, many Americans are discontented with criminal justice because they are unhappy about high crime rates. Yet the causation apparently also runs the other way: homicide goes up when belief in the effectiveness and fairness of criminal justice goes down.[28] According to Roth, high American homicide rates also reflect our relative lack of social solidarity and insecurity about social status. Roth explains the emergence of distinctively high American homicide rates during the second half of the nineteenth century as a result of two events. First, the Civil War left a legacy of animosity between southerners and northerners and between whites and blacks, and left the South alienated from the national government. Second, a precipitous decline in levels of self-employment left many American men without hope of escaping a condition of economic dependence they had been taught to see as shameful. According to Roth, these developments spawned an enduring culture of belligerence. Against this background, our interest in criminal justice can be understood as anxiety over who will control a powerful weapon that we have no confidence will remain impartial.

Criminal law is also important because the criminal justice system affects many more people in the United States than in comparable societies. The real impact of anti-crime sentiment has been felt in longer and more frequent incarceration rather than in execution. Since 1970 the number of incarcerated

---

26. Jonathan Simon, Governing through Crime: How the War on Crime Transformed American Democracy and Created a Culture of Fear 61–62 (2007).

27. *Id.* at 69.

28. Randolph A. Roth, American Homicide 300 (2009); Gary LaFree, Losing Legitimacy: Street Crime and the Decline of Social Institutions in America 79–81 (1998).

offenders has increased sevenfold. Our incarceration rates are the highest in the world (with the possible exception of North Korea).[29]

Also striking is the racial demography of both crime and punishment in America. African Americans face both a homicide rate and an incarceration rate about six times that of whites.[30] Hispanic Americans are also overrepresented on both sides of the criminal justice process. It seems clear that both crime and punishment are major dimensions of racial stratification of American society. This suggests that the criminal justice system must be highly salient in the experience of many members of racial minorities in the United States. Yet if white Americans see themselves as less vulnerable to crime and punishment by virtue of their racial identity, the criminal justice system may be highly salient for them too. In a society where many people worry about violence and incarceration, not having to do so may seem a perquisite of privilege.

The distribution of crime and punishment may be very important in shaping social status and identity along other dimensions as well. Men are far more likely to commit crimes of violence than women, and are incarcerated in far greater numbers. Men are also more likely to suffer crimes of violence, but women are particularly vulnerable to sexual assault and domestic violence. It is probably true in most societies that persons of higher social class are better protected against crime.

Our society's highly unequal distribution of the risks of crime and punishment may explain some of the disproportionate interest and anxiety Americans bring to the criminal justice issue. If these risks are perceived as important tokens of status in a professedly egalitarian society, exposure to even a minor risk of crime may be experienced as degrading. The hypothesized relationship between social status and the distribution of the risks of crime may explain the entertainment value of crime dramas, enjoyed in safety. Each time we imagine that someone else has been victimized or punished, without being threatened with such consequences ourselves, we can experience a gratifying superiority of status. This suggests a rather uncomfortable cultural explanation for our high rates of both crime and punishment. Perhaps we leave some sectors of society harshly but ineffectively policed because we find the resulting distribution of risk entertaining.

---

29. James Q. Whitman, Harsh Justice: Criminal Punishment and the Widening Divide between America and Europe 3 (2003); David Garland, The Culture of Control: Crime and Social Order in Contemporary Society 14 (2001).

30. Bureau of Justice Statistics, Correctional Populations in the United States, 2010, NCJ 236319 (2011); Bureau of Justice Statistics, Homicide in the U.S. Known to Law Enforcement, 2011, NCJ 243035 (2013).

In sum, criminal law is important because it is a useful institution for controlling violence. Violence is important to us collectively because a society that fails to control violence is miserable for everyone. The control of violence is therefore an essential responsibility of the state, crucial to its legitimacy. Violence is important to us as individuals and as group members because the distribution of violence within society is an important determinant of relative social status. To the extent that we are vulnerable to violence, we may feel a sense of degradation that pervades our daily experience and shapes our social interactions. Thus the control and fair distribution of violence is essential to achieving a liberal society that affords all of its members at least some measure of dignity. In short, criminal law matters because it is important to both the descriptive and normative legitimacy of the legal system as a whole.

VI. Conclusion

This chapter has defined criminal law as law forbidding conduct and imposing state punishment. It has argued that proscription expresses disapproval, and is often directed at conduct that intentionally injures known victims. Such intentional injury is likely to be socially costly and personally demeaning. This chapter has also defined punishment as affliction because of blame for forbidden conduct, and argued that blame attaches to voluntary, culpable, wrongful conduct. It has argued that blame for defying a prohibition implies the legitimate authority of the proscribing and punishing power over the wrongdoer. The capacity of such a power to impose authoritative blame differentiates punishment from revenge, as alternative strategies for restoring the degraded status of victims. The chapter argued that state proscription and punishment of unauthorized violence is essential to producing the public good of a rule of law. By asserting and maintaining this monopoly on legitimate violence, the state protects the dignity of its citizens more stably and reliably than they could do on their own. Yet because criminal punishment legimates law and motivates compliance by distributing social status, criminal law is also a powerful political weapon and is inevitably the object of political contention. In the United States, with its unfortunate history of slavery and segregation, the misuse of criminal law to recreate racial hierarchy is a particularly troubling danger. Indeed, it has been argued that the tremendous growth in incarceration since the civil rights era is "the new Jim Crow."[31]

31. Michelle Alexander, The New Jim Crow: Mass Incarceration in the Age of Colorblindness 185–87 (2012).

TWO

The American Criminal Justice System

I. Introduction

In the previous chapter we defined criminal law as the law of state punishment, and identified it as a usual feature of modern liberal states, useful in establishing a rule of law. This chapter focuses in on criminal law as part of the development of the American state. It describes how the United States came to have a criminal justice system, the development of that system, and how that system currently processes criminal cases. Although much of the law described in this chapter is procedural, this description of the American criminal justice process is offered as a frame for the discussions of substantive criminal law to follow. We want to understand how questions of substantive criminal law arise in the American criminal justice process, and to distinguish these substantive questions from procedural issues that may also determine the outcome of a criminal case.

Because the existence and effectiveness of a system of criminal law is a matter of degree, such a system need not have a very definite beginning. We can say that criminal law is in force where a governing power proscribes conduct, acts as an aggrieved party when such conduct is committed, and imposes noncompensatory sanctions. There is no necessary connection among these features of criminal law, and so they can be established piecemeal. They will usually coexist alongside civil compensation, and they may or may not succeed in displacing private vengeance and suppressing violence. A criminal justice system might be effective in some regions or among certain communities only. Different governing authorities might assert criminal jurisdiction over the same people and places.

The American criminal justice system is descended from colonial legal systems that were partially transplanted from England. The particular rules of American criminal law derive primarily from American statutes. But the basic understanding of criminal law as a distinct field of law, and many of its defining procedures and concepts, are adapted from the English background. Thus the story of how America came to have a system of criminal law includes the story of how England developed such a system.

Quite different historical accounts could be given of English and American criminal justice, emphasizing the role that criminal justice institutions played in the everyday lives of ordinary people, or in the distribution of power between strong and weak. However this chapter has a more modest ambition. It simply recounts the creation, over time, of the institutions and procedures that now define criminal law as a distinct body of law.

II. The English Origins of Criminal Law

The establishment of a royal criminal justice system in England unfolded over the course of centuries, in tandem with a system of civil liability and compensation to injured private parties. Yet this system had remarkably early beginnings, because of the unusual stability and durability of central government in England. From the seventh century, Anglo-Saxon kings, in consultation with leading lords and clerics, presided over a system of courts, and promulgated laws for them to apply.[1]

For much of the Anglo-Saxon period, victims could seek redress for acts of violence and other wrongs in county or "shire" courts.[2] The procedure usually involved the parties and their supporters swearing oaths. The remedies for most offenses were payments of compensation to the plaintiff, and fees or fines to the court. Such payments represented what we might call a state interest in law enforcement. Anglo-Saxon kings issued schedules of compensation, and encouraged victims to seek legal redress, rather than revenge.[3] A defendant unable to pay would likely have to serve the plaintiff as a slave. Some serious offenses were not compensable and would be punishable by death, with the defendant's property going to the court.[4] Such wrongs may have been understood as expressions of disrespect for the king, who extended his protection against such injuries.

1. John H. Langbein, Renee Lerner & Bruce Smith, History of the Common Law: The Development of Anglo-American Legal Institutions 6 (2009).
2. John Hudson, The Formation of the English Common Law: Law and Society in England from the Norman Conquest to Magna Carta 37, 39 (1996).
3. Alfred William Brian Simpson, "*The Laws of Ethelbert*," *in* On the Laws and Customs of England: Essays in Honor of Samuel E. Thorne 14 (1981).
4. Theodore Frank Thomas Plucknett, A Concise History of the Common Law 442 (5th ed. 1956).

By the tenth century, the Anglo-Saxon kings took a more proactive role in investigating and prosecuting crime. The adult male population was organized into tens and hundreds and required to swear oaths to eschew and to report offenses.[5] Offenses were now clearly forbidden as wrongs against the king, violations of his "peace" and betrayals of the subjects' sworn obligations to him. Such wrongs came to be divided into trespasses in violation of the king's peace, and capital offenses, dubbed "felonies." The latter term suggests that these capital offenses were conceived as fundamental violations of a feudal relation, justifying the forfeiture of property held in feudal tenure. Eventually, felonies would be distinguished from treasons, which were attacks on the king and his interests, rather than the interests of others subject to his protection. Treasons were also subject to death and forfeiture.

At times it was generally known that a serious offense had been committed, and by whom, but no accuser or other witness would come forward to vindicate the royal interest. If no one of sufficient status or credibility would clear the suspect with an oath, the suspect could be tested with an ordeal, such as dunking or burning, presided over and interpreted by a priest.[6] James Whitman has argued that reluctance to accuse was a common problem throughout the medieval period.[7] In a devoutly Christian culture, complicity in punishment of the innocent was a moral catastrophe, recalling the betrayal and judicial execution of Christ. Moreover, accusation could provoke counter-accusation or violent revenge. For aggrieved victims, accusation was a dishonorable alternative to vengeance, and involved the religious risks of swearing an oath and usurping divine judgment. The ordeal provided a path to punishment without witnesses, while also insulating the judge against moral and spiritual responsibility in a dubious case. For the accused, the ordeal provided an opportunity to show honor and courage, to accept physical suffering but possibly escape the ignominy of guilt.

After the Conquest, Norman kings built on late Anglo-Saxon practices, binding the population to report crimes and produce suspects through the institution of "frankpledge," or face fines.[8] Fines were especially heavy for the failure to identify the slayer of a Norman. Citizens were obliged to arm themselves and pursue suspects in a "hue and cry," and were expected to summarily execute killers and thieves caught in the act. Most prosecutions were still initiated by

---

5. John P. Dawson, A History of Lay Judges 181–82 (1960).
6. Charles Warren Hollister, The Making of England to 1399, at 217 (8th ed. 2001).
7. James Q. Whitman, The Origins of Reasonable Doubt: Theological Roots of the Criminal Trial 3 (2008).
8. John H. Langbein, Renee Lerner & Bruce Smith, History of the Common Law: The Development of Anglo-American Legal Institutions 27 (2009).

victims, however, through a process called "appeal of felony." The Normans preferred trial by battle in such cases, so that successful prosecutions typically created an opportunity for court-supervised revenge. Defendants were apparently sometimes allowed to purchase judgment by an "inquest"—a sworn verdict of local villagers—in substitution for a battle. Many appeals of felony were settled privately, so as to avoid the risks of battle and the burdens of payment to the Crown.

Two major developments altered this system substantially by the early thirteenth century, and created the outlines of the modern system of state accusation and jury fact-finding. In 1166, at the Assize of Clarendon, King Henry II ordered villages and hundreds to provide juries of "presentment" to report offenses, under oath, to royal sheriffs and justices.[9] Because the accusation was not initiated by a victim willing to seek revenge, trial by battle was not available. Defendants presented by a jury would be obliged to swear their innocence and suffer an ordeal, which might avail them the mild sanctions of banishment or a bond securing future good behavior. Henry failed in efforts to assert such criminal jurisdiction over clerics, who were subject to the church's canon law system. In 1215 the church—which by now had developed methods of investigation and fact-finding based on interrogation and testimony—forbade priests from participating in ordeals throughout Europe.[10] This withdrawal of religious sanction defeated the purpose of the ordeal, which was not to find fact, but to immunize fact-finders against the spiritual risks of error. English royal justices responded by replacing ordeals with the jury inquest procedure as the means of adjudicating the accusations of juries of presentment.

During the same period a civil jury system developed to provide private compensation for trespassory offenses. Trespasses were of two main forms: trespasses by force of arms, which were batteries against the person; and a trespass by breach of an enclosure, which was an invasion of property. Upon presentation of appropriate allegations by a plaintiff, a royal official would issue a writ of trespass requiring the defendant to explain before a jury why he should not pay compensation. This procedure became popular with disputants and would be expanded during the fourteenth century to include claims for wrongful injuries that were not seen as violations of the king's peace.[11] These were claims "on the case," and would later be classified as claims of negligence. These three types of claims for compensation were the beginnings of a system of tort law

9. *Id.* at 35–42.

10. Disciplinary Decrees of the General Council 258 (H.J. Schroeder ed., 1937).

11. John H. Langbein, Renee Lerner & Bruce Smith, History of the Common Law: The Development of Anglo-American Legal Institutions 103–04 (2009).

distinct from criminal law. Nevertheless, because compensation, fees and fines, and physical punishment had traditionally been available at the same proceedings, successful jury adjudication of civil claims for trespass would have made it seem sensible to use juries in determining criminal responsibility as well.

Yet jury trial of criminal cases had traditionally been at the option of the defendant, because the defendant's assent absolved the judge and jurors of bloodguilt. Defendants had two reasons to withhold this assent. First, until the middle of the fourteenth century, the membership of the inquest jury often overlapped with that of the presenting jury that had accused him. Second, a felon convicted by jury stood to lose not only his life, but also his estate. Courts were sometimes obliged to torture defendants—not to induce confession, as in continental legal systems, but to induce submission to a jury trial.[12]

Another important feature of the emerging system was detention in county jails, at their own expense, of those charged by the presenting jury. The sheriff would hold those charged with minor offenses until they paid him bail or were tried in his court. Those charged with the most serious offenses would not be bailed. The sheriff would hold them for trials to be conducted by visiting royal justices. The development of serviceable jails enabled the Crown to suppress the custom of popular summary execution of felons caught in the act.

During the fourteenth century, juries of presentment assumed a standard form as countywide grand juries, typically composed of complainants, witnesses, and local officials such as coroners and constables who were likely to have knowledge of serious crimes. Two mid-century statutes established that felony and treason offenses could not be punished without grand jury "indictment or presentment" and trial (presumably by jury).[13] A statute of 1368 referred to this required sequence as "due process."[14] Treasons were distinguished from felonies and narrowly defined. These pronouncements apparently reassured the restive knightly class by limiting the emerging criminal jurisdiction of the king's council. Thus royal jurisdiction over serious crimes expanded during this period, but also became better regulated.

At the same time, a shift occurred in the processing of lesser offenses. Local courts were now presided over by local gentry commissioned by the Crown as "justices of the peace."[15] Justices of the peace tried charges brought by either the indictment of presenting juries, or—increasingly—by the "information" supplied by village constables or, occasionally, complainants. Justices of the peace

---

12. John H. Langbein, Torture and the Law of Proof: Europe and England in the Ancien Regime 75–76 (1977).
13. 25 Edw. 3 st. 5 c.4 (1351).
14. 42 Edw. 3 C.3 (1368).
15. Charles Warren Hollister, The Making of England to 1399, at 353 (2001).

were responsible for enforcing labor and other "police regulations" imposed by either parliamentary legislation of royal edict, often by summary proceedings, without a jury. They, rather than the sheriffs, supervised the village constables and directed the popular pursuit of suspects. This system helped preserve some of the social authority of the landholding class despite the declining value of land and the increasing independence of the peasantry. In so doing it kept the landed gentry beholden to the king for their social position.

The trial was far less formal than it is today, and very little is known about trial procedure before the middle of the sixteenth century. For minor offenses, justices of the peace operating without juries conducted investigations and summoned witnesses. In felony cases, parties sometimes offered witnesses in court, but sometimes contacted jurors in advance of trial to inform them about the case. These witnesses were not always sworn. Although civil litigation was conducted by attorneys, attorneys rarely appeared in criminal cases. Defendants were not allowed attorneys and had no right to compel the appearance of witnesses. Attorneys rarely prosecuted except in treason trials. In felony cases, the victim would ordinarily appear as both an accuser and a witness. If the offense were a homicide, the complainant might be the victim's family, or a local coroner. The judge might summon additional witnesses and question them. The defendant, although unsworn, would be expected to answer to the evidence throughout the trial. It does not appear that judges ordinarily instructed the jury or commented on the evidence, some of which was known only to the jurors.

Juries were required to issue a unanimous verdict. The jury would sometimes issue a "special verdict," finding particular facts rather than drawing a conclusion on the charge. This was an important option in homicide cases, where exculpatory circumstances for a killing warranted the opportunity to purchase a pardon rather than an outright acquittal. Another procedure for sparing a guilty felon, increasingly relied upon, was to deem him a priest and grant "benefit of clergy."[16] The fictive priest would be branded and perhaps fined or briefly imprisoned, but then released. The brand served as a record that would preclude a second benefit of clergy for recidivists. Although royal pardons were sometimes available upon recommendation of the judge, there were no appeals from a jury verdict. An acquittal was final, and the defendant could not be retried. However the jury could be sanctioned for a decision against the evidence. From the late fifteenth to the mid-seventeenth centuries, the king's council sitting as the court of Star Chamber investigated and punished official

---

16. John H. Langbein, *Shaping the Eighteenth-Century Criminal Trial: A View from the Ryder Sources*, 50 U. CHIC. L. REV. 1, 37–41 (1983).

malfeasance (although not capitally).[17] This court had the power to punish jurors, although it was likely to be exercised only in politically significant cases.

Beginning in the mid-sixteenth century, justices of the peace were required to receive criminal complaints, hear supporting witnesses and bind them to appear at the itinerant royal courts called "assizes," question the defendant, determine bail, and record a report for the royal justices.[18] The first modern criminal law treatises were manuals to help justices of the peace identify offenses and frame charges. At the assizes, the accuser and supporting witnesses would appear before the grand jury. If the grand jury approved their claims as a "true bill," they stood trial. At trial, assize judges, who were now better informed about the case than the jurors, would question the witnesses.

An important development was the passage of statutes eliminating benefit of clergy for the worst homicides (dubbed murders, as distinguished from mere manslaughters) and other grievous felonies. This was probably a response to increasing rates of homicide, as urbanization and commerce created new opportunities for crime, while the pacific ethic of Christianity yielded to a classically inspired ethic of martial honor and virtue. The restriction of benefit of clergy made the pardon process more important. Executions were frequent at the end of the sixteenth century, as many as 800 a year among a population of only 4 million.[19] Another sixteenth-century innovation was a practice of reserving some doubtful convictions for further review by a panel of assize judges. If these judges determined that a legal error had been made, they would recommend a pardon. This was not truly an appeal, as the power to reserve a case vested in the trial judge, not the defendant.

III. The Transformation of English Criminal Law during the Colonial Period

The political crises of the seventeenth century occasioned important changes in the roles of jury and judge. Parliamentary disaffection with the king provoked a 1641 statute depriving his council of criminal jurisdiction and shifting the power to commission courts to Parliament.[20] This statute arguably altered

---

17. John H. Langbein, Renee Lerner & Bruce Smith, History of the Common Law: The Development of Anglo-American Legal Institutions 562–87 (2009).
18. 2 English Historical Documents: 1042–1189, at 440–43 (D.C. Douglas & G.W. Greenway eds., 2d. ed. 1981).
19. Leon Radzinowicz, A History of English Criminal Law: The Movement for Reform 153 (1948).
20. 16 Charles I, c. 10 (1641).

the character of courts as agents of the king's protection, although criminal cases were still considered "pleas of the crown," and judges continued to see themselves as servants of the kings who appointed them.

Nevertheless the long struggle over lawmaking power in seventeenth-century England that culminated in the Glorious Revolution prompted a debate over the source of legal authority. Mediating the competing claims of royal and popular sovereignty, politically and intellectually ambitious jurists such as Edward Coke offered themselves as exponents of the wisdom and reason of the common law.[21] The leading jurist of the later seventeenth century, Matthew Hale, developed an influential account of English law as a contract between king and people that required the reason of jurists to rationalize and explain. Anticipating Locke, Hale saw property interests as natural, and law as fundamentally an instrument for their protection. Hale's ideas would later be repeated in Blackstone's *Commentaries on the Laws of England* (1765–1769), which were greatly influential in America.[22] It is important to understand that the claims about English law made by Coke, Hale, Blackstone, and similar authorities in the seventeenth and eighteenth centuries were opinionated and speculative. Courts had little reason to define criminal law with any precision before this era. Early American lawyers may have read these works as descriptive of English law, but they were often prescriptive efforts to influence the law. Indeed, the revolutionary generation likely embraced these works as expressions of a congenial Whig ideology, charting a path toward enlightened reform.

With the end of the Star Chamber's power to punish jurors, trial judges asserted such a power themselves. Courts invoked this power primarily to coerce unwilling jurors to enforce unpopular royal policies against religious and political dissent. In ordinary cases, juries were happy to take direction from judges, who began to summarize the evidence and instruct juries on the law. This practice gave increasing precision to the law, and further encouraged the production of a treatise literature. Hale's treatise *History of Pleas of the Crown* was much concerned with the proper instruction of juries.[23]

The 1670 decision in *Bushell's Case* held that jurors could not be punished for a verdict contrary to the evidence and the judge's instructions.[24] The court reasoned that jurors might decide on the basis of their own knowledge rather than evidence produced in court, and that judges themselves often held divergent views of law. This case established the jury's famous power to "nullify" the law

21. Edward Coke, Institutes of the Laws of England (1644).
22. William Blackstone, Commentaries on the Laws of England (4 vols.) (Oxford 1765–1769).
23. Matthew Hale, History of Pleas of the Crown (1736).
24. Vaughan 135, 124 Eng. Rep. 1006, 6 St. Tr. 999 (C.P. 1670).

by acquitting. The trial judge could resist an acquittal he deemed unwarranted by questioning the jurors on their views, reinstructing them, and requiring them to redeliberate. Once recorded, however, an acquittal was final. The tolerance of jury nullification reflected the influence of puritanical religion, which placed great emphasis on the claims of individual conscience and the continuing spiritual importance of avoiding complicity in spilling blood. The pious Hale's treatise repeatedly urged acquittal in the face of doubt. Jury instructions during this period often told jurors they should not convict without a "satisfied conscience." Professor James Whitman has argued that the requirement of proof beyond a reasonable doubt, although not formally imposed until the late eighteenth century, became part of the popular understanding of jury service after *Bushell's Case*.[25]

Jury nullification worked primarily to the defendant's benefit, because only an acquittal was final. A faulty conviction could be overturned in two ways: by recommending a pardon on the evidence, and by reserving a case for review of legal error. Pardons became increasingly important during the seventeenth and eighteenth centuries, as the number of felons executed declined. By the eighteenth century, reviewing judges issued written opinions for publication.

The Glorious Revolution at the seventeenth century's end brought three key developments. First, a Bill of Rights precluded excessive bail and fines and cruel and unusual punishment, provisions repeated in the U.S. Constitution's Eighth Amendment.[26] Second, the Crown was deprived of power to remove judges.[27] Third, legislation granted defendants new procedural protections in treason cases, including a right to counsel at trial, a right to be informed of the charges in advance of trial, and a right to compel defense witnesses to appear.[28] These rights would later be afforded all defendants.

The eighteenth century brought two dramatic changes to the English criminal justice system. First, the development of transportation to America as a penal sanction intermediate between benefit of clergy and execution greatly reduced capital punishment and sped the growth of the American population. More important for our purposes, the English trial became an adversary process conducted by lawyers.

The state took an increasing hand in prosecution through a number of devices. In London and its vicinity justices of the peace took on more

---

25. James Q. Whitman, The Origins of Reasonable Doubt: Theological Roots of the Criminal Trial 25 (2008).
26. Furman v. Georgia, 408 U.S. 238, 242–44 (1972).
27. 12 & 13 Wil. 3, c. 2, § 3 (1701).
28. John H. Langbein, Renee Lerner & Bruce Smith, History of the Common Law: The Development of Anglo-American Legal Institutions 654 (2009).

responsibility to investigate crime and began to employ informers and investigators. The Crown offered rewards for the successful private prosecution of serious crimes, which created a profession of mercenary investigators.[29] In addition, justices of the peace offered defendants immunity to serve as "crown witnesses" against other offenders. These bounty hunters and Crown witnesses—sometimes habitual criminals themselves—were widely viewed with suspicion, as having motives to frame the innocent. Prosecuting attorneys appeared on behalf of government agencies prosecuting counterfeiting, forgery, and theft of government property. Government solicitors gathered evidence, which was presented in court by hired barristers. Royal solicitors were sometimes appointed to assist the prosecution in high-profile crimes of violence as well.

In the 1730s, judges began to respond to these new prosecutorial practices by permitting defendants to use counsel to examine witnesses and argue points of law. The participation of defense counsel divided the trial into distinct prosecution and defense cases. The defendant was no longer obliged to respond to prosecution witnesses, but left his counsel to question their veracity and motives. Defense counsel could put on witnesses, and often sought to prevent the defendant from speaking at all. Judges also policed the prosecution case by developing three restrictive rules of evidence.[30] They excluded coerced confessions, the uncorroborated testimony of confederates, and evidence of bad character, including prior offenses. Defense attorneys of course vocally demanded the enforcement of these restrictions. The trial had shifted from a test of the defendant's credibility to a test of the prosecution's case. By the last quarter of the eighteenth century, juries were often being instructed that guilt must be proved beyond reasonable doubt, while prisoners assisted by counsel often stood silent. Yet our hindsight should not exaggerate these developments. Lawyers were expensive, and the great majority of criminal defendants, even at the end of the eighteenth century, had none.

IV. Colonial American Criminal Justice

Did American criminal law incorporate English criminal law and institutions as American law upon our independence? Not exactly. Such incorporation

29. Allen Steinberg, *From Private Prosecution to Plea Bargaining: Criminal Prosecutions, the District Attorney, and American Legal History*, 30 CRIME & DELINQUENCY 568, 571 (1984).

30. John H. Langbein, *Historical Foundations of the Law of Evidence: A View from the Ryder Sources*, 96 COLUM. L. REV. 1168, 1172 (1996).

would have required that the colonies had remained subject to English law, through all its vicissitudes and changes, throughout the colonial period; and that American colonists, upon rejecting English rule, were happy to submit to English law. Neither assumption applies. English criminal law had limited and changing authority in colonial America and limited and contested prestige in post-revolutionary America.

English constitutional law, as reflected in the 1608 decision in *Calvin's Case* and the 1693 decision in *Blankard v. Galdy*, did not extend English law to conquered territories.[31] Instead, such colonies were governed either by local law, or by such law as the king made for them. The 1702 English decision in *Smith v. Brown and Cooper* rationalized Virginia slavery on just this basis.[32] Some colonial charters required local authorities to promulgate laws as compatible with English law as was convenient. Others colonies were simply left unmolested to develop their own law. There were very few persons with legal training in seventeenth-century America, and those few were generally not permitted to appear in court. Bradley Chapin, historian of colonial criminal justice, concludes that the first colonists perceived England as "disorderly, immoral and crime-ridden," and its legal system as "archaic, inefficient and capricious." In short, "they shared the common knowledge that the criminal law of England was infamous."[33] Recall that at the end of Elizabeth's reign, homicide was rampant and execution very frequent in England.

The New England and Pennsylvania colonies of religious dissenters saw themselves as spiritual communities with distinctive apprehension of a higher law. The tidewater plantation colonies preferred autonomy to manage their large population of bound labor without interference, although their governors were under more constraint to apply English law. The formerly Dutch settlements adapted the institutions they inherited. Chapin estimates that early colonial codes drew slightly more than half their content from English law.[34] Yet they left out much that English law included, promulgating simple and accessible codes in English, meant to be known. They greatly reduced the number of capital crimes. The colonies of religious dissenters eliminated capital punishment of property crimes. The plantation colonies largely limited these to crimes by bound laborers.

Colonial criminal law was also initially informal and expeditious, reflecting the low population density and the difficulty of holding or transporting a

31. Blankard v. Galdy, 91 Eng. Rep. 356 (K.B. 1693).
32. Smith v. Brown, 91 Eng. Rep. 566 (K.B. 1705).
33. Bradley Chapin, Criminal Justice in Colonial America, 1606–1660, at 3 (1983).
34. *Id.* at 14.

malefactor for trial. Informality and orality were also desirable so as to avoid inviting imperial oversight and interference. Summary justice and corporal punishment were common, and vigilante justice not unknown in newly settled areas. Grand jury presentment and jury trials were initially rare.

Punishment was often imposed for contempt rather than violation of a code provision. Courts were not always distinct from other governing authorities. They sometimes issued and enforced personal directives, or enforced the discipline of masters over servants. In the New England colonies, religiously authorized leaders exercised an intrusive and paternalistic scrutiny. Peace bonds (with propertied citizens often standing surety for propertyless neighbors) were an important method of social control, and expulsion an important sanction.[35] In the plantation colonies, magistrate justice reinforced private governance and corporal punishment. The imposition and extension of indentures were important sanctions.[36] Other colonial sanctions included whipping and mutilation (usually of the poor), fines (usually of the propertied), admonitions, and other shaming rituals. Forfeiture of estate was explicitly banned in several colonies and was employed very rarely where permitted.[37]

Capital punishment was reluctantly imposed in societies suffering from labor shortage. Indeed, Pennsylvania permitted capital punishment only for "wilful murder."[38] The New England colonies threatened, but rarely imposed, capital punishment for morals offenses. The bloody Salem witchcraft trials provided a spectacular exception to this pattern, but one with a chastening effect.

Where early colonial procedure was formalized, it was a simplified replica of English procedure. Constables could arrest a suspect caught in the act or upon the warrant of a magistrate. Suspects arrested for noncapital crimes were permitted to post bail. Grand jury presentment became common in the major settlements, although written indictments were sometimes confined to capital cases. Jury trials were generally available for capital and sometimes for lesser offenses, and became more common in the eighteenth century. As in England, the accused was not sworn but was expected to answer his accusers, and without the aid of counsel. Indeed, in the New England colonies, defendants were under considerable pressure to confess their sins and hope for mercy. By the eighteenth century, out-of-court confessions were treated with suspicion, as in England.

---

35. Jack Marietta & Gail Stuart Rowe, Troubled Experiment: Crime and Justice in Pennsylvania, 1682–1800, at 43–45 (2006).
36. *Id.* at 93.
37. Bradley Chapin, Criminal Justice in Colonial America, 1606–1660, at 59 (1983).
38. Stuart Banner, The Death Penalty: An American History 98 (2002).

An important American innovation was the development of public prosecution. By the early eighteenth century, such prosecutors commonly presented felony cases to the grand jury, and in some colonies tried them as well. The Dutch colonies had local public prosecuting attorneys in the second half of the seventeenth century. After the English takeover, county sheriffs replaced them. By the early eighteenth century, deputy attorney generals had taken over this role. In 1732, New York required each county to pay a salary for such an official.[39] Connecticut in 1704 eliminated private prosecution by statute and required appointment of an attorney for the Crown in each county.[40] By 1711 Virginia had turned prosecution of all felonies over to attorneys general.[41] The Carolinas soon also reserved prosecution in County Courts to deputy attorneys general. Over the course of the eighteenth century Massachusetts developed a system of county prosecutors. By the 1820s most states had public prosecutors, and by the 1840s many of these prosecutors were popularly elected.[42]

In the eighteenth century, the empire exerted some pressure on the colonies to conform their criminal law to the English model, particularly in Pennsylvania, which adopted a new English-influenced criminal code in 1718 and declared the applicability of parliamentary laws.[43] The new code increased the number of capital offenses, but was still far more humane than contemporaneous English law. Eighteenth-century judges were more likely to have some knowledge of English law, and defense attorneys began to participate in some criminal trials. In colonial America as in England, juries asserted the power to determine law as well as fact in political cases. In the famous 1735 trial of John Peter Zenger in New York, a jury accepted truth as a defense to a charge of seditious libel, in defiance of the judge's instruction.[44] The verdict was left undisturbed, and the result was widely celebrated. Andrew Hamilton, Zenger's trial attorney, was not sanctioned, even though Zenger's first defense attorney had been disqualified and sanctioned for contempt. By the late eighteenth century, criminal defendants were far more often represented by counsel at trial in America then in England. Yet many offenders still could not afford counsel.

---

39. 1 THE SOCIAL HISTORY OF CRIME AND PUNISHMENT IN AMERICA: AN ENCYCLOPEDIA 473 (5 vols.) (Wilbur Miller ed. 2012).
40. Jack M. Kress, *Progress and Prosecution,* 423 ANNALS. AM. ACAD. POL & SOCIAL SCI. 99, 103 (1976).
41. *Id.*
42. Robert Ireland, *Privately Funded Prosecution of Crime in the Nineteenth Century United States,* 39 AM. J. LEGAL HIST. 43, 43 (1995).
43. JACK MARIETTA & GAIL STUART ROWE. TROUBLED EXPERIMENT: CRIME AND JUSTICE IN PENNSYLVANIA, 1682–1800, at 7 (2006).
44. 17 How. St. Tr. 675 (1735).

By the time American colonies became independent of Britain they had long developed their own laws and procedures. In the meantime, as we have seen, English criminal law went through dramatic developments throughout the colonial period. When many colonies were settled, English criminal law, which had long been enforced without counsel, jury instructions, or appeals, was not well defined. Lawyers became important in American society during the eighteenth century—including a majority of the framers. As the revolution approached, leading American lawyers were reading the English treatise literature, particularly the works of visionary Whigs such as Hale and the instantly popular Blackstone. Thus the idea of the English common law as the rational articulation of the contract between government and people was a source of intellectual influence during the revolutionary period. That does not mean that revolutionary Americans saw themselves as bound to follow English law.

V. Criminal Justice in the New Republic

Although the Revolution spawned a new federal government, criminal justice was primarily a matter of state law. Federal criminal law was largely limited to the protection of federal governmental interests, and the policing of interstate and international transportation and commerce. Some of these federal crimes were important and controversial—criminalizing sedition and interference with the capture of fugitive slaves, for example—but Congress passed no general criminal code.[45] The emerging dispute over slavery exerted a constant pressure to localize legal issues that might bear on labor relations. Given the violence inherent in the institution of slavery, it cannot easily coexist with a criminal justice system unless that system actively supports it. Recall too, that the states with the strongest antislavery sentiments were those emerging from the colonies of religious dissenters with their own strong traditions of local autonomy. The power to criminalize and punish came to be seen as part of a police power inhering in states and communities, rather than as a defining feature of national sovereignty.

The federal constitution set limits to its criminal law, forbidding ex post facto laws, legislative condemnation or "attaint" of individuals,[46] cruel and unusual punishment, and excessive bails and fines.[47] It also forbade unreasonable

---

45. Act of February 12, 1793, 1 Stat. 302; Act of September 18, 1850, 9 Stat. 462 (collectively known as the fugitive slave acts).
46. U.S. CONST. art. I § 9, 10.
47. U.S. CONST. amend. VIII.

searches, seizures, and arrests and vague warrants that might allow them.[48] It barred compulsory self-incrimination, double jeopardy, and deprivation of life, liberty, or property without "due process."[49] The Constitution also conferred rights to grand jury indictment, jury trial, counsel, and cross-examination of witnesses, and made available a "writ of habeas corpus" process to challenge imprisonment as unlawful.[50] Apart from the prohibitions on ex post facto and attainder laws, these limits applied only to the federal system, but most state constitutions ensconced similar rights.

After the Revolution, some states and territories adopted English common law as it stood in 1776, as authoritative in default of legislation.[51] However, most adopted statutes continuing in force either preexisting law, or the common law as previously applied in that jurisdiction.[52] American editions of Blackstone's Commentaries held that the common law was locally enacted and therefore different in content in each American jurisdiction.[53] Pennsylvania, which had accepted English influence before the Revolution, quickly reformed its homicide law to reduce reliance on capital punishment, and joined many states in forbidding reliance on post-independence English law.[54]

The application of English criminal law was particularly controversial in the new republic. Many Americans considered English criminal law, with its abundance of capital crimes, as barbaric, or associated it with repressive sedition prosecutions during the run up to the Revolution. [55] There was strong sentiment to define crimes by legislation rather than leaving the definition of criminal liability to judges. The 1812 decision of the U.S. Supreme Court in *United States v. Hudson & Goodwin* quashed a federal indictment for the common law crime of seditious libel, on grounds that federal courts lacked the power to define crimes.[56] The case arose only a few short years after the Alien & Sedition Acts had met popular repudiation in the election of 1800, and been allowed to lapse. Thus the case dramatized how a judicial power to criminalize could

---

48. U.S. Const. amend. IV.
49. U.S. Const. amend. V.
50. U.S. Const. amend. VI; U.S. Const. art. I § 9. cl. 2.
51. N.Y. Const. art. I, § 14.
52. Guyora Binder, Felony Murder 125 (2012).
53. St. George Tucker, Blackstone's Commentaries: With Notes of Reference to the Constitution and Laws of the Federal Government of the United States, and of the Commonwealth of Virginia 1803, at 430 (1803).
54. Jack Marietta & Gail Stuart Rowe, Troubled Experiment: Crime and Justice in Pennsylvania, 1682–1800, at 210–16 (2006).
55. St. George Tucker, Blackstone's Commentaries: With Notes of Reference to the Constitution and Laws of the Federal Government of the United States, and of the Commonwealth of Virginia 1803, at 438–39 (1803).
56. United States v. Hudson, 11 U.S. 32 (1812).

frustrate popular will. Judicial lawmaking was almost as controversial at the state level as well. Most of the original states codified their criminal law within a few decades, and newer states codified criminal law shortly after statehood.

These codes often borrowed offense definitions from Blackstone's influential treatise. Yet there were other influences as well. Jeremy Bentham had advocated codification of criminal law, arguing that clear communication of criminal prohibitions to the public would have a deterrent effect.[57] Edward Livingston, author of Louisiana's criminal code, was a vocal exponent of Bentham's ideas. Bentham and his follower John Austin developed a conception of offenses as divisible into discrete elements, including acts and mental states.[58] Influential treatises on criminal law published at mid-century by Francis Wharton and Joel Prentiss Bishop incorporated these ideas.[59]

The codification process was associated with another important American innovation, the penitentiary. The American codes were often passed in conjunction with legislation mandating the construction of penitentiaries. These codes greatly reduced the number of capital felonies, and assigned penalties in terms of years of imprisonment. They often arranged offenses in graded hierarchies, with longer prison terms triggered by aggravating elements. In this way, Americans sought to implement the recommendations of penal reformers such as Beccaria and Bentham, who advocated mild but certain punishment in preference to harsh penalties haphazardly applied. The new penitentiaries imposed a monastic discipline and aimed at repentance and, ultimately, character reform.[60] Felonies were typically reconceptualized as crimes meriting incarceration in a state penitentiary. Misdemeanors or other petty offenses were punished by fines or short- term incarceration in local jails. Jury trials were not always made available for such offenses.

Grand juries or coroner's juries were generally required for charging felonies through most of the nineteenth century. Private prosecution was forbidden in some jurisdictions, and simply diminished over time in others. Yet this left an important gap, because the understanding persisted that public prosecutors had largely unreviewable discretion to decide not to prosecute. The trial court

---

57. Jeremy Bentham, A Fragment on Government (1776); Jeremy Bentham, Traités de Législation, Civile et Pénale (1802).

58. Jeremy Bentham, "*Specimen of a Penal Code*," 1 Works of Jeremy Bentham 164 (2005); Jeremy Bentham, An Introduction to the Principles of Morals and Legislation 70–80 (1876); John Austin, Robert Campbell, and Sarah Austin Lectures on Jurisprudence: Or, the Philosophy of Positive Law 1093–94 (1880).

59. Francis Wharton, A Treatise on the Criminal Law of the United States (1846); Joel Prentiss Bishop, Commentaries on the Criminal Law (1856–1858).

60. David Rothman, The Discovery of the Asylum: Social Order and Disorder in the New Republic 82 (1971).

had the power to dismiss an indictment that failed to set out the requisite elements of an offense. Grand juries often resisted prosecutors and refused to approve charges in a significant minority of cases during the nineteenth century.[61] Eventually, some jurisdictions created the option of charging by information in order to evade such resistance, with the approval of the U.S. Supreme Court.[62]

During the early nineteenth century, American judges followed the English practice of commenting on the evidence. They also drew on an increasingly available treatise literature in instructing on the law. In the 1820s it became common to instruct juries on the requirement of proof beyond a reasonable doubt. Lawyers criticized judicial summing up of the evidence as trespassing on the jury's power, and by the second half of the nineteenth century, a number of states had forbidden this by statute.[63] The result was a compromise recognizing a firm distinction between fact and law, and allocating these spheres to juries and judges, respectively. Yet judges still endeavored to use their dominion over law to police jury decision-making. For a time, they accepted or even sought information from jurors and set aside verdicts for improper deliberation. However they soon concluded that juror testimony about deliberation was unreliable, and that this practice invited corruption. Instead, trial judges simply overturned jury convictions they saw as unwarranted by the evidence or at odds with their instructions. There was no remedy for an improper acquittal, and conviction rates were low by modern standards. A few states explicitly permitted juries to decide on the law as well as the facts, but juries often asserted their power to acquit despite the evidence.[64]

By the early decades of the nineteenth century, most jurisdictions had appellate courts. Appellate judges were generally trained and experienced as lawyers. Between the Jacksonian period and the Civil War, most states moved to an elected judiciary, although election of appellate judges was more controversial and less prevalent. By the 1840s criminal appeals were generally available, although rarely employed. The prosecution could appeal the dismissal of an indictment or a particular charge. Only the defense could appeal from a jury verdict. Convictions could be overturned for insufficient evidence, and new trials could be awarded for erroneous jury instructions, admission of irrelevant inculpatory evidence, or failure to admit relevant exculpatory evidence.

---

61. John H. Langbein, Renee Lerner & Bruce Smith, History of the Common Law: The Development of Anglo-American Legal Institutions 750 (2009).
62. Hurtado v. California, 110 U.S. 516 (1884).
63. John Langbein, The Origins of Adversary Criminal Trial 323 (2003).
64. Albert W. Alschuler & Andrew G. Diess, *A Brief History of the Criminal Jury in the United States*, 61 U. Chic. L. Rev. 867, 911 (1994).

VI. Criminal Justice after the Civil War

The Civil War of course began a long process of transforming the structure of the federal constitution and the nature of the federal state. The Civil War amendments extended federal protections of life, liberty, property, free status, and the privileges and immunities of citizenship against states. They also authorized the federal government to enforce these and other rights, thereby expanding the scope of the federal criminal law power.[65] The federal government assumed a direct role in maintaining order and in supervising local administration of law enforcement during the occupation and reconstruction of the South, but the U.S. Supreme Court soon interpreted the Civil War amendments to allow little direct federal role in enforcing civil rights. An unrealized potential implication of the Fourteenth Amendment's due process and privileges and immunities clauses was their "incorporation" of the federal bill of rights as checks against the states. Although federal courts had no power to define crimes they, like state courts, retained the inherent power to criminally punish contempt of court. This power was repeatedly used by both federal and state courts to suppress labor strikes between 1880 and 1930, after which such powers were curbed by federal and state legislation.[66]

Although jury trial was common at the beginning of the nineteenth century, it became increasingly rare in the second half of the century, as the distinctive American institution of plea bargaining became the dominant mode of disposing of criminal charges. In his study of the emergence of plea bargaining in Massachusetts, George Fisher has argued that prosecutors resorted to it unilaterally wherever relatively determinate sentencing gave them the power to determine punishment by bargaining over the charge.[67] The graded structure of some criminal codes facilitated such plea bargaining, as the offenses charged often "included" less-aggravated offenses. In addition, prosecutors' unreviewable discretion to drop prosecution made such plea bargaining possible. Fisher argues that rising civil caseloads pressured trial judges to join the bargaining process by offering to exercise their sentencing discretion to reward guilty pleas. In this way prosecutors avoided review by juries and judges avoided review by appellate courts. Fisher adds that once defendants acquired the right to give sworn testimony in the later nineteenth century, jury trials became perilous for

---

65. U.S. CONST. amend. XIV.

66. WILLIAM FORBATH, LAW AND THE SHAPING OF THE AMERICAN LABOR MOVEMENT 59–97 (1991).

67. GEORGE FISHER, PLEA BARGAINING'S TRIUMPH: A HISTORY OF PLEA BARGAINING IN AMERICA 111–14 (2003).

career criminals.[68] Despite instructions to the contrary, jurors would often infer the guilt of defendants who declined to testify. Yet experienced criminals who did testify would be impeached by their criminal records.

Prosecutors and judges were eventually able to also offer less-experienced defendants a powerful incentive to plead. Late nineteenth-century legislatures gave judges the power to place convicted defendants on probation with suspended sentences. Probation was promoted by progressive era reformers as a humane policy that could rehabilitate offenders in the community, yet it was also supported by prosecutors. Many prosecutors had begun to operate their own informal systems of probation by suspending prosecution in return for a guilty plea to be placed on file for use in the event the defendant reoffended. Prosecutorial discretion and plea bargaining eased the prosecutor's burden in processing cases, and created the appearance of high conviction rates, although that appearance was often illusory.

Plea bargaining was also facilitated by the prevalence of defense counsel. Although a right to counsel was widely recognized in the nineteenth century, this was not a right to free counsel for the indigent. Some jurisdictions provided such counsel for capital cases, and charitable organizations provided some free counsel in some cities during the nineteenth century. By the end of that century New York and California undertook to provide counsel for all felonies. Fisher's data indicates that about half of criminal defendants were represented by counsel in Massachusetts during most of the nineteenth century.[69] Lawrence Friedman and Robert Percival found that 85 percent of defendants had counsel for serious offenses in late nineteenth-century Oakland.[70] A number of urban jurisdictions established public defender services during the first half of the twentieth century. Fisher has shown that supporters of public defense of the indigent argued that public defenders would increase the efficiency of criminal justice by working with prosecutors to negotiate pleas.[71] The 1932 Supreme Court decision in *Powell v. Alabama* required the provision of counsel in capital cases, and in the 1963 case of *Gideon v. Wainwright* the Supreme Court expanded this right to all serious criminal charges.[72] This holding required the creation of public defender services or assigned counsel programs everywhere.

---

68. *Id.*
69. *Id.* at 164.
70. Lawrence M. Friedman & Robert V. Percival, The Roots of Justice: Crime and Punishment in Alameda County, California 1870–1910 (1981).
71. George Fisher, Plea Bargaining's Triumph: A History of Plea Bargaining in America 170 (2003).
72. Powell v. Alabama, 287 U.S. 45 (1932); Gideon v. Wainwright, 372 U.S. 335(1963).

Prosecutor and juror discretion were not the only barriers to effective law enforcement in late nineteenth-century America. Perhaps the greater difficulties were (1) the slow development of effective policing and, even more important, (2) the underlying political conflicts that retarded that development. The decentralization of criminal justice meant there could be no national police force. Early nineteenth-century law enforcement institutions had included volunteer watchmen and elected constables in the towns, and county sheriffs with very limited resources. In the rural south landowners participated in or supported slave patrols, and similar vigilante groups developed in frontier areas. There was a good deal of political resistance both to empowering the state and paying for it.[73] This did not, of course, eliminate coercive social control, but meant that its legitimacy was not universally accepted, and that those targeted by or left unprotected against unofficial violence had little recourse beyond self-help.

Police forces were organized in cities only in the middle decades of the nineteenth century in response to urban riots. These forces were designed to consolidate in one body the functions of keeping order, arresting suspects, and—eventually—investigating crime. Yet there was a good deal of unease about these police forces. Propertied citizens demanded protection, but the forces developed to provide it would inevitably be controlled by the immigrant groups the gentry wanted protection from. Recruited by urban political machines, police were often poorly trained, supervised, and armed, and were sometimes corrupt. Few of these forces performed effectively before the end of the nineteenth century.[74] They had little capacity to investigate crime beyond the resource of coercive interrogation. Their activity focused less on felony offenses then on public order misdemeanors—public drunkenness, vagrancy, prostitution, disorderly conduct, and the like. Arrest for these offenses led to summary trials in magistrate courts, and short jail sentences or fines.

The ineffectuality of law enforcement permitted or provoked a good deal of organized private violence. Businesses hired or organized private security forces that clashed with laborers, vigilante groups flourished in some areas, ethnic and racial tensions provoked urban riots that police did little to suppress, and many individuals carried arms.[75] In particular, African Americans faced lynching and other vigilante violence in the South and mob violence in northern cities, without effective police protection, and sometimes with police participation. Randolph Roth's research indicates that the second half of the

73. Samuel Walker, Popular Justice: A History of American Criminal Justice 59–64 (1980).

74. *Id.* at 63–64.

75. *Id.* at 56–58; Randolph Roth, American Homicide 315–20 (2009); Lawrence Friedman, Crime and Punishment in American History 175 (1993).

nineteenth century saw a rise in violence among unrelated adults in the United States, at a time when other industrialized states were effectively reducing such violence. Roth argues that political conflicts both provoked intergroup violence and discouraged political support for empowering the state as an agent for conflict resolution.[76] It is not so much that the criminal justice system failed to solve the problem of crime. It is rather that the same political conflicts that generated violence also discouraged the development of effective institutions.

With the turn of the century, crime became the object of academic research by the new social sciences, which conceptualized it as one of many social problems associated with circumstances such as poverty, immigration, and alcohol abuse. This more deterministic view of crime encouraged the amelioration of criminal sanctions, inspiring agitation against capital punishment. Progressive reformers proposed institutions that would subject afflicted urban populations to the intervention of trained experts, rather than placing individuals in custody. These new institutions included juvenile and family courts, and public and private social service agencies. For adult offenders, these new institutions included supervised release on probation and parole. Thus progressives attempted to make punishment more rehabilitative by promoting indeterminate sentencing, and shifting discretion over the disposition of offenders from a judge at the stage of sentencing to a correctional professional at a later point.[77]

One implication of this program was to redesign prisons as therapeutic and educational institutions, preparing and evaluating prisoners for release. Such prisons would be dubbed "reformatories" and modeled on residential reform schools for wayward youth. Yet reformatories operated much like other prisons. Indeterminate sentencing laws often limited the discretion correctional officials could exercise, or made indeterminate sentencing an option judges could evade. Parole boards often left their discretion unused by adopting inflexible policies. Limited public investment in rehabilitation insured that once released on parole, prisoners received little supervision or social services. As actually institutionalized, parole did little to individualize sentencing, to rehabilitate offenders, or to check the power of judges and prosecutors to negotiate sentences.[78] Later criticisms of indeterminate sentencing charged that the discretion it conferred on correctional officials invited them to discriminate on the basis of race or politics or to exploit their power over inmates. Yet there is little evidence that indeterminate sentencing actually resulted in the exercise of much discretion or contributed very much to the persistent problems of

---

76. Randolph Roth, American Homicide 300 (2009).

77. David Rothman, Conscience and Convenience: The Asylum and Its Alternatives in Progressive America 89–92 (1980).

78. *Id.*

race discrimination and prisoner abuse in the correctional system. The critique instead reflected the distrust of discretion and faith in process that animated legal reformers in the 1960s and 1970s. Parole probably made far less difference than its proponents hoped and its detractors assumed.

Progressive reformers also sought to professionalize police forces through civil service reform of recruitment practices, training in police academies, and scientific management.[79] Eventually, modern communication and transportation technology would greatly improve the organization and efficiency of police—but also of the criminals they combatted. In addition, conflicts developed between the investigative and order-maintenance functions of police. Supervision, pooling of information, and collaboration with prosecutors all tended to concentrate the work of police in administrative offices, and interfere with patrolling.[80]

Progressive regulation of commerce, industry, and property led to the proliferation of regulatory offenses at both the state and federal levels. Most of these were petty offenses, enforced by fines. Controversy attended the conditioning of more severe penalties on oversights and omissions, however.

VII. Crime as a National Political Issue

Crime became an explicit focus of national politics in the twentieth century. The "red scare" following World War I led to the use of federal anti-espionage powers against domestic radicals and labor leaders, particularly the newly formed Communist Party. The adoption of the national prohibition of alcohol by constitutional amendment provoked the emergence of far-flung criminal enterprises and created a law enforcement problem of national scope. The use of violence to secure lucrative liquor markets against rivals and uncooperative law enforcement caused homicide rates to spike and created the perception of a national crime wave. This prompted the organization (or at least the renaming and expansion) of the Federal Bureau of Investigation. Organized crime became a special focus of federal criminal law. Crime commissions were formed to study the causes of crime and the performance of the criminal justice system. Pressure to ameliorate punishment dissipated.[81]

---

79. Samuel Walker, Popular Justice: A History of American Criminal Justice 133–35 (1980).
80. *Id.* at 189–91.
81. William Stuntz, The Collapse of American Criminal Justice 186–89 (2011); Jonathan Simon, Governing through Crime: How the War on Crime Transformed American Democracy and Created a Culture of Fear 46–49 (2007); Samuel Walker, Popular Justice: A History of American Criminal Justice 169–70 (1980).

During the interwar years national advocacy groups such as the ACLU, the NAACP, and the Communist Party brought national attention to the issue of race discrimination in the South, including the systematic denial of basic criminal procedure rights to African-American defendants. Some of the legal challenges they brought or supported induced the U.S. Supreme Court to begin to use the Fourteenth Amendment to apply federal constitutional protections against the states.[82]

After World War II, America's leadership in prosecuting leaders of the Nazi regime, and its Cold War competition with the Soviet Union, prompted American leaders to contrast the American state with these dictatorial governments. Historian Mary Dudziak has shown that one consequence was the elite repudiation of racial discrimination, as reminiscent of Nazi genocide, and as an impediment to American influence in the developing world.[83] Another consequence was an effort to identify the American state with the rule of law by emphasizing individual rights and procedural formality as constraints on government action. The discretion once embraced by progressive reformers was now increasingly seen as a potential source of dictatorial abuse.

One expression of this new "legal process" perspective was the more complete constitutionalization of criminal procedure and, to a lesser extent, substantive criminal law. Beginning in the 1960s the Supreme Court "incorporated" most federal criminal procedure rights into the Fourteenth Amendment's due process constraints on the states. The Court proceeded to draw the ire of critics by applying the Sixth Amendment to require provision of counsel to the indigent for all serious criminal charges, the Fourth and Fifth and Sixth Amendments to exclude evidence obtained through unreasonable searches and coercive interrogations, and the Fifth Amendment to require notice of rights to silence and to counsel during questioning.[84] The Court further constrained police discretion by striking down many public order offenses as vague or overbroad.[85] It also struck down statutes punishing dangerousness or criminality as such, without punishing past conduct.[86] It set national standards precluding retroactive criminalization by courts.[87] In constraining courts from creating or

82. Powell v. Alabama, 287 U.S. 45 (1932); Norris v. Alabama, 294 U.S. 587 (1935); Moore v. Dempsey, 261 U.S. 86 (1923).

83. Mary Dudziak, Cold War Civil Rights: Race and the Image of American Democracy 206–09 (2000).

84. Mapp v. Ohio, 367 U.S. 643 (1961); Gideon v. Wainwright, 372 U.S. 335 (1963); Massiah v. U.S., 377 U.S. 201 (1964); Griffin v. California, 380 U.S. 609 (1965); Miranda v. Arizona, 348 U.S. 436 (1966).

85. Papachristou v. City of Jacksonville, 405 U.S. 156 (1972).

86. Robinson v. California, 370 U.S. 660 (1962).

87. Bouie v. City of Columbia, 378 U.S. 347 (1964).

expanding liability retroactively, the Court also indirectly checked efforts by police and prosecutors to target political enemies or unpopular groups by prosecuting their previously innocent conduct. In addition, the Court ruled that the Sixth Amendment required that the prosecution had the burden to prove all the facts, or "elements," defining the offense beyond a reasonable doubt.[88] It further held that the defense could not be required to disprove such facts, and the jury could not be instructed to presume them.[89] In the area of corrections, the Court struck down capital sentencing laws permitting unguided jury discretion to select among first degree murderers.[90] A few years later, the Court approved laws permitting capital sentencing on the basis of enumerated aggravating factors.[91]

The other important expression of legal process thought in criminal justice was criminal code reform. Columbia Law Professor Herbert Wechsler, after assisting the Nuremberg Tribunal, became a major exponent of the legal process school, and principal reporter for the American Law Institute's Model Penal Code project. Wechsler's Model Penal Code began with an articulation of purposes, precise definition of general concepts, and general rules of construction.[92] It proceeded to provide precise definition of offenses and exculpatory defenses, to require subjective (i.e., mental) criteria of culpability for all offenses, to impose demanding burdens of proof on the prosecution, and to grade offenses on the basis of increasing levels of mental culpability. In particular, the Code analyzed offense definitions, separating their material and mental elements; divided material elements into conduct (acts or neglected duties), circumstances, and results; classified mental criteria into culpable mental states of purpose, knowledge, recklessness, or negligence; and required that the offense definition assign a required culpable mental state to each conduct, circumstance, and result element.[93] The Code required the prosecution to prove all material and mental offense elements.

Approved by the American Law Institute in 1963, the Code proved greatly influential. Over the next two decades three-fourths of the states revised their codes in response.[94] They did not all follow the Code on all issues, but adopted its basic organization and scheme of element analysis. State supreme courts have also adopted the Code's solutions to many problems unresolved by state

88. *In re* Winship, 397 U.S. 358 (1970).
89. Sandstrom v. Montana, 442 U.S. 510 (1979); Mullaney v. Wilbur, 421 U.S. 684 (1975).
90. Furman v. Georgia, 408 U.S. 238 (1972).
91. Gregg v. Georgia, 428 U.S. 153 (1976).
92. American Law Institute Model Penal Code §§ 1.02 (Official Draft 1962).
93. *Id.* at §§ 1.13, 2.01, 2.02.
94. Wayne LaFave, Criminal Law 5 (2010).

statutes.[95] Some of the U.S. Supreme Court's criminal law decisions during this era—notably the ones on burden of proof, capital punishment, and police use of force—reflected the Code's influence as well.

The liberal program of formalizing the criminal justice process eventually collided with an ascendant conservative politics. The social turmoil of the 1960s was accompanied by rising crime rates, urban riots, and white flight. All of these contributed to a racially tinged politics of law and order at the national and state levels. Anti-crime sentiment initially focused on resisting the Supreme Court's imposition of Fourth, Fifth, and Sixth Amendment constraints on police investigation, a viewpoint captured by the popular 1971 Clint Eastwood film *Dirty Harry*.[96] Anti-crime politics later shifted to the aims of reinstating the death penalty and reducing or eliminating parole and probation. A majority of states reinstated their death penalties, following the Model Penal Code's guided discretion model. The officials elected on a platform of reinstating the death penalty also supported other anti-crime measures, including recidivist sentencing enhancements, tougher drug laws, mandatory incarceration, and funding for prison construction.[97] Many states adopted laws imposing life sentences on offenders convicted of three or more felonies. Such laws were approved by the Supreme Court as compatible with the Eighth Amendment's proscription of excessive punishment, on the grounds that they advanced the legitimate penal purpose of incapacitating dangerous offenders.[98] Consistent with the Court's approval of such incapacitative sentencing, the Court also permitted pretrial detention without bail of defendants deemed dangerous.[99]

Because legal process liberals now mistrusted discretion as an arena for the expression of bias or petty authoritarianism, they joined the critique of indeterminate sentencing and its associated rehabilitative aspirations. Parole was eliminated in some jurisdictions, and probation was less relied upon. The federal system and a substantial minority of states adopted sentencing guideline schemes. These schemes typically incorporated recidivist sentencing principles, enhancing sentences on the basis of the defendant's prior criminal record. Thus both judges and correctional officials lost discretion in the move to guideline sentencing. Liberal elected officials also collaborated with conservative colleagues by proposing their own anti-crime initiatives, targeting hate crimes, domestic violence, rape, and child abuse, or providing funds to hire additional

---

95. *Id.* at 6.
96. DIRTY HARRY (Malpaso Productions 1971).
97. JONATHAN SIMON, GOVERNING THROUGH CRIME: HOW THE WAR ON CRIME TRANSFORMED AMERICAN DEMOCRACY AND CREATED A CULTURE OF FEAR 61–62 (2007).
98. Ewing v. California, 538 U.S. 11(2003); Lockyer v. Andrade, 538 U.S. 63 (2003).
99. United States v. Salerno, 481 U.S. 739 (1987).

police. Conservative and liberal politicians competed to show solicitude for crime victims. Victims' rights legislation in various jurisdictions mandated consultation of victims in plea bargaining and sentencing, and sometimes provided funds for restitution and social services for victims.[100] Moral philosophers responded to the national mood by developing a sudden interest in retributive theories of punishment. In an era of attacks on welfare, taxation, and government, perhaps the most effective way to advocate for expanded social services or public employment was to package them as crime control initiatives.

The combined effect of these developments was to increase the number of offenders incarcerated and the length of their terms. By the end of the century, the American prison population had increased sevenfold, and America's incarceration rate had become the highest in the world.[101] This massive increase in incarceration also had a disturbing racial valence. African Americans, already dramatically overrepresented in the criminal justice system, went to jail and prison in ever-greater numbers.[102] African Americans were particularly overrepresented among the growing inmate population imprisoned for drug offenses, relative to their representation among drug users.[103]

Although the federal sentencing guidelines were much criticized by sentencing judges, the U.S. Supreme Court initially upheld the constitutionality of transferring decision-making to an appointed sentencing commission.[104] One focus of controversy was the federal sentencing guidelines requirement that federal judges use alleged but unproven criminal conduct to enhance sentences. Eventually the Court ruled that the Sixth Amendment barred this practice. In *Blakely v. Washington* it held that any facts (other than the defendant's prior convictions) permitting judges to impose a higher penalty than would otherwise be authorized, or requiring a higher sentence than would otherwise be permitted, are offense elements.[105] Accordingly, the Court held, such facts must be proven beyond a reasonable doubt at trial. In *United States v. Booker*, however, the Court held that federal judges could continue to sentence on the basis of unproven conduct as long as they were not required to do so.[106] The

100. Markus Dubber, Victims in the War on Crime: The Use and Abuse of Victims' Rights 167–70 (2002).
101. James Q. Whitman, Harsh Justice: Criminal Punishment and the Widening Divide between America and Europe 3 (2003); David Garland, The Culture of Control: Crime and Social Order in Contemporary Society 14 (2001).
102. Michelle Alexander, The New Jim Crow: Mass Incarceration in the Age of Colorblindness 185–87 (2012).
103. *Id.* at 98, 278 n.3.
104. Mistretta v. United States, 488 U.S. 361 (1989).
105. Blakely v. Washington, 542 U.S. 296 (2004).
106. United States v. Booker, 543 U.S. 220 (2005).

federal guidelines are now advisory rather than mandatory, but federal judges follow them in the great majority of cases.

Despite the integrative influence of national politics, and of federal constitutional standards on all American criminal justice systems, these systems remain largely independent. Substantive criminal law is almost entirely statutory. Each state and the federal system have their own statutes. Thus, judicial decisions in each jurisdiction have no binding authority on other jurisdictions (apart from federal decisions on issues of federal constitutional law governing the states). Each American jurisdiction is a separate system with a separate law.

VIII. The Processing of Criminal Cases Today

Today, violations of criminal law come to the attention of law enforcement when reported by victims or witnesses, observed by police on patrol or in surveillance or undercover work, or discovered by government officials in gathering information required by regulatory regimes. Law enforcement agencies as a whole, and particularly local police, can devote only limited resources to investigation. Thus the decision how to deploy those resources is an important exercise of discretion over criminal justice policy.

A criminal case may begin with either the arrest or a charging of a suspect. Once arrested, a suspect must be cautioned as to her Fifth Amendment rights to remain silent and to consult an attorney before answering questions. Yet police can proceed to question a suspect who waives these rights, as most do. The Fourth Amendment has been held to require that an arrest must be justified by a judicial determination of probable cause to believe the suspect committed a crime, as soon as practicable, generally within 48 hours.[107] If the crime charged is one for which a sentence of incarceration is possible, the suspect acquires a Sixth Amendment right to the assistance of counsel (at public expense, if the defendant is indigent) at certain critical stages, including questioning by police, hearing the charges, pleading, and lineups.[108]

There is no explicit federal constitutional right to pretrial release. The Eighth Amendment requires only that if release is conditioned on bail, the amount be reasonably related to its purpose, which is usually to ensure appearance. A majority of state constitutions do recognize a right to conditional release on bail. Moreover, most jurisdictions provide by statute for the prompt consideration of pretrial release. In addition, the Article I, Section 9 guarantee

107. Gerstein v. Pugh, 420 U.S. 103 (1975); Cty. of Riverside v. McLaughlin, 500 U.S. 44 (1991).
108. Gideon v. Wainwright, 372 U.S. 335 (1963); Massiah v. United States, 377 U.S. 201 (1964).

of habeas corpus and the due process clauses of the U.S. Constitution imply that pretrial detention must be justified by some legitimate government purpose. Presumably, pressuring defendants to waive their rights to silence or to trial would not be a legitimate purpose for pretrial detention, although this is surely its effect on some suspects. In many jurisdictions, release and bail may be denied altogether if the charged crime is very serious and the court determines that the defendant is likely to commit violence if released. Moreover, the Supreme Court has upheld the constitutionality of pretrial detention for the sole purpose of preventing crime.[109]

In the federal system and about half the states, a felony charge must be approved by a grand jury. In other jurisdictions, charges may be approved by a judge "on information." In either case, the standard is probable cause to believe the defendant committed the crime.[110] This standard applies to each required element of the offense charged. Apart from this requirement, the prosecutor exercises relatively unrestricted discretion whether to charge any offense for which there is evidence. If evidence supports an aggravated offense, such as assault with intent to injure, the prosecutor may choose to charge only a lesser-included offense, such as simple assault. This power to determine the charges of course permits the prosecutor to reward guilty pleas, testimony against other suspects, or participation in rehabilitative "diversion" programs. A demonstrably corrupt or discriminatory failure to charge could give rise to civil or criminal liability, however.

The charging instrument must identify the offense and specify the offense elements the prosecution expects to prove. These elements are the required facts—acts or omissions, circumstances, results, and intentions or other mental states—defining the offense. A purpose of the charging instrument is to inform the defendant of the type of offense charged, with enough specificity as to time, place, and other persons, to enable him or her to prepare a defense. A charge that does not specify all the offense elements the prosecution must prove is legally deficient. A charge not supported by evidence showing the probability of each of these elements is factually deficient. The initial determination of probable cause by a grand jury or judge is often made without the participation of defense counsel.

Once a grand jury or judge has approved a charge on the basis of a finding of probable cause, the defendant is either summoned or brought (if already in custody) to court to hear the charge and plead guilty or not guilty. This "arraignment" may or may not coincide with the hearing concerning probable cause to

---

109. United States v. Salerno, 481 U.S. 739 (1987).
110. Hurtado v. California, 110 U.S. 516 (1884).

arrest. If the defendant is in custody, a determination on bail may be made at this point. The defendant must have the opportunity to be assisted by counsel before entering a plea. A defendant cannot be sentenced to any term of incarceration without being afforded this right.[111]

Once charged, the defendant has a Sixth Amendment right to a reasonably "speedy" trial, which he or she can waive by requesting more time to prepare. This right is defined by statute or by case law in each particular jurisdiction. During the interim between charging and trial, both parties have discovery obligations. Each may be obliged to exchange lists of witnesses, and the prosecution is required to share any exculpatory evidence in its possession. The defense may have to alert the prosecution if it intends to offer certain defenses. In addition, both sides may offer motions concerning the admissibility of evidence, and procedural matters such as venue, discovery, or the mental competence of the defendant to stand trial. The defense may move to dismiss some or all of the charges as legally deficient. If granted, such a motion to "quash" a charge would not prevent the prosecution from recharging the defendant with a legally adequate charging instrument.

The prosecution may appeal adverse pretrial rulings before trial, because this is its only opportunity. Once a jury acquits, the prosecution is barred by the Fifth Amendment prohibition on double jeopardy from contesting legal errors that may have caused the acquittal. The defense must wait until after conviction to appeal legal errors. A jury acquittal would obviate any appeal. The remedy for a wrongful failure to dismiss a charge would be to overturn a conviction on that charge. The remedy for a wrongful evidentiary ruling favoring the prosecution would be a new trial.

Trials are the exception. According to Donald Dripps, "it would not be uncommon for half of all arrests to result either in no charges or in charges that are later dismissed, for 80% of the cases that are not dismissed to end in guilty pleas, and for the remaining cases to be tried. . . . [A] 70% conviction rate at trial would not be unusual."[112] In some jurisdictions over 90 percent of cases that are not dismissed end in plea bargains.[113]

If the accused goes to trial he has a waivable Sixth Amendment right to be tried by a jury for any offense with a possible sentence of incarceration for six months or more.[114] Bench trials pose some disadvantages. The judge will be aware of inculpatory but inadmissible evidence, may be less likely to nullify the

---

111. Argersinger v. Hamlin, 407 U.S. 25 (1972).

112. DONALD DRIPPS, *Criminal Justice Process*, in 1 ENCYCLOPEDIA OF CRIME AND JUSTICE 369 (Joshua Dressler ed., 2d ed. 2002).

113. *Id.* at 370.

114. Duncan v. Louisiana, 391 U.S. 145 (1968).

law in the defendant's favor, and may be easier for the prosecution to convince than 12 jurors. On the other hand, defense counsel with an unsympathetic client, or who intends to offer highly technical evidence, may prefer trial by a sophisticated fact-finder.

The judge and attorneys select a jury, which may be a lengthy process or a short one, depending on the jurisdiction. The judge or attorneys may question prospective jurors. The judge may, either spontaneously or at the request of attorneys, dismiss jurors who seem unlikely to judge impartially. In some jurisdictions attorneys are given the power to dismiss a limited number of jurors for any reason other than their race or gender. Once a jury is impaneled, "jeopardy" attaches, for purposes of the Fifth Amendment. In a bench trial, jeopardy attaches after the first witness is sworn. Once jeopardy attaches, the defendant can never again be charged with the same or a "lesser included" offense, although he may be retried on the same charge in the event of a mistrial or a legal error at trial.[115] The court may declare a mistrial at any point if an event occurs that irreparably impairs the fairness of the trial, such as a lawyer referring to excluded evidence within the hearing of the jury. Either party may move for a mistrial.

After the jury is impaneled, the trial begins with the prosecution's opening statement describing what it intends to prove. The defense may respond with its opening statement or may wait until the prosecution has completed its case. The prosecution then proceeds to examine witnesses, and present any physical or documentary evidence. The prosecution will attempt to offer evidence proving each required element of every offense charged, beyond a reasonable doubt. The defense has a Sixth Amendment right to cross-examine each prosecution witness.

When the prosecution has completed its case, the defense may move for dismissal of any charged offense on grounds that the evidence was insufficient to prove any of its constituent elements. If the trial court concludes that no reasonable fact-finder could find a required offense element beyond a reasonable doubt, it must dismiss that charged offense. Because jeopardy has attached, a successful motion to dismiss at this stage functions as an acquittal, and prevents recharging.

If any charges remain, the defense can simply rest, hoping that the jury will conclude that the prosecution has not proven its case. Alternatively, the defense may now examine its own witnesses and introduce physical and documentary evidence. The prosecution may cross-examine these witnesses. The

115. Blockburger v. United States, 284 U.S. 299 (1932); United States v. Perez, 22 U.S. 579 (1824).

defendant is under no obligation to testify, and the prosecution may not treat such silence as evidence of guilt. The defense may introduce evidence for two general purposes: (1) to rebut or cast doubt on the prosecution's proof of the offense elements, or (2) to support an affirmative defense.

An affirmative defense is an argument that the defendant should be acquitted of one or more charged offenses, even if the prosecution succeeded in proving its case. The argument depends upon proof of certain facts—we may call these elements as well. If the accused produces some evidence supporting each of these elements, roughly equivalent to the probable cause needed to establish a charge, the judge will instruct the jury on the exculpatory effect of this defense. The Sixth Amendment requires the prosecution to prove offense elements, but not to disprove defenses.[116] Nevertheless, the penal code of a particular jurisdiction may impose a burden on the prosecution to disprove a particular defense beyond a reasonable doubt, once the defendant has supported it with evidence.

Affirmative defenses are of two general types: justifications and excuses. Justification defenses deny that the defendant's offense was wrong under the circumstances. Justification defenses include self-defense, reasonable use of force to prevent crime or effect arrest, and necessity or lesser evils. The burden of proof is on the prosecution to disprove justification defenses in most jurisdictions. Because law enforcement officers depend on justification defenses to absolve them of liability for doing their duty, otherwise tough-on-crime legislators are generally willing to burden the prosecution with disproving such defenses.

Excuse defenses concede that the defendant's offense was wrong under the circumstances, but insist that the defendant is not responsible for that wrong. Excuse defenses include duress, insanity, and sometimes reasonable mistakes of law. In most jurisdictions defendants bear the burden of proof on excuses. Some defenses are only partial: they mitigate liability rather than acquitting altogether. Provocation and extreme emotional disturbance, both lowering liability for intentional killings from murder to manslaughter, are examples of such defenses.

One defense that is neither a justification nor an excuse is entrapment, acquitting defendants who were persuaded by law enforcement officers to commit crimes they otherwise were not disposed to commit.[117] Such

---

116. Patterson v. New York, 432 U.S. 197 (1977) (excuses); Martin v. Ohio, 480 U.S. 228 (1987) (justifications).

117. Saunders v. People, 38 Mich. 218 (1878); O'Brien v. State, 6 Tex. App. 665 (1879); Jacobson v. United States, 503 U.S. 540 (1992); Rebecca Roiphe, *The Serpent Beguiled Me: A History of the Entrapment Defense*, 33 SETON HALL L. REV. 257 (2003). The defense is unavailable for persuasion by private actors. United States v. Maddox, 492 F. 2d 104 (5th Cir. 1974).

entrapment is arguably no excuse, as the offender is still at fault for choosing to commit the crime. Such a defense provides a relatively mild but enforceable sanction against overzealous law enforcement. The more straightforward sanction—denying a justification defense for the officer's complicity in the offender's crime—has two disadvantages. First, it might chill legitimate undercover work against targets actively seeking opportunities to offend. Second, such a remedy would often be undermined by the exercise of prosecutorial discretion in favor of law enforcement, whereas an entrapment defense is administered by courts. Entrapment is often considered a doctrine of criminal procedure.

After both sides have concluded their cases, each side offers a closing argument. In a jury trial, the judge then instructs the jury on the elements of the offenses charged, any available defenses, and the allocation of the burden of proof. In a bench trial, the judge decides the case under the same standards a jury would employ.

Jury instructions come from three sources: (1) "pattern" jury instructions, published by appellate courts; (2) instructions requested by the defense or prosecution; and (3) the judge's own understanding of the law. If the judge rejects an instruction proposed by the defense, or selects an instruction over the defense's objection, and the defendant is then convicted, the defendant may appeal. After instruction, the jury deliberates until it reaches a verdict, or until the judge is convinced that the jury cannot reach a verdict on some charges. Most jurisdictions require unanimity in felonies. If the jury cannot agree on a charge, the judge will declare a mistrial as to that charge, permitting the prosecution to begin another trial.

In a bench trial, the judge may, depending on local rules, create an appealable record of the legal basis for his or her decision, for example by issuing a memorandum detailing conclusions of law and findings of fact, and give an opportunity for motions before finalizing it as a judgment.

If a jury or judge convicts on any charge, the judge will usually proceed to schedule a sentencing hearing. The sentence will be within the range of penalties permitted for that offense by statute. Ordinarily, it will be informed by a pre-sentence report on the defendant's record and background, and the arguments or evidence presented by both sides at the sentencing hearing. In jurisdictions with sentencing guidelines, the judge may be quite constrained. As noted, a fact requiring a higher penalty than would otherwise be required, or permitting a higher penalty than would otherwise be permitted, must now be proven beyond a reasonable doubt to a jury at trial (unless conceded as part of a plea bargain). Juries often serve as both sentencing fact-finders and sentencers in capital cases under guided discretion capital sentencing laws.

After a jury verdict of conviction, the defendant may move for a judgment notwithstanding the verdict—again, arguing that no reasonable jury could have been convinced beyond a reasonable doubt based on the evidence, or could have rationally rejected the defendant's affirmative defense.

After conviction by jury or judge, the defendant may appeal to a higher court, if he or she has "preserved error" by first giving the trial judge the opportunity to correct it. Such appeals may be based on procedural or evidentiary issues beyond the scope of this book. Substantive questions most often arise on appeal in one of the following ways:

1. Before trial, the trial court has dismissed a charge as accusing the defendant of conduct that is not constitutionally punishable, or not proscribed. The prosecutor appeals from this decision, requesting a direction to the trial judge to reinstate the charge.
2. Before trial, the defendant has made a motion for dismissal on one of these grounds, which the court has denied. After conviction, the defendant appeals the denial of this motion. The requested remedy would be to overturn the conviction with prejudice, thereby dismissing the underlying charge so that the defendant could not be recharged or retried.
3. During the trial, the defendant has moved for the dismissal of one or more charges for insufficient evidence to persuade any rational factfinder as to one or more offense elements, or to disprove a proffered defense that the prosecution bears the burden to disprove. Alternatively, after trial, the defendant has moved unsuccessfully for a judgment notwithstanding the verdict, on similar grounds. After conviction, the defendant appeals the denial of one of these motions. The remedy would again be to overturn the conviction as to any such charge, with prejudice.
4. The judge gave the jury instructions on the elements of charged offenses or proffered defenses, or on the parties' burdens of proof, that the defense objected to as erroneous. The defendant now appeals on the ground that the judge's instructions were erroneous. The requested remedy would be to overturn the conviction without prejudice, thereby granting the defendant a right to a new trial, with directions to the trial court not to repeat the error. The prosecution might then elect to retry the defendant, or drop charges, or offer a plea to a lesser charge. The appellate court may, however, rule that the instruction was erroneous, but determine that proper instructions would have given the jury no reason to change its verdict. If it deems the error "harmless," the conviction will stand.

5. After conviction in a bench trial, the defendant appeals from the conclusions of law, or the denial of a motion on the substantive law governing the case. Again, the remedy would be to vacate the conviction without prejudice, unless the error was harmless.
6. Finally, the defendant may appeal an evidentiary ruling made before or during the trial on the ground that it was premised on an error of substantive criminal law. Thus, the defendant may appeal the exclusion of evidence supporting a defense the trial court improperly deemed unavailable, or the exclusion of evidence negating an offense element the court improperly deemed not part of the prosecution's burden to prove. The requested remedy would be to overturn the conviction without prejudice. The defendant would get an opportunity to present the excluded evidence at a new trial, should the prosecution opt to continue the case.

Substantive criminal law is the product of court decisions in appeals like these, as well as the criminal code and constitutional provisions such decisions apply.

IX. Conclusion

The conception of criminal law as the punishment of offenses against the state is very ancient, and criminal law has long been understood to involve a symbolic substitution of the state for the victim of crime. We have seen that the substitution of public punishment for private redress did in fact play an important role in the suppression of interpersonal violence and feuding in English and American history. Yet this symbolic substitution of state for victim can be a double-edged sword. When the legitimacy of state power is under attack—as occurred during Reconstruction, Prohibition and the 1960's—the identification of the state as crime victim can have a perversely criminogenic effect. Accordingly, state officials are constantly tempted to bring the victim back into view to legitimate law enforcement. All criminal justice systems face a dilemma: the visibility of too many victims undermines the state's claim to efficacy in protecting citizens; on the other hand, if victims become too invisible, the state can no longer present itself as their champion.

THREE

Why Punish?

I. Introduction

This chapter is about normative theories of punishment—theories intended to answer the question of why we should punish. Theories of punishment matter in criminal law because they identify the considerations of policy and morality that can guide both the definition and application of the law.

Why does criminal law need normative theories? After all, insofar as criminal law is positive law, we are subject to it whether or not we think it is just. Yet criminal law needs normative theories for three reasons.

First, punishment deprives offenders of freedoms deemed fundamental in liberal society. A state claiming to be founded on liberal principles must therefore justify and limit its power of punishment. In a democracy, the people are ultimately responsible for making law. Normative theories offer us criteria to use in evaluating law and deliberating over its reform.

Second, as we saw in Chapter 1, the effectiveness of criminal law depends a great deal on popular support. Because the coercive power of criminal law is not sufficient to induce general compliance, to some extent we *are* subject to criminal law insofar as we accept it. In a democracy criminal law is made by collective consent, and it aspires to inspire in each of us a sense of obligation to comply. Law enforcement must also rely on public cooperation to investigate and prosecute crime. Most fundamentally, criminal law denounces offenders in our name, and claims to repair the damaged dignity of victims by influencing communal judgments of right and wrong. These expressive aspects of criminal punishment require popular participation to be effective. If criminal law is to fulfill the function described in Chapter 1, it must offer the public persuasive reasons to support and participate in punishment.

Finally, criminal law needs normative theories for the same general jurisprudential reasons that all law needs normative theories. Lawmakers cannot write rules precise enough to anticipate all cases. Constitutional framers and legislators must rely on other actors—courts, prosecutors, and the public—to apply the law in light of purposes those actors will accept. These actors cannot apply criminal law without discretion. If they are going to exercise that discretion rationally and conscientiously, as public servants and citizens, they need normative theories.

One source of imprecision is necessarily vague constitutional standards. American criminal law is limited by prohibitions on ex post facto laws, cruel and unusual punishment, and deprivation of life and liberty without due process, as well as rights to notice of charges and to jury trials. In addition, civil liberties provisions limit punishment of speech, worship, travel, contracting, bearing arms, and other basic liberties. A theory of just punishment is needed to make sense of what liberty is protected, what process is due for its deprivation, and what punishment is cruel and unusual for what offenses.

Statutory provisions defining offenses and defenses also require interpretation. Is self-defense "reasonable" when retreat is possible? Is a fatal assault with intent to injure "malicious?" Must "consent" to sexual intercourse be manifest? Courts must have some way of resolving these questions. In most American jurisdictions statutory offenses are grouped together in codes, also containing general provisions with definitions, defenses, rules of joint liability, schemes for grading penalties, and so on. The adoption of a code presumes some set of principles by virtue of which the separate provisions cohere. A theory of punishment supplies principles a legislature might use in ordering a code, and a court might use in interpreting it.

Indeed, most American codes begin with provisions stating purposes to guide interpretation. The New York Penal Law, declaring that its provisions must be construed "to promote justice and effect the objects of the law" identifies these purposes as follows:

1. To proscribe conduct which unjustifiably and inexcusably causes or threatens substantial harm to individual or public interests;
2. To give fair warning of the nature of the conduct proscribed and of the sentences authorized upon conviction;
3. To define the act or omission and the accompanying mental state which constitute each offense;
4. To differentiate on reasonable grounds between serious and minor offenses and to prescribe proportionate penalties therefor;
5. To provide for an appropriate public response to particular offenses, including consideration of the consequences of the offense for the victim, including the victim's family, and the community; and
6. To insure the public safety by preventing the commission of offenses through the deterrent influence of the sentences authorized, the rehabilitation of those convicted, the promotion of their successful and

> productive reentry and reintegration into society, and their confinement when required in the interests of public protection.[1]

Notice that this provision does not offer a single purpose to guide interpretation, but several. Sections 1 through 3 set limits to the proscriptive function of the criminal law. They identify the basic requisites of blameworthiness developed in Chapter 1. Offenses require proscription, conduct, mental culpability, wrongfulness (the absence of justification), and responsibility (the absence of excuse). Section 1 embraces Mill's harm principle as a limit on offenses.

The last three sections set limits to the punitive function of the criminal law. Section 4 introduces a principle of proportionality as a limit on punishment. Offenses must be graded and punishments determined on the basis of the purposes of punishment. Sections 5 and 6 identify those purposes. Section 5 identifies the purposes of punishment as the expression of blame deserved by offenders and recognition owed victims. Section 6 identifies the purposes of punishment as the prevention of crime through deterrence, reform, and incapacitation of potential offenders. Yet here we encounter an interesting difficulty. The two sections identify two different types of purposes that seem inconsistent.

The purposes invoked in Section 5 conceive punishment as corrective, a retrospective response to offenses that have already occurred. Section 5 describes punishment as necessitated by propriety, a social obligation similar to an apology, a condolence, or a greeting. Punishment is proper insofar as deserved. By this measure, the suffering of the offender is intrinsically desirable, just as it is better to suffer remorse after wrongdoing than to feel gratified.

The purposes expressed in Section 6 conceive punishment as preventive, a prospective prophylactic against future offenses. Section 6 describes punishment as instrumentally rational, dictated by efficacy. Punishment is efficacious insofar as its benefits in preventing crime outweigh its costs. By this measure, the suffering of the offender counts as an intrinsic cost that the preventive consequences of punishment must outweigh, not an intrinsic benefit.

II. Corrective and Preventive Theories

Moral philosophers have seen corrective and preventive approaches to punishment as fundamentally inconsistent. According to John Rawls,

> [T]here are two justifications of punishment. What we may call the retributive view is that punishment is justified on the grounds that

1. N.Y. PENAL LAW § 1.05 (2015).

> wrongdoing merits punishment. It is morally fitting that a person who does wrong should suffer in proportion to his wrongdoing. That a criminal should be punished follows from his guilt, and the severity of the appropriate punishment depends on the depravity of his act. The state of affairs where a wrongdoer suffers punishment is morally better than the state of affairs where he does not; and it is better irrespective of any of the consequences of punishing him.
>
> What we may call the utilitarian view holds that on the principle that bygones are bygones and that only future consequences are material to present decisions, punishment is justifiable only by reference to the probable consequences of maintaining it as one of the devices of the social order. Wrongs committed in the past are, as such, not relevant considerations for deciding what to do. If punishment can be shown to promote effectively the interest of society it is justifiable, otherwise it is not.[2]

Rawls here distinguished between a retributive view of punishment as properly imposed on the basis of desert, and a utilitarian view of punishment as properly imposed on the basis of future social welfare. Writing as a moral philosopher, Rawls saw each conception of punishment as premised on a different view of ethics. Retributive punishment presupposed a deontological ethics, based on duties to fulfill commitments and to treat others impartially, regardless of consequences. By contrast, utilitarian punishment presupposed a consequentialist ethics, based on the goal of maximizing benefits and minimizing costs, regardless of the means. When looked at in this way, the purposes of the New York Penal Law seem contradictory.

But are deserved punishment and crime prevention really inconsistent purposes? Some philosophers have tried to reconcile them by arguing that punishment prevents crime most effectively, or with the least social cost, when it is deserved. Other philosophers have objected that these arguments make the reconciliation of prevention and desert contingent on social conditions that could be different, leaving the two aims opposed at the level of fundamental principle.

Because this is a book about criminal law, however, we are not going to take the approach of starting with a contestable moral theory and then using it to determine whether criminal law is permissible. After all, if our conclusion were negative, the book would be over before it began! Instead, we started with the observation that criminal law has proved itself a useful and perhaps even

2. John Rawls, *Two Concepts of Rules*, 44 PHIL. REV. 3, 5 (1955).

necessary institution in liberal societies such as ours, and we will approach the problem of normative theory in this chapter by asking: What goals and values are implicit in an institution of this type? This approach takes its inspiration in part from Michael Walzer's contextualist conception of value in *Spheres of Justice*, and Ronald Dworkin's method of "constructive interpretation" in normative legal theory.[3] Walzer argues that freedom is well served when society is governed by a collection of autonomous institutions, each distributing different goods for different reasons, and when decision-makers act on reasons appropriate to their institutional roles. Dworkin argues that officials act most lawfully when they exercise discretion on the basis of the normative principles that best justify the law as it has developed. Both thinkers try to identify the values immanent in particular institutions rather than starting from a universally valid definition of the good.

If we think about crime prevention and deserved punishment as particular goods rather than conceptions of the good, they are reconcilable. If we think of them as practices, we may find that certain institutions enable us to do both. Arguably both practices are necessary features of a rule of law, as described in Chapter 1. Law, as we have defined it, is a complex institution that often relies on both authority and force to achieve compliance. A rule of law discourages violence in part by providing a substitute for the expressive and dignitary effects of vengeance. If citizens are more willing to obey and help enforce a criminal law they see as just, then deserved punishment can have an important preventive effect. At the same time, citizen perceptions of law's justice will inevitably be influenced by its success in preventing violence. Unless law protects it will probably lack the authority to speak for the public in denouncing offenders and vindicating victims.

When we return the utilitarian and retributive theories of punishment to their origins among enlightenment era reformers, we may see their similarities as more important than their differences. Eighteenth-century European criminal justice relied on haphazardly administered capital and corporal punishment, publicly performed with elaborate ceremony and supplemented by informal networks of social control. Punishment even for petty crimes was severe if inflicted, but could often be avoided by those in favor with the rich, well born, or influential. Eighteenth-century liberals saw this situation as scandalous. Colonial Americans were particularly critical of English criminal justice.

In 1764 the Italian reformer Cesare Beccaria published the immediately influential *On Crimes and Punishments*, in which he argued for penalties that

---

3. Ronald Dworkin, Law's Empire 49–55 (1986); Michael Walzer, Spheres of Justice: A Defense of Pluralism and Equality 7–8 (1983).

were moderate but regular, certain, swift, and proportioned to the threat the offense posed to society.[4] Beccaria drew on social contract theory in arguing that no self-governing people would agree to capital punishment or other forms of excessive punishment. By contrast, moderate punishment was rationally justified as necessary to protect life and liberty. Beccaria drew on the utilitarianism of the Swiss philosopher Baron Helvetius[5] in arguing that penalties—fines and terms of imprisonment—should be just sufficient to deter: excessive punishment was contrary to the interests of society and the rights of its members.

The English legal philosopher and reformer Jeremy Bentham developed Beccaria's utilitarian arguments into a systematic theory of law: laws should take the form of legislatively enacted codes, aiming to achieve the greatest happiness and least pain for the greatest number.[6] Bentham's ideas, most fully expressed in his 1789 *Introduction to the Principles of Morals and Legislation*, achieved influence in England, France, and America.[7] Utilitarian thought held that punishment's sole aim was to prevent crime, and that it could do so by deterring, reforming, and incapacitating offenders. The nineteenth century witnessed the proliferation of penitentiaries, criminal codes, and regular police forces utilitarians had called for. In these important ways our contemporary criminal justice system is the realization of their vision.

Retributivism dates from the same period but had less influence on law reform at the time. Retributivist thought is generally traced to the writings of the eighteenth-century German philosopher Immanuel Kant, especially the *Groundwork of the Metaphysic of Morals* (1785) and the *Metaphysic of Morals* (1797).[8] Like Beccaria, Kant was much influenced by social contract theory. He saw law as necessary to the exercise of liberty. Yet he sternly objected to Beccaria and Bentham's utilitarian account of punishment:

> Juridical punishment can never be administered merely as a means to promoting another good either with regard to the criminal himself or to civil society, but must in all cases be imposed only because the individual on whom it is inflicted has committed a crime. For one man ought never to be dealt with merely as a means subservient to the purpose of

---

4. Cesare Beccaria, On Crimes and Punishments (1764).
5. Guyora Binder & Nicholas J. Smith, *Framed: Utilitarianism and Punishment of the Innocent*, 32 Rutgers L.J. 115, 156 (2000); Claude A. Helvetius, De L'esprit: Or Essays on the Mind and Its Several Faculties (1758).
6. Guyora Binder & Nicholas J. Smith, *Framed: Utilitarianism and Punishment of the Innocent*, 32 Rutgers L.J. 115, 166–68 (2000).
7. Jeremy Bentham, Introduction to the Principles of Morals and Legislation (1789).
8. Immanuel Kant, Metaphysics of Morals (1797); Immanuel Kant, Groundwork of the Metaphysics of Morals (1785).

> another. . . . He must first be found guilty and punishable, before there can be any thought of drawing from his punishment any benefit for himself or his fellow citizens. The penal law is a categorical imperative; and woe to him who creeps through the serpent-windings of utilitarianism to discover some advantage that may discharge him from the justice of punishment, or even from the due measure of it. . . .[9]

Kant's view of punishment flowed from his account of morality as fairness. To act morally was to respect the equality of all persons as autonomous, by pursuing only those ends that could be realized equally for everyone. Thus moral reasoning involved imagining rules that could fairly reconcile the conflicting desires of all persons. Moral action involved following such rules, whether or not others did likewise. Kant saw law as a fair social contract securing each person's freedom by the coercive enforcement of moral rules according a similar freedom to all. To exercise liberty was to enjoy the benefits of legal rights, and so to incur an obligation to respect and enforce the legal rights of others. This duty of cooperation included a duty to suffer punishment for culpably violating the rights of others. The exercise of legally protected liberty therefore implied a promise to respect rights or suffer punishment. Retributive punishment repaid a debt incurred by enjoying the benefits of a cooperative institution as a free-rider.[10]

Kant's insistence that the social consequences of punishment are irrelevant to its justice may seem puzzling, as he credited the rule of law with offering benefits unavailable in a state of nature. Yet for Kant, the most important benefit of the rule of law was not the security from violence it provided, but the dignity of legal personality. Law clothed the citizen with legal rights, and so legitimized the pursuit of desire as the exercise of freedom. Kant's claim about the benefits of punishment was similarly conceptual rather than consequential. Liability to deserved punishment was the price of enjoying legal rights and so was a mark of dignity. This dignitary benefit required that punishment be deserved but did not depend on its effectiveness in preventing crime. From Kant's viewpoint, a system of punishment may serve other desirable aims, but no other aim than justice can determine the distribution of punishment.

Although Kant and Bentham disagreed about the ultimate purpose of punishment they agreed about several key goals of reform. First, like Beccaria, both

---

9. Immanuel Kant, The Philosophy of Law: An Exposition of the Fundamental Principles of Jurisprudence as the Science of Right 195 (W. Hastie trans., 1887).

10. Guyora Binder, *Punishment Theory: Moral or Political?*, 5 Buff. Crim. L. Rev. 321, 350–66 (2002).

were democrats. Kant felt that law was an expression of freedom only insofar as people imposed it on themselves, which they could do collectively. Bentham eventually concluded that officials would only serve public welfare if they were answerable to the electorate. Second, Kant and Bentham both thought punishment should be proportionate to the expected harm of the crime. For Kant, greater wrongdoing deserved more reprobation. For Bentham, it merited more deterrence. Neither approved hanging petty thieves. Third, both favored certainty of punishment and more generally valued rules. For Kant, fidelity to law was a matter of principle. For Bentham, officials could not be trusted to serve the public unless they were constrained and monitored. Neither approved the corrupt and arbitrary use of pardons prevailing in eighteenth-century criminal justice. Fourth, both valued transparent government. For Kant, honesty was a moral imperative. For Bentham, publicity was necessary for official accountability. Kant and Bentham would likely have agreed about most questions of criminal justice policy.

By adopting a mixed theory many modern thinkers have accommodated the Kantian constraint that only desert determine the distribution of punishment. They reason that the aim of crime prevention justifies having the institution of punishment but that desert properly constrains its distribution.[11]

One argument for such a mixed theory is that retributivism and utilitarianism are not incompatible, because they answer different questions. Recall that punishment combines two features, blame and deprivation. Retributivism explains why and when the imposition of blame is justified: blame is justified when, and because, it is deserved. On the other hand, utilitarianism explains why and when suffering is justified. For utilitarians suffering is only justified by the prospect of preventing greater suffering. Because, by definition, punishment requires both blame and suffering, both retributivist and utilitarian constraints must arguably be met for punishment to be justified.

Another argument for a desert-constrained utilitarianism emphasizes the "utility of desert." Noting the efficacy of legitimacy in motivating compliance, Paul Robinson and John Darley have argued that punishment best prevents crime by conforming to popular notions of desert.[12] Our discussion of the rule of law in Chapter 1 suggested that other benefits accompany the crime-preventive effects of deserved punishment. State punishment of violence humbles wrongdoers and restores the injured dignity of victims more reliably than vengeance, and without the risk of further retaliation. By making dignity dependent on

11. H.L.A. Hart, Punishment and Responsibility: Essays in the Philosophy of Law 1–27 (1968); John Rawls, *Two Concepts of Rules*, 44 Phil. Rev. 3, 5 (1955).

12. Paul H. Robinson & John M. Darley, *The Utility of Desert*, 91 Nw. U. L. Rev. 453 (1997).

state protection rather than self-help, deserved punishment gives those subject to the criminal law a motive to comply with law and a substantial stake in its success. Deserved punishment therefore provides enhanced security of status for individuals, and enhanced authority and legitimacy for the state. These benefits indirectly prevent crime. Separating the coercive use of force from the expression of deserved blame would preclude these benefits.

III. Preventive Purposes

Utilitarians argued that crime prevention could justify punishment only if the expected benefits of crime prevention outweighed the aggregate expected costs—including the certain costs to the offenders themselves and those who depended on them. Bentham regarded punishment as undesirable unless it actually achieved prevention substantial enough to outweigh its considerable social costs and to exceed the net benefits of alternative strategies of prevention. Thus, one implication of utilitarianism is a limiting principle, permitting punishment only insofar as necessary to improve social welfare. Nevertheless, utilitarians identified three mechanisms by which punishment could prevent crime: deterrence, rehabilitation, and incapacitation.

A. Deterrence

Deterrence prevents crime by reducing the incentive to commit it. It is common to distinguish general deterrence (discouraging all potential offenders) from special deterrence (discouraging the person punished). Special deterrence is one method of changing the behavior of past offenders and reducing their recidivism; it relies on raising the expected cost or opportunity cost of offending. By contrast, rehabilitation seeks to discourage offending by changing preferences rather than changing costs. For Beccaria and Bentham, reducing recidivism was an ancillary benefit of punishment. General deterrence was the main purpose of criminal punishment.

Punishment is not the only method of deterring crime. Policymakers can adjust the incentives facing potential offenders by making crime less attractive or alternative pursuits more attractive. We can discourage crime by using locks, guards, cameras, etc. to make it harder to achieve its rewards. We can also make crime harder to achieve—and so more costly—by putting fences around potential offenders rather than their targets. Thus incapacitation strategies, discussed below, overlap with this strategy of deterring crime by securing its targets. There are also several ways to make alternative pursuits more appealing. Policymakers can offer education, jobs, cash, or status-enhancing honors to those who avoid crime. In short, policymakers can deter crime through positive as well as negative sanctions.

On what assumptions may negative sanctions—penalties—be expected to deter crime? According to political scientist James Q. Wilson, deterrence requires that (1) potential offenders choose whether to offend on the basis of a rational calculus of costs and benefits, (2) punishment is relatively swift and certain, and (3) potential offenders are aware of expected penalties. If these assumptions apply, potential offenders will calculate that crime does not pay, and avoid it.[13]

Deterrence theory, thus described, addresses crime and compliance caused by circumstances—the incentives facing the offender—rather than individual character. Deterrence strategies can only make a difference insofar as actors are greedy and self-regarding. Thus deterrence theory imagines legal subjects as disposed to offend whenever they can get away with it, and compliant only out of complacency or cowardice rather than conscience. In this respect, the premises of deterrence theory are at odds with a defining feature of punishment, the implication of blame. Ironically, however, the expression of blame may be the feature of punishment with the greatest power to deter. Reflecting on widespread resistance to Prohibition and the Vietnam draft, Louis Michael Seidman concluded that "large numbers of people are willing to play the crime game when the threatened punishment no longer communicates moral disapproval."[14] Psychologist Tom Tyler has found that compliance is best predicted by belief in the law's legitimacy, whereas criminologist Gary LaFree and historian Randolph Roth have both found that American homicide rates rise and fall with distrust in government.[15]

Although Wilson claims that deterrence depends on a high probability of punishment, some economists have assumed the opposite. They reason that because the expected cost should be the severity of punishment multiplied by its probability, rational actors should be indifferent between a high probability of a low penalty and a low probability of a high penalty. Assuming the public can save by investigating and prosecuting fewer crimes, it should be cost-effective

---

13. James Q. Wilson, Thinking about Crime 145–48 (1975).

14. Louis M. Seidman, *Soldiers, Martyrs, and Criminals: Utilitarian Theory and the Problem of Crime Control*, 94 Yale L.J. 315, 332–34 (1984).

15. Tom R. Tyler, Why People Obey the Law 178, 269–70 (2006); Gary LaFree, Losing Legitimacy: Street Crime and the Decline of Social Institutions in America (1998); Randolph Roth, American Homicide 1–26 (2009).

to punish a few offenders very severely.[16] Indeed, if threatened penalties are sufficiently extreme it should never be necessary to inflict them, and the combined cost of crime and punishment should drop to zero.

Despite this tempting free-lunch logic, empirical studies generally show a preventive effect only for increases in the probability of punishment, not for increases in severity.[17] Several related explanations have been offered for diminishing returns to sentence length. Perhaps the status degradation implied by conviction and imprisonment is a more important deterrent than the day-to-day deprivation entailed by incarceration. People tend to find a loss of status traumatic, but may adapt to misfortune as time passes.[18] In addition, most people discount their future welfare, and offenders may be more shortsighted than the average. Similarly, offenders may be risk-preferring and may be attracted to a high stakes gamble.[19] Very long determinate sentences also undermine deterrence of offenses in prison, by delaying and reducing any resulting penalties. Conversely, mild but consistent punishment may motivate compliance by signaling the effectuality and fairness of law enforcement institutions. Certainly Beccaria and Bentham expected that mild but certain punishment would strengthen public confidence in law, and would better deter crime. We will see that this basic tenet of deterrence theory—that certainty of punishment is more efficacious then severity—has important implications across a wide range of policy issues.

How well do the assumptions of deterrence theory apply to the American criminal justice system? Wilson notes that a majority of offenders escape punishment,[20] while the severity of American punishment is extremely high by global standards. From the standpoint of deterrence theory, these very severe sentences are a waste of resources and of suffering. Criminologists note that many crimes, including some of the crimes of violence we most want to deter, often seem impulsive or expressive, rather than calculated. Even such apparently economic crimes as bank robbery are hard to explain on instrumental grounds, as perpetrators face an 80 percent chance of apprehension and often

16. Richard Posner, Economic Analysis of Law 164–72 (1977); Gary Becker, *Crime and Punishment: An Economic Approach*, 76 J. Pol. Econ. 169, 183–85, 191–93 (1968).

17. Anthony N. Doob & Cheryl M. Webster, *Sentence Severity and Crime: Accepting the Null Hypothesis*, 30 Crime & Just. 143, 181–89 (2003).

18. Jeremy A. Blumenthal, *Law and the Emotions: The Problems of Affective Forecasting*, 80 Indiana L.J. 155, 168–69 (2005).

19. Louis M. Seidman, *Soldiers, Martyrs, and Criminals: Utilitarian Theory and the Problem of Crime Control*, 94 Yale L.J. 315, 332–34 (1984); Michael K. Block & Robert C. Lind, *An Economic Analysis of Crimes Punishable by Imprisonment*, 4 J. Legal Stud. 479, 481 (1975).

20. James Q. Wilson, Thinking about Crime 117–19 (1975).

squander the proceeds of their crimes immediately.[21] Some offenders court rather than shun risk and notoriety. Roth notes that killers are often depressed or suicidal, and speculates that people who want to die are not easily deterred by threats.[22]

Of course it could be that punishment is doing its job of deterring the instrumentally rational majority, and that a residue of expressively motivated crime is exactly what we would expect. Yet studies such as Tyler's suggest that compliance with law is usually no more instrumentally motivated than offending. Thus, it is hard to be confident that the threat of punishment deters anyone.

The possibility that offenders typically lack the capacity to be influenced by deterrent threats raises a conundrum. Is deterrence advanced by punishing those who could not have been deterred? Utilitarians have offered two contradictory answers. Bentham insisted that threatening the undeterrable was pointless and punishing them wasteful. He argued that they should be excused.[23] H.L.A. Hart argued that others might be deterred by such punishment. He reasoned that potential offenders may not know the capacities of those punished, or may hope to escape punishment by faking incapacity.[24] Punishing the undeterrable arguably raises the certainty of punishing the deterrable. Hart's argument is disturbing because it suggests that deterrence theory justifies punishing those who are not truly blameworthy. Indeed, Louis Michael Seidman has sharpened this point by arguing that a rational system of general deterrence will deter the deterrable, and will therefore punish only the helplessly undeterrable.[25] If so, Bentham's approach of sparing the undeterrable would leave criminal law with no one to punish. Hart's argument also points to another problem with efforts to increase deterrence at the margins by fine-tuning legal doctrine. Potential offenders may know very little about the law.[26]

B. Rehabilitation

Like deterrence, rehabilitation was an important aim of punishment, inspiring reformers in the late eighteenth and early nineteenth centuries. In proposing

---

21. Jack Katz, Seductions of Crime: Moral and Sensual Attractions in Doing Evil 164–65 (1988).
22. Randolph Roth, American Homicide 10 (2009).
23. Jeremy Bentham, The Theory of Legislation 322 (1931).
24. H.L.A. Hart, Punishment and Responsibility: Essays in the Philosophy of Law 41–44 (1968).
25. Louis M. Seidman, *Soldiers, Martyrs, and Criminals: Utilitarian Theory and the Problem of Crime Control*, 94 Yale L.J. 315, 329 (1984).
26. Paul H. Robinson & John M. Darley, *The Utility of Desert*, 91 Nw. U. L. Rev. 453, 460 (1997).

that imprisonment replace execution as the principal penal sanction, Bentham imagined the prison as a social science laboratory, a "Panopticon" in which prisoner conduct would be constantly observed and evaluated. Knowing they were being observed, prisoners would become habituated to docile and industrious behavior.[27] According to the well-known argument of Michel Foucault, Bentham's prison became a model for the organization of many modern institutions, including schools, factories and offices, and mental hospitals, all premised on the expectation that monitoring would inculcate self-discipline.[28]

American reformers and legislators combined Bentham's techniques with their own evangelical optimism. Beginning at the end of the eighteenth century, almost every new American state adopted a new criminal code organized around terms of imprisonment, and built an expensive new penitentiary to house the prisoners. They imagined penitentiaries as refuges from the corrupting influences of urban life, where prisoners could quietly labor, read scripture, and repent. American penitentiaries were anticipated with great interest and greeted with enthusiasm. De Tocqueville traveled to the United States to see its prisons, not its democracy. Although we may today think of prisons as hellish emblems of societal failure, they were originally seen as symbols of enlightened optimism about humanity's perfectibility. Rehabilitation was the American prison's original program and purpose.[29] Moreover, this program was initially seen as successful. The new criminal justice system of codes, prisons, and police coincided with an emergent industrial society that achieved new forms of social order. As far as it is possible to tell, violent crime decreased during the first half of the nineteenth century in America, and continued to decline thereafter in Europe.[30]

By the late nineteenth century, social reformers were less enthusiastic about prisons, which were often administered with much more concern for cost and revenue than the well-being of prisoners. Prison administrators cut rehabilitative programs to save money or to simplify the task of guarding the inmates. Many gave prisoners mind-numbing industrial work in hope of turning a profit. Yet progressive era reformers remained committed to rehabilitation as a central goal of punishment. Progressive penology reflected a new confidence in the

---

27. Michel Foucault, Discipline and Punish: The Birth of the Prison 243 (1975); Jeremy Bentham, Panopticon, or the Inspection House 1–3 (1791).
28. Michel Foucault, Discipline and Punish: The Birth of the Prison 288 (1975); David J. Rothman, The Discovery of the Asylum 107 (1971).
29. Edward L. Rubin, *The Inevitability of Rehabilitation*, 19 Law & Inequality 343, 347 (2001); David J. Rothman, The Discovery of the Asylum 79–88, 105, 107 (1971).
30. Samuel Walker, Popular Justice: A History of American Criminal Justice 105–07, 221–22 (1980).

potential of social science to understand, and of social policy to improve urban life. Accordingly, reformers came to believe that many offenders could be better managed and rehabilitated in the community, and that the hope of returning home would incentivize prisoners to reform. Rehabilitation remained the goal, with probation and parole now the favored means.[31] Yet few resources were devoted to implementing these reforms until after World War II. By that time ideas about rehabilitation were increasingly influenced by Freudian psychoanalysis and other models of abnormal personality. Rehabilitation came to be more associated with psychotherapy than with repentance or social reform.

In the 1970s the American consensus that rehabilitation was a central purpose of punishment suddenly collapsed. A number of factors contributed to this development. One was a widespread feeling that the criminal justice system had failed, as violent crime rates began to increase markedly in the 1960s, at the same time that incarceration rates had diminished, new criminal procedure rights had been recognized, capital punishment fell into disuse, and tensions between urban African-American communities and police boiled over into riots. Conservative politicians began to attack indeterminate sentencing and parole as part of a broader law-and-order agenda.

Law-and-order conservatives encountered little resistance to their attack on parole and indeterminate sentencing. Liberal reformers saw the highly discretionary institutions of indeterminate sentencing and parole as incompatible with the new due process rights they had fought for in criminal justice and other arenas. They saw rehabilitative aims as often specious pretexts for the reign of prejudice, corruption, and authoritarianism. Indeed, some civil libertarians objected that conditioning parole on participation in rehabilitative programs amounted to compulsory medical treatment.[32] Left-wing activists criticized the therapeutic orientation of rehabilitation as blaming criminality on the personalities of the poor and doing nothing to address the unjust social conditions they saw as causes of crime. Criminologists and criminal justice professionals lost confidence in the rehabilitative ideal when empirical studies suggested that rehabilitative programs in prison had no effect on recidivism.[33] A new generation of retributivist philosophers and legal theorists argued that respecting the autonomy of offenders required holding them accountable for their voluntary acts rather than viewing their offenses as symptoms of disease.

---

31. DAVID J. ROTHMAN, CONSCIENCE AND CONVENIENCE: THE ASYLUM AND ITS ALTERNATIVES IN PROGRESSIVE AMERICA 43–45 (1980).
32. Francis A. Allen, *Criminal Justice, Legal Values, and the Rehabilitative Ideal*, 50 J. CRIM. L. & CRIMINOLOGY 226, 229–30 (1959).
33. Robert Martinson, *What Works?—Questions and Answers about Prison Reform*, 35 PUB. INT. 22, 25 (1974).

Retributivist theorists noted that rehabilitative concerns could justify incarcerating petty offenders far longer than they deserved, if their backgrounds and circumstances indicated their prospects for rehabilitation were poor. Retributivist scholars formed common cause with due process liberals and law-and-order conservatives in pressing for determinate sentencing reforms.[34] The result was the adoption of determinate sentencing schemes that—in combination with other factors, such as higher penalties for drug offenders and recidivists—greatly lengthened sentences and increased incarceration rates. Over the next 35 years, the population in prisons and jails increased by some sevenfold,[35] contrary to the intentions of liberal proponents of determinate sentencing. It continued to increase even after violent crime rates began to decrease during the 1990s. Eventually the prison population stabilized, and has even dropped in some states in recent years.

C. Incapacitation

While legal theorists showed a new interest in retribution during the last decades of the twentieth century, political leaders more commonly emphasized the goal of incapacitation. Rational skepticism about the efficacy of rehabilitation and deterrence combined with demagoguery to popularize an image of offenders as incorrigible predators. This demonization of offenders certainly reflected late twentieth-century racial politics. The success of the civil rights movement in discouraging the overt expression of prejudice by public officials did not eliminate racial animus among the public, or the electoral benefits of appealing to it. Because violent crime was increasing, because offenders were disproportionately black, because riots had associated black protest with violence, and because the Warren Court was associated with both civil rights and criminal justice reforms, crime became one of a number of proxy issues by which political leaders could make a coded appeal to race.[36]

Political leaders implied that criminality was an immutable characteristic of offenders, so that nothing but force could prevent crime. On this logic, releasing prisoners made recidivism inevitable, and showed greater concern

34. Kate Stith & Jose Cabranes, Fear of Judging: Sentencing Guidelines in the Federal Courts 34 (1998); *see* Richard Singer, Just Deserts: Sentencing Based on Equality and Desert (1979); Andrew Von Hirsch, Doing Justice: The Choice of Punishments (1976); Twentieth Century Fund, Fair and Certain Punishment (1976).

35. Michelle Alexander, The New Jim Crow 6 (2010).

36. Jonathan Simon, Governing through Crime: How the War on Crime Transformed American Democracy and Created a Culture of Fear 141–76 (2007).

for criminals than victims. In an era of political competition over toughness on crime, both parties collaborated on lengthening sentences. New sentencing guidelines typically based sentences on prior convictions as well as the offense of conviction. In many jurisdictions repeat offenders could face life sentences for relatively minor offenses. When harsh recidivist sentences were challenged in court as disproportionate, they were upheld not as deserved, but as justifiably aimed at incapacitating dangerous offenders.

On what assumptions do prison terms incapacitate offenders? According to Wilson, incapacitative incarceration presupposes that (1) past offenders are more likely than the rest of the population to offend in the future if left at large; (2) if removed, they will not be replaced by others drawn to exploit newly available opportunities to offend; and (3) they will not become more dangerous in prison and commit more or worse crimes upon subsequent release than they otherwise would have.[37] Notice that the first and second assumptions of incapacitation theory, that risk inheres in offenders rather than situations, is somewhat contrary to the assumptions of deterrence theory. The second assumption of incapacitation theory seems particularly inapt for drug trafficking offenses, where we would expect a substantial replacement effect.[38] Yet increased drug enforcement is a substantial factor in the higher incarceration rates of recent decades.[39] About 34 percent of state prison inmates were serving time for drug offenses in 2004.[40]

Criminologists distinguish between collective incapacitation (incapacitation of all offenders) and selective incapacitation (incapacitation of those most likely to offend again). Collective incapacitation will be most cost-effective when past offenders are few in number and all very likely to offend again if released. Conversely, if offending is widely distributed, collective incapacitation becomes prohibitively costly. In fact, a substantial portion of adult males offend over the course of their lifetimes.[41] Under such conditions, incapacitation can only be cost-effective if applied selectively to a subset of offenders. This requires the additional assumptions that some offenders are far more likely to commit crimes than others, and that these offenders can be identified.

There is reason to think selective incapacitation can work. A 1982 Rand Corporation study of prisoners found that a relatively small group of

---

37. JAMES Q. WILSON, THINKING ABOUT CRIME 133–35 (1975).
38. RYAN S. KING ET AL., INCARCERATION AND CRIME: A COMPLEX RELATIONSHIP 6 (2005).
39. WILLIAM J. STUNTZ, COLLAPSE OF AMERICAN CRIMINAL JUSTICE 267–69 (2011); MICHELLE ALEXANDER, THE NEW JIM CROW 60 (2010).
40. BUREAU OF JUSTICE STATISTICS, DRUGS AND CRIME FACTS, 2007, NCJ165148.
41. Alfred Blumstein & Jacqueline Cohen, *Characterizing Criminal Careers*, 237 SCI. 985, 987 (1987).

offenders had committed a majority of crimes committed by the group as a whole. Moreover, the study claimed it could predict with 80 percent probability who would be a low and who would be a moderate to high rate offender. Predictive factors were recent unemployment, and a history of crime, incarceration, and drug use, both recently and as a juvenile.[42]

Although these findings suggested that selective incapacitation was possible, they did not necessarily justify the high rates of incarceration and lengthy recidivist sentences that are often defended as incapacitative. The Rand study showed that we already had a lot of the "right" people in prison, and could have reduced the financial and human cost of incapacitation by imposing less punishment on the predicted low rate offenders. It did not show we should imprison more offenders, because it did not tell us how many high rate offenders remained at large. Nor did it justify the assumption that unapprehended offenders with risk factors were as likely to offend as apprehended offenders with risk factors. It stands to reason that the highest rate offenders are also the offenders most likely to be apprehended.[43] If so, offenders outside of prison with risk factors should be less dangerous than those already in prison.[44] Nor did the Rand study imply that we can achieve cost-effective incapacitation by lengthening prison terms, because it did not demonstrate a power to predict individuals' rates of offending in the distant future. Criminals tend to offend at much lower rates as they get older, so indicators of high rate offending in the recent past do not predict high rate offending decades down the road.

One controversial feature of selective incapacitation is the possible disconnect between risk factors and culpability. Thus, unemployment is certainly not criminal, and probably not blameworthy. Youthful offenses and drug involvement may reflect the absence or incapacity of parents rather than the fault of the child. More fundamentally, risk of future offending does not necessarily depend on guilt for a recent offense. Thus, it is not obvious why the incapacitation theorist should restrict incarceration to the guilty, or accompany it with denunciation. Indeed, incapacitation appears to justify preventive detention better than it justifies punishment.

Yet, on closer inspection, the idea of incapacitative incarceration incorporates hidden judgments of blame and desert. First, incapacitation strategies assign causal responsibility for crime to offenders rather than their situations or social environments, often without much empirical evidence. Second, the

---

42. Peter W. Greenwood & Allan Abrahamse, Selective Incapacitation xv–xii (1982).
43. Ryan S. King et al., Incarceration and Crime: A Complex Relationship 6 (2005).
44. Franklin Zimring & Gordon Hawkins, Incapacitation: Penal Confinement and the Restraint of Crime 83–84 (1995).

unexamined equation of incarceration with incapacitation reflects indifference to the welfare of offenders. This equation entails either the empirical assumption that offenders cannot reoffend in prison, or the normative assumption that such offending does no harm.

We can easily dismiss the first of these possibilities. Although reliable statistics on crime in prison are notoriously difficult to gather, all evidence indicates violent crimes against the person are disturbingly common in American prisons. While formerly high homicide rates have fallen, victim-reported rates of assault and sexual assault remain extraordinarily high.[45] The concentration of aggressive young men in close quarters with no escape from confrontation may make crimes of violence more rather than less likely for this population.

Thus, incarceration "incapacitates" only if all this crime committed against prisoners does not count. From the perspective of utilitarianism, which weighs the welfare of all persons equally, however, crime against prisoners cannot be ignored. If prisoners offend at the same rates they would outside of prison, incarceration merely redistributes the risk of victimization to offenders. This redistribution of crime risk is advantageous only on the assumption that we need not prevent crime against offenders, because they deserve it. When put baldly in this way, the claim that prisoners deserve to be assaulted or raped is disturbing. If officially imposed, such corporal punishment would be barred by the Eighth Amendment as inherently inhumane.

It is also difficult to justify lengthy recidivist sentences as deserved. In upholding a sentence of 25 years-to-life for stealing three golf clubs imposed under California's "three strikes" law, the Supreme Court instead justified it as conducive to "public safety," because incapacitative.[46] George Fletcher has argued that retributivism offers no convincing account of why a second offense deserves more punishment than an equally culpable and equally harmful first offense.[47] We might punish the recidivist for failing to rehabilitate himself, but this verges on punishing the offender for having a bad character rather than committing a bad act. We will see in Chapter 4 that punishing propensities violates constitutional due process. Although incapacitative sentences arguably violate desert, incapacitation theory's implicit exclusion of prisoners from the "public" is a desert concept, not a utility one. It seems doubtful that

---

45. ALLAN J. BECK & PAIGE M. HARRISON, SEXUAL VICTIMIZATION IN PRISONS & JAILS REPORTED BY INMATES 2008–09, at 6 (2010); HUMAN RIGHTS WATCH, NO ESCAPE: MALE RAPE IN U.S. PRISONS 1–2 (2001); Daniel Lockwood, *Issues in Prison Sexual Violence*, *in* PRISON VIOLENCE IN AMERICA 97–102 (Michael C. Braswell et al. eds., 1994).

46. Ewing v. California, 538 U.S. 11, 26 (2003).

47. GEORGE P. FLETCHER, RETHINKING CRIMINAL LAW 460–66 (1978).

incapacitation as currently conceptualized and put into practice can be justified on either utilitarian or retributive premises.

IV. Retribution

Like utilitarianism, retributivism provides both a limiting principle and an affirmative justification for punishment. The limiting principle forbids undeserved (rather than inefficacious) punishment. The affirmative justification is that deserved punishment is fair (whether or not it is beneficial).

Retributivists have offered three sorts of arguments to demonstrate the fairness of deserved punishment: intuitionist arguments, contractarian arguments, and dignitary arguments.

A. The Intuitionist Argument

Intuitionist arguments try to show that desert is the only proper consideration in deciding whether to punish, by posing hypothetical cases requiring readers to choose whether to pursue social welfare by treating identifiable individuals in undeserved ways.

Philosophers have imagined scenarios in which utilitarianism would require punishing the innocent. Thus E.F. Carritt argued that if authorities were unable to apprehend killers, utilitarianism would justify framing and hanging an innocent to deter murder.[48] H.J. McCloskey imagined a racist mob in the Jim Crow era South gathering in response to a crime against a white by an unidentified African American. He speculated that if a sheriff were unable to identify the offender, he might maximize utility by framing and punishing an innocent African American to prevent a riot that might kill many African Americans.[49] Both philosophers urged readers to reject a utilitarian justification for punishing the guilty, on the grounds that it could also justify punishing the innocent.

Critics of utilitarianism have also tried to mobilize moral intuitions against utility as a limiting principle. Legal theorist Michael Moore imagined a robber and rapist who inherited wealth and became physically disabled before sentencing, with the result that he posed little danger of recidivism. He argued that if it were possible to cheaply and effectively fool the public into believing the robber and rapist had been punished, it would be utility maximizing to

48. E.F. Carritt, Ethical and Political Thinking 65 (1947).
49. H.J. McCloskey, *A Non-utilitarian Approach to Punishment*, 9 Inquiry 249, 253 (1965).

do so, as this would achieve the deterrent benefits of punishment without the costs. Moore argued deserved punishment maintains its appeal even when it will have no beneficial effect.[50]

These intuitionist arguments share a common flaw. All three hypotheticals involve well-meaning officials achieving utility by deceiving the public. They have to make the public believe that the guilty are being punished in order to achieve deterrence. An announced policy of punishing the innocent and sparing the guilty would be counterproductive.[51] Would it maximize utility to empower officials to deceive the public in this way? Certainly Bentham did not think so. He offered public utility as a criterion for testing publicly monitored government policy in open debate before a democratic electorate. He assumed that public officials are governed by the same selfish motives as potential offenders, and will serve the public welfare only insofar as properly incentivized and monitored. Moreover, he saw insecurity about government repression and corruption as frequent impediments to happiness.[52] Thus a publicly announced policy of permitting officials to deceive the public would be destructive of utility. A secret policy would violate the preconditions for the pursuit of utility and would be detected and punished in a properly utilitarian state.

Much of the critical force of these examples derives from their misattribution of dishonesty and lawlessness to utilitarianism. One could create a similarly unfair portrait of retributivism by identifying it with a character such as the detective in *A Touch of Evil* who frames the guilty,[53] or the officers in *Magnum Force* who secretly execute murderers.[54] Kant, who took both honesty and obedience to law very seriously, would not have approved. Both Bentham and Kant were very committed to a rule of law. They just had different accounts of why that was a good thing.

The charge that utilitarianism can justify punishing the innocent is also unfair because *both* utilitarianism and retributivism require that we sometimes punish the innocent and sometimes spare the guilty. Any criminal justice system will make errors, regardless of how it allocates the burden of proof. Punishing the innocent is the inevitable price of punishing the guilty, while sparing the guilty is the inevitable price of sparing the innocent. We cannot decrease false positives without increasing false negatives, or decrease false negatives without increasing false positives. Retributivism cannot view

50. MICHAEL S. MOORE, LAW AND PSYCHIATRY: RETHINKING THE RELATIONSHIP 233–43 (1984).
51. John Rawls, *Two Concepts of Rules*, 44 PHIL. REV. 3, 12 (1955).
52. Guyora Binder & Nicholas J. Smith, *Framed: Utilitarianism and Punishment of the Innocent*, 32 RUTGERS L.J. 115, 153–54 (2000).
53. TOUCH OF EVIL (Universal Pictures 1958).
54. MAGNUM FORCE (Warner Brothers 1973).

punishing all the guilty and sparing all the innocent as absolute duties, because they are in conflict and cannot both be achieved.

In addition, retributivists may intentionally impose deprivation on known innocents. Thus, they permit defensive force against aggressive psychotics.[55] They may preventively detain the dangerous who have not yet chosen aggression. Such preventive uses of violence and detention are acceptable to the retributivist as long as they are not called punishment.[56] The U.S. Supreme Court illustrated this attitude in upholding Kansas's scheme to preventively detain sex offenders on release from prison, on the ground that constitutional limits on punishment do not apply to a purely preventive use of force.[57] Why does retributivism permit coercion or deprivation of the innocent, but not punishment? Because the retributivist is primarily concerned about blame and denunciation, not suffering. What retributivism cannot permit is dishonest denunciation, blaming one who is known to be innocent.[58]

The kernel of truth in the intuitionist argument is that utilitarians may value the institution of blaming as a potent deterrent, but they cannot sincerely participate in it. Believing as they do that individuals are destined to pursue self-interest, and can only behave prosocially with the help of institutions, utilitarians may be too deterministic in their outlook to impose blame. If so, perhaps utilitarians do pretend to punish, and willingly afflict those they cannot genuinely regard as guilty.

B. The Contractarian Argument

The contractarian argument can be traced back to Kant. For Kant, the problem of justifying punishment was how to reconcile state coercion with moral freedom. His general approach was to identify freedom with responsiveness to reason rather than desire. Kant identified moral reason with impartiality. One freed oneself from selfish desire by acting in conformity to fair or universalizable rules. Kant saw just laws as a great blessing, because they would secure to each person not just what that person might want, but what that person was fairly entitled to. By accepting an obligation to obey just laws, citizens could achieve moral freedom and acquire legal rights. As penal enforcement of law

---

55. George P. Fletcher & Luis E. Chiesa, *Self-Defense and the Psychotic Aggressor*, *in* CRIMINAL LAW CONVERSATIONS 369–72 (Paul H. Robinson et al. eds., 2009).
56. Michael Corrado, *The Abolition of Punishment*, 35 SUFFOLK L. REV. 257, 265–72 (2001).
57. Kansas v. Hendricks, 521 U.S. 346, 369 (1997).
58. Dishonest exoneration would be problematic as well, but acquittal and dismissal of charges in our system implies only lack of proof, not exoneration.

against others was the condition for being secure in one's rights, the exercise of legal rights implied a duty to accept penal enforcement of the law. By exercising their rights citizens implicitly consented to the coercive enforcement of the laws enabling their freedom. They were morally obliged to suffer punishment for violating the law and to cooperate in imposing punishment. The proper measure of punishment owed was the injury or suffering imposed on a victim, so that punishment would dramatize the hypothetical self-defeat implicit in universalizing the offender's selfish behavior.

The modern legal philosopher Herbert Morris offered an influential reformulation of this argument.[59] Morris posited a civic duty to accept punishment for offending, analogous to the modern citizen's duties to pay taxes, serve in the military, or dispose of trash. Thus he conceived of security of persons and property as public goods generated by the cooperation of citizens in respecting one another's rights. Next Morris conceived of this cooperative scheme as a transaction, a contract binding each citizen to obey the law in return for receiving its protection. He characterized this compliance as a price, and characterized offenders as free-riders, enjoying the benefits of the rule of law without paying for them. This failure to earn their freedom left offenders indebted. Morris observed that the resulting unfairness might undermine the commitment of those otherwise disposed to comply. Punishment would not only coerce compliance among the selfish, it would also motivate compliance among the cooperative by reassuring them that this compliance would be effectual, and that the burdens of producing public goods would be shared. Punishment would pay the debt, thus restoring a fair "balance" of burdens and benefits.[60]

By analogizing security against crime to other public goods, Morris's argument assimilated together crimes infringing rights and crimes violating public duties, such as evading taxation, conscription, or sanitation regulations. All of these involved taking an unfair advantage by failing to share the burdens of cooperation. Some readers objected that talk of unfair advantages implied that the proper measure of punishment was the perpetrator's pleasure—which might be negligible for crimes of careless injury—rather than the victim's injury. Morris perhaps intended that punishment internalize the external costs of antisocial conduct, but this would have the odd consequence of permitting, for a price, crimes unusually gratifying to a particular offender.

Moreover, Morris's argument also invited scrutiny into the relationship between retributive justice and distributive justice. Was the overall balance of benefits and burdens in society fair? The poor have less property to protect

---

59. Hebert Morris, *Persons and Punishment*, 52 MONIST 475 (1968).
60. *Id.* at 483.

than the wealthy, and are often less well protected against personal violence. If the poor benefit less from the criminal justice system, are they less obliged to comply with it? Suppose their poverty can be ascribed to inadequate provision of public goods such as education, public transportation, and healthcare that would benefit all. Why should they cooperate in producing the public goods of property and personal security when others refuse to cooperate in producing public welfare? Suppose further that their poverty is a continuing effect of past injustices such as slavery or the expropriation of Native American lands. What if distributive unfairness contributes to the causes of crime, reducing the personal culpability of offenders, and spreading responsibility for crime more broadly? Does distributive injustice then undermine retributive justice, absolving the downtrodden of any duty to obey law, and depriving society of the moral standing to punish?[61] We can sharpen this problem by considering a pair of particularly troubling cases.

Alex Cabarga's parents moved with him to a commune when he was five. When he was nine, they abandoned him to the custody of Luis ("Tree Frog") Johnson, who beat and sexually molested Cabarga daily for many years. At age 17, Cabarga helped Johnson kidnap an 11-year-old boy and a 2-year-old girl. Cabarga and Johnson held these two children prisoner for 10 months, using beatings and starvation to repeatedly coerce the children into performing sex acts with both of them. The children were freed and Cabarga and Johnson were arrested, the day after Cabarga turned 18. Cabarga was convicted of multiple crimes and ultimately sentenced to 25 years in prison.[62]

In Jack Abbott's bestselling 1981 book, *In the Belly of the Beast: Letters from Prison*, he described his life as a "state-raised convict": in foster care from age 9, in detention from age 12 where he suffered physical abuse and spent two or three years of his childhood in solitary confinement.[63] Shortly after his release at 18 Abbott was imprisoned again for a petty offense and faced attacks from older prisoners. He soon killed a fellow prisoner in repelling a sexual assault. He earned a 3- to 20-year sentence. As an adult prisoner, Abbott claimed, he spent more than a decade in solitary confinement, and was beaten, starved, shackled, tear-gassed, drugged, kept in total darkness, and deprived of clothing, bedding, and sanitation. He wrote that long confinement with other violent offenders trained him to view any dispute as potentially fatal, and to view retreat as futile and dangerous. Abbott's eloquent writing attracted the attention and support

---

61. Jeffrie Murphy, *Marxism and Retribution*, 2 PHIL. & PUB. AFFAIRS, 217–43 (1973).
62. PAUL H. ROBINSON, WOULD YOU CONVICT?: SEVENTEEN CASES THAT CHALLENGED THE LAW 196–216 (1999).
63. JACK ABBOTT, IN THE BELLY OF THE BEAST (1981).

of Norman Mailer who helped win his release on parole at the age of 37. On the morning that his book was celebrated by the *New York Times*, Abbott misunderstood a waiter's efforts to lead him into an alley to relieve himself (the café had no restroom). Fearing an ambush, Abbott stabbed the waiter fatally in the chest. Charged with murder, Abbott's crime was mitigated to manslaughter as a result of his defense of extreme emotional disturbance. Yet he was sentenced under a recidivist sentencing scheme to 15 years to life, with no realistic prospect of ever being released again, and committed suicide in prison.[64]

Both defendants committed terrible crimes against innocent victims. Yet both suffered significant injustice. Cabarga was not afforded the protection of the very laws he violated. Abbott was abused by the criminal justice system itself. Moreover, in both cases, injustice played a causal role in the crimes and arguably diminished the offenders' responsibility. It is fair to say that neither offender had much opportunity to develop into a moral agent. Fairness seems an odd value to invoke in explaining their predictably severe punishment.

Do these considerations demonstrate that Cabarga and Abbott did not deserve punishment? Surely social injustice that also diminishes the victim's moral agency greatly attenuates blame. Moreover, Abbott and Cabarga are particularly vivid examples of a larger pattern of underprivileged children left unprotected by responsible adults, and reliant upon criminal associates for physical and economic security. David Simon's carefully researched TV dramas *The Corner*[65] and *The Wire*[66] powerfully illustrate this dynamic. Abbott and Cabarga make visible the submerged iceberg of determinism that threatens the coherence of retribution. If, as Kant claimed, we can only act autonomously pursuant to a moral law, how can we be blamed for our transgressions?

Must we then conclude that the only reasons to punish are utilitarian considerations of crime control? Not necessarily. First, the utilitarian case for punishing Abbott and Cabarga is no stronger than the retributive case. Although Abbott seemed very dangerous, his account of prison violence and his record remind us that dangerous offenders are no less dangerous in prison. Cabarga seemed unlikely to offend once out of the thrall of his abuser, and seemed a likely target for abuse in prison himself.

On the other hand, there are additional retributive considerations in favor of punishing both defendants, which Morris's contractarian argument does not quite capture. Failure to punish Abbott and Cabarga would surely have

---

64. John Kaplan, Robert Weisberg & Guyora Binder., Criminal Law: Cases and Materials 525–27 (2012).
65. The Corner (HBO 2000).
66. The Wire (HBO 2002–2008).

provoked popular outrage focusing on the victims of their crimes. Recall the New York Penal Law's formulation of its retributive aims recognized an obligation to provide "an appropriate public response" to crime "including consideration of the consequences of the offense for the victim, including the victim's family, and the community." Kant insisted that "even if a civil society resolved to dissolve itself . . . the last murderer lying in the prison ought to be executed . . . in order that . . . blood-guilt may not remain upon the people; for otherwise they might all be regarded as participators in the murder."[67] We have not adequately explained retributive punishment until we have accounted for this strange idea that a failure of government to punish makes other citizens complicit in wronging victims.

C. The Dignitary Argument

The dignitary argument is aimed at explaining this aspect of retribution. The philosopher Jean Hampton most fully developed such a dignitary account of retributivism. According to Hampton, justice requires us to do more than treat each other fairly. It requires that we recognize each other's equal worth as autonomous agents and treat each other with equal respect. Hampton saw social esteem as an important dimension of social life, often more important to humans than material goods. She saw subordination as inconsistent with freedom, and reinterpreted Kantian fairness as a concern with equal dignity. For Hampton, a liberal state was legitimate insofar as it achieved a liberal society, a society of equal dignity. She saw the achievement of such a society as a collective responsibility of all citizens, however, because social status is collectively produced. Hampton's liberal society was a cooperative social contract among citizens conferring dignity on each in return for respecting all.[68]

In Hampton's view, crime violates such a social contract by expressing disrespect for others. The intentional infliction of an injury demeans a victim. Other parties to the social contract are implicated in this degradation because even our awareness of victimization adds to the victim's humiliation. By tolerating such treatment we participate in constructing the victim's subordinate status as one who can be degraded. A failure to prevent or punish subordination accepts it as society's view of the victim. Society shares responsibility in much

---

67. IMMANUEL KANT, THE PHILOSOPHY OF LAW: AN EXPOSITION OF THE FUNDAMENTAL PRINCIPLES OF JURISPRUDENCE AS THE SCIENCE OF RIGHT 198 (W. Hastie trans., 1887).

68. Jean Hampton, *Correcting Harms versus Righting Wrongs: The Goal of Retribution*, 39 UCLA L. REV. 1659 (1991).

the way that we are implicated by failing to object to a racist joke or a malicious slander. Punishment cannot repair or correct the victim's physical injury, but it repairs the dignitary injury by publicly and authoritatively reasserting the victim's worth. It also checks the offender's claim to an undeserved status of superiority:

> Those who wrong others ... demean them. They incorrectly believe or else fail to realize that others' value rules out the treatment their actions have accorded the others, and they incorrectly believe or implicitly assume that their own value is high enough to make this treatment permissible. So, implicit in their wrongdoings is a message about their value relative to that of their victims.... A retributivist's commitment to punishment is ... a commitment to asserting moral truth in the face of its denial. If I have value equal to that of my assailant, then that must be made manifest after I have been victimized. By victimizing me, the wrongdoer has declared himself elevated with respect to me, acting as a superior who is permitted to use me for his purposes. A false moral claim has been made.... The retributivist demands that the false claim be corrected.[69]

On Hampton's view, punishment does not humiliate or degrade the offender, but humbles him by rejecting his claim to superiority. Hampton follows Hegel in insisting that retributive punishment recognizes the dignity of the offender by treating him as a self-determining voluntary actor, capable of recognizing the dignity of others and owing a responsibility to do so.[70]

Hampton's account of retributivism has the advantage of acknowledging the widespread sentiment that punishment of the offender is owed to the victim, and that punishment is a substitute for revenge. It explains why authoritative denunciation of offenders is obligatory. Yet it does not solve the problem of determinism or explain how it benefits the offender to pretend he is more autonomous than he truly is.

Hampton's dignitary argument also provokes other questions. Why does the vindication of the victim require that denunciation of the offender be accompanied by suffering? A possible answer is that it remedies the offender's undeserved gratification in the victim's suffering. The offender's gloating would compound the victim's humiliation. Yet this seems too neat: offenders often

---

69. JEFFRIE MURPHY & JEAN HAMPTON, FORGIVENESS AND MERCY 124–25 (1988).
70. Markus Dubber, *The Right to Be Punished: Autonomy and Its Demise in Modern Penal Thought*, 16 L. & HIST. REV. 113, 116–17 (1998).

seem myopically narcissistic rather than sadistic, and may not be thinking about their victims at all. It just seems to be an arbitrary convention of many cultures that no currency but the perpetrator's compelled suffering can pay for the indignity of being victimized by violence. Yet proponents of "restorative justice" point to communitarian cultures, in which an offender's sincere apology to the victim and other community members can restore the victim's dignity and begin the offender's rehabilitation and reintegration. They argue that such a process could better redress the victim's dignitary injury, while permitting a reduction in the offender's suffering.[71] Hampton's focus on the victim's dignity implies that the connection between the offender's suffering and the aim of retribution is highly contingent.

Moreover, although Hampton's argument explains the appeal of retribution for intentional injuries to individuals, not all crimes demean individuals. Crimes of reckless endangerment may place many unknown people at risk without harming any. Crimes against public institutions such as taxation and military service do not demean individuals. Here punishment negates an offender's implicit claim to undeserved superiority, but does not negate any victim's subordination. The dignitary argument at best justifies punishment of such crimes as permissible, not obligatory.

Finally, Hampton's account of retributive punishment as a means to equal dignity invites the same rejoinder as Morris's account of retributive punishment as a means of fairly sharing the burdens of social cooperation. Just as society distributes resources through a variety of institutions, it also confers dignity and status in many arenas. What if society fails its obligation to foster equal dignity in these other areas? Is retributive punishment still justified for offenders who have not enjoyed the equal dignity promised by the social contract? When society disproportionately punishes members of otherwise subordinated groups does it express a clear message of support for equal dignity? Might it not appear that offenders are being demeaned for their group membership rather than their offenses?

In sum, retributivism provides an illuminating account of why offenses are wrong and why offenders deserve to be denounced, but one that is undermined when social conditions are distributively unfair and criminogenic. Retributivism provides a less convincing account of why offenders deserve to suffer. The most compelling reasons for imposing suffering seem to be

71. *See* Erik Luna, *Punishment Theory, Holism, and the Procedural Conception of Restorative Justice*, 2003 UTAH L. REV. 207, 229–30 (2003); John Braithwaite, *A Future Where Punishment Is Marginalized*, 46 UCLA L. REV. 1727 (1999).

consequentialist—that this satisfies our culture's sense of justice, and failure to do so would erode support for the rule of law.

V. Proportional Punishment and Sentencing Process

The U.S. Supreme Court has brought theories of punishment to bear in determining whether the Eighth Amendment's prohibition on "cruel and unusual punishment" bars certain punishments as disproportionate,[72] and in determining the constraints on sentencing procedure imposed by the Sixth and Eighth Amendments.

A. Proportionality

Disproportionality of punishment is distinct from other violations of the Eighth Amendment. Thus torture and denaturalization have been held inherently cruel, regardless of the crime for which it is imposed. A punishment may be inherently "unusual" in the sense of not being authorized by statute or otherwise within the powers of the sentencing court. Punishment of any kind is impermissible unless imposed for criminal conduct.[73] Persons may be preventively detained because of their dangerousness alone, but may not be punished without a determination of guilt.[74] These limits are not proportionality requirements.

A proportionality limit concerns the severity or quantity of punishment. Disproportionate punishments are otherwise permissible punishments applied to otherwise punishable crimes. They are disproportionate if they are excessive in relation to the crime or the particular defendant's guilt for committing it. The Supreme Court first identified proportionality as a constraint on punishment in the 1910 case of *Weems v. United States*, overturning the sentence of an official in the Philippines to 15 years of hard labor for falsifying a public record. The Court applied the Eighth Amendment to require that "punishment for crime should be graduated and proportioned to offense."[75] Yet the

72. The Eighth Amendment's prohibition on "excessive fines" clearly imposes a proportionality limit. *See* United States v. Bajakajian, 524 U.S. 321, 324 (1998) (forfeiture of entire $350,000 taken out of United States "grossly disproportionate" for failure to report it to customs authorities).
73. Robinson v. California, 370 U.S. 660, 666–67 (1962).
74. Kansas v. Hendricks, 521 U.S. 346, 363 (1997).
75. Weems v. United States, 217 U.S. 349, 367 (1910).

Weems decision said nothing about how punishment should be proportioned to the offense.

Thus an important question is whether the Eighth Amendment adopts either retributivism or utilitarianism as principles limiting the amount of punishment. May offenders be punished more than they deserve? May offenders be punished more than is beneficial? May either utility or desert justify the severity of punishment (a disjunctive test), or must both be satisfied (a conjunctive test)? The Supreme Court has not adopted any one of these positions for all punishments and offenders. Instead it has applied two different multifactor tests. In its capital punishment cases, the Court developed a more demanding test, comparing sentences to those imposed by other jurisdictions and those imposed by the same jurisdiction for other crimes. This test appears to require a conjunction of desert and deterrence. In its cases on terms of incarceration, the Court developed a more lenient test. This test is disjunctive, permitting any rationale, including incapacitation, to justify a sentence, and insulates the sentence from comparison. Moreover, the boundary between the domains of these two tests has become fluid. There is currently no clear rule for determining which test applies in a given case.

Until recently, the Court divided proportionality issues into those involving death sentences and those involving sentences of incarceration. The proportionality test applied to capital punishment is derived from the Court's 1976 decision in *Gregg v. Georgia*, holding that capital punishment is not inherently cruel. A plurality of the Court adopted a two-part test for inherent cruelty (and most of the other justices followed a similar analysis without explicitly requiring it). First, the plurality required that penalties comport with "evolving standards of decency" as reflected in "contemporary community attitudes."[76] The plurality held (and a majority of justices agreed) that capital punishment met this test because the great majority of American jurisdictions had recently passed capital punishment statutes. Second, the plurality required that penalties comport with the "dignity of man" by not being "grossly out of proportion" and by avoiding unnecessary pain.[77] The determination of gross excessiveness involved comparison of the harm and culpability involved in the crime to the severity of punishment. One scholar has argued that any such judgment requires comparison to penalties imposed for other crimes in the same jurisdiction,[78] a comparison the Court made in later precluding capital punishment for rape.[79] According to the plurality, avoiding unnecessary pain meant

76. Gregg v. Georgia, 428 U.S. 153, 173, 190 (1976).
77. *Id.* at 173.
78. Youngjae Lee, *Constitutional Right against Excessive Punishment*, 91 VA. L. REV. 677, 693 (2005).
79. Coker v. Georgia, 433 U.S. 584, 600 (1977).

excluding punishments excessive relative to any crime, or useless relative to any legitimate purpose.

The plurality upheld capital punishment as potentially serving deterrence and retribution. A majority of justices agreed, while three justices opined that capital punishment also served incapacitation, although without specifying whether this purpose would have sufficed to justify capital punishment.[80] A deterrence justification for our current system of capital punishment seems unlikely: we would not expect a tiny risk of execution rather than life imprisonment to deter, and states without capital punishment as a group have much lower homicide rates than death penalty states do. Although a majority of the Court in *Gregg* acknowledged that there was no conclusive evidence that capital punishment increased deterrence, it held that legislatures could rationally believe that it did. The plurality added that retribution was a legitimate purpose of punishment necessary to maintain the rule of law by discouraging vengeance. The opinion left unclear whether the aim of deterrence alone would suffice to reconcile a penalty with human dignity.

Subsequent decisions applied this framework in holding capital punishment disproportionate for certain crimes. First, capital punishment was limited to murders accompanied by at least one statutorily enumerated aggravating circumstance that would narrow the class of death-eligible murderers. Second, the Court rejected mandatory death sentences even for aggravated murder. The court reasoned that mandatory death sentencing had been repudiated by a historical consensus, and that sentencing should reflect variations in culpability among cases of the same offense, and differences in an offender's criminal records and character.[81] Third, the Court ruled that accomplices in felony murderer (and possibly felony murderers themselves) must act with at least reckless indifference to a danger of death, in order to be death eligible.[82] The Court reasoned that absent this requirement the defendant was neither sufficiently culpable to deserve death, nor sufficiently aware of the risk of liability to be deterred by the penalty. Finally, the Court held the death penalty disproportionate for nonhomicidal crimes against individuals, because (1) public attitudes generally opposed its use for these crimes, and (2) it was, in the opinion of

---

80. *Gregg*, 428 U.S. at 226 (citing Roberts v. Louisiana, 428 U.S. 325, 350 (White, J., dissenting) (1976)).

81. Lockett v. Ohio, 438 U.S. 586, 606 (1978); Roberts v. Louisiana, 428 U.S. 325, 333 (1976); Woodson v. North Carolina, 428 U.S. 280, 304 (1976).

82. Tison v. Arizona, 481 U.S. 137, 158 (1987); Enmund v. Florida, 458 U.S. 782, 801 (1982). *Enmund* required either actual killing or intent to kill. *Tison* lowered the culpability requirement to recklessness, but perhaps extended it to those who actually killed, by implication. One decision reading these cases as requiring recklessness for the killer is Loving v. Hart, 47 M.J. 438 (1998).

the justices, undeserved for such crimes, which involved less harm and culpability than unaggravated premeditated murder (which could not be punished capitally).[83] In one such case the Court also argued that application of the death penalty to nonhomicides would have the perverse consequence of undermining the deterrence of murder by providing offenders in nonhomicidal capital crimes with an incentive to kill witnesses.[84]

In addition the Court has applied the *Gregg* framework to bar execution for crimes committed by certain classes of offenders, specifically juveniles and those with developmental intellectual disabilities. Again the Court relied on evidence of a consensus against executing such offenders. It also viewed such offenders as lacking sufficient culpability to deserve the most extreme penalty, and as less capable than typical adults of being deterred by consequences.[85]

In decisions concerning both the types of crimes and the types of offenders that are death eligible, the Supreme Court has repeatedly stated that capital punishment must be limited to "those offenders who commit 'a narrow category of the most serious crimes' and whose extreme culpability makes them 'the most deserving of execution.'"[86] Yet it has also repeatedly argued that the same considerations that reduced a defendant's culpability also reduced his deterrability. Indeed, the gravity of the offense, the desert of the punishment, and the deterrent necessity of the punishment have often seemed like barely distinguishable questions. Sometimes the justices argue that an offense deserves more punishment because it is more harmful; typically they add that it merits greater deterrence for this reason. Sometimes they argue an offender deserves less punishment because he or she is less culpable; almost invariably they add that deterrent threats will be less effective against such an actor. Accordingly, the cases on the proportionality of the death penalty are systematically ambiguous as to whether desert is an independent "side-constraint"[87] on death eligibility, or whether deterrence can justify execution of the undeserving. Further obscuring the Court's standard is the fact that the Court never finds descriptive disproportionality without normative disproportionality, and vice versa. Thus the Court treats a consensus against execution of a certain class of offenders as a sine qua non for finding execution undeserved or unnecessary for deterrence. Only under circumstances where a consensus eschews

83. Kennedy v. Louisiana, 554 U.S. 407, 420 (2008); *Coker*, 433 U.S. at 592, 598.
84. *Kennedy*, 554 U.S. at 445–46.
85. Roper v. Simmons, 543 U.S. 551, 571–75 (2005); Atkins v. Virginia, 536 U.S. 304, 321 (2002); Thompson v. Oklahoma, 487 U.S. 815, 836–39 (1988).
86. *Kennedy*, 554 U.S. at 420; *Roper*, 543 U.S. at 568; *Atkins*, 536 U.S. at 319.
87. Youngjae Lee, *Constitutional Right against Excessive Punishment*, 91 VA. L. REV. 677, 721–24 (2005).

capital punishment does the Court also find capital punishment grossly excessive and unnecessary.

In cases concerning terms of imprisonment, the court has developed a different and less demanding standard. Recall that the Eighth Amendment's proportionality limit was first applied in *Weems v. United States* to strike down a 15-year sentence to hard labor for a nonviolent offense.[88] Although the *Weems* Court described the standard of proportionalilty as progressive, contemplating that improvements in penology would decrease the suffering needed to prevent crime, the Court's standards instead became less demanding as sentences lengthened and prison populations rose in the last decades of the twentieth century. The court upheld a life sentence for a third petty fraud offense in the 1980 case of *Rummel v. Estelle*,[89] a sentence of 40 years for dealing marijuana in the 1982 case of *Hutto v. Davis*,[90] a sentence to life without parole for possessing two-thirds of a kilo of cocaine in the 1991 case of *Harmelin v. Michigan*,[91] and a recidivist sentence of 25 years to life for stealing three golf clubs in the 2003 case of *Ewing v. California*.[92]

To be sure a 1983 decision struck down a recidivist sentence of life without parole for a petty fraud offense.[93] The court considered the penalty undeserved for the crime, and compared it to sentences imposed by other jurisdictions or for other crimes. Later decisions repudiated this test, however, judging sentences by comparison only upon first finding gross disproportionality.[94] Yet, it is hard to see how the proportionality of a term of years could be judged without comparing it to sentences for more and less grave offenses. The only other metric, a Kantian requirement of equivalence between the suffering imposed on the offender and the harmfulness of the offense (discounted by any culpability less than purpose) would condemn all of the sentences under discussion.

How did the gross proportionality required for sentences of incarceration differ from the gross proportionality required for death sentences? In *Harmelin*, and especially in *Ewing*, the court seemed not to require retributive proportion or deterrent efficacy in particular, but instead to require that the sentence advanced any of the traditional purposes of punishment. Thus the Court included incapacitative and rehabilitative aims as justifications for prison terms.[95] Moreover, the required penological justifications for incarceration

88. Weems v. United States, 217 U.S. 349, 362–63 (1910).
89. Rummel v. Estelle, 445 U.S. 263, 264–65 (1980).
90. Hutto v. Davis, 454 U.S. 370, 370–72 (1982).
91. Harmelin v. Michigan, 501 U.S. 957, 961–62, 994–95 (1991).
92. Ewing v. California, 538 U.S. 11, 30–31 (2003).
93. Solem v. Helm, 463 U.S. 277, 281–84 (1983).
94. *Ewing*, 538 U.S. at 30; *Harmelin*, 501 U.S. at 1005.
95. *Ewing*, 538 U.S. at 26, 29; *Harmelin*, 501 U.S. at 999.

were clearly disjunctive. The Court justified recidivist sentences, in particular, on the basis of incapacitation alone, without regard to desert or deterrence. Indeed, life sentences for nonviolent offenses arguably create perversely anti-deterrent incentives to use violence to eliminate witnesses or resist arrest.

More recently the Court destabilized its proportionality jurisprudence by applying the proportionality requirement used in death penalty cases to terms of imprisonment. In *Graham v. Florida*, the Court barred application of a penalty of life without parole to a juvenile for a nonhomicide defense.[96] The Court found a consensus among sentencers to avoid such sentences, and rationalized that consensus primarily on the basis of desert. Thus the Court reasoned that young people are too impulsive to be as culpable as adults, and that nonhomicide crimes are less deserving of punishment than homicide crimes. In addition, the Court found juveniles less deterrable than adults due to the same characteristics that made them less culpable. Finally, the Court added that considerations of incapacitation and rehabilitation do not justify the permanent imprisonment of minors capable of further maturation.

Does the *Graham* decision signal the repudiation of the indulgent disjunctive standard for terms of imprisonment? Not quite, not yet. Justice Kennedy purported to distinguish the previous imprisonment decisions as applying to particular sentences rather than "categories" of "sentencing practice." Yet this distinction is elusive. Comparative review of any particular sentence requires us to treat the offense, the offender, and the penalty as tokens of types, and to see how often those types correlate. Thus, comparative review of any particular sentence necessarily identifies a category of sentencing practice so that Justice Kennedy's test does not exclude any sentences from review. Certainly Kennedy's distinction fails to distinguish *Graham* from previous proportionality challenges to terms of imprisonment. The category of "life without parole for juveniles committing nonhomicide offenses" is more specific than the category of "life without parole for nonviolent offenses." Thus, if Graham's sentence of life without parole for a violent home invasion requires full proportionality review, why not Harmelin's sentence of life without parole for drug possession? It remains to be seen whether *Graham* leads to reconsideration of the proportionality of recidivist and drug sentences. If it does, *Graham's* gratuitous discussion of incapacitation could be invoked to argue that incapacitation can still justify grossly undeserved terms of imprisonment for adults.

---

96. Graham v. Florida, 560 U.S. 48, 82 (2010).

B. Sentencing

The purposes of punishment also bear on another related constitutional issue: how sentencing decisions should be made. A punishment can be challenged, not because it is excessive per se, but because it was determined by an unreliable procedure. Yet the appropriate process depends in part on what defendants are being punished for.

If punishment is purely retributive, it should be determined entirely by the defendant's guilt for committing a particular wrong, rather than for the defendant's character or likelihood of committing future crimes. The most straightforwardly retributive sentencing process would simply mandate the same sentence for every instance of the same offense. If the sentencer distinguishes among those committing the same offense, the criteria should be restricted to the considerations used in grading offenses—that is, actual or expected harm of the offense, culpability, and partially justifying or excusing circumstances. Because a purely retributive sentence expresses the precise measure of society's condemnation, it should arguably be made by the same decision-maker that determines guilt at trial, and according to the same standards of proof. Finally, because post-conviction behavior is irrelevant, there is no obvious reason for retributive sentencing to be indeterminate.

General deterrence is also compatible with a fairly rigid sentencing process. Because certain punishment deters most effectively, deterrence favors mandatory punishments, publicized in advance, with no subsequent discretion to adjust the sentence based on post-offense conduct. On the other hand, because deterrence is premised on the broader utilitarian aim of cost-effective crime prevention, it can accommodate competing preventive considerations such as rewarding cooperation with law enforcement, or preventing further crime by the particular offender. This could justify a discretionary process and an indeterminate sentence.

Special prevention—embracing special deterrence, rehabilitation, and incapacitation—requires a highly individualized process. An incapacitative or rehabilitative sentence depends on speculative predictions of the offender's future behavior rather than the offense of conviction. Post-offense behavior may be relevant. Moreover, special prevention may be best served by suspending a portion of the sentence. Thus special prevention may call for indeterminate sentences.

The Supreme Court has considered constitutional constraints on sentencing process in two contexts: application of the cruel and unusual punishment clause to capital sentencing, and application of the Sixth Amendment right to a jury trial to sentencing guidelines.

In the area of capital sentencing, the Supreme Court struck down unguided jury discretion to sentence first degree murderers to death as unconstitutional in 1972's *Furman v. Georgia*.[97] This system resulted in the execution of a tiny portion of first degree murderers. The selection of the losers in this lottery seemed arbitrary at best, and often racially discriminatory. Yet, as noted above, the Court later rejected mandatory capital sentencing for any form of murder, no matter how narrowly defined. The Court instead upheld guided discretion statutes that conditioned capital sentences on juries finding one or more statutorily enumerated aggravating circumstances and weighing them against mitigating circumstances. The Court reasoned that sentencing necessarily involved consideration of the defendant's background. In the 1978 case of *Lockett v. Ohio*, the Court required consideration of any mitigating circumstance, including the offender's rehabilitative potential.[98] There appeared to be a contradiction between the Court's view on the purposes of capital punishment, and its views on the proper process. Although the justifying purposes of retribution and general deterrence arguably require mandatory sentencing based on offense characteristics, the Court insisted on discretionary sentencing based on offender characteristics.

Critics have argued that this effort to individualize capital sentencing restored much of the arbitrariness of the old system. The national rate of execution is so low—about .3 percent of criminal homicides—and varies so much between states with similar statutes, it seems unlikely that the current system distributes death on any principled basis.[99] In a 1987 decision, the Court rejected a challenge based on statistical evidence that race—especially the race of the victim—still influenced capital sentencing decisions.[100] The Court essentially abandoned its earlier aspiration to preclude race discrimination in capital sentencing.

In the area of sentencing guidelines, the Court also resisted a purely retributive view of sentencing. As part of the rise of determinate sentencing, a majority of jurisdictions reduced sentencing discretion by adopting guideline systems. The federal guidelines, created pursuant to the Sentencing Reform Act of 1984, became particularly controversial, because of their severity and because they enhanced sentences on the basis of uncharged and unproven criminal conduct. The guidelines are credited with the virtual disappearance of jury trials in

---

97. Furman v. Georgia, 408 U.S. 238, 239–40 (1972).
98. Lockett v. Ohio, 438 U.S. 586, 604–05 (1978).
99. Executions averaged 39 per year in 2012 to 2014 according to the Death Penalty Information Center; homicides numbered 13,483 in 2013. FBI UNIFORM CRIME REPORTS, CRIME IN THE UNITED STATES 2013 tbl. 16 (2013).
100. McCleskey v. Kemp, 481 U.S. 279, 292 (1987).

the federal system, because the "relevant conduct" enhancements in combination with substantial recidivist enhancements mean the particular offense of conviction makes little difference to the penalty.

The Court eventually held, in *Apprendi v. New Jersey* and *Blakely v. Washington*, that any factual finding that required a higher sentence would be treated as an offense element rather than a sentencing factor.[101] The addition of a mandatory aggravating factor would turn the offender's conduct into a different offense. As a consequence, the prosecution would have to prove such an offense element at trial. Yet in *United States v. Booker* the Court declined to treat the federal conduct enhancements as offense elements requiring proof. Instead, it simply held that the guidelines are not mandatory,[102] resulting in little if any reduction in the severity of sentences. Indeed the Court currently permits appellate courts to overturn sentences for unreasonableness, while deferring to guideline-compliant sentences as presumptively reasonable. There is some evidence that appellate courts are particularly likely to overturn below-guideline sentences.

The *Booker* decision is puzzling. It seems fair to say that Congress intended the guidelines system to reduce judicial sentencing discretion. Although this feature of the guidelines system clearly does not offend the Sixth Amendment right to a jury trial, the Supreme Court struck it down. On the other hand, the Sentencing Commission intentionally removed from jury consideration and set a low burden of proof for facts that could increase liability. Even though this feature of the guideline system seemed to offend the Sixth Amendment right recognized by the Court in *Blakely*, the Court preserved it. In justifying this strange choice, the Court invoked a conception of sentencing as inherently discretionary and individualized. In this context, as in the capital sentencing context, the Court chose a guided discretion process over a purely retributive model of sentencing.

VI. Conclusion

In this chapter we saw that the normative theories of punishment available in liberal states like ours are of two general types: utilitarian and retributive. Although these theoretical approaches seem based on incompatible premises, our codes and cases rely on both. This chapter explained this apparent

---

101. Blakely v. Washington, 542 U.S. 296, 303–05 (2004); Apprendi v. New Jersey, 530 U.S. 466, 490–92 (2000).

102. United States v. Booker, 543 U.S. 220, 226 (2005).

inconsistency by showing that each approach offers a persuasive justification for a different aspect of the institution of punishment.

Utilitarianism, aimed at minimizing suffering, helpfully addresses the question of why and when the state should afflict offenders with suffering. Deterrence provides a rationale for swift, certain, and moderate sanctions. Increasingly severe sanctions yield little marginal benefit. Dramatic increases in the frequency and duration of incarceration have been rationalized as incapacitative, but utilitarianism does not justify indiscriminate or lengthy incarceration as preventive.

Retributivism, concerned with equalizing dignity, helpfully addresses the question of why and when the state should denounce offenders as blameworthy. Although the intuitionist argument mischaracterizes the differences between retributivism and utilitarianism, the contractarian argument explains why blame is deserved, and the dignitary argument explains why the public is obliged to join in imposing it. Yet these arguments imply that we cannot complacently accept the justice of retribution without evaluating the overall distribution of freedom and dignity in our society.

Bearing in mind that deterrence is not served by severe sanctions, and that authoritative proscription and denunciation are the most effective deterrents, it seems that the pursuit of desert and deterrence will often be compatible. However, given the dubious effectiveness of incarceration in either rehabilitating or incapacitating offenders, and the morally troubling premises of incapacitation theory, these are not good reasons to punish. Instead, persuading people not to offend and securing potential targets of crime are as desirable aims in prison as they are in the rest of society.

In applying theories of punishment, the Supreme Court has repeatedly placed itself in contradiction. It justifies capital punishment on the basis of deterrence and desert, but is unwilling to see it applied regularly enough to deter or fairly enough to be deserved. It acknowledges that life sentences for nonviolent offenses serve neither desert nor deterrence, but insulates them from scrutiny. These contradictions do not result from combining utilitarianism and retributivism, which often limit punishment in similar ways. Instead they arise from the Court's willingness to condone wilfully unrestrained punishment seemingly aimed at demeaning offenders as worthless. Such punishment violates a common premise of both utilitarianism and retributivism: the equal worth of all persons.

FOUR

The Criminal Act

I. Introduction

This chapter begins our examination of the concept of a criminal offense. It explores two related propositions: that an offense must be defined in advance by law, and that such a definition must specify a wrongful act. A third important proposition, that such a definition requires a guilty mind, is more controversial and will be addressed in a separate chapter.

We saw in Chapter 1 that the idea of punishment presupposes prior prohibition. A criminal offense is a punishable violation of a legal prohibition. Recall that in American constitutional law, a criminal offense consists of those elements the prosecution must allege in the charging instrument and prove beyond a reasonable doubt at trial, even if the accused offers no evidence or argument in his own defense. Thus an offense is an event that conforms to a legal offense definition. This chapter will explore the reasons for and implications of this requirement that offenses be defined by law.

Offense elements are of two kinds: (1) objective elements defining the required conduct, and any required antecedent or concurrent circumstances, or results; (2) subjective elements, defining the offender's beliefs, desires, or mental states at the time of his or her conduct. Blackstone reasoned that

> to make a complete crime, cognizable by human laws, there must be both a will and an act. For though, in *foro conscientiae*, a fixed design or will to do an unlawful act is almost as heinous as the commission of it, yet, as no temporal tribunal can search the heart, or fathom the intentions of the mind, otherwise than as they arc demonstrated by outward actions, it therefore cannot punish for what it cannot know. For which reason in all temporal jurisdictions an overt act, or some open evidence of an intended crime, is necessary, in order to demonstrate the depravity of the will, before the man is liable to punishment. And as a vitious will without a vitious act is no civil crime, so, on the other hand, an unwarrantable act without a vitious will is no crime at all. So that to constitute

> a crime against human laws there must be, first, a vitious will; and, secondly, an unlawful act consequent upon such vitious will.[1]

This chapter discusses the requirement of an objective element. We have seen that both retributive and utilitarian theories justify conditioning punishment on public judgments of blame. Because an offender is blamed for her offense, the offense must be a voluntary choice. You cannot be blamed for the circumstance that you are 30 years old, or female. You cannot be blamed for the circumstance that another person is a police officer. Certainly we might blame you for bringing about a circumstance, or for acts you commit in the presence of a circumstance, but we cannot hold you responsible for a state of affairs without some such account of your choices. Some would argue that even your disposition to do wrong is merely a circumstance for which you cannot be blamed unless you choose to act on it. Conditioning liability on choice is also sensible if prohibition and punishment are to have a deterrent function. From a utilitarian perspective, punishment that cannot influence behavior is pointless.

Following Blackstone, criminal lawyers and judges often express the requirement of chosen behavior as an "act requirement." Originally, English criminal law required not just an action, but an action of a particularly forceful kind. A crime was a breach of the royal peace and, if committed against a private party, was ordinarily also actionable as a trespass. Such trespasses were originally of two kinds: those committed against a person by force and arms, and those committed against property by breach of enclosure. The violence of these acts made them unlawful in the sense of being overt challenges to the authority of law.

Today, however, the criminal law no longer focuses so much on physical movement. An involuntary movement such as a sneeze or convulsion cannot be the object of blame, while sedentary neglect of a duty can be. Remaining in place on a battlefield is a static exertion of willpower that may incur either honor or ignominy, depending on the circumstances. The Model Penal Code uses the term "conduct" to cover both acts and omissions.[2] This expansion of what counts as conduct coincided with an expansion in the perceived function of criminal law, from regulating violence to deterring a broad range of harmful conduct. This expansion meant that criminal conduct no longer had to bear the earmarks of unlawfulness. One might commit a crime by failing to properly

1. 4 William Blackstone, Commentaries on the Laws of England 20–21 (1765–1769).
2. Model Penal Code § 1.13 (1962).

label or safely package a product, or by providing or withholding information in a business transaction.

The gradual emergence of a more abstract conception of criminal conduct in England and America probably followed developments in tort law. Prior to the nineteenth century, torts had been divided into trespasses, requiring direct physical force, and trespasses on the case, causing injury indirectly from the breach of a duty of care. In the 1830s English courts reclassified unintended trespasses as trespasses on the case, thereby creating the broad category of negligence liability and leaving a smaller category of intentional torts. The distinction between these two categories now turned on mental states rather than different types of conduct. By the later nineteenth century American courts reached similar conclusions. The 1850 case of *Brown v. Kendall* was an action in trespass vi et armis for the tort of assault and battery.[3] Chief Justice Lemuel Shaw ruled that the plaintiff could recover for injuries inflicted with a stick only if they were caused intentionally or negligently. That they were caused directly by violence meant that trespass was the proper procedural form for seeking recovery, but had no significance for the standard of liability.[4] The wrong consisted in culpable injury, not unauthorized violence. Shaw cited the opinion in the 1803 English case of *Leame v. Bray*, which described a fatal carriage collision as both a trespass and a felony if resulting from negligent driving.[5]

With the disappearance of trespassory forms of action, it no longer seemed natural to identify crimes as trespasses. The proliferation of transportation and industrial accidents encouraged the attribution of responsibility for remote risks in both civil and criminal law. Thus, in *The Common Law*, Oliver Wendell Holmes Jr. denied that there could be any difference in kind between trespasses and acts causing harm remotely: "An act is always a muscular contraction and nothing else. The chain of physical sequences which it sets in motion or directs to the plaintiff's harm is no part of it."[6] In a 1914 article on causation in tort, Henry Terry employed this same conception of acts in arguing that trespass necessarily imposed liability for the results of conduct.[7] At the turn of the century William Clark and William Marshall concluded that the crime of battery could be based on negligently causing remote harm.[8]

The more criminal conduct resembles law-abiding conduct, the harder criminal law is to obey and to apply. If the category of conduct that *can* be

---

3. 60 Mass. 292 (1850).
4. *Id.* at 295–96.
5. *Id.* at 295 (citing Leame v. Bray, 5 Esp. 18 (1803)).
6. Oliver Wendell Holmes, Jr., The Common Law 91 (1881).
7. Henry Terry, *Proximate Consequences in the Law of Tort*, 28 Harv. L. Rev. 10 (1914).
8. 1 William Clark & William Marshall, A Treatise on the Law of Crimes 421 (1900).

criminalized expands, it becomes more important to precisely define and publicly communicate particular criminal prohibitions. Thus the requirement of an act and the requirement of a legal prohibition have overlapping functions.

Punishing voluntary conduct arguably requires advance proscription in a world where we do not entirely trust officials. If we wish to ensure that lawmakers target conduct, not identities or other circumstances, we should require them to forbid conduct prospectively. If instead we permit lawmakers to decide what conduct is punishable after it occurs, they may simply choose to criminalize whatever conduct was committed by persons with certain characteristics.

To warrant blame, voluntary conduct must also be wrongful. At the very least, an offense must be something forbidden by law at the time committed. Arguably, to be worthy of blame the offender must also have had reason to know it was forbidden. Thus wrongfulness in the sense of illegality implies not only that the conduct has been prohibited in advance, but that the prohibition has been communicated in advance. This compound requirement of prospectivity and publicity, recognized in many legal systems, is referred to as the "principle of legality."

This principle of legality cannot be applied without a lot of normative judgments. Because criminality implies blameworthiness, we cannot make sense of the idea of a criminal prohibition without a normative theory of criminalization. Prior communication of a prohibition is not enough to satisfy legality, because a legislature could fulfill that minimal requirement by proscribing all voluntary conduct. Such a broad proscription would not be adequate to define wrongful conduct, for three reasons. First, violating such a broad prohibition would not be blameworthy because it would be unavoidable. Second, such a broad prohibition would collide with the civil liberties protections that any liberal state must have. Third, assuming authorities would not actually prosecute and punish all conduct, the breadth of a comprehensive prohibition would negate its prospectivity. Discretion to criminalize would be shifted to prosecutors and courts, and exercised after the offending conduct had occurred. For all of these reasons, criminal prohibitions must have limits. The requirements of prospectivity and publicity serve no purpose unless criminal prohibitions are also limited by substantive criteria of wrongfulness.

If the concept of a criminal offense requires that prohibitions be limited in content, this has implications for their form. Suppose that instead of proscribing all conduct, a legislature proscribed "any antisocial conduct." Like a comprehensive prohibition, a vague prohibition shifts discretion to decision-makers who judge conduct retrospectively, and so negates the requirements of prospectivity and voluntary conduct. In addition, vague prohibitions undermine civil liberties. Even if courts later determine that the exercise of civil liberties is not punishable, fear of being charged and punished might "chill" protected conduct. Moreover, because vague prohibitions are effectively retroactive, we might rationally fear that exercise of civil liberties might provoke prosecutors to charge us with other antisocial conduct as pretexts for punishment. Thus legality requires that criminal prohibitions be not only prospective, public, and substantively limited, but also specific. Moreover, what criminal prohibitions have to be specific about is the required *conduct*. Otherwise we are back to punishing identity or other circumstances, or protected conduct. Thus, the principle of legality and the act requirement are linked.

How should wrongful conduct be defined? As a logical matter, specific prior proscription need not take the form of generally applicable rules. After all, courts routinely issue injunctions imposing particular duties and constraints on particular individuals. But if the main purpose of criminal law is to secure equal dignity by protecting certain basic entitlements and public goods, it is important that criminal prohibitions be general and impersonal (although they might apply only to persons in certain offices or situations). Proscribing types of conduct is also necessary for general deterrence so that prospective offenders will know what punishment to expect for the contemplated conduct. Thus a criminal proscription should not be directed against particular persons, or against particular acts at particular times and places. Instead, it should be directed against a type of act, an act that fits a general description. A criminal prohibition should be expressed as a rule.

On this view of criminal law, an offense is wrong, not just because it is harmful, or badly motivated, but because it attacks some type of individual entitlement or collective interest law has undertaken to protect. Blackstone defined offenses as "public wrongs" and classified them according to the interests they threatened.[9] Jeremy Bentham reasoned that a criminal offense could only be the violation of a legal right or duty already recognized in some other branch of law, such as tort or property.[10] In his view, criminal law merely added an additional sanction. Bentham conceived a criminal offense as a type of conduct committed under a type of circumstance that made injury to a legally protected interest a probable result. Today, most American criminal codes are organized into offenses against different kinds of interests, such as the person, property, or government administration. In this respect, an offense definition is not just a description of an act, but a normative characterization of it as antagonistic to a public interest.

---

9. 4 William Blackstone, Commentaries on the Laws of England 1–2 (1765–1769).
10. Jeremy Bentham, Theory of Legislation 239–40 (R. Hildreth trans., 5th ed. 1887).

We usually think of enacting prospective rules of general application as a legislative function. Legislatures are also seen as the most democratically responsive branches of government. Insofar as compliance with criminal law depends upon its popular legitimacy, offenses are best defined legislatively.

In sum, the principle of legality requires prospective, public, specific, regular, and (usually) legislative definition of offenses, while the act requirement requires that offense definitions include voluntary wrongful conduct.

II. Legality

The "principle of legality" is commonly expressed by the maxim "no crime, no punishment, without a law." Punishment requires a crime, defined by law. As we have seen, legality has at least five components: prospectivity, publicity, specificity, regularity, and legislativity. Prospectivity requires that conduct be prohibited before it is committed, not judged after the fact. Regularity requires that law be made generally and impartially, applying to categories of conduct rather than particular actors or acts. Publicity requires that those subject to punishment receive notice of conduct forbidden, so they have a fair opportunity to avoid liability, and society gets the benefit of the resulting deterrence. Specificity is really an implication of prospectivity and publicity. Vagueness in a prohibition defers lawmaking discretion to the retrospective stages of prosecution and adjudication and obscures its content from public view. In this way, it frustrates publicity and prospectivity, and also diminishes legislativity.

Legislativity is a principle of separation of powers. It requires that crimes be defined by legislators rather than courts. Why does it matter who makes criminal law? The English common law of crimes was largely (though not exclusively) judge-made before the eighteenth century. It was presumed to be customary law, consisting of discretionary standards administered by popular juries. Judges seemed best positioned to observe, summarize, and rationalize jury behavior. Even after revolution established the ultimate lawmaking authority of Parliament, Blackstone still regarded legislation as either declaratory of the common law, or in furtherance of its purposes.[11] Lockean liberalism ultimately derived the authority of law from natural rights rather than collective will, and popular ideas continued to identify the common law with such rights.

A preference for legislative lawmaking is more associated with Rousseauean democratic theory, which saw natural liberty as necessarily extinguished by

---

11. 1 WILLIAM BLACKSTONE, COMMENTARIES ON THE LAWS OF ENGLAND 86 (1765–1769).

collective subjection to a self-made law. Utilitarian reformers were particularly critical of judge-made law, which they viewed as obscure, contradictory, and excessively discretionary. If law was to be consistent, coherent, clear, and transparent, it needed to be made by a single supreme authority, not a decentralized system of common law adjudication. If it was to be regular, precise, and prospective, there would be little scope for jury participation in lawmaking. Accordingly, democratic legitimation of a criminal law achieving the other requisites of legality could only take the form of election of a supreme lawmaking body. Of course judges can be elected, too. Nevertheless, the same populist sentiments that motivated the adoption of judicial election in the antebellum United States also motivated codification of criminal law.

Two dimensions of legality, regularity and prospectivity, are explicitly required by the American Constitution. Regularity is guaranteed by constitutional provisions precluding bills of attainder at the federal[12] and state[13] levels of government. Combined with the Sixth Amendment right to a jury trial for serious offenses (now incorporated into the Fourteenth Amendment due process obligations of the states), the bill of attainder provisions ensure that individuals will be judged by courts, not by legislatures. Criminal legislation must define crimes, not identify criminals. Indeed, one could plausibly derive a constitutional requirement of an act from these bill of attainder clauses.

Prospectivity is also required by Article I, Sections 9 and 10, which forbid the federal government and the states from passing "any ex post facto law." In the case of *Calder v. Bull*, Justice Chase reasoned that this forbade laws making conduct committed before their enactment an offense, or increasing the penalty of prior offenses, or reducing the required proof.[14]

Is retroactive criminalization also barred when accomplished by judicial decision rather than legislation? Common law courts had long applied doctrines precluding expansive interpretation of criminal legislation. They developed these to resist the legislative expansion of capital liability. During the sixteenth century, Parliament had eliminated benefit of clergy for many felonies, and execution rates rose very high. Accordingly, courts developed, and treatises endorsed, a doctrine that criminal statutes were to be strictly construed against the Crown. Coke, for example, wrote that "Acts of Parliament . . . are to be so construed, as no man that is innocent, or free from injury or wrong, be by a literal construction punished or endamaged."[15] Invoking this doctrine,

---

12. U.S. CONST. art. I, § 9.
13. *Id.* art. I, § 10.
14. Calder v. Bull, 3 U.S. 386, 390 (1798).
15. 2 EDWARD COKE, THE FIRST PART OF THE INSTITUTES OF THE LAWES OF ENGLAND 360 (18th ed. 1823).

courts sometime adopted hypertechnical constructions to avoid capital liability for minor offenses.[16] This canon of construction is today known as the *rule of lenity*. It remains authoritative in the federal system, which has no systematic criminal code. In adopting comprehensive penal codes, however, many state legislatures concluded that the rule of lenity was unnecessary. By the early twentieth century about half the states had adopted rules of construction requiring courts to interpret codes in accord with their purposes rather than to interpret them strictly against the state.[17] The Model Penal Code adopts a similar standard, and proceeds to identify those purposes.[18] On the other hand, some modern codes incorporate a rule of lenity. Ohio's criminal code provides that code sections "defining offenses or penalties shall be strictly construed against the state, and liberally construed in favor of the accused."[19]

The Supreme Court has also identified constitutional constraints on judicial criminalization. In the 1812 case of *United States v. Hudson and Goodwin*, the Court rejected retroactive judicial criminalization, but not on the basis of the ex post facto law clauses.[20] The defendants had been charged with libel of the U.S. president. Such a crime had formerly been proscribed by the hated Sedition Act of 1798, but this had been allowed to lapse after its proponents lost the election of 1800. A federal court had accepted an indictment against Hudson and Goodwin for this offense based on the common law. The Court held that lower federal courts had only those powers granted to them by Congress, which did not include the power to define crimes. The Court conceded that any grant of judicial power implied a further power to enforce decisions by punishing for contempt of court. Yet the Court denied lower federal courts the power traditionally exercised by English courts to define a common law of crimes. Thus the Court's decision required legislativity of federal criminal law, while leaving each state free to determine whether its courts could define crimes.

In fact, most states adopted criminal codes during the early nineteenth century, and leading jurists argued that criminal legislation was superior to judicial criminalization in notice, deterrence, consistency, and democracy.[21] Yet not all jurists agreed. Francis Wharton's 1846 treatise on American criminal law offered the interesting argument that statutes had largely displaced the

16. Livingston Hall, *Strict and Liberal Construction of Criminal Statutes*, 48 HARV. L. REV. 748, 751 (1935) (citing MICHAEL FOSTER, CROWN CASES 357–59 (1765); MATTHEW HALE, HISTORIA PLACITORUM CORONOAE 335 (1736); WILLIAM HAWKINS, A TREATISE OF PLEAS OF THE CROWN 343 (1716); The King v. Page & Harwood, 82 Eng. Rep. 550 (1648)).
17. *Id.* at 753–54.
18. MODEL PENAL CODE § 1.02 (1962).
19. OHIO REV. CODE ANN. § 2901.04 (West 2015).
20. 11 U.S. 32 (1812).
21. Guyora Binder, *Origins of American Felony Murder Rules*, 57 STAN. L. REV. 59, 117–18 (2004).

common law of crimes in England well before the American Revolution.[22] As these statutes were not binding, American courts had been obliged to develop and apply their own common law rules of criminal law. Wharton argued that the common law empowered courts to punish as misdemeanors any conduct that (1) disturbed the public peace, (2) maliciously injured property, (3) harmed the general public welfare, (4) offended sexual mores, or (5) threatened to lead to other crimes.[23] Yet he also acknowledged that American common laws of crime were being rapidly replaced by legislative codes.

Many states have adopted statutory provisions limiting offenses to those created by statute, as the Model Penal Code recommends.[24] Others have done so by judicial decision.[25] Yet a number of jurisdictions permit courts to punish common law crimes. Thus, Florida and DC statutes declare the common law of crimes to be in force except as superseded by subsequent legislation.[26] Even without such statutes, courts in Maryland, Massachusetts, North Carolina, and South Carolina have recognized nonstatutory offenses in recent decades.[27] These courts consistently deny that they are creating retroactive liability. Instead, they characterize the common law as having been fixed at the outset of colonization or the beginning of independence, so that they are applying preexisting law.[28] Yet this claim conflicts with the modern understanding of common law adjudication as an evolutionary process of adapting precedent to new problems. Application of an ancient common law of crimes is difficult given how vague its content was in England before colonization began in 1607, and how little we know of its subsequent modification in the rustic conditions of colonial America. Inevitably, exercise of jurisdiction to punish common law crimes involves broad discretion that defeats the values of publicity and specificity and threatens the value of prospectivity.

In the twentieth century, the Supreme Court began to apply the due process clause against state criminal legislation that it deemed excessively vague. These cases were famously cryptic: indeed, their rationales were often at least as vague as the statutes they struck down.[29] However, it seems likely that the

---

22. FRANCIS WHARTON, TREATISE ON AMERICAN CRIMINAL LAW 2–3 (1846).
23. *Id.* (citing United States v. Hart, 1 Peters C.C. 390 (1816)).
24. MODEL PENAL CODE § 1.05(1) (1962).
25. Ledgerwood v. State, 134 Ind. 81 (1893).
26. D.C. CODE § 45-401 (2015); FLA. STAT. § 775.01 (2015).
27. *In re* May, 584 S.E.2d 271 (N.C. 2003); Commonwealth v. Triplett, 686 N.E.2d 195 (Mass. 1997); State v. Prince, 447 S.E.2d 177 (S.C. 1993); *In re* Antoine H., 570 A.2d 1239 (Md. 1990).
28. State v. Egan, 287 So. 2d 1 (Fla. 1973); *see* Rogers v. Tennessee, 532 U.S. 451 (2001) (Scalia, J., dissenting).
29. *See* Anthony Amsterdam, *The Void for Vagueness Doctrine in the Supreme Court*, 109 U. PA. L. REV. 67 (1960).

requirement of legislative specificity was in part a judicial response to legislative rejection of the rule of lenity.

The early void-for-vagueness cases, decided during the heyday of "substantive due process," generally involved economic regulation. Thus, in *Connally v. General Construction Co.* the Court struck down a minimum wage ordinance imposing fines on government contractors paying less than the prevailing local wage.[30] Justice Sutherland wrote "the terms of a penal statute [...] must be sufficiently explicit to inform those who are subject to it what conduct on their part will render them liable to its penalties ... and a statute which either forbids or requires the doing of an act in terms so vague that men of common intelligence must necessarily guess at its meaning and differ as to its application violates the first essential of due process of law."[31] Postwar decisions enforcing the "void-for-vagueness" doctrine generally involved regulations of speech. Thus, the Court seemed concerned that courts might apply vague statutes against constitutionally protected conduct, or that they would discriminate by applying such statutes expansively against those who exercised constitutional rights, or that these possibilities would chill the exercise of constitutional rights.

Indeed, a statute might be insufficiently specific in either of two ways: vagueness and overbreadth. The concept of vagueness applies when a prohibition proscribes conduct that can be criminalized but does not sufficiently define that conduct to give fair warning of prohibited conduct and prevent discriminatory exercises of discretion by law enforcement. The concept of overbreadth applies where a prohibition covers constitutionally protected conduct as well as constitutionally criminalizable conduct. An overbroad statute interferes with the exercise of a constitutional right. Even if courts refrain from enforcing the statute against exercise of a right, the mere existence of the statute infringes the right by deterring or "chilling" its exercise. The Court has most often deemed statutes unconstitutionally overbroad when their prohibitions include speech protected by the First Amendment[32] but has sometimes applied the concept to other rights, such as the right to travel or abortion rights.[33] Yet the Court has expressed reluctance to do so,[34] with the result that it sometimes references the concept of vagueness in condemning statutes that clearly

30. 269 U.S. 385 (1926).

31. *Id.* at 391; *see also Int'l Harvester Co. v. Kentucky*, 234 U.S. 216 (1914) (vagueness in statute punishing combinations to exact a higher than "normal" price).

32. Broadrick v. Oklahoma, 413 U.S. 601 (1973).

33. Aptheker v. Sec'y of State, 378 U.S. 500 (1964); *Planned Parenthood of Central Mo. v. Danforth*, 428 U.S 52, 82–83 (1976).

34. Schall v. Martin, 467 U.S. 253, 268n. (1984); New York v. Ferber, 458 U.S. 747, 768–74 (1982); Chicago v. Morales 527 U.S. 41, 52 (1999).

proscribe constitutionally protected conduct.[35] Of course, a statute that does not clearly communicate whether it proscribes constitutionally protected conduct is arguably both vague and overbroad.

The distinction between vagueness and overbreadth is illustrated by the divergent analyses in two New Deal Court decisions striking down vagrancy statutes. The statute at issue in *Lanzetta v. New Jersey* provided that "[a]ny person not engaged in any lawful occupation, known to be a member of any gang consisting of two or more persons, who has been convicted at least three times of being a disorderly person, or who has been convicted of any crime in this or any other State, is declared to be a gangster. . . .".[36] The Court decreed that "[n]o one may be required, at peril of life, liberty or property, to speculate as to the meaning of penal statutes. All are entitled to be informed as to what the State commands or forbids."[37] It then noted that both "gang" and "member" were undefined, and that the statute did not specify to whom the defendant must be "known" as a gang member. Finally, the Court objected that the statute punished "no act or omission" but simply the circumstance of being a gangster. The statute enabled the state to punish merely on suspicion that the defendant intended to engage in some criminal act in the future. If we think of an act as an event occurring at some particular time and place, a failure to specify an act makes it difficult to determine whether the crime took place within the spatial and temporal limits of the court's jurisdiction. The Court held that the statute's vagueness made it "repugnant" to due process "on its face."[38]

Thornhill v. Alabama struck down a statute forbidding any person "without a just cause or legal excuse, to go near to or loiter about . . . any place of . . . lawful business, for the purpose of . . . influencing or inducing other persons not to trade with . . . or be employed by such . . . firm . . . for the purpose of . . . hindering . . . any lawful business. . . ."[39] The Court found this statute to be a First Amendment violation on its face regardless of whether it was enforced only against those who threatened violence. The Court reasoned that

> It is not merely the sporadic abuse of power by the censor, but the pervasive threat inherent in its very existence that constitutes the danger to freedom of discussion. . . . A like threat is inherent in a penal statute, . . . which does not aim specifically at evils within the allowable area of state control but, on the contrary, sweeps within its ambit other activities that,

---

35. Kolender v. Lawson, 461 U.S. 352 (1983).
36. 306 U.S. 451, 452 (1939).
37. *Id.* at 453.
38. *Id.* at 458.
39. 310 U.S. 88 (1940).

> in ordinary circumstances, constitute an exercise of freedom of speech or of the press. The existence of such a statute, which readily lends itself to harsh and discriminatory enforcement by local prosecuting officials, against particular groups deemed to merit their displeasure, results in a continuous and pervasive restraint on all freedom of discussion that might reasonably be regarded as within its purview.[40]

Although the *Thornhill* statute was overbroad, vagueness also factored into the decision, because a reasonable restriction of speech for public safety would have been permissible, if sufficiently precise to preclude discriminatory enforcement and a chilling effect on permissible speech. Yet the limitation of the statute's prohibition to picketing "without just cause or lawful excuse" failed to communicate what speech remained permissible. Thus, the statute might have been upheld had it applied only within some specified distance from an entrance to a place of business, in order to permit advocacy while preventing physical confrontations. However a vague regulation of constitutionally privileged conduct would necessarily be overbroad.

During the civil rights era, when the Supreme Court greatly expanded its supervision of state criminal justice systems through the due process clause, it brought its retroactivity case law together with its specificity case law. In the 1964 case of *Bouie v. City of Columbia*, the Court addressed the problem of expansive judicial interpretation of a precise criminal prohibition.[41] Here, African-American civil rights activists protested a segregated restaurant by refusing to leave. They were convicted of trespass, defined by statute to require entering after notice of exclusion, not remaining after such notice. The court reasoned that an important purpose of the ex post facto law clause was to give fair notice of the risk of liability, and drew on the void-for-vagueness cases to hold that due process also required notice as to judicial application of law. Thus, the Court concluded that due process precluded an "unforeseeable and retroactive" judicial "enlargement of a criminal statute" by interpretation. Here the Court's notice argument seemed disingenuous: the defendants surely knew the restaurant was segregated, and that this segregation was permitted and enforced by state law. Instead, the Court's primary concern appeared to have been the use of judicial discretion to target defendants because of their race and dissident views, rather than any unfair surprise. The challenge in *Bouie* was to the statute as applied rather than the statute itself.

---

40. *Id.* at 97–98.
41. 378 U.S. 347 (1964).

The California case of *Keeler v. Superior Court* combined two different objections to judicial expansion of the criminal law: an objection to judicial lawmaking and an objection to retroactive lawmaking.[42] Upon encountering his ex-wife, in an advanced state of pregnancy, Keeler announced that he would "stomp it out" of her.[43] He then proceeded to kick her, causing the death of her fetus. He was charged with murder, defined under a California code provision passed in the mid-nineteenth century, which proscribed killing a human being with malice. The California Supreme Court ruled that the charge had to be quashed. First, the court drew on legislative history in arguing that "human being" had meant a person born alive when the murder statute was framed. Next, the court noted that the California Penal Code restricted criminal offenses to those found in the Code or other statutes, and concluded that "there are no common law crimes in California." Third, citing *Bouie*, the court held that even if a court could expand the scope of the murder prohibition prospectively, it could not apply that expanded prohibition retroactively to Keeler's act without violating due process. One may argue that there were no strong reasons to cabin judicial discretion here. After all, Keeler could hardly have been surprised to learn that his conduct was criminal, and he was not targeted because of his race. And yet there was a sense in which Keeler could have been unfairly targeted for political reasons, even if not because of his own political views. Such a prosecution could have been brought to achieve a controversial increase in the penalty for abortion, without going through the elected legislature.

We may contrast *Keeler* and *Bouie* with another case in which judicial expansion of criminal liability did not seem unfair, discriminatory, or undemocratic. In *Rogers v. Tennessee*, the defendant was convicted of murder after he stabbed his victim in the heart, and the victim died of the wound after 15 months.[44] Rogers appealed on the grounds that Tennessee courts had long instructed juries that killing required that death follow the injury within a year and a day. The failure to give such an instruction, he argued, amounted to retroactive punishment. The Court reasoned, however, that the statute provided Rogers adequate notice that fatally stabbing a victim in the heart with the intent to kill was murder. The year-and-a-day limitation, although once common, had been widely rejected as pointless because medical understanding of temporally remote causes of death had improved. The Court held that judicial interpretation of a criminal statute could be deemed unconstitutionally retroactive only if it was "unexpected and indefensible" on the basis of existing legal sources.[45]

---

42. 470 P.2d 617 (Cal. 1970).
43. *Id.* at 623.
44. 532 U.S. 451 (2001).
45. *Id.* at 462.

In what way was judicial abrogation of the year-and-a-day rule in *Rogers* more expected and defensible than judicial abrogation of the requirement of notice of exclusion upon entry in *Bouie*? The requirement of notice upon entry was in the statutory offense definition, whereas Tennessee's year-and-a-day rule was not. Moreover, some index of exclusion from property arguably needs to be part of the definition of a trespass offense. Recall that the original conception of a trespass was a breach of the peace. A trespass against property has traditionally meant not just being in the wrong place, but defying an expressed will to exclude. Specifying a criterion for exclusion helps define the forbidden conduct and so enhances the behavior-guiding function of the law. By contrast, a criterion for attributing causal responsibility for a result is arguably not a conduct rule directed at potential offenders. Instead it is a "decision" rule to be applied by a court after the fact.[46] Accordingly, it is not crucial that the public have prior notice of criteria of causal responsibility.

Is *Rogers* distinguishable from *Keeler*? One might argue that the born-alive rule, like the year-and-a-day rule, was (1) a judicial gloss not required by the statutory text, and (2) an arbitrary formal test rendered obsolete by advancing medical knowledge and skill. By the time *Keeler* was decided, a late-term fetus had a 90 percent chance of surviving until birth. Yet against the background of the controversy over abortion, the court could not presume societal consensus that a fetus was a person protected by the murder statute. The debate over the status of a fetus was not a medical debate, but a moral one, implicating the rights of the mother. The question of whether the lingering death of an adult was caused by an intentional stabbing, by contrast, posed no controversial value question requiring democratic resolution. Moreover, whether a victim is a human being is part of the conduct rule, because it affects the question of how wrong it is to attack the victim. If so, this question must be resolved and publicized prospectively to fulfill the behavior guiding function of the law.

During the civil rights era, the U.S. Supreme Court was more concerned about the dangers of police discretion than the dangers of judicial discretion. This was a major theme of its criminal procedure jurisprudence as it subjected law enforcement officers to judicial supervision by conditioning searches and seizures on judicial findings of probable cause. Yet the Court also pursued this agenda in substantive criminal law by systematically striking down the vagrancy statutes police used to arrest suspicious persons. Indeed, the requirement of probable cause to believe the defendant had committed a crime was meaningless if police could arrest for the "crime" of being out in public, or being

---

46. Meir Dan-Cohen, *Decisions and Conduct Rules: On Acoustic Separation in Criminal Law*, 97 HARV. L. REV. 625, 626–30 (1984).

the object of police suspicion. Drawing on *Lanzetta* and *Thornhill*, the Court therefore struck down vagrancy statutes permitting arrest and conviction on suspicion of future criminality. The two key cases were *Shuttlesworth v. City of Birmingham*[47] and *Papachristou v. Jacksonville*.[48]

In *Shuttlesworth*, the defendant was convicted of violating an ordinance punishing "loitering or standing" after being ordered by police to move on. The Court held the ordinance unconstitutional as applied in the case, with no requirement of proof that the defendant's refusal to move caused any harm. Although "overbreadth" is usually thought of as a facial deficiency, the Court's critique of the statute as applied in *Shuttlesworth* was that, as construed, it was overbroad. Thus, the Court defined the freedom to move or remain in public as part of the liberty of person that is protected by the due process clause, and treated a police order to move as violating that liberty unless justified by a sufficient reason. Hence, a criminal sanction for violating such an order criminalized constitutionally protected conduct. Yet if the state needs a justifying reason for criminalizing inactivity, it would seem to need a justifying reason for criminalizing action as well. *Shuttlesworth* implies that due process requires that punishable conduct be wrongful rather than innocent.

The statute challenged in Papachristou was based on an Elizabethan labor statute, and punished

> [r]ogues and vagabonds, or dissolute persons who go about begging; common gamblers, persons who use juggling or unlawful games or plays, common drunkards, common night walkers, thieves, pilferers or pickpockets, traders in stolen property, lewd, wanton and lascivious persons, keepers of gambling places, common railers and brawlers, persons wandering or strolling around from place to place without any lawful purpose or object, habitual loafers, disorderly persons, persons neglecting all lawful business and habitually spending their time by frequenting houses of ill fame, gaming houses, or places where alcoholic beverages are sold or served, persons able to work but habitually living upon the earnings of their wives or minor children. . . .[49]

Similar statutes were introduced in much of the South during the Jim Crow era, giving police broad discretion to arrest African Americans, or threaten them with arrest. Justice Douglas's opinion for the court presented the statute

47. 382 U.S. 87 (1965).
48. 405 U.S. 156 (1972).
49. *Id.* at 156 n.1.

as overbroad, characterizing it as infringing a liberty to move about that was fundamental in a free society, and that needed no justifying purpose. He emphasized the harmlessness of much activity covered by the statute. As in *Lanzetta*, the statute punished identities rather than acts—being a thief rather than stealing, being a lascivious person rather than selling sexual services. In essence, it punished the future disposition to commit a crime rather than the crime itself.

The Court revisited the vagrancy problem in *Chicago v. Morales*, striking down a Chicago ordinance punishing remaining in public for no apparent purpose with at least one person police reasonably suspect of being a gang member, after being warned to disperse and remove themselves from the area.[50] The decision was somewhat surprising for three reasons. First, the law provided notice to the defendants of their potential liability in the form of orders to disperse. Second, the law seemed to punish conduct—the omission to fulfill a duty to disperse—rather than an identity such as reputed gang membership. Third, the political context of the law's passage gave little reason to fear it would provide a pretext for racial discrimination. Although the ordinance was clearly intended for use in crime-ridden African-American neighborhoods, it was passed by a city council with substantial African-American representation, at the request of leaders of those communities. The affected communities appeared to have the power to protect themselves from police abuse by political means, without resort to the courts. Thus it seemed that the law did not offend the values of fairness or equality usually invoked in void-for-vagueness cases.

Indeed, the Court's decision seemed more motivated by a concern to protect liberty against an overbroad prohibition, as in *Shuttlesworth*. Yet Justice Stevens's opinion for the Court denied this, assuming that overbreadth was only applicable to First Amendment rights.[51] Stevens instead argued that the statute was defectively vague in two ways. First, the duty to disperse and remove oneself from the area lacked spatial and temporal definition. Second, the element of lack of apparent purpose specified no indicia of purposelessness, nor did it require proof of any illegitimate purpose. Thus it depended on the virtually untrammeled subjective judgment of an officer.

The uncertainty of the spatial and temporal scope of the required dispersal and removal does indeed generate a problem of notice. For example, are members of a group given such an order subject to arrest if some move down the block and across the street? These uncertainties also give police a great deal of discretion in making an arrest.

---

50. 527 U.S. 41 (1999).
51. *Id.* at 52–53.

The vagueness of the lack of apparent purpose element does not deprive the offender of notice that he is at risk of punishment, however. The offender cannot be punished until he receives and disobeys the order to disperse. Instead, the vacuity of this element is objectionable because the resulting prohibition unjustifiably offends liberty.

Suppose the statute dispensed with the dispersal order process, and simply forbade standing anywhere in public. Such an oppressive prohibition would grossly interfere with liberty for little benefit. Indeed, citing *Shuttlesworth*, Justice Stevens argued that police cannot arbitrarily require citizens to move, adding that "[i]f the loitering is in fact harmless and innocent, the dispersal order itself is an unjustified impairment of liberty."[52] The liberty involved is the "'right to remove from one place to another according to inclination' [recognized] as 'an attribute of personal liberty' protected by the Constitution" in *Williams v. Fears*.[53] But let us narrow our hypothetical statute to preclude remaining in a public place with a gang member. Even this narrower statute is an unreasonable interference with liberty, if the liberal state should allow us to associate with willing adults for innocent purposes. The dispersal order is impermissible because it simply does to an individual what a general prohibition on standing in public would do to a population. Perhaps a requirement of criminal purpose would justify such interference with liberty, but a lack of apparent purpose is drastically overinclusive (and sometimes underinclusive, when a criminal purpose is apparent). So the lack of apparent purpose element is defective because it is an overbroad restriction on the freedoms to move about and to associate.

Now, suppose that instead of authorizing the issuance of dispersal orders, the statute barred certain named individuals from standing about in public. This would make the statute more, not less defective, as it would arguably be a bill of attainder. Yet if the legislature cannot impose prohibitions on particular individuals, it seems they should not be able to delegate this power to police. The situation changes if police make a reasonable finding that the individual is about to commit a crime. In *Terry v. Ohio*, the Court permitted police to temporarily detain and question persons in public, but only on the basis of reasonable suspicion they had committed or would soon commit a crime.[54] Thus, it seems likely that punishment for defying orders to move along would be upheld if such orders were conditioned on demonstrably reasonable suspicion that the offender was engaged in some other crime. To be sure, discriminatory

52. *Id.* at 58–59 (citing *Shuttlesworth*, 382 U.S. at 90).
53. *Morales*, 527 U.S. at 53 (citing Williams v. Fears, 179 U.S. 270, 274 (1900)).
54. 392 U.S. 1 (1968).

exercise of police discretion remains a danger with such a statute, as it has been established that *Terry* stops are deployed disproportionately against African Americans.[55] Yet the Chicago statute was defective because it did not even require a pretense of reasonable suspicion to trigger interference with an individual's liberty.

Our review of legality shows that it is a complex idea, requiring a prospective, public, and specific criminal prohibition, usually enacted by a legislature. We have also seen that the requirement of such a criminal prohibition cannot be isolated from normative views about the appropriate content of a criminal prohibition. Offense definitions must be prospective and specific about the required types of conduct. Yet they must define rules sufficiently general to ensure that offenders are punished for their acts and not their identities. These rules must be especially precise when they define exceptions to constitutional liberties, and the degree of precision required cannot be separated from normative judgments about the relative value of the interests protected and the liberties infringed by the criminal prohibition.

III. Wrongful Acts

What is a criminal act, and why require it?

Consider the 1918 Oklahoma case of *Proctor v. State*, overturning a conviction for the offense of acquiring or keeping a place with the intent to sell liquor therein.[56] Proctor had discussed plans with contractors to remodel a building he owned for use as a bar. The court reasoned that punishing this offense would violate due process because the offense did not require any criminal conduct. The court explained this conclusion in two somewhat contradictory ways. First, ownership of property was a relationship recognized by law—a status—not an act committed by the owner. In other words, the law was defective because it punished no act. Second, even if the acquisition and continued possession of property was conduct, it was inherently "innocent" conduct, not conduct that could be criminalized. By this, the court might have meant that owning property was by itself harmless and blameless conduct. Alternatively, it might have meant that ownership of property was a right specifically protected by the Fourteenth Amendment due process clause. In either case, the law was defective because the act it punished was not wrongful.

---

55. Andrew Gelman et al., *An Analysis of the New York City Police Department's "Stop-and-Frisk" Policy in the Context of Claims of Racial Basis*, 102 J. AM. STAT. ASS'N 813, 814 (2007).
56. 176 P. 771 (Okla. Crim. App. 1918).

Finally, the court reasoned that if ownership of property was not a punishable act, the only remaining basis for criminalizing the offense was the intention to sell liquor. Thus, the court concluded, the defendant was being improperly punished for his thoughts alone.

But why not punish evil thoughts? It cannot be because they are hard to prove. All crimes are hard to prove, by design. The reasonable doubt standard is meant to be exacting. Although thoughts can be concealed, that is no reason to forgo punishing evil thoughts when they are expressed. Yet there are other, better reasons for not punishing mere thoughts. Punishment for unexecuted thoughts arguably violates both utility and desert. Presuming that we cannot choose our thoughts and desires, but we can choose whether to act on them, bad thoughts cannot be deterred by the threat of punishment. Moreover, there is no reason to deter bad thoughts because, unless they are acted on, they do no harm.[57] Similarly, if bad thoughts are unchosen, we cannot deserve blame for having them. In a liberal society we should arguably be free to harbor any thought we like. Moreover, punishing thought threatens privacy. The investigations required to uncover criminal thoughts might also uncover other thoughts, such as political opinions, religious beliefs, or sexual desires, that the individual should be free to express or keep secret.

A. Wrongfulness

What makes an act wrong? Does the wrongness of a criminal offense inhere in disobedience to law, so that the mere fact of prior proscription renders an act wrong? Or must an offense merit proscription by violating some other important value such as utility or fairness? Through much of the history of the common law, criminality was associated with defying royal authority, but specifically by engaging in unauthorized violence in public, in violation of the king's peace. Crimes were generally trespasses by force of arms or by breach of an enclosure. Thus, when early modern courts and scholars referred to "unlawful" acts they probably meant trespasses. The manifest violence of such acts evinced their illegality.

Blackstone adapted the idea of the king's peace to the newly established parliamentary supremacy, by defining crimes as injuries to public interests.[58]

---

57. *But see* MEIR DAN-COHEN, HARMFUL THOUGHTS: ESSAYS ON LAW, SELF, AND MORALITY (2002) (arguing that a low opinion of a person injures her reputation even if she never learns about it).

58. 4 WILLIAM BLACKSTONE, COMMENTARIES ON THE LAWS OF ENGLAND 1–2 (1765–1769).

He incorporated Lockean rights theory by identifying the protection of certain individual entitlements, such as property and personal security, as the essential justifying purpose of law. Such private interests were therefore invested with the public interest. Once this reinterpretation occurred, a requirement of publicly manifest violence was no longer ideologically necessary, although it maintained a continuing vestigial influence.

For Bentham, law's purpose was to prevent injuries or coordinate action to achieve benefits.[59] Crimes were not fundamentally different from other legal wrongs. They were simply those injuries to legal entitlements or omissions to carry out legal duties that were sufficiently costly and sufficiently deterrable to warrant punishment. Following Bentham, Holmes conceived crimes as acts committed under circumstances offering a reasonably apparent risk of harm.[60]

In his widely admired essay "On Liberty," John Stuart Mill argued that a liberal government could only punish conduct harmful to others.[61] Perhaps Proctor's ownership of property was "innocent" because harmless. One premise of Mill's harm principle was the utility principle. He thought suffering should only be imposed in order to deter the infliction of greater suffering. He also thought punishment should be directed at action harming others rather than one's self, because each person likely had better information about her own welfare, and more reason to consider it, than did the legislature. Mill also relied on libertarian premises: he thought each individual should be free to define her own ends.

What does the harm principle exclude? In an influential work on criminalization, the philosopher Joel Feinberg contrasted punishment for harm to others with (1) paternalistic punishment for harm to self, (2) punishment for conduct offending others' taste without inflicting tangible harm (such as public consensual sex acts), and (3) punishment for conduct discreetly violating others' moral beliefs (such as consensual deviant sex acts in private).[62] The harm principle does not exclude punishment for acts that create a risk of harm, as this might be the most effective way to prevent harm itself.

To what extent does American criminal law embrace the harm principle? When criminal codes announce social protection or deterrence as their aim, they imply that a concern with preventing harm has informed offense definition, but not in any way that a defendant could invoke as a bar to prosecution. On the other hand, First Amendment freedoms of speech and worship exclude certain motives for punishing conduct, and effectively require that prohibitions

59. Jeremy Bentham, Theory of Legislation 1–3 (R. Hildreth trans., 1887).
60. Oliver Wendell Holmes, Jr., The Common Law 75–76 (1881).
61. John Stuart Mill, On Liberty 21–22 (1859).
62. Joel Feinberg, Harm to Others: The Moral Limits of the Criminal Law (1984).

that inhibit the exercise of First Amendment freedoms must be justified by danger to a public or private interest.

In *Lawrence v. Texas* the Supreme Court arguably embraced a limited constitutional harm principle extending to constitutionally protected conduct.[63] Here the Court, recognized a right of consensual sexual conduct in private among adults, overturned a statute criminalizing homosexual sodomy, and held that such conduct could not be criminally punished unless it endangered a person or a public institution protected by law. Private consensual sexual conduct was therefore a liberty protected by the due process clause against unreasonable punishment, and only harm provided a sufficient reason to punish it. This was a striking decision, with surprising implications. *Lawrence* seems to forbid criminalizing consensual incest and prostitution among adults in private on the basis of mere moral disapproval. It does not preclude criminalizing consensual incest to preserve the institution of the family, or criminalizing prostitution to protect public health or as a prophylactic against violations of consent.

It is important to recognize that *Lawrence*, like the overbreadth cases of *Thornhill* and *Shuttlesworth*, only concerns the punishment of harmless conduct that is otherwise constitutionally protected. Yet when we exempt private consensual sexual conduct as well as the political and religious conduct protected by the First Amendment, we have covered much of the conduct that anyone might wish to punish for moral reasons alone. Moreover, requiring a harm rationale for the punishment of constitutionally protected conduct could have broader implications. Recall that *Shuttlesworth* suggested that a general liberty of person, including freedom of movement, may not be infringed absent some danger of harm. Yet this general freedom of movement is arguably infringed by all government coercion and all incarceration. It seems that due process should require a weighty justification for any such interference with liberty. Thus the harm principle invoked selectively in *Shuttlesworth* and *Lawrence* might come to be seen as a requirement for any criminal prohibition.

Even if the harm principle were clearly binding, however, this would leave open large questions about what counts as harm. Bernard Harcourt has shown that as the harm principle has become increasingly accepted, "vices" formerly seen as immoral or offensive, such as prostitution, have now been recharacterized as threats to public health or economic welfare.[64] A constitutional harm principle could be undermined by a posture of judicial deference toward specious legislative claims that proscribed conduct is dangerous or costly.

---

63. 539 U.S. 558 (2003).
64. Bernard Harcourt, *The Collapse of the Harm Principle*, 90 J. CRIM. L. & CRIMINOLOGY 109, 109–13 (1999).

Before leaving the requirement of wrongfulness, we should recall that offense definition is not the only stage at which criminal law ensures that punishable conduct is wrongful. Even if a particular offense harms or endangers an interest worthy of legal protection, its commission might be justified in order to prevent some other injury or to achieve some other good. A claim of justification is a defense that denies the wrongfulness of conduct satisfying an offense definition.

B. Conduct

Why should a criminal offense be an act? Why not punish bad thoughts or bad persons? Retributivism offers a ready answer for this question: we deserve blame only for what we choose, not for what we are. Utilitarianism offers a more ambivalent answer. On the one hand, punishment is most likely to achieve general deterrence if it is conditioned on choice. On the other hand, conditioning incarceration on harmful dispositions might serve the goals of incapacitation and rehabilitation. So the requirement of an act reflects the view that the primary purposes of criminal punishment are retribution for, and deterrence of, wrongful choices.

Yet perhaps we do choose our desires and characters. We commend people for laboriously developing skills that bring them satisfaction once mastered, and disapprove of people who indulge themselves by pursuing addictive desires. Observing these judgments, virtue ethicists have argued that we have a duty to habituate ourselves to desire what is beneficial.[65] To the extent we are the predictable products of our choices, we can be blamed for desires and dispositions to do wrong. Yet the causal chains connecting our choices to the dispositions we later develop are long and tangled. Punishing these choices would be inconsistent with the focus on temporally and spatially discrete events required by legality. If the defendant is charged with responsibility for having developed a bad character over the course of a life, we cannot be certain whether this "crime" occurred within the jurisdiction trying him, or after passage of the law forbidding it. One reason for defining offenses is to ensure that the charges communicate to defendants how they can defend themselves. Yet the "crime" of having developed a bad character would require the defendant to answer for his entire life. Finally, in a liberal society that encourages people

---

65. Kyron Huigens, *Virtue and Inculpation*, 108 HARV. L. REV. 1423 (1995).

to define their own visions of the good,[66] we may be reluctant to coerce people to develop virtuous characters.

We have related reasons for protecting unexecuted thoughts from punishment. It seems that we cannot deliberate morally about what to do, or deliberate politically about what to permit, without thinking about wrongful acts. Moreover, commitment to freedom of speech and thought would seem to require us to protect even antisocial thoughts from punishment. In addition, privacy concerns militate against criminalizing unexecuted desires because of the intrusions that might be required to detect them.

Thus the requirement of an act fulfills some of the same functions as legality. By directing punishment at spatially and temporally discrete past choices, an act requirement gives potential offenders a fair opportunity to avoid liability and to defend themselves at trial, and prevents illiberal punishment on the basis of a person's identity or ideology.

IV. Omissions

Ensuring that punishment is tied to spatially and temporally definite choices does not require conditioning punishment on physical movement. I can make a spatially and temporally discrete choice by failing to pay taxes due at a certain place and time, by failing to feed my infant for a day, or by remaining in a neighbor's home after I have been asked to leave. In other words, I can choose by knowingly omitting to fulfill a duty. The omission occurs at the time when and the place where I should have acted, but chose not to.

Nevertheless, there is an important difference between an act and an omission. It seems that I can commit an act regardless of whether someone has forbidden it, but I can only commit an omission if there is a norm requiring me to do something. Thus, in the case of *Jones v. United States*, the defendant was convicted of manslaughter for the death of an infant left in her care by the mother.[67] She was found to have caused the death, not by assaulting or poisoning the child, but by the passive conduct of failing to feed him adequately. Yet the conviction was reversed and remanded because of the trial court's failure to instruct the jury that the prosecution would have to prove that the defendant had a legal duty to care for the child. A neighbor who was aware of the child's hunger and who could have prevented the child's death by alerting child welfare authorities would not be liable for choosing not to do so,

---

66. *See generally* BRUCE ACKERMAN, SOCIAL JUSTICE IN THE LIBERAL STATE (1980).
67. 308 F.2d 307 (D.C. Cir. 1962).

because lacking any legal duty to do so. The court noted four potentially applicable sources of a duty to care for an infant. First a statute might impose such a duty—for example, a school employee might be legally required to report evidence of malnutrition in a pupil. Second, such a duty might inhere in a status-relationship, such as parenthood. Third, such a duty might voluntarily assumed by contract. Fourth, such a duty might be voluntarily undertaken, thereby inviting others to rely on the volunteer's implicit or explicit assurance. It was fairly clear that Jones had assumed a duty either by contract or undertaking, but a jury had to decide this.

The scope of duties of care and rescue are matters of moral controversy. Utilitarianism would seem best served by requiring anyone who knows she can avert harm to do so. Others counter that fear of liability would then discourage witnesses from reporting they had seen people in need. Some retributivists argue that the law rationally distinguishes between those who cause harm by commission and those who cause harm by omission. According to legal philosopher Michael Moore, prohibitions on conduct leave us many more alternative courses of action than affirmative duties to act.[68] Thus, a general duty to prevent death burdens autonomy far more than a general duty to avoid acts causing death.

Although there is controversy about the proper scope of duties to prevent harm to others, this controversy presupposes that blame for passive conduct depends on a duty to act. One cannot choose to neglect a duty without having such a duty. The Model Penal Code therefore requires that "[l]iability for the commission of an offense may not be based on an omission unaccompanied by action unless: (a) the omission is expressly made sufficient by the law defining the offense; or (b) a duty to perform the omitted act is otherwise imposed by law."[69] In addition, liability for omission requires that fulfillment of the neglected duty is possible. This condition renders the omission voluntary.

Because omissions require duties, there appears to be an asymmetry between acts and omissions. The former seem like facts of nature that exist independent of any legal or moral norms, whereas the latter seem like normative judgments. Thus Moore, following Oliver Wendell Holmes Jr., defines acts as willed muscular contractions.[70] Yet the criminal law theorist George Fletcher disagrees that acts are physical phenomena. He points out that standing on

68. Michael S. Moore, Act and Crime: The Philosophy of Action and Its Implications for Criminal Law 54–56 (1993).

69. Model Penal Code § 2.01(3) (1962).

70. Michael S. Moore, Act and Crime: The Philosophy of Action and Its Implications for Criminal Law 78–86 (1993); Oliver Wendell Holmes, Jr., The Common Law 131–32 (1881).

guard and participating in a "sit-in" are acts, not omissions, yet they do not involve movement.[71] Moreover, as with omissions, our ability to identify acts depends upon our understanding of the social practices that give them normative meaning. Before it became common to require separate proof of a mental element at the end of the eighteenth century in England, evidence of a crime was expected to include indicia of violence or stealth that made the conduct "manifestly criminal."[72] Homicide required not just causing death, but using a means recognizable as a weapon. Theft required not just acquiring control of goods, but doing so in a way recognizable as a "trespass." Such a trespass involved conforming to cultural expectations for criminal behavior.

Today, many of the acts required by offense definitions are acts of communication. This is particularly true when criminal liability depends on collaboration, as in conspiracy or accomplice liability; or exploitation or intimidation of a victim, as in fraud, extortion, harassment, sexual assault, or witness tampering; or consensual transaction, as in the sale or purchase of contraband; or concealment of information, as in obstruction of justice or perjury. We cannot identify the act without interpreting its meaning. Some crimes, such as that in *Proctor*, require proof of possession, acquisition, or control, all of which depend on interpretive judgments about legal relationships or expected future conduct. We may, like the *Proctor* court, reasonably question whether legal relationships such as ownership and possession are acts at all. In any case, many of the "acts" required by contemporary criminal law require normative judgment to identify, and, in this respect, resemble omissions.

Because criminal omissions require a duty to act, the definition of a crime of omission cannot satisfy the principle of legality unless the imposition of the duty also satisfies that principle. Thus, the duty must be imposed prospectively. Arguably, it should also be imposed publicly and specifically, to provide fair notice, avoid chilling protected conduct, and prevent discriminatory prosecution. If criminal prohibitions should be imposed legislatively, it would seem that duties should also be defined legislatively. Yet many of our legal duties are defined by judicially developed tort law, which sometimes applies very flexible standards. Tort law is particularly relevant in defining duties to prevent injury. Thus when defendants are charged with causing harm by omission, their liability may turn on unpredictable exercises of judicial discretion.

71. George P. Fletcher, *On the Moral Irrelevance of Bodily Movements*, 142 U. PA. L. REV. 1443, 1445–47 (1994).

72. Guyora Binder, *The Meaning of Killing*, *in* MODERN HISTORIES OF CRIME AND PUNISHMENT 88, 89–90 (Markus D. Dubber & Lindsay Farmer eds., 2007); George P. Fletcher, *The Metamorphosis of Larceny*, 89 HARV. L. REV. 469, 501–10 (1976).

In *Commonwealth v. Levesque*, the defendants negligently started a fire in a warehouse where they were squatting illegally.[73] They failed to report the fire, presumably hoping to escape responsibility for damage to the warehouse. They were held liable for recklessly causing the deaths of six firefighters, who died fighting the blaze when a portion of the structure collapsed. The court reasoned that Massachusetts law imposed a general duty to act with reasonable regard of the welfare of others. The court then found a duty on the part of those who negligently create a danger to prevent resulting harm. Such a duty was endorsed by the American Law Institute's Restatement of Torts, but had never been recognized as a basis for civil or criminal liability in Massachusetts.[74]

By contrast, in *State v. Lisa* the defendant's manslaughter charge was quashed where the defendant failed to seek medical aid for a victim who passed out in his apartment during a party and died of a drug overdose hours later.[75] The defendant had supplied some of the drugs, had led the victim to a bedroom, and excluded other guests so that he could have sex with her (and indeed sexually assaulted her after she was unconscious). The indictment had based a duty to seek medical care on his having caused the danger, and isolated the victim from other sources of aid, relying on the authority of the Restatement of Torts. The court held that because these duties had not previously been established by New Jersey case law, the defendant lacked adequate notice of them. Such a requirement of notice of a duty may be understood not only as a requirement of legality, but also as a requirement that liability be conditioned on culpability.

Does due process require notice of duties? At least sometimes. In *Lambert v. California*, the U.S. Supreme Court overturned a conviction for the omission of failure to register as a felon within five days of entering Los Angeles, because of the failure to require proof of "the probability" of the defendant's knowledge of a duty to register.[76] The Court emphasized that the harmlessness of the only conduct involved, entering a city, gave the defendant no reason to inquire into any attendant duties. Professor Alan Michaels has argued that a decisive factor in the decision is that travel is not merely harmless conduct, but constitutionally protected, so that notice is necessary to prevent the chilling of a protected liberty.[77]

---

73. 766 N.E.2d 50 (Mass. 2007).
74. RESTATEMENT (SECOND) OF TORTS § 321(1) (1965).
75. 919 A.2d 145 (N.J. Super. Ct. App. Div. 2007).
76. 355 U.S. 225 (1957).
77. Alan C. Michaels, *Constitutional Innocence*, 112 HARV. L. REV. 828, 862–67 (1999).

V. A Constitutional Requirement of Conduct

With the understanding that conduct can include both acts and omissions, does constitutional due process require such conduct? It does. We have seen that the Court in *Lanzetta* objected to a statute punishing having a criminal record and being known as a member of gang, because the statute did not require any act or omission. The Court reached a similar conclusion in the important case of *Robinson v. California*, which overturned a statute punishing "being addicted to the use of narcotics."[78] The judge in the case instructed the jury that the defendant could be convicted if he exemplified the "status" of addiction, which he described as the chronic condition of one who had become addicted until he reformed. Justice Stewart observed that the statute, thus construed,

> is not one which punishes a person for the use of narcotics, for their purchase, sale or possession, or for antisocial or disorderly behavior resulting from their administration. It is not a law which even purports to provide or require medical treatment. Rather, we deal with a statute which makes the "status" of narcotic addiction a criminal offense, for which the offender may be prosecuted "at any time before he reforms." California has said that a person can be continuously guilty of this offense, whether or not he has ever used or possessed any narcotics within the State, and whether or not he has been guilty of any antisocial behavior there.[79]

In condemning this statute as imposing cruel and unusual punishment in violation of the Eighth Amendment, Stewart likened it to punishment for mental illness or leprosy, and noted that it was possible to become addicted involuntarily. He implied, however, that the state could punish use of drugs, and could order the civil commitment of addicts to a treatment facility or criminalize their failure to accept treatment.

Justice Douglas joined Stewart's opinion, but his separate concurrence emphasized the possibility of involuntary addiction, the ill health effects of addiction, the physiological basis of the resulting cravings, and the difficulty of overcoming it without assistance. He argued for the superior wisdom of combatting addiction with medical treatment rather than punishment, and opined that the use of criminal punishment, "with its resulting stigma and irreparable damage to the good name of the accused,"[80] for the purpose of treatment rather

78. 370 U.S. 660 (1962).
79. *Id.* at 666.
80. *Id.* at 667 (Douglas, J., concurring).

than the expression of blame violated the Eighth Amendment. Yet he conceded that punitive measures could justifiably be imposed on an addict "when they relate to acts of transgression."[81] He emphasized that the California statute instead punished "being an addict."[82]

Justice Harlan's concurrence rejected the instruction but not the statute. He reasoned that the use of drugs by an addict could be voluntary and that punishing addiction would therefore be acceptable if the instructions required proof of drug use within the jurisdiction. However "since addiction alone" is nothing "more than a compelling propensity to use narcotics, the effect of this instruction was to authorize criminal punishment for a bare desire to commit a criminal act."[83] This, he held, was beyond the constitutional power of the state.

Justice Clark dissented, arguing that because California required commitment to a treatment facility for addicts incapable of self-control, the criminal statute at issue applied only to addicts who took drugs voluntarily. Accordingly, he concluded, the addiction punished was not "an involuntary status."[84] Moreover, he argued, the purpose of incarceration was medical rather than penal, to deny addicts access to the drug.

Justice White added in dissent that he might support the decision "[i]f appellant's conviction rested upon sheer status, condition or illness or if he was convicted for being an addict who had lost his power of self-control...."[85] However, he saw the conviction as one for the repeated use of narcotics and understood the statute as reasonably absolving the state of the difficult task of proving that the use took place within the jurisdiction. Justice White argued that the majority opinion had the undesirable implication that punishment for drug use itself was unconstitutional.

Thus the opinions considered five interrelated questions: the permissibility of punishment for (1) statuses or conditions, (2) desires or propensities, (3) conduct committed at an unknown time and place, (4) involuntary conduct, and (5) the purpose of treatment alone. Which of these five uses of punishment did the *Robinson* decision actually forbid?

Contrary to Justice White's claim that the decision barred punishment for drug use, all six of the justices in the majority conceded the right of California to punish drug use within the state. Both of the dissenting justices seemed to concede that involuntary drug use should not be punished, but argued that Robinson had used drugs voluntarily and could be punished for it under the

81. *Id.* at 674 (Douglas J., concurring).
82. *Id.* (Douglas, J., concurring).
83. Robinson v. California, 370 U.S. 660, 679 (1962) (Harlan, J., concurring).
84. *Id.* at 684 (Clark, J., dissenting).
85. *Id.* at 685 (White, J., dissenting).

statute. Justice Harlan agreed, objecting only to the instruction permitting punishment for addiction rather than use. Justice White argued that addiction was nothing more than repeated use, but the justices in the majority did not agree.

How did the majority think the proscribed offense differed from voluntary use? Both dissenting justices sought to characterize the majority's objection as confined to the punishment of what Justice Clark called "an involuntary status."[86] To be sure, Justices Stewart and Douglas both characterized addiction as a disease that might be developed involuntarily. Justice Douglas also emphasized that an addict's cravings, however developed, are bodily needs. The addict might resist gratifying them, but is powerless to avoid feeling them. Yet, as Justice Harlan's concurrence pointed out, the analogy of addiction to disease interweaves two distinct critiques of punishing addiction.

The disease analogy expresses that addiction is a physiological condition distinct from the actions causing it. Although addictive cravings might result from voluntary action, they are involuntary in that the defendant cannot simply wish them away. They require prolonged abstinence to overcome. Moreover, the addiction itself makes such abstinence difficult. Thus addiction influences and is influenced by behavior, but is not reducible to behavior. It is both a physical state and a constraint on volition.

Douglas used the disease analogy to argue that incarceration and the threat of incarceration were unlikely to deter addictive cravings, and the involuntariness of these cravings made it unfair to blame addicts for having them. At the root of these arguments lay a commitment to the harm principle and a view of addicts as primarily harming themselves. If addicts were incapable of reforming despite their misery and ill health, threatening them with more misery was backward and inhumane.

Stewart drew a different point from the disease analogy. Addiction was a condition of the body, but one that might or might not have been caused by voluntary "antisocial" acts. Such voluntary acts might or might not have occurred within the jurisdiction and subsequent to their proscription. Stewart objected not to punishing drug use within California, but to California's evasion of its responsibility to proscribe and prove such conduct. Of course to be an addict in California one must have either taken drugs in California or entered California in a condition of addiction. Yet entering the state is not "antisocial" conduct, and is indeed an exercise of the constitutional right of interstate travel, related to the right of personal mobility invoked in *Shuttlesworth* and *Papachristou*. The

86. *Id.* at 684 (Clark, J., dissenting).

condition of addiction itself is not an act, but a circumstance. The same would be true of insanity, or of having been previously convicted of crime.

Harlan also viewed the statute as an evasion of the state's burden, but he characterized that evasion differently. For him, addiction was not a physiological condition, but a pejorative description of character, like vagrancy. Rather than viewing addiction as an effect of past criminalizable conduct, Harlan characterized it as a desire or disposition to commit crime in the future. Like the *Proctor* court, Harlan objected to punishing unexecuted thoughts. There was perhaps also an implication that such criminal dispositions are easily ascribed by law enforcement. For Harlan, the statute in *Robinson* was defective in the same way as the statutes overturned in *Lanzetta* and the later case of *Papachristou.* Such habitual offender statutes enabled the state to punish people for what they might do, without having to prove they had actually done it.

In short, the Douglas opinion condemned the cruel punishment of conduct that was blameless because involuntary and harmless to others; the Harlan opinion condemned the punishment of status, identity, and disposition rather than conduct; and the controlling Stewart opinion gestured in both directions. Thus, the *Robinson* case can be read as standing for two principles: a requirement that every offense include a conduct element, not merely circumstances and mental elements; and a further requirement that the conduct be performed voluntarily. Both requirements are expressed in the Model Penal Code's Section 2.01(1): "A person is not guilty of an offense unless his liability is based on conduct which includes a voluntary act or the omission to perform an act of which he is physically capable." Yet the *Robinson* decision left large questions concerning the scope of both principles.

VI. A Constitutional Requirement of Voluntariness?

The later case of *Powell v. Texas* put Douglas's voluntariness principle to the test.[87] Powell challenged his conviction for public drunkenness on the grounds that he was an alcoholic, helpless to control his drinking, and helpless to restrain himself from going in public once drunk. Hence, he concluded, application of the statute to him cruelly punished involuntary conduct in violation of the Eighth Amendment. Four justices (Douglas, Stewart, Brennan, and Fortas) agreed. Another group of four justices (Harlan, Black, Marshall, and Warren) reasoned that drinking and going in public were acts, and that as the statute

87. 392 U.S. 514 (1968).

did not single out alcoholics for punishment, it did not define a status crime. The deciding vote fell to Justice White, who agreed with the Douglas group that the *Robinson* case had forbidden the punishment of involuntary conduct and could therefore be applied to bar punishment of an alcoholic for drinking. But White argued that the statute as applied did not violate this voluntariness principle because alcoholism did not cause an irresistible compulsion to go in public. So which of the two interpretations of *Robinson* did the *Powell* decision endorse—the requirement of voluntariness, or the requirement of conduct? We cannot say, because while White treated the voluntariness requirement as the holding of *Robinson*, he had dissented from the result in *Robinson*, and criticized the voluntariness principle as bad policy. There is no way to know whether White would have resolved an addict's challenge to a conviction for drug use by favoring precedent or policy.

Nor have subsequent cases resolved this question. In *Pottinger v. City of Miami*, a federal court found the City of Miami liable for violating the Eighth Amendment rights of homeless persons arrested or convicted for the "harmless" offense of sleeping in public.[88] Invoking *Robinson* and *Powell*, the court reasoned that sleeping in public was involuntary for homeless persons, and that homelessness itself was generally an involuntary consequence of mental illness or involuntary unemployment. Yet in *Joyce v. San Francisco*, another federal court refused to adopt this reasoning, conceding that *Robinson* would preclude punishing the status of homelessness, but not conduct made probable by that condition.[89]

The issue left open by *Robinson* and *Powell* is not whether punishable conduct must be voluntary, but how voluntary it must be. Courts interpret statutory definitions of punishable conduct as requiring volition on the part of the actor. For example, in the Alabama case of *Martin v. State*, the defendant was convicted of public drunkenness after he was arrested in his home while in an intoxicated state, and taken outside by police.[90] The Alabama Court of Appeals overturned the conviction on the grounds that the statutory language "appears in any public place" implied a voluntary act of going in public.[91] The Model Penal Code does not define its requirement of a voluntary act but provides that voluntary acts do not include reflexes, convulsions, and unconscious movements including those occurring while asleep, or under hypnosis.[92] It also excludes any other "bodily movement that . . . is not a product of the effort or

88. 810 F. Supp. 1551 (S.D. Fla. 1992).
89. 846 F. Supp. 843 (N.D. Cal. 1994).
90. 17 So. 2d 427 (Ala. Ct. App. 1944).
91. *Id.* at 427.
92. Model Penal Code § 2.01(2) (1962).

determination of the actor, either conscious or habitual."[93] This would certainly preclude liability for movements compelled by physical force, or legal compulsion, as in *Martin*. It would not preclude liability for the habitual decisions we make when our attention wanders while driving or doing dangerous work.

Claims of unconsciousness pose two kinds of difficulties.

First, when an accused moves in ways that appear purposeful, it is natural to assume that conduct is conscious, and to mistrust a defendant's subsequent claims of automatism as self-serving. Defendants have sometimes explained acts of violence involving elaborate preparation or concealment as instances of somnambulism. Yet, the act element of an offense is an issue on which the prosecution bears the burden of proof beyond a reasonable doubt. Thus claims of automatism put the prosecution in the difficult position of refuting expert claims about exotic psychological states. A famous case illustrating this problem was *People v. Newton*.[94] During an arrest, Black Panther leader Huey Newton was shot in the stomach and both arresting officers were shot, one fatally. A witness claimed to have seen Newton shooting at the officers, while Newton claimed to have lost consciousness after being shot. A medical expert testified that a gunshot in the abdomen could have caused an unconscious state in which Newton would still have been capable of shooting the officers. Newton's manslaughter conviction was overturned for failure to instruct the jury on the prosecution's burden to prove Newton's consciousness. Thus on a claim of automatism, the defense faces only a burden of production, to supply some evidence. Meeting this burden shifts the burden to the prosecution to disprove the claim beyond a reasonable doubt. By contrast, when the defendant claims insanity, he or she must prove it by a preponderance of the evidence in most jurisdictions. Newton's charges were eventually dropped, largely because of a lack of evidence that he had fired any of the shots.

A second problem raised by claims of automatism is one of "time-framing" where the defendant causes his unconsciousness or anticipates that he may become unconscious.[95] In *People v. Decina*, the defendant had an epileptic seizure while driving, resulting in the death of four girls walking home from school.[96] He was convicted of a negligent homicide offense, on the theory that he knew he was prone to such seizures and acted negligently in driving while aware of this condition. An appellate court agreed, rejecting the defendant's argument that he could not drive negligently while he was unconscious. The

---

93. *Id.* § 2.01(2)(d).

94. 87 Cal. Rptr. 394 (Cal. Ct. App. 1970).

95. Mark Kelman, *Interpretive Construction in the Substantive Criminal Law*, 33 STAN. L. REV. 591 (1981).

96. 138 N.E.2d 799 (N.Y. 1956).

court reasoned that Decina's negligent act took place when he got behind the wheel knowing of a risk of sudden unconsciousness. The court transferred voluntariness from the conscious decision to drive to the later involuntarily dangerous driving. A dissenting judge objected that the defendant had not fulfilled a statutory element of driving carelessly because at the time of the accident he could not be said to have been driving at all. This judge also objected to the majority's implication that the defendant was guilty of dangerous driving every time he drove without incident and asked "how many of this State's 5,000,000 licensed operators are subject to such penalties for merely driving the cars they are licensed to drive? . . . It is no answer that prosecutors and juries will be reasonable or compassionate. A criminal statute whose reach is so unpredictable violates constitutional rights."[97] Once again we see the interrelatedness of considerations of legality, wrongfulness, and volition. Because driving is a common activity and licensed by the state, it seems, as the *Proctor* court said of ownership of property, "innocent." The offense in question, causing death by means of negligent driving, defined the punishable conduct vaguely, and the court applied it in an unexpected way.

In the Illinois case of *People v. Grant*, the defendant was convicted of assault against a police officer and sentenced to prison for three to nine years.[98] Although he offered evidence that he was unconscious during the assault because of an epileptic seizure, the trial court instructed the jury to consider this evidence only in determining whether the defendant had established an excuse of insanity. An appellate court held this to be erroneous and awarded a new trial to determine whether the prosecution had proven the required element of a voluntary act. Yet after noting that defendant seemed to have a history of violence during seizures, the court held that

> Although a voluntary act is an absolute requirement of liability under . . . our Code . . . there is no requirement that every act preceding the actual commission of the offense be voluntary. Thus the jury may, on remand, determine that the jury attacked [the officer] . . . while in a state of automatism, but that he nevertheless committed an offense . . . if he had prior notice of his susceptibility to engage in violent involuntary conduct brought on by drinking . . . or by some other conscious causal behavior.[99]

---

97. *Id.* at 148 (Desmond, J., dissenting in part).
98. 360 N.E.2d 809 (Ill. App. Ct. 1977).
99. *Id.* at 815.

Both the *Decina* and *Grant* courts are ready to transfer voluntariness from a conscious decision to risk unconscious movement to a subsequent unconscious proscribed act. Transferring voluntariness is subject to at least three objections. First, from the standpoint of legality, the conduct of risking automatism will generally be quite different from the conduct proscribed, so that the proscription does not give adequate notice that it may cover unconscious conduct. Second, whether a voluntary act of risking unconsciousness results in harm is, from an ex ante standpoint, a matter of moral luck. Thus, from the standpoint of desert, the defendant who causes harm unconsciously is no more blameworthy than the one who harmlessly risks becoming unconscious. Although hindsight bias may make the ex ante likelihood of the proscribed conduct seem much greater than it was, the voluntary act of risking unconsciousness is much less blameworthy than voluntarily committing the proscribed conduct. Third, severely punishing a low probability result is inefficient from the standpoint of deterrence theory. Because increases in the certainty of punishment have greater deterrent effect than increases in the severity of punishment, it would be more effective to impose a modest punishment on every instance of the conscious risk-taking rather than those very few instances where the defendant becomes unconscious and causes harm while in that state.

Decisions such as *Decina* and *Grant*, holding defendants responsible for managing the effects of an illness are rare. On the other hand, criminal law routinely broadens the time frame for assessing the voluntariness of conduct when it holds offenders responsible for unconscious conduct they commit after voluntarily intoxicating themselves. Thus in *Davidson v. State*, self-intoxication with Ambien did not render a shooting involuntary.[100] Self-induced unconsciousness will ordinarily negate a required mental element of knowingly or purposefully causing some injury. Yet the Model Penal Code provides that self-induced intoxication cannot negate a required mental element of recklessness with respect to a result even if it in fact renders an actor unaware of the risk of causing that result.[101] Thus a culpable attitude of carelessness can be transferred along with voluntariness. We will return to this problem of transferred culpable mental states in Chapter 5.

Unless voluntariness transfers from a conscious act of risk-taking to a later unconscious act, claims of unconsciousness clearly negate a requirement of voluntary conduct rooted in constitutional due process. The same is true of claims of physical or legal compulsion, such as those involved in *Martin v. State*.

---

100. 849 N.E.2d 591 (Ind. 2006).

101. Model Penal Code § 2.08(3) (1962).

What remains unclear is whether any influences on conscious choice such as addiction, poverty, coercive threats, or social pressure can negate voluntariness. Ordinarily an argument based on such an influence would be framed as an excuse, conceding a voluntary actus reus, but denying the defendant's responsibility for the choice he or she made. If so, the defendant would usually bear the burden of proof on the issue. In some cases, such an influence might result in an impairment of perception or judgment that would negate the culpable mental state required for the offense. As noted, many jurisdictions allow evidence of voluntary intoxication to support a claim that the defendant acted without expecting or intending certain harmful consequences. The prosecution bears the burden to prove required mental states.

VII. Possession

The principle established in *Robinson*, that criminal offenses must include conduct, not merely statuses or circumstances, seems at odds with an obvious feature of our contemporary criminal justice system. A substantial portion of the inmates filling American jails and prisons have been convicted of drug possession. Moreover, constitutional rules of criminal procedure encourage police to focus on these offenses, by permitting police to detain and question those they "reasonably" suspect of drug offenses, search them for weapons they reasonably suspect them to be carrying, and thereby uncover any drugs.[102] Yet possession seems like a legal relationship to an object, or perhaps the circumstance of proximity to the object, combined with an intention to exercise control. Thus, in *Proctor* the court argued that mere possession of real property was not an act. How, then, can we square possession offenses with the prohibition on punishing status? The Model Penal Code does so by providing that possession is only voluntary conduct when "the possessor knowingly procured or received the thing possessed or was aware of his control thereof for a sufficient period to have been able to terminate his possession."[103] Thus the punishable conduct is either acquisition of the contraband or the omission to dispose of it.

The federal law of possession is well illustrated by the case of *United States v. Maldonado*, in which the defendant's conviction for possession of cocaine with intent to distribute was upheld.[104] A police informant named Santos had been recruited by one drug dealer to deliver the cocaine to another dealer

102. Terry v. Ohio, 392 U.S. 1, 27 (1968).
103. Model Penal Code § 2.01(4) (1962).
104. 23 F.3d 4 (1st Cir. 1994).

named Palestino, in a hotel room. On arriving at the room, Santos was instead met by the defendant, who told him Palestino would come. The defendant suggested that Santos place the cocaine in a different room in the hotel, but Santos refused, and continued to wait. Eventually Santos suggested they both get soft drinks in the hotel lobby, to which the defendant agreed. Santos and the defendant left the hotel room together, with Santos leaving the cocaine in the room. The defendant was arrested at that point, without ever touching the cocaine, being alone with it, paying for it, or being told he could have it. Nevertheless, the court concluded that he had "constructive possession."[105] The court defined constructive possession as "the power and intention to exercise control" over an object.

In considering the control element, the court reasoned that Maldonado had power over the drugs when they were left in a hotel room he had access to. It conceded that he might have faced resistance from Santos if he had attempted to exclude Santos from the room and assume control of the drugs. But it then reasoned that he could have resisted any effort by Santos to leave with the drugs (although without claiming he intended to do so), and characterized this hypothetical mutual veto as "joint" constructive possession. The court also chose to ignore the fact that Maldonado was surrounded by police, who had no intention of letting him leave with the drugs. Yet the court concluded that he was guilty of actual possession, not merely attempted possession.

In considering the intent element, the court reasoned not that Maldonado actually intended to resist Santos's departure with the drugs, but simply that he intended to facilitate their transfer to Palestino. Yet surely he could intend to facilitate someone else's possession without intending to possess the drugs himself. Again, he was convicted of possessing them himself, not as an accomplice to Palestino or Santos.

Constructive possession can involve an act where the defendant intentionally excludes others from access. But this must be his intent. In *State v. Casey*, the court ruled that an ex-felon's effort to exclude police from his trailer did not constitute possession of the weapon a friend had left inside, as there was no evidence that Casey intended to access the weapon or keep it away from the police.[106] Moreover, if the defendant merely had the means to exclude others from accessing the good, and would have done so if necessary, we have only a circumstance combined with a disposition. This does not seem to involve any conduct.

105. *Id.* at 7–8.
106. 203 P.3d 202 (Or. 2009).

Another critique of possession statutes is that they violate not the act requirement, but the harm principle, which limits punishment to offenses that impose harm or a risk of harm on others. Thus, the mere possession of a gun or drugs does no harm. Accordingly, possession offenses may involve conduct, but not sufficiently wrongful conduct to warrant punishment. Possession can be thought of as an inchoate crime, where the possession of a gun is criminalized to prevent its use in a crime of violence. The possession of large amounts of drugs might be criminalized to prevent their distribution to addicts who will harmfully self-administer with diminished voluntariness. In this respect possession offenses resemble attempts. Yet attempt liability requires far more than an opportunity to complete the crime. It requires proof of intent to commit the harmful crime, and an act that manifests the offender's commitment to complete the crime. Conduct falling short of this threshold is "mere preparation." Possession offenses, however, seem to criminalize potentially preparatory conduct and nothing more. A teacher who seizes drugs from a middle school student and retains them until they can be safely destroyed commits the offense of possession, and—like Santos, the police agent—can only avoid liability by offering a justification defense.

The resulting divergence between legal proscription and social harm raises problems of overbreadth and legality. In *United States v. Teemer*, a court held that even momentarily moving another's gun to free up a chair would constitute possession.[107] The alternative, reasoned the court could "exculpate a bank robber who . . . upon request picked up another bank robber's gun from the table and handed it to him." The court acknowledged that its conception of possession would inculpate an ex-felon who took a loaded gun from a child and disposed of it, but hoped that "prosecutors and—failing that—most juries would show good sense in such situations."[108] Note that the court's hypothetical clearly involves a voluntary act. The injustice the court here hopes jury nullification or prosecutorial discretion will prevent is the punishment of harmless conduct.

VIII. Conclusion

A criminal act is ordinarily a legally proscribed voluntary choice to endanger a public interest. We have seen that many aspects of this conception of a criminal act have been incorporated into the requirements of due process of law. Thus

---

107. 394 F.3d 59 (1st Cir. 2005).
108. *Id.* at 64.

due process requires that punishment be conditioned on a past wrongful voluntary act or omission to perform a legal duty, publicly and prospectively proscribed by law. If conduct is the exercise of a constitutionally protected liberty, it cannot be punished unless it is wrongful in endangering a public interest. In most American jurisdictions, the institution proscribing the conduct must be an electorally responsive legislature rather than the judiciary. Respecting the principles of legality, harm, and choice in defining criminal conduct helps us create a criminal law worthy of popular compliance and support.

FIVE

The Criminal Mind

I. Introduction

In Chapter 4, we explored the concept of a criminal act and the proposition that such an act is a necessary element of every criminal offense. In this chapter, we examine the concept of criminal *culpability* and the proposition that a guilty mind or *mens rea* is also a necessary element of every criminal offense. We will also discuss the related concept of *strict liability*, or liability without culpability.

It seems clear that wrongdoing must be intentional or careless both to justify blame and to be responsive to deterrent threats. Yet a requirement of a mental element is less clearly established in American law than the requirement of an act. Three difficulties contribute to this uncertainty.

First, a mental element is not always necessary to condition punishment on culpability, because culpability may be implicit in the act element. The act of "torture" implies an intention to inflict pain and an attitude of cruelty. The circumstance that the victim of battery is an "infant" implies cruelty and awareness of a risk of injury. A demand accompanied by a "threat" implies an intent to intimidate, and knowledge that the victim does not consent. "Causing" a result is often defined as committing an act necessary to the result and from which it was foreseeable. If so, causation implies some knowledge. In all these cases, proof of the conduct element implies some culpability even if the prosecution is not required to prove a mental element. Thus it is not clear that a constitutional requirement of culpability necessitates charging and proof of a mental element. Proof of a mental element is a *formal* test of culpability, but one could condition liability on *substantive* culpability by requiring an inherently culpable act. And just as we can distinguish *formal culpability* (proof of a required mental state) from *substantive culpability* (moral fault), we can also distinguish *formal strict liability* (no required mental state) from *substantive strict liability* (no requirement of fault). So even if we agree that punishment should be conditioned on substantive culpability, it remains an open question whether punishment should be conditioned on formal culpability.

Second, proof of a mental element by the prosecution is not the only way to get the question of the defendant's culpability before the fact-finder. The defendant may be permitted to offer the absence of culpability as an excuse from responsibility. Historically, questions of culpability were first raised as excuses, based on insanity, accident, and mistake. The idea that the prosecution should prove culpability as part of the offense emerged only gradually and has been accepted incompletely. Insanity, involuntary intoxication, extreme emotional disturbance (as a defense to murder), and reasonable mistake of law are all excuses that might be seen as mens rea issues. We will consider mistake of law in this chapter, extreme emotional disturbance in Chapter 6 (on homicide), and insanity in Chapter 9 (on justification and excuse).

Third, even when a court requires formal culpability, it may not clearly identify the principle requiring this result. When statutory offense definitions specify no mental element, courts may nevertheless interpret the statute as requiring proof of a mental element. They might do so on the ground that the Constitution requires it, either in general, or for some types of offenses or penalties. Alternatively, courts might read a mental element into a statute for other reasons: because they believe this would serve desert or utility, or because they believe the legislature so intended, or because they think uncertainty should always be resolved in the defendant's favor. We will see that the Supreme Court has often invoked the principle that punishment should depend on culpability, but avoided deciding whether and when the Constitution requires this.

Assuming that punishment should depend on a culpable mental state, we must decide what kind of mental states will suffice. Surely a mental state must be malign to help justify punishment as deserved. Blackstone held that all crime required a "vitious will." But is that enough, or must the mental state be malign in a specific way? Perhaps there should be some connection between the reasons we punish, and the mental states we require. A utilitarian might equate culpability with an expectation of net cost, whereas a Kantian retributivist might conceive culpability as a quality of selfish unfairness. The eighteenth-century judge Michael Foster defined "malice" as a "heart regardless of social duty and deliberately bent on mischief."[1]

Yet this kind of antisocial disposition seems like a quality of the offender rather than the offense. In our last chapter we saw that an important purpose of requiring a particular criminal act is to ensure that we are imposing blame for a past choice, not making a prediction about future behavior. When we punish (and therefore blame) an offender for a particular criminal act, it seems we

1. MICHAEL FOSTER, CROWN LAW 257 (1762).

should show him to be at fault *for that act.* Arguably then, the culpable mental state should *correspond* with the criminal act. Suppose Nosy picks up a brightly colored pill from a sidewalk and puts it in his wallet. Unbeknownst to him it contains illegal drugs. It seems he has intended no wrong and should not be liable for possessing illegal drugs. But now suppose Sneaky steals Nosy's wallet and so acquires the pill. Unlike Nosy, Sneaky has intended wrong, but is it the right wrong? It seems that Sneaky deserves punishment for theft, but not drug possession. Moreover, punishing unforeseeable drug possession as a collateral consequence of theft seems more likely to deter theft than to deter drug possession. So both desert and deterrence arguably support correspondence between a culpable mental state and a proscribed injury.

Assuming that a culpable mental state must indeed correspond to the proscribed criminal act, *how* culpable must I be with respect to that criminal act? Is careless wrongdoing enough to justify punishment? Arguably purposeful or knowing wrongdoing justifies more severe punishment than careless wrongdoing. If we should not punish without culpability, it seems we should also not punish in disproportion to the degree of culpability. If so, we will need to rank different mental states. It seems that someone who expects to cause a substantial injury is more culpable than one who expects to impose a small risk of a minor injury. Thus the quantity of culpability is arguably a function of the cost the actor expects to impose as a result of his or her conduct.

Should it matter whether the defendant *wants* to impose cost? For a utilitarian, the answer must be no. Other things being equal, the fulfillment of desire is always a good thing, not something to be punished. On this utilitarian conception, culpability is purely cognitive rather than volitional. But this purely cognitive view of culpability has some counterintuitive implications. Suppose Farmer Jane fires a rifle across a field at her neighbor Farmer Millie, hoping to kill her, although Jane knows the odds of success are very low. Farmer Bob lives closer to Farmer Millie and shoots his rifle in Farmer Millie's direction to test its recoil. He knows his odds of hitting Farmer Millie are low, although they are higher than Farmer Jane's. From a utilitarian perspective Farmer Bob's act is more culpable. Yet many will say that Farmer Jane acted with intent to kill, whereas Farmer Bob acted with at most recklessness. Thus a purely cognitive conception of culpability appears to rank these cases backward.

Next, consider a famous pair of philosophical hypotheticals: In Phillippa Foot's version, an engineer diverts a trolley from a track where it will run over five workers, to another where it will kill one.[2] In a variation offered by Judith

2. Phillippa Foot, *The Problem of Abortion and the Doctrine of Double Effect*, 5 OXFORD REV. 1 (1967).

Jarvis Thomson, a surgeon kills a healthy patient to harvest organs that will save five dying patients.[3] From a utilitarian perspective the two acts are equally justifiable, knowingly causing one death to save five. But most people feel that the second act is not justifiable, and one explanation for this discrepancy is that the surgeon purposefully causes a death, whereas the engineer knowingly causes one.[4] Alan Michaels has argued that even when an offender knowingly causes an injury, we blame him not for expecting harm, but for his willingness to bring it about.[5] So should we condition punishment on cognitive states or volitional states?

What mental state should we require when an offense has multiple act elements? Consider an offense requiring (1) a battery, (2) of a minor, (3) leading to injury. Suppose Bruiser intentionally pushes Loudmouth in a barroom argument. Unbeknownst to Bruiser, Loudmouth is a teen in the bar illegally. To Bruiser's surprise, Loudmouth falls awkwardly over a chair and breaks a bone. Are we justified in punishing Bruiser for injuring a minor if he is culpable with respect to the battery element only, but not the age of the victim or the injury? Following the criminal law theorist Ken Simons, we may call liability that is conditioned on no culpable mental states at all *pure strict liability*.[6] We may call liability conditioned on culpable mental states with respect to some act elements, but not others, *impure strict liability*.[7] We may call an act element without a corresponding culpable mental state a *strict liability element*. If we agree that punishment should always be conditioned on a culpable mental state, we reject pure strict liability. But should we also reject impure strict liability? Should we require a culpable mental state with respect to each act element?

In sum, although mens rea is a central concept of the criminal law, it is an ambiguous one. This chapter will explain that ambiguity historically. We will see that over the course of two centuries a utilitarian reform movement developed and promoted the idea that every offense should have a statutorily defined mental element. This movement has had considerable influence on American law, especially through the promulgation of the Model Penal Code and decisions of the U.S. Supreme Court constructing federal offense definitions, requiring proof of offense elements to satisfy due process, and occasionally requiring a mental element to satisfy due process. Yet the Model Penal Code's reception

---

3. Judith Thomson, *The Trolley Problem*, 94 YALE L.J. 1395 (1985).
4. ITZHAK KUGLER, DIRECT AND OBLIQUE INTENTION IN THE CRIMINAL LAW 37–41 (2002).
5. Alan Michaels, *Acceptance: The Missing Mental State*, 71 S. CAL. L. REV. 953 (1998).
6. Kenneth W. Simons, *When Is Strict Liability Just?*, 87 J. CRIM. L. & CRIMINOLOGY 1075, 1081 (1997).
7. *Id.*

has not been uniform, and the Supreme Court has been reluctant to intervene in the primarily legislative process of criminal lawmaking.

II. The Idea of Mens Rea in Ancient and Medieval Law

The notion that a crime involves a guilty mind is very ancient. The translation of this notion into a duty to find a particular mental state before imposing punishment is modern, however.

Roman law sources as early as the third century B.C. conditioned liability for damage on *culpa*, that is, fault or negligence. O.F. Robinson provides us this overview of intent in the Roman law of public delicts, or crimes:

> For the commission of a crime, ... guilty intention—*dolus* ... —was normally required.... An accident did not impose criminal liability. ... [C]rimes such as pasturage at night on another's land presume a guilty intention... [b]ut the intention was specifically relevant in cases of incendiarism and death.... Ignorance of the law, unlike ignorance of the facts, was culpable; it was the duty of the citizen to know the law.[8]

Robinson describes the mental dimension of Roman homicide law as follows:

> An intention to kill was necessary and it was this intention which made someone who ordered a killing a murderer; an infant or a madman could not be liable since they could not form a murderous intention. The motive was irrelevant; a mercy killing would have counted as a murder.[9]

If death was intended, even a nonfatal wounding might still be murder, for, as Hadrian wrote, "in crimes it is the intention that is regarded, not the issue."[10] Yet intention was also inferred from objective indicia so that death resulting from a blow with a weapon was presumed intentional, while death resulting from a blow with a household implement was deemed unintended.[11]

Christian sources suggested that blame presupposed sinful desires. Discussing perjury, Augustine wrote that "words make not guilt without a guilty mind." Elsewhere, Augustine wrote "Accidents which, without our will, happen

8. O.F. Robinson, The Criminal Law of Ancient Rome 16 (1995).
9. *Id.* at 44.
10. *Id.*
11. *Id.*

to others through good and lawful actions of ours . . . must not be imputed to us."[12] For Augustine, a properly governed soul yearned only to serve God. A will moved by impious desires was in a state of alienation from God, and actions motivated by such desires were sinful. Thus for Augustine, mens rea meant a disloyal disposition, manifested in improperly motivated action. The action might do injury, but its sinfulness inhered in its motive rather than its effects.

In the thirteenth century Aquinas complicated this scheme by distinguishing between consequences intended directly because desired as ends or as necessary means and consequences intended indirectly, because foreseen as collateral results of the ends achieved or the means employed. If the end was lawful and the means chosen were lawful and necessary, collateral harm was permissible although intended indirectly.[13] The diversion of the trolley discussed above provides an example of permissible indirect intent. The killing of a patient to harvest organs is an example of impermissible direct intent.

Christian ethical ideas were incorporated into canon law, and thereby influenced the clerics who recorded and compiled medieval English law. The early twelfth-century compilation *Leges Henrici Primi* coined the maxim "no guilt without a guilty mind."[14] Henry de Bracton, a contemporary of Aquinas, wrote that accidental killing was no homicide "because a crime is not committed unless the intention to injure exists" and "[i]n crimes the intention is regarded, not the result."[15] Bracton added that killers should not be pardoned if they had acted carelessly or unlawfully.[16] At the time all killings were capital offenses unless pardoned, and it is not clear how much culpability influenced pardon decisions. Bracton also conditioned liability for theft on intent to steal, although this was not the law of his day. The 1278 Statute of Gloucester provided that the king, at his pleasure, could pardon those found to have killed accidentally (or in self-defense).[17] In 1389 the Crown agreed to refuse pardons to those who committed "murder" (i.e., killed stealthily) or killed with "malice prepense" (i.e., not accidentally or in self-defense).[18] Case reports from the later fifteenth century offer several examples of lawyers invoking a principle that felony requires intent.[19] In the most famous of these, the court found theft

12. Augustine, *Epistle 47: To Publicola, reprinted in* 33 PATROLOGIAE CURSUS COMPLETUS, SERIES LATINA 184, 187 (J.P. Migne ed., 1861).
13. AQUINAS, SUMMA THEOLOGICA PART II–II Q. 64 arts. 7–8.
14. L.J. DOWNER, LEGES HENRICI PRIMI 94 (c. 5, 28b) (1972).
15. 2 HENRY DE BRACTON, ON THE LAWS AND CUSTOMS OF ENGLAND, 384 (folio 136b) (Samuel Thorne transl., 1977).
16. *Id.* at 341 (folio 120b).
17. 6 Edw. 1 c. 9 (1278).
18. 13 Rich. 2 (1389).
19. Francis Sayre, *Mens Rea*, 45 HARV. L. REV. 974, 991 (1932).

partly on the basis of a carrier's dishonest intent in misappropriating goods he had been given to deliver.[20]

III. Transferred and Presumed Intent in Early Modern English Law

Only in the sixteenth century did criminal offenses begin to take on a more definite shape. As justices of the peace became responsible for framing charges, a treatise literature arose to assist them by defining the various offenses. During the same period, statutes were passed excluding those who killed with malice from benefit of clergy, and a number of decisions began to work out criteria for such malice. In one, the famous case of *R. v. Saunders*, a defendant was held liable for murder when he gave a poisoned apple to his wife, who unwittingly fed it to her daughter.[21] The court held that Saunders' malice transferred from his intended to his actual victim, so that the killing was not accidental.[22] In a late sixteenth-century work Francis Bacon generalized this holding into a conception of the criminal offense as combining an injury with a criminal intent: "all crimes have their conception in a corrupt intent, and have their consummation and issuing in some particular fact; which though it be not the fact at the which the intention of the malefactor levelled, yet the law giveth him no advantage of the error, if another particular ensue of as high a nature."[23] He added that intent was required for capital crimes.[24] Edward Coke's 1628 Institutes refreshed the maxim of the *Leges Henrici*, stating that "the act makes no guilt unless the mind is also guilty."[25] Matthew Hale agreed with Bacon that "it is the will and intention that regularly is required, as well as the act and event, to make the offense capital."[26] The 1638 decision in *Levett's Case*[27] acquitted the defendant of the manslaughter of an intruder he erroneously thought was a burglar. This case was cited by Hale as an example of the excuses of both "ignorance" and "infortunium."[28]

On the other hand, seventeenth and eighteenth century English homicide trials rarely turned on proof of intent. Certain kinds of conduct were seen as

---

20. Carrier's Case, Y.B. Pasch 13 Edw. IV, f.9, pl. 5 (1473).
21. R v. Saunders, 75 Eng. Rep. 706 (Q.B. 1576).
22. *Id.*
23. 1 FRANCIS BACON, LAW TRACTS 80 (2d ed. 1741).
24. *Id.* at 60.
25. EDWARD COKE, THE THIRD PART OF THE INSTITUTES OF THE LAWS OF ENGLAND 107 (1797).
26. 1 MATTHEW HALE, THE HISTORY OF THE PLEAS OF THE CROWN 38 (1736).
27. Cro. Car. 538 (1638).
28. 1 MATTHEW HALE, THE HISTORY OF THE PLEAS OF THE CROWN 42, 474 (1736).

highly incriminating, and obviated proof of intent. A revealing example is the "Statute of Stabbing," enacted in 1603, which imposed capital liability without benefit of clergy for any fatal stabbing of a victim who had neither drawn a weapon nor struck a blow.[29] Although criticized for not requiring any mental state, this statute punished killings that would likely have been punished as murder anyway. Juries typically convicted all defendants of murder who inflicted fatal wounds with weapons, unless the victim had initiated or agreed to combat.[30]

In the early eighteenth century William Hawkins applied Bacon's idea of transferred intent in proposing murder liability for unintended killings in the course of a felony. Hawkins wrote "it is a general rule, that where-ever a man intending to commit one felony, happens to commit another, he is as much guilty as if he had intended the felony which he actually commits."[31] In *R. v. Woodburne*[32] Judge Sir Peter King set limits to this transfer of intent. The defendants were charged with maiming with intent to disfigure. They claimed they lacked the requisite intent because they instead had intended to kill. Rather than inviting the jury to transfer intent from killing to the actual injury, the judge instructed the jury to convict only if they believed the defendants had intended to kill by means of disfiguring. "There are some cases where an unlawful or felonious intent to do one act, may be carried over to another act, done in prosecution thereof, and such other act will be felony, because done in prosecution of an unlawful or felonious intent.... But now the indictment on this statute is for a certain particular intent...." Where a statute conditioned liability for a felony on proof of a "particular intent," the intent to commit some other felony would not transfer.

A half a century later, this dichotomy between crimes requiring proof of intent and other crimes was colliding with an emergent sense that criminal liability should always depend on intent. Blackstone's Commentaries restated Coke's maxim of no guilty act without a guilty mind as a positive requirement that every offense include "first, a vitious will; and, secondly, an unlawful act consequent upon such vitious will."[33]

Yet culpability still was not a distinct element of liability to be proven in every case. In his discussions of specific offenses, Blackstone defined only about half the felonies as requiring some particular mental state. As a procedural

---

29. 1 Jac. 1 cl. 8 (1603).
30. Guyora Binder, *The Meaning of Killing*, *in* MODERN HISTORIES OF CRIME AND PUNISHMENT 101–02 (Markus D. Dubber & Lindsay Farmer eds., 2007).
31. 1 WILLIAM HAWKINS, A TREATISE OF THE PLEAS OF THE CROWN 74 (1716).
32. 16 St. Tr. 53 (1722).
33. 4 WILLIAM BLACKSTONE, COMMENTARIES ON THE LAWS OF ENGLAND 21 (1769).

matter, a "vitious will" was presumed from the performance of an unlawful act. Blackstone pointed to *Oneby's Case* (1727),[34] in which the judges considered a special verdict finding simply that the defendant had killed, without indicating whether or not he was provoked. The judges convicted him of murder, reasoning that "[i]f A kills B and no sudden quarrel appears, it is murder; for it lies on the party indicted to prove the sudden quarrel" that would preclude malice and thereby reduce the killing to manslaughter.[35] Blackstone generalized this holding to all disputes over mens rea. However fundamental it may have been to criminal guilt, culpability could only be placed in issue by the defense in the form of an excuse. "All the several pleas and excuses . . . may be reduced to this single consideration, the want or defect of will."[36]

Blackstone divided these excuses into three kinds: an incapacity for "understanding" based on infancy or insanity; compulsion based on necessity, duress, or legal command; and an inability to exercise understanding and will as a result of either "mistake" or "misfortune." Mistake (Hale's "ignorance") meant either ignorance of a required circumstance or mistaken belief in a justifying circumstance: "when a man intending to do a lawful act does that which is unlawful." Blackstone cited *Levett's Case* to illustrate this excuse. Blackstone added "but this mistake must be . . . a mistake of fact and not an error in point of law . . . . For a mistake in point of law, which every person of discretion . . . is bound and presumed to know is in criminal cases no sort of defence. . . ."[37] "Misfortune" (Hale's "infortunium") meant the unintended causation of a required result. The excuse of misfortune or accident was unavailable, however, for unintended injuries resulting from some other offense: "for, being guilty of one offence, in doing antecedently what is in itself unlawful, he is criminally guilty of whatever consequence may follow."[38] Blackstone seemed to conceive of a "vitious will" as simply a capacity for voluntary action, exercised in committing an offense.

Blackstone's contemporary, Lord Mansfield, redefined this will as an intention, but one sometimes established by legal presumption rather than proof. In *Rex v. Woodfall* (1770), Mansfield held that a criminal libel did not require intent to injure a victim's reputation, but only the intent to publish a document, combined with an injurious result. Mansfield reasoned "when an act, in itself indifferent, becomes criminal if done with a particular intent, then the intent must be proved and found; but when the act is in itself unlawful, the proof of justification and excuse lies on the defendant, and in failure thereof, the law implies a

34. 92 Eng. L. Rep. 465 (K.B. 1727).
35. *Id.* at 473.
36. 4 William Blackstone, Commentaries on the Laws of England 20–22 (1769).
37. *Id.* at 27.
38. *Id.*

criminal intent."[39] Thus every offense required a criminal intent, but this intent only needed to be proved for inchoate offenses such as attempts, where a harm is planned but not accomplished. When an offender caused harm, intent was presumed and the burden to disprove it fell on the defendant. Here it is important to appreciate that Mansfield made this claim when inchoate crimes were unusual. In 1770 there was no general common law doctrine that the attempt to commit any offense was also an offense. Indeed, Mansfield himself originated that doctrine 14 years later in *Rex v. Scofield*,[40] holding a defendant liable for the novel offense of attempted arson.

IV. The Idea of a Mental Element in Nineteenth-Century England and America

Bentham bitterly criticized the common law's obscurity and proposed the enactment of a lucid penal code using a consistent vocabulary for defining offenses, so as to ensure the law's publicity. He saw the function of criminal punishment as enhancing confidence in private entitlements and public goods by deterring injuries and being seen to do so. What made offenses wrongful was harm (or danger) to these interests rather than disobedience to the king or unauthorized use of violence. Bentham insisted on a culpability term as part of each offense definition in order to ensure that the injury punished was deterrable through the prospect of punishment. Thus, he defined each offense by identifying the interest protected, the proscribed injury to it, and the required expectation of causing such an injury. Conduct was culpable if one committed it knowingly, and with knowledge of circumstances rendering a proscribed injury likely.[41] The mental element of each offense had to correspond with the proscribed injury. This requirement of correlation between act elements and mental elements is sometimes referred to as the "correspondence principle."[42] Thus, intent could not be transferred from an intended harm to an unexpected injury of a different kind. If, in intentionally inflicting one injury, the actor foresaw or should have foreseen a risk of causing a second injury, the actor might be liable for the second injury on that basis.

---

39. 5 Burrows 2667 (1770).
40. Cald. 397 (1784).
41. Guyora Binder, *Foundations of the Legislative Panopticon: Bentham's Principles of Morals and Legislation*, *in* FOUNDATIONAL TEXTS IN MODERN CRIMINAL LAW 79, 91–95 (Markus D. Dubber ed., 2014); JEREMY BENTHAM, OF LAWS IN GENERAL 32–33 (H.L.A. Hart ed., 1970); JEREMY BENTHAM, PRINCIPLES OF MORALS AND LEGISLATION 70–96 (1948).
42. JEREMY HORDER, HOMICIDE AND THE POLITICS OF LAW REFORM 20 (2012).

For Bentham, mental culpability was cognitive, not volitional. Like Aquinas, Bentham distinguished between direct and indirect intention, but treated them as equally culpable. What mattered was the expectation of causing harm, not the desire to do so. By contrast with Augustine, Bentham saw nothing wrong with selfish desire. Indeed, because Bentham saw all human action as necessarily motivated by the same desire to seek pleasure and avoid pain, he believed law could only influence choices, not desires. Thus criminal law should punish "intention" (the choice to act with an expectation of causing injury) but not "motive" (the desire to bring about the proscribed injury or some other wrong).[43] Moreover, it should describe culpable mental states in a neutral descriptive language, rather than using normatively fraught terms such as "malicious" or "corruptly."

The Benthamite legal philosopher John Austin further subdivided culpability into intent, rashness, and heedlessness. Intent was an expectation of causing harm, rashness was knowledge of a probability of harm, whereas heedlessness was knowledge of circumstances making danger of harm reasonably apparent. These terms correspond to the Model Penal Code's later terms of knowledge, recklessness, and negligence. Austin used the term "motive" to refer to purpose and, like Bentham, considered motives as such irrelevant to liability.[44]

In early nineteenth-century England increasing sentiment favored restricting capital punishment and conditioning liability on culpability. The Statute of Stabbing was repealed in 1828. In 1833 the Benthamite lord chancellor Henry Brougham appointed a Criminal Law Commission, including several Benthamites, to compile and codify existing law.[45] Because the commissioners were not authorized to propose reforms, they could not overtly urge that mental elements be added to the definitions of offenses. Instead, building on Coke's and Blackstone's claims that the common law had traditionally required a guilty mind, they often presumed that offenses already had mental elements. They therefore reinterpreted objective elements of liability as evidentiary presumptions of culpability, and argued that the common law had traditionally presumed that everyone intended the natural and probable consequences of his or her actions. Thus, a traditional requirement of a fatal blow with a weapon to prove the objective element of "killing" could be reinterpreted as

---

43. Guyora Binder, *The Rhetoric of Motive and Intent*, 6 BUFF. CRIM. L. REV. 1 (2002).
44. 1 JOHN AUSTIN, LECTURES ON JURISPRUDENCE 422–36 (1869); 2 JOHN AUSTIN, LECTURES ON JURISPRUDENCE 1093 (1869).
45. Lindsay Farmer, *Reconstructing the English Codification Debate: The Criminal Law Commissioners, 1833–45*, 18 L. & HIST. REV. 397, 411–22 (2000); K.J.M. SMITH, LAWYERS, LEGISLATORS AND THEORISTS: DEVELOPMENTS IN ENGLISH CRIMINAL JURISPRUDENCE 1800–1957, at 121–38 (1998).

an evidentiary presumption that one who uses a weapon intends to kill. A traditional requirement of a wound or injury as proof of causation of death could be reinterpreted as a presumption that the infliction of a grievous wound was intended. Massachusetts chief justice Lemuel Shaw used this strategy in a notorious 1850 murder trial, instructing the jury that

> a person must be presumed to intend to do that which he voluntarily and wilfully does in fact do, and . . . he must intend all the natural, probable, and usual consequences of his own acts. Therefore, when one person assails another violently with a dangerous weapon, likely to kill and which does in fact destroy the life of the party assailed, the natural presumption is, that he intended death or other great bodily harm.[46]

Once these objective criteria of liability had been reinterpreted as evidence of intent, then the excuses of mistake and accident could be reinterpreted as negating the intent element.

By reinterpreting traditional objective requirements as constructive evidence of subjective elements the English commissioners were able to read an intent element into almost any offense. Having thus rooted the requirement of a mental element in tradition, the commissioners could then turn around and critique these "presumptions" of intent as formalistic and artificial. They also criticized transfers of intent from an intended injury to a different unintended injury, and especially murder liability for unintended killing during a felony. Such transfers wrongly punished motive rather than intent and violated the principle of correspondence.[47]

Nineteenth-century Americans were also interested in codifying criminal law, but their codes mostly adopted Blackstone's terminology rather than Bentham's. Judges also relied on Blackstone and other treatises as guides in interpreting statutory offense definitions. Numerous early- and mid-nineteenth century American cases read a mental element into statutes, on the ground that a guilty intent was a requirement for every crime. Thus a Connecticut court decided that punishment for providing nonemergency Sunday carriage service was precluded by honest belief in an emergency. This result was required by "the maxim that a criminal intent is essential to every crime."[48] An

46. Commonwealth v. Webster, 59 Mass. 295, 305 (1850).

47. Lindsay Farmer, *Reconstructing the English Codification Debate: The Criminal Law Commissioners, 1833–45*, 18 L. & Hist. Rev. 397, 411–22 (2000); K.J.M. Smith, Lawyers, Legislators and Theorists: Developments in English Criminal Jurisprudence 1800–1957, at 121–38 (1998); Thomas Starkie, First Report from His Majesty's Commissioners on Criminal Law 29 (1834).

48. Myers v. State, 1 Conn. 502, 504 (1816).

Ohio court reversed a fine for harboring a fugitive slave for failure to charge knowledge of the guest's slave status, citing Hale's statement that "*Ignorantia facti* doth excuse."[49] An Alabama court conditioned punishment for supplying contaminated water on knowledge of its defect because "a criminal intent is a necessary ingredient of every indictable offense."[50] A New York court similarly required knowledge that meat sold was rotten because "the essence of every legal crime is the wrongful intent combined with a wrongful act."[51]

At mid-century, Francis Wharton and Joel Prentiss Bishop published the first treatises on American criminal law. Wharton's 1846 treatise followed Blackstone in organizing his discussion of mens rea around personal capacity, concentrating on insanity, infancy, and intoxication, and devoting only a paragraph to mistake and accident. Wharton held that ignorance of law would not excuse unless there was no opportunity to know the law.[52] He added that "in a few instances ... mistake of fact will be an excuse ... [b]ut if an unforeseen consequence ensue from an act which was in itself unlawful, and its original nature wrong and mischievous, the actor is criminally responsible for whatever consequence may ensue."[53]

Quite different in emphasis, Bishop's 1856 treatise embraced Blackstone's requirement of a guilty mind, and endorsed a sweeping doctrine of exculpatory mistakes: "The wrongful intent ... being the essence of every crime, it follows that in all cases where the party, without fault or carelessness is misled concerning facts, and acts as would be justified in doing if the facts were what he believes them to be he is legally, as he is morally, innocent."[54] Rather than accepting the transfer of unlawful intent from any crime to another, Bishop deployed King's distinction between transferable and non-transferable intentions, and Mansfield's distinction between inherently unlawful acts and innocent acts rendered criminal by a particular intent. Bishop reasoned that crimes ordinarily required both an intention to "do a forbidden thing" and a harmful result. Yet the harm produced need not always be the specific harm intended: A "general" intent to commit some crime ordinarily sufficed to make the offender criminally responsible for any harm caused. As long as the intended result was roughly as bad as the result produced, the unlawful intent would "transfer" to the actual, but unintended, result. Yet Bishop excepted certain crimes from this doctrine of a transferable or "general" intent to do wrong.

---

49. Birney v. State, 8 Ohio Rep. 230, 238 (1837).
50. Stein v. State, 37 Ala. 123, 132 (1861).
51. People v. Parker, 38 N.Y. 85, 86 (1868).
52. Francis Wharton, A Treatise on American Criminal Law 23 (1846).
53. *Id.* at 23–24.
54. 1 Joel Prentiss Bishop, Commentaries on the Criminal Law § 242 (1856).

These crimes required a "specific" intent that could only transfer to a result of the same kind intended:

> The doctrine of the transfer of the intent to the unintended act . . . is limited in its application; because of the peculiar character of many of the specific offenses. Thus . . . to constitute some crimes . . . there must exist a precise and specific intent, for which no other, however heinous in itself, will be a substitute. So there are certain acts, which are not in their nature wrong, but only wrong when done with some particular intent . . . There are some crimes requiring . . . the concurrence of two or more separate intents; as, an intent to do wrong in general, or to do a particular wrong, with an ulterior purpose beyond. Thus, in larceny there must be, first, an intent to trespass on another's personal property; secondly . . . the further intent to deprive the owner of his ownership therein. So burglary consists in the intent, which must be executed, to break in the night-time into a dwelling house; and the further concurrent intent, which may be executed or not, to commit therein some crime which is a felony. In these and other like cases, the particular or ulterior intent must be proved, in addition to the more general one, in order to make out the offence.[55]

Under this formulation, "specific" intent offenses included all inchoate crimes involving an unfulfilled purpose, and all other crimes for which common law courts or statutes had defined an intent element. All other offenses were "general" intent offenses, meaning that they required mens rea, but required proof only of the proscribed act rather than any mental state.

Later works by Wharton borrowed Bishop's terminology of general and specific intent, but used these terms to refer to different psychological states rather than different standards of liability. For Wharton, general intent meant the intent to impose a risk of a type of injury, which rendered one liable for all injuries within the class. Specific intent was an intent to cause a particular injury, which could not transfer.[56]

American judges and jurists tried to use the dichotomy between general and specific intent to solve a wide array of problems involving claims of mistake and accident. The typical pattern of argument was that a mistake about a circumstance or the accidental (i.e., unintended) causation of a result should relieve the defendant of liability for a "specific intent" crime, but not for a

---

55. *See id.* § 229, 220–22.
56. Francis Wharton, Philosophy of Criminal Law 156–57 (1880).

general intent crime. Thus, a general intent crime required an intentional act, but did not require intent with respect to any circumstances or consequences. A crime requiring intent with respect to some circumstance or result was a specific intent crime. Sometimes it is argued that a general intent crime must involve conduct malum in se, so that unknown circumstances and unexpected harms can only aggravate an already culpable act.

Yet the distinction between specific and general intent did not take judges very far, because they still had to decide which offenses were specific intent and which were general intent, and, for specific intent offenses, which circumstances and results required specific intent. In addition, judges had to decide whether mistakes had to be reasonable and accidents unforeseeable to negate either type of intent. Until the latter question was resolved, one could argue that any particular mistake or accident should not negate even specific intent because culpable or unreasonable, or that it should negate even general intent because innocent or reasonable.

One response to this problem was to carve out certain categories of mistakes or accidents as inherently wrongful. Courts often held that mistakes and accidents would not negate general intent if they resulted from voluntary intoxication, or in committing another crime. Similarly, mistakes of law could not negate general intent. Yet these rules left other important questions unresolved. Would all other mistakes and accidents negate general intent, or only reasonable ones? Could unreasonable (i.e., reckless or negligent) mistakes and accidents negate specific intent? Were accidents and mistakes subject to the same standards?

Because it was used in so many different ways, the dichotomy between general and specific intent took on a variety of different meanings. Thus, "specific intent" could refer to the mental element of any crime, whereas "general intent" could refer to the defendant's blameworthiness or responsibility. Alternatively, "specific intent" could mean the intent to commit a particular crime whereas general intent meant the intent to commit any crime. Third, "specific intent" could mean an intention the prosecution must prove, whereas "general intent" would mean an intention presumed from the proof of some other fact. Fourth, "specific intent" could mean purpose or knowledge, whereas "general intent" would mean recklessness or negligence.

Similar questions confronted English courts over the course of the nineteenth century. Utilitarian reformers steadily pressed their view that every offense should be defined as including a mental element, consisting of knowledge of some probability of a proscribed injury. Although the criminal law commissioners were content to reinterpret objectively defined offenses as having presumptive or transferred mental elements, later reformers rejected these presumptions and constructions of intent as fraudulent fictions. In the meantime, however, the older conception of mistake and accident as excuses to responsibility persisted. In the 1870s a famous trio of cases in England's criminal appeals court dramatized this controversy.

In *R. v. Pembliton*,[57] the defendant threw a rock at a crowd, unintentionally smashing a window. His conviction for malicious damage to property was overturned on the ground that the "malice" required by the statute had to be directed to the proscribed injury to property. A majority of the justices held that awareness of the danger of breaking the window—in other words recklessness—would have sufficed to make the damage malicious even if it was not purposeful, although one judge reasoned that malicious damage had to be intentional. Yet the justices confined their ruling to the particular statute, reserving the question of whether the malice required for murder under the common law could transfer from another offense such as robbery. Thus the holding was compatible with a scheme such as Bishop's in which intent could transfer for some offenses and not others.

In *R. v. Prince*,[58] the defendant was convicted of taking "an unmarried girl, being under the age of 16, out of the possession and against the will of her father," although the jury found the defendant reasonably believed her to be 18. Here the majority noted the absence of any such term as "knowingly" or "maliciously," and so denied that the defendant's mistake negated a statutory offense element. Instead, Judge Blackburn treated the defendant's claim of mistake as an "excuse" presuming that notwithstanding the statute, "a guilty mind is an essential ingredient in a crime." Here, a "guilty mind" appears to signify responsibility rather than a proscribed offense element. Writing for the majority, Judge Blackburn reasoned that the proscribed wrong was taking a young girl from her parent's custody and that her consent could only excuse him if she were in fact of age. Judge Denman added that if she had been between the ages of 16 and 20 the interference with parental custody would still have been unlawful although not criminal. Judge Bramwell denied that such an act was illegal, but held it to be a wrong, the type of injury the statute aimed at preventing (where not justified by some exigency). He concluded that because the offender's act both violated the terms of the statute and was morally wrong, no excuse was warranted and the requirement of a guilty mind was satisfied. Only Judge Brett would have overturned the conviction, arguing that the act the defendant honestly and reasonably believed he committed was not criminal. Even Brett would have convicted if Prince had believed he was committing some other

57. L.R. 2 C.C.R. 119 (1874).
58. L.R. 2 C.C.R. 154 (1875).

crime, by transferring Prince's intent. Notice that, in Bishop's terminology, none of the judges saw the offense as a specific intent offense.

Finally, in *R. v. Faulkner*,[59] a sailor accidentally set his ship on fire by sneaking into the hold and breaking into a cask of rum while holding a lighted match. He was convicted of malicious damage on the theory that his intent to steal the rum constituted the required malice, because theft is a felony. The prosecution argued that malice should transfer among all felonies, but the court rejected this position. In overturning the conviction, the judges cited *Pembliton*.[60] Judge Fitzgerald concluded that "the intention of the accused forms an element in the crime" but considered the element satisfied if "the defendant intended to do the very act with which he is charged, or . . . it was a necessary consequence of some other felonious or criminal act in which he was engaged, or . . . having a probable result which defendant foresaw or ought to have foreseen, he nevertheless persevered in such other criminal act."[61] Thus, Fitzgerald defined "malicious" as including not only intention with respect to the injury charged, but also the intention to commit some other crime combined with knowledge, recklessness, or negligence toward the injury charged. Rather than requiring intent with respect to the injury or transferring intent from another crime to the injury, Fitzgerald combined both. The intent to commit another crime reduced the culpability required with respect to the injury but did not replace it entirely. Fitzgerald's complex definition of malicious damage demonstrates the inadequacy of any simple dichotomy between general and specific intent offenses. If malicious damage requires either intentional damage or negligent damage combined with the intention to commit another crime, does that make it a specific intent offense or a general intent offense?

How can we reconcile the acquittals in *Pembliton* and *Faulkner* with the conviction in *Prince*? After all, the court held Prince responsible for unwittingly abducting a minor on the basis of his merely immoral motive, while absolving Pembliton and Faulkner of unintended harm despite their criminal motives. One difference is that *Prince* was a case about mistake rather than accident, and the court may have been more inclined to require culpability with respect to a result than a circumstance. Yet the more important difference is that the court interpreted the statutory offenses differently. In *Pembliton* and *Faulkner*, the court determined that malicious damage required at least some culpability with respect to damage, and as such culpability was not proved, the defendants could not be convicted. By contrast, the court in *Prince* found that the

59. 13 Cox C.C. 550 (1877).
60. *Id.* at 559 (O'Brien, J., concurring).
61. *Id.* at 557 (Fitzgerald, J., concurring).

abduction offense required no culpability with respect to the age of the victim. Having determined that the prosecution had proven the offense, the court proceeded to consider whether Prince's mistake could nevertheless excuse him for responsibility for his offense. Only at this stage in the analysis did his immoral motive became relevant.

Pembliton and *Faulkner* had their American equivalent in the 1873 Massachusetts case of *Commonwealth v. Adams*,[62] which held that it was not assault and battery for the driver of a sleigh to run down a pedestrian inadvertently, while driving at an excessive speed in violation of a traffic ordinance. The court reasoned that the willful violation of a speeding ordinance does not supply the necessary intent for assault and battery. Nevertheless, the court did express a willingness to transfer intent from an offense malum in se, an approach that might have yielded the opposite outcomes in *Pembliton* and *Faulkner*.

Pembliton, Prince, and *Faulkner* were decided against the background of another effort to codify English law. During the 1870s and 1880s the Benthamite reformer and judge James F. Stephen produced a digest of English criminal law, a draft code based on the digest, and a history of English criminal law. Although Stephen's code was not adopted in England (it was adopted in Canada), his digest and history influenced courts' and scholars' understanding of English criminal law. Stephen's digest did not explicitly require that every offense include a mental element, but he later made this premise explicit in his judicial opinion in *Regina v. Tolson*.[63] In this case the court held that an honest and reasonable belief that one's first spouse was dead should acquit a defendant of bigamy although the statute identified no required mental state with respect to the spouse's survival. Stephen reasoned that the absence of an explicit mental element in the statute did not mean the offense lacked one, as the statute also lacked any explicit requirement of consciousness, sanity, or maturity. He concluded that "the full definition of every crime includes explicitly or by implication a proposition as to a state of mind. Therefore if the mental element of any conduct alleged to be a crime is proved to have been absent . . . the crime so defined is not committed."[64] In his *History of English Criminal Law*, Stephen reiterated that "the definition of all or nearly all crimes contains . . . a mental element," and he equated mens rea with these mental elements.[65] Stephen expressed the Benthamite view that these mental elements were properly

62. 114 Mass. 323 (1873).
63. 23 Q.B.D 168 (1889).
64. *Id.*
65. 2 James Fitzjames Stephen, A History of the Criminal Law of England 94–95 (1883).

defined in cognitive terms, as "intentions" rather than "motives."[66] Accordingly, Stephen denied that the "malice" required for murder involved any hostility toward the victim. Instead, malice was a technical term encompassing several mental states involving awareness of a risk of death. Stephen interpreted the maxim that everyone is presumed to intend the probable consequences of her actions as meaning simply that everyone is presumed to choose the consequences she expects as a result of her actions.[67]

Stephen's digest defined many offenses as committed "willfully," "knowingly," "maliciously," "fraudulently," or "with intent" to achieve some further aim. Citing *Levett's Case*, it also provided a general doctrine of mistake similar to Bishop's: "[a]n alleged offender is in general deemed to have acted under that state of facts which he in good faith and on reasonable grounds believed to exist when he did the act alleged to be an offense."[68] This curious formulation treated actors as committing only those actions they reasonably believed themselves to have committed. This clearly meant that a reasonable mistake about a required circumstance element would "excuse." It also appeared to imply that the unforeseeability of a required result would also preclude liability. If so, this represented a default rule conditioning liability on a culpable mental state of at least negligence with respect to each objective element of offenses defined by the common law. It was not clear to whom Stephen assigned the burden of proof on this issue. For statutory offenses, Stephen expected the court to determine whether the legislature intended to excuse reasonable mistakes. Stephen's digest provided that although voluntary intoxication could not excuse, evidence of intoxication could be offered to show the defendant lacked a specific intention required by an offense definition.[69] Similarly, he pronounced that ignorance of a law could be offered to negate a specific intention (such as the intent to take property of another) but not to excuse the offense.[70] Stephen implied that voluntary intoxication and mistake of law were unreasonable per se.

The future Supreme Court justice Oliver Wendell Holmes Jr. shared Stephen's utilitarian premises. As noted in the last chapter, Holmes rejected the identification of crime with trespassory conduct and instead saw crime as any conduct creating a reasonably apparent danger of proscribed harm. He began his discussion of criminal law in *The Common Law* by quoting Stephen's definition of malice.[71] Holmes then proceeded to try to define mens rea. Holmes saw

66. *Id.* at 110.
67. *Id.* at 111–12.
68. JAMES FITZJAMES STEPHEN, A DIGEST OF THE CRIMINAL LAW 27 (4th ed. 1887).
69. *Id.* at 22.
70. *Id.* at 26.
71. OLIVER WENDELL HOLMES, JR., THE COMMON LAW (1881).

intent as a traditional requirement of criminal law, reasoning that the excuse of accident had long been a defense to trespass in criminal prosecutions, but not always in civil suits. Yet Holmes conceptualized criminal intent in objective terms, as action in the face of apparent danger. Although he did not use the terms "general" and "specific intent," he offered an account of this distinction. Holmes reasoned that most crimes were defined by injury or a failed attempt to injure. For such crimes, proof of apparently dangerous conduct sufficed to satisfy the deterrent aims of the criminal law. Where, however, criminal liability was conditioned on conduct involving little inherent risk of injury, proof of a purpose to injure should be required. Holmes offered larceny and burglary as examples of offenses combining relatively minor intrusions upon property with purposes to inflict greater harm.[72]

V. Public Welfare Offenses and the Question of Strict Liability

During the period when Stephen wrote, Parliament passed many new statutes criminally enforcing commercial and health regulations on businesses. English courts often construed these regulatory offenses as imposing liability regardless of fault.[73] By contending that the common law had traditionally conditioned criminal liability on a mental element, Stephen implied that such strict liability was a modern legislative innovation. Yet some of the first cases imposing strict liability for endangering the public involved the common law offense of nuisance.[74] Moreover, the novelty consisted in imposing liability for remote causation and diffuse injury, rather than the lack of a mental element. In *R. v. Stephens*, the court justified strict nuisance liability by arguing that a nuisance prosecution was a necessary substitute for a private lawsuit, where the injury was diffuse. Thus, culpability seemed unnecessary where the penalty was a fine rather than incarceration, and the purpose of liability was to internalize the external costs of businesses to the public welfare. Even if businesses injured the public innocently, they had no just claim to profit by it. Criminal enforcement was needed to recover the public's losses because private enforcement was precluded by a collective action problem. Thus, the court considered such offenses criminal only in form, but civil in function, in the sense that they aimed at compensation and deterrence, but not blame. This rationale for strict

72. *Id.* at 39–76.
73. Francis Sayre, *Public Welfare Offenses*, 33 COLUM. L. REV. 55, 60 (1933).
74. R v. Stephens, L.R. 1 Q.B. 702 (1866); R v. Medley, 6 Car. & P. 292 (K.B. 1834).

liability restricted it to offenses punishing diffuse endangerment of the public welfare with fines.

American courts during this period developed a similar doctrine concerning public welfare offenses, but without always articulating a similarly limiting rationale. Many of the first American strict liability offenses involved highly contested moral issues. In the 1850s, as the slavery crisis deepened, some slave jurisdictions imposed strict liability on persons unwittingly assisting fugitive slaves.[75] One of these decisions offered the surprising argument that as between an innocent carrier and an innocent slaveholder, the carrier should bear the loss from unwittingly assisting a runaway slave. This argument, frequently offered for strict liability in tort, seems inapt for criminal law, which imposes blame but not compensation. In the 1840s Massachusetts courts punished adultery and bigamy even if defendants honestly and reasonably believed their spouses to be dead.[76] By the 1860s, Massachusetts courts cited these cases in punishing the unwitting sale of liquor,[77] and only then applied them to food safety regulations. The Massachusetts approach to liquor regulations was soon imitated in other states.[78] New York developed a more cautious endorsement of strict liability offenses similar to England's, limiting its use to minor offenses,[79] involving "moderate fines."[80]

In the early twentieth century the U.S. Supreme Court considered several cases on the constitutionality of strict criminal liability. In 1910 the Court approved imposing monetary penalties without proof of intent. In *Shevlin-Carpenter v. Minnesota*[81] the Court rejected a due process challenge to a statute imposing double damages on loggers who unwittingly felled trees on public land without a permit. The following year the Court observed in passing in a civil case that "The power of the legislature to declare an offense, and to exclude the elements of knowledge and due diligence from any inquiry as to its commission, cannot, we think, be questioned."[82] Yet in the 1921 case of *Baender v. Barnett*,[83] the Court hinted that due process sometimes required culpability. The defendant brought a due process challenge to a charge of possessing counterfeiting equipment, based on the failure of the statutory offense definition to specify a mental element. The Court rejected the challenge, on the ground that

---

75. *E.g.*, State v. Baltimore & Susquehanna Steam Co., 13 Md. 181 (1859).
76. Commonwealth v. Mash, 7 Met. 472 (Mass. 1844); Commonwealth v. Elwell, 2 Met. 190 (Mass. 1840).
77. Commonwealth v. Boynton, 2 Allen 160 (Mass. 1861).
78. Francis Sayre, *Public Welfare Offenses*, 33 COLUM. L. REV. 55, 66.
79. Tenement House Dept. of City of New York v. McDevitt, 109 N.E. 88, 90 (N.Y. 1915).
80. People *ex rel.* Price v. Sheffield Farms Co., 225 N.Y. 25, 32–33 (1918).
81. 218 U.S. 57 (1910).
82. Chicago, Burlington, & Quincy Ry. Co., v. United States, 220 U.S. 559, 578 (1911).
83. 255 U.S. 224 (1921).

the trial court had properly interpreted the statute as conditioning the offense on a mental element. The Court explained:

> The statute is . . . to be taken in a reasonable sense, and not in one which works manifest injustice or infringes constitutional safeguards. In so holding, we but give effect to a cardinal rule of construction recognized in repeated decisions of this and other courts. . . . In *Margate Pier Co. v. Hannam,* 3 B. & Ald. 266, 270, Abbott, C.J., quoting from Lord Coke, said: "Acts of Parliament . . . are to be so construed, as no man that is innocent, or free from injury or wrong, be by a literal construction punished or endamaged." . . . And in *United States v. Jin Fuey Moy,* 241 U.S. 394 . . . we said: "A statute must be construed, if fairly possible, so as to avoid, not only the conclusion that it is unconstitutional, but also grave doubts upon that score."[84]

Here the Court linked together two different canons of statutory construction: a rule of lenity, requiring criminal statutes to be interpreted restrictively against the prosecution so as to prevent punishment of the blameless; and the rule that statutes are to be interpreted as constitutional if possible. Thus the Court implied that substantive culpability was a requirement of due process, and a mental element an appropriate means of satisfying it.

Yet the following year, in the case of *United States v. Balint,* the Court upheld a conviction for unlicensed sale of controlled narcotics without proof that defendant knew the drugs were controlled, an offense punishable by a prison sentence of up to five years.[85] Citing *Shevlin-Carpenter,* the Court reasoned that although the common law required mens rea, the legislature defining a statutory offense was free to require mens rea or not. Thus the judicial decision whether to require a mental element depended on the judicial understanding of legislative intent rather than the requirements of due process. The Court went on to describe categories of offenses where strict liability was typical. These included statutes imposing duties to facilitate public benefits, such as paying taxes, and also statutes imposing safety standards to protect a diffuse public interest. Concluding that drug regulation fit the latter pattern, the Court construed the offense as requiring no proof of culpability, despite its substantial penalty. In the contemporaneous case of *United States v. Behrman,* the Court held that if a statutory offense definition specifies no mental element, an indictment need not supply one.[86]

Stephen's Benthamite conception of mens rea as a mental state corresponding to injury influenced American legal scholars, perhaps in combination with

---

84. *Id.* at 225–26.
85. 258 U.S. 250 (1922).
86. 258 U.S. 280 (1922).

nineteenth-century German scholarship requiring various forms of "dolus."[87] Wharton invoked the English debates of Stephen's code commission as evidence of a new view of malice as a mental state regarding injury.[88] He also embraced the principle that criminal liability ordinarily required mens rea in this sense.[89] As noted, Holmes also saw mens rea as a normal requirement of criminal liability, and viewed Stephen's conception of malice as paradigmatic. In the twentieth century, the most important American exponents of Stephen's ideas were Francis Sayre and Herbert Wechsler. Sayre's promotion of the concept of a mental element and his critique of strict liability influenced interpretation of federal statutes and due process doctrine in the Supreme Court, as well as informing Wechsler's work. Wechsler developed a system for defining offenses that influenced code reform in the states.

VI. Strict Liability, Statutory Interpretation, and Due Process in the U.S. Supreme Court

Sayre's 1932 article "Mens Rea" argued that mens rea was an ancient requirement of criminal liability in the common law.[90] He added that in the common law this requirement had been satisfied by a criminal or immoral motive. With the growth of criminal legislation, however, mens rea had taken on a technical meaning as the mental element of an offense. Sayre analyzed mens rea questions and divided them into four issues. One concerned the incapacity to act culpably (based on infancy, insanity, or perhaps intoxication). This issue continued to raise large questions of moral principle amenable to judicial resolution. The other three questions were quite different, however. They included whether offenses required specific intentions to cause a type of result; whether mistakes about a circumstance could exculpate, and whether exculpatory mistakes had to be reasonable; and whether the intention to commit some other offense sufficed to criminalize a proscribed but unintended result. For Sayre, these were all questions about the mental element defining a particular offense, in a particular jurisdiction. Each mental element consisted of one or more mental states or "intentions" accompanying the criminal act. There was no single quality of mens rea unifying all offenders or offenses, and no moral principles dictating what the mental elements of all offenses should be. Instead,

---

87. Greg Taylor, *Concepts of Intention in German Criminal Law*, 24 OXFORD J.L. STUD. 99 (2004).
88. FRANCIS WHARTON, A TREATISE ON THE LAW OF HOMICIDE IN THE UNITED STATES § 29 (1875).
89. FRANCIS WHARTON, PHILOSOPHY OF CRIMINAL LAW (1880).
90. Francis Sayre, *Mens Rea*, 45 HARV. L. REV. 974 (1932).

the mental states defining each offense in each jurisdiction were matters to be resolved by legislative will. Thus, Sayre concluded, mens rea had shifted from a motive to an intention.

In his 1933 article "Public Welfare Offenses,"[91] Sayre explored the contradiction between the supposedly ancient requirement of mens rea and the prevalence of public welfare offenses punished on the basis of strict liability. He rejected a resolution that would arbitrarily require culpability for common law offenses while permitting strict liability for any statutory offense. Nor was he satisfied with requiring culpability only for crimes malum in se, while permitting strict liability for mala prohibita. One could hardly claim that conviction of a regulatory offense carried no moral stigma if the penalty was imprisonment. Nor was imprisonment needed for social protection if the offender had manifested no willingness to offend. "Crimes punishable with prison sentences, therefore ordinarily require proof of a guilty intent," Sayre concluded.[92] Although willing to compromise this principle in some instances[93] for reasons of deterrence, he warned that

> [t]he modern rapid growth of a large body of offenses punishable without proof of a guilty intent is marked with real danger. Courts are familiarized with the pathway to easy convictions by relaxing the orthodox requirement of a *mens rea*. The danger is that in the case of true crimes where the penalty is severe and the need for ordinary criminal law safeguards is strong, courts following the false analogy of the public welfare offenses may now and again similarly relax the *mens rea* requirement, . . . as the easiest way to secure desired convictions. The moral obloquy and the social disgrace incident to criminal conviction are whips which lend effective power to the administration of criminal law. When the law begins to permit convictions for serious offenses of men who are morally innocent and free from fault, who may even be respected and useful members of the community, its restraining power becomes undermined. Once it becomes respectable to be convicted, the vitality of the criminal law has been sapped.[94]

Although basically utilitarian in his orientation, Sayre regarded the restriction of punishment to the deserving as necessary to win allegiance to a rule of law.

---

91. Francis Sayre, *Public Welfare Offenses*, 33 Columbia L. Rev. 55 (1933).
92. *Id.* at 72.
93. Notably, for statutory rape. *See id.* at 73.
94. *Id.* at 79–80.

Sayre offered his critique of public welfare offenses at an inauspicious time: during the Depression, when the Supreme Court faced mounting criticism for subjecting commercial regulation to due process review, and just a few years before the Court largely abandoned the practice. In 1943 the Court reiterated its endorsement of strict liability for regulatory offenses in *United States v. Dotterweich*,[95] upholding a misdemeanor conviction for shipping mislabeled drugs for a subordinate employee, without proof the defendant had any reason to believe the drugs were mislabeled. Citing *Balint*, Justice Frankfurter concluded that this regulation fit it into a category of legislation that

> dispenses with the conventional requirement for criminal conduct—awareness of some wrongdoing. In the interest of the larger good, it puts the burden of acting at hazard upon a person otherwise innocent but standing in responsible relation to a public danger. . . . Balancing relative hardships, Congress has preferred to place it upon those who have at least the opportunity of informing themselves of the existence of conditions imposed for the protection of consumers before sharing in illicit commerce, rather than to throw the hazard on the innocent public who are wholly helpless. It would be too treacherous to define or even to indicate by way of illustration the class of employees which stands in such a responsible relation. . . . In such matters, the good sense of prosecutors, the wise guidance of trial judges, and the ultimate judgment of juries must be trusted.[96]

Frankfurter's argument assumed that prosecutors and jurors would confine liability to employees with authority to decide what was shipped, and who were therefore negligent for any mislabeling. Yet he required neither proof of negligence as a mental element nor proof of such authority as an act element. This reliance on unreviewable enforcement discretion to limit liability to the deserving was vulnerable to overbreadth and legality objections, and illustrates that requiring specificity and requiring culpability can be alternative strategies for legitimating punishment.

Although the notion that the government could burden the innocent for the general good seemed attractive in the midst of World War II, it may have seemed far less so in the postwar era, when the United States sought to identify itself with the rule of law, in contrast to its Soviet rival. Although the Court fell short of requiring a mental element for every criminal offense, or even for every

95. 320 U.S. 277 (1943).
96. *Id.* at 281–85.

severely punished offense, it interpreted many offense definitions as requiring culpability that were silent on the subject, and identified some circumstances where the constitution required proof of culpability.

In the 1952 case *Morissette v. United States*,[97] the Court interpreted a statute punishing theft of federal property as requiring knowledge that the material taken was property of another. The defendant in the case took rusting, used bombshells from a military target range to sell as scrap, believing they had been abandoned. The court below, citing *Balint* and *Behrman*, had argued that it was precluded from requiring knowledge of the ownership of the goods unless the statutory language so specified. Justice Jackson's opinion held *Balint* and *Behrman* inapplicable to a statute of this kind. Relying heavily on Sayre's scholarship, Jackson reasoned that fundamental principles compelled courts to interpret the statute as requiring intent, without his clarifying whether these principles were constitutional. Jackson claimed that an intent requirement was both a broadly recognized requirement of justice and an assumption of the common law:

> The contention that an injury can amount to a crime only when inflicted by intention . . . is as universal and persistent in mature systems of law as belief in freedom of the human will and a consequent ability and duty of the normal individual to choose between good and evil. . . . Unqualified acceptance of this doctrine by English common law in the Eighteenth Century was indicated by Blackstone's sweeping statement that to constitute any crime there must first be a "vicious will." . . . Crime, as a compound concept, generally constituted only from concurrence of an evil-meaning mind with an evil-doing hand . . . took deep and early root in American soil. As the state codified the common law of crimes, even if their enactments were silent on the subject, their courts assumed that the omission did not signify disapproval of the principle, but merely recognized that intent was so inherent in the idea of the offense that it required no statutory affirmation. Courts, with little hesitation or division, found an implication of the requirement as to offenses that were taken over from the common law.[98]

Jackson proceeded to identify public welfare offenses such as those involved in *Balint* and *Behrman* as an exceptional category, typically involving (1) a statutory rather than a common law origin, (2) omission rather than action,

---

97. 342 U.S. 246 (1952).
98. *Id.* at 250–52.

(3) the imposition of risk rather than harm, and (4) a situation where "penalties commonly are relatively small, and conviction does not grave damage to an offender's reputation."[99] He then posed the question whether the Court should "expand the doctrine of crimes without intent."[100]

This formulation contained an ambiguity. Because *Balint* held both that due process permitted Congress to impose strict liability, and that Congress had intended to do so, the "doctrine of crimes without intent" could have meant an exception to a due process requirement of mens rea, or an exception to a presumption of congressional intent to require mens rea. That Jackson never mentioned due process suggests the latter meaning. He went on to note that the common law traditionally required mens rea for theft, and to argue that Congress should be presumed to have retained this requirement absent explicitly contrary language.[101] The climax of his argument invoked several constitutional principles—the right to a jury trial, the privileges and immunities of citizenship, the presumption of innocence, the limits of federal judicial power recognized in *United States v. Hudson and Goodwin*—but without saying that any one of them would prevent Congress from explicitly imposing severe punishment on the basis of strict liability:

> The Government asks us by a feat of construction radically to change the weights and balances in the scales of justice. The purpose and obvious effect of doing away with the requirement of a guilty intent is to ease the prosecution's path to conviction, to strip the defendant of such benefit as he derived at common law from innocence of evil purpose, and to circumscribe the freedom heretofore allowed juries. Such a manifest impairment of the immunities of the individual should not be extended to common law crimes on judicial initiative. The spirit of the doctrine which denies to the federal judiciary power to create crimes forthrightly admonishes that we should not enlarge the reach of enacted crimes by constituting them from anything less than the incriminating components contemplated by the words used in the statute.[102]

Subsequent decisions have applied *Morissette* to require proof of culpability for several federal crimes. In *United States v. U.S. Gypsum*,[103] the Supreme Court held that the offense of price-fixing required an intention, rather than

99. *Id.* at 256.
100. *Id.* at 260.
101. *Id.* at 262.
102. *Id.* at 263–64 (citing United States v. Hudson & Goodwin, 11 U.S. 32 (1812)).
103. 438 U.S. 422 (1978).

merely an effect, of fixing prices, and that the intent could not be conclusively presumed from proof of the effect. The Court's opinion invoked the principle that "'ambiguity concerning the ambit of criminal statutes should be resolved in favor of lenity,'" and concluded that

> *Morissette* can be fairly read as establishing, at least with regard to crimes having their origin in the common law, an interpretative presumption that *mens rea* is required.... While strict liability offenses ... do not invariably offend constitutional requirements, ... the limited circumstances in which Congress has created and this Court has recognized such offenses ... attest to their generally disfavored status.[104]

In *Liparota v. United States*,[105] the Court deemed an offense of illegally acquiring food stamps to require proof of knowledge of illegality, citing *United States v. U.S. Gypsum*. The Court reasoned that requiring intent "is particularly appropriate where ... to interpret the statute otherwise would be to criminalize ... apparently innocent conduct." In *Staples v. United States*,[106] an offense of failure to register certain firearms, punishable by up to 10 years in prison, was held to require knowledge of the features subjecting the gun to registration. Justice Thomas interpreted *U.S. Gypsum* and *Morissette* as requiring evidence of congressional intent to dispense with mens rea,[107] and added that "the penalty imposed under a statute has been a significant consideration in determining whether the statute should be construed as dispensing with *mens rea*."[108]

Some lower courts have interpreted *Morissette* as setting due process limits on the permissibility of strict liability. In *Holdridge v. United States* the U.S. Court of Appeals for the Eighth Circuit ruled that due process did not require that an offense of repeated trespass on a government base be predicated on an additional unlawful purpose, because the penalty was slight and the offense was not derived from the common law.[109] Writing for the court, the future Justice Blackmun implied that due process had required the contrary result in *Morissette*:

> where a federal criminal statute omits mention of intent and where it seems to involve what is basically a matter of policy, where the standard

104. *Id.* at 437.
105. 471 U.S. 419 (1985).
106. 511 U.S. 600 (1994).
107. *Id.* at 606.
108. *Id.* at 616.
109. 282 F.2d 302 (8th Cir. 1960).

> imposed is, under the circumstances, reasonable and adherence thereto properly expected of a person, where the penalty is relatively small, where conviction does not gravely besmirch, where the statutory crime is not one taken over from the common law, and where congressional purpose is supporting, the statute can be construed as one not requiring criminal intent. The elimination of this element is then not violative of the due process clause.[110]

This principle was applied by the U.S. Court of Appeals for the Sixth Circuit in striking down a statute imposing up to two years imprisonment for selling migratory bird parts, without requiring knowledge that the goods sold contained protected bird parts.

> [I]n order for one to be convicted of a felony . . . unknown to the common law which carries a substantial penalty, Congress must require the prosecution to prove the defendant acted with some degree of scienter. Otherwise, a person acting with a completely innocent state of mind could be subjected to a severe penalty and grave damage to his reputation. This, in our opinion, the Constitution does not allow.[111]

Although the line of statutory interpretation cases from *Morissette* to *Staples* did not clearly bind legislatures to condition punishment on mens rea, other decisions did set due process limits to strict liability, as a means of enforcing other constitutional rights. In the fascinating 1945 case of *United States v. Screws,*[112] the Court was obliged to apply Fifth Amendment due process standards to a criminal statute punishing violations of Fourteenth Amendment due process rights. Constrained to interpret this vague statute to conform to the Constitution if possible, the Court held that a specific intent to violate a particular constitutional right was constitutionally required to cure the vagueness of the offense of wilfully depriving the victim of constitutional rights. In *Smith v. California,*[113] the Court reversed a conviction for possession of obscene literature where no knowledge of its obscene character had been required. The Court reasoned that as possession and dissemination of literature were protected by the First Amendment unless the literature was obscene, strict liability with respect to obscenity would chill protected activity by requiring

---

110. *Id.* at 310.
111. United States v. Wulff, 758 F.2d 1121, 1125 (6th Cir. 1985).
112. 325 U.S. 91 (1945).
113. 361 U.S. 147 (1959).

booksellers to examine their wares, thereby greatly raising their costs. In the later case of *United States v. X-Citement Video*[114] the Court used very similar reasoning in requiring proof of knowledge of the age of performers depicted on film for an offense of distribution of child pornography.

The 1957 decision in *Lambert v. California* held that due process required that the offense of failure to register as an ex-felon within five days of entering Los Angeles required proof of probable knowledge of a duty to register. The decision's rationale was mysterious. Justice Douglas, writing for a five-judge majority, began by denying "that 'a vicious will' is necessary to constitute a crime ...." Indeed, he conceded that "[t]here is wide latitude in the lawmakers to declare an offense and to exclude elements of knowledge and diligence from its definition."[115] Yet, he described that latitude as limited by a requirement of publicity, or "notice." Because the conduct element of the offense was an omission, Douglas held that knowledge of the duty was necessary. "Notice is required in a myriad of situations where a penalty or forfeiture might be suffered for mere failure to act ... But the principle is equally appropriate where a person, wholly passive and unaware of any wrongdoing, is brought to the bar ... in a criminal case."[116]

A requirement of knowledge of the duty for all omissions would contradict the suggestion in *Morissette* that punishing omissions is a factor weighing in favor of strict liability. However Douglas restricted his requirement of knowledge to a smaller class of omissions. He reasoned that most requirements of licensing or registration are triggered by some underlying activity, such as operating a business that exposes the public to risk. By contrast, violation of the felon-registration statute "is unaccompanied by any activity whatever, mere presence in the city being the test."[117] Thus individuals are subjected to the requirement of registration, not by any conduct, but by a circumstance, the status or identity of being an ex-felon. In this way the *Lambert* decision anticipated the prohibition on status crimes in *Robinson v. California*.

For criminal law theorist Alan Michaels, the key to understanding the holding in *Lambert* is not the absence of any activity being licensed, but the nature of the activity being licensed: entering or remaining within the city. Licensing this conduct is objectionable because criminalizing it is impermissible. As we observed in the context of vagrancy statutes, freedom to move about is part of the liberty of person protected by the due process clause. Similarly, the right

114. 513 U.S. 64 (1994).
115. 355 U.S. 225, 228 (1957).
116. *Id.* at 228.
117. *Id.* at 229.

to travel within the United States is one of the privileges and immunities of citizenship. Michaels offers the following due process test for strict liability:

> Strict liability is constitutional when, but only when, the intentional conduct covered by the statute could be made criminal by the legislature . . . [This] principle flows from two relatively uncontroversial propositions. The first is that the legislature normally may not punish the exercise of a fundamental right. . . . The second is that punishment must be predicated on some voluntary act or omission covered by a statute.[118]

By "strict liability," Michaels means what we have called impure strict liability. Thus, Michaels asserts that pure strict liability is unconstitutional. On Michaels's view, not only must every offense include some voluntary conduct that is not constitutionally protected, but that conduct must be culpable. Once the state has identified one element involving voluntary, culpable, punishable conduct, it can narrow liability further by adding strict liability elements. Thus, because the state can punish the intentional sale of alcohol, it can punish the intentional sale of alcohol when, unbeknownst to the seller, the purchaser is a minor. Yet it cannot criminalize the intentional sale of literature where, unbeknownst to the seller, the literature is obscene, because it cannot punish the sale of literature. From this perspective, the problem with the registration statute in *Lambert* was the absence of any intentional conduct element other than the protected conduct of entering or remaining in Los Angeles.[119]

Another line of cases established that required mental elements had to be proven beyond a reasonable doubt and could not be presumed from conduct. In the late nineteenth-century decision in *United States v. Davis*,[120] the Court required proof beyond a reasonable doubt of "every fact necessary to constitute the crime charged" as a "fundamental principle deemed essential for the protection of life and liberty." It permitted the jury to presume sanity, but not conclusively. As a matter of federal law, but not constitutional law, it deemed sanity to be an offense element, and so placed the burden on the prosecution to rebut any evidence of insanity introduced by the defense, beyond a reasonable doubt. In the 1952 case of *Leland v. Oregon*,[121] the Court held that states were not obliged to make sanity an offense element, but did not deny that offense elements had to be proved beyond a reasonable doubt. Thus, *Leland* recognized

---

118. Alan Michaels, *Constitutional Innocence*, 112 HARV. L. REV. 828, 834, 877–78 (1999).
119. *Id.* at 862–64.
120. 160 U.S. 469 (1895).
121. 343 U.S. 790 (1952).

two distinct categories of mental criteria of liability: the mental element of the offense, on which the prosecution had to bear the burden of proof; and mental excuses, which the Constitution did not require prosecutors to disprove. The Court's decision in *Tot v. United States*[122] set due process limits to legislative creation of presumptions, requiring that the fact presumed must bear some rational connection to the fact proven.

In the 1970s, the Court decided several more cases on the prosecutorial burden of proof. The *In re Winship* decision[123] confirmed that proof beyond a reasonable doubt of every offense element was a requirement of due process. In *Mullaney v. Wilbur*,[124] the Court applied the presumption of innocence to question the practice of presuming or constructing mental states. The Court struck down a murder statute that presumed malice, the mental element of murder, from proof of intent to kill, the mental element of the lesser-included offense of manslaughter. The statute imposed on the defense the burden of disproving malice by proving provocation or heat of passion by a preponderance of the evidence, thereby limiting the defendant's guilt to manslaughter. The Court reasoned that this scheme allowed the prosecution to avoid proving an essential offense element, in violation of the presumption of innocence required by *Winship*. Yet the *Mullaney* Court denied that anything turned on calling malice an offense element or a factor bearing on sentencing:

> if *Winship* were limited to those facts that constitute a crime as defined by state law, a State could undermine many of the interests that decision sought to protect without effecting any substantive change in its law. It would only be necessary to redefine the elements that constitute different crimes, characterizing them as factors that bear solely on the extent of punishment. . . . *Winship* is concerned with substance, rather than this kind of formalism.[125]

Thus observers were surprised when, two years after *Mullaney*, the Court upheld a statute defining intent to kill as the mental element of murder, and allowing the defendant to mitigate liability down to manslaughter by proving the excuse of extreme emotional disturbance.[126] This decision made the "formalistic" distinction between an excuse and the absence of a mental element determinative of the prosecutor's burden of proof. In *Sandstrom v Montana*,[127]

---

122. 319 U.S. 463 (1943).
123. 397 U.S. 358 (1970).
124. 421 U.S. 684 (1975).
125. *Id.* at 698–99.
126. Patterson v. New York, 432 U.S. 197 (1977).
127. 442 U.S. 510 (1979).

however, the Court reasserted the principles of *Winship* and *Mullaney*, while also drawing on *Morissette* and *U.S. Gypsum*. The Court in *Sandstrom* precluded instructions requiring or even permitting juries to presume that defendants intended the natural and probable consequences of their actions. In *Francis v Franklin*,[128] the Court confirmed that even rebuttable presumptions of intent were forbidden.

In sum, although the Supreme Court never adopted the broad prohibition on strict liability proposed by Sayre, it held that a mental element was required in many circumstances. Thus, it held that federal courts must presume a mental element absent clear congressional intent to impose strict liability, especially when the offense has a common law origin and a substantial penalty. It held that a mental element is sometimes required to preclude a criminal prohibition from chilling the exercise of protected liberty. If Professor Michaels is right, it held that at least one culpable mental state is required for every criminal offense. Finally the Court has held that once the legislature defined a mental element, it could not shift the burden of proof on that issue to the defense, or permit juries to presume the mental element from proof of other facts.

The uncertain import of these various lines of precedent was recently put to the test by a drug trafficking statute in Florida that imposes penalties of up to 30 years incarceration on the basis of strict liability for possession or delivery of drugs, presumes knowledge of the illicit nature of drugs from the fact of possessing them, and permits defendants to offer an affirmative defense of lack of knowledge of their illicit nature. In *Shelton v. Secretary, Department of Corrections*,[129] a federal district court granted habeas relief on the theory that this statute violates due process. The court interpreted *Morissette, U.S. Gypsum*, and *Lambert* as implying that strict liability is permitted only when the conduct knowingly engaged in is dangerous, or likely to be regulated, and the penalty and associated stigma are small. The court reasoned that delivery of packages is generally harmless conduct not likely to be regulated while the penalty for committing drug delivery was great.

In *State v. Adkins*,[130] however, the Florida Supreme Court rejected a similar due process argument. The Florida court determined that the offense required knowledge of the "presence" of the substance possessed, but not of its illicit nature. The court therefore concluded that the statute did not impose pure strict liability. It cited *Balint* as support for treating the illicit nature of a drug

128. 471 U.S. 307 (1985).
129. 802 F. Supp. 2d 1289 (M.D. Fla. 2011).
130. 96 So. 3d 412 (Fla. 2012).

as a strict liability element, and *Patterson* as support for defining the absence of culpability as an affirmative defense.

In reviewing the District Court's decision in *Shelton*, the U.S. Court of Appeals for the Eleventh Circuit did not choose between these positions, observing that the Supreme Court's case law leaves the constitutionality of strict liability uncertain. Reasoning that habeas corpus is available only for an obvious and unreasonable violation of federal law, however, it overturned the District Court's decision.[131]

VII. The Model Penal Code's Culpability Scheme

Whereas Sayre's writing influenced federal courts to read mental elements into statutory offenses, Herbert Wechsler's work influenced state legislatures to define mental elements more systematically and precisely. If anything, Wechsler was even more insistent on conditioning sentences of incarceration on culpable mental states. Wechsler's influential 1937 article, "A Rationale of the Law of Homicide,"[132] written with Jerome Michael, drew heavily on Stephen's discussions of homicide in his digest and history. Like Stephen, Wechsler denied that malice, the mental element of murder, embodied any quality of mind or character. Instead, malice was simply a disparate collection of mental states. Like Stephen, Wechsler regarded only expectations with respect to the proscribed injury as truly relevant to culpability. Thus conditioning murder liability on an intent to grievously injure or an intent to rob was sensible only insofar as these other aims entailed an apparent danger of death. Wechsler reconciled felony murder rules with his expected-injury theory of culpability by treating certain felonies as presumptive evidence of recklessness. If culpability is expected injury, the motive for inflicting or risking the injury should not matter. Accordingly, Wechsler rejected the traditional understanding of provocation as negating the mental element of murder. Instead, a provoking assault was just one circumstance that might partially excuse culpable wrongdoing, by explaining an emotional disturbance leading to a loss of self-control. To the extent possible, Wechsler sought to confine moral judgment to the consideration of defenses and to define offenses in neutral descriptive language.

Wechsler's proposed reform of homicide became the prototype for the Model Penal Code he drafted for the American Law Institute. The decision to

---

131. Shelton v. Sec'y, 691 F.3d 1348 (11th Cir. 2012).

132. Herbert Wechsler & Jerome Michael, *A Rationale of the Law of Homicide*, 37 COLUM. L. REV. 701 (1937).

draft such a code was made in 1950, and the Code was drafted between 1952 and 1962. Wechsler described deterrence as the ultimate aim of his draft of the Model Penal Code, and its scheme of culpability.[133] The Code defined its own purposes along the lines of Bentham's conception of a criminal code: to deter conduct threatening net harm to public and private interests, to publicly define and proscribe such conduct, to identify dangerous persons, "to safeguard conduct that is without fault from blame," and to "differentiate on reasonable grounds between serious and minor offenses." Thus, the Code was designed to condition liability on fault with respect to harming or endangering protected interests, and to grade liability on the basis of different degrees of fault or expected harm.[134]

Wechsler's aims included entrenching a requirement of mens rea and clarifying what that requirement entailed. He also sought to replace the confusing concepts of general and specific intent with a more precise taxonomy of mental states. His strategy was to eliminate mistake and accident as general defenses, and instead to define a mental element for each offense. Thus the Code required the prosecution to prove one of four possible culpable mental states with respect to each circumstance or result included in the offense definition. By assigning each offense a particular mental element, the Code obviated the protean distinction between general and specific intent. All intent was now "specific" as every fact comprising the actus reus of the offense would require a corresponding mental state. An inchoate intent to commit another crime might be used to aggravate an offense, but it could not substitute for a culpable mental state corresponding to each actus reus element. The Code eschewed the concepts of general and specific intent for determining the exculpatory consequences of mistake of law or involuntary intoxication, instead focusing inquiry on whether the mental state in question negated the mental element of the offense.

The Code distinguished between crimes, subject to prison sentences, and violations, for which only fines and forfeitures could be imposed. It required proof of all offense elements beyond a reasonable doubt,[135] although the defendant would bear the initial burden of production for an "affirmative defense."[136] Generally applicable affirmative defenses included all justifications, and the excuses of insanity, involuntary intoxication, duress, and military orders. Infancy was not an excuse, but age was a jurisdictional element the

133. Herbert Wechsler, *The Challenge of a Model Penal Code*, 65 HARV. L. REV. 1097, 1105, 1108 (1952).
134. MODEL PENAL CODE § 1.02(1) (1962).
135. *Id.* § 1.12 (1).
136. *Id.* §§ 2.02(1), 2.05(1).

prosecution bore the burden to prove. In addition to affirmative defenses, the code provided for a few defenses that the defendant was obliged to prove by a preponderance of evidence. These included certain reasonable mistakes of law not negating offense elements, entrapment by law enforcement agents, and reasonable mistake as to the age of a victim of sexual abuse. The Code also provided that offense definitions could include permissive presumptions of material elements from other facts.[137] The jury would be instructed that it could, but need not, accept such facts as proof beyond a reasonable doubt of the material element. Such presumptions are rare in the Code. Notable examples are a presumption of recklessness and extreme indifference to human life from causing death in the course of certain dangerous felonies,[138] a presumption of knowledge of the age of a child taken from the custody of its parent,[139] a presumption of knowledge that property received is stolen from an unusually low price or a record of receiving stolen property,[140] and a presumption of knowledge that a check will bounce from a subsequent failure to cover it.[141]

The Code defined "material elements" as consisting of conduct, attendant circumstances, or results included in an offense definition, or negating a defense of justification or excuse.[142] One purpose of dividing the actus reus into discrete elements was to permit the organization of offenses into hierarchies of greater and lesser offenses. For example, the Code defines simple burglary as entry of a building not open to the public, with the purpose to commit a crime.[143] It defines aggravated burglary as simple burglary with (1) the additional circumstances that it is committed in a dwelling and at night, (2) the additional circumstance that it is committed while armed with a deadly weapon, or (3) the additional conduct of attempting to inflict injury. Circumstance or result elements that are different only in quantity can also be ranked, permitting offenses with otherwise identical elements to be arranged into a hierarchy of lesser-included offenses. Examples of grading hierarchies are drug possession offenses, identical apart from the quantity of the drug; and sexual molestation of minors, where the grade is determined solely by the age of the victim. Stacking offenses in this way permits plea bargains or compromise verdicts, so that an offender charged with the more aggravated offense can be convicted of the lesser-included offense under the same charging instrument. Another purpose of classifying the actus reus into discrete elements was to permit greater

---

137. *Id.* § 1.12(5).
138. *Id.* § 210.2.
139. *Id.* § 212.4.
140. *Id.* § 223.6.
141. *Id.* § 224.5.
142. *Id.* § 1.13(9)–(10).
143. *Id.* § 221.1(1).

precision in defining mental elements, as each actus material element could be assigned a different corresponding culpable mental state.

If the offense was a crime (rather than a violation), and was defined in the Code (rather than some other statute), the prosecution would have to prove a culpable mental state corresponding to each material element.[144] In other words, for such offenses the Code forbade formal strict liability, including impure strict liability. The Code permitted no strict liability elements in the crimes it defined. For offenses defined in other statutes, the Code permitted strict liability only if a legislative purpose to impose it for the offense or some particular element "plainly appears"[145] and required that such an offense be punished as a violation.[146] If the prosecution failed to prove the mental state corresponding to a material element, that element would not be proven. The Code made one exception to this general requirement of proof of culpability. For sexual abuse of a child under 10, the age of the victim was a strict liability element. For sexual abuse of a minor above that age, the age of the victim was also a strict liability element, but the defendant could prove a defense of reasonable mistake of age by a preponderance of the evidence.[147]

Although (with this one exception) the Code required a culpable mental state corresponding to every act, circumstance, and result element for any crime, these mental states varied in gravity. The Code identified four culpable mental states: purpose, knowledge, recklessness, and negligence. Purposely had its conventional meaning for conduct and result elements. Belief or hope that a circumstance was present was sufficient for purpose. "Knowingly" had its obvious meaning for conduct and circumstance elements, but for a result element it meant with practical certainty of causing the result. "Recklessly" meant "consciously disregard[ing] a substantial and unjustifiable risk that the . . . element exists or will result." The disregard had to be a gross deviation from the standard of a law-abiding person. "Negligently" meant disregarding a risk the actor should have been aware of, involving gross deviation from the standard of a reasonable person.[148]

These culpable mental states involve a combination of cognitive and volitional elements. Thus purpose is largely volitional (although purpose with respect to a circumstance is satisfied by belief it exists). Knowledge is purely cognitive. Recklessness is primarily cognitive ("consciously disregarding . . . risk"), but also involves some evaluation of the actor's ends (the risk must be "unjustifiable,"

144. *Id.* §§ 2.02(1), 2.05(1).
145. *Id.* § 2.05(1)(b).
146. *Id.* § 2.05(2).
147. *Id.* § 213.6.
148. *Id.* § 2.02(2).

meaning that "considering the nature and purpose of the actor's conduct" it violates the standard of a law-abiding person). Negligence is also largely cognitive, as the actor is being judged by the risk apparent to a reasonable person in her situation. However, the risk must again by unjustifiable in light of the actor's purposes. Despite this interweaving of cognitive and volitional standards, the Model Penal Code has been criticized for unduly emphasizing the cognitive dimension of culpability.[149] Its taxonomy of culpable mental states excludes a volitional state employed by many continental legal systems, "dolus eventualis," which combines the expectation of harm with its acceptance.[150] It rarely requires the purely volitional mental state of purpose with respect to result elements, for example, providing that purposeful conduct committed with an expectation of causing a result constitutes an attempt to cause that result.[151]

The Model Penal Code's culpable mental states constitute a hierarchy, with purpose as the most culpable and negligence the least. Thus, negligence can be proven by evidence of recklessness, knowledge, or purpose; recklessness could be proven by evidence of knowledge or purpose, but not negligence; knowledge could be proven by evidence of purpose, but not recklessness or negligence; and purpose could not be proven by evidence of any other mental state.[152] A consequence of this was that otherwise identical offenses could be graded based on the "lowest" culpable mental state required to accompany a particular material element.[153] These offenses would "stack," so that the lower-graded offenses would be a lesser-included offense of the higher-graded ones. The classic example of such stacking was the Code's hierarchical arrangement of homicide offenses. Once again, this stacking arrangement would facilitate plea bargaining and compromise verdicts.

The Code used the culpable mental states required for each material element to replace the traditional defenses of accident and mistake.

Instead of offering a defense of accident, the Code simply provided that "[w]hen purposely or knowingly causing a particular result is an element . . . [it] is not established if the actual result is not within the purpose or the contemplation of the actor," and that "[w]hen recklessly or negligently causing a result is an element . . . [it] is not established if the actual result is not within the risk of which the actor is aware, or . . . of which he should be aware."[154] Although the Code did not permit harmful intent to be transferred from one type of injury

149. Kenneth W. Simons, *Rethinking Mental States*, 72 B.U. L. REV. 463 (1992).

150. Alan Michaels, *Acceptance: The Missing Mental State*, 71 S. CAL. L. REV. 953, 1025–26 (1998).

151. MODEL PENAL CODE § 5.01(1)(b) (1962).

152. *Id.* § 2.02(5).

153. *Id.* § 2.02(10).

154. *Id.* § 2.03(2)–(3).

to another, it did permit transferring intent among injuries that satisfied the same offense definition, as in *R. v. Saunders*, the poison apple case.[155] Thus, the required culpable mental state with respect to a result element always concerned injury to a certain type of interest rather than injury to a particular person or thing. The Code did, however, permit intent to transfer from an intended injury to a less serious injury. Thus on the facts of *R. v. Woodbourne*, the Code would have held the defendants liable for assault with intent to maim on the basis of their admission they intended to kill.

Instead of treating mistake as an excuse, the Code provided that a mistake of fact or law was a "defense"—but *not* an "affirmative defense"—if it negated the required culpable mental state corresponding to a material element of the offense.[156] Of course, if the defendant had a lower level of culpability corresponding to the material element he could be liable for a lesser-included offense. If the defendant's mistaken belief would have made him liable for some other crime of lesser grade if the belief were true, he would be liable for an offense of that grade.[157]

The Code's general approach to mistake applied to mistakes of law as well. Thus, if the offense definition made some legal circumstance a material element, an offender would have to have a culpable mental state with respect to that legal circumstance. For the most part, a mistake of law would acquit the defendant if and only if it negated a culpable mental state required by the offense definition.[158] The defendant would not have to prove a mistake of fact or law negating such a required mental element. Instead, the prosecution would have to prove the mental element beyond a reasonable doubt. Under two circumstances, a mistake of law could provide a defense even if it did not negate the mental element of the offense, however. Proof by a preponderance of the evidence that the defendant believed his conduct to be legal would provide a defense if that belief was based on (1) a misleading official statement of law, or (2) an official failure to publicize the legal prohibition.[159] Assuming this defense negates the blameworthiness of the offense it appears to be an excuse.

The Code adopts a similar, but slightly more punitive approach to voluntary intoxication. Involuntary intoxication is treated as the equivalent of a mental disease or defect and so can provide the basis for an excuse of insanity.[160] Voluntary intoxication "is not a defense unless it negatives an element of the

155. *Id.* §§ 2.03(2)(a)–(b), 2.03(3)(a)–(b).
156. *Id.* § 2.04.
157. *Id.* § 2.04(2).
158. *Id.* § 2.02(9).
159. *Id.* § 2.04(3), § 2.04(4).
160. *Id.* § 2.08(4).

offense."[161] Yet in an important class of cases, the Code precludes voluntary intoxication from negating an offense element: "When recklessness establishes an element of the offense, if the actor, due to self-induced intoxication, is unaware of a risk of which he would have been aware had he been sober, that unawareness is immaterial."[162] Such an offender is treated as actually aware, and so reckless, rather than merely as at fault for being unaware, or negligent.

VIII. The Model Penal Code's Default Rules

Although the Code requires a culpable mental state for every material element, that does not mean that offense definitions have to enumerate each required mental state. Instead the Code provides default rules enabling a court to assign a culpable mental state to each material element whether or not one is specified in the provision defining the offense. We have seen that federal law interprets ambiguous offense definitions by means of a standard considering multiple factors, including the severity of punishment, the common law or legislative origins of the offense, whether the offense inflicts injury or imposes risk, and whether it is malum in se. The Model Penal Code scheme of default rules is similar in one respect: it requires culpability for all elements if the punishment may include incarceration. Once that threshold is passed, the only issue is which culpable mental state should be assigned to each element. The Code answers this question with a pair of technical rules.

If the offense definition assigns one culpable mental state to the offense "without distinguishing among the material elements thereof" that mental state applies to each material element.[163] We may call this the *distributive default rule.* Thus, if the offense is described as "knowingly battering and causing injury to a police officer," it appears to require knowledge that the victim is a police officer and an expectation of physical injury, because the culpable mental state is not restricted to one particular element. If, on the other hand, the offense is described as "battering and knowingly causing injury to a police officer," the requirement of knowledge does not distribute to the conduct of battery and the circumstance that the victim is a police officer. The distributive default rule does not apply because even though only one culpable mental state is mentioned, it is not assigned to the offense as a whole. Suppose the offense is described as "knowingly battering and negligently causing injury to

---

161. *Id.* § 2.08(1).
162. *Id.* § 2.08.
163. *Id.* § 2.02(4).

a police officer." Because two different culpable mental states are assigned to particular elements, the distributive rule does not apply and so no culpable mental state is distributed.

When no culpable mental state is explicitly assigned to a material element by the provision defining the offense, or distributed to it by application of the distributive rule, which culpable mental state is required? This question is answered as follows: "when the culpability sufficient to establish a material element of an offense is not prescribed by law, such element is established if a person acts purposely, knowingly, or recklessly with respect thereto."[164] As recklessness is the "lowest" level of culpability listed, and is included in purpose and knowledge, the required culpable mental state is recklessness. We may call this the *recklessness default rule*. The Code does not presume strict liability if no culpable mental state is specified, nor does it presume negligence, the lowest permitted level of culpability. Instead, legislatures (which have adopted the Code's default rules) wanting to condition incarceration on negligence must do so explicitly.

To illustrate the operation of these rules, consider the Model Penal Code's definition of burglary: "A person is guilty of burglary if he enters a[n] . . . occupied structure with the purpose to commit a crime therein, unless the premises are at the time open to the public or the actor is . . . privileged to enter. . . . Burglary is a felony of the second degree if . . . perpetrated in the dwelling of another at night or if . . . the actor . . . recklessly inflicts . . . bodily injury. Otherwise burglary is a felony of the third degree."[165] This definition explicitly assigns purpose to the element of commission of another crime, and recklessness to the aggravating element of injury; it assigns no mental state to the elements of entry, the structure being occupied, the structure being closed to the public generally and the actor in particular, and the aggravating elements of the structure being a dwelling and the entry occurring at night. Which default rule applies? The distributive rule does not apply because the first mental state mentioned, purpose, applies to the element of commission of another crime rather than the offense as a whole. Thus the recklessness rule applies. The guilty defendant must be at least reckless with respect to all elements as to which no mental state is assigned.

Although the Model Penal Code inspired code reform in almost three-fourths of the states,[166] only about half the states have adopted parts of the

---

164. *Id.* § 2.02(3).
165. *Id.* § 221.1.
166. WAYNE R. LAFAVE, CRIMINAL LAW 5 (2010).

Code's default rule scheme.[167] As of this writing, 21 states have selected one culpable mental state as a default standard, with recklessness the most popular choice. Sixteen states either forbid strict liability, or permit it only on the basis of a clear statement by the legislature, and almost as many have adopted the distributive default rule.

We can get an idea of how courts use default rules by comparing cases from New York, Rhode Island, and Ohio. In *People v. Ryan*,[168] defendant was charged under a provision of the New York Penal Law punishing "knowingly and unlawfully possess[ing] 625 milligrams of a hallucinogen." The evidence showed that an associate-turned-informant delivered to him a quantity of psilocybin mushrooms, which he variously described as "about two pounds" and "a shit load of mushrooms." The New York Penal Law forbids impure strict liability absent a clear legislative statement, and includes a distributive rule, but not a recklessness default rule. On the basis of the Penal Law's default rules, the Court of Appeals reversed defendant's conviction for failure to prove his knowledge of the weight of the drugs. The court reasoned as follows:

> Read in context, it seems evident that "knowingly" does apply to the weight element. Indeed, given that a defendant's awareness must extend not only to the fact of possessing something ("knowingly ... possesses") but also to the nature of the material possessed ("knowingly ... possesses ... a hallucinogen"), any other reading would be strained. Inasmuch as the knowledge requirement carries through to the end of the sentence, eliminating it from the intervening element—weight—would rob the statute of its obvious meaning....
>
> That reading is fortified by two rules of construction ordained by the Legislature itself. First, a "statute defining a crime, unless clearly indicating a legislative intent to impose strict liability, should be construed as defining a crime of mental culpability" (Penal Law § 15.15[2]). If any material element of an offense lacks a mens rea requirement, it is a strict liability crime (Penal Law § 15.10). Conversely, a crime is one of "mental culpability" only when a mental state "is required with respect to every material element of an offense" (id.).
>
> By ruling that a defendant need not have knowledge of the weight, the Appellate Division in effect held, to that extent, that second degree criminal possession is a strict liability crime (see, Penal Law § 15.10). That is

167. Guyora Binder, *Felony Murder and Mens Rea Default Rules: A Study in Statutory Interpretation*, 4 BUFF. CRIM. L. REV. 399, 400 (2000).

168. 626 N.E.2d 51 (N.Y. 1993).

> an erroneous statutory construction unless a legislative intent to achieve that result is "clearly indicat[ed]" (Penal Law § 15.15[2]).
>
> In a similar vein, the Legislature has provided in Penal Law § 15.15(1): "When . . . some element of an offense, requires a particular culpable mental state, such mental state is ordinarily designated in the statute defining the offense by use of the terms "intentionally," "knowingly," "recklessly" or "criminal negligence," . . . . When one and only one of such terms appears in a statute defining an offense, it is presumed to apply to every element of the offense unless an intent to limit its application clearly appears."
>
> Accordingly, if a single mens rea is set forth, as here, it presumptively applies to all elements of the offense unless a contrary legislative intent is plain.[169]

Finding no such legislative intent, the court held that knowledge was required. The legislature then manifested its contrary intent by revising the statute in response to this decision, to punish one who "knowingly possesses a hallucinogen, and the hallucinogen weighs 625 milligrams."[170]

The Rhode Island case of *State v. Lima*[171] illustrates application of a recklessness default rule. The defendant was charged with child abuse causing injury under a statute specifying no mental state with respect to injury. The defendant was convicted after the trial court rejected her requested jury instruction requiring intent to injure. On appeal, the court awarded a new trial and, invoking the Model Penal Code, directed the trial court to instruct the jury that recklessness was required with respect to the injury.

The Model Penal Code's default rule scheme clearly precludes impure strict liability by specifying a corresponding mental state for every material element. But what if a code does not clarify whether the default rule applies to every material element, or only to the offense as a whole? Prior to 2015 the Ohio code precluded liability unless the defendant had "the requisite degree of culpability for each element as to which a culpable mental state is specified by the section defining the offense."[172] The code added that "When the section defining an offense does not specify any degree of culpability, and plainly indicates

169. *Id.* at 54.

170. N.Y. PENAL LAW § 220.18 (2015). The legislature also provided that "notwithstanding the use of the term 'knowingly' in. . .defining an offense in which the aggregate weight of a controlled substance. . . is an element, knowledge. . .of the aggregate weight. . . is not an element . . . ." *Id.* at § 15.20 (4)(2015)

171. 546 A.2d 770 (R.I. 1988).

172. OHIO REV. CODE ANN. § 2901.21(A) (2000).

a purpose to impose strict criminal liability for the conduct described in the section, then culpability is not required for a person to be guilty of the offense. When the section neither specifies culpability nor plainly indicates a purpose to impose strict liability, recklessness is sufficient culpability to commit the offense."[173] Thus the Ohio code provided a recklessness default rule with a clear statement exception, for sections that specify no culpability at all. It included no distributive rule, however, or any other default rule indicating how courts should construe offense definitions including one culpability term and multiple material elements.

One such offense in Ohio is unlicensed weapons possession, which requires knowing possession without a license or while under one of several disabilities that invalidate a license. In a 2008 decision, the Ohio Supreme Court applied the recklessness default rule to these disabilities.[174] Yet just two years, later the court reversed itself, reasoning that the recklessness default rule applied only to entire sections bereft of culpability terms, not to elements within offense definitions assigning a culpable mental state to other elements.[175] The majority's decision presumed a default rule of strict liability for material elements with no mental state assigned. In 2015, the Ohio legislature overruled this decision with a new provision applying the recklessness default rule to elements without culpability terms rather than to sections without culpability terms. The revised language provided that "[w]hen language defining an element of an offense . . . neither specifies culpability nor plainly indicates a purpose to impose strict liability, the element of an offense is established only if a person acts recklessly."[176]

The Model Penal Code approach to offense definition has helped many jurisdictions resolve two vexing problems concerning mens rea: mistake of law, and mental incapacity. The Code resolves these issues by differentiating between required culpable mental states and mental states excusing the defendant from responsibility. If the defendant lacked a culpable mental state required by an offense definition, regardless of why, she has not committed the offense. On the other hand, deficits of cognition or volition may absolve the defendant of responsibility even if they do not affect the required culpable mental states. Whether these deficits excuse the defendant, however, may depend on whether the defendant was at fault in causing them.

---

173. *Id.* § 2901.21(B).
174. State v. Clay, 900 N.E.2d 1000 (Ohio 2008).
175. State v. Johnson, 42 N.E.2d 347 (Ohio 2010).
176. OHIO REV. CODE ANN. § 2901.21(C) (2015).

IX. Mistake of Law

Should mistakes of law absolve an actor of guilt? It seems an actor cannot deserve blame for conduct he does not know is wrong. That is one reason the state is obliged to publicize its criminal prohibitions. Yet many criminal prohibitions track widely shared moral norms, such as those against killing and rape. Such offenses are "mala in se:" their wrongness does not depend upon state prohibition. An actor's failure to recognize these norms is itself subject to blame. So perhaps ignorance of criminal prohibitions should exculpate only if they are "mala prohibita." But if the state has publicized its prohibitions, why should not citizens be expected to know them? On the other hand, an actor might be aware of a criminal prohibition and yet violate it because of a mistake about some other law. Thus, one could recognize the wrongness of theft without knowing some rule determining the assignment and lawful transfer of property rights. Similarly, one could recognize the wrongness of homicide without knowing one has a particular legal duty to prevent another's death.

The Model Penal Code discusses mistakes of law in its general rule on mistake: "Ignorance or mistake as to a matter of fact or law is a defense if the ignorance or mistake negatives the ... [culpable mental state] required to establish a material element of the offense."[177] This approach is exemplified by the English case of *R. v. Smith*,[178] in which the defendant removed fixtures he had attached to the walls of his apartment when he moved out, mistakenly believing they belonged to him rather than the landlord. The Court dismissed charges for damaging property of another on the view that the intent required for this crime entailed knowledge that the affected property belonged to someone else. Similarly, the decision in *People v. Bray*[179] awarded a new trial for the offense of possessing a weapon while an ex-felon, to determine if the defendant reasonably believed his prior offense was not a felony. The court deemed mistake as to the legal classification of his prior offense to be a mistake about one of the "facts" bringing his conduct within the offense definition. The jury instruction endorsed in this decision requires at least unreasonableness, or negligence, with respect to all circumstance elements, whether or not they depend on a legal rule.

A second Model Penal Code provision holds that "neither knowledge nor recklessness or negligence as to whether conduct constitutes an offense or as to the existence, meaning or application of the law determining the elements of

---

177. Model Penal Code § 2.04(1)(a) (1962).
178. 2 Q.B. 354 (1974).
179. 52 Cal. App. 3d 494 (1975).

an offense is an element of such offense, unless the definition of the offense . . . so provides."[180] Thus, a mistake about whether conduct is a crime negates a mental element only if the statutory offense definition identifies culpability with respect to the offense definition as included in the mental element. Let us consider two federal cases illustrating this approach. In *United States v. Baker*,[181] the U.S. Court of Appeals for the Fifth Circuit upheld a conviction for selling fake Rolex watches. The statute punished intentionally selling goods, knowing they bear a counterfeit trademark. The trial court had refused the defendant's requested instruction that he could only be convicted if it was his intention to disobey the law. The appellate court approved this refusal, because awareness of violating the law was not an element of the offense. By contrast, in *Cheek v. United States*,[182] the U.S, Supreme Court held that "willfully" evading the tax imposed by the Internal Revenue Code, means doing so defiantly. Such defiance of the tax code requires awareness of the tax code provision evaded. Thus, unlike the trademark forgery offense in *Baker*, the tax evasion offense in *Cheek* did require knowledge of the legal rule violated. Yet the Supreme Court also held that Cheek was not required to know or believe that the income tax he avoided was constitutional, because the mental element of the offense required only knowledge that his conduct violated the statute, not knowledge that it was criminal. *Both* decisions are consistent with the rule recommended by the Model Penal Code.

Assuming the mental element of the offense does not require knowledge that the conduct violates law, is it *fair* to punish for an offense the defendant believes is legal? In *Hopkins v. State*,[183] a minister was convicted of erecting a sign with the intention of soliciting work performing marriages, for putting up highly visible signs stating his name and profession. The trial court refused to allow Hopkins to introduce evidence that he had erected the signs in reliance on an assurance from the local prosecutor that the signs were legal. The court reasoned that "[w]hile ignorance of fact may sometimes be admitted as evidence of lack of criminal intent, ignorance of the law ordinarily does not give immunity from punishment for crime, for every man is presumed to intend the necessary and legitimate consequences of what he knowingly does." Thus the court assumed that mens rea meant intentional wrongdoing, but relied on a blanket prohibition on the exculpatory use of mistakes of law, and a presumption that one who intends an act intends its legal consequences. Yet notice

180. MODEL PENAL CODE § 2.02(9)(1962).
181. 807 F.2d 427 (5th Cir. 1986).
182. 498 U.S. 192 (1991).
183. 69 A.2d 456 (Md. 1950).

that the Model Penal Code rules reach the same result by different means. The Code does not condition guilt on an intention to offend, but on fulfillment of the mental element of the offense. The mental element here was the intention to solicit marriages, which the jury found. The act element required simply the posting of a sign, which Hopkins performed. Thus Hopkins would have been guilty under Model Penal Code Sections 2.04(1)(a) and 2.02(9). His belief that the signs were legal was irrelevant to the offense elements.

Yet, a different provision of the Model Penal Code could have offered Hopkins an excuse, notwithstanding his satisfaction of all the offense elements. Section 2.04(3) provides: "A belief that conduct does not legally constitute an offense is a defense when . . . (a) the . . . enactment defining the offense . . . has not been published or reasonably made available . . .; or (b) [the actor] acts in reasonable reliance upon an official statement of the law, afterwards determined to be . . . erroneous, contained in . . . a statute . . . a judicial decision . . . an administrative order . . . or an official interpretation of the public officer . . . with responsibility for the interpretation, administration or enforcement of the law defining the offense."[184] This would apply to Hopkins if we deem the prosecutor's advice an "official interpretation."

Such a defense was made available in the Massachusetts case of *Commonwealth v. Twitchell*,[185] which overturned the manslaughter conviction of parents who permitted the death of their child by failing to provide medical treatment for a surgically correctable bowel defect. The parents were observant Christian Scientists and relied on a pamphlet issued by their church indicating that they could not be deemed negligent for "the sole reason" that for religious reasons they provided treatment only by spiritual means. The pamphlet in turn quoted a law absolving such parents of liability for child neglect, and also relied on an official opinion by the state's attorney general stating that parents would not be prosecuted for such neglect. The court determined that the parents' immunity from child neglect prosecution did not preclude prosecution for manslaughter based on reckless causation of death. As the parent's reasonable mistake about their legal responsibilities did not negate the recklessness toward death required by the offense definition, the parents committed the offense. However, the court remanded for a new trial to consider an excuse of reasonable reliance on an official statement of law, as provided in Model Penal Code Section 2.04(3), even though the Massachusetts criminal code lacked such a provision.

---

184. Model Penal Code § 2.04(3) (1962).
185. 617 N.E.2d 609 (Mass. 1993).

By contrast, the New York Court of Appeals refused to grant such a defense in *People v. Marrero*,[186] despite the fact that New York Penal Law includes a provision very similar to the Model Penal Code's.[187] Marrero, a federal corrections officer, was convicted of possessing an unlicensed firearm despite a statutory exemption for peace officers, then defined as including "correction officers of any state correction facility or of any penal correctional institution."[188] Marrero, like the trial judge and two judges of an appellate court, believed federal correctional officers were included within this exemption. The New York Court of Appeals held that he was not, and that his therefore mistaken belief that he was exempted by the statute was not "founded on" the statute as required for the defense. The court bolstered this conclusion by invoking the common law maxim that ignorance of law is no excuse, as explained by Justice Oliver Wendell Holmes Jr. Holmes reasoned that such an excuse would subvert deterrence by encouraging ignorance and lying and that the law therefore "sacrifices the individual to the general good."[189] A dissent retorted that as the Model Penal Code and the New York Penal Law had afforded such an excuse in some circumstances, it must have rejected this sacrifice. Both arguments beg the question. An excuse for mistakes based on an official statement of law is one of several possible compromises between excusing all mistakes of law and excusing none. The legislative adoption of such a compromise therefore cannot in itself signify legislative endorsement of either extreme, or justify interpreting that excuse narrowly or broadly.

Even if interpreted to excuse Marrero, the Model Penal Code's mistake of law excuse excludes many reasonable mistakes, including those based on legal advice. In the case of *Long v. State*,[190] the defendant got an out-of-state divorce and then, advised incorrectly by counsel that the divorce was valid in Delaware, he remarried. He was convicted of bigamy at trial. The Delaware Supreme Court held that although the defendant's belief that his ex-wife was dead would have negated the "specific intent" required for bigamy, his belief he was legally divorced did not. Nevertheless, the court held that a mistake of law can negate "general criminal intent," meaning that it can excuse him from responsibility for his offense. Invoking Holmes, however, the court reasoned that excusing mistakes of law would encourage ignorance and lying. Accordingly, the court

186. 69 N.Y.2d 382 (1987).

187. N.Y. Penal Law § 15.20(2) (2015) (applying to conduct committed "under a mistaken belief that it does not . . . constitute an offense . . . founded upon an official statement of the law" in a statute, executive order, court decision, or official interpretation).

188. *Marreo*, 69 N.Y.2d at 397 n.7.

189. *Id.* at 403 (citing Oliver Wendell Holmes, Jr., The Common Law 48 (1881).

190. 65 A.2d 489 (Del. 1949).

concluded, an excuse of reasonable mistake of law should be granted only where the defendant can demonstrate a good faith effort to learn the law and can corroborate his or her mistake. As a record of erroneous advice from an attorney documents both the defendant's diligence and his mistaken belief, reasonable reliance on advice of counsel arguably warrants an excuse even on Holmes's utilitarian premises.

The Model Penal Code's excuse for reliance on an official statement of law is narrow insofar as it excludes some reasonable mistakes involving mala prohibita. Yet it is surprisingly broad in excusing mala in se if such offenses are permitted by an official statement of law. Indeed, this risk is illustrated by the *Twitchell* case, which applies the excuse to manslaughter.

X. Incapacity for Culpability

Like mistakes of law, psychological impairment can negate both the culpable mental states required for a particular offense and the responsibility requisite for blame. Like almost all American jurisdictions, the Model Penal Code provides an excuse conditioned on a mental disease or defect.[191] It also provides that evidence of these conditions is "admissible whenever it is relevant to prove that the defendant did or did not have a state of mind which is an element of the offense."[192]

In *Hendershott v. People*, the Colorado Supreme Court considered a statutory provision permitting the use of psychiatric evidence to negate specific intent only.[193] The defendant had been charged with an offense requiring reckless infliction of bodily injury, and offered testimony that a personality disorder marked by impulsiveness precluded the consideration of risk required for recklessness. In Colorado, specific intent crimes are only those requiring a mental element of purpose. The court ruled that precluding the defendant from offering evidence tending to disprove the mental element of the offense violated due process. Despite the court's persuasive argument that the Supreme Court's decisions in *Sandstrom* and *Mullaney* require this result, only about 10 states have adopted the Model Penal Code's blanket rule permitting the use of psychiatric evidence to negate any mental element. The most common approach is to permit psychiatric evidence to negate "specific" but not "general intent." And a few jurisdictions permit such evidence only to support an insanity excuse.

---

191. *Id.* § 4.01.
192. *Id.* § 4.02.
193. 653 P.2d 385 (Colo. 1982).

The majority rule, allowing psychiatric evidence to negate specific intent but not general intent, involves two difficulties.

First, as we have noted, the meanings of these terms are uncertain. If specific intent just means "the mental element of the offense," the majority rule converges with the Model Penal Code rule. "Specific intent" could also mean purpose with respect to any element, as it did in the Colorado code applied in *Hendershott.* Yet "specific intent" can also encompass purpose, knowledge, or recklessness (as opposed to negligence); or any culpable mental state with respect to a result or circumstance element (as opposed to a conduct element); or any culpable mental state with respect to an inchoate element, or a secondary injury.

Assuming we have assigned a definite meaning to general and specific intent, we face a second difficulty: How do we justify considering psychiatric evidence to negate some required mental states but not others? One solution to both of these difficulties is to interpret "general intent" as not truly a mental state at all, but a normative expectation of reasonable foresight and care, absent which the actor is negligent. Then, if the psychiatric evidence is offered to show it is unfair to hold the actor to that standard of reasonableness, it is properly treated as an excuse from responsibility.

If we hold that due process requires jury consideration of any evidence corroborating the absence of required culpable mental states, it follows that a defendant should be able to use even voluntary intoxication in this way. Yet the *Hendershott* court rejected this implication, endorsing earlier decisions allowing voluntary intoxication only to negate purpose, but not knowledge, recklessness, or negligence.[194] The court reasoned that unlike insanity, voluntary intoxication itself implies choice and therefore fault. Yet it did not justify equating the choice to impair one's perceptions and judgment with the choice to knowingly cause a particular injury. Instead it merely invoked the Colorado code's definition of general intent as encompassing knowledge.

The Model Penal Code also differentiates voluntary intoxication from insanity as a source of incapacity to harbor culpable mental states. The Code includes *involuntary* intoxication that substantially impairs cognition or volition within its mental disease or defect excuse.[195] It also provides that evidence of voluntary intoxication can be used to negate purpose or knowledge, but not recklessness.[196] The Code also presumes that voluntary intoxication cannot

194. *Id.* at 396–97.
195. MODEL PENAL CODE § 2.08(4)(1962).
196. *Id.* § 2.08(2).

negate negligence, as it defines negligence as the failure to perceive a risk one should have perceived.

It seems justifiable to treat voluntary intoxication as irrelevant to negligence, but how is it justifiable to treat it as irrelevant to recklessness, which requires actual awareness of risk? Impairing one's risk perception may increase the odds one will inflict some type of injury, but probably not enough to constitute recklessness with respect to such injury.

If we cannot rationally equate voluntary intoxication with knowledge or recklessness with respect to injury, it seems that excluding evidence of voluntary intoxication offered to negate these mental states must violate due process. The U.S. Supreme Court considered this question in *Montana v. Egelhoff*,[197] but gave an equivocal response.

Egelhoff was convicted of knowingly causing death. Evidence of Egelhoff's intoxication was excluded pursuant to a statute precluding jury consideration of intoxication in determining the existence of any mental element of an offense. The Montana Supreme Court reversed the conviction and struck down the statute as violating due process by excluding evidence necessary for contesting a required offense element.

A four-justice plurality plurality of the U.S. Supreme Court agreed, in an opinion authored by Justice O'Connor. In an opinion drafted by Justice Scalia, another four-justice plurality denied that due process requires admitting evidence of intoxication when relevant to disprove offense elements. Justice Scalia reasoned that due process generally permitted the exclusion of relevant evidence for reasons of public policy, and as the common law at the time of Blackstone excluded intoxication as an excuse, admission of evidence of intoxication could not be a fundamental requirement of justice. The latter argument ignored the point that in Blackstone's time there was no general requirement that the prosecution prove mens rea, an issue usually then introduced by the defendant in the form of an excuse. The constitutional jurisprudence requiring prosecutorial proof of all offense elements is a departure from eighteenth-century law.

The decisive fifth vote to restore the conviction was cast by Justice Ginsburg, who avoided the due process question by denying that the Montana statute excluded evidence relevant to the proof of a mental element. She interpreted the provision excluding evidence of intoxication in determining the existence of mental states as actually defining the offense disjunctively to require either an expectation of death or voluntary intoxication combined with the

197. 518 U.S. 37 (1996).

appearance that the defendant expected death. This tortuous interpretation of the Montana statute overruled the Montana Supreme Court's own authoritative interpretation. Ginsburg's justification for doing so was the novel proposition that state courts are somehow required by federal law to interpret state statutes to avoid conflict with the federal constitution rather than overturning them. The point of this rule seemed to be to save the U.S. Supreme Court from having to clarify the requirements due process. It seems that on the issue of excluding evidence of incapacity to act culpably, as on the questions of strict liability and voluntariness, the Court has preferred to keep the constitutional limits of the criminal law well hidden.

XI. Conclusion

The idea of mens rea may be ancient, but the principle that every act element requires a corresponding mental state is relatively modern.

Conditioning punishment on fault helps ensure it is deserved, while punishment best deters harm by targeting conduct the actor expects to be harmful. Requiring proof of culpable mental states corresponding to act elements is only one way to achieve these goals, however. Thus, a legal system may also condition punishment on mens rea by (1) restricting act elements to manifestly culpable conduct, or (2) holding defendants responsible to excuse themselves by introducing evidence of mistake or accident. We have seen that the English criminal law first addressed fault primarily, although not exclusively, through the act element and excuses. Contemporary American law addresses culpability primarily, although not exclusively, by requiring proof of a mental state.

American criminal law scholarship has been influenced by the ideas of utilitarian reformers, including Bentham and Stephen, who urged the precise legislative definition of offenses to achieve deterrence, regularity, and publicity. These utilitarians conceived culpability in value-neutral terms as a cognitive state corresponding to each objective element. In the nineteenth century this movement successfully promoted a reinterpretation of the common law's primarily objective criteria of liability as a series of presumptions of culpability. The cumbersome terminology of general and specific intent was part of that reinterpretation, with general intent often signifying a mental element that was presumed rather than proven. The awkwardness of general intent as a way of describing a normative standard of behavior rather than a mental state, and its fictive status as a mental element, made it vulnerable to critique.

In the twentieth century, reform proceeded along two tracks.

First, the Supreme Court developed a practice of reading a mental element into federal offense definitions outside of an elusive category of regulatory offenses. In addition, it determined that due process sometimes required a mental element to ensure that a criminal prohibition did not chill constitutionally protected conduct. Indeed, in *Lambert* it arguably implied that it must be foreseeable to the actor that he is committing some conduct that is not constitutionally protected. If so, the Court forbade pure strict liability. Perhaps most significantly, the Court constitutionalized the concept of offense elements, requiring proof beyond a reasonable doubt of any mental states deemed offense elements. At the same, the Court fell short of forbidding impure strict liability, and shied away from clarifying the requirements of due process.

Second, the Model Penal Code influenced most state legislatures to define offenses and clarify their mental elements. The Code required a culpable mental state corresponding to each objective offense element for offenses punishable by incarceration, thereby precluding impure strict liability. It replaced the terminology of general and specific intent with Austin's taxonomy of culpable mental states. It provided influential definitions of culpable mental states, and provided default rules to assign culpable mental states to each objective element. The great majority of state legislatures revised their codes in light of the Model Penal Code, although not all of them rejected impure strict liability. Nevertheless, the new codes generally defined the mental elements of more offenses, by identifying culpable mental states and linking them to objective elements.

When combined with the Supreme Court's constitutional jurisprudence of offense elements, the reform of criminal codes largely transformed the issue of mens rea into a series of technical questions about statutory offense definitions. In short, culpability became formal culpability. Residual arguments that offenders were not substantively at fault despite having fulfilled the mental element of the offense were now analyzed as excuses, which the defendant could be required to prove.

SIX

Homicide, From Killing to Causing

I. Introduction

We have explicated the concept of a criminal offense in American law, including its component parts, criminal conduct and culpability. In this chapter we will apply these concepts in exploring homicide, the paradigmatic offense of causing harm.

Regulating homicide is a central responsibility of criminal law. Punishing homicide discourages violence, vindicates victims, expresses social solidarity, and obviates revenge. It is fundamental to the monopoly on legitimate force that defines the sovereign state.

And yet, public punishment of homicide provokes resistance. In most societies the majority of homicides are the unlucky consequences of broadly tolerated routines of violence rooted in disputes over social status and justified by norms of sociability, loyalty, or honor.[1] There is constant pressure to narrow liability to some imagined class of the wholly antisocial who kill for completely unsympathetic reasons. There is predictable political contestation over who will be thus demonized, and whose violence will be minimized and explained away.

A seemingly neutral solution is to grade homicides according to the killer's expectation of death. Yet social and cognitive biases undermine the neutrality of such judgments. Given a sympathetic victim or an unsympathetic defendant, jurors are easily persuaded to equate intentional violence with intentional killing. Yet we cannot infer intent to kill from a gunshot.[2] Shots can be fired to frighten or wound and are often inaccurate. Gunshot wounds cause death only about one-tenth of the time. Hindsight also disposes jurors to overattribute

1. T.A. Green, *The Jury and the English Law of Homicide, 1200–1600*, 74 MICH. L. REV. 413, 415–16 (1976); JACK KATZ, THE SEDUCTIONS OF CRIME (1990); RANDOLPH ROTH, AMERICAN HOMICIDE (2012).
2. Colbert v. State, 66 S.E. 2d 836 (Ga. 1951).

recklessness or negligence when death results, especially if the conduct is something illegal such as resisting arrest or selling drugs.[3]

Because death is fortuitous, punishing homicide poses a theoretical problem. Why should the harmful results of culpable conduct matter to criminal liability? If our purpose in punishing is retributive, it seems we should punish chosen conduct and ignore fortuitous results. If our purpose is efficient deterrence we should attach a certain penalty to culpable risk rather than conditioning a severe penalty on an uncertain result.[4] That every legal system punishes actual injury more severely than endangerment shows that neither desert nor deterrence exhaust the purposes of criminal punishment. Criminal law punishes homicide to vindicate victims and suppress vengeance.

Because of its centrality to social order and government authority, homicide law casts a long shadow over criminal law. It is the paradigmatic criminal offense and tends to influence the way all other offenses are defined. In early America, Pennsylvania's legislative reform of homicide law inspired the passage of comprehensive codes.[5] In nineteenth-century England also, legislative reformers such as the Criminal Law Commission and Judge J.F. Stephen paid particular attention to homicide law.[6] The Model Penal Code applied a system of crime definition Herbert Wechsler had first proposed for homicide.[7] Throughout this development, Anglo-American reformers remade homicide law in light of the new utilitarian conception of law. Thus, over the course of 200 years, homicide shifted from a crime of malicious killing to a crime of culpably causing harm.

By the end of the sixteenth century, capital liability was mandatory for murder, which required "killing" with "malice." Killing involved not just a fatal result, but a distinctive kind of conduct, a trespass by force and arms that breached the king's peace.[8] Such a trespass required a battery—injurious or offensive contact. Indeed, the medieval meaning of "kill" was to strike.[9] This restrictive conception of the conduct required for killing largely obviated inquiry into

---

3. Donald Dripps, *Fundamental Retribution Error*, 56 VAND. L. REV. 1383 (2000).
4. Herbert Wechsler & Jerome Michael, *A Rationale of Homicide: I*, 37 COLUM. L. REV. 701, 731 (1937).
5. Edwin R Keedy, *History of the Pennsylvania Statute Creating Degrees of Murder*, 97 U. PA. L. REV. 759, 760–61 (1949).
6. R. CROSS, THE REPORTS OF THE CRIMINAL LAW COMMISSIONERS (1833–1849); R. Cross, *The Abortive Bills of 1853, in* RESHAPING THE CRIMINAL LAW 5 (P.R. Glazebrook, ed. 1978); 2 J.F. STEPHEN, HISTORY OF THE CRIMINAL LAW OF ENGLAND 118–21 (1883).
7. Herbert Wechsler & Jerome Michael, *A Rationale of the Law of Homicide*, 37 COLUM. L. REV. 701, 1261 (1937).
8. Guyora Binder, *The Meaning of Killing, in* MODERN HISTORIES OF CRIME AND PUNISHMENT 91–95 (Markus Dubber & Lindsay Farmer, eds. 2007).
9. *Id.*

causation and intention. The required malice was not an intention to cause death. Instead, it was the absence of contributory conduct on the part of the deceased—aggression or agreed combat—that would at least partially excuse the defendant's breach of the peace. As Blackstone conceptualized this structure, malice was presumed from the act of killing, and it was incumbent on the defendant to place it at issue by proving an excuse.

Early American reformers sought to reduce capital punishment by dividing murder into degrees, and restricting capital punishment to first degree murder, requiring premeditated intentional killing, or murder in the course of certain grievous felonies. In England, Benthamite reformers reconceptualized homicide as causing death, combined with a culpable mental state. As transportation and industrial accidents became more common, it was increasingly apparent that death could be caused remotely. Homicide liability was more often imposed based on negligently or recklessly causing death. These changes coincided with the rise of negligence and the decline of trespass in tort. Plaintiffs recovered for a wider array of remotely caused injuries but were obliged to prove fault. So too homicide was reconceived as an injury caused with fault. By the late nineteenth century, J.F. Stephen had redefined malice as a set of different culpable mental states.

Today, most American codes that define homicide offenses follow the general approach of the Model Penal Code: they impose liability based on causing death with a culpable mental state, and grade the offense primarily on the basis of the culpable mental state. Even when codes retain the terminology of killing and malice, courts interpret these terms as Stephen did, equating killing with causing death, and malice with culpable mental states.

Causation is usually divided into two issues. First, causal responsibility for results is limited to "factual" causes—usually conduct necessary to the result. Second, criminal law applies standards of "legal causation" to screen factual causes for normative salience. Legal causation standards are of two kinds. An older direct cause test requires that an injury not depend too much on independent factual causes—especially human acts—subsequent to the defendant's conduct. The foreseeability test proposed in the Model Penal Code requires that the injury be sufficiently probable as a result of the defendant's act. The direct cause test reflects a retributivist view that blame and punishment presuppose that human acts are ordinarily autonomous. From this it follows that actors should not be punished for injuries resulting from the independent volition of other actors. The foreseeability test reflects a utilitarian view that deterrent sanctions should be conditioned on expected harm. Proper assessment of expected harm includes consideration of the predictable behavior of others. As deterrence need not presuppose free will, utilitarianism can more easily treat one person's act as the cause of another's.

Assuming causation of death is established, the defendant's liability will depend on whether and how much he is culpable. The culpable mental states usually required for homicide liability are of three kinds: (1) intent to kill, (2) culpable indifference toward a risk of death, or (3) an intent to commit some other crime. American homicide law has diverged markedly from English homicide law, which conditions murder liability on intent to grievously wound. Thus, in England, a fatal intentional shooting is murder. In most American jurisdictions it is murder only if additional requirements are met.

Intentional killing is usually second degree murder, but can be aggravated to first degree murder by premeditation and mitigated to manslaughter by adequately provoked emotion. Culpably indifferent homicides are usually graded as second degree murder if grossly reckless, and manslaughter if reckless or negligent. Grossly reckless murder usually requires either the endangerment of multiple victims, or a cruel or otherwise antisocial motive. Sometimes negligent homicide is a lesser offense. Homicides are often graded as first degree murder when committed in the course of a statutorily enumerated predicate felony. Other dangerous felonies may trigger second degree murder liability, while in a minority of jurisdictions misdemeanors trigger manslaughter liability. Felony murder often does not require proof of a mental state with respect to death, but usually requires a dangerous felony and foreseeable causation of death.

In most states and the federal system, murders can be capitally punished if certain aggravating circumstances are proved, and all mitigating evidence has been found insufficient. This scheme of guided discretion is constitutionally required for capital sentencing. Although the American death penalty has been the focus of great public controversy, only a tiny fraction of American homicides are capitally punished.

The evolution of American homicide law reflects the effort of utilitarian reformers to purge the law of moral judgment and calibrate punishment according to expected harm. Yet this aim seems at odds with the inherently normative practice of punishing homicide, which serves to vindicate victims by assigning blame for actual results.

II. Origins of English Homicide Law

Although Anglo-Saxon law determined levels of compensation for most injuries, it regarded stealthy killings as unrectifiable by these means. These "murders" triggered execution and forfeiture of property to the court.[10] By the second century of Norman rule, all killings were deemed offenses against the king, subject to appeal of felony, and finally execution unless justified or pardoned.[11] Felonious killing probably required death from a visible wound or injury inflicted with a weapon. At this juncture, the word "kill" meant to strike a blow.[12] Paraphrasing Bracton, Pollock and Maitland observed that "'blind blows' which neither break bone nor draw blood are no sufficient foundation for a charge of felony."[13] Although felony charges were heard in the royal courts, clerics successfully resisted appearing before them.

The law of homicide developed in defining exceptions to the capital punishment of killers. The 1278 Statute of Gloucester provided for routine pardons of killings by accident or self-defense. Juries could spare killers by issuing special verdicts finding these excuses.[14] Judges also had the power to spare killers by determining that they were clergymen and therefore exempt from royal jurisdiction. The Crown could also issue pardons at its own discretion. However a 1390 statute objected to pardons for stealthy "murders," killings by ambush, and killings with "malice prepense."[15] Malice aforethought was not required for capital liability, but would ensure it insofar as it precluded purchasing a pardon. This term may have invoked Aristotle's conclusion that "acts due to sudden anger are . . . not . . . done of malice afore-thought, for it is the man who gave the provocation that began it . . . ."[16]

The sixteenth century brought passage of statutes eliminating benefit of clergy for various crimes, including murders "of malice prepensed."[17] Killings that remained subject to benefit of clergy were now referred to as manslaughters. Further limits were imposed by the 1603 "Statute of Stabbing," which excluded benefit of clergy for those who killed by stabbing one who had drawn no weapon and struck no blow.[18] Most such killings would have been considered murders rather than manslaughters anyway. These restrictions on benefit of clergy were probably a response to increasing rates of homicide, as

---

10. Naomi D. Hurnard, The King's Pardon for Homicide before A.D. 1307, at 1 (1969).
11. *Id.* at 6.
12. Guyora Binder, *The Meaning of Killing*, *in* Modern Histories of Crime and Punishment 91 (Markus Dubber & Lindsay Farmer eds., 2007).
13. 2 Frederick Pollock & Frederic William Maitland, The History of English Law before the Time of Edward I, at 467–68 (1895) (citing Bracton).
14. Naomi D. Hurnard, The King's Pardon for Homicide before A.D. 1307, at 281–82 (1969).
15. Statute the Second, 1389–1390, 13 Rich. 2, c. 1 (Eng.).
16. Aristotle, "*Nicomachean Ethics*," *in* Aristotle in 23 Volumes, vol. 19, 1135b.20 (Harris Rackham transl., 1934).
17. 3 James Fitzjames Stephen, A History of the Criminal Law of England 44–45 (1883).
18. 1 Jac. I c. 8. (1603).

urbanization created new opportunities for crime, while the pacific ethics of Christianity yielded to a classically inspired ethic of martial honor and virtue.[19]

Several court decisions delineated the boundary between manslaughters and murders with malice aforethought. If the victim had provoked violence by striking a blow, or had willingly joined in combat, the defendant's offense was diminished. Otherwise the infliction of a fatal wound was malicious. The 1535 case of *R. v. Oneby* held that: "if A kills B and no sudden quarrel appears, it is murder; for it lies on the party indicted to prove the sudden quarrel."[20] Malice was not a mental state transforming killing into murder, but was inherent in killing itself, absent circumstances that diminished the defendant's responsibility for breaching the peace. The 1611 decision in *MacKalley's Case* explained that "if one kill another without provocation, and without any forethought malice, which can be proved, the Law will adjudge the same murder, and implieth malice."[21] Malice was also implied in the killing of a victim by a thief and the killing of an arresting officer. Additional cases held that members of a band who resolved to overcome resistance to robbery with deadly force were all guilty of murder for a killing by any;[22] and one who joined in a gang attack was guilty of murder when he threw a stone that fatally struck a bystander.[23] The use of arms or other violence constituted malice,[24] but the malicious killer had to start things. Assailants who joined an ongoing affray and struck fatal blows were guilty only of manslaughter, as were participants in mutual combat who killed their fleeing antagonists.[25] Malice could be transferred to unintended victims. Thus, in the 1573 decision of *R. v. Saunders*, the defendant was liable when he gave his wife a poisoned apple, which she passed on to their daughter.[26] If malice is a quality of action rather than a kind of intention, there is nothing mysterious about ascribing malice to unintended results of such action.

The combination of increasing homicide and decreasing access to benefit of clergy produced a high rate of execution. During the reign of Elizabeth, England executed about 800 a year among a population of only 4 million. [27]

---

19. J. HORDER, PROVOCATION AND RESPONSIBILITY (1992).
20. 92 Eng. Rep. at 473 (K.B. 1535). This case concerned a special verdict. George Fletcher has argued that the decision does not preclude burdening the prosecution with disproving provocation alleged by the defendant in a case tried to a general verdict. GEORGE FLETCHER, RETHINKING CRIMINAL LAW 527–29 (1978).
21. 9 Coke Rep. 65b, 67b.
22. Lord Dacre's Case, 72 Eng. Rep. 458 (K.B. 1535).
23. Mansell and Herbert's Case, 73 Eng. Rep. 279, 2 Dyer 128.
24. Holloway's Case, 79 Eng. Rep. 715 (K.B. 1628).
25. R. v. Salisbury, 1 Plow 100 (1553); J.M. KAYE, *The Early History of Murder and Manslaughter*, 83 LAW Q. REV. 568, 589 (1967).
26. R. v Saunders, 2 Plowd 473 (1573).
27. JOHN LANGBEIN, RENEE LERNER & BRUCE SMITH, HISTORY OF THE COMMON LAW 616 (2009).

III. English Homicide Law in the Age of Blackstone

Over the next two centuries, jurists explicated homicide law in treatises. They generally used "murder" to signify the entire category of nonclergyable felonious homicide and "manslaughter" to designate felonious but clergyable homicide. They defined "murder" as killing with malice aforethought. Matthew Hale defined "killing" as ordinarily a fatal "stroke" with a weapon.[28] Malice aforethought involved a prior plan to "offer hurt to the person of the other,"[29] but not necessarily to kill. [30] Hale added that malice could be directed at a group or population as well as an individual.

These authors divided malice aforethought into two categories. Malice could be manifested or "expressed" by threats, lying in wait, ordering an attack, or administering poison.[31] It was "implied" by a sudden attack without provocation or mutual combat. Mitigation on the basis of mutual violence arguably reflected a classically inspired ethos of honor and martial virtue that emerged during the Renaissance.[32] Yet certain reasons for fighting were disqualifying. Thus lawful arrest and resistance to robbery did not qualify as provocations, so that killing arresting officers and robbery victims implied malice.[33] On the other hand, killing to resist or prevent a wrong of sufficient gravity, such as a felony, was excusable as necessary defense.

Thus Hale treated manslaughter as an intermediate category between murder and necessary defense. Where killing could be avoided by retreat, or where the threatened offense was not grave enough, a defensive killing was manslaughter. Offenses not warranting deadly force included trespass against property and adultery:

> A. commits adultery with B. the wife of C. who . . . takes them in the very act, and with a staff kills the adulterer upon the place; this is manslaughter, and neither murder, nor under the privilege of se defendendo; but if A. had been taken by C. in the very attempt of rape upon the wife, and she crying out, her husband had come and killed A. in the act of his ravishment, it had been within the privilege of se defendendo, because it was a felony; the former case was judged manslaughter by the court . . . . [34]

---

28. 1 Matthew Hale, History of the Pleas of the Crown 426 (1736).
29. William Lambard, Eirenarcha: or Of the Office of the Justices of Peace 233–34 (1581).
30. Matthew Hale, Pleas of the Crown 41 (1678).
31. Michael Dalton, The Countrey Justice 242 (1635).
32. Jeremy Horder, Provocation and Responsibility 5–59 (1992).
33. Michael Dalton, The Countrey Justice, 238 n.18 (1635).
34. Matthew Hale, Historia Placitorum Coronae 486 (1736).

Hale considered adultery to mitigate the killing of the wife's paramour, because it was a legal wrong against the husband. The force had to be used at the scene because it had to be preventive in aim. Yet an early eighteenth-century decision on this issue equivocated between characterizing such killings as justified prevention of wrongdoing and as excused expression of strong emotion:

> [j]ealousy is the rage of a man, and adultery is the highest invasion of property . . . . If a thief comes to rob another, it is lawful to kill him. And if a man comes to rob a man's posterity and his family, yet to kill him is manslaughter. So is the law though it may seem hard . . . Although this is the highest possible invasion of property, a man is not justifiable in killing another, whom he taketh in adultery with his wife; for it savors more of sudden revenge than of self-preservation; but this law hath been executed with great benignity.[35]

These discussions concerned only killings of male paramours by husbands.

A persistent problem in the treatise literature was the relationship between the unlawfulness and the dangerousness of conduct resulting in death. Michael Dalton held that acts obviously dangerous to others implied malice whether or not unlawful. Fatalities resulting from unlawful acts without such danger were manslaughters. An unintended death resulting from a lawful act without apparent danger was nonfelonious death by "misadventure."[36]

Although Edward Coke defined murder as killing with malice,[37] he surprisingly characterized unlawful act killings without malice (such as a shooting accident while poaching) as murders.[38] Apparently Coke failed to distinguish murder from manslaughter. In calling unlawful act killings murders he meant only that they were felonious, not that they were excluded from benefit of clergy. A pair of mid-seventeenth century cases rejected an unlawful act murder rule.[39]

In the eighteenth century, several jurists proposed a narrower "felony murder" rule. In a 1701 opinion, Chief Justice Holt tried to reconcile Coke's unlawful act murder rule with the traditional requirement of malice by treating the commission of a felony as a form of malice.[40] William Hawkins reasoned that killing in the course of any offense likely to provoke resistance implied malice, and then treated all felonies as provocative in this way.[41] Hawkins limited this

35. R. v. Mawgridge, 84 Eng. Rep. 1107 (1707).
36. *Id.* at 237–42.
37. EDWARD COKE, THE THIRD PART OF THE INSTITUTES OF THE LAWS OF ENGLAND 47 (1644).
38. *Id.* at 57.
39. Chichester's Case, 82 Eng. Rep. 888 (K.B. 1647); R. v. Hull, 84 Eng. Rep. 1072 (K.B. 1664).
40. R. v. Plummer, 84 Eng. Rep. 1103, 1105–07 (K.B. 1701).
41. 1 WILLIAM HAWKINS, A TREATISE OF THE PLEAS OF THE CROWN 86 (1716).

rule to felonies "principally intended for some other purpose, and not to do a personal injury to him in particular who happens to be slain."[42]

Michael Foster's 1762 treatise viewed killing as presumptive evidence of malice, placing a burden on the defendant to prove accident or some other defense.[43] This presumption made sense if "killing" meant striking a fatal blow with a weapon, and malice meant an intention to injure. Yet Foster also introduced a broader conception of malice as a defective moral sensibility, a "heart regardless of social duty and deliberately bent on mischief." Foster supported both a felony murder rule, and an unlawful act manslaughter rule, but limited predicate crimes to those "malum in se." He added that an unlawful act done heedlessly was manslaughter, but that an unlawful and fatal act done with the intent to inflict "mischief or great bodily harm" would be murder, because it manifested a depraved moral sense.[44] Foster gave, as an example, driving a cart through a crowd, knowing it would likely inflict harm.

William Blackstone's influential discussion of homicide in his *Commentaries* relied heavily on Foster. He divided homicide into three kinds: justified, excused, and felonious.[45] Homicide was justified if required by law, or necessary in enforcing it. Homicide was excusable on grounds of self-defense and misadventure. Felonious homicide included murder with malice, express or implied, and manslaughter, which could be either voluntary or involuntary. Express malice was a prior commitment to inflict grievous bodily harm, expressed by such indicia as lying in wait or conspiring with others. Implied malice was simply any killing that was not explicable on the basis of sudden passion or careless inattention. Yet even sudden anger was compatible with malice if it led to gratuitous cruelty.[46] Like Foster, Blackstone treated all killing as presumptively malicious, forcing the defendant to justify, excuse, or mitigate any killing or face execution. Malice aforethought embraced "any evil design" reflecting a "wicked, depraved, and malignant heart."

Voluntary manslaughter required an intent to injure arising from sudden anger. A quarrel leading to a killing in mutual combat was manslaughter— not self-defense— because the killer could have retreated.[47] Similarly, a homicidal response to a provoking blow, or to the sight of adultery would mitigate

42. *Id.* at 87.

43. MICHAEL FOSTER, A REPORT OF SOME PROCEEDINGS ON THE COMMISSION FOR THE TRIAL OF THE REBELS IN THE YEAR 1746, *at* 255 (1792).

44. *Id.* at 261.

45. 4 WILLIAM BLACKSTONE, COMMENTARIES ON THE LAWS AND CUSTOMS OF ENGLAND 177 (1765).

46. *Id.* at 199.

47. *Id.* at 184–85.

murder to manslaughter, provided there was no "cooling time" for rage to be replaced with resolve. The provocation could not be a verbal insult. Blackstone described the sight of adultery as mitigating the killing of the paramour and did not discuss homicide of the adulterous spouse.[48]

Involuntary manslaughter was distinguished from death by misadventure because the negligent and fatal act was unlawful—a trespass, such as dueling, throwing stones on a crowded city street, performing unlicensed surgery, or beating a pupil excessively.[49] Such unlawful acts included an otherwise lawful act performed in a very careless fashion.[50] Where the offender expected grievous injury to some unknown person, however, a resulting death to anyone would be murder.

Whereas a killing in the course of a trespass was manslaughter, a killing in pursuit of a felony was murder. Yet Blackstone illustrated this felony murder rule with cases in which the defendant unintentionally killed a bystander while targeting another victim.[51] Thus it seems possible he understood the rule to transfer malice only among violent felonies.

A study of homicide law applied in London's Old Bailey court during the seventeenth and eighteenth centuries offers a simpler account than the treatises. The concept of malice did not seem to be the focus of much controversy. Trials rarely focused on proof of intent. What mattered was whether death resulted from the infliction of a wound with a conventional weapon, or some humble tool; and whether there was any evidence of provocation or mutual combat.[52] The novel theories of murder with implied malice that appeared in the treatises—based on killing during a felony or recklessly dangerous conduct—were apparently not applied by courts.

Homicide indictments typically charged that the defendant assaulted the victim with a certain weapon, with malice aforethought, causing a wound in a certain spot, from which the defendant died. They did not include allegations of intent to kill, extreme indifference to human life, or another felony. Nor did they describe killings as having been committed in the course of a felony, or in resisting lawful arrest, although some of these killings clearly fit these scenarios.[53] It seems that the infliction of a wound by means of a weapon defined the

48. *Id.* at 191–92.
49. *Id.* at 197.
50. *Id.* at 192.
51. *Id.* at 201.
52. Guyora Binder, *The Meaning of Killing*, *in* MODERN HISTORIES OF CRIME AND PUNISHMENT 88, 93 (Markus Dubber & Lindsay Farmer eds., 2007).
53. *Id.* at 94.

offense, while malice was not a required mental state constituting the offense, but a normative conclusion about the offense, like guilt.

Almost all murder convictions were killings with a weapon.[54] More than half involved a sword or knife. Others used a gun, club, or ax. Typically there was no evidence of intent to injure or kill other than the use of the weapon. Fatal assaults with a tool resulted in murder liability only if sufficiently persistent to manifest an intention to injure seriously. There were no murder convictions arising from child-neglect, medical malpractice, traffic or construction accidents, or unintended fires.

In sum, intent to kill, extreme indifference to human life and killing in the course of felonies were not required for murder liability. When death resulted from an unprovoked armed attack, the participants were guilty of murder, whether or not they intended to kill. The intent to commit a felony did not substitute for the intent to kill, because none was required. On the other hand, a felony also did not turn accidental death into murder. Its only significance was to preclude provocation.

Manslaughters were generally fatal assaults with weapons where victims had offered provocation. This provocation, in turn, could take three forms: an unarmed blow, drawing on a defendant who could have retreated, or agreeing to armed combat. If the victim drew where retreat was impossible, or struck an armed blow, the defendant would be excused altogether on grounds of self-defense. Cases of witnessing adultery were rare but not unknown. Manslaughter liability was also the norm where there was no provocation, but the defendant attacked with a tool rather than a weapon, and the attack was limited to a single blow rather than a sustained assault. A third manslaughter scenario was an unprovoked but unarmed attack. Yet such cases could also lead to outright acquittals, particularly when the fatal injury resulted from a fall rather than directly from a blow. Physical chastisement of subordinates was common in early modern society, and juries probably had difficulty seeing unarmed blows as killings, even when they had fatal consequences. Carelessly inflicted fatal injuries sometimes led to manslaughter liability, and sometimes to outright acquittal.[55]

---

54. *Id.* at 95–101.
55. *Id.* at 101–04.

IV. American Codification of Homicide

By the time of the Revolution about half the colonies had enacted homicide statutes, usually simply imposing death for "willful" or "malicious" murder.[56] After the Revolution, Americans moved to codify their criminal law. Several jurisdictions initially adopted simple homicide statutes such as those enacted during the colonial period. However most eventually adopted statutes modeled on the Pennsylvania homicide statute of 1794.[57] Influenced by Quaker religious sentiment and enlightenment reformism, Pennsylvania legislators sought to reduce capital punishment by dividing murder into degrees. Although the bill's original proponents hoped to limit capital murder to "deliberate assassination," the ultimate legislation graded both "wilful, deliberate and premeditated" murder and murder "committed in the perpetration or attempt" of arson, rape, robbery or burglary as first degree murder, subject to capital punishment at the discretion of the jury.[58] All other "murder" was second degree murder, subject only to terms of incarceration. The statute did not define murder itself, but merely incorporated prior understandings of the crime. By the 1820s Pennsylvania courts held that killings in the course of felonies were murders, but probably used "killing" to refer only to fatal attacks with weapons or poison.[59]

Pennsylvania's grading scheme was adopted by about two-thirds of the states during the nineteenth century.[60] Some states added a simple definition of murder as killing with malice. Most interpreted these statutes to make unintended killing in the course of enumerated felonies first degree murder. Some interpreted them to make killings in the course of unenumerated felonies second degree murder. A few imposed second degree murder liability for maternal deaths in the course of illegal abortions.[61] At mid-century, treatises by Joel Bishop and Francis Wharton read a felony murder rule into these grading statutes.[62]

Georgia's 1817 homicide statute, which drew on Blackstone and Foster, also proved to be an influential model. Georgia defined murder as killing with malice aforethought, express or implied, adding that malice was expressed by

56. Guyora Binder, Felony Murder 123 (2012).
57. Guyora Binder, *The Origins of American Felony Murder Rules*, 57 Stan. L. Rev. 59, 119 (2004).
58. Act of Apr. 22, 1794, ch. 1766, § 2, 1794 Pa. Laws 186, 187.
59. Guyora Binder, *The Origins of American Felony Murder Rules*, 57 Stan. L. Rev. 59, 145 n.44 (2004).
60. *Id.* at 120.
61. State v. Smith, 32 Me. 369 (1851); State v. Leeper, 70 Iowa 748 (1886); State v. Minard, 96 Iowa 267 (1895).
62. Joel P. Bishop, Commentaries on the Criminal Law (1858); Francis Wharton, A Treatise on the Law of Homicide in the United States (1855).

intentional killing and implied by killing without provocation or under circumstances showing an "abandoned and malignant heart."[63] The Georgia code defined manslaughter as including voluntary killing with provocation and involuntary killing in an unlawful act, or a lawful act committed in an unlawfully careless way. It explicitly adopted a felony murder rule, defining murder as including involuntary killing in an unlawful act "which, in its consequences, naturally tends to destroy the life of a human being, or is committed in the prosecution of a felonious . . . intent." [64] Illinois and several other states adopted such statutes and many western states, including California, combined Georgia's provisions on malice, abandoned and malignant heart murder, and felony murder, with Pennsylvania's on grading. In the late nineteenth century, courts began applying these statutes to impose murder liability where dangerous conduct caused death indirectly. In *Mayes v. People* defendant angrily threw a beer mug at his wife, shattering an oil lamp she carried and causing her fatal burns.[65] He was convicted of murder for killing with an abandoned and malignant heart, with no requirement of intent to grievously injure. In *People v. Adams*, several defendants were liable for felony murder when they forced a robbery victim off a train, causing a fatal head injury.[66] The court refused an instruction that murder required that death was intended or probable. Even jurisdictions without such statutes developed the doctrines of abandoned heart murder and felony murder by statutory construction.

A few states adopted codes providing that unintended killing in the course of any felony was murder, but without conditioning all murder on malice. An issue arose in these states whether murder could be predicated on felonious assault, such as a beating aimed at severe injury. Courts in New York and Missouri held that such assaults could not constitute predicate felonies.[67] Why not? The Missouri case was particularly surprising. The defendant had administered a prolonged beating with a chain to a defenseless child. In another state, this might have been punished as "abandoned and malignant heart" murder, but Missouri lacked this form of murder. Why not instead predicate murder on aggravated assault? The court drew on Hawkins's idea that felony murder should be predicated on a felony intended at some purpose other than personal injury. Thus, it reasoned that the statutory term "other felony" referred to "some collateral felony, and not to those acts of personal violence which are

---

63. 1817 Ga. Laws 95.
64. *Id.* at 96.
65. Mayes v People, 106 Ill. 306 (1883).
66. People v. Adams, 109 Ill. 444 (1884).
67. People v. Rector, 19 Wend. 569(N.Y. 1838); State v. Shock, 68 Mo. 552 (1878).

necessary and constituent elements of the homicide itself, and are therefore, merged in it. . . ."[68]

The late nineteenth century witnessed a wave of highly publicized "honor killings" of the paramours of adulterous wives. Although the law of most jurisdictions classified such killings as manslaughters, many jurors acquitted such killers, sometimes under a fictive insanity defense.[69] Georgia courts endorsed killings to prevent adultery or fornication as justified,[70] and a Texas statute justified killings of paramours, but was held not to justify the killings of adulterous wives.[71] A Mississippi court did mitigate the killing of an adulterous wife, however, in a case where the defendant fired at the paramour and killed his wife by mistake. The court explained the mitigation of paramour killings as due to sudden emotion that "unsettles reason," and so argued that "in principle there can be no difference in the degree of the crime whether the betrayed husband slays the faithless wife or her guilty paramour."[72] This shift in the conception of provocation from partial justification, to partial excuse made it easier to mitigate domestic killings as crimes of passion.

By the end of the nineteenth century, the homicide law of most American jurisdictions arrayed killings into a graded hierarchy of offenses of three different kinds. *Intentional killings* were voluntary manslaughters if provoked, second degree murders if unprovoked, and first degree murders if unprovoked and premeditated. *Fatally dangerous acts* were involuntary manslaughters if merely careless, but became second degree murders if they manifested depraved indifference to human life. *Killings in the course of crime* were involuntary manslaughters if committed in the course of a misdemeanor, second degree murders if committed in the course of unenumerated felonies, and first degree murders if committed in the course of enumerated felonies. This basic Blackstonean structure of homicide law remains in place in most jurisdictions today. Yet the conception of homicide that prevails today, as the causation of death with a culpable mental state, owes more to Bentham and other utilitarian reformers than to Blackstone.

68. State v. Shock, 68 Mo. 552, 556 (1878).

69. *See generally* W. Lewis Roberts, *The Unwrittten Law*, 10 KY. L.J. 456 (1922); Comment, *Recognition of the Honor Defense under the Insanity Plea*, 43 YALE L.J. 809 (1934); Robert Ireland, *The Libertine Must Die: Sexual Dishonor and the Unwritten Law in the Nineteenth Century United States*, 23 J. SOC. HIST. 27 (1992).

70. Biggs v. Georgia, 29 Ga. 723 (1860); Miller v. State, 9 Ga. App. 599 (1911),

71. Billings v. State, 102 Tex. Crim. 338 (1925); Reed v. State, 59 S.W. 2d 122 (1933).

72. Rowland v. State, 35 So. 826 (1904).

V. The Utilitarian Critique of Homicide Law

Utilitarian reformers critiqued the homicide law described in treatises such as Blackstone's as being irrational. For Bentham, criminal law was fundamentally aimed at deterring harm through the threat of punishment rather than imposing a state monopoly on violence or suppressing private revenge. As we have seen, Bentham conceived crime as conduct predictably injurious to societal interests. Deterrable offenders would have to know they would likely cause injury and therefore face punishment. From this perspective, it was sensible to define homicide as causing death with the expectation of doing so, rather than as an unexcused fatal trespass. Bentham reasoned that a subjective expectation of a result could be proven by showing that circumstances rendering such a result probable were apparent to the offender. The higher the expectation of death proven in this way, the more punishment was justified by a deterrent benefit. John Austin would ultimately divide such expectations of harm into the hierarchy of increasingly culpable mental states familiar from our discussion of the Model Penal Code.[73]

Bentham's conception of a legal wrong as the predictable causation of harm to a protected interest achieved influence in English and American tort law. Traditionally, a trespass against the person by force and arms required infliction of harm by direct physical contact, and usually no further proof of causal responsibility. The defendant was liable unless he could demonstrate extraordinary care. Where injury was caused indirectly, however, the defendant was liable only if negligently violating a duty of ordinary care. By the 1830s, however, English courts had begun to abandon this distinction.[74] They replaced it with one between intentional torts and negligent torts. The key difference was in the culpable mental state rather than the type of action. American courts adopted a similar approach after the influential 1850 opinion of Massachusetts Chief Justice Lemuel Shaw in *Brown v. Kendall*.[75] As tort was reconfigured around culpability and causation of injury, rather than violent conduct, it also became natural to think of crime as culpable causation rather than a trespassory breach of the peace.

Recall that in the 1830s a commission was appointed to study English criminal law and propose reforms. Staffed by Benthamites, the Commission critiqued homicide law as practiced and described in the treatises. Their general

73. 2 John Austin, Lectures on Jurisprudence 1093–94 (1869).
74. John C. Goldberg & Benjamin C. Zipursky, The Oxford Introductions to U.S. Law: Torts 14 (2010).
75. Brown v. Kendall, 60 Mass. 292 (1850).

strategy was to interpret traditional rules as legal presumptions that some fact could prove either causation of an injury, or the expectation of causing injury. In this way they could validate the Benthamite model of criminal offenses as rooted in the common law, and then use the model to critique that common law tradition as formalistic. Thus, the commissioners interpreted "malice" as an imprecise term for intent to kill, understood "kill" as meaning to cause death by any means, and so denied that malice could be presumed from killing. On the other hand, they treated the traditional requirements of a stroke with a weapon and a mortal wound as evidentiary presumptions of intent to kill. They critiqued the felony murder rule proposed in the treatises as a legal fiction substituting intent to commit a felony for the intent to cause death.[76]

The partial influence of these ideas was apparent in Lemuel Shaw's jury instruction in the Massachusetts case of *Commonwealth v. Webster*, in which he offered this subjectivist gloss on Blackstone's presumption of malice from killing:

> the implication of malice arises in every case of *intentional homicide*; and, the fact of killing being first proved, all the circumstances of accident, necessity, or infirmity, are to be satisfactorily established by the party charged.... [A] person must be presumed to *intend* to do that which he voluntarily and wilfully does in fact do, and that he must *intend* all the natural, probable, and usual consequences of his own acts. Therefore, when one person assails another violently with a dangerous weapon, likely to kill and which does in fact destroy the life of the party assailed, the natural presumption is, that he *intended* death or other great bodily harm . . . [emphasis supplied][77]

A Benthamite Code was proposed for India by Thomas Macaulay in 1837 and enacted in 1862.[78] Macaulay defined murder simply as causing death with knowledge one is likely to do so, absent provocation, unjustified defense, or consent, all of which could reduce knowing homicide to manslaughter. Negligent homicide was a lesser offense.

In the 1870s Judge James F. Stephen unsuccessfully proposed a penal code for the UK, in which he strove to package Benthamite outcomes in the familiar vocabulary and categories of the common law. He redefined killing as causation of death: killing, he concluded, had always meant "causing death directly,

---

76. KEITH J.M. SMITH, LAWYERS, LEGISLATORS AND THEORISTS 127–38 (1998).
77. Commonwealth v. Webster, 59 Mass. 295, 305 (1850).
78. THOMAS MACAULAY ET AL., A PENAL CODE PREPARED BY THE INDIAN LAW COMMISSIONERS (1837).

distinctly, and not too remotely."[79] Stephen argued that malice, as developed in the common law, had referred to five alternative mental states: intent to kill, recklessness of a probability of death, intent to grievously injure, intent to commit any felony, and intent to resist arrest or lawful confinement. Stephen argued that only two of these, intent to kill and recklessness of death, were defensible as a basis for punishing homicide, because guilt for an injury should be based on the expectation of causing that injury. Because intent to kill entailed recklessness of death, Stephen concluded that murder should be conditioned simply on recklessness of death, a standard similar to Macaulay's. Stephen therefore proposed conditioning intent-to-injure murder, felony murder, and resisting-arrest murder on recklessness of death or enumerated reckless acts.[80]

Although clever, Stephen's argument obscured more than it illuminated. Intent to kill had not traditionally been required as proof of malice, for which intent to injure sufficed. Recklessness of death had not been sufficient without such an intent to injure. Finally, the intent to commit a felony or resist law enforcement had not been substitutes for the intent to injure, but merely precluded claims of provocation and self-defense where intent to injure was present. Thus Stephen could have simplified existing law by defining malice as intent to injure. Yet his Benthamite premises made intent to injure an unacceptable measure of culpability for death.[81]

Stephen did not succeed in persuading Parliament to adopt his definition of murder, and it is not clear that English law ever did accept his view that recklessness with respect to death sufficed for murder. Nevertheless, Stephen promoted his approach to felony murder through his decision in *Regina v. Serné*,[82] requiring that a predicate felony be manifestly dangerous to human life.

Bentham and Stephen influenced Oliver Wendell Holmes Jr.'s conception of homicide. Invoking *Brown v. Kendall*, Holmes denied that trespass was a distinctive category of action, and so argued against strict liability for injuries directly caused by trespassory conduct.[83] For Holmes, as for Bentham and Austin, acts were no more than muscular movements, and any events following such movements were consequences. Accordingly, Holmes adopted a Benthamite view of crime as conduct committed under circumstances predictably causing harm. Like Stephen, he rejected a conception of murder as killing without excuse, and instead saw it as causing death with the expectation of such result.[84] Rather

---

79. 3 JAMES F. STEPHEN, HISTORY OF THE CRIMINAL LAW OF ENGLAND 3 (1883).
80. 2 JAMES F. STEPHEN, HISTORY OF THE CRIMINAL LAW OF ENGLAND 118–21 (1883).
81. 1 JAMES F. STEPHEN, HISTORY OF THE CRIMINAL LAW OF ENGLAND 112–14 (1883).
82. 16 Cox C.C. 311 (1887).
83. OLIVER WENDELL HOLMES, JR., THE COMMON LAW, 52–60, 92–94 (1881).
84. *Id.* at 51–60.

than presuming intent from dangerous conduct, Holmes argued that culpability was reducible to apparent danger, and that differences in degree were quantitative.

In 1937 Herbert Wechsler, future drafter of the Model Penal Code, coathored a pivotal article, "A Rationale of Homicide," proposing a comprehensive reform of homicide law along the lines proposed by Stephen.[85] A central feature of this proposed reform was the definition of homicide offenses as the causation of death accompanied by various culpable mental states regarding a risk of death.

VI. The Emergence of Causation as an Element of Homicide

By the time Wechsler proposed replacing killing with causation of death as the actus reus of homicide, most scholars and judges had come to equate killing with causing death.

In early modern law, the objective limits of the trespassory conception of wrongdoing usually obviated inquiry into causation of death. Nevertheless, we have seen that as early as the sixteenth century the defendant could become responsible for indirect injury. This was one implication of the famous *Saunders* case, in which an innocent actor passed on a poisoned apple to an unintended victim. The 1773 trespass case of *Scott v. Shepherd* similarly extended tort liability for injuries to an unintended victim from a firecracker thrown in a crowded market and then successively thrown away by two potential victims. One judge treated the injury as the instantiation of a general risk attributable to the act. "The natural and probable consequence of the act done by the defendant was injury to somebody, and, therefore, the act was illegal ... Being, therefore, unlawful, the defendant was liable to answer for the consequences, be the injury mediate or immediate."[86] The 1662 decision in *Rew's Case* imposed homicide liability when a wound was a necessary condition to death, even if the victim's failure to have the wound treated was also necessary to his death: "if one gives wounds to another who neglects to cure of them ... yet if he die it is murder or manslaughter ... because if the wounds had not been given he would not have died."[87]

---

85. HERBERT WECHSLER & JEROME MICHAEL, *A Rationale of the Law of Homicide: I*, 37 COLUM. L. REV. 701 (1937).
86. Scott v Shepherd, 96 Eng. Rep. 525 (K.B. 1773).
87. Rew's Case, 84 Eng. Rep. 1066 (1662).

The seventeenth-century jurist Matthew Hale was the first to offer a scholarly discussion of causation in criminal law. Hale conditioned homicide on a stroke or other violence, a wound or injury, and death within a year. He agreed with *Rew's Case* that an assailant was responsible for death from neglect of a treatable wound. On the other hand, if the victim would have recovered without any treatment, but died only because of subsequent maltreatment, the assailant was not causally responsible. Hale also denied that law could impose liability for causing death by influencing the emotions of the victim, because of the lack of any trespass. Thus, "death without the stroke or other violence makes not the homicide."[88]

The infliction of a wound or injury was a requirement for a homicide indictment, still recognized—although criticized—by Stephen in the late nineteenth century.[89] The 1773 decision in *R. v. Lad* overturned a conviction for the murder of a nine-year-old girl who died from lacerations sustained in a brutal rape, because of the indictment's failure to allege a mortal wound.[90] Even in cases of poisoning, early modern witnesses described visible symptoms such as swelling or bleeding wounds, bespeaking a broadly shared assumption that murder required a visible wound or injury.[91]

Only in the nineteenth century did physicians begin to appear as witnesses in homicide cases to testify about the cause of death.[92] In most nineteenth-century homicide prosecutions, the act in question was an armed battery, fulfilling the traditional requirement of a trespass by force and arms. Yet by the second half of the nineteenth century several American homicide cases arose from careless acts of endangerment.[93] Like tort liability, criminal liability had expanded beyond the bounds of trespass, and so criminal lawyers had to explain wrongdoing in a different way: as causing harm, rather than engaging in unauthorized violence.

Lawyers first began to think about causal responsibility in negligence cases where damages could be assessed for remote harm, without visible violence. Nineteenth-century lawyers conceptualized these problems in spatiotemporal terms. Events had multiple causes, linked in sequences. Causes could be

---

88. 1 Matthew Hale, History of the Pleas of the Crown 426 (1736).
89. 3 James F. Stephen, A History of the Criminal Law of England 4 (1883).
90. R. v. Lad, 168 Eng. Rep. 150 (K.B. 1773).
91. Guyora Binder, *The Meaning of Killing*, *in* Modern Histories of Crime and Punishment 88, 91 (Markus Dubber & Lindsay Farmer eds., 2007).
92. Malcolm Gaskill, Crime and Mentalities in Early Modern England 254 (2000).
93. United States v Warner, 4 McLean 463 (C.C.D. Ohio 1848); Mayes v. People, 106 Ill. 306 (1883); Belk v. People, 125 Ill. 584 (1888); White v. State, 84 Ala. 421 (1888); People v. Buddenseick, 103 N.Y. 487 (1886); Grimes v. State, 63 Ala. 166 (1879); Combes v. Commonwealth, 93 Ky. 313 (1892); Hennessee v. People, 21 How. Pr. 239 (N.Y. 1861).

directly adjacent to their consequences, or connected through intervening causes, and so could be more or less remote. Counsel in an 1830 English case argued that "A man is liable only for the natural and proximate consequence of his actions, and not for remote consequences resulting directly from some intermediate agent."[94] The American scholar Simon Greenleaf offered a similar formulation in his 1848 treatise on evidence.[95] On this view, when an injury followed unlawful action immediately, or "directly," causation was self-evident. Intervening causes diminished causal responsibility, particularly if these were the actions of another person. Yet the original wrongdoer might be held responsible for these intervening actions if his wrongdoing had caused them. To break the proverbial chain of causation, intervening actions would have to be sufficiently voluntary or independent.

John Stuart Mill criticized this distinction between direct and remote causes. Mill argued that no single event could be the cause of another. Instead, the "real Cause" of an event is the whole

> set of antecedents . . . but for which it would not have happened. . . . and we have, philosophically speaking, no right to give the name of cause to one of them, exclusively of the others. . . . [Sometimes] the appearance is presented of a more immediate and close connection between the effect and . . . one antecedent. . . . But though we may think proper to give the name of cause to that one condition, the fulfillment of which completes the tale, and brings about the effect without further delay; this condition has really no closer relation to the effect than any of the other conditions has. All the conditions were equally indispensable to the production of the consequent. . . .[96]

From this perspective, no single event was truly the cause of death.[97] Moreover, among acts necessary to a death, the nearer and more remote acts made an equal contribution. This suggested that the law's ascription of causal responsibility for death to one necessary condition among many was not a scientific fact but a normative judgment. According to Nicholas St. John Green, proximate cause in negligence actions simply meant whatever results seemed normatively ascribable to the defendant's negligence. Thus, "In actions for negligence, a defendant is held liable for the natural and probable consequences of

---

94. Ward v. Weekes, 7 Bing. 211, 212 (1830).

95. SIMON GREENLEAF, A TREATISE ON THE LAW OF EVIDENCE 258 (1848).

96. JOHN STUART MILL, A SYSTEM OF LOGIC 399–400 (1843).

97. Nicholas St. J. Green, *Proximate and Remote Cause*, 4 AM. L. REV. 201 (1870); Jeremiah Smith, *Legal Cause in Actions of Tort*, 25 HARV. L. REV. 103, 104 (1911).

his misconduct. In this class of actions his misconduct is called the proximate cause of those results which a prudent foresight might have avoided."[98]

Accordingly, by the early twentieth century legal scholars distinguished factual causation from legal causation.[99] An act was a factual cause of any result for which it was a necessary condition. Yet it was only a legal cause if it satisfied additional normative criteria. "Proximate causation" was now identified as a standard of legal causation, but there was disagreement among courts and commentators as to what it required.[100] Some views emphasized the idea of a causal chain, in which the defendant's act is necessary to all subsequent events necessary to the result. Others emphasized the idea of probability, requiring that the result be foreseeable to the offender.

As judges and scholars developed criteria of factual and legal causation in tort, they were available for use in criminal law as well. In the next two sections we will see how American courts defined factual and legal causation in criminal cases during the century between *Brown v. Kendall* and the drafting of the Model Penal Code.

VII. Factual Causation

Although the concept of a necessary condition seems straightforward, its application could become complicated when death followed assaults by two different independent actors. If the victim would not have died without both wounds, both assaults were necessary, and so both were factual causes. If only one wound was necessary for death and the other was not, only the necessary one would be a factual cause.[101] Yet suppose A inflicted a mortal wound, and B inflicted a wound not mortal by itself, but which accelerated the fatal effect of A's assault. Under these circumstances, both A and B were factual causes. The accepted reasoning is that because death is inevitable, an act necessary to death must mean an act necessary to death at a particular time. If the combination of the two attacks accelerates death, both are factual causes.[102] Some authors have seen such implications as reason to reject a necessary condition

98. Nicholas St. J. Green, *Proximate and Remote Cause*, 4 AM. L. REV. 201 (1870).
99. Jeremiah Smith, *Legal Cause in Actions of Tort*, 25 HARV. L. REV. 103, 104 (1911); James Angell McLaughlin, *Proximate Cause*, 39 HARV. L. REV. 149, 153–55 (1925).
100. Joseph H. Beale, *The Proximate Consequences of an Act*, 33 HARV. L. REV. 633 (1920); Henry W. Edgerton, *Legal Cause*, 72 U. PA. L. REV. 211 (1924); James Angell McLaughlin, *Proximate Cause*, 39 HARV. L. REV. 149 (1925).
101. People v. Brown, 62 Cal. App. 96 (1923).
102. Comm. v. Costley, 118 Mass. 1 (1875).

test and instead define factual causes as "substantial factors" in causing a result.[103]

A further implication of the necessary condition test is that if one attack is independently sufficient to cause death when it occurs, the other is not a factual cause, even if it was sufficent to cause death later. Thus, if A stabbed a victim, but B subsequently shot the victim in the head, the shot would preempt the stabbing.[104] The stabbing would only count as necessary to death occurring when it did if it was necessary to the shooting, for example by immobilizing a victim who otherwise would not have encountered the shooter. Under these circumstances the shooting might still be sufficiently independent of the stabbing that the stabbing was not a legal cause of death. Nevertheless, the stabbing would be a factual cause.

If the sufficiency of one of two wounds to cause death when it occurred can preclude any causal role for the other wound, it is challenging to prove the causal responsibility of either wound. For example, in the English case of *R. v. Dyos*, the defendant was acquitted of homicide despite being found to have inflicted one of two potentially mortal head wounds to a victim who died. The medical testimony indicated that death was probable from each blow, and that each blow might have been sufficient to cause death. Yet because the death might have occurred without his blow, the defendant's attack was not a factual cause of death.[105]

What if both wounds are independently sufficient to cause death at the same time? In *Jones v. Commonwealth*,[106] two officers fired without provocation on a suspect, each inflicting a necessarily lethal chest-wound. The jury was given the straightforward instruction that each assailant was causally responsible for death if his shot "caused or hastened death," and found both defendants guilty. The court upheld the verdict because the instruction was correct, and regarded its application as a jury question.

Yet how could either wound have caused the death if neither was necessary to it?[107] Professor Joseph Beale long ago argued that both shooters are causally responsible,[108] and this has become the prevailing opinion among

---

103. Jeremiah Smith, *Legal Causae in Actions of Tort*, 25 HARV. L. REV. 303, 309 (1912); J. HALL, GENERAL PRINCIPLES OF CRIMINAL LAW 283 (1960); ROLLIN PERKINS & RONALD BOYCE, CRIMINAL LAW 72–78 (1982).

104. State v. Scates, 50 N.C. 420 (1858); People v. Ah Fat, 48 Cal. 61 (1874); State v. Wood, 53 Vt. 558 (1881); People v. Elder, 100 Mich. 515 (1894); Walker v. State, 116 Ga. 537 (1902); State v. Angelina, 73 W.Va. 146 (1913).

105. Crim. L. Rev. 660–662 (1979).

106. Jones v. Commonwealth, 281 S.W.2d 920 (Ky. 1955).

107. James Angell McLaughlin, *Proximate Cause*, 39 HARV. L. REV. 149 (1925).

108. Joseph H. Beale, *The Proximate Consequences of an Act*, 33 HARV. L. REV. 633 (1920).

scholars.[109] It was endorsed in the official Commentaries on the Model Penal Code,[110] even though the Code defines a cause as "an antecedent but for which the result would not have occurred."[111] Scholars have offered three rationales for this view, but none seems satisfactory.

One approach is simply to abandon the requirement that a cause be necessary to death, and replace it with the substantial factor test.[112] This was the approach taken in the torts case of *Andersen v. Minneapolis-St. Paul & Sault St. Marie Railway*, in which the plaintiff's house was destroyed by two fires from two different sources.[113] This is an appealing standard in tort, where damages for loss can be apportioned among multiple actors. It seems ill-suited however to the all-or-nothing judgment of criminal liability for a death.

A second approach is Beale's. Beale argued that each shooting is necessary to the death. According to this argument, the identity of a death depends not just on to whom it occurs and when it occurs, but also on *how* it occurs. It follows that both shots are necessary to this particular death because a death from two wounds happens in a different way than a death from one wound.[114] Yet this argument begs the question. If what we mean by a death from two wounds is a death *caused* by two wounds, we have not yet determined whether the death in *Jones v. Commonwealth was* caused by two wounds. If instead we mean only that the death in Jones followed two wounds, we have not distinguished it from a death following one wound necessary to cause death and a superfluous second wound.

A third response is that the two shootings are members of a set of events, one of which is necessary to the death.[115] It proposes that instead of defining a cause as necessary to a result, we should define a cause as a necessary element of a set of events sufficient to cause death. Because if we "subtracted" either shot the other shot would be necessary, both shots satisfy this test.[116] The problem with this test is that it also seems to recognize as a cause a mortal wound inflicted at T1 even when followed by an independent and immediately fatal wound at T2. As the superfluous first wound becomes necessary to death if we "subtract" the second, the first wound is a necessary element of a sufficient set.

---

109. Glanville Williams, Textbook of Criminal Law 379–80 (1983); Markus Dubber, Criminal Law: Model Penal Code 130 (2002).
110. Model Penal Code Commentaries 259 (1985).
111. Model Penal Code § 2.03(1) (1962).
112. Wayne LaFave, Criminal Law 354 (2010).
113. Anderson v. Minneapolis, St. P. & S. S. M. Ry. Co., 179 N. W. 45. (Minn. 1920).
114. Joseph H. Beale, *The Proximate Consequences of an Act*, 33 Harv. L. Rev. 633,639 (1920); Rollin Perkins & Ronald Boyce, Criminal Law, 773 (1982); Markus Dubber, Criminal Law: Model Penal Code 130 (2002); Model Penal Code Commentaries, pt. 1, § 2.03, at 259 (1985).
115. Eric Johnson, *Criminal Liability for Loss of a Chance*, 91 Iowa L. Rev. 59 (2005).
116. Markus Dubber, Criminal Law: Model Penal Code 130 (2002).

Yet courts have repeatedly denied the causal responsibility of the first assailant in these situations.[117]

VIII. Legal Causation

Where factual causation is proven, the prosecution must also prove legal causation. In the late nineteenth and early twentieth centuries courts conceptualized legal causation as a sequence of necessary conditions linking the defendant's act to the death, unbroken by certain intervening causes. These intervening causes were unusual natural events, or human acts that were independent of the defendant's act.

Why differentiate natural events from human acts? If we start with the utilitarian view of acts as voluntary muscular contractions, it is entirely expected that a dangerous act will be mediated by other events before eventuating in injury. To a utilitarian, then, all causation is remote. Accordingly, intervening events are not necessarily exculpatory, and this should remain true even if the intervening events are additional human acts, as these too are natural events subject to causal laws. Indeed deterrence presupposes that human acts are subject to prediction and manipulation.

Yet nineteenth-century courts had two reasons to differentiate acts from natural events. First, they were accustomed to a traditional conception of homicide as killing, a practice encompassing an armed stroke inflicting a wound, followed by death. One nineteenth-century court objected to the idea that multiple actors could independently cause death, as entailing the "absurdity of saying that the deceased was killed twice."[118] Second, religion and morality taught that human action was ordinarily freely willed rather than dictated by causal laws. As Paul Ryu later explained, "the doctrine that a voluntary human agent interrupts causation was influenced by . . . Kant's view that man's voluntary action always starts a new chain of causation and can never be the effect" of another person's earlier act.[119]

Courts struck a compromise between these opposing conceptions of action and their corresponding accounts of punishment as retributive or deterrent. Accordingly they held that subsequent acts interrupted the causal responsibility of prior actors only if the subsequent acts were sufficiently "independent." Yet this independence standard merely relocated the causation question from the injury to the intermediate act necessary to the injury.

---

117. Paul Robinson, Criminal Law 164–65 (1997).
118. State v. Scates, 50 N.C. 420, 423 (1858).
119. Paul Ryu, *Causation in Criminal Law*, 106 U. Pa. L. Rev. 773, 782 (1958).

Over time, courts increasingly saw both natural events and human acts as intervening insofar as unforeseeable.[120] Once foreseeability tests prevailed, it seemed simpler to ignore intervening events and just focus on the foreseeability of the result itself.

A. Intervening Natural Events

Canonical examples of intervening natural events include the late nineteenth-century cases of *Bush v. Commonwealth*[121] and *People v. Rockwell*.[122] Bush's victim recovered from his gunshot but died of scarlet fever contracted from the doctor. The court observed that "the fever was not the natural consequence of the wound, nor was . . . it necessary to have the wound treated by a physician just recovering from the scarlet fever . . . . If the death was not connected with the wound in the regular chain of causes and consequences, . . . it cannot be said that the wound was the natural or proximate cause of the death."[123] Rockwell knocked the victim down with a punch, whereupon a horse inflicted a fatal injury by stepping on him. The court overturned the conviction: "It is impossible to maintain such a charge without making every one liable not only for natural and probable consequences, but for all possible consequences and circumstances which immediately follow a wrongful act. There was no necessary connection between the act of respondent and the conduct of the horse. . . ."[124] The result would be different if the defendant's act foreseeably subjected the victim to danger.

However unusual a natural event, it would not break the causal chain linking an assault to death if it preceded the assault. Thus, if a minor assault fatally aggravated a preexisting illness or injury, the assailant was causally responsible. In *Hopkins v. Commonwealth*,[125] the defendant fatally shot a victim weakened by tuberculosis. The court approved an instruction imposing causal responsibility if the defendant "hastened death" by inflicting a wound not inherently mortal. In *State v Frazier*, a court imposed causal responsibility for death resulting from a single punch cutting the mouth of a hemophiliac, declaring "immaterial that defendant did not . . . reasonably anticipate that his act would cause death."[126]

---

120. *Id.* at 790.
121. Bush v. Commonwealth, 78 Ky. 268 (1880).
122. People v. Rockwell, 39 MICH. 503 (1878).
123. Bush v. Commonwealth, 78 Ky. 268, 271–72 (1880).
124. People v. Rockwell, 39 Mich. 503, 504 (1878).
125. Hopkins v. Commonwealth, 117 Ky. 941 (1904).
126. State v. Frazier, 339 Mo. 966 (1936).

There was less consensus about causal responsibility when a fatal heart attack or seizure followed an assault. On the one hand, a heart attack might be seen as an injury caused by the assault's aggravation of a preexisting illness. On the other hand, a heart attack might be attributed to the victim's emotions following the assault. If so, liability would violate traditional rules requiring a mortal wound and barring responsibility for emotional effects.

In the 1880 New York case of *Cox v. People* the victim probably died of asphyxiation from being left bound and gagged. Nevertheless the court held that if defendant's "violence so excited the terror of deceased that she died from the fright. . . then the prisoner's act was in law the cause of her death."[127] The 1910 decision in *Ex Parte Heigho* cited *Cox* in ruling that defendant could lawfully be charged with manslaughter where his attack on a victim provoked the victim's mother to suffer a fatal heart attack.[128] By contrast, in the 1908 Kentucky case of *Commonwealth v. Couch*, the defendant's unlawful gunshot startled a pregnant woman, leading to a fatal miscarriage. The court upheld the dismissal of a manslaughter indictment because such a death was not a "natural and probable consequence" of the unlawful act.[129] In the later case of *Hubbard v. Commonwealth*, the same court overturned a manslaughter conviction for the death of a jailer who suffered a fatal heart attack while attempting to force the resisting defendant into a cell. The court concluded that causation required either a physical blow or an act from which death was probable.[130]

B. Intervening Acts

Intervening actions have often been divided into those independent of the defendant's act, and responses to the defendant's act. Independent acts necessary to death have often been treated like natural events, and considered superseding causes if unforeseeable at the time of the original attack. Accordingly, an assailant was liable when he left his helpless victim lying wounded in a road to be foreseeably struck by traffic.[131] Conversely an assailant was not liable where an unrelated attacker appeared and fatally kicked his prostrate victim.[132] Courts have often treated intervening fatal acts as causally dependent on the

127. Cox v. People, 80 N.Y. 500 (1880); State v. O'Brien, 81 Iowa 88 (1890).
128. *Ex parte* Heigho, 18 Idaho 566 (1910); People v Studer, 59 Cal. App. 547 (1922) (causation if assault "contributed to" fatal heart attack).
129. Commonwealth v. Couch, 106 S.W. 830, 831 (Ky., 1908).
130. Hubbard v. Commonwealth, 202 SW 2d 634 (KY, 1947).
131. People v Fowler, 178 Cal. 657 (1918).
132. People v. Elder, 100 Mich. 515 (1894).

defendant's act if they are "normal" responses.[133] They have treated endangerment as the cause of flight, rescue, medical care, and efforts to reduce or relocate the danger; and treated assault as the cause of defensive force. Such responses may be attributed to the defendant even if unnecessarily dangerous.

Most cases raising the intervening actor problem involve one of two scenarios: inadequate medical treatment or victim self-endangerment.

There has long been agreement that neither failure to treat nor inept treatment would supersede a wound as a cause of death. Some courts reasoned that inadequate medical treatment simply left the victim in his original peril.[134] Other courts reasoned that inept treatment was a foreseeable outcome of inflicting a wound.[135] On such reasoning some courts imposed liability for death from merely negligent treatment even if the original wound was not mortal.[136] Thus, one court imposed homicide liability on the assailant when such a wound became fatally septic because sewn up rather than being allowed to drain.[137] Presumably, an assailant had no right to a skillful solution to a problem he had created. Yet criminally negligent or malicious medical care would not be deemed normal, and so would be a superseding cause.

Neither would the victim's refusal of treatment break the causal chain. Defendants were causally responsible where victims exacerbated injuries by removing bandages,[138] or refused necessary amputations.[139] Yet these results could be explained on two very different rationales: (1) the victim had a right to refuse treatment, or (2) the refusal was irrational, but this irrationality was an effect of physical injury.

What if the victim inflicted injury on himself? Defendants were responsible for deaths in dangerous flight from a violent assault. This included not only victims ordered into danger,[140] but endangered victims who opted to leap into a ditch,[141] or from a speeding car,[142] or into a river.[143]

---

133. WAYNE LAFAVE, CRIMINAL LAW, 364–67 (2010); ROLLIN PERKINS & RONALD BOYCE, CRIMINAL LAW 813 (1982).
134. Parsons v. State, 21 Ala. 300 (1852); Com v. Hackett, 84 Mass. 136 (Mass, 1861); Hamblin v. State, 81 Neb. 148 (1908); Johnson v. State, 64 Fla. 321 (1912).
135. People v. Whithurst, 2 LaBatt 178 (Cal. 1858).
136. State v. Morphy, 33 Iowa 270 (1872).
137. Downing v. State, 114 Ga. 30 (1901).
138. Stanton's Case, 2 City Hall Rec. 164 (NY 1817); United States v. Hamilton, 182 F. Supp. 548 (D.D.C. 1960).
139. Franklin v. State, 41 Tex. Crim. 21 (1899).
140. Adams v. People, 109 Ill. 444 (1884); Keaton v. State, 41 Tex. Cr. R. 621 (1900).
141. Thornton v. State, 107 Ga. 683 (1899).
142. Sanders v. Commonwealth, 244 Ky. 77 (1932); Patterson v. State, 181 Ga. 698 (1936); Whaley v. State, 157 Fla. 593 (1946).
143. Letner v. State, 156 Tenn. 68 (1927) (defendant's gunshot provoked one victim to leap into river capsizing boat and drowning another victim).

Yet courts sometimes absolved defendants when fleeing victims took unnecessary risks. A captain who crashed a ship was held blameless for the deaths of passengers who tried to swim ashore rather than await rescue.[144] Two nineteenth-century cases held abusive husbands blameless when their severely battered wives fled their rural homes at night in winter and died of exposure. In both cases, courts faulted the victims for not having sought shelter in nearby homes.[145] One court concluded that leaping from a car was not a normal response to simple assault.[146]

Several courts were unwilling to hold defendants responsible for deaths from defensive fire or the use of deadly force by police.[147] Many courts conditioned felony murder liability on a participant in the felony killing or directly causing death. This specialized causation rule is often called an "agency" rule (the killer must be the defendant or his agent). By the middle of the twentieth century, however, some courts rejected this restriction, holding participants in robberies liable for foreseeable deaths, including those resulting from defensive force.[148]

Courts often held arsonists causally responsible for the deaths of firefighters entering burning buildings.[149] In the 1929 case of *State v. Leopold,* a Connecticut court determined that entering a blaze to save property was a sufficiently "natural and ordinary course of conduct" to render an arsonist responsible for the fatal result.[150] Yet courts were less willing to extend causal responsibility for such deaths to offenders who caused fires negligently.[151] Thus, the independence of the victim's self-endangerment from the defendant's act turned not only on the foreseeability of the victim's conduct, but also on the wrongfulness of the defendant's conduct.

This normativity of causal attribution was also apparent when victims injured themselves gratuitously. In *People v. Lewis,*[152] the defendant shot his brother-in-law in the abdomen, inflicting a wound that would have caused death in an hour. The victim, in great pain and expecting to die, cut his own throat and died within minutes. The court saw the gunshot as necessary to

144. United States v. Warner, 4 McLean 463 (C.C.D. Ohio 1848).
145. State v. Preslar, 48 N.C. 421 (1856); Hendrickson v. Commonwealth, 85 Ky. 281 (1887).
146. Patterson v. State, 181 Ga. 698 (1936).
147. Commonwealth v. Campbell, 89 Mass. 541 (1863); Butler v. People, 125 Ill. 641 (1888); Commonwealth v. Moore, 121 Ky. 97 (1905); State v. Oxendine, 187 N.C. 658 (1924).
148. People v. Payne, 359 Ill. 246 (1935); Commonwealth v. Moyer, 357 Pa. 181 (1947); Commonwealth v. Almeida, 362 Pa. 596 (1949).
149. State v. Glover, 330 Mo. 709 (1932).
150. State v. Leopold, 110 Conn. 55 (1929).
151. Carbo v. State, 4 Ga. App. 583 (1908).
152. People v. Lewis, 124 Cal. 551 (1899).

the self-inflicted wound, but not its cause, because a shooting does not lead to a suicide "in the natural course of events."[153] Yet, the court concluded that the gunshot combined with the knife wound to hasten death, if only by seconds:

> when the throat was cut, Farrell was not merely languishing from a mortal wound. He was actually dying—and after the throat was cut he continued to languish from both wounds. Drop by drop the life current went out from both wounds, and at the very instant of death the gunshot wound was contributing to the event.[154]

The difficulty is that this reasoning would yield the same result if the knife wound had not been a mortal or even a serious injury. The decision has been criticized for evading the question of Lewis's causal responsibility for the victim's unforeseeable suicide.[155]

In *Stephenson v. State*,[156] a Ku Klux Klan leader abducted, beat, bit, and attempted to rape the victim. The victim, while under the control of the defendant's henchmen, purchased and ingested poison. She died about 10 days after being returned home, apparently from the combined effects of the poison and an infected bite wound. Rather than relying on any causal contribution from the bite wound, the court offered two different accounts of the defendant's causal responsibility for the victim's ingestion of poison. First, citing cases of victims injured in flight from sexual assault, the court reasoned that the victim's suicide was the "natural and probable consequence" of the defendant's threat to harm her.[157] Second, the court reasoned that if Stephenson's "conduct rendered the deceased distracted and mentally irresponsible, and that such was the natural and probable consequence of such unlawful and criminal treatment" he was causally responsible for a resulting suicide.[158]

Could a defendant also cause death without inflicting any injury, merely by aiding or encouraging suicide? Some courts imposed liability on the basis of complicity in the crime of suicide, rather than causal responsibility for the death.[159] Others held that suicide was no crime and the victim's voluntary act precluded causal responsibility for one who aided or encouraged.[160] Yet

153. *Id.* at 555.
154. *Id.* at 559.
155. Jerome Hall, General Principles of Criminal Law 267 (1960).
156. Stephenson v. State, 205 Ind. 141 (1932).
157. *Id.* at 186.
158. *Id.* at 189.
159. Commonwealth v. Bowen, 13 Mass. 356 (1816); Commonwealth v. Hicks, 118 Ky. 637 (1904).
160. Sanders v. State, 54 Tex. Crim. 101 (1908) (suicide not a crime and so aiding or encouraging it is no crime).

a number of courts concluded that the intentional provision of the means for suicide caused death, on the view that the victim's act was the expected response.[161]

On similar reasoning, one court upheld a manslaughter conviction for the surviving participants in a game of Russian roulette. The court found the defendant's participation

> . . . to be a cause and not a mere condition of Stewart Britch's death. . . . The testimony does not require a ruling that when the deceased took the gun from Atencio it was an independent or intervening act . . . . There could be found to be a mutual encouragement in a joint enterprise.[162]

On the other hand, other decisions rejected homicide liability for drag racers whose competitors suffered fatal crashes. [163] One such decision argued that imposing liability on fellow participants reflected a misapplication to criminal law of a concept of proximate cause drawn from tort. Whereas this tort concept made each of us responsible for any harms foreseeable as a result of our conduct, criminal law required "a more direct causal connection."[164]

C. Causation by Omission

Inaction may be a necessary condition for death. Death may be prevented by feeding another, providing or summoning medical care, rescuing from danger, supervising a person dangerous to himself, or summoning police or fire services to abate a danger. We have seen that liability for omission depends upon a legal duty,[165] and that legality may require prior imposition and notice of such a duty.[166] Assuming that a legal duty has been imposed constitutionally, that a person neglected to fulfill this duty, and that this omission was necessary to death, the omission is a factual cause of death. Must the omission satisfy additional criteria of legal causation?

A well-known case posing this problem is *Palmer v. State*,[167] in which the defendant was held liable for manslaughter when her boyfriend and housemate

---

161. Blackburn v. State, 23 Ohio St. 146 (1872); Burnett v. People, 204 Ill. 208 (1904); People v Roberts, 211 Mich. 187 (1920); Persampieri v. Commonwealth, 343 Mass. 19 (1961).
162. Commonwealth v. Atencio, 345 Mass. 627, 629–30 (1963).
163. Commonwealth v. Root, 403 Pa. 571 (1961); Thacker v. State, 103 Ga. App. 36 (1961).
164. Commonwealth v. Root, 403 Pa. 571 (1961),
165. Jones v. United States, 308 F. 2d 307 (1962); Model Penal Code § 2.01(3) (1962).
166. Lambert v. California, 355 U.S. 225 (1957); State v. Lisa, 919 A. 2d 145 (2007).
167. Palmer v. State, 164 A. 2d 467 (Md. 1960).

repeatedly beat her baby, ultimately inflicting fatal injuries. The court concluded that the defendant's failure to remove the child from the home was both a factual and a proximate cause of death. Despite the fact that the boyfriend was a voluntary actor, who was also criminally responsible for the death, the court denied that he was an "intervening actor" breaking the chain of responsibility. The court reasoned that his continued endangerment of the child's life was a foreseeable result of Palmer's failure to remove the child. In a jurisdiction treating voluntary criminal acts as inherently independent, the defendant might not have been held causally responsible for her child's death.

IX. The Model Penal Code's Causation Test

In criminal cases, nineteenth- and early twentieth-century courts generally denied that intervening acts or events were superseding causes if they were "foreseeable," "probable," or "normal" consequences of the defendant's act. This invited utilitarians to argue that it would be simpler to ignore intervening acts or events and rest causal responsibility on the foreseeability of the result itself. Thus Nicholas St. John Green in 1870 identified proximately caused results as "those . . . which a prudent foresight might have avoided."[168] Holmes argued in 1881 that it was irrelevant whether unforeseeable factual causes preceded or succeeded defendant's act. The only important question was whether the defendant could have foreseen the result of his action.[169] In a 1914 article, Henry Terry argued that standards of proximate causation should correlate with standards of culpability. Thus, the defendant should be causally responsible for all intended consequences no matter how occurring or how improbable. Negligent acts should be deemed the cause of injuries of a kind sufficiently probable to warrant care to avoid, no matter how unlikely the particular way in which the injury occurred. Intervening events should block causal responsibility only for injuries for which the defendant would be held strictly liable.[170] In their article "A Rationale of Homicide," Wechsler and Jerome Michael discussed the act element of homicide, which they conceived to be the causation of death. They concluded that causation required not only that the act was a necessary condition to the result, but also that it was of a kind that generally makes such a result more probable. At mid-century, criminal law theorists Jerome Hall and

---

168. Nicholas St. J. Green, *Proximate and Remote Cause*, 4 AM. L. REV. 201 (1870).
169. OLIVER WENDELL HOLMES, JR., THE COMMON LAW, 93 (1881).
170. Henry T. Terry, *Proximate Consequence in the Law of Torts*, 28 HARV. L. REV. 10, 19, 20 (1914).

Paul Ryu each agreed that legal causation should be reconceptualized as the attribution of injury to the defendant's culpability.[171]

Drawing on these ideas, Wechsler and the other drafters of the Model Penal Code redefined legal causation in terms of culpable mental states. Their official commentary explained that

> When the requirement of "proximate causation" dissociates the actor's conduct from a result of which it is a but-for cause, the reason is always a judgment that the actor's culpability with respect to the result, i.e. his purpose, knowledge, recklessness or negligence, is such that it would be unjust to permit the result to influence his liability or the gravity of his offense. Consequently the Code proceeds on the assumption that issues of this sort ought to be dealt with as problems of the culpability required for conviction and not as problems of "causation.[172]

Thus, the Model Penal Code adopted different causation standards depending on the culpable mental state required for causing a result. In essence, the defendant was liable for causing any result for which he had the requisite culpable mental state.

Model Penal Code Section 2.03(1) distinguished factual from legal causation: "[c]onduct is the cause of a result when: (a) it is an antecedent but for which the result in question would not have occurred; and (b) the relationship between the conduct and the result satisfies any additional causal requirements imposed by the Code. . . ."[173] Model Penal Code Section 2.03(2) provided that an act necessary to a result caused it purposely or knowingly if the result was "within the purpose or contemplation" of the actor. Such an act also caused the result purposely or knowingly if the result (a) "differ[ed] from that designed or contemplated . . . only in the respect that a different person or . . . property . . .[was] injured" or was less severe than the injury intended or expected; or (b) was of the same kind as that intended or expected and was "not too remote or accidental . . . to have a [just] bearing on the actor's liability. . . ."[174] Model Penal Code Section 2.03(3) applied this same approach to crimes of causing a result recklessly or negligently. For such crimes, the actor was responsible for results he caused factually that were "within the risk" he was or should have been aware of. He was also responsible for factually caused

171. Jerome Hall, General Principles of Criminal Law 247–95 (1960); Paul Ryu, *Causation in Criminal Law*, 106 U. Pa. L. Rev. 773 (1958).
172. Model Penal Code Commentaries, pt. 1, § 2.03, at 258 (1985).
173. Model Penal Code § 2.03(1) (1962).
174. *Id.* §2.03 (2).

results that (a) differed from the probable result "only" in that a different person or different property was injured, or that (b) were less severe than the probable result. In addition the actor was responsible for factually caused results of the same kind as the probable results and that occurred in "not too remote or accidental a way to have a [just] bearing on liability."[175] Finally, Model Penal Code Section 2.03(4) conditioned strict liability for causing a result on the result being "a probable consequence of the actor's conduct."[176]

This scheme holds actors who culpably impose a risk causally responsible for injuries within the scope of that risk. Let us apply this to *Bush v. Commonwealth*, in which the defendant shot the victim with intent to kill, but the victim died of scarlet fever contracted from a doctor treating the wound. This death from scarlet fever was arguably not "within the purpose or contemplation" of the actor. Was the death "too remote or accidental to have a just bearing" on the defendant's liability? Death seems too accidental if Bush had no reason to expect that the shooting substantially increased the victim's chances of dying of scarlet fever. Thus, the "not too accidental" standard convicts a defendant charged with intentional or reckless homicide on the basis of a merely foreseeable death, as long as he intended or consciously risked that death would occur in some other fashion.

Now let us consider a more difficult case. While Officer #1 grapples with Suspect, Officer #2 unjustifiably shoots Suspect in the abdomen. Suspect survives, but goes into shock and unconsciously wrests a gun from Officer #1 and shoots him fatally. Did Officer#2 recklessly cause the death of Officer#1 under Model Code Section 2.03?

Officer #2 was certainly reckless with respect to death in shooting Suspect. He may also have been negligent with respect to the death of Officer #1 in aiming a shot dangerously close to him. Conceivably Officer #2 should have foreseen that Suspect might defend himself by using deadly force against either officer. Yet Officer #2 probably could not have anticipated Suspect killing Officer #1 unconsciously. Thus the particular way in which Officer #1 was killed was arguably not within a risk toward which Officer #2 was reckless.

Was this killing different "only" in that another person died? If Officer #2's shot had missed Suspect and killed Officer #1 he would have been guilty under this test. Yet this substitution of victims is *not* the only difference—the shooter is different, and the shooting was unconscious.

Next, was the death too remote or accidental to justly attribute to Officer #2? Was causation "too remote" because mediated by an intervening actor?

---

175. *Id.* §2.03(3).
176. *Id.* §2.03 (4).

A defensive response to an assault is arguably normal and therefore dependent. Unconscious defense is abnormal, yet the unconsciousness was arguably caused by the defendant—unless we consider it too unforeseeable to attribute to the defendant. To determine whether the death was "too accidental" to justly attribute to the defendant it seems we must decide whether the defendant was at least negligent with respect to such a death. Yet, as we have already seen, whether Officer #2 was negligent with respect to such a death depends on how we describe it. He was reckless with respect to the risk of death, negligent with respect to the risk of hitting his partner, perhaps negligent with respect to the risk of someone being killed by defensive fire, and perhaps blameless with respect to the risk of someone being killed by an unconscious victim.

Both examples illustrate a problem with any test conditioning causal responsibility on probability. The problem is that probability is a relationship between classes of events, not between particular events. As a result, the probability of a particular result following particular conduct depends on how we describe both, or in other words how we classify them.[177] Generally, the more detail we fill in about the actual circumstances of the actor's conduct, the more probable the actual result will seem to have been ex ante; while the more detail we fill in about the result, the less probable it will seem to have been ex ante. Remember that the odds of death from an intentional shooting are surprisingly low. If we define the result as the death of a particular person, by a particular causal pathway, the odds become quite low. Because multiple true descriptions are always available, the probability of any particular event is indeterminate.

It would seem we could address this multiple description problem by (1) describing the conduct as including whatever circumstances the defendant was or should have been aware of, and (2) describing the result as any instance of the proscribed injury—death, in the case of homicide. If the Model Penal Code test were this simple, a culpable defendant would be causally responsible for any death that would not have occurred but for his culpable conduct. But this seems implausible. Suppose that Officer #2's shot hits no one, but that a pregnant woman in a nearby apartment is startled and has a fatal miscarriage. The death would not have occurred but for the officer's culpable act, yet it seems arbitrary to attribute the death to him.

The fatal miscarriage seems "too remote or accidental" to attribute to Officer #2, but recall that the Model Penal Code only applies this standard in

177. Clarence Morris, *Duty, Negligence and Causation*, 101 U. PA. L. REV. 189, 198 (1952); H.L.A. HART & A. HONORE, CAUSATION IN LAW 256–57 (1985); MICHAEL MOORE, PLACING BLAME, 363–99 (1997); Mark Kelman, *Interpretive Construction in the Substantive Criminal Law*, 33 STAN. L. REV. 591, 595–96, 640–42 (1981); GUYORA BINDER, FELONY MURDER 50–51 (2012).

assigning causal responsibility for results outside the risk for which the actor is culpable. It seems that the Code must not view the risk of death for which the actor is culpable as the entire risk that the act will factually cause death.

Why is this? The answer is that because of the Code's utilitarian premises, it does not actually fault the offender for imposing a risk of death. Instead, it faults the offender for imposing a risk of *harm*. Recall that the Code makes us reckless or negligent only with respect to risk of death that is substantial and *unjustifiable* in light of the "nature and purpose of the actor's conduct."[178] This standard presumes that all conduct generates costs and benefits. Conduct is therefore culpable not because it is of a kind expected to result in some deaths, but because it is of a kind expected to result in too many deaths in light of its benefits and other harms. Culpability for death is therefore based on expected net harm rather than expected death per se.

The assessment of causal responsibility for particular injuries on the basis of expected net harm raises some puzzling questions. Note that we tolerate thousands of traffic fatalities to enjoy the convenience of automobile travel. Suppose a car manufacturer makes design changes that sacrifice passenger safety in order to lower pollution and price. If the safety risks are small enough and the expected economic and environmental benefits great enough, we might find the safety risks justified. But as the numbers change, at some point the new design becomes negligent. Is the car manufacturer now liable for all the traffic fatalities in which the car is involved, or only for the excess above what is justified by the car's benefits? And if so, which ones? We may use juries to pick out particular cases that seem to dramatize the car's dangers, but in fact it is the expected aggregate harm that is negligent, not any particular deaths the jury picks out.[179]

Ultimately, the Model Penal Code was a utilitarian document aimed at deterring harm rather than punishing past injury.[180] Utilitarianism conceives harm in aggregate and comparative terms as the net disutility for all persons at all future times of all consequences of choosing an act over the optimal alternative. But because the actual future is always incomplete, and the alternative future to which it is compared never materializes, the actual harm resulting from any act can never be known. Accordingly, utilitarianism can only evaluate acts prospectively, on the basis of the expected net harm of such acts under such circumstances. Paradoxically, from this perspective the occurrence of

178. MODEL PENAL CODE § 2.02(2)(c), § 2.02 (2)(d) (1962).

179. LEO KATZ, BAD ACTS AND GUILTY MINDS 249–50 (1987).

180. Herbert Wechsler, *The Challenge of a Model Penal Code*, 65 HARV. L. REV. 1097, 1105, 1108 (1952); Herbert Wechsler, *Codification of Criminal Law in the United States: The Model Penal Code*, 68 COL. L. REV. 1425, 1432 (1968).

any particular injury does not effect the harmfulness of the conduct. Thus, as Herbert Wechsler explained

> [f]rom the preventive point of view, the harmfulness of conduct rests upon its tendency to cause the injuries to be prevented far more than on its actual results; results, indeed, have meaning only in so far as they may indicate or dramatize the tendencies involved. Reckless driving is no more than reckless driving if there is a casualty and no less if by good fortune nothing should occur. . . . [I]f the criminality of conduct is to turn on the result, it rests upon fortuitus considerations unrelated to the major purpose to be served by the declaration that behavior is a crime. . . . A major issue to be faced, therefore, is whether penal law ought to be shaped to deal more comprehensively with risk creation, without reference to actual results.[181]

The movement of Anglo-American homicide law from a focus on unexcused killing to a focus on culpable causing reflects the influence of utilitarian ideas. Yet the logical extension of these ideas would be to condition liability on culpability alone, dispensing with causal responsibility and indeed with homicide liability itself. Nevertheless, rather than eliminating homicide offenses, the Model Penal Code reformulated them. Indeed, reforming homicide was a major aim of the Code.

X. The Model Penal Code's Homicide Scheme

From the utilitarian viewpoint, the homicide provisions of nineteenth-century American criminal codes remained unsatisfying. Their traditional Blackstonean terminology did not make clear whether homicide was a crime of culpably causing death by any means, or a crime of causing death by particular forbidden acts. To a utilitarian, the only reason to punish deaths caused by felonies or dangerous acts was that these acts evidenced some degree of expectation of causing death. Thus it was preferable to condition liability on proof of such expectations rather than incorporating some inculpatory circumstance or conduct into the act element of the offense. Terms such as "malice" and "abandoned and malignant heart" did not define the required expectations with

181. Herbert Wechsler, *The Challenge of a Model Penal Code*, 65 HARV. L. REV. 1097, 1106 (1952).

sufficient precision, and invited juries to convict of killing where the defendant acted from bad motives, rather than with an expectation of death.

The utilitarian approach to crime definition gained authority among American scholars in the late nineteenth century. In the second edition of his treatise on homicide, Wharton identified himself with a modern reform movement, represented by Macaulay and Stephen, viewing malice as an actual mental state regarding the prospect of death. He therefore rejected a view of malice as a presumption of culpability triggered by certain acts. More specifically, he repudiated his earlier support for felony murder liability.[182] Oliver Wendell Holmes Jr. also invoked Macaulay in disapproving felony murder liability.[183] Holmes reasoned that felony murder liability would be applied too infrequently to deter the predicate felony, and could not deter killing by felons who did not expect to cause death. Like Stephen, Holmes argued that malice could be reduced to a single mental state of foresight of death, although Holmes preferred objective foreseeability rather than subjective foresight.[184]

Similarly utilitarian ideas informed Wechsler and Michael's article "A Rationale of Homicide."[185] Wechsler and Michael reviewed American homicide law and advocated its systematic reorganization in order to better achieve the goal of "prevention," and with the express hope that their work would provide a model for criminal law reform generally.

They began by invoking Stephen's conclusions about the mental states required for murder at common law, and his rejection of felony murder.[186] They proceeded to critique the division of murder into degrees, arguing that premeditation and deliberation were not distinguishable from simple intent to kill.[187] They endorsed distinguishing abandoned heart murder from involuntary manslaughter on the quantitative basis of the expected probability of death, so that murder would require "gross recklessness," while manslaughter would require recklessness or negligence. They also invoked the authority of the English Criminal Law Commissioners and Stephen, against that of Holmes, in arguing that gross recklessness murder should require subjective foresight of a risk of death, rather than just an apparent risk. They disparaged alternative approaches to unintended murder that would condition abandoned heart

182. FRANCIS WHARTON, A TREATISE ON THE LAW OF HOMICIDE IN THE UNITED STATES, at iii–iv, 39–45, 153–54 (1875).

183. OLIVER WENDELL HOLMES, JR., THE COMMON LAW 48–50 (1881).

184. *Id.* at 51–53.

185. Herbert Wechsler & Jerome Michael, *A Rationale of the Law of Homicide: I*, 37 COLUM. L. REV. 701, 730–31 (1937).

186. *Id.* at 701–03.

187. *Id.* at 707–09.

murder on endangerment of multiple victims, or on a particularly antisocial motive.[188] Next, they embraced Stephen's proposal to limit felony murder to cases where the predicate felonies were committed in a way dangerous to life, but preferred replacing it with gross recklessness murder.[189] They also rejected a requirement of a felonious purpose independent of physical harm to the victim for felony murder.[190] The only relevant form of culpability for harm was the expectation of causing that type of harm.

Turning to voluntary manslaughter, Wechsler and Michael purported to identify two competing standards in the common law. One restricted mitigation of intentional killing to particular provoking acts of violence such as assaults or unlawful arrests. The other rule conditioned mitigation on any circumstances that would likely cause strong emotion on the part of a reasonable person. Using the familiar pattern of utilitarian argument that viewed required circumstances as proxies for mental states, they reasoned that a provocative violence standard only made sense on the empirical assumption that acts of violence tend to provoke strong emotion.[191] In so doing, they presumed that the function of a provocation defense could not be to identify victims meriting less vindication. Instead it was to identify offenders who were less deterrable and perhaps in need of treatment to reduce their emotional distress.

Wechsler and Michael insisted that involuntary manslaughter should be distinguished from noncriminal homicide by a higher risk of death, and so should require at least gross negligence. They raised, but did not resolve, an issue as to whether involuntary manslaughter should also require subjective foresight of a risk of death, so as to require recklessness.[192] They objected to unlawful act manslaughter on the same basis that they rejected felony murder: the unlawful act was relevant only if it manifested an expectation of death.[193]

Finally, as discussed above, Wechsler and Michael addressed the act element of homicide, which they conceived to be the causation of death. They concluded that causation required not only that the act was a necessary condition to the result, but also that it was of a kind that generally makes such a result more probable.[194]

These ideas provided the foundation for the Model Penal Code Wechsler later drafted. The Code required proof beyond a reasonable doubt of every

188. *Id.* at 709–13.
189. *Id.* at 713–15.
190. *Id.* at 715–17.
191. *Id.* at 717–20.
192. *Id.* at 720–22.
193. *Id.* at 722–23.
194. *Id.* at 723–24.

offense element, which included any required conduct and associated culpable mental states. The Code allowed only permissive presumptions. Thus, juries could be instructed that they might infer a required mental state from certain circumstances, such as the use of a deadly weapon, but not that they must.[195] All offenses had to include conduct elements, whether acts or omissions to fulfill duties.[196] Yet for many offenses, including homicide, causing a harmful result was the only required conduct. The Code defined homicide as causation of death with purpose, knowledge, recklessness, or negligence with respect to death.[197] As these four mental states constituted a hierarchy, homicide offenses were graded from more to less culpable, with the lesser offenses included within the greater.

The Code conditioned murder on purpose or knowledge of causing death, or recklessness and "extreme indifference to the value of human life," which it did not define.[198] Recklessly causing death without extreme indifference was manslaughter. Knowing and extremely indifferent killing were also reduced to manslaughter if committed "under the influence of extreme emotional disturbance" reasonably excused by the circumstances as perceived by the killer.[199] This mitigating condition replaced provocation, and was conceptualized as a partial excuse based on the offender's diminished self-control rather than a partial justification based on the victim's wrongdoing. Because the Code refers to this as an "excuse" based on "the actor's situation as he perceived it to be,"[200] it appears to be "a matter of excuse . . . peculiarly within the knowledge of the defendant" and therefore an "affirmative defense," requiring the production of evidence by the defendant to trigger a prosecutorial burden to disprove the excuse beyond a reasonable doubt.[201] Manslaughter did not include negligent homicide, which was graded a lesser offense. The Code also mitigated murder to manslaughter (or negligent homicide) on the basis of recklessly (or negligently) unreasonable self-defense.[202] Manslaughter was a unitary offense, subjected to the same penalties, regardless of how committed.

The Code gave only halfhearted expression to Wechsler's disapproval of felony murder liability, providing that participation in enumerated felonies permitted an inference of recklessness and extreme indifference.[203] This provision

195. Model Penal Code § 1.12(5) (1962).
196. *Id.* § 1.12, § 2.01.
197. *Id.* § 210.
198. *Id.* § 210.2(1).
199. *Id.* § 210.3(1)(b).
200. *Id.*
201. *Id.* § 1.12 (1), § 1.12 (2)(a), § 1.12 (3)(c).
202. *Id.* § 3.02(2).
203. *Id.* § 210.2(1)(b).

did not merely aggravate reckless killing from manslaughter to murder on the basis of the felony: it allowed jurors to infer recklessness where it was not otherwise proven. Such an inference is dubious: Wechsler's commentary acknowledged that killings occur in only about 1 percent of robberies and far less frequently in burglaries.[204] On the other hand, the Code's causation scheme required at least foreseeability of death for any form of homicide liability. Notably, the Code departed from prevailing doctrine in making participants in the felony liable for the killing only if they caused death or aided or encouraged an act causing death.

Consistent with Wechsler's views in the *Rationale*, the Code eliminated any distinction between first and second degree murder.[205] Yet it created a category of capitally punishable murder based on a finding of at least one of several enumerated aggravating circumstances involving recidivism, multiple victims, criminal motives, or unusual cruelty; and a finding that none of several enumerated mitigating factors was substantial enough to warrant leniency.[206] After such findings, the court was obliged to weigh the evidence of aggravating and mitigating circumstances and any other relevant evidence in determining whether to impose a capital sentence.[207]

XI. American Homicide Statutes after the Code

The Model Penal Code reshaped the way American homicide law was conceptualized and taught but had less effect on the substance of its rules. The Code provoked criminal code revision in over 30 jurisdictions.[208] Many new codes defined homicide in greater detail than their predecessors. They often defined the act element of homicide as causing death rather than killing, adopted the Code's hierarchy of mental states, and replaced malice with particular mental states with respect to death. Yet most retained a felony murder rule, a distinction between first and second degree murder, and a distinction between voluntary and involuntary manslaughter.

The Model Penal Code also influenced homicide law indirectly, by influencing the U.S. Supreme Court's incorporation into due process of a requirement of

---

204. MODEL PENAL CODE COMMENTARIES, pt. II, §210.2 at 38 n.6 (1980).
205. MODEL PENAL CODE § 210.2 (1962).
206. *Id.* § 210.6.
207. *Id.* § 210.6(2).
208. Charles McClain & Dan M. Kahan, *Criminal Law Reform: Historical Development in the U.S.*, *in* 1 ENCYCLOPEDIA OF CRIME AND JUSTICE 424 (J. Dressler, ed. 2002).

prosecutorial proof beyond a reasonable doubt of offense elements. American courts could no longer instruct juries that they must presume that the natural and probable consequences of an action were intended, or presume intent to kill from the use of a deadly weapon.[209] Similarly, the Court held that if a statute defines murder as killing with malice, and malice as intent to kill without provocation, the prosecution must disprove provocation beyond a reasonable doubt to win a murder conviction.[210] This shows that the Court substantially adopted not only the Code's allocation of the burden of proof and its conception of the presumption of innocence, but also the Code's premise that the function of a criminal statute was to define offenses by identifying their constituent act and mental elements. In a subsequent decision the Court permitted New York to require defendants to prove the Model Penal Code's excuse of extreme emotional disturbance, in order to mitigate murder to manslaughter. The Court held that the statute defined the mental element of murder as intent to kill rather than malice, while classifying extreme emotional disturbance as an excuse rather than as disproof of the mental element.[211] In shifting the burden of proof on this issue onto the defendant, the New York Penal Law deviated from the Model Penal Code. The Court was criticized by scholars for permitting this.

A. The Act Element

Today there are four general approaches to defining the act element of homicide offenses, roughly equal in popularity: (1) defining homicide as causing death, and defining causal responsibility by statute;[212] (2) defining homicide or particular homicide offenses as causing death, but leaving the definition of causation to judicial elaboration;[213] (3) defining homicide offenses as killing;[214] and (4) leaving such offenses as "murder" and "manslaughter" undefined by statute.[215] Thus, about half the states have adopted the Model Penal

---

209. *In re* Winship, 397 U.S. 358 (1970); Sandstrom v. Montana, 442 U.S. 510 (1979); Francis v. Franklin, 471 U.S. 307 (1985).
210. Mullaney v. Wilbur, 421 U.S. 684 (1975).
211. Patterson v. New York, 432 U.S. 197 (1977).
212. N.J. STAT. ANN. §§ 2C:11-2(a), 2C:2-3 (2013); 18 PA. CONS. STAT. ANN. §§ 2501(a), 303 (2013); TEX. PENAL CODE ANN. §§ 19.01(a), 6.04 (2013).
213. GA. CODE ANN. §§ 16-5-1 ff. (2013); N.Y, PENAL LAW § 125.00 (2013); OHIO REV. CODE ANN. § 2903 (2013).
214. CAL. PENAL CODE § 187(a) (2013); FLA. STAT. § 782.04(1)(a) (2013).
215. MICH. COMP. LAWS ANN. § 750.316 (2013); VA. CODE ANN. § 18.2-30 (2013); N.C. GEN. STAT. ANN. § 14-17 (2013).

Code's conception of the actus reus of murder as causing death, but most states leave basic questions of causal responsibility for judicial resolution. Judicially developed standards of causal responsibility remain much as they were in the middle of the twentieth century: in other words, such standards are divided between a focus on intervening events and one on foreseeable results. A widely publicized case illustrating the persistent view that an intervening actor supersedes a prior actor's causal responsibility was the Michigan Supreme Court's dismissal of a murder indictment against Dr. Jack Kevorkian for providing suffering patients with the means of suicide.[216] The court noted the absence of any evidence that the suicides were involuntary. In the still substantial number of jurisdictions with codes using the terms "kill" or "murder" rather than "cause death," the question arises whether these terms have some narrower meaning, for example excluding causation by omission, by assisting suicide, or by provoking defensive force.

B. Intentional Homicide

A substantial minority of jurisdictions condition murder liability on the intent to grievously injure, including such populous states as Illinois, Michigan, New Jersey, and Texas.[217] In these jurisdictions, a fatal intentional shooting would seem to be murder absent provocation or other mitigation.

Yet most American jurisdictions condition at least some forms of murder liability on intentional killing. For example, California, New York, and Ohio punish intentional killing as second degree murder.[218] Florida, North Carolina, and Virginia define premeditated intentional killing as first degree murder.[219] Pennsylvania punishes intentional killing as first degree murder, but defines it as requiring premeditation.[220] Under the strict terms of these statutes, fatal intentional shootings are not murders. Yet juries are probably often willing to find intent to kill on such facts, even though only a small fraction of intentional gunshots lead to death.[221] Indeed, some courts still instruct juries that they

216. People v. Kevorkian, 447 Mich. 436 (1994).

217. 720 Ill. Comp. Stat. 5/9-1(a)(1) (2013); N.J. Stat. Ann. § 2C:11-3(1, 2) (2013); Tex. Penal Code Ann. § 19.02(b)(2) (2013); People v. Aaron, 409 Mich 672, 709 (1980).

218. Cal. Penal Code §§ 188, 189 (2013); N.Y. Penal Law § 125.25(1) (2013); Ohio Rev. Code Ann. § 2903.02 (2013).

219. Fla. Stat. § 782.04 (2013); N.C. Gen. Stat. Ann. § 14-17 (A) (2013); Va. Code Ann. § 18.2-32 (2013).

220. 18 Pa. Cons. Stat. Ann. § 2502(a), (d) (2013).

221. Guyora Binder, Felony Murder 190 n.43 (2012); Donald A. Dripps, *Fundamental Retribution Error*, 56 Vand. L. Rev. 1383 (2003).

may infer intent to kill from the use of a deadly weapon when death results.[222] Moreover, many of these jurisdictions also punish depraved indifference murder,[223] while others leave murder incompletely defined.[224] Thus courts in such jurisdictions may still read intent to injure into the concepts of depraved indifference or murder itself.

Most American jurisdictions continue to divide murder into degrees, and most of these grade premeditated murder as first degree.[225] Such standards continue to draw criticisms such as those offered by Wechsler and Michael. As courts generally deny that premeditation requires any temporal interval between thought and action, it is unclear how an intentional killing could fail to be premeditated. On the other hand, if premeditation is taken to imply a calm or "cold-blooded" affect, it is not clear that the calmest killings are the most culpable.[226] A mercy killing may result from calm resolution,[227] while a sadistic killing of a child may result from a frenzied rage, precluding a finding of "premeditation and deliberation."[228] Nevertheless, premeditation may be a sensible reason to aggravate murder liability if we are correct in assuming that juries often find intent to kill where the facts only show intent to injure or use of a deadly weapon. Where findings of premeditation rely on evidence of a motive to kill, they may pick out genuine cases of intentional killing.

Although only a few jurisdictions mitigate murder on the ground of imperfect self-defense, most mitigate intentional killing (or fatal intentional injury) to manslaughter on the basis of strong emotion. They generally require that emotion sufficient to impair self-control accompanied the killing, and that the killer faced circumstances that either justify or commonly produce such emotion.[229] In such jurisdictions, courts confront a number of issues. Must the emotion be anger, or may it include other emotions such as fear or despair? Does a claim of "provocation" or "heat of passion" require that the victim have actually wronged the defendant? Does it suffice if the defendant reasonably

---

222. WAYNE LAFAVE, CRIMINAL LAW 775 (2010).

223. N.Y. PENAL LAW § 125.25 (2013); CAL. PENAL CODE §§ 187–189 (2013); FLA. STAT. § 782.04 (2013); N.C. GEN. STAT. ANN. § 14-17 (B)(1) (2013); GA. CODE ANN. § 16-5-1(B) (2013).

224. 18 PA. CONS. STAT. ANN. § 2501(a) (2013); VA. CODE ANN. §§ 18.2-30, 18.2-31 (2013).

225. CAL. PENAL CODE § 189 (2013); FLA. STAT. § 782.04 (2013); MICH. COMP. LAWS. ANN. §§ 750.316, 750.317 (2013); N.Y. PENAL LAW §§ 125.27, 125.25 (2013); N.C. GEN. STAT. ANN. § 14-17 (2013); 18 PA. CONS. STAT. ANN. § 2501(a) (2013); VA. CODE ANN. §§ 18.2-32 (2013).

226. SAMUEL PILLSBURY, JUDGING EVIL, RETHINKING THE LAW OF MURDER AND MANSLAUGHTER 101–06 (2003).

227. John KAPLAN, ROBERT WEISBERG & GUYORA BINDER, CRIMINAL LAW 355–56 (2012) (discussing case of Dorothy Healy).

228. People v. Anderson, 70 Cal. 2d 15 (1968).

229. People v. Berry, 18 Cal. 3d 509 (1976).

believes such a wrong to have taken place? May the defendant base mitigation on upsetting circumstances unrelated to the victim?

The Model Penal Code's extreme emotional disturbance defense focuses more on the defendant's loss of self-control than on the circumstances justifying it. Although only a minority of jurisdictions have adopted this statutory language,[230] the case law has moved toward more subjective standards of mitigation that resemble the extreme emotional disturbance standard. For example, in the California case of *People v. Berry*, the court determined that murder liability could be mitigated on the basis of any strong emotion that the defendant's circumstances would provoke in an ordinarily reasonable person. It therefore awarded a heat-of-passion instruction to a defendant who strangled his recently wed wife 10 days after she told him she had become sexually involved with another man and asked for a divorce. The court found it significant that the victim alternately invited and refused sexual intimacy, implying that sexual frustration could partially excuse murder.[231] Victoria Nourse has criticized highly subjective standards such as the Model Penal Code's as condoning domestic homicides "provoked" by the victims' efforts to escape abuse or resist control. [232] Some scholars argue that mitigation is only merited for morally justifiable emotions, in opposition to the utilitarian view that motives should not be evaluated.[233]

C. Homicide by Risk-Taking

Most American jurisdictions continue to condition either unitary murder or second degree murder on extreme indifference to human life.[234] Such provisions often leave unexplained how this form of murder differs from reckless manslaughter. Some jurisdictions have required endangerment of multiple victims;[235] and some have required an antisocial motive.[236] Where negligence suffices for manslaughter, recklessness might constitute extreme indifference.

---

230. *E.g.*, N.Y. PENAL LAW § 125.27(2.)(a) (2013).
231. *E.g.*, People v. Berry, 18 Cal. 3d 509 (1976).
232. Victoria Nourse, *Passion's Progress: Modern Law Reform and the Provocation Defense*, 106 YALE L.J. 1331–448 (1997).
233. Dan M. Kahan & Marth C. Nussbaum, *Two Conceptions of Emotion in Criminal Law*, 96 COLUM. L. REV. 270 (1996); Kyron Huigens, *Virtue and Inculpation*, 108 HARV. L. REV. 1423 (1995).
234. CAL. PENAL CODE § 189 (2013); FLA. STAT. § 782.04 (2013); GA. CODE ANN. §§ 16-5-1 (2013); 720 ILL. COMP. STAT. 5/9-1, 5/9-2 (2013); N.C. GEN. STAT. ANN. § 14-17 (2013): N.Y. PENAL LAW §§ 125.27, 125.25 (2013).
235. People v. Suarez, 6 N.Y. 3d 202 (2005).
236. Ramsey v. State, 114 Fla. 766 (1934); People v. Protopappas, 201 Cal. App. 3d 152 (1988).

A majority of jurisdictions also punish involuntary manslaughter, either as a distinct lower grade of manslaughter, or as one form of a unitary manslaughter offense. Involuntary manslaughter is defined in three ways: as reckless killing,[237] as negligent killing,[238] or as killing in the course of an offense that is not a predicate for felony murder.[239] Reckless manslaughter generally requires subjective foresight of death, but occasionally objective foreseeability of a very great risk suffices.[240] Negligent manslaughter now usually requires objective foreseeability of death, rather than the simple violation of a duty of care.

A notorious case conditioning manslaughter liability on the mere failure to take ordinary care was that of *State v. Williams*. In this 1971 case the Washington Court of Appeals upheld a manslaughter conviction for a couple who failed to get timely medical care for an infant suffering from an abscessed tooth, with fatal consequences. The Native American parents were unaware of any risk to the child's life and feared that a doctor would contact child welfare authorities, who often seized Native American children without cause.[241] The Court reasoned that Washington's criminal code required only "simple" negligence for manslaughter. However the Washington code now divides manslaughter into two degrees, requiring recklessness toward death, and "criminal negligence" toward death,[242] defined as the Model Penal Code defines negligence.[243]

D. Homicide in the Course of Crime

Few of the new codes abolished felony murder, but a handful of states now condition felony murder on extreme indifference to human life.[244] Most felony murder rules are effectively conditioned on objective foreseeability of death. A majority of felony murder jurisdictions limit predicate felonies to a list that usually includes robbery, rape, arson, kidnapping, and burglary.[245] These traditionally enumerated felonies are often described as inherently dangerous, but

237. 720 ILL. COMP. STAT. 5/9-3 (Westlaw 2013); N.J. STAT. ANN. § 2C:11-4(a.)(1) (Westlaw 2013); N.Y. PENAL LAW § 125.15(1) (2013); TEX. PENAL CODE ANN. § 19.04(a) (2013).
238. CAL. PENAL CODE § 192(b) (2013); FLA. STAT. § 782.07(1) (2013); 18 PA. CONS. STAT. ANN. § 2504(a) (2013).
239. CAL. PENAL CODE § 192(c) (2013); GA. CODE ANN. §§ 16-5-3 (2013); OHIO REV. CODE ANN. § 2903.04 (2013).
240. Commonwealth v. Welansky, 316 Mass. 383 (1944).
241. State v. Williams, 484 P. 2d 1167 (1971).
242. REV. CODE WASH. §§ 9A.32.060, 9A.32.070 (2011).
243. *Id.* § 9A.08.010 (1)(d).
244. GUYORA BINDER, FELONY MURDER 184 (2012).
245. *Id.* at 190.

burglary is far less dangerous than the others.[246] Jurisdictions with graded murder usually define killing in the course of enumerated felonies as first degree murder. A substantial minority of felony murder jurisdictions permit felony murder predicated on non-enumerated felonies. This is often second degree murder, and the predicate felonies are usually limited to those committed in a foreseeably dangerous way.[247] Most jurisdictions also require foreseeability as a criterion of the actor's causal responsibility for death, or of causal linkage between the felony and the death.[248] These various requirements of danger effectively condition felony murder liability on criminal negligence, even though statutes rarely identify negligence toward death as the mental element of the offense.[249] A substantial minority of jurisdictions employ an "agency" rule, excluding liability for deaths caused by acts resisting the felony. An agency requirement and a foreseeability requirement are compatible, and several jurisdictions have both.[250] Few jurisdictions impose felony murder liability for deaths of co-felons.

An additional limitation on predicate felonies is a requirement that the felony be independent of the death. Thus, robbery aims at theft, rape aims at sexual violation, and arson aims at destruction of property. The danger to the person is incidental to these independent aims. About half of the jurisdictions that permit felony murder predicated on non-enumerated felonies preclude predicate felonies, such as assault, that aim at physical harm to the victim and therefore "merge" with the killing.[251] Some jurisdictions include egregious forms of assault such as aggravated child abuse or drive-by shooting as predicate felonies. Such felonies might be seen as entailing depraved indifference to human life even though they do not aim at a wrong independent of the death.

How are we to explain the persistence of felony murder liability in the face of the utilitarian critique of the felony murder doctrine? The persistence of felony murder liability in America reflects a rejection of utilitarianism's purely risk-oriented conception of culpability as overly narrow. Utilitarians defined culpability for causing a result as narrowly limited to expectations of causing such a result, yet American legislatures have apparently considered felonious purposes as also relevant to a killer's culpability for death. American courts have generally explained felony murder liability in one of two ways: (1) the intentional commission of a felony particularly dangerous to life *implies* a high

---

246. *Id.* at 193–94.
247. *Id.* at 199.
248. *Id.* at 209.
249. State v. Martin, 119 N.J. 2 (1990).
250. Guyora Binder, Felony Murder 209 n.43 (2012).
251. *Id.* at 245–46.

expectation of death, or (2) the intent to commit a particularly grave felony can "*transfer*" to an unintended death because it is morally equivalent to a high expectation of death. Neither account is convincing *on its own* because neither the danger nor the gravity of a predicate felony seems great enough *by itself* to equal the culpability toward death involved in intentional or grossly reckless murder. Yet if we *combine* the expectation of death entailed in a dangerous predicate felony with an independent felonious purpose, we arguably have sufficient culpability to warrant severe punishment.[252] Thus, experimental subjects elected to punish negligent homicide with incarceration for less than a year, but chose a term of more than 20 years for negligent homicide in the course of armed robbery.[253] A felonious purpose of robbing or raping arguably aggravates the culpability of killing negligently, just as, in some jurisdictions, an antisocial purpose aggravates reckless manslaughter to depraved indifference murder. The dual culpability required by this rationale for felony murder liability explains why many jurisdictions require an independent felonious purpose, and therefore bar felony murder predicated on aggravated assault.

A particularly vexed issue is the responsibility of felons for killings by co-felons. Interestingly, experimental subjects who assigned substantial penalties to armed robbers who killed negligently assigned lower terms to their co-felons.[254] Most codes explicitly impose felony murder liability only on those who kill or cause death. Accomplices in the felony are held liable for the felony murder only if they meet judicially developed criteria of complicity in felony murder. The most common test holds co-felons of the killer responsible for deaths foreseeable as a result of the felony, and resulting from acts in furtherance of the felony.[255] A substantial minority of felony murder statutes make all participants in a felony liable for any deaths caused by the felony.[256] If applied to implicate co-felons for deaths foreseeable only to the killer, these provisions would unfairly impose strict liability. But if interpreted to condition the liability of each participant on the foreseeability of death to him or her as a result of the felony, these provisions require the same culpability for killers and their accomplices. Several jurisdictions with such statutes offer an affirmative defense for unarmed accomplices who had no reason to expect the use of deadly force.[257]

252. Guyora Binder, *The Culpability of Felony Murder*, 83 Notre Dame L. Rev. 965 (2008).
253. Paul Robinson & John Darley, Justice, Liability and Blame: Community Views and the Criminal Law 169–81 (1995).
254. *Id.* at 176–78.
255. Guyora Binder, Felony Murder 216 (2012).
256. *Id.* at 221–25.
257. N.Y. Penal Law § 125.25(3) (2013).

Although felony murder liability remains prevalent, most jurisdictions have dispensed with the doctrine of unlawful act manslaughter and now condition involuntary manslaughter simply on recklessness or negligence. Nevertheless, some jurisdictions have defined homicide crimes predicated on violations of motor vehicle laws. A recent development has been the legislative definition of special homicide crimes predicated on drug delivery. Liability for deaths resulting from voluntary self-administration of drugs is obviously problematic from the standpoint of causation. The victim is an intervening actor, and although drug use is a normal and foreseeable consequence of supplying drugs, fatal overdoses are low-probability events. Thus far, charges under these statutes have been infrequent, but with rising opioid overdose rates, that may change.

XII. Death Penalty Law after the Code

One of the areas of law where the Model Penal Code has had the greatest influence is on capital sentencing. Until 1972, juries in most states had largely uncabined discretion to condemn or spare defendants convicted of first degree murder (or murder in states without degrees). The NAACP Legal Defense Fund charged that this system enabled race discrimination in sentencing, and that particularly in Southern states, capital punishment amounted to a system of authorized lynching. In a carefully planned litigation campaign, the Legal Defense Fund argued that capital punishment violated the evolving standards of decency determining the meaning of the cruel and unusual punishment clause of the Constitution's Eighth Amendment. The Legal Defense Fund asserted that capital punishment was tolerated by the white majority only because it was used discriminatorily.[258] This campaign achieved a major success with the Supreme Court's 1972 decision in *Furman v. Georgia*, striking down on Eighth Amendment grounds all existing capital punishment statutes as being excessively discretionary, and potentially discriminatory.[259] However, because the Court had not held that capital punishment was unconstitutional per se, most states quickly repassed capital sentencing statutes that addressed the problems of arbitrariness and excessive discretion in one of two ways: either by making execution mandatory for all convicted of the highest degree of murder, or by following the Model Penal Code's scheme of balancing aggravating and mitigating circumstances.

---

258. Michael Meltsner, Cruel and Unusual 180–185, 268–278 (1973).
259. Furman v. Georgia, 408 U.S. 238 (1972).

In a series of 1976 decisions, the Court held that capital punishment could be justified by the legitimate penal purposes of retribution and deterrence,[260] accepted the Model Penal Code's guided discretion approach,[261] and rejected mandatory execution of any class of murderers because insufficiently individualized.[262] In a subsequent case the Court required sentencers to consider any mitigating evidence offered by the defense, including evidence of the defendant's rehabilitative potential and lack of dangerousness.[263] The Court also required that each jurisdiction narrow the class of death-eligible murderers by requiring proof of at least one aggravating circumstance, either at the guilt phase or the sentencing phase.[264]

As explained in Chapter Three on the purpoes of punishment, the Court has also imposed some categorical limits on the use of the death penalty. Thus, the Court has limited capitally punishable offenses against persons to murder.[265] It has limited capital punishment of accomplices to felony murder to those who acted with intent to kill or who played a major role in the felony and acted with reckless indifference to human life.[266] It has also limited capital punishment to normally functioning adults by precluding execution of minors and those with developmental mental disabilities.[267]

Taken together, the decisions on the sentencing process seem to contradict themselves. On the one hand, the Court has objected to sentencing discretion as inviting arbitrariness and discrimination, and justified capital punishment on the basis of considerations of deterrence and desert that seemed realizable through rules defining conduct and culpable mental states. Yet it has also demanded discretionary sentencing based on individualized assessment of the offender's character and capacity. The Court's requirement of narrowing and its rejection of mandatory sentences for any category of murder seemed to confirm the Legal Defense Fund's claim that regular application of capital punishment to persons from all social groups and classes would seem intolerably cruel. The Court seems determined to limit capital punishment to a very small number of cases. In recent years, there has been about 1 execution for every 400 homicides.[268] It seems unlikely that any process could possibly select

---

260. Gregg v. Georgia, 428 U.S. 153 (1976).
261. Jurek v. Texas, 428 U.S. 262 (1976).
262. Woodson v. North Carolina, 428 U.S. 280 (1976), Roberts v. Louisiana, 428 U.S. 325 (1976).
263. Lockett v. Ohio, 438 U.S. 586 (1978).
264. Lowenfield v. Phelps, 484 U.S. 231 (1988); Zant v. Stephens, 462 U.S. 862 (1983); *Ring v. Arizona*, 536 U.S. 584 (2002).
265. Coker v. Georgia, 433 U.S. 584 (1977), Kennedy v. Louisiana, 554 U.S. 407 (2008).
266. Enmund v. Florida, 458 U.S. 782 (1982), Tison v. Arizona, 481 U.S. 137(1987).
267. Roper v. Simmons, 543 U.S. 551 (2005); Atkins v. Virginia, 536 U.S. 304 (2002).
268. John Kaplan, Robert Weisberg & Guyora Binder, Criminal Law 339, 471 (2012).

such a small percentage of murderers for execution on a principled basis. If so, there is a dilemma between fewer executions and fairer executions. A society's choice of the former over the latter does indeed raise doubt that it still accepts capital punishment as decent.

Thus it seems that the Court rather quickly gave up on the ambition, articulated in its *Furman* decision, of preventing arbitrary execution.[269] With its 1987 decision in *McCleskey v. Kemp*,[270] the Court also seemed to abandon any effort to prevent race discrimination in capital sentencing. Here the Court rejected an equal protection challenge to Georgia's death penalty statute, despite evidence of a great statistical disparity in sentencing based on the race of the victim. The Court offered the troubling argument that accepting such statistical disparities as evidence of unconstitutional race discrimination could invalidate much of the American criminal justice system.

XIII. Conclusion

The contemporary American law of homicide reflects the sustained influence of a utilitarian reform movement. That movement organized legal thought around a conception of human action as risking or causing results, and a conception of law as minimizing costly results, with clear rules conditioning sanctions on dangerous conduct. Within this framework, homicide was conceptualized as the expected causation of death. From this perspective, traditional definitions of homicide emphasizing manifestly violent acts or antisocial motives were seen as archaic and confused. Under the influence of these ideas homicide changed from a crime of unexcused killing to one of culpable causing. Causation was also reconceived, from direct infliction of injury to the creation of risk followed by injury within the scope of that risk.

Yet the logic underlying these reforms pushed in the direction of dispensing with homicide liability altogether and simply punishing the imposition of risk. The persistence of homicide liability shows that criminal law serves aims beyond the deterrence of net cost. It also serves to vindicate victims by imposing blame for actual injury. This judgmental function is also implicit in the persistence of doctrines evaluating actors' purposes and motives: the felony murder rule, the conditioning of reckless murder on cruelty or antisocial motive, the selective attribution of intervening actions to defendants, and the

269. Robert Weisberg, Deregulating Death, Sup. Ct. Rev. 305–95 (1983).
270. McCleskey v. Kemp, 481 U.S. 279 (1987).

consideration of motive in capital sentencing. Moreover, normative judgment is entailed in the attribution of the finely calibrated culpable mental states that utilitarianism makes essential to liability for endangerment. Given the low probability of death from even such purportedly dangerous conduct as firing guns, and the scarcity of any other evidence of subjective intent, juries are probably attributing mental states on the basis of hindsight and prejudice. As long as we are committed to punishing actual results, utilitarian rationality will be frustrated by the facts that most homicide does not result from a conscious decision to kill, and that assessments of justified risk are inherently subjective.

SEVEN

Rape and Theft, From Force to Non-consent

I. Introduction

Our previous chapter explored the problem of criminal liability for harm by examining the evolution of the offense of homicide in American law. We saw that the English common law had conceived homicide as a crime of violent conduct, triggering royal jurisdiction by breaching the king's peace. Under the influence of a utilitarian reform movement, lawyers in both England and America reconceptualized homicide during the nineteenth century as a crime of subjective expectation. The focus shifted from the conduct element to a newly important mental element. Moreover, even the offending conduct—causation of harm—came to be defined in terms of expectations.

This chapter further pursues this theme of the transformation of the idea of a criminal offense from a trespassory breach of the peace to a culpable choice. It turns to crimes defined not by a harmful result, but by violation of a victim's will. We will look at two important types of offense—sexual assault and theft—that threaten different interests, but that nevertheless both involve a violation of consent. Both offenses involve conduct affecting another person that can be benign if the other party genuinely authorizes it. Indeed, consensual sexual contact is central to social practices—family and household formation, reproduction, romantic love, self-expression—that are greatly valued. Similarly, consensual transfer of property is also central to social practices—allocation through market exchange and gift—that are greatly valued. Because the laws of rape and theft police the boundaries of these central social practices, they are almost as important to social order as the law of homicide. In a modern liberal society, the boundaries of sex and commerce are defined by consent. We might say that today, where the essential element of homicide is a result element—death—the essential element of both rape and theft is a circumstance element: the lack of consent or authorization.

Like homicide, rape and theft formerly required conduct that is no longer required. Homicide formerly required killing (which usually meant an armed attack inflicting a wound or injury). Rape formerly required force by the assailant overcoming the physical resistance of the victim. Theft formerly required trespass, a forcible taking from possession by the thief. Indeed, the historic linkage between sexual assault and theft offenses is suggested by the common etymology of the words "rape" and "robbery." Just as culpable causation of death now suffices for homicide, sexual intercourse with a sufficiently culpable violation of consent now often suffices for sexual assault, and acquisition with a culpable violation of the owner's consent is usually enough for theft. Thus all three offenses expanded in scope as traditional requirements of manifestly violent conduct were abandoned or de-emphasized. In all three cases, these shifts reflected a broad redefinition of the public interest vindicated by punishment. Crime was formerly conceived as a martial challenge to the governing authority of a sovereign. In a modern liberal state, however, crime is seen as an attack on a legal entitlement. Individuals and associations participate in sovereignty not only through democratic politics, but also through public adoption and vindication of private interests.

Because private interests conflict, however, the transformation of private interests into legal rights is an outgrowth of political contestation. The differential social power of different interests might explain why the transformations of homicide, theft, and rape—although similar in form—occurred at different times. Thus, the evolution of rape law differed significantly from the development of homicide and theft, in that the movement from manifest violence to an infringement of autonomy occurred much later. The expansion of theft began as early as the fifteenth century, under pressure from the growing activity and influence of merchants. Homicide and theft law changed profoundly during the nineteenth century, whereas the transformation of rape awaited the emergence of a feminist reform movement in the late twentieth century, and remains incomplete. Thus, force often remains a requirement, and other violations of consent such as fraud and nonphysical coercion are rarely criminalized. In addition, prosecutor and jury discretion can undermine reforms.

It seems obvious that the persistence of anachronistic requirements of force and resistance for rape both reflected and reinforced the subordinate social position of women. In her influential book on rape law, Susan Estrich drew several invidious comparisons between the law of rape and the law of theft. Thus, she noted that theft victims are not ordinarily required to physically resist thieves and robbers for the prosecution to prove they did not consent to the taking of their property.[1] Moreover, if a thief grasped the victim, pushed her to the ground, and lay on top of her, no one would doubt that his theft

---

1. SUSAN ESTRICH, REAL RAPE (1987).

was sufficiently forcible to constitute robbery.[2] And yet, where rape requires force, such conduct is often considered insufficient to satisfy the force element. These disparities suggested to Estrich that the sexual autonomy of women is valued less than the security of property.

II. Reflections on Consent

Is a violation of consent essential to criminal liability? Yes, in one sense: all crimes violate the state's prohibition. Yet many crimes are also violations of the interests of persons or organizations. Must these crimes be forbidden by the victims as well as by the state?

Not necessarily. Some crimes against persons can be committed with the consent—even the competent consent—of the victim. These include homicides and other crimes inflicting physical damage. The crime of battery is usually defined as requiring physical contact that is *either* offensive or physically injurious. Consensual contact—including sexual contact—cannot be offensive, but it can be injurious. Consent can authorize some physical injuries—for example, if they are minor, if they are foreseeable risks inhering in a lawful sport or contest, or inflicted for the purpose of medical treatment by licensed professionals. The Model Penal Code makes consent a defense to physical injury in these three circumstances.[3] Apart from these exceptions, inflicting physical harm is criminal, regardless of the victim's consent. The same principle applies even to unsuccessful attempts to injure or wound.

Causing damage and violating consent are two different ways of violating the rights of a victim. According to the terminology introduced in Chapter One, criminal prohibitions confer entitlements of two kinds on victims: property entitlements and inalienable entitlements. Rights against injury regardless of consent are inalienable entitlements. Alienable or waivable rights enforced by criminal liability are property entitlements. In this sense, crimes against consent such as theft, assault, and even sexual assault are violations of property entitlements. It should be noted that the alienability of a property right does not necessarily imply the transferability of the right to another. Thus, I might have property rights over access to my own labor and person, but that does not mean I can transfer these rights to someone else. My powers to control access to my labor and my person are inalienable, even though their exercise allows me to confer temporary access to my labor and person.

---

2. *Id.* at 40.
3. Model Penal Code §2.11 (2) (1962).

So criminal violations of consent depend on the will of the victim in a way that criminal injuries do not. Nevertheless, the will of the victim can play some role in determining liability for criminal injuries as well. Thus, the formal inalienability of rights against injury is somewhat diminished in substance by prevailing criteria of causal responsibility. Recall that a drug dealer will generally not be causally responsible for a customer's fatal overdose. The victim's voluntary act of self-endangerment breaks the chain of causal responsibility. To be sure, the dealer can be liable if he administers the overdose with the victim's consent. Nevertheless, an intervening actor rule means that some manifestations of victim consent will also preclude causal responsibility for harm.

Why should consensual physical damage be punished? The conventional response is that criminal law protects a public interest in life and health transcending the interests of a victim. For example, the public can punish self-injury with the purpose of evading the military draft. It can also punish consensual injury for paternalistic reasons. A utilitarian may take the view that individuals are usually the best judges of their own welfare without making their preferences constitutive of their welfare. Perhaps willingness to injure one's self is evidence of incompetence to judge one's welfare. We might view the freedom to make irrational self-regarding choices as one source of welfare but nevertheless balance it against other welfarist considerations. Finally, the ideal of a rule of law gives us reasons to regulate consensual physical damage. Insofar as we conceive the state's power to govern as a monopoly on violence, the state has an interest in either preventing or licensing intentional physical injury of others.

Assuming the state will punish violations of consent, how can we tell when consent has been violated? Force offers an obvious index of non-consent. Yet force can have a narrower or broader meaning. If I hit you with a club and ride off on your bike, I have obviously taken the bike by force. But what if I boldly take it from your front porch in your presence, while you are too frightened to interfere? What if you are not present, but I break the lock securing the bike?

I can also violate consent by means of fraud, as when I ask to borrow your bike and don't bring it back. I can violate consent by exploiting the trust of a child or other person incompetent to consent. Finally, I can violate consent by means of nonphysical coercion. Thus, I might buy my employee's bicycle for a pittance, by threatening—explicitly or implicitly—to fire him.

In protecting consent against deception, exploitation, and coercion, we face a common difficulty. All three of these violations of consent may also be described more benignly as influences on consent. Liberal societies are also market societies, in which we view voluntary transactions as not only cooperative, but also competitive. We expect that markets will reward those with better information, greater wisdom, and less economic need (i.e., lower demand). Indeed, this competition incentivizes individuals to learn, calculate, produce, and accumulate, and thereby enables markets to allocate goods and labor efficiently—all to the benefit of the general welfare. But if markets are desirably competitive, differences in knowledge, skill, and power inhere in market transactions, and the beneficiaries of these differences are arguably behaving prosocially. Once we move beyond overt violence as an index of non-consent, there is no bright line separating competition from theft. Indeterminate standards of consent may be acceptable in the realm of civil liability, but they are problematic in criminal law, where legality requires specific and prospective definition of offenses.

As reformers have redefined sexual assault as a crime against consent, they have—for better or worse—likened sexual relations to market transactions. To a great extent, sexual relations are infused with the ethos of the marketplace in our society. Cultural historians tell us that in the nineteenth century new amusements such as novel-reading and card playing encouraged a speculative and calculative attitude toward not only investments and careers, but also marriages. Today prostitution itself is discouraged, but products are routinely marketed to both men and women as enhancing their attractiveness and thereby giving them an edge in sexual competition.

A benefit of characterizing sexual assault as a violation of consent is its implicit insistence that individuals are free to determine their own sexual partners and practices. People should not have to demonstrate adherence to cultural norms regarding sex or gender to be protected against sexual assault. Yet because it evokes the competitive ethos of the marketplace, a focus on consent also has important costs. Viewing sexual interactions as competitive legitimizes a measure of deception, coercion, and exploitation as inevitable. It makes inequalities of power seem like an outgrowth of individual choices, thereby obscuring systematic gender hierarchy. Finally, a focus on the mental event of consent obscures the physicality of sex and the violence of sexual assault.

III. The "Metamorphosis" of Theft

Today we think of theft as an economic crime. Yet theft was originally criminalized as a breach of the peace.[4] In Roman law and other ancient legal systems,

---

4. 2 FREDERICK POLLOCK & FREDERIC WILLIAM MAITLAND, THE HISTORY OF ENGLISH LAW BEFORE THE TIME OF EDWARD I, at 462–63 (1898).

including early English law, a "manifest" thief—one caught with the stolen goods, or within an enclosure at night—could be summarily killed with impunity.[5] This public authorization of vengeance presumed that the problem posed by theft was the risk of blood feud rather than insecurity of property. Theft was criminal insofar as it was seen as a provocation to violence.

The Leges Henrici recognized open theft as an unemendable offense,[6] and the 1166 Assize of Clarendon named theft along with murder and robbery as indictable offenses. Yet the common law historians Pollock and Maitland report that appeals of larceny—that is, prosecution of theft as a felony—were rare during the medieval period. Instead, victims generally sought recovery of property, or its value, through civil actions,[7] whereas an appeal of felony could lead to forfeiture of the stolen goods and the thief's property. Robbery, by contrast, was a frequent ground for appeal of felony from the introduction of that process in the twelfth century.[8] It has been suggested that the appeal of robbery provided a source for the civil action of trespass vi et armis that developed after the 1278 statute of Gloucester.[9] The requirement of armed force quickly became a fiction. By the time larceny prosecutions became more common, larceny was identified with this civil claim.

In his book *Theft, Law and Society*, Jerome Hall traced the expansion of theft liability in English law from the fifteenth to the nineteenth century. He explained this expansion as reflecting increasing commerce in moveable goods and, ultimately, in intangible property interests. The expansion of theft perhaps also reflected the rising political and economic strength of the merchant class. In the century following the English Revolution, the newly sovereign Parliament passed many new theft statutes.[10] In his important article *The Metamorphosis of Larceny*, George Fletcher showed that this expansion of theft liability also involved a rather sudden transformation in the structure of liability, reflecting a modern conception of crime itself as the culpable violation of a legal right rather than a manifest breach of the peace.

According to Fletcher, the older model of theft presupposed two principles, which he calls possessorial immunity and manifest criminality. Possessorial immunity meant that an actor lawfully acquiring possession of goods was

5. George Fletcher, *The Metamorphosis of Larceny*, 89 HARV. L. REV. 462, 475–79 (1976); BARRY NICHOLAS, AN INTRODUCTION TO ROMAN LAW 211–12 (2008).
6. 2 FREDERICK POLLOCK & FREDERIC WILLIAM MAITLAND, THE HISTORY OF ENGLISH LAW BEFORE THE TIME OF EDWARD I, at 458 (1898).
7. *Id.* at 494–95.
8. Percy Bordwell, *Property in Chattels*, 29 HARV. L. REV. 501, 505–08 (1916).
9. *Id.*
10. JEROME HALL, THEFT, LAW AND SOCIETY (1935).

immune from criminal liability for misappropriating them. The owner of the goods might have a civil action for recovery of the goods based on a breach of trust, but such dishonesty was a private matter that did not engage the royal interest in peace and order. As Blackstone explained,

> no delivery of goods from the owner to the offender, upon trust, can ground a larceny. As if A lends B a horse and he rides away with him; or if I send goods by a carrier and he carries them away; these are no larcenies.... Neither by the common law was it larceny in any servant to run away with the goods committed to him to keep, but only a breach of civil trust.[11]

Larceny—as felonious theft was called—had to be an unlawful taking from possession. Manifest criminality meant that an unlawful act had to manifest criminality by means of force or stealth to trigger criminal liability. Larceny required not just a taking from possession, but a trespassory taking—an open violation of the will of the owner, traditionally signified by force, or the breach of an enclosure. As theft liability expanded to encompass commercial dishonesty, the concepts of taking and trespass were stretched to the breaking point. Once broken, they seemed nonsensical, and the older conception of criminal law as the enforcement of a royal monopoly on force was forgotten.

Three key cases illustrate the shift: the *Carrier's Case* (1473),[12] *Chisser's Case* (1678),[13] and *Pear's Case* (1779).[14] All had a common structure: A acquired temporary control of moveable property at time 1, with the consent of the owner B; then A misappropriated the property at time 2, in manifest violation of B's will. In each case, there were two obstacles to liability: A could not take possession at time 2 of what he had already acquired at time 1, and A could not steal at time 1 without a trespass. Over the course of these cases, the meaning of trespass shifted from physical violence to a mere violation of consent. Later, trespass ceased to be required at all.

In the *Carrier's Case*, a carrier was hired by a Flemish merchant to deliver bales of dyed cloth to Southampton, but instead took them elsewhere, opened the bales, and hid their contents. The sheriff of London recovered the cloth and seized it as stolen property, forfeit to the Crown. The merchant sued unsuccessfully for recovery of the cloth, arguing that it had not been stolen. The Court of

---

11. 4 William Blackstone, Commentaries on the Laws of England 230 (1765).
12. "The Carrier's Case", (1473) 13 Edw. IV, f. 9, pl. 5.
13. Rex v. Chisser, (1678) 83 Eng. Rep. 142 (K.B).
14. The King v. Pear, (1779) 168 Eng. Rep. 208 (C.C.).

Star Chamber held that the goods had indeed been stolen, but could not agree on a rationale. The problem was that the carrier had possessorial immunity, which precluded the trespassory taking required for larceny.

As explained by Judge Bryan, where "the party has possession by . . . lawful delivery, there cannot . . . be felony or trespass . . .; and there can be no felony except with violence and vi et armis. But such things as he himself holds, he cannot take vi et armis."[15]

Judge Chokke offered the theory that the carrier had only received the bales, but not their contents, so that he took possession of the contents only when he broke bulk. This theory had the implication that he could have sold the unbroken bales without committing theft. Judge Nedeham of the Court of Exchequer offered two theories. One was that the carrier had lawful possession of the goods as a bailee until he violated his instructions by breaking open the bales. This terminated his bailment, causing possession to return to the merchant. According to the other theory, the carrier never had even temporary possession of the cloth, but only custody—just as silverware set on a table by a servant would never leave the possession of a householder. In either case, the carrier took the cloth from the possession of the owner after he broke the bales. Under all of these theories, it seemed that the breaking open of the bales was the violent act supplying the necessary trespass vi et armis.[16] Blackstone later explained this breaking as necessary because it rendered the furtive intent "manifest."[17]

Two hundred years later, Chisser inspected two ties in a clothing shop and then asked their price. Upon hearing it, he offered a lower one, but then ran from the shop, ties in hand. The judge ruled this a larceny, reasoning that he took the goods with felonious intent "for the act subsequent, viz. his running away with them, explains his intent precedent." According to this reasoning, the theft took place at time 1, when the shopkeeper placed the ties in Chisser's hands. Yet theft was impossible at time 1 because there was not yet any trespass, or even any violation of consent. Accordingly, the judge offered a second argument, reasoning that "although these goods were delivered to Chisser by the owner, yet they were not out of her possession by such delivery, till the property should be altered by the perfection of the contract. . .; and when Chisser run away with the goods, it was as if he had taken them up, lying in the shop, and run away with them."[18] This second explanation contradicts the first, by locating the theft at time 2, when he trespassed against the owner's consent

15. "The Carrier's Case", (1473) 13 Edw. IV, f. 9, pl. 5.
16. *Id.*
17. 4 William Blackstone, Commentaries on the Laws of England 230 (1765).
18. Rex v. Chisser, (1678) 83 Eng. Rep. 142 (K.B).

by openly taking the ties from her premises. On this view, the shopkeeper did not consent to Chisser's possession of the ties at time 1, but only his custody.

A century later, a court found larceny on an even more difficult set of facts. Pear hired a horse to go to Sutton, giving a false address. Instead of going to Sutton he proceeded to Smithfield Market and sold the horse. The jury found that Pear had intended to steal the horse when he hired it. A panel of judges concluded that if the defendant's purpose in hiring the horse had been fraudulent, his conduct was larceny. This seemed to locate the theft at time 1, the fraudulent hiring of the horse. Yet the court's explanation located the theft at time 2, the moment of conversion. Because of Pear's fraud, the stable retained possession. Thus, "the parting with the property had not changed the nature of the possession, but . . . it remained unaltered in the [owner] at the time of the conversion; and . . . the prisoner was therefore guilty of felony."[19] The deception of the owner at time 1 vitiated the owner's consent to transfer of possession. Thus Pear's control over the horse after leaving the stable was mere custody, while the stable owner retained constructive possession even though the horse was off his premises and out of his sight. Only when Pear converted the horse by selling it did he take the horse from the owner's possession.

The difficulty with this theory was not only that Pear appeared to have possession of the horse before he sold it, but that it is hard to identify a manifest trespass at time 2. In *Chisser's Case*, we could view Chisser's open defiance of the shopkeeper and his taking of the goods from the premises as the trespassory taking. But Pear took the horse from the stable without open conflict at time 1. The sale at time 2 was a trespass only in the sense that it violated the owner's consent. It made Pear's dishonesty subsequently manifest to a court, but that dishonesty would not have been apparent to a contemporaneous witness.

Perhaps for this reason, *Pear's Case* was quickly reinterpreted. Edward East's 1803 account of the case identified the theft as taking place at time 1, the hiring of the horse. According to East's account, the significance of Pear's fraud was not that it prevented possession from transferring at time 1, but that "fraud supplied the place of force" to provide the necessary trespass at time 1.[20] Yet if fraud can satisfy the element of trespass, trespass has changed meaning, from a manifest breach of the peace to any violation of consent, including one that is surreptitious. East similarly reinterpreted *Carrier's Case* and *Chisser's Case*, shifting the moment of trespassory taking back to the initial acquisition at time 1, with fraud supplying the trespass.[21]

---

19. The King v. Pear, (1779) 168 Eng. Rep. 208 (C.C.).
20. 2 Edward East, Pleas of the Crown 688 (1806).
21. *Id.* at 687, 696–97.

After these developments, larceny acquired a settled definition, in both England and America, as a trespassory taking from the possession of another and carrying away of tangible, moveable property of another, with the intent to permanently deprive the owner of the property and without a claim of right to it. The trespass was now any violation of the consent of the owner to the transfer of possession.[22] The fraudulent acquisition of possession, as in *Pear's Case*, became known as larceny by trick. By the end of the nineteenth century, larceny came to include even finding lost property or receiving mistakenly delivered property with the intention to keep it, providing one knew or believed he could discover the identity of the rightful owner.[23]

These expansions of larceny criminalized some forms of deception. Yet because larceny was confined to the unlawful acquisition of possession, it left other ruses unpunished. Accordingly, Parliament developed three additional forms of theft: theft by false token,[24] theft by false pretenses,[25] and embezzlement.[26]

Suppose that rather than renting the horse, Pear had purchased the horse with a forged bank draft. He could not be guilty of larceny, because—having acquired title along with possession—he would not have taken possession of property of another. Yet he would be liable for the statutory misdemeanor of theft by false token, which required acquisition of property by means of a false token or counterfeit letter. False token was an expansion of the medieval common law misdemeanor of "cheat," which punished use of a deceptive device such as a false measure or crooked dice.[27]

Suppose instead that Pear purchased the horse on credit, giving false information about his identity and address so as to avoid payment of the purchase price or repossession of the horse. As a purchaser, he would again be innocent of larceny. However, he would have been guilty of the statutory offense of theft by false pretenses, which required inducing the owner of property to transfer title by knowingly misrepresenting a material past or current fact with the intent to defraud.

Next, suppose that Pear hired the horse and returned it to a groom employed by the stable—who then sold it, pocketing the proceeds. The groom could not have been guilty of larceny, for he acquired possession of the horse lawfully.

---

22. 2 WILLIAM L. CLARK & WILLIAM L. MARSHALL, A TREATISE ON THE LAW OF CRIMES 649–98 (1900).
23. R. v. Thurborn, (1848) 169 Eng. Rep. 293 (Cr.), State v. Levy, 23 Minn. 104 (Minn. 1876) (finders); The Queen v. Middleton, (1873) L.R. 2 Cr. Cas. Res. 38, Wolfstein v. People, 6 Hun 121 (N.Y. Sup. Ct. 1875) (mistaken delivery).
24. 33 Hen. VIII, c. 1 (1541).
25. 30 Geo. II, c. 24 (1757).
26. 39 Geo. III, c. 85 (1799).
27. R. v. Maddocke, (1619) 2 Roll Rep. 107.

Thus, in *Bazeley's Case*, the defense successfully argued that a bank teller could not commit larceny by pocketing a customer's deposit. The court reasoned that Bazeley (1) acquired possession from the customer without trespass, and (2) could not take possession from the bank because it never acquired possession.[28] In response to that case, Parliament defined the new offense of embezzlement, which required that an employee fraudulently convert (sell or consume) money or goods he received on behalf of his employer. Eventually, embezzlement was broadened to include the fraudulent conversion of property of another by anyone in lawful possession of it. By this definition, if Pear rented a horse in good faith and later sold it, he would be guilty of embezzlement.

In addition to these forms of deceptive misappropriation, theft also came to include coercive misappropriation. This development had a number of sources. The English common law imposed liability for the misdemeanor of extortion on a public official who demanded any payment under color of office that he was not due.[29] Statutes were passed in the sixteenth and eighteenth centuries punishing threats to destroy property unless payment was made.[30] A 1757 statute imposed misdemeanor liability for threatening accusation of certain offenses in order to extort money. Several eighteenth-century cases extended robbery liability for threats to accuse victims of sodomy, or to destroy their homes.[31] In 1843, the English Libel Act defined as a misdemeanor an extortionate threat to expose embarrassing truths.[32] The Larceny Act of 1861 made it a felony to demand money by menace, and by the early twentieth century, this provision had been interpreted to include any threat that would impair consent.[33]

In America, extortionate threats to expose crimes were criminalized by statute in New Jersey in 1796, Kentucky in 1802, Georgia in 1816, and eventually, in almost every state.[34] Illinois extended this in 1827 to threats to expose any embarrassing information, and this eventually became the majority rule.[35] Many statutes eventually included extortionate threats to inflict bodily injury or destroy property, as well.[36]

---

28. Bazeley's Case, (1799) 2 East P.C. 571 (Cr. Cas. Res.).
29. 4 William Blackstone, Commentaries on the Laws of England 141 (Oxford 1765).
30. [1567] Scot. Parl. Acts, ch. 27; 9 Geo. I, ch. 22, § 1 (1722).
31. Rollin M. Perkins & Ronald N. Boyce, Criminal Law 448–49 (1982).
32. Lord Campbell's Libel Act, 1843, 6 & 7 Vict., c. 96, § 3.
33. R. v. Boyle and Merchant, 3 K.B. 339 (K.B. 1914).
34. N.J. Laws ch. 108, § 57 (1796); Ky. Acts 115, §14 (1802); Ga. Laws ch. 178, § 27 (1816); A. Griep, *Comment, Criminal Law: A Study of Statutory Blackmail and Extortion in the Several States*, 44 Mich. L. Rev. 461, 464–65 (1945).
35. Ill. Laws ch. 145, § 108 (1827); Chen Yehudai, *Informational Blackmail: Survived by Technicality?*, 92 Marq. L. Rev. 779, 818 (2006).
36. A. Griep, *Comment, Criminal Law: A Study of Statutory Blackmail and Extortion in the Several States*, 44 Mich. L. Rev. 461, 464 (1945).

The distinctions among larceny, embezzlement, false pretenses, and extortion depended on the blurry lines separating custody, possession, and title, and between deceptive and coercive influence. This created a net with gaps through which malefactors could escape. In *Commonwealth v. O'Malley*, the victim handed O'Malley a wad of bills to count for her. She invited him to take one dollar as a loan, yet he ran off with the entire amount. A jury acquitted him of larceny, likely doubting whether he had formed the intent to steal before receiving possession of the bills with consent. He was then charged and convicted of embezzlement. Yet the conviction was overturned on the ground that having received the funds for a limited purpose in the owner's presence, O'Malley had only custody, not lawful possession. Thus O'Malley escaped liability altogether.[37] In *Norton v. United States*, the defendant demanded support from film star Clark Gable for a child Gable allegedly fathered, although—as Gable knew—he had not been in the country where and when the child was allegedly conceived. The defendant's conviction for attempted fraud was overturned on the ground that the scheme was intended to extort payment through the implied threat of adverse publicity, rather than to induce payment by deceiving Gable.[38]

To prevent a defendant from escaping liability for one theft offense by arguing that he had committed another, the Model Penal Code, and many state codes, consolidated these various offenses into one offense of misappropriation that could be committed in a variety of ways. For example, the Ohio code provides that

> No person, with purpose to deprive the owner of property or services, shall knowingly obtain or exert control over either the property or services in any of the following ways: (1) without the consent of the owner or person authorized to give consent; (2) beyond the scope of the consent of the owner or person authorized to give consent; (3) by deception; (4) by threat; (5) by intimidation.[39]

The Model Penal Code Section 223 provides that "[a]n accusation of theft may be supported by evidence that it was committed in any manner that would be theft under this Article, notwithstanding the specification of a different manner in the indictment or information."[40] Section 223 identifies theft by "unlawful taking" (including "exercis[ing] unlawful control), "deception," "extortion,"

37. Commonwealth v. O'Malley, 97 Mass. 584, 586 (1867).
38. Norton v. United States, 92 F. 2d 753, 755 (9th Cir. 1937).
39. OHIO REV. CODE ANN. § 2913.02 (1993).
40. MODEL PENAL CODE §223.1(1) (1962).

misappropriation of property lost or mistakenly delivered, "receiving stolen property," "theft of services," and "failure to make required disposition of funds received."[41]

Most codes condition all forms of theft on the intent to permanently deprive the owner of property. Thus, joyriding or other intended temporary use without consent is not theft. However, prolonged use of or damage to property that deprives the owner of the bulk of its economic value suffices as permanent deprivation. The mental element of theft often includes knowledge that the goods taken are property of another. This requirement is often described as the availability to the defendant of a "defense" of claim of right. For example, the Model Penal Code permits the defendant to allege that he was unaware the property belonged to another, or honestly believed he was entitled to use it as he did, or took property offered for sale, intending to pay the offered price. If the defendant alleges any of these claims of right, the burden is on the prosecution to disprove it.[42]

IV. Frauds

The acquisition of possession by deception, as in *Pear's Case*, is called larceny by trick. Now that larceny and embezzlement have been combined in most jurisdictions, however, unlawful acquisition of possession is no longer necessary, and possession confers no immunity from theft liability. Accordingly, larceny by trick is no longer an important category of theft. Theft by deception now takes two main forms: theft by false pretenses, and scheme to defraud.

Theft by false pretenses traditionally requires (1) acquisition of title (2) as a result of the owner's reliance on a (3) material (4) misrepresentation (5) of past or current fact (6) made with fraudulent intent. Fraudulent intent here means that the defendant knew her representations were false and intended that these misrepresentations would cause the victim to part with property. These requirements are designed to distinguish such theft from sales or gifts. Consider *People v. Sattlekau*,[43] in which the defendant, identifying himself as one "Ernest Paul," advertised for a hotel housekeeper, offering a "possibility of matrimony." Upon answering the ad, the victim learned that the defendant intended to sell a hotel in Pennsylvania for $6,000 and combine the proceeds with other funds to purchase a hotel in New York City for $20,000. The defendant and the victim

---

41. *Id.* § 223.
42. *Id.* § 223.1(3)
43. People v. Sattlekau, 104 N.Y. S. 805 (1907).

went on several dates, and made plans to marry, whereupon the defendant asked the victim for a short-term loan of $1,000 to enable him to close the transaction. After the victim had given the defendant this money, he telegrammed her that the Pennsylvania Hotel had burned down and that he was ruined. She never heard from him again. Eventually, it was determined that he had lied to her about his identity, his ownership of a hotel, and his other sources of funds. Although he received the funds in the form of a loan, the defendant was guilty of theft because possession of money is treated as ownership. His false promise to marry the victim and his fictional plans to buy a hotel were not seen as misrepresentations of past or present material facts (although one might argue that his intentions regarding the future are present facts). Nevertheless, his identity, his wealth, and his ownership of a hotel were all present facts, and all material in assessing his ability to repay a loan. The defendant argued, however, that the victim might have relied, not on his material misrepresentations, but his false promises; and that the defendant might have intended these false promises to procure the money. Thus he denied that the elements of reliance and fraudulent intent had been proven. Nevertheless the court concluded that the jury had been correctly instructed on reliance and fraudulent intent, and that sufficient evidence of those elements had been presented.

Since the late nineteenth century, federal law has punished an offense consisting of an element establishing federal jurisdiction such as use of the mail, in service of a "scheme or artifice to defraud, or... obtaining money or property by... false... pretenses."[44] In contrast to theft by false pretenses, scheme to defraud is an inchoate offense. It requires fraudulent intent, but does not require successful transfer of property, or actual reliance by any victim. Moreover, it does not require a misrepresentation of past or present fact. In the early case of *Durland v. United States*,[45] the defendant advertised a Ponzi scheme by offering bonds with a promise to pay an ever-increasing return. The defendant had no business or investment plans for raising this money, and made no representation that he did. The defendant was held liable, even though the offending advertisements consisted of nothing more than false promises to pay.[46] On the other hand, a scheme to defraud must target multiple victims or contemplate multiple deceptive transactions. The offense has been characterized as a descendant of the common law offense of cheat, aimed at punishing systematic deception.[47]

---

44. 18 U.S.C. § 1341 (1948).
45. Durland v. United States, 161 U.S. 306 (1896).
46. *Id.* at 315.
47. Courtney Genco, Note, *Whatever Happened to Durland?: Mail Fraud, RICO, and Justifiable Reliance*, 68 NOTRE DAME L. REV. 333, 344–47 (1992).

As with false pretenses, the deception must be "material to the bargain," and the intent must be to inflict economic "injury" in order to count as fraudulent.[48] Thus, in *United States v. Regent Office Supply*,[49] a U.S. Court of Appeals overturned a conviction for scheme to defraud, where stationery supply salesmen falsely claimed (1) to have been referred by friends or business associates of the buyer, or (2) to be doctors or other professionals trying to dispose of unneeded supplies, or (3) to have undertaken to sell unneeded supplies after a death, as a favor to the surviving family members and in order to relieve their economic distress. The court deemed such deceptions immaterial as long as the defendant was honest about the nature of the goods sold and the price charged.[50] The decision may be criticized in two respects. First, most of these misrepresentations were economically material in suggesting that the seller had a motive to offer the goods for less than the prevailing market price. Second, some of the misrepresentations offered altruistic reasons for buying the goods. Either of these considerations might be important to a buyer.

The requirement of a tangible economic injury has been greatly attenuated in cases involving employee corruption. Two key cases were decided in 1987. In *Carpenter v. United States*,[51] a *Wall Street Journal* columnist provided a friend advance information about the content of his influential articles on stocks, enabling the friend to profit by trading in anticipation of the article's expected effects on stock prices. Although it is hard to identify any tangible loss to the *Journal* or to any particular investor from this scheme, the Supreme Court upheld a scheme-to-defraud conviction. Rather than candidly basing liability on the columnist's breach of a fiduciary duty to his employer, the Court offered the strained rationale that the *Journal* had a "property interest" in the content of the columns as "confidential business information."[52] In *McNally v. United States*,[53] the Supreme Court ruled that corrupt state and local officials could not commit a scheme to defraud by, for example, accepting a bribe to route a highway or to site a government facility in one place or another. To constitute fraud, the corrupt decision would have to cause the public fiscal loss, rather than merely deprive the public of its "intangible right to honest government."

Congress responded to these cases in 1988 by defining scheme to defraud as including "a scheme or artifice to deprive another of the intangible right to honest services."[54] The courts applied this statute to punish the acceptances of

48. United States v. Regent Office Supply, 421 F. 2d 1174, 1182 (2d Cir. 1970).
49. *Id.* at 1176.
50. *Id.* at 1182.
51. Carpenter v. United States, 484, U.S. 19 (1987).
52. *Id.* at 26–27.
53. Mcnally v. United States, 483 U.S. 350 (1987).
54. 18 U.S.C. § 1346 (1988).

bribes by public or private employees, regardless of whether it occasioned any financial loss to the employer. Thus, in *United States v. Rybicki*, a U.S. court of appeals punished a scheme whereby lawyers would bribe insurance adjusters to expedite resolution of their claims, even though there was no evidence that they resolved them any more favorably, or that the practice cost the insurance company any money.[55]

On the other hand, the Supreme Court sharply limited "honest services" fraud in a trio of cases decided in 2010. In *Skilling v. United States*, the court overturned convictions for an Enron executive who had maintained the price of company stock by inflating earnings, in order to maintain his high compensation, and the value of his own holdings. The Court reasoned that punishing any conduct beyond outright bribery would violate due process requirements of specificity.[56] On the basis of this decision, the Court held that self-dealing by a corporate officer could not be punished as honest services fraud.[57] Finally, the Court also implied that a conflict of interest on the part of a public official falling short of actual bribery could not be punished as a scheme to defraud.[58]

V. Extortion

In ordinary language, "extortion" is taken to mean gaining something to which one is not entitled by means of coercion. "Coercion" is generally thought of as inducement to do something by physical compulsion or a threat. It is common to say that a threat communicates a conditional intention to harm, in contrast to an offer, which communicates a conditional intention to benefit. Yet thus defined, the concept of threat is no more determinate than the concept of harm itself. Does the collection of a debt inflict harm? Does one jeweler harm another by locating across the street? Does one romantic partner harm another by ending a relationship? In all these cases, we are uncertain whether anyone has been made worse off by losing something they value, but to which they were not entitled. Thus, we are uncertain whether a proposal to deprive someone of something to which he or she is not entitled is a threat or an offer. Hence, we cannot be sure whether combining such a proposal with a request

55. United States v. Rybicki, 354 F. 3d 124 (2d Cir. 2003).
56. Skilling v. United States, 130 S. Ct. 2896 (2010).
57. Black v. United States, 130 S. Ct. 2963 (2010).
58. Weyrauch v. United States, 130 S. Ct. 2971 (2010).

for something to which the proposer is not entitled is wrongful extortion or permissible bargaining.

This uncertainty leads to a problem in moral and legal philosophy known as the "paradox of blackmail." We can easily identify conditional proposals to disadvantage others in legal ways that intuitively seem extortionate, and that are criminally punished. This surely includes "informational blackmail"—threats to expose guilty secrets, such as crimes, private breaches of faith, or facts damaging to reputation. Somewhat more controversially, this includes "spite blackmail"—threatening any act expected to lower another's utility without raising the actor's utility. Still more controversially, it might include "opportunistic blackmail"—using monopoly power over particularly desperate buyers to charge very high prices. The question raised by these various forms of blackmail is how two legal acts—lawfully disadvantaging another, and requesting money—can become illegal upon being combined.[59]

A great variety of "solutions" have been offered to this problem. Legal economists William Landes and Richard Posner view blackmail based on threats to expose crime as a form of private law enforcement, and argue that it deters less effectively than state punishment.[60] This conclusion is not obvious: supplementing public punishment with private punishment would seem to raise the overall certainty of punishment, and so the effectiveness of deterrence. If, however, we assume that public punishment deters primarily through denunciation, condoning cover-ups would undermine deterrence as well as retribution. In any case, Landes and Posner's theory is deficient in leaving other forms of blackmail unexplained.

James Lindgren provides a general account of informational blackmail as a form of corruption, in which the blackmailer misappropriates another party's power to harm the target.[61] On Lindgren's theory, the true victim of blackmail is not the target, but the third party—law enforcement, the deceived spouse, potential employers—denied access to the information. Yet in many cases of informational blackmail, the third party—perhaps a general public titillated by scandal—has no real right to the information. Moreover, Lindgren's corruption theory does not explain what is wrong with spite blackmail or opportunistic blackmail.

Leo Katz argues that blackmail requires that the threatened act be immoral even if legally permissible.[62] Katz's theory accounts for opportunistic blackmail

---

59. James Lindgren, *Unraveling the Paradox of Blackmail*, 84 COLUM. L. REV. 670 (1984).
60. William Landes & Richard Posner, *The Private Enforcement of Law*, 4 J. LEGAL STUD. 1, 42 (1975).
61. James Lindgren, *Unraveling the Paradox of Blackmail*, 84 COLUM. L. REV. 672 (1984).
62. Leo Katz, *Blackmail and Other Forms of Arm-Twisting*, 141 U. PA. L. REV. 1567 (1993).

and spite blackmail. From the standpoint of utilitarian ethics, any spiteful act is immoral by definition. Katz's theory accounts well for threats to expose embarrassing but noncriminal acts. Yet it has some difficulty accounting for the core case of blackmail, the threat to expose a crime, which is presumably a laudable rather than an immoral act. He would have to respond that the spiteful motive for informing on the target would render doing so immoral even if it would benefit society. The real difficulty with Katz's theory is that it leaves undefined the moral criteria needed to distinguish blackmail from lawful bargaining.

George Fletcher proposes a moral standard for distinguishing extortionate from permissible bargains: a proposed act is extortionate if it infringes the equal dignity of persons by enabling the blackmailer to "dominate" the target.[63] The difficulty with this standard is that all bargaining is coercive insofar as it exploits economic demand to force others to give more and accept less than they otherwise would.

Extortion offenses take two forms in American law: (1) acquisition of something of value by means of a threat (that does not suffice for robbery), and (2) the solicitation of bribes by public officials.

A revealing example of the first category is the case of *People v. Dioguardi*.[64] Two different locals of the Teamsters Union attempted to organize workers at the same shipping company by establishing picket lines, thereby shutting down the company's operations (as delivery drivers refused to cross these lines). The company could not satisfy the demands of both locals and so could not remove both obstacles. Officers of the company were then approached by a Teamsters Union official who promised that both locals would desist if the company made substantial payments to each local and made monthly payments thereafter to a "consulting firm" that would effectively guarantee labor peace. The Teamster's official and others were convicted of extortion. The conviction was overturned on appeal on the ground of insufficient evidence that the defendants were responsible for the picketing by the locals. The New York Court of Appeals reinstated the charges (while awarding a new trial), on the ground that the defendant did not have to inflict harm on the victim, but merely to have the power to prevent harm and to threaten to remove it. Thus, the Court effectively held that extortion includes opportunistic blackmail as well as spite blackmail. Yet the decision is problematic in imposing causal responsibility for an omission to prevent harm without a legal duty to do so. If the defendants

---

63. George Fletcher, *Blackmail: The Paradigmatic Crime*, 141 U. PA. L. REV. 1617 (1993).
64. People v. Dioguardi, 203 N.Y.S. 2d 870 (1960).

truly had not been responsible for the picketing, it is not clear why they should not expect compensation for ending it.

Although the offenses of blackmail and soliciting bribes have completely different origins, they have considerable overlap. Consider four possible circumstances in which an official solicits a bribe. The official: (1) threatens to illegally exercise an official power to the detriment of another, perhaps to arrest the other unlawfully, unless paid; (2) threatens to legally exercise an official power to the detriment of another, perhaps to arrest an obviously guilty suspect, unless paid; (3) offers to exercise official discretion to award another a benefit for which the other is eligible, but has no right to, perhaps a government contract; (4) offers to exercise an official power to provide a benefit to another who is legally ineligible for it, if paid. The first case is clearly extortion in the ordinary language sense of theft by coercion. The fourth is clearly not: the officer is offering to benefit the other, and the only victim of the official's conduct is the public, which has been deprived of the official's honest service. The second might be thought extortionate because the demand for payment renders the otherwise lawful arrest unlawful. The third might be thought extortionate on the ground that the victim is being deprived of an opportunity to fairly compete for a benefit.

The federal Hobbs Act, by its terms, simply punishes "extortion" including "the obtaining of property from another, with his consent . . . under color of official right."[65] Initially, federal courts included solicitation of bribes by public officials only when accompanied by a threat to inflict harm.[66] Today, federal courts punish solicitation or acceptance of bribes, even if the bribes are paid willingly.[67] Yet if there is no extortionate threat, liability generally requires an explicit conditioning of a benefit on payment. Thus, Robert McCormick was a West Virginia legislator who had supported legislation relaxing licensing criteria for foreign doctors, because of his concern about a persistent shortage of doctors in his district. A lobbyist for these doctors approached him about extending this legislation, and he made plans to propose such an extension in the next session. During his re-election campaign, McCormick contacted the lobbyist and asked for money. He pointed out that his campaign was expensive, that he had paid campaign expenses out of his pocket, and that he had received no contributions from the foreign doctors. As a result of this discussion, the lobbyist delivered several envelopes of cash from the foreign doctors (which

65. 18 U.S.C. § 1951(a), 18 U.S.C. § 1951(b)(2) (1948).
66. United States v. Addonizio, 451 F. 2d 49 (3d Cir. 1971).
67. United States v. Kenny, 462 F. 2d 1205 (3d Cir. 1972).

were not reported as campaign contributions). In reversing a conviction under the Hobbs act, the Supreme Court concluded that

> [w]hatever ethical considerations and appearances may indicate, to hold that legislators commit . . . extortion when they act for the benefit of constituents or support legislation benefitting some of their constituents, shortly before or after campaign contributions are solicited and received from those beneficiaries, is an unrealistic assessment of what Congress could have meant by "extortion under color of official right."[68]

The Court required either the explicit offer of a quid pro quo, or a threat, for a request for a campaign contribution to be considered extortion.

VI. Robbery and Burglary

Robbery was a frequent ground for appeal of felony from the inception of that practice.[69] Blackstone defined robbery as requiring the "felonious and forcible taking from the person of goods or money to any value, by putting him in fear."[70] Thus, he conceptualized robbery as larceny plus the additional elements of the (1) presence of the victim, and (2) violence or the threat of violence to his person.

Modern law has maintained this basic conception of robbery as aggravated theft. Thus, the mental element of robbery includes the mental element of larceny: the intent to permanently deprive another of property, without a claim of right. Robbery does not generally require that this intention to steal accompany the use of force. Thus, an assailant who takes advantage of his victim's prostration by helping himself to the victim's possessions is usually guilty of robbery.[71] In this sense, robbery is fundamentally a theft aggravated by violence, rather than an assault aggravated by a larcenous purpose.

The Model Penal Code defines robbery as the infliction or threat of serious bodily injury, or the threat of some other very serious offense such as kidnapping, rape, or arson, "in the course of committing a theft."[72] The Code defines "the course of" theft as including both attempted theft and flight with the stolen goods. A similar result was reached in *Coleman v. State*, when the Indiana

---

68. McCormick v. United States, 500 U.S. 257, 272 (1991).
69. 2 Frederick Pollock & Frederic William Maitland, The History of English Law before the Time of Edward I, at 494 (1898).
70. 4 William Blackstone, Commentaries on the Laws of England 241 (1765).
71. Wayne LaFave, Criminal Law 1060 (2010).
72. Model Penal Code § 222.1(1962).

Supreme Court affirmed the robbery conviction of a shoplifter who brandished a knife only upon being confronted by a store manager after exiting the store. The court concluded that the taking continued while the defendant remained in the presence of persons in charge of the store.[73]

A crucial question in the law of robbery concerns the degree of force or threat required. The prevailing view is that the force required for robbery is more than that required for physically removing the object stolen from the person or presence of the victim. Thus, in *Lear v. State*, the defendant's robbery conviction was overturned, where he grabbed a bag of silver out of the hands of a shopkeeper with no additional violence. The court held that the force required for robbery had to be sufficient to overcome or preclude resistance.[74] Thus pocket-picking and purse snatching are not robbery. Where the defendant acquires by threat rather than force, courts must determine how explicit the threat must be. Many cases arise in which the defendant simply demands money from a teller or cashier without an explicit threat or the display of a weapon. In the Maryland case of *Spencer v. State*, the court overturned a conviction on the ground that a reasonable person would not understand the phrase "don't say nothing" to constitute a threat.[75] On the other hand, an earlier decision in *Dixon v. State* upheld a robbery conviction where the defendant merely demanded money with a rolled-up newspaper and a "cold, hard look."[76]

Burglary was not one of the original grounds for appeal of felony enumerated in the Assize of Clarendon. It seems to have grown out of an earlier offense of robbery in the home and to have achieved no stable form in the medieval period.[77] Coke defined it as breaking and entering the house of another at night with the intent to commit a felony, whether or not the felony was committed.[78] In this sense, burglary may be seen as an inchoate offense, a primitive form of attempt liability. The attempted crime was usually theft, but might be any felony.

Modern statutes often expand burglary in two ways. First, just as the law of theft reconceived trespass as a violation of consent rather than a use of force, burglary statutes have replaced the required breaking with a violation of consent. Second, they often expand the mental element from the intent to commit a felony to the intent to commit any crime. The Model Penal Code's provision defines burglary as entering "a building or occupied structure, or separately

73. Coleman v. State, 653 N.E. 2d 481 (Ind. 1995).

74. Lear v. State, 39 Ariz. 313 (1931).

75. Spencer v. State, 30 A. 3d 891, 898–99 (Md. 2011).

76. Dixon v. State, 488 A. 2d 962, 970 (Md. 1985).

77. 2 Frederick Pollock & Frederic William Maitland, The History of English Law before the Time of Edward I, at 493 (1898).

78. Edward Coke, Third Part of the Institutes of the Laws of England 67 (1644).

secured occupied portion thereof, with purpose to commit a crime therein, unless the premises are . . . open to the public or the actor is privileged to enter."[79] Under the Model Penal Code's default culpability rules, the actor must probably be reckless with respect to the lack of privilege to enter. Burglary is aggravated to a higher grade if committed in a dwelling at night, or if the defendant recklessly inflicts or attempts to inflict injury, or is armed with a deadly weapon.[80]

Although most burglary prosecutions arise from theft-motivated break-ins, burglary liability can also be imposed for illegal entries for purposes of crimes against persons. Because penalties for burglary are high, burglary liability is a powerful means of deterring and punishing domestic violence. Often the penalty for burglary is much higher than the penalty for assault. Yet its application in this context poses several thorny issues. First, intra-familial and other domestic violence can destabilize living arrangements, creating ambiguity as to whether an assailant is a cohabitant or invitee who is privileged to enter the victim's home. Even if the assailant's entry is deemed unprivileged, the assailant may lack sufficient awareness that he is entering without privilege to satisfy the mental element of burglary.[81] This difficulty is avoided when a victim of domestic abuse has won an order of protection, providing notice to the potential assailant that he is excluded from the home. Yet this situation poses a further difficulty. If the estranged domestic partner enters in violation of the order, he has entered illegally and also committed the offense of violating the order. Is this burglary? A Minnesota court determined that it was not: the illegal entry and the violation of an order precluding entry merged.[82] Yet if an order precludes both entry into the home and contact with the victim, entering to talk to the victim would constitute burglary. This possibility poses a further difficulty concerning proportionality of punishment. A protective order is a prophylactic against violence, but an offender can often violate such an order without committing or intending an act of violence. Although the penalties for violating a protective order are generally slight, the penalties for burglary can be considerable: up to 20 years incarceration in Minnesota. Should the potential assailant face such a penalty for merely violating a prophylactic rule?

This last issue reflects a larger problem with the offense of burglary. Burglary is an inchoate offense, punishing an attempt to commit another crime, with unlawful entry as a means to that goal. Ordinarily the penalty for attempting an offense correlates with, and falls somewhat below, the penalty for the completed

---

79. MODEL PENAL CODE § 221.1(1) (1962).
80. *Id.* § 221.1(2).
81. State v. McMillan, 973 A. 2d 287 (2009).
82. State v. Colvin, 645 N.W. 2d 449 (2002).

offense. Yet the penalty for burglary does not depend on the penalty for completing the intended offense, and may greatly exceed that penalty. Civilian jurisdictions have no such crime, instead simply adding a small penalty for trespass to property to the penalty for committing or attempting another crime. Some scholars have accordingly argued that burglary liability should be abolished.[83]

VII. The Emergence of Rape Liability

Before sexual assault was recognized as a breach of the king's peace or an attack on a particular victim, it was treated primarily as an offense against the interests of families in controlling kinship and property. In the early medieval period, heads of households sought justice for the abduction of marriageable women, regardless of their consent. After the assizes of Clarendon, sexual assaults were proceeded against in one of two ways. They might be prosecuted by the Crown as a trespass, or by the victim, by means of appeal of felony. The penalty for trespass was a payment or imprisonment, while the felony could lead to death or maiming. Pollock and Maitland report that appeals of rape were rarely successful. Some were settled by marriage between the parties.[84] According to Bracton, appeals of felony required the complainant to report the crime immediately, display wounds or torn clothing, and repeat her story consistently on several occasions. The accused might defend himself by alleging consent. Bracton also reported that the penalty varied with the marriageability of the victim, with the greatest penalties if she was a virgin of high birth; less for a wife, widow, or nun; and still less for a concubine or prostitute.[85] In the late thirteenth century, the Statutes of Westminster extended the period for appeals of felony, and provided two years imprisonment as the penalty for the trespass procedure, and death as the penalty for the felony. These offenses applied to any who would "ravish or take with force" any woman "against her will," whether or not a "maiden," or any girl "within age" regardless of her consent.[86]

Little is known about how these statutes were enforced in ensuing centuries. In the sixteenth century, benefit of clergy was excluded for rape.[87]

---

83. Wayne LaFave, Criminal Law 1079–81 (2010).
84. 2 Frederick Pollock & Frederic William Maitland, The History of English Law before the Time of Edward I, at 490–91 (1898).
85. 2 Henry De Bracton, On the Laws and Customs of England 414–15 (Samuel E. Thorne transl., 1968).
86. Statute of Westminster the First, 1275 c. 5 (Regnal. 3 Edw. 1); Statute of Westminster the Second, 1285 c. 1 (Regnal. 13 Edw. 1).
87. 18 Eliz. I, c. 7 (1576).

Seventeenth- and eighteenth-century treatises agreed on the contours of the offense: it required unlawful "carnal knowledge" of a female above the age of 10 by force and against her will.[88] The most common view was that this required penile penetration of the vagina. The requirement of "unlawfulness" referenced Hale's assertion that husbands could legally force sexual intercourse upon unwilling wives.[89] Hale, in a passage later incorporated into jury instructions, also warned that "rape . . . is an accusation easily to be made and hard to be proved, and harder to be defended by the party accused, tho never so innocent."[90] He proposed a variety of corroborating circumstances, such as the victim's good reputation, contemporaneous outcry, and physical injuries, without which the jury might presume her testimony "false or feigned."[91]

Seventeenth century Massachusetts statutes provided that "whosoever shall . . . have carnal copulation with any . . . [woman] Childe under ten years old. . . he shall be put to death,"[92] and "[i]f any man shall ravish any maid or single woman, committing carnal copulation with her by force, against her will, that is above the age of ten years, he shall be either punished with death, or with some other grievous punishment."[93]

Several questions are raised by the common law's traditional definition of rape. First, what is meant by "against her will:" that the act was unwanted, expressly objected to, or physically resisted? Second, what is meant by "force?" Can unwanted sexual penetration be other than forcible? If something additional is required, what must it be? Third, no culpable mental state is mentioned. Yet the offense is severely punished. Is a culpable mental state therefore required implicitly? The ensuing sections examine how these questions were answered in English and American law.

VIII. The Requirement of Resistance

It appears that eighteenth-century English courts treated rape as requiring not only unwillingness on the part of the victim, but also physical resistance.[94]

---

88. Edward Coke, The Second Part of the Institutes of England 180 (1642); 1 Matthew Hale, History of Pleas of the Crown 628 (1736); William Hawkins, A Treatise of the Pleas of the Crown 108 (1716); 4 William Blackstone, Commentaries on the Laws of England 210 (1765); 1 Edward East, Pleas of the Crown 43–44 (1803).
89. 1 Matthew Hale, History of Pleas of the Crown 629 (1736).
90. *Id.* at 635.
91. *Id.* at 633.
92. The Laws and Liberties of Massachusetts (1672) 16 (1669)
93. *Id.* at 15 (1649).
94. Bruce MacFarlane, *Historical Development of the Offence of Rape*, *in* 100 Years of the Canadian Criminal Code (Richard C.C. Peck & Josiah Wood eds., 1993).

Thus, in a 1751 case, the defendant was acquitted although the complainant protested that she was terrified and had "no power" to resist.[95] Another defendant was acquitted for raping his 12-year-old daughter because she only resisted verbally rather than physically, and acquiesced when he threatened to stop visiting her.[96] In the American colonies, vigorous prosecution of fornication and adultery exposed rape complainants to the risk of criminal liability unless they could prove they were blameless for the unlawful sexual intercourse.[97] Indeed, noting that fornication was the largest category of criminal cases in pre-revolutionary New England, Professor Anne Coughlin has argued that claims of rape often arose as exculpatory claims of duress during the colonial period, and so were viewed skeptically.[98]

During the nineteenth century, two conceptions of rape contended with one another. One conception defined rape as requiring force overcoming the will of the victim. On this view, force meant something like what it meant in the context of robbery. Carnal knowledge without consent was a trespass, like that involved in purse-snatching or pickpocketing, and constituted a battery. Like robbery, however rape required additional force, sufficient to overcome or prevent resistance. On the other hand, as Professor Coughlin has pointed out, rape differed from robbery in the important respect that it excused the victim from criminal liability for consensual nonmarital sex. To perform this exculpatory function the force had to do more than interfere with the victim's freedom—it had to extinguish it entirely.[99] Many courts therefore interpreted "by force and against her will" as requiring unyielding physical resistance.

An alternative view of rape interpreted "against her will" as meaning simply "without consent." The traditional requirement of force might refer simply to the force inherent in nonconsensual sexual penetration. Overcoming physical resistance was not necessary to the offense, but was simply one way of violating consent. Consent could also be violated by exploiting unconsciousness, insanity, mental impairment, youth, and possibly even deception or intoxication.

This more expansive view of rape achieved currency in England by the late nineteenth century. Thus, the 1845 decision in *R. v. Camplin* upheld the conviction of a defendant who had sexual intercourse with a 13-year-old girl whom he had gotten drunk.[100] An 1859 decision upheld a rape conviction for

---

95. R. v. Adkins, Old Bailey proceedings, no. 532 (Sept. 11, 1751).
96. R. v. Sherwin, Old Bailey proceedings, no. 129 (Jan. 13, 1779).
97. Anne Coughlin, *Sex and Guilt*, 84 VA. L. REV. 1, 44–46 (1998); CORNELIA HUGHES DAYTON, WOMEN BEFORE THE BAR: GENDER, LAW & SOCIETY IN CONNECTICUT, 1639–789 (1995)
98. Anne Coughlin, *Sex and Guilt*, 84 VA. L. REV. 1, 44 (1998).
99. *Id.* at 29.
100. R. v. Camplin, (1845) 1 Cox C.C. 220.

sexual intercourse with a mentally disabled 13-year-old. Chief Judge Lord Campbell wrote:

> The question is, what is the proper definition of the crime of rape? Is it carnal knowledge of a woman against her will, or is it sufficient, if it be without the consent of the prosecutrix? If it must be against her will, then the crime was not proved in this case; but if the offense is complete where it was by force and without her consent, then the offense was proved . . .[101]

A decision imposing rape liability for intercourse with a sleeping victim followed in 1872.[102] Rape liability was also imposed for sexual intercourse achieved by impersonating the victim's husband,[103] or pretending to probe with an instrument during a medical examination.[104]

By contrast, American courts often insisted that rape required force and utmost resistance. An 1838 New York decision invoked Hale in concluding that

> Any fact tending to the inference that there was not the utmost reluctance and the utmost resistance, is always received. That there was not an immediate disclosure, that there was no outcry, though aid was at hand. . . , that there are no indications of violence to the person, are . . . circumstances . . . throwing distrust upon the assumption that there was a real absence of assent, 1 Hale, P. C., 633.[105]

An 1856 California decision used identical language in overturning a conviction for failure to allow evidence of the 13-year-old complainant's "lewd acts" with other men.[106] An 1877 Connecticut decision reasoned that "carnal knowledge by force and nonconsent thereto . . . are essential elements, and the jury must be fully satisfied of their existence by the resistance of the complainant, if she had the use of her faculties and physical powers at the time, and was not prevented by . . . the exhibition of brutal force."[107] An 1879 Wisconsin decision found resistance insufficient if it ended at any point during the crime:

> if the woman resist, but finally consent, no offense is committed. . . . voluntary submission of the woman, while she has power to resist, no

101. R. v. Fletcher, (1859) 8 Cox C.C. 131, 134.
102. R. v. Myers, (1872) 12 Cox C.C. 311.
103. R. v. Case, (1850), 1 Den. 580.
104. R. v. Flattery, (1877), 2 Q.B.D. 410.
105. People v. Abbott, 19 Wend. 192, 194–95 (1838).
106. People v. Benson, 6 Cal. 221 (1856).
107. State v. Shields, 45 Conn. 256, 264 (1877).

> matter how reluctantly yielded, removes from the act an essential element of rape . . . If the carnal knowledge was with the voluntary consent of the woman, no matter how tardily given, no matter how much force had theretofore been employed, it is no rape.[108]

An 1897 Georgia decision agreed: "She must have resisted with all her power and kept up that resistance as long as she had strength."[109]

This utmost resistance standard effectively required that non-consent be manifested continuously, throughout the assault. The 1874 New York decision of *People v. Dohring* overturned a conviction for raping a 14-year-old victim on the grounds of insufficient resistance. The court commented:

> The resistance must be up to the point of being overpowered by actual force . . . or . . . there must be fear of duress or death. . . . Certainly if a female . . . remaining conscious, does not use all her own powers of resistance and defense . . . and does yield before being overcome by greater force, or by fear, or being surrounded by hostile numbers, a jury may infer that, at some time in the course of the act, it was not against her will. . . . Can the mind conceive of a woman . . . revoltingly unwilling that this deed should be done upon her, who would not resist so long and hard as she was able? And if . . . she does not, must it not be that she is not entirely reluctant?[110]

Such skepticism about the sincerity of non-consent could become insurmountable when combined with medical testimony that penetration of a resisting victim was physically impossible.[111] Thus ineffectual resistance became evidence of consent. A 1906 Wisconsin decision overturned a conviction where the complainant professed to have screamed and struggled to escape, and to have been forcibly silenced and held in place. The court noted

> [W]e cannot conceive it possible that one whose mind and exertions had . . . been set on resistance, . . . would in narrative mention nothing but escape or withdrawal. . . . [S]he is equipped to interpose most effective obstacles by means of hands and limbs and pelvic muscles. Indeed, medical writers insist that these obstacles are practically insuperable in absence of more than the usual relative disproportion of age and strength

108. Conners v. State, 47 Wis. 523, 527 (1879).
109. Matthews v. State, 29 S.E. 424, 426 (Ga. 1897).
110. People v. Dohring, 59 N.Y. 374, 384 (1874).
111. Susan Edwards, Female Sexuality and the Law 122–26 (1981).

> . . . In addition to the interposition of such obstacles is the ability and tendency of reprisal, of counter physical attack. It is hardly within the range of reason that a man should come out of so desperate an encounter as the determined normal woman would make necessary, without signs thereof on his face, hands, and clothing. . . . Resistance is opposing force to force, not retreating from force.[112]

The requirement of force overcoming resistance disqualified other forms of non-consent. A Michigan court explained that sexual intercourse with an insane woman was not rape, which required "not only that there should be force, but that the utmost reluctance and resistance on the part of the woman, should appear."[113] On the same reasoning, a doctor could not attempt rape by telling his 15-year-old patient that submitting to sexual intercourse was medically necessary.[114] An Alabama court held that a fraudulent marriage ceremony did not make the subsequent intercourse rape,[115] while courts in North Carolina and Tennessee denied that husband impersonation could be rape.[116] An Arkansas court held rape did not include sexual intercourse with a sleeping—and therefore unresisting—victim.[117] In all these cases, the requisite force and resistance were missing.

The utmost resistance standard persisted into the twentieth century.[118] As late as 1975, the New York decision of *People v. Yanik* reaffirmed the standard. The court overturned a conviction in which the victim verbally refused the defendant's invitation to spend the night, the defendant threw the victim on the bed and got on top of her, the victim kicked the defendant, and the defendant then punched the victim in the nose and tore her dress, before proceeding with sexual intercourse. The court rejected the trial court's instruction even though it quoted the statutory definition of "forcible compulsion" as "physical force that overcomes earnest resistance, or a threat either expressed or implied, that places a person in fear of either death or a serious physical injury." Citing *Dohring*, it required an instruction that "forcible compulsion" must overcome utmost resistance.[119]

---

112. Brown v. State, 127 Wis. 193, 199–200 (1906).
113. People v. Crosswell, 13 Mich. 427, 433 (1865).
114. Don Moran v. People, 25 Mich. 356 (1872).
115. State v. Murphy, 6 Ala. 765 (1844).
116. Wyatt v. State, 2 Swan 394 (Tenn. 1852); State v. Brooks, 76 N.C. 1 (1877).
117. Charles v. State, 11 Ark. 389 (1850); *but see* Commonwealth v. Burke, 105 Mass. 376 (1870).
118. Model Penal Code Commentaries, pt. II, § 213, at 304n. (1980).
119. People v. Yanik, 55 A. 2d 164, 167–68 (1975).

This decision provoked criticism from feminist groups, who argued that this standard placed rape complainants on trial and added insult to injury by blaming victims for causing their own rapes. The New York legislature concluded that a requirement of utmost resistance forced women to take unnecessary risks as the price of legal protection. The legislature passed a statute explicitly rejecting the utmost resistance standard in favor of a reasonable resistance standard, "so that the amount of resistance must be proportional to the attack, [considering factors] such as the relative strength of the parties and the futility of resistance."[120] Applying this standard in *People v. Dorsey*, a New York upheld the conviction of a 200-pound teen who trapped a much smaller middle-aged woman in an elevator and ordered her to undress, even though she did not resist and he made no explicit threat (until after the sexual assault ended). The court reasoned that a threat of violence was implicit, and that resistance was futile and hazardous, and held that she was not obliged to determine what he would do if she refused his demands.[121]

Yet a reasonable resistance standard still can acquit a defendant who forces sex by means of violence or threats, because of insufficient resistance. Thus, in *State v. Powell*, a Louisiana court overturned a conviction where the complainant testified that she asked the defendant for a ride to the nearby home of her cousin, whereupon he drove her to a secluded location, slapped her repeatedly, claimed he was armed, and threatened to kill her unless she submitted to sex acts. The court noted that she was uninjured, and ruled that she was unreasonable in concluding that resistance would have been futile.[122] An unstated premise of the opinion appears to be that the complainant could have most effectively resisted sexual intercourse at time 2 by not getting into the defendant's car at time 1. Yet surely consent to a ride is not consent to sex, any more than it is consent to part with one's wallet.

The distinction between the *Dorsey* and *Powell* cases illustrates a claim made by legal scholar Susan Estrich: that regardless of the legal standard adopted, legal decision-makers view rape complaints more skeptically when the accused is an acquaintance of the complainant. Moreover, complainants often feel intense social pressure not to incriminate members of their social circle. These effects combine to suppress reporting of rapes by acquaintances,[123] although victim studies indicate that rapes by acquaintances outnumber rapes by strangers by a factor of three or four to one.[124] The traditional focus on

---

120. N.Y. State Legislation, ch. 692, § 2 (1977).
121. People v. Dorsey, 429 N.Y.S. 2d 828 (1980).
122. State v. Powell, 438 So. 2d 1306 (La. App. 1983).
123. Susan Estrich, *Rape*, 95 Yale L.J. 87, 88, 92–93 (1986).
124. U.S. Department of Justice, Criminal Victimization 9 (2010).

stranger rapes can be seen as a legacy of the medieval conception of criminal law as enforcing peace in public, while leaving private households unregulated. This conception of criminal law proved inadequate to protect property in a market society premised on commercial exchange. It is equally inapt for protecting sexual autonomy in a liberal society of social equals.

IX. Reform Standards: Force or Non-consent?

The drafters of the Model Penal Code saw the resistance requirement as fundamentally misguided in focusing on the behavior of the victim rather than the offender. Given the Code's aim of identifying and treating dangerous persons, it seemed that punishment should not depend on victim behavior, or even on harm to a victim. The drafters understood the resistance requirement as an objective index of non-consent, required by courts in order to overcome the difficulty of proving a subjective mental state. Yet they saw the violation of consent as harm to the victim, and so irrelevant. What mattered was whether the defendant had behaved dangerously, and how dangerously. Indeed, the drafters adopted a fashionably Freudian view of sexual desire as omnipresent but repressed, so that consent to sex was ultimately indeterminate, and reported violations of consent were unreliable:

> emphasis . . . upon the nonconsent of the victim as opposed to the overreaching of the actor . . . would compress into a single statute a diversity of conduct ranging from "brutal attacks to half won arguments . . . in parked cars." . . .[O]ften the woman's attitude may be deeply ambivalent. She may not want intercourse, may fear it, or may desire it but feel compelled to say "no." Her confusion at the time may later resolve into nonconsent. Some have expressed the fear that a woman who subconsciously wanted to have sexual intercourse will later feel guilty and "cry rape."[125]

Based on this thinking, the Code eliminated non-consent as an element of sexual offenses, instead criminalizing various acts achieved by means of force, coercion, incapacity, or fraud. The drafters were also convinced that the high penalty and stigma imposed for rape made judges and juries reluctant to convict. This combination of excessive severity and low certainty undermined the

---

125. MODEL PENAL CODE COMMENTARIES, pt. II, § 213, at 302–303 (1980) quoting Comment, *Forcible and Statutory Rape: An Exploration of the Operation and Objectives of the Consent Standard*, 62 YALE L.J. 55, 67, 74, 82 (1952).

deterrent effect of rape laws. In response to these concerns, the Code set forth a graded hierarchy of sexual offenses defined by the conduct of the accused, without regard to a victim's subjective mental state.

Section 213.1 defined felonies of three degrees. Second degree rape involved sexual penetration (1) by force; (2) by threat of serious injury, extreme pain, or kidnapping; (3) by intoxication of the victim without her knowledge for the purpose of preventing resistance; (4) of an unconscious victim; or (5) of a victim under 10. First degree rape added to the elements of second degree rape one of two aggravating circumstances: (1) the offender inflicted serious injury, or (2) the victim had neither consented to associate with the offender at the time, nor previously consented to sexual contact with the offender. The third degree felony was not called rape, but "gross sexual imposition." It consisted of sexual intercourse (1) by means of a "threat that would prevent resistance by a woman of ordinary resolution," (2) with knowledge the victim is mentally ill, or (3) with knowledge the victim believed she was not having sex or mistakenly believed the sexual partner was her husband.[126] All these offenses excluded liability for husbands and domestic partners. Conviction was precluded if a rape was not reported within three months or if the victim's testimony was uncorroborated. In addition, juries were to be instructed to view victim testimony skeptically "in view of the emotional involvement of the witness and the difficulty of determining the truth with respect to alleged sexual activities carried out in private."[127]

Today, almost all jurisdictions impose rape liability for sexual penetration by force. A significant minority have followed the Model Penal Code in ceasing to require the additional element of non-consent. Courts in jurisdictions of both kinds have generally rejected any requirement of resistance. In 1980, California replaced its statutory language requiring resistance overcome by force and violence with a requirement of force and non-consent. In the subsequent case of *People v. Barnes*, the California Supreme Court explained this reform as motivated by the recognition that resistance can be dangerous and passivity can reflect fear rather than consent. The accused prevented the victim from leaving his home by blocking her way, shouting, arguing, raising his fist, and pointing out his strength. Becoming afraid, the victim allowed the assailant to hug and kiss her. When she refused to remove her clothes, he threatened to become angry, whereupon she disrobed and submitted to sexual intercourse. The Court upheld the conviction despite the lack of resistance, or even an explicit threat.[128]

---

126. Model Penal Code § 213.1 (1962).
127. *Id.* § 213.6.
128. People v. Barnes, 42 Ca. 3d 284 (1986).

Yet other courts have read the requirement of force as requiring resistance. In the North Carolina case of *State v. Alston*, the complainant had lived with the accused despite his physical abuse, but finally moved out one time after he struck her. A month later the accused came to her school, grabbed her, demanded to know where she was living, and threatened to "fix her face." He then demanded that they have sex. The complainant accompanied him to the house of a mutual friend. The complainant expressed that she did not want to have sex, but Alston undressed her and had sexual intercourse with her, while she cried. The North Carolina Supreme Court overturned Alston's conviction, even though acknowledging that the victim expressed the requisite non-consent, and submitted because of her fear that Alston would hurt her. The court reasoned that Alston did not employ force or threats of violence at the time of the sexual intercourse to overcome her resistance.[129]

Susan Estrich's influential 1986 article "Rape" drew on *Alston, Powell* and similar cases, in critiquing the Model Penal Code's approach to reforming rape law. Such cases illustrated persistent social attitudes trivializing rapes by acquaintances of the victim, particularly in the context of courting. Such attitudes treated consent to companionship as implying consent to sex, presumed that fear of violence from an acquaintance was unwarranted, and reflected worry that men might be severely punished for innocently misinterpreting women's desires. The Model Penal Code arguably embraced such attitudes in denying that women knew their own minds, and in treating forcible sexual penetration by a stranger as more harmful and less likely to be consensual than the same conduct committed by a "voluntary social companion" or a former lover.[130]

Estrich observed that as a result of such attitudes, standards requiring resistance or injuries were more likely to be applied in favor of an accused who was an acquaintance of the victim. By contrast, when the accused was a stranger, the assailant's violent intentions and the victim's non-consent were presumed. For these reasons, Estrich predicted that juries applying a force standard would likely not see a date as using force or threat without evidence of physical resistance, weapons, or injuries.

Estrich concluded that a standard permitting assailants to knowingly violate the consent of victims as long as they did not explicitly threaten violence was unacceptable. Yet she reasoned that fact-finders would only be willing to punish—and could only fairly punish—date rape if liability were conditioned on culpability with respect to non-consent.[131] Thus she proposed a reasonable

129. State v. Alston, 312 S.E.2d 470 (N.C. 1984).

130. MODEL PENAL CODE COMMENTARIES, pt. II, § 213, at 307 (1980).

131. Susan Estrich, *Rape*, 95 YALE L.J. 1087, 1098–101 (1986).

notice standard. One would be liable if he sexually penetrated a victim who had made her non-consent apparent to a reasonable observer. "If reasonableness is defined . . . according to a rule that 'no means no' . . . it is not unfair to hold those men who violate the rule criminally responsible."[132] Persistence in the face of verbal resistance or other manifest non-consent would be negligent per se.[133]

A well-known decision adopting Estrich's approach is the Connecticut case of *State v. Smith*.[134] The complainant met the accused at a bar through mutual friends, and returned with him to his apartment, although expecting her friends to join them. When the accused hugged and kissed her, she said "I really don't want to do anything." When he persisted and held her down, she tried to push him off, spat in his face, and said "you're a big man to have to force a woman." He replied that he could make it hard for her or she could make it easy on herself. She then allowed him to perform sexual intercourse. Smith was convicted under a statute punishing compulsion to engage in sexual intercourse by force or the threat of force that would reasonably cause a person to fear physical injury. The defendant argued that the conviction was not supported by sufficient evidence of the victim's non-consent, or sufficient evidence of the defendant's knowledge of her non-consent. The Connecticut Supreme Court conceded that the prosecution was obliged to prove the culpable violation of consent as part of its burden of proving compulsion, but denied that this entailed proving the mental state of either victim or assailant. Instead, non-consent was an objective circumstance:

> The law of contract has come to recognize that a true "meeting of the minds" is no longer essential to the formation of a contract and that rights and obligations may arise from acts of the parties, usually their words, upon which a reasonable person would rely. . . . Similarly, whether a complainant has consented to intercourse depends upon her manifestations of such consent as reasonably construed.[135]

Accordingly, the court required that "the state must prove beyond a reasonable doubt that the conduct of the complainant would not have justified a reasonable belief that she had consented."[136] The court concluded that the prosecution had met that burden: "only by entertaining the fantasy that 'no' meant 'yes'

132. *Id.* at 1104.
133. *Id.* at 1104–05.
134. State v. Smith, 210 Conn. 132 (1989).
135. *Id.* at 140.
136. *Id.* at 141.

... could the defendant believe that T's behavior ... indicated consent."[137] The *Smith* decision is sometimes described as requiring proof that the accused disregarded the victim's expressed objections. In fact, it requires only proof that the accused proceeded without the victim's express permission.[138]

With greater explicitness, the New Jersey decision of *In re M.T.S.* also defined rape as sexual penetration without objectively manifest consent. The offense charged was sexual penetration by force or coercion. According to the New Jersey Supreme Court, "the juvenile, a seventeen year old boy, engaged in consensual kissing and heavy petting with a fifteen year old girl and thereafter engaged in actual sexual penetration of the girl to which she had not consented. There was no evidence or suggestion that the juvenile used any unusual or extra force or threats to accomplish the act of penetration."[139] The court upheld the defendant's juvenile conviction, reasoning that physical force is inherent in sexual penetration without consent. The court characterized such penetration as a battery, an unauthorized touching. The New Jersey court treated consent as a communicated authorization.

The New Jersey court characterized the applicable statute, passed in 1978, as a reform statute, intended to eliminate the disadvantages traditionally facing rape victims. According to the court, the New Jersey legislature rejected the Model Penal Code approach in favor of a model endorsed by the National Organization for Women.[140] According to the court, "[r]eformers ... shared the goals of facilitating rape prosecutions and sparing victims ... degradation .... Some ... advocated ... defining rape as unconsented-to intercourse; others urged the elimination of any reference to consent.... Nonetheless, all ... shared a central premise: that the burden of showing non-consent should not fall on the victim of the crime."[141]

The court interpreted the statute's lack of "any reference to the victim's will or resistance" as reflecting an aim to prevent guilt from being conditioned on the victim's mental state or behavior. The court concluded that

> [A]ny act of sexual penetration engaged in by the defendant without the affirmative and freely given permission of the victim ... constitutes the offense of sexual assault. Therefore, physical force in excess of that inherent in the act of sexual penetration is not required for such penetration to be unlawful. The definition of physical force ... is satisfied if the

137. *Id.* at 143.
138. *Id.* at 142.
139. *In re* M.T.S., 129 N.J. 422, 425 (1992).
140. *Id.* at 439–41.
141. *Id.* at 438.

> defendant applies any . . . force. . . in the absence of what a reasonable person would believe to be affirmative and freely given permission. . . . Permission to engage in an act of sexual penetration can be . . . indicated through physical actions rather than words. Permission is demonstrated when the evidence . . . is sufficient to demonstrate that a reasonable person would have believed that the alleged victim had affirmatively and freely given authorization to the act.[142]

The court was explicit that rape law should reform rather than reflect existing norms of sexual conduct and communication:

> The role of the factfinder is not to decide whether reasonable people may engage in acts of penetration without the permission of others. The Legislature answered that questions when it enacted the reformed sexual assault statute: reasonable people do not engage in acts of penetration without permission, and it is unlawful to do so. The role of the factfinder is to decide . . . only whether the defendant's belief that the alleged victim had freely given affirmative permission was reasonable.[143]

In contrast to the rule adopted by Connecticut and New Jersey, defining non-consent as the absence of expressed permission, New York has adopted a definition of non-consent as expressed objection. Rape in the third degree is defined as sexual intercourse where "the victim clearly expressed that he or she did not consent to engage in such act, and a reasonable person in the actor's situation would have understood such person's words and acts as an expression of lack of consent to such act under all the circumstances."[144] This is a true "no means no" rule, where the Connecticut and New Jersey rules might better be characterized as a "yes means yes" rule.

Before leaving our analysis of the act element of rape in contemporary law, we should note some other common reforms. Today, the marital exemption has been uniformly abandoned for forcible rape. Most jurisdictions have created similar protections against sexual assault for both men and women, either by defining sexual assault in gender-neutral terms and encompassing (usually penetrative) sex acts beyond vaginal intercourse, or by creating parallel crimes of forcible sodomy. Courts seldom instruct juries to be skeptical of complainant testimony. Few jurisdictions require corroboration or prompt complaints.

---

142. *Id.* at 444–45.
143. *Id.* at 448.
144. New York Penal Law § 130.05(2)(d) (2000), § 130.25(3) (2000).

Rape shield laws prevent defense attorneys from questioning complainants about past sexual activity with partners other than the defendant, absent some unusual circumstance making such evidence relevant.

X. The Mental Element of Rape

The divergent conceptions of the conduct required for rape in England and America were accompanied by divergent standards of culpability.

As English courts increasingly conceptualized rape as a violation of consent, they considered the problem of the assailant's mistaken belief in consent. In two mid-nineteenth century cases, judges instructed juries that rape required an intent to have sexual intercourse by force and against the victim's will.[145] In *R. v. Flattery*, one of the judges suggested that a reasonably mistaken belief in consent would acquit.[146] In *R. v. Tolson*, Judge Stephen opined that "mens rea means ... in the case of rape, an intention to have forcible connection to a woman, without her consent."[147] Nevertheless, the decision in this case (which concerned bigamy rather than rape) exculpated only reasonable mistakes about circumstance elements. Thus, by the start of the twentieth century, English law conditioned rape on negligence toward non-consent.

The required culpability was increased to recklessness in 1976, in the controversial case of *D.P.P v. Morgan*. This decision upheld the conviction of three men who attacked a protesting and struggling woman at the invitation of and with the cooperation of her husband. Yet it held erroneous the trial judge's instruction that the defendants should be convicted if they honestly, but unreasonably believed the victim consented. A majority of the court held that a proper jury instruction would have required them to be at least indifferent as to whether the victim consented (and concluded that a properly instructed jury would have so found).[148] This recklessness standard was incorporated into the statute defining rape later that year, but a 2003 reform restored a mental element of negligence.

Nineteenth-century American courts drew their definitions of rape from common law treatises, which identified no required mental state. Moreover, as a victim's utmost resistance made non-consent manifest, and as overcoming such resistance manifestly required force, the utmost resistance standard obviated proof of culpability. By the end of the nineteenth century, American

145. Reg. v. Stanton (1844) 1 Car. & K. 415; Reg. v. Wright (1866) 4 F. & F. 967, 968.
146. R. v. Flattery, (1877) 2 Q.B.D. 410.
147. R. v. Tolson, (1889) 23 Q.B.D. 168, 185.
148. D.P.P. v. Morgan, (1976) A.C. 182.

lawyers had given almost no thought to the problem of mistake regarding consent.[149] As late as 1982, a leading American criminal law treatise did not address the question at all.[150]

The Model Penal Code uses culpability terms in defining some sexual assault offenses. Rape includes sexual intercourse by intoxicating the victim for the purpose of overcoming resistance. The third degree felony of gross sexual imposition includes sexual intercourse knowing the victim is insane, or is unaware that she is having sexual intercourse with someone who is not her husband. Crimes mentioning no mental element include sexual intercourse by forcible compulsion, with an unconscious victim, or by means of a "threat that would prevent resistance by a woman of ordinary resolution." None of these crimes require culpability with respect to non-consent, because non-consent is not an act element. However, they require application of the recklessness default rule to the objective elements of forcible compulsion, unconsciousness, and preventing resistance.[151] Ohio also punishes forcible rather than nonconsensual sexual intercourse, but requires more culpability. Rape requires purposeful compulsion to engage in various sex acts by force or threat, whereas "sexual battery" requires knowingly coercing the other person to submit to such acts by means preventing resistance by a person of ordinary resolution.[152]

Most American jurisdictions require non-consent, even if they also require force. In 1975, California became the first American jurisdiction to require proof of culpability with respect to non-consent. In *People v. Mayberry* the California Supreme Court held that rape requires negligence with respect to the victim's non-consent—even though the California rape statute at that point still required force overcoming or preventing resistance. The court reasoned that the California Penal Code requires a union of act and intent or criminal negligence for every crime, and that as the intent or negligence must be wrongful, the relevant intent or negligence was not merely to have sexual intercourse, but to violate consent. The court added that the high penalty and stigma imposed by a rape conviction precluded the inference that the legislature had intended to except rape from this general requirement of culpability. Accordingly, a defendant testifying that he believed the victim consented was entitled to a jury instruction that a reasonable belief that the victim consented would acquit the defendant.[153] This remains the law in California, now that resistance is no longer required.

---

149. 1 William L. Clark & William L. Marshall, A Treatise on the Law of Crimes 636–48 (1900).
150. Rollin Perkins & Ronald Boyce, Criminal Law 197–212 (1982).
151. Model Penal Code Commentaries, pt. II, § 213, at 313, 319 (1980)
152. Ohio Rev. Code Ann. § 2907.02(A)(2) (1972); Ohio Rev. Code Ann. § 2907.03(A)(1) (1972).
153. People v. Mayberry, 15 Cal. 3d 143 (1975).

Few other American jurisdictions require culpability with respect to non-consent. Some courts explain this by describing rape as a "general intent offense" so that intent is required only for the act of sexual intercourse, but not the additional circumstance of non-consent.[154] This seems acceptable if the conduct element requires violence on the part of the assailant, or resistance on the part of the victim, making the non-consent of the victim obvious. Fulfilling the act element then implies culpability toward non-consent. Yet reformers have rightly criticized act elements requiring victims to resist physically or endure injury before they can vindicate their rights in court. Can rape still be a "general intent" crime once reformers have redefined it simply as nonconsensual sexual intercourse? Without some culpability toward non-consent, it is hard to see how intentional intercourse could merit blame and punishment. On this basis, Susan Estrich concluded that the elimination of the requirement of force should be legitimated by the introduction of a requirement of culpability.[155]

The Alaska Supreme Court saw reform of the act element of rape as necessitating expansion of the mental element of rape in conditioning rape on reckless disregard of non-consent. The court concluded that the legislature, having "enhanced the risk of conviction . . . by eliminating the requirement that the state prove 'resistance'" had "counteracted this risk through its treatment of mens rea."[156] The statute made lack of consent a "'surrounding circumstance' which under the Revised Code, requires a complementary mental state. . . ."[157] Because no mental state was mentioned in the offense definition, the court assigned the statutorily required default mental state of recklessness.

In redefining force as the absence of affirmatively expressed consent, the New Jersey Supreme Court added a requirement of negligence with respect to this absence. The court reasoned that when "the State does not allege . . . force extrinsic to the act of penetration, the factfinder must decide whether the . . . penetration was undertaken in circumstances that led the defendant reasonably to believe that the alleged victim had freely given affirmative permission . . . ."[158] The court added that "[i]f there is evidence to suggest that the defendant reasonably believed that such permission had been given, the State must demonstrate either that defendant did not actually believe that

---

154. People v. Langworthy, 416 Mich. 630, 643–45 (1982); People v. Witte, 115 Ill. App. 3d 20 (1983).

155. Susan Estrich, *Rape*, 95 YALE L.J. 1087, 1094–132.

156. Reynolds v. State, 664 P. 2d 621, 625.

157. *Id.*

158. *In re* M.T.S., 129 N.J. 422, 447-448 (1992).

affirmative permission had been freely-given or that such a belief was unreasonable under all of the circumstances."[159] Courts in Connecticut and New York adopted similar requirements of negligence regarding the victim's non-consent. However, both courts resisted calling the required unreasonableness a mental element, for fear that defendants would argue they were too intoxicated to notice the victim's expression of her preferences.[160]

In Pennsylvania, legislative reform of the act element of rape created uncertainty about the mental element of rape. In 1972, Pennsylvania adopted a criminal code closely based on the Model Penal Code. It conditioned rape on forcible compulsion, or threat of forcible compulsion that would prevent resistance by a person of reasonable resolution. Pennsylvania's provisions on culpability were almost identical to the Model Penal Code's—requiring a culpable mental state of intent, knowledge, recklessness, or negligence corresponding to all elements, and requiring recklessness in default of a statutorily specified mental state.[161] In the 1982 case of *Commonwealth v. Williams*, a Pennsylvania appellate court defined the force required for rape confusingly as whatever was necessary "to establish lack of consent and to induce the woman to submit."[162] The court rejected an instruction on reasonable mistake regarding consent, on the ground that rape was not defined by the statute as including any element of belief regarding consent.[163] The court made no reference to Pennsylvania's recklessness default rule, and referred to rape as an offense of general intent.

In the 1986 case of *Commonwealth v. Rhodes*, the Pennsylvania Supreme Court applied the rape statute to an adult who had molested a compliant eight-year-old child, reasoning that forcible compulsion included "not only physical force or violence, but also moral, psychological, or intellectual force," which could encompass exploitation of a child's trust and deference to adult authority.[164] In the 1994 case of *Commonwealth v. Berkowitz*, however, the court reversed the conviction of a college student who fondled, undressed, and sexually penetrated another student in his dorm room while she repeatedly objected. The court acknowledged that the victim had not consented, but reasoned that force required "something more than a lack of consent."[165] In reaction to criticism of this decision, the legislature—rather than redefining rape as sexual intercourse

159. *Id.* at 448.
160. People v. Newton, 8 N.Y. 3d 460, 463–65 (2007); State v. Smith, 210 Conn. 132, 138.
161. 18 Pa. C. S. § 302(a)(c) (1972).
162. Commonwealth v. Williams, 294 Pa. Super. 93, 97 (1982).
163. *Id.* at 100.
164. Commonwealth v. Rhodes, 510 Pa. 537, 555 (1986).
165. Commonwealth v. Berkowitz, 641 A. 2d 1161, 1165 (Pa. 1994).

without consent—defined "forcible compulsion" to include "intellectual, moral, emotional or psychological force, either express or implied."[166]

In the 1998 case of *Commonwealth v. Fischer*, another college student was convicted of rape after a dormitory encounter in which he held a fellow student's arms over her head and forced his penis into her mouth. This followed a consensual sexual encounter between the two earlier in the day. The defendant appealed, arguing that his attorney provided ineffective assistance in failing to request an instruction on reasonable mistake regarding consent. Citing Pennsylvania's recklessness default rule, an appellate court agreed that an instruction on mistake would be warranted in a case without physical resistance. However, the court denied that the instant case met this requirement, and also denied that failure to request an instruction could be ineffective assistance of counsel before any court had ruled that the instruction was required.[167] Pennsylvania courts have expressed uncertainty as to whether a mistake instruction must now be given in some cases.[168]

If rape is defined simply as nonconsensual sexual intercourse, there are some constitutional considerations in favor of requiring some culpability with respect to non-consent. Recall that Professor Alan Michaels read the classic Supreme Court cases of *Lambert v. California*[169] and *Smith v. California*[170] to imply that each offense must include culpable conduct that is constitutionally punishable.[171] Intentional sexual intercourse alone does not satisfy this test. At one time, sex acts outside of marriage were regarded as constitutionally punishable, so that it might be argued that the circumstance of non-consent merely aggravated the already criminal conduct of fornication. In criticizing the *Morgan* decision, George Fletcher argued that intimate sex acts are invasions that should, like surgeries, be considered presumptively unlawful unless justified by consent.[172] After *Lawrence v. Texas*, however, consensual sex acts with adults in private are not constitutionally punishable. The *Lambert* principle implies that an offense of nonconsensual sexual intercourse can only be punished with proof of culpability with respect to the circumstance rendering the sexual intercourse constitutionally punishable—non-consent.

166. 18 PA. C. S. § 3101 (1995).
167. Commonwealth v. Fischer, 721 A. 2d 1111 (Pa. Super. 1998).
168. Commonwealth v. Hairston, 2014 Pa. Dist. & Cty. Dec. LEXIS 147.
169. Lambert v. California, 355 U.S. 225 (1957).
170. Smith v. California, 361 U.S. 147 (1959).
171. Alan Michaels, *Constitutional Innocence*, 112 HARV. L. REV. 828 (1999).
172. GEORGE FLETCHER, RETHINKING CRIMINAL LAW 698–707 (1978).

XI. Rape by Incapacity, Extortion, and Fraud

We have examined standards designed to punish offensive sexual penetration. Yet nonconsensual sexual penetration can also occur because the victim lacks the capacity to authorize it, or has been coerced or deceived.

Incapacity can be based on unconsciousness, mental incapacity, or age. Sex acts with an unconscious victim are punished severely: almost all states grade it at the same level as forcible rape, as does the Model Penal Code.[173] Some describe the relevant state in cognitive terms as unawareness, while others describe it in motor terms as physical helplessness. There is variation as to whether a culpable mental state is required with respect to unconsciousness. As the Model Penal Code specifies no mental state with respect to unconsciousness, the default requirement of recklessness applies. Perhaps half the states require knowledge, with substantial minorities requiring negligence and not requiring any mental state.

When we turn to mental disabilities short of unconsciousness, it is useful to divide these into enduring disabilities and temporary intoxication. Typically, sexual intercourse based on insanity, retardation, or other mental disability is punished as a lesser grade of offense. Most states require negligence with respect to the disability, while some require knowledge. The disability is certainly significant enough to trigger liability if it prevents understanding that sexual intercourse is occurring. Yet disability can also trigger liability if it impairs the victim's evaluation of sexual intercourse. A number of states retain a marital exemption for this form of sexual assault.

Almost all jurisdictions criminalize sexual penetration achieved by means of the intentional involuntary intoxication of the victim. This is commonly graded on par with forcible rape, and sometimes it is simply included within forcible rape by judicial interpretation. On the other hand, sexual intercourse with a partner who is voluntarily intoxicated but conscious and able to express her preferences is generally not criminalized, even when it is apparent that the intoxication has impaired evaluative judgment. The Model Penal Code Commentaries argued that because consumption of alcohol and drugs is a "common. . . ritual of courtship" that inherently risks "intoxication and insensibility," it would be "unrealistic and unfair to assign to the male total responsibility for the end result."[174] Defendants have sometimes offered intoxication as evidence of consent, or justification for their belief that the victim consented.[175]

---

173. MODEL PENAL CODE § 213.1(1) (1962).
174. MODEL PENAL CODE COMMENTARIES, pt. II, §213.1, at 315 (1980).
175. Karen Kramer, *Rule by Myth*, 47 STAN. L. REV. 115 (1994).

The most frequently charged form of sexual assault by incapacity involves an underage partner. Typically this form of offense is divided into two or three grades. Most codes will have a relatively minor offense requiring sexual intercourse with a partner in the age range of around 14 to 16, when the offender is at least three or four years older than the victim. A more severe offense will apply to sexual intercourse with younger victims, and sometimes there is a highly aggravated offense involving victims under 10 or 11.

In contrast to other forms of incapacity, age is typically a strict liability element. The traditional rationale for this was that because fornication was unlawful, the conduct was already culpable, and the victim's youth was just an aggravating circumstance. With the reconceptualization of this type of sexual assault as a crime against autonomy rather than morality, this rationale failed. Accordingly, the Model Penal Code required proof of negligence with respect to age, except for the aggravated sexual assaults predicated on the victim being under 10.[176] For these very young victims, the traditional rationale for strict liability still applied: even if the offender reasonably believed the victim was 10, his intended conduct was still highly culpable. After promulgation of the Code, a number of states began to require negligence, or to afford the defendant an affirmative defense of reasonable mistake.[177]

Although sexual abuse of young children is investigated systematically and prosecuted vigorously, sexual intercourse with older teens is prosecuted selectively. Prosecutors are more likely to pursue such charges where the difference in age between sexual partners is greater, or where the suspect has abused a position of trust or authority. According to some observers, prosecutors often use "statutory rape" charges as substitutes for forcible rape charges where they believe sexual intercourse was nonconsensual but lack compelling evidence, or to force a guilty plea and spare the victim a trial.[178]

Another increasingly important category of rape by incapacity is based on the relational statuses of assailant and victim. Thus, custodians of prisons and mental institutions are sometimes liable for sex with inmates. In some jurisdictions medical care-givers, psychotherapists, and even pastors can be criminally liable for sex with persons they are treating or counseling. Parents, foster-parents, guardians, and teachers of adolescents may face liability that exceeds that applied for statutory rape. All of these status offenses involve exploitation of authority, and in this sense are premised more on coercion than

---

176. Model Penal Code §1.12(2)(a), § 213.6 (1) (1962)..
177. People v. Hernandez, 61 Cal. 2d 529 (1964); State v. Guest, 583 P. 2d 836 (Alaska 1978).
178. Michelle Oberman, *Turning Girls into Women: Reevaluating Modern Statutory Rape Law*, 85 J. Crim. L. & Criminology 15 (1994).

on incapacity to consent. Like bribery, however, these offenses are punished not only as violations of the consent of victims, but also as corruptions of office that endanger the public interests for which authority is granted.

A status of incapacity to consent may be seen as a prophylactic rule to guard against coercion or deception, as well as to ease proof. In many instances, the exploitation of a vulnerable or dependent victim may combine coercion and deception with the betrayal of trust. Nevertheless, prosecutions for inducing participation in sex by means of nonviolent coercion or deception are rare, and codes do not uniformly proscribe such conduct. No doubt fraud and extortion are difficult to define precisely, but this does not preclude American law from doing so in the context of theft.

The Model Penal Code proscribes sexual intercourse achieved by some kinds of deception. Thus, gross sexual imposition includes sexual intercourse with knowledge that the victim "is unaware that a sexual act is being committed upon her or that she submits because she mistakenly supposes that ... [the accused] is her husband."[179] The controversial California decision in *Boro v. People*[180] illustrates this approach, and its disadvantages.

Impersonating a doctor, Boro called the victim to tell her that blood tests had revealed that she had contracted a life-threatening and highly infectious disease, which would require health officials to warn all of her friends and contacts. Boro explained that the disease could only be cured in one of two ways: through painful and ruinously expensive surgery and hospitalization, or by having sexual intercourse with a medicated "donor," for which she would have to pay a much smaller sum. She met Boro at a motel, gave him the requested funds, and had sex with him. Boro was charged under a provision criminalizing sexual intercourse with a partner "unconscious of the nature of the act." The charge was quashed on the basis that Boro had only deceived the victim about reasons to have sexual intercourse, not about the nature of the act. The court distinguished this case from the earlier case of *People v. Minkowski*, in which a physician disguised sexual intercourse as a probe with a gynecological instrument, inserted for the ostensible purpose of treating menstrual cramps.[181] Such fraud in the fact sufficed for rape, whereas Boro's fraud in the inducement did not. The court added that the California code treated husband impersonation as fraud in the fact, because it conceals the nature of the proposed act as unlawful adultery. Impersonation of a nonmarital sexual partner

179. Model Penal Code § 213.1(2) (1962).
180. Boro v. People, 210 Cal. Rptr. 122 (1985).
181. People v. Minkowski, 204 Cal. App. 2d 832 (1962).

would not have been rape on the view that the identity of the partner is merely an inducement, but not essential to the act.

In reaction against this decision, the California Penal Code today specifies that the victim is unconscious of the nature of the act when the perpetrator fraudulently misrepresents sexual intercourse as serving a professional purpose.[182] The code also now defines rape as including sexual intercourse induced by the defendant's impersonation of anyone known to the victim.[183] Although the vast majority of American jurisdictions criminalize sex with an unconscious victim, only a minority use California's broader formulation, including deception as to the nature of the act. Instead, to punish acts such as Minkowski's, they must rely on general provisions against sex by force, or specific provisions punishing sexual exploitation of patients. Few would punish Boro for sexual assault, as opposed to theft by false pretenses.

Today, most American codes condition sexual assault on some forms of coercion. Some states proscribe sex acts accomplished by threats of "retaliation," which is usually defined narrowly to include future violence or abduction. Others proscribe sex coerced by threats of arrest or other adverse official conduct. A few states punish sex acts achieved by abuse of supervisory or disciplinary authority. Presumably the latter category would include sexual demands by employers. The Model Penal Code proscribed coerced sex generally, defining "gross sexual imposition" as including "[compulsion] to submit by any threat that would prevent resistance by a woman of ordinary resolution."[184] The Model Penal Code Commentaries elaborated:

> Examples might include threat to cause her to lose her job or to deprive her of a valued possession. This provision . . . rests on the judgment that using one's ability to cause harm in order to override the will of a reluctant female is wrongful and should be punished. . . . Yet there are obvious dangers in extending the prospect of criminal sanctions into the shadow area between coercion and bargain. To take an extreme example, the man who "threatens" to withhold an expensive present unless his girlfriend permits his advances is plainly not a fit subject for punishment under the law of rape.[185]

---

182. CAL. PENAL CODE, § 261(4)(D) (1986).
183. *Id.* § 261(5).
184. MODEL PENAL CODE § 213.1(2)(a) (1962).
185. MODEL PENAL CODE COMMENTARIES, pt. II, § 213.1(2)(a), at 312 (1980).

Some states have followed the Code's approach. Ohio defines sexual battery as sexual penetration coerced "by any means that would prevent resistance by a person of ordinary resolution."[186] New Jersey proscribes sex acts compelled by "coercion," defined to include threats to accuse of crime, expose a secret, testify or withhold testimony in a legal proceeding, or inflict any harm without benefitting the actor.[187] Pennsylvania's convoluted rape provision punishes sexual intercourse "by forcible compulsion" or "threat of forcible compulsion that would prevent resistance by a person of reasonable resolution," where "force" includes "physical, intellectual, moral, emotional or psychological force, either express or implied."[188]

This Pennsylvania statute was adopted in light of criticism of earlier decisions, including a case involving coercion, *Commonwealth v. Mlinarich.*[189] Mlinarich pressured his 14-year-old foster daughter into repeated sex acts by threatening to have her confined in a juvenile detention center. The Court concluded that forcible compulsion included "psychological duress," as in the *Rhodes* case, where an adult easily influenced a small child. However, the court distinguished this from "appeals to the intellect and morals of the victim."[190] The court reasoned that, although the option of return to detention was "repugnant" to the victim, she was "left with a choice and therefore the submission was a result of deliberate choice and was not an involuntary act."[191] The prosecution argued that such a threat—coming from a guardian—was one that a 14-year-old could not reasonably be expected to resist. The court responded that the "person of reasonable resolution" was an objective standard, while minors were sufficiently protected from exploitation by the lesser offense of statutory rape. The legislature added the otherwise cryptic terms "moral" and "intellectual" force to the statute in part to punish conduct like Mlinarich's as rape.

One decision following the Model Penal Code's approach is *Lovely v. Cunningham.*[192] This federal decision upheld a New Hampshire conviction under a statute punishing sex coerced by threats of retaliation, defined as including "threats of future physical or mental punishment, kidnapping, false imprisonment, extortion or public humiliation or disgrace."[193] Lovely paid a homeless man for work he did not perform, provided him lodging, and paid

---

186. 29 OHIO REV. CODE ANN., § 2907.03(A)(1972)
187. N.J.STAT. ANN. 2(c):14:2(c)(1) (1978).; N.J. STAT. ANN. 2(c):13-5(a) (1978).
188. 18 PA. C. S. § 3101, §3121 (1995).
189. Commonwealth v. Mlinarich, 518 Pa. 247 (1988).
190. *Id.* at 252.
191. *Id.*
192. Lovely v. Cunningham, 796 F. 2d 1 (1st Cir. 1986).
193. N.H. REV. STAT. § 632-A:1 (1975).

restitution for a theft he committed. He then pressured the victim to perform sex acts by threatening to fire him, kick him out of his house, sue him for debt, and perhaps make trouble for him with the police. Lovely appealed his conviction on the ground that the statute was unconstitutionally vague and that its application to his conduct would retroactively expand it. The First Circuit Court of Appeals disagreed, finding that the threats to fire the homeless man and make legal trouble for him amounted to more than a threat to "withhold an expensive present" and thereby satisfied the Model Penal Code's test. Yet that test is indeterminate insofar as it incorporates the Commentaries' express ambivalence about sexual bargaining. Accordingly, we might wonder whether the statute would have been applied in the same way if the victim had been female, and the coerced sex had been heterosexual.

Application of the concepts of fraud and coercion to sexual assault reflects the redefinition of sexual assault as a crime against autonomy rather than a crime against morals. In applying these transactional concepts to sexual assault, however, courts and legislatures constantly confront the anxiety that they are "assigning to the male total responsibility" for an immoral bargain. Perhaps for this reason, they seem to prefer incapacity rules, which forbid sexual assault by forbidding certain victims from having sex.

XII. Conclusion

The prohibition and punishment of theft and rape help define important institutions. With the emergence of a liberal society, theft and rape were redefined as attacks on the entitlements of individuals to make autonomous choices. This was reflected in a decreased emphasis on manifest violence and an increased emphasis on the culpable violation of consent, for offenses of both kinds. In the development of each offense, a requirement of forcible trespass was reinterpreted as a violation of consent. Eventually, the law recognized that such violations of consent can be accomplished by such diverse means as intimidation, fraud, coercion, or the exploitation of incapacity, as well as physical force. Nevertheless, this transformation began earlier and has been accomplished more thoroughly in the law of theft than in the law of rape. Unfortunately, in the law of rape, the requirement of force persists explicitly, and the requirement of resistance persists implicitly. This implicit requirement of resistance is most influential in discouraging prosecution and punishment of "acquaintance rapes," which we now know are more common than "stranger rapes."

EIGHT

Anticipatory and Participatory Liability

I. Introduction

This chapter examines doctrines that attribute liability for an offense to an actor who has not fulfilled all of its objective elements. These doctrines impose anticipatory liability for trying to commit crimes, or participatory liability for helping to commit crimes. The first category includes the inchoate offenses of attempt, solicitation, and conspiracy to commit some other offense. The second category consists primarily of liability for another's offense as an accomplice, but also includes liability as a co-conspirator, a perpetrator by means, or a supervisor.

Attempts generally require a purpose of completing a crime, and at least some substantial conduct in pursuit of that purpose. Depending on the jurisdiction the conduct must corroborate or manifest the intent to complete the crime, or create a danger of completing the crime, or constitute part of the conduct required for the crime, or constitute all of the conduct without achieving the result. Solicitation requires a purpose that a crime be committed, and an invitation or command to someone else to commit the offense. Conspiracies generally require an agreement with one or more persons that one of the parties will commit a crime, and sometimes require some conduct in pursuit of that goal, but less than would be required for an attempt.

These offenses are "inchoate offenses" in that (1) they all have one or more inchoate elements, subjective elements without a corresponding objective element; and (2) the occurrence of the "missing" objective element would transform these offenses into another offense—a "completed" offense. Thus, inchoate offenses are thought of as incomplete offenses, "included" within other completed offenses. Ordinarily an inchoate offense "merges" with the completed offense so that one cannot be punished for both. Yet, as we shall see, the status of conspiracy as an inchoate offense is contested or problematic—sometimes offenders are punished for conspiracies and also for offenses in furtherance of the conspiracy. Sometimes conspiracies are not considered to be "included" within complete offenses.

Complicity in an offense generally requires that one aids or encourages someone else to commit the offense, with the purpose that they commit it. The accomplice is then liable for the offense committed by the perpetrator. A perpetrator by means, acting with the culpability required for the offense, induces a person to commit the conduct required for an offense, although that person either lacks the culpability required for the offense or has an excuse. The perpetrator by means is also liable for the offense. Some jurisdictions classify this way of offending as a form of complicity. Co-conspirator liability makes conspirators liable for offenses committed in furtherance and foreseeably as a result of a conspiracy. Some jurisdictions extend liability to accomplices for secondary crimes committed as a foreseeable result of the crimes they encouraged or aided. These jurisdictions often condition such liability on the existence of a "common plan" but without requiring a formal finding of conspiracy. Vicarious liability and corporate liability requires a crime to have been committed by an agent (often an employee) of the person or enterprise found liable. The agent may or may not have been culpable, but the employer is usually liable on the basis of negligence or strict liability.

These doctrines are all relatively modern. Attempts were not generally punishable in English law until the late eighteenth century. A misdemeanor of soliciting any crime was first recognized in the early nineteenth century. Conspiracy was originally a doctrine confined to the Star Chamber, and was not widely used before the labor disputes attending industrialization. Liability for inchoate offenses was unnecessary before the development of law enforcement institutions with investigatory and prosecutorial capacity. A reactive criminal justice system will naturally focus on actual harms. A preventive system, by contrast, will aim at identifying dangerous persons, often using undercover agents and making arrests before harm is done. Preventive systems therefore criminalize inchoate offenses.

Although accomplice liability is an old doctrine, it broadened at the start of the twentieth century to include acts of support that are spatially and temporally remote from the offense. Accomplice liability and (especially in the federal system) co-conspirator liability became important tools of the new law enforcement institutions, providing leverage to induce suspects to inform against each other. Liability for causing the conduct of an innocent agent, or "perpetration by means," is a new doctrine, reflecting an extension of the modern idea of causal responsibility to the acts of others. Vicarious (including corporate) liability for the acts of employees is an outgrowth of the modern regulatory state.

Most of the doctrines imposing liability for trying to offend and for helping others to offend share a common structural feature. As noted, the inchoate offenses generally have the culpability required for the completed offense, but they are missing a conduct or result element. Because accomplice, perpetrator-by-means and co-conspirator liability require culpability with respect to objective elements achieved by others, they resemble inchoate offenses. To be sure, accomplices and conspirators do something—aid, encourage, solicit, agree—but they do not personally fulfill the conduct elements of the offense for which they are punished. Thus, almost all the doctrines considered here condition liability primarily on subjective elements. The emergence and increasing importance of anticipatory and participatory liability are part of the larger movement toward a more subjective conception of offending described in the preceding chapters. Corporate liability and vicarious liability do not fit this pattern, as they involve little or no subjective culpability, but they rarely impose severe punishment.

Because anticipatory and participatory offending generally involve the same culpability as standard offending, but with less conduct or consequence, they pose a common problem: Should they be punished as severely? Should attempters and conspirators be punished as severely as those who complete offenses? Should accomplices be punished as severely as perpetrators? Underlying these dilemmas is a fundamental question about whether objective elements should make a difference to punishment.

Both the retributive and utilitarian approaches to punishment offer reasons to think that punishment should depend primarily on culpability. From a retributive perspective, the results of conduct—whether effectual or ineffectual, harmful or harmless—may seem like a matter of luck, morally irrelevant to desert. From a utilitarian perspective, deterrence should be aimed at discouraging all conduct expected to cause harm, and incapacitation should be directed at all persons disposed to offend. Thus utilitarianism also has reason to punish on the basis of culpability, with little regard to what offenders have accomplished. Yet actual conduct and its results continue to matter to the public, which perhaps expects criminal law not only to discourage crime and assign blame, but also to vindicate victims. American law resolves these dilemmas differently with respect to anticipatory and participatory liability: inchoate offenses are often punished less than completed offenses, but accomplices are subject to the same punishments as perpetrators.

Additional issues cut across anticipatory and participatory liability doctrines. Although anticipatory liability and participatory liability are based primarily on subjective criteria, they are still governed by criminal law's requirement of an act. This poses the question: How much conduct should be required by these doctrines? How substantial and effectual must efforts to offend be to count as attempts? How effectual must aid be to establish complicity? Can aid alone show the agreement required for conspiracy, and if so, how substantial must it be? What if the defendant, having done barely enough to attempt, or aid, or encourage, or agree, then renounces her criminal purpose before the crime is complete?

Because offenders liable for trying and helping to commit crimes may have committed no self-evidently criminal breach of the peace, these doctrines test the limits of criminal law. This chapter will explore this problem by first discussing the inchoate offenses of attempt, solicitation, and conspiracy; and then the accessorial doctrines of complicity, perpetration by means, co-conspirator liability, and—albeit briefly—vicarious and corporate liability.

II. Punishment of Attempt

During the seventeenth and eighteenth centuries a handful of criminal prosecutions were brought in England for attempting to commit crimes. Lord Mansfield's 1784 decision in *Rex v. Scofield*, convicting the defendant of an attempted arson, reasoned that "the completion of an act, criminal in itself, [was not] necessary to constitute criminality."[1] Thus the attempt of any crime could be charged as a misdemeanor, whether the underlying offense was a felony or a misdemeanor. Solicitation of other crimes was soon identified as a misdemeanor as well, in the 1801 British case of *R. v. Higgins*,[2] and in the 1834 federal case of *United States* v. Lyles.[3]

In contrast to these traditional rules, the Model Penal Code treats the attempt or solicitation of an offense as a crime of the same grade as that offense for all except the highest grade of offenses. Thus, an attempted murder is graded the same as a completed manslaughter, but an attempted manslaughter (an attempt to kill accompanied by extreme emotional disturbance) is also graded the same as a completed manslaughter.[4] Most state codes, however, grade attempts one level below the completed crime, or divide offenses into groups, providing a range of penalties for the attempts lower than those available for the completed offenses.

Should attempts be punished as much as completed offenses? As we have seen, attempt liability is usually explained on grounds of desert, deterrence, and incapacitation. From a retributive perspective, it may seem that offenders should be punished based on their beliefs and expectations, not events beyond their control. Once an actor has done all he can to bring about harm, the actual

1. Cald. 397 (1784).
2. 102 Eng. Rep. 269 (1801).
3. 4 Cranch C.C. 469 (1834).
4. MODEL PENAL CODE § 5.05 (1962).

occurrence of harm seems a matter of *moral luck*, irrelevant to desert. It would follow that attempts to cause harm should be punished as severely as completed offenses.

On the other hand, perhaps the successful attempter deserves more punishment than the failed attempter to counteract the undeserved gratification he derives from achieving his wrongful aim. Moreover, if retribution means giving victims as well as offenders their due, we need to punish achieved injury more severely than attempt or endangerment.[5] The goal of vindicating victims also explains why many codes punish failed attempts, while leaving reckless and negligent endangerments unpunished. An intentional attack is personal, expressing antagonism toward a particular victim.[6] By contrast, although we may condemn carelessness as antisocial, we do not see it as antagonistic to a particular individual.

Utilitarians also have some reasons to punish both attempt and endangerment as severely as equally culpable achieved harm. Assume that Al and Betty have made equally culpable choices to do an act creating a 50 percent risk of injury, but that only Betty's act results in injury. Consider two approaches to deterring the imposition of such risks. One policy would jail Betty for two years, because she caused harm, and leave Al unpunished because he caused no harm. The other would jail both Al and Betty for one year, because they both imposed the same risk. The policy of punishing risk rather than harm lowers the severity and increases the certainty of punishment for the same conduct. If increases in certainty of punishment are more deterrent than increases in severity, it follows that equal punishment of expected harm is more deterrent than a *punishment lottery* conditioning punishment on actual harm. If our goals are incapacitative, it also seems sensible to sentence on the basis of expected rather than actual harm. If two offenders are equally likely to cause harm in the future, it seems equally necessary to reform and restrain each of them.

Yet utilitarianism also offers reasons to punish completed offenses more severely than partial or failed attempts. If the successful offender is gratified by success, he arguably needs a greater penalty to achieve the same deterrent effect. In addition, we might want the law to influence the offender who has arranged or tried to cause harm, but not yet succeeded. If the attempter is

5. *See* Guyora Binder, *Victims and the Significance of Causing Harm*, 28 PACE L. REV. 713 (2008); Leo Katz, *Why the Successful Assassin in More Wicked than the Unsuccessful One*, 88 CAL. L. REV. 791 (2000); Sanford H. Kadish, *The Criminal Law and the Luck of the Draw*, 84 J. CRIM. L. & CRIMINOLOGY 679 (1994); David Lewis, *The Punishment That Leaves Something to Chance*, 18 PHIL. & PUB. AFFAIRS 53 (1989); Stephen J. Schulhofer, *Harm and Punishment: A Critique of the Emphasis on the Results of Conduct in the Criminal Law*, 122 U. PA. L. REV. 1497 (1974).

6. Guyora Binder, *Victims and the Significance of Causing Harm*, 28 PACE L. REV. 713, 736 (2008); R.A. DUFF, CRIMINAL ATTEMPTS 132, 141 (1996).

already fully liable for the completed offense, however, law offers no deterrent for persisting. This provides a reason for differential punishment for inchoate and completed offenses.

Most jurisdictions compromise these competing considerations by punishing attempts and other inchoate offenses, but less severely than the completed offense.

III. Mental Element of Attempt

What mental state is required for attempt liability? From a Benthamite perspective, the purpose of attempt liability is to correlate liability with expected harm rather than actual outcomes. If this is our aim, it seems that the mental element for attempt should be the same as the mental element for the completed offense. Moreover, if liability should be based on expected harm, culpable mental states for both attempts and completed crimes should be confined to cognitive states rather than desires. On this reasoning, attempts could be predicated on negligence, recklessness, or knowledge—but not purpose.

Conversely, if the purpose of attempt liability is to vindicate victims targeted by failed attacks, attempt liability should require purpose. Moreover, as a matter of ordinary language, to attempt some task or result implies a purpose to achieve it. The law of attempt is premised on this association of attempt with purpose. To be sure, most jurisdictions have adopted regulatory schemes proscribing particular acts of careless endangerment, such as driving recklessly or while drunk, or possessing controlled drugs and munitions. Yet there is no general doctrine of attribution creating an offense of reckless or negligent endangerment as an inchoate analog for every offense of injury. The general doctrine of attempt liability is limited to the most culpable acts of endangerment. Thus, the great majority of American jurisdictions treat "attempt" as implying and requiring "intent." There is less consensus as to whether the required intent must always be what civilian lawyers call "direct intent" (purpose), or whether "indirect intent" (knowledge or belief) suffices.

One implication of conditioning attempt on intent is that an assault imposing a risk of death is not an attempted murder without a purpose or a confident expectation of causing death. Thus, several appellate courts have overturned attempted murder convictions for assailants who knowingly exposed victims to HIV, for failure to prove a purpose of causing death,[7] or belief that death would result.[8]

---

7. Smallwood v. State, 680 A.2d 512 (Md. 1996); Brock v. State, 555 So. 2d 285 (Ala. Crim. App. 1989).
8. Brock v. State, 555 So. 2d 285 (Ala. Crim. App. 1989).

A further implication of the proposition that attempt implies intent is that there can be no attempt to commit a careless injury. An illustrative case is that of *State v. Lyerla.*[9] Lyerla recklessly fired three shots at a pickup truck, hitting and killing one of three passengers, and causing an accident that injured the other two. He was convicted of second degree murder, which required that death result from a dangerous act committed with depraved indifference to human life. Yet he was also convicted of two counts of attempted second degree murder. The South Dakota Supreme Court reversed these attempt convictions, joining the courts of other states in holding "attempted reckless homicide a logical impossibility."[10]

The same result would be reached on these facts under Model Penal Code Section 5.01(1), which defines attempt as follows:

> A person is guilty of an attempt to commit a crime if, acting with the culpability otherwise required for the commission of the crime, he: (a) purposely engages in conduct which would constitute the crime if the attendant circumstances were as he believes them to be; or (b) when causing a particular result is an element of the crime, does or omits to do anything with the purpose or causing or with the belief that it will cause such result, without further conduct on his part; or (c) purposely does or omits to do anything that, under the circumstances as he believes them to be, is an act or omission constituting a substantial step in a course of conduct planned to culminate in his commission of the crime.

Under Section 5.01(1)(b), Lyerla would have had to fire the gun with the purpose or expectation of causing death to be guilty of attempting any form of homicide.

Although Section 5.01(1) generally follows the principle that "attempt implies intent," it requires different culpable mental states for different kinds of objective elements. For conduct elements, it always requires purpose. For result elements, belief that the result will occur suffices (but not recklessness or negligence of a risk). Finally, for circumstance elements that are fulfilled, Section 5.01(1) requires only the culpability otherwise required for the offense. The offender must believe circumstance elements to be fulfilled to be liable for an attempt when the circumstance is unfulfilled, however. Assume that statutory rape requires negligence with respect to the age of the victim. An offender charged with attempted statutory rape must believe the victim to be underage if she is not, but need only be negligent of the risk she is underage if she is underage in fact.

9. 424 N.W.2d 908 (S.D. 1988).
10. *Id.* at 913.

The Model Penal Code's equation of purpose and belief with respect to results is consistent with the position taken in recent California cases. In *People v. Bland*, the defendants fired a barrage of shots at a car, purposefully killing the driver and wounding two passengers.[11] Here the Court permitted liability for the attempted murder of the two passengers, if the defendants intended to kill the driver by killing everyone in the car.[12] A later California decision added that "if a person placed a bomb on a commercial airline intending to kill a primary target, but also ensuring the death of all the passengers, the person could be convicted of the attempted murder of all the passengers" even though that was not his objective.[13] Like Section 5.01(1)(b), these decisions condition attempted murder on expected killing as well as intended killing.[14]

Scholars have not agreed with the Model Penal Code's treatment of culpability with respect to circumstance elements in attempts. Both Antony Duff and Gideon Yaffe have suggested that a defendant aware of but indifferent to a circumstance element should be guilty of a completed crime, whereas a defendant mistakenly believing a circumstance element present, but indifferent to it, should not be liable for an attempt. Thus, a consumer who pays a low price for a product, mistakenly believing it stolen, should not be liable for attempted possession of stolen goods. A hunter who mistakenly believes the hunting season is over would not be guilty of attempted hunting out of season. Yet if the goods are in fact stolen and the hunting season is in fact over, both defendants are liable for the completed crimes notwithstanding their indifference.[15] For these authors, purpose and knowledge (i.e., true belief) both suffice as required mental states for circumstance elements of an attempt, but false belief does not. As we will see, other authors have treated the absence of a circumstance element as relevant only to the act element of attempts, making some attempts "impossible." We will consider such claims below.

IV. The Act of Attempting

What conduct should be required for attempt liability? If the sole purpose of attempt liability were to equalize the deterrent and retributive punishment of

11. People v. Bland, 48 P.3d 1107 (Cal. 2002).
12. *See id.* at 1110.
13. People v. Stone, 205 P.3d 272, 275 (Cal. 2009).
14. A rare case imposing attempt liability on the basis of recklessness is *People v. Thomas*, 729 P.2d 972 (Colo. 1986).
15. Gideon Yaffe, Attempts: In the Philosophy of Action and the Criminal Law 158–61 (2010); R.A. Duff, Criminal Attempts 208–11 (1996).

harm and risk, we would expect criminal attempts to be complete attempts, in which the offender tried and failed, for example by shooting and missing. Thus complete attempters and complete offenders would be punished equally, because their conduct and culpability would be equal. From a deterrent standpoint, it is important that complete attempts be punished more severely than incomplete attempts so as to give those who are planning crimes an incentive to desist before taking the final step. One might achieve this aim by leaving incomplete attempts unpunished, or by punishing them only partially.

Yet attempt liability serves a third purpose, which is to identify and incapacitate the dangerous before they have caused harm. Indeed, the drafters of the Model Penal Code considered this the main purpose of attempt liability. This aim counsels punishing incomplete attempts. Indeed, incapacitation is arguably best served by arresting and incarcerating as soon as a dangerous disposition has been reliably identified, without regard to the suspect's conduct. From the incapacitative perspective, an intention to cause harm—if reliably identified—should suffice to trigger police intervention. Yet such purely preventive detention would run afoul of the principle that criminal liability requires an actus reus, and its related prohibitions on status offenses and vague and overbroad offenses. Accordingly, some conduct is required.

Moreover, just as vagrancy offenses provoke worries about discriminatory exercise of police discretion, inchoate liability poses similar dangers. As inchoate offenses do not involve actual harm, undercover police agents can participate in these offenses for purposes of investigation without incurring liability. Yet this enables police to entice targets to commit crimes they otherwise would not, by offering money to the poor, work and purpose to the idle, friendship to the lonely, or drugs to the addicted. It might be especially tempting to accommodate a pushy friend by insincerely professing willingness to commit a crime. Producing criminality by recruiting the hapless may frustrate rather than serve the goal of prevention, but may nevertheless serve the professional, political, or personal interests of law enforcement by boosting arrest and crime statistics, by harassing political enemies or social pariahs, or by generating opportunities for corruption.

Thus the problem of defining the act element of attempt may be seen as a conflict between the aim of incapacitating the criminally disposed at the earliest possible point and requirement of an act, as well as the retributive and deterrent aims of punishing the choice to impose danger, which is most evident at the latest possible point.

Courts have devised several tests to determine whether criminal plans have gone far enough to merit attempt liability. An influential early formulation was that of the future U.S. Supreme Court justice Stephen Field in the California case of *People v. Murray*.[16] Justice Field determined that the defendant had not yet attempted an incestuous marriage by summoning a magistrate to perform it:

> [S]omething more than mere intention is necessary to constitute the offense charged. Between preparation and the offense itself there is a wide difference. The preparation consists in devising or arranging the means or measures necessary for the commission of the offense; the attempt is the direct movement toward the commission after the preparations are made. . . . [A] party may purchase and load a gun, with the declared intention to shoot his neighbor; but until some movement is made to use the weapon upon the person of his intended victim, there is only preparation and not an attempt. . . . The attempt . . . must be manifested by acts which would end in the consummation of the particular offense, but for the intervention of circumstances independent of the will of the party.[17]

This test distinguishes preparatory acts from acts of commission and requires that the defendant start committing the conduct required for the offense. The defendant must do all he can before he is thwarted by some external circumstance. Yet this test may embrace two very different kinds of interrupting circumstances: (1) the defendant completes all his planned actions, but is thwarted in achieving his goals by an event beyond his control; or (2) the defendant does as much as he can before he is interrupted by resistance or arrest. The former conception of an interrupting circumstance would allow conviction only for a completed attempt; however, the latter conception of an interrupting circumstance would allow conviction after very early arrest.

An influential New York decision, *People v. Rizzo*, overturned the conviction of four men who unsuccessfully looked for a courier said to be delivering wages from a bank.[18] The court offered this formulation, very similar to that in *Murray*:

> The law . . . has recognized that many acts in the way of preparation are too remote to constitute the crime of attempt. The line has been drawn between those acts that are remote and those that are proximate and near to the consummation. The law must be practical and therefore considers those acts only as tending to the commission of the crime that are so near to its accomplishment that in all reasonable probability the crime itself would have been committed, but for timely interference.[19]

16. 14 Cal. 159 (1859).
17. *Id.* at 159–60.
18. 246 N.Y. 334 (1927).
19. *Id.* at 337.

The *Rizzo* court then went on to reason that even without the arrest, the crime would not have been committed because the courier "was not found . . . no attempt to rob him could be made until he came in sight. . . . There was no man . . . whom these defendants could rob. . . . In a word, these defendants had planned to commit a crime, and were looking around the city for an opportunity to commit it. . . ."[20]

These decisions offer a number of potentially inconsistent tests. The attempt must be complete, or must at least be proximate to the completion of the crime, or must have led to the completion of the crime but for an interruption; or it must commence after the defendant secured everything needed for completing the crime. In addition to thus surfeit of standards, both opinions implicitly rely on images of trespassory violence to illustrate the distinction between preparation and attempt. Thus, an attempt seems to require something like a shot or a blow that breaches the peace and marks the conduct as criminal.

As we saw in previous chapters, nineteenth-century reformers reinterpreted requirements of trespassory conduct as evidentiary presumptions of criminal intent. In the early twentieth century, a number of theorists conceptualized the conduct element of attempt similarly, proposing that attempt liability depend on conduct unequivocally manifesting the intent to commit the crime,[21] and several American courts adopted such standards.[22] Some decisions, such as that in *Rizzo*, treated the absence of an "indispensable element," such as the targeted person or property, or a required weapon, as precluding an attempt.[23] Several courts required a finding that the defendant would have persisted and completed the offense but for the intervention of some external force, without requiring an unequivocal act.[24] One scholar, R.H. Skilton, proposed an abnormal step test, requiring an act after which the defendant would likely persist.[25] By contrast to the probable persistence and abnormal step tests, an unequivocality standard had the advantage of identifying a predictor of probable persistence. Inculpatory conduct showed the actor was sufficiently committed to the offense to risk apprehension. As the Model Penal Code Commentaries put it, "once the actor must desist or perform acts that he realizes would incriminate him if all external facts were known, in all probability a firmer state of mind exists."[26]

---

20. *Id.* at 338.
21. GLANVILLE L. WILLIAMS, CRIMINAL LAW: THE GENERAL PART 629 (1961); J.W. Cecil Turner, *Attempts to Commit Crimes*, 5 CAMBRIDGE L.J. 230 (1934); JOHN SALMOND, JURISPRUDENCE, OR THE THEORY OF THE LAW 404 (7th ed. 1924).
22. *E.g.*, People v. Buffum, 256 P.2d 317 (Cal. 1953); State v. Mandel, 278 P.2d 413 (Ariz. 1954).
23. State v. Fielder, 109 S.W. 580 (Mo. 1908); State v. Wood, 103 N.W. 25 (S.D. 1905).
24. *See, e.g.*, People v. Gibson, 210 P.2d 747 (Cal. Dist. Ct. App. 1949); State v. Brown, 95 N.C. 685 (1886).
25. Robert H. Skilton, *The Requisite Act in a Criminal Attempt*, 3 U. PITT. L. REV. 308 (1937).
26. MODEL PENAL CODE COMMENTARIES, pt. 1, § 5.01, at 329 (1985).

The drafters of the Model Penal Code distinguished and rejected six different tests for the objective element of attempt. They dismissed proximity tests, requiring an act sufficiently close to a completed attempt, as completely indeterminate and as ill-serving the goal of incapacitating the dangerous. They rejected Justice Holmes's proposal to modify this test by requiring greater proximity for attempts to commit less harmful crimes, on grounds that it was aimed at optimally deterring harmful conduct rather than incapacitating persons with criminal dispositions. They objected to tests requiring probable persistence, or probable success but for external interruption. Such tests failed to identify the required evidence of probable persistence, and so replicated the indeterminacy of proximity tests. They conceded the determinacy of tests requiring the presence of all requisites for the commission of the crime, but objected that they would exclude many dangerous individuals. In particular, such tests would interfere with police stings by precluding liability for attempted transactions with fictitious persons or for fictitious goods. They objected to the proposed abnormal step test as inadministrable, because requiring a hypothetical judgment about the probable behavior of an unidentifiable class of persons contemplating but then desisting from crimes. The one test the Model Penal Code drafters found sensible required conduct unequivocally manifesting the intent to commit the completed offense. Nevertheless, they objected that this standard also set the bar too high for prosecutorial proof.[27]

It sufficed, the Model Penal Code drafters concluded, to require that the conduct "corroborate" rather than prove the intent. "Substantial steps" corroborating such intent included following or lying in wait for a victim, enticing a victim to the intended site of the crime, surveying the intended site of the crime, entering the intended site unlawfully, securing means to commit the crime having no innocent purpose, and soliciting an innocent agent to carry out part of the criminal act. The Model Penal Code test did not require that the defendant would have succeeded but for external interruption, or that all the requisites for commission of the offense were present. As long as the defendant believed that circumstances obtained that permitted success, and committed a substantial step, he fulfilled the act element of attempt. A substantial minority of jurisdictions has adopted the substantial step test by statute.[28] Many states define attempts as requiring an act "beyond preparation."[29] When more

---

27. *Id.* at 321–29.

28. GA. CODE ANN. § 16-4-1 (2015); 720 ILL. COMP. STAT. 5/8-4(a) (2015); N.J. STAT. ANN. § 2C:5-1(a)(3) (2015); 18 PA. CONS. STAT. § 901(a) (2015).

29. TEXAS PENAL CODE ANN. § 15.01(a) (2015) ; Enix v. State, 69 So. 3d 354 (Fla. Dist. Ct. App. 2011); State v. Mack, 589 S.E.2d 168 (N.C. Ct. App. 2003); People v. Jones, 504 N.W.2d 158 (Mich. 1992); Sizemore v. Commonwealth, 243 S.E.2d 212 (Va. 1978).

specific tests are used to distinguish attempt from preparation, the probable persistence test appears to be the most prevalent.

The different tests vary along two dimensions: whether an attempt requires that objective circumstances enabling success be present, and how far the defendant must proceed in committing planned conduct. Consider a case where the defendant (1) exchanges sexually explicit emails with a person represented to be a 12-year-old girl, (2) proposes having sex, (3) acquires an obscene image, (4) sends the obscene image, (5) agrees to meet in a public place proposed by the putative 12-year-old, (6) drives to the meeting place, (7) enters the meeting place, (8) proceeds to a secluded place with the victim, and finally (9) molests the victim. At what point does the defendant's conduct suffice for attempt to distribute obscenity to a minor? At what point is there an attempt to molest a child? What if the "victim" is actually an adult police officer (so that steps 8 and 9 can never occur)?

Under a last-step test, if the putative victim is an adult, the defendant is guilty of attempted distribution of obscenity to a minor at step 4, but never becomes guilty of attempted child-molesting (because the sequence must end at step 7). Under a proximity test, the defendant may be guilty of attempted distribution at step 3, but is probably not liable for attempted molestation until step 8 because the crime requires direct contact with a victim and privacy. If so, a proximity test, like a last-step test, precludes a successful sting for this offense. On the other hand, a dangerous proximity test might find liability at an earlier point, such as step 6.[30]

Under an indispensable-element test, there is probably also liability for attempted distribution at step 3, but again, no liability for attempted molestation before step 8, thus precluding a successful police sting. We might argue that if the "victim" is a police officer, the defendant cannot attempt either offense, because an actual child is a requisite for both offenses. However, the better interpretation of this test acquits the defendant only if—like Rizzo—he is aware that more needs to be done to find a target, or a suitable means of attacking it.

Under a test requiring probable success but-for-interruption,[31] if the victim is a police decoy, the defendant might not be liable for attempting either crime, because the absence of a victim precluded either offense. Conversely, the prosecution could argue that the absence of a victim was an obstacle independent of the defendant's will. Arguably the better version of this test requires probable persistence rather than probable success. We cannot infer probable

---

30. Van Bell v. State, 775 P.2d 1273, 1275 (Nev. 1989).
31. *See, e.g.,* State v. Spies, 672 N.W.2d 792 (Iowa 2003).

persistence from electronic communication alone, which could merely be fantasy. Accordingly this test probably does not permit attempt liability before step 6 or 7.

Under an unequivocality test, liability for attempted child-molestation might crystallize at step 5, when the defendant arranges the meeting, although the defense could argue that this is still only "talk" that might remain in the realm of fantasy. If so, step 6, driving to the meeting place, probably shows sufficient seriousness. Under an abnormal-step test, the defendant may be guilty of attempted child-molestation as step 4 when he sends the photos, as he has exposed himself to criminal liability at that point.[32] Under the Model Penal Code's substantial-step test, the defendant is clearly guilty of attempted child-molestation at step 5 when he agrees to meet the victim ("seeking to entice the contemplated victim . . . to go to the place contemplated for commission"[33]), but he could be guilty as early as step 2, when he proposes sex ("under the circumstances as he believes them to be"[34] . . . "soliciting an innocent agent to engage in conduct constituting an element of the crime"[35]).

In rejecting the last-act, proximity, indispensable-element, and but-for-interruption tests, the Model Penal Code shows its rejection of a conception of attempt as an attack on a particular victim. If the purpose of attempt liability is to permit early arrest, on the basis of strong evidence of intent but without much conduct, attempt liability will often depend on police solicitation of the criminally disposed. Yet police are (hopefully) reluctant to encourage harm to real victims. Thus police stings will tend to focus on crimes of endangerment such as drug possession and bribery. The Model Penal Code's approach to attempt liability, insofar as it enables police stings, will often generate liability for doubly inchoate crimes—futile attempts to create risks of social harm.

V. Impossible and Abandoned Attempts

Our hypothetical case illustrates two other issues concerning the act element of attempts: impossibility and abandonment.

For a brief period in the mid-nineteenth century, courts in several countries barred attempt liability where the defendant used ineffective means, or targeted a person or property that was absent. In the United States, the conviction

---

32. *See* People v. Mahboubian, 543 N.E.2d 34 (N.Y. 1989) for such reasoning.
33. Model Penal Code § 5.01(2)(b) (1962).
34. *Id.* § 5.01(1)(c).
35. *Id.* § 5.01(2)(g).

of a slave for attempted poisoning was reversed for failure to allege that the substance employed was dangerous.[36] In England, defendants were acquitted of burglary for entering an empty house with intent to steal,[37] and of attempted larceny for thrusting a hand into an empty pocket.[38] Yet the English decisions were soon overruled,[39] and almost all American courts agreed.[40] A consensus soon prevailed that "factual impossibility" does not preclude attempt liability. The Illinois code, for example provides that "[i]t is not a defense to a charge of attempt that because of a misapprehension of the circumstances it would have been impossible for the accused to commit the offense attempted."[41]

It may seem that a rule precluding liability for "factually impossible attempts" is functionally similar to an "indispensable element" test for preparation versus attempt. Thus, if we say that a prospective offender remains at the preparation stage until he has created the conditions necessary for success, it would seem that an attempt is logically impossible at this stage. Note, however, that a defendant such as Rizzo, acquitted because he was still looking for the victim, knew that he had not yet secured an indispensable condition for success. We can explain the acquittal of the slave on a similar basis—she was not alleged to have believed the ingredient she used was dangerous to life. By contrast, defendants who try to steal from empty receptacles expect or hope to find them full. We can have an indispensable element test for distinguishing preparation from attempt, but require that a missing indispensable element be reasonably apparent to the prospective offender. Such a test would make "impossibility" exculpatory only insofar as reasonably apparent.

If an attempt is impossible whenever a circumstance precludes success, every attempt—which is a failure by definition—is arguably impossible. Although American courts agree that "factual impossibility" will not preclude attempt liability, they often add that "legal impossibility" will. This proposition is uncontroversial if it means that mistakenly believing one's act is proscribed cannot make one guilty of an attempt. For example, an 18-year-old who votes, mistakenly believing he is 17, can be guilty of attempted election fraud. Yet an 18-year-old who votes, mistakenly believing the voting age is 19, cannot be. Model Penal Code Section 5.01(1)(a) adopts this position by imposing attempt liability for one who "purposely engages in conduct that would constitute [a] crime if the attendant circumstances were as he believes them to be."

---

36. The State v. Clarissa, A Slave, 11 Ala. 57 (1847).
37. R. v. M'Pherson, 169 Eng. Rep. 975 (1857).
38. R. v. Collins, 169 Eng. Rep. 1477 (1864).
39. R. v. Ring, 17 Cox C. C. 491 (1892).
40. *E.g.,* State v, Mitchell, 71 S.W. 175 (Mo. 1902); Clark v. State, 8 S.W. 145 (Tenn. 1888).
41. 720 Ill. Comp. Stat. 5/8-4(b) (2015).

Yet some courts have employed a broader conception of legal impossibility, defining it as the successful commission of an act that is not a crime. On such reasoning, courts have acquitted in two cases of receiving recovered property, believing it stolen;[42] one of shooting a stuffed deer outside the hunting season, believing it real;[43] one of selling procaine, perhaps believing it to be heroin;[44] and one of offering a bribe to a person mistakenly believed to be a juror.[45] All of these cases involved law enforcement stings, which may have provoked judicial concerns about entrapment. Nevertheless, all these defendants satisfied the Model Penal Code standard for attempts by trying to commit acts that would have been crimes if the circumstances were as they believed them to be.[46]

These decisions have been much criticized. A number of scholars and courts have argued that the conception of legal impossibility on which they rely is as indeterminate as the concept of factual impossibility.[47] Thus, any conduct can be described in multiple ways. By including the circumstance precluding success in our description of any failed attempt, we can portray it as factually impossible. Similarly, by describing any failed attempt to commit an offense as a successful effort to do something legal, we can portray it as legally impossible. Thus neither test can reliably distinguish possible from impossible attempts. Yet the precluding circumstance is exculpatory only if known to the actor, and the act is a success only if completing the offense was not the actor's goal. Both tests fail because we cannot choose an apt description of the act without knowing the actor's mental state.

Several theorists have argued for a narrower test of impossibility that could exculpate in cases of receiving recovered goods and selling phony narcotics, but convict in the cases involving empty receptacles. According to George Fletcher, the proper test is to determine if a hypothetical rationally motivated defendant would still commit the act, knowing it would not be criminal.[48] Thus, a rationally motivated purchaser buys goods because they are cheap, not

42. Booth v. State, 398 P.2d 863 (Okla. Crim. App. 1964); People v. Jaffe, 185 N.Y. 497 (1906).
43. State v. Guffey, 262 S.W.2d 152 (Mo. 1953).
44. United States v. Oviedo, 525 F.2d 881 (5th Cir. 1976).
45. State v. Taylor, 133 S.W.2d 336 (Mo. 1939).
46. In three of these cases the statutory definition of the offense may have made a difference. In one, the underlying offense was defined as "receiving stolen property, knowing it to be so." The court reasoned that the defendant could not have attempted this offense without actually knowing the property to be stolen. People v. Jaffe, 185 N.Y. 497, 501 (1906). The Court made a similar argument in *Booth v. State*. 398 P.2d 863, 872 (Okla. Crim. App. 1964). In another case, the statutory offense was "to corrupt or attempt to corrupt a summoned juror." State v. Taylor, 133 S.W.2d 336, 337 (Mo. 1939). Here the court reasoned that the person one *attempted to corrupt* must in fact be a summoned juror. *See id.* at 340.
47. *E.g.*, United States v. Hsu, 155 F.3d 189, 199 (3d Cir. 1998).
48. George P. Fletcher, Rethinking Criminal Law 161–65 (1978).

because they are stolen. A rationally motivated drug dealer who sells a drug profitably is (arguably) indifferent to its actually being a controlled substance.[49] We have noted that any failed attempt can be described as factually or legally impossible. Fletcher's rational motivation test instructs us to select a description of the conduct that explains it as rationally motivated. Note that Fletcher's rational motivation test for impossible attempts is implicit in an unequivocality test for distinguishing attempts from preparations. If a rationally motivated actor would be indifferent to whether his act fulfilled the offense definition, an act that does not fulfill the offense definition is equivocal.

Other theorists such as R.A. Duff and Gideon Yaffe have proposed tests for impossibility that would focus on the motives of the actual defendant rather than a hypothetical rational actor.[50] Their tests convict of an attempt only if the defendant would have completed the offense if the circumstances were as he *wished* them to be, not as he believed them to be. If he mistakenly believed the goods he purchased were stolen, but did not care, he would not be guilty of attempting to receive stolen goods. If he mistakenly believed the drug he sold was heroin but did not care, he would not be guilty of an attempt to distribute heroin. This actual motivation test is not a test of the act element of attempt at all, but of the mental element. It requires knowledge for a fulfilled circumstance element, but purpose for an unfulfilled one.[51]

Finally, let us reconsider our hypothetical pedophile. If his "victim" is a police decoy, are his attempts to distribute obscenity and molest a child impossible? If his conduct stops at step 4, his conduct is equivocal—he might be seeking gratification from fantasizing and be indifferent to whether the person he communicates with is a child or a role-playing adult. Of course this indifference is reprehensible, and poses a danger to children. For these reasons, the Model Penal Code would convict. Yet if attempt requires intent, the prosecution should arguably have to prove purpose with respect to the age of the victim, as the Duff and Yaffe tests would require. If they do so, why should the equivocality of the defendant's conduct acquit him, as Fletcher's test would require? One answer is that the danger posed by manipulable defendants may be minimal and evidence of their resolve may be scripted by police. If there are few real 12-year-olds interested in encouraging the sexual interest of reclusive adults, or

49. *See id.*

50. Gideon Yaffe, Attempts: In the Philosophy of Action and the Criminal Law (2010); R.A. Duff, Criminal Attempts (1996).

51. Gideon Yaffe, Attempts: In the Philosophy of Action and the Criminal Law 129–66 (2010); R.A. Duff, Criminal Attempts 378–80 (1996); J.C. Smith, *Two Problems in Criminal Attempts Reexamined-II*, 1962 Crim. L. Rev. 212, 216–22 (Yaffe would convict Jaffe on the facts, but his approach is similar to Duff's).

real terrorists interested in entrusting responsibility and information to emotionally dependent simpletons, law enforcement stings may not be identifying the truly dangerous. An alternative strategy for dealing with this concern is an entrapment defense, which usually acquits defendants who show they were induced to commit the crime by law enforcement, unless the prosecution can prove they were predisposed.[52] In this way, an entrapment defense imposes a sanction when police participate in crime that is not justified by crime prevention.

Suppose our hypothetical pedophile reaches the meeting place (step 6), becomes nervous on seeing many witnesses there, and drives home. Under the substantial step, abnormal step, and unequivocality tests, he is arguably already guilty of attempted child molestation when he reaches the meeting place. Should we nevertheless acquit him on grounds of abandonment? In the well-known California case of *People v. Staples*, a mathematician rented an office above a bank for a month, stored tools and blowtorches there, and drilled partway through the floor, with the plan of burglarizing the bank.[53] The defendant contended that he abandoned the plan as absurd after two weeks. When the rental period was over, the landlord informed the police about the tools and the holes in the floor. The defendant urged the court to employ a probable-persistence test, and argued that his voluntary abandonment showed the he would not have completed the crime without interruption. The trial court found him liable under this test, on the dubious ground that he abandoned the plan involuntarily when the rental period ended. An appellate court affirmed the conviction, but rejected the probable-persistence test in favor of a proximity test. It concluded that he had moved beyond preparation by starting to drill, thereby performing part of the breaking element of burglary. Having fulfilled the elements of attempt, his subsequent abandonment was irrelevant.[54] It seems that only a probable- persistence test and a last-step test make even last minute abandonment exculpatory. Under a probable-persistence test, the abandonment must be voluntary.

The defendant certainly committed a substantial step by "possession . . . of materials to be employed in the commission of a crime, at or near the place contemplated for its commission, where such possession . . . serves no lawful purpose of the actor."[55] Yet Model Penal Code Section 5.01(4) provides an affirmative defense for any attempter who "abandoned his effort to commit the

52. Jacobson v. United States, 503 U.S. 540 (1992).
53. 6 Cal. App. 3d 61 (1970).
54. *Id.* at 69.
55. Model Penal Code § 5.01(2)(f) (1962).

crime . . . under circumstances manifesting a complete and voluntary renunciation of his criminal purpose," while excluding renunciations "motivated . . . in part, by circumstances not . . . apparent at the inception of the actor's course of conduct, that increase the probability of . . . apprehension or which make [completion of the offense] more difficult. . . ." It adds that "renunciation is not complete if it is motivated by a decision to postpone the criminal conduct . . . or to transfer the criminal effort to another . . . objective or victim."[56] Several jurisdictions have adopted this defense.[57]

How can we reconcile the Model Penal Code's defense of abandonment with its substantial-step test? Recall that the primary purpose of the substantial-step test is incapacitation of the dangerous. A conscientiously motivated abandonment negates the inference of dangerousness from the commission of a substantial step. In addition, recall that the Model Penal Code equates liability for attempts and completed offenses. This has the antideterrent effect of encouraging those who have committed a substantial step to persist (as they are already fully liable). An abandonment defense counteracts this antideterrent effect by incentivizing desistance. It is unnecessary for jurisdictions that draw the line between preparation and attempt closer to the completion of the crime, and that punish completed crimes more severely than attempts.

VI. Solicitation

The offense of solicitation was originally seen as a form of corruption. The 1801 case of *Rex v. Higgins* approved a charge for the common law misdemeanor of soliciting a servant to steal from his master, and cited cases on bribery and perjury.[58] The Model Penal Code defines solicitation as encouraging or requesting conduct that would constitute an offense or complicity in an offense, with the "purpose of promoting or facilitating its commission."[59] With its usual emphasis on subjective intention, the Code imposes solicitation liability even for failed attempts to communicate encouragement or a request to another party.[60] The Code treats the solicitation of an innocent agent to commit a conduct element as an attempt, however.[61]

56. *Id.* § 5.01(4).
57. N.J. Stat. Ann. § 2C:5-1(d) (2015) ; Ohio Rev. Code Ann. § 2923.02(d) (2015); 18 Pa. Cons. Stat. § 901(c) (2015).
58. 102 Eng. Rep. 269 (1801).
59. Model Penal Code § 5.02 (1962).
60. *Id.* § 5.02(2).
61. *Id.* § 5.01(2)(g).

Today, most jurisdictions impose liability for soliciting all offenses, or all felonies.[62] A few limit solicitation to enumerated crimes.[63] Generally, the act required for solicitation is simply to encourage, request, or command the commission of a pertinent crime, although one state restricts solicitation to the offering of money to induce a criminal offense.[64] The required mental element is usually intent that a crime be committed,[65] or sometimes intent that conduct constituting crime be committed.[66] A few jurisdictions allow a defense of renunciation.[67]

In most jurisdictions, punishment for solicitation is less than that for attempt. For example, in New York, punishment for solicitation is generally two grades below that of the offense solicited, while punishment for attempt is generally one grade below. By contrast, a few jurisdictions treat solicitations as attempts. Thus New Jersey cases treat "bare" solicitation as a substantial step.[68] Defining solicitation as an offense may be thought of as a compromise between treating solicitation as an attempt to commit the crime solicited, and leaving solicitation unpunished.

A number of courts have wrestled with the question as to whether and when solicitation suffices to constitute an attempt. Some have treated solicitation as sufficient for an attempt when accompanied by additional conduct such as payment or the provision of aid. In the California case of *People v. Decker*, the defendant paid an undercover police officer a $5,000 deposit to kill his sister; gave information about her location, habits, and appearance; insisted he had "never been more sure" of any decision; and urged the officer to eliminate witnesses as well.[69] The court emphasized not only the payment and aid, but also the strong evidence of intent, reasoning that "[w]henever the design of a person to commit crime is clearly shown, slight acts in furtherance of the design will constitute an attempt."[70]

Whether one can attempt an offense by merely urging an agent to commit it may depend on whether the offense requires particular conduct, or only the causation of a result. This is because of the different mental element required

62. Fla. Stat. §777.04(2) (2015) ; 720 Ill. Comp. Stat. 5/8-1(2015) ; N.Y. Penal Law § 100 (2015); 18 Pa. Cons. Stat. § 902 (2015); Ga. Code Ann. § 16-4-7 (2015); Mich. Comp. Laws § 750.157b (2015) ; N.C. Gen. Stat. § 14-2.6 (2015); Va. Code Ann. § 18.2-29 (2015) .
63. Cal. Penal Code § 653f (2015); Tex. Penal Code Ann. § 15.03 (2015).
64. Mich. Comp. Laws § 750.157b (2015).
65. Cal. Penal Code § 653f (2015).
66. N.Y. Penal Law § 100.00 (2015).
67. Mich. Comp. Laws § 750.157b (2015).
68. *See, e.g.*, State v. Sunzar, 751 A.2d 627 (N.J. Super. Ct. 1999).
69. People v. Decker, 157 P.3d 1017 (Cal. 2007).
70. *Id.* at 1022.

for attempting these two types of offenses. Let us assume that attempt requires purpose with respect to conduct and result elements. If an offense requires only the causation of a result, one can attempt it by soliciting another to commit the offense with a purpose to cause the result. If the offense requires certain conduct, however, one can only attempt the offense with the purpose of committing that conduct. But one cannot intend to personally commit conduct by inducing another to commit it.[71] Thus, insofar as we conceive offenses as requiring trespassory conduct, an attempt must involve an attempt to commit such conduct. Insofar as we conceive offenses as requiring only results, we will require only an attempt to cause such results. Such an attempt to cause a proscribed result could be committed by soliciting another to bring it about—at least if we define proximate causation as including foreseeably inducing the voluntary action of others.

VII. Punishing Conspiracy

Conspiracy is today conceptualized as a type of inchoate crime, requiring an agreement that some other crime will be committed. Yet conspiracy was not initially seen as an anticipatory offense adaptable to any crime.

At its origins in the fourteenth century, conspiracy was confined to successful plots to corrupt justice: "Conspirators be they that do confeder or bind themselves . . . that every of them shall aid and support the Enterprise of each other falsely and maliciously to indite, or cause to be indited . . . or falsely to move or maintain Pleas; . . . and such as retain Men . . . to maintain their malicious Enterprises . . . as well the Takers as the Givers."[72] In the seventeenth century the Star Chamber imposed liability for unsuccessful conspiracies to bring false charges, and by the late seventeenth century common law courts punished agreement to commit any crime.[73]

The 1721 case of *Rex v. Journeymen Taylors of Cambridge* went further, convicting tailors of conspiring to withhold their labor in order to raise their wages.[74] Although such a strike violated a recent statute prohibiting tailors from organizing, the indictment had failed to charge a violation of the statute. The court concluded that the charge was for a common law offense, explaining that "a conspiracy of any kind is illegal, although the matter about which they

71. *See* GIDEON YAFFE, ATTEMPTS: IN THE PHILOSOPHY OF ACTION AND THE CRIMINAL LAW 203–11 (2010).
72. THIRD ORDINANCE OF CONSPIRATORS, 33 Edw. 1 (1304).
73. Francis Sayre, *Criminal Conspiracy*, 35 HARV. L. REV. 393, 399–400 (1922).
74. 88 Eng. Rep. 9 (1721).

conspired might have been lawful for them . . . to do, if they had not conspired to do it."[75] Thus, conspiracy began to shift from a crime of corruption to one of collective action.

Similar prosecutions were brought in the United States during the nineteenth century[76] and some labor historians have concluded that "the conspiracy doctrine was the primary legal remedy for regulating industrial conflict between 1806 and 1896."[77] Conspiracy prosecutions were controversial in the antebellum United States, because they charged conspiracy as a common law offense in an era of codification.[78] Defense attorneys often argued that most English conspiracy convictions had been for statutory crimes, and challenged judicial authority to charge common law crimes.[79] They argued further that unless the object of the conspiracy violated a statute, conspiracies were indistinguishable from any other voluntary associations. This implied in turn that common law conspiracy liability violated legality by affording prosecutors and courts discretion to define and punish criminal conduct retroactively and thereby take sides in political and economic disputes. That conspiring required only the communication of thoughts increased the risk that conspiracy liability would be used to punish dissent.

These arguments put pressure on courts to connect conspiracy liability to existing criminal law, by requiring that either the object of the conspiracy or the intended means were criminal. Thus, in most labor conspiracy cases, prosecutors were required to prove that the intended tactics for organizing a strike or closing a shop to nonunion employees involved unlawful acts of violence or destruction.[80] American courts frequently cited Lord Denman's dictum that a conspiracy indictment must "charge a conspiracy either to do an unlawful act or a lawful act by unlawful means,"[81] but sometimes denied that "unlawful" meant criminal.[82] Writing in the early twentieth century, Sayre argued that logic required that a criminal conspiracy involve an agreement to commit a crime, whether as a means or an end, and read most of the precedent as consistent with this view.[83]

---

75. *Id.* at 10.
76. State v. Donaldson, 32 N.J.L. 151 (1867); Commonwealth v. Hunt, 45 Mass. 111 (1842); Commonwealth v. Pullis (Philadelphia Mayor's Ct. 1806), 3 Doc. Hist. Am. Indus. Soc'y 59 (John R. Commons et al., eds. 1910).
77. Victoria C. Hattam, Labor Visions and State Power: The Origins of Business Unionism in the United States 36 (1993).
78. *Id.* at 45–53.
79. *Id.* at 52–53.
80. *Id.* at 36, 57.
81. Rex v. Jones, 110 Eng. L. Rep. 485, 487 (1832).
82. Commonwealth v. Hunt, 45 Mass. 111 (1842); *State v. Burnham*, 15 N.H. 396 (1844).
83. Francis Sayre, *Criminal Conspiracy*, 35 Harv. L. Rev. 393, 416 (1922).

Yet some twentieth-century courts continued to define conspiracies as agreements to commit acts "corrupt, dishonest, fraudulent or immoral," but not necessarily criminal.[84] Thus, a 1906 South Carolina court punished conspiracy to disrupt a picnic.[85] A 1933 Kentucky decision upheld an indictment for conspiracy to violate usury laws that were otherwise enforceable only through civil restitution.[86] Many noncriminal delicts punished by means of conspiracy liability were obstructions of justice or acts of official corruption that are now covered by criminal statutes. Yet conspiracy was also used to suppress unpopular speech. The Supreme Court cast doubt on the constitutionality of punishing conspiracy to commit noncriminal conduct in the 1948 case of *Musser v. Utah*, when it considered a First Amendment challenge to a conviction for advocating polygamy under a statute punishing conspiracy to injure public morals.[87] Rather than determining whether the conduct punished was protected by the First Amendment, it remanded to the Utah Supreme Court for a determination of whether the statutory offense definition was void for vagueness.[88] The Utah Supreme Court indeed found it unconstitutionally vague.[89]

Because conspiracy liability did not always require the intention to commit some other offense, it was not simply a lesser-included offense as was attempt. This posed a problem when a defendant conspired to commit an offense and then did so. In England, the traditional rule had been that the misdemeanor of conspiracy would "merge" with any felony committed pursuant to the conspiracy, but conspirators could be punished for the conspiracy as well as misdemeanors committed in its pursuit. Most American jurisdictions permitted punishment for both the conspiracy and the offenses committed pursuant to it.

The Model Penal Code adopted Sayre's view of conspiracy as an inchoate offense, the criminality of which depended on the proscription of some other offense. The Code provided that "[a] person is guilty of conspiracy with another person . . . to commit a crime if with the purpose of promoting or facilitating its commission he . . . agrees" to its commission, attempt, or solicitation, or to aid in planning or committing these offenses.[90] The penalty for conspiracy was the same as that imposed for the attempt, solicitation, or completion of the gravest offense planned.[91] If all the planned offenses were completed,

84. State v. Parker, 158 A. 797, 799 (Conn. 1932).
85. State v. Ameker, 53 S.E. 484 (S.C. 1906).
86. Commonwealth v. Donoghue, 63 S.W.2d 3 (Ky. Ct. App. 1933).
87. 333 U.S. 95 (1948).
88. *Id.* at 97.
89. Musser v. Utah, 223 P.2d 193, 194 (Utah 1950).
90. Model Penal Code § 5.03(1) (1962).
91. *Id.* § 5.05.

the conspiracy would merge into the completed offenses and would not be punished.[92] Similarly, if an actor committed an attempt, solicitation, and conspiracy to commit the same offense, the defendant could be punished for only one such inchoate offense.[93] This regime presumed that punishing conspiracy served deterrent aims insofar as conspiracy created a danger of commission of a planned offense, and served incapacitative aims insofar as conspiring revealed the dangerous propensity of the defendant to commit offenses. All inchoate offenses, including conspiracy, were considered lesser-included offenses of a completed crime. Yet they were as punishable as the completed crime because equally culpable.

Should an agreement to commit a crime—consisting merely of words and thoughts—be seen as comparably dangerous to an attempt to commit the crime? That may depend on how we define an attempt. Recall that the Model Penal Code required little action for an attempt—only a substantial step to corroborate the seriousness of intent. In comparison, the Model Penal Code required some action for conspiracy as well—an overt act in pursuit of the conspiracy by one of the conspirators.[94] Moreover, a conspiracy poses some additional dangers that the planned offense will be successfully committed. As Justice Frankfurter wrote, "[c]oncerted action both increases the likelihood that the criminal object will be successfully attained and decreases the probability that the individuals involved will depart from their path of criminality. Group association for criminal purposes often . . . makes possible the attainment of ends more complex than those which one criminal could accomplish."[95] In addition, a conspiracy might lead to additional crimes beyond those planned.

Today, American criminal codes generally define conspiracy liability, so there is very little scope for charging conspiracy as a common law crime. Almost all of these statutes confine the object of conspiracy to a criminal offense.[96] Thus conspiracy has come to be seen as a form of derivative liability similar to attempt or solicitation, depending on the proscription of some other offense. In most cases the punishment is similar to that imposed for attempt—less than that imposed for the completed offense and more than that imposed for solicitation. Yet most jurisdictions reject the Model Penal Code's practice of

92. *Id.* § 1.07(1)(b).
93. *Id.* § 5.05.
94. *Id.* § 5.03(5).
95. Callanan v. United States, 364 U.S. 587, 593 (1961).
96. The criminal codes of the 12 most populous states all impose conspiracy liability. Of these, only Michigan's code punishes conspiracies to commit illegal acts that may not be criminal offenses.

merging conspiracy with the completed offense, instead adhering to the federal rule that "it has been long and consistently recognized by the Court that the commission of the substantive offense and a conspiracy to commit it are separate and distinct offenses."[97]

One rationale for punishing both the conspiracy and the completed offense is that conspiracy to commit a crime is not really a lesser-included offense of that crime. Conspiracy includes an additional element—the agreement—not required for that crime. Thus, just as one can conspire to commit an offense without completing or attempting it, one can attempt or commit an offense without conspiring to do so.[98]

A second rationale is that the agreement to commit a crime creates a potentially durable criminal organization, and so creates danger of further offenses. "Combination in crime makes more likely the commission of crimes unrelated to the original purpose for which the group was formed."[99] Collaboration multiplies the number of people with motives to commit secondary crimes such as coercing victims, resisting law enforcement, or intimidating witnesses. Because offenders cannot use legal remedies to enforce criminal agreements, they may employ violence to do so. Successful collaboration enables collaboration on further crimes by building trust and reducing search costs. Because criminal collaboration improves the odds of success, collaboration on one crime gives conspirators the means to offend more successfully in the future, and thereby encourages such offending. [100] Professor Neal Katyal has drawn on institutional economics literature to argue that just as legitimate businesses can achieve efficiencies by being organized as firms, so can criminal enterprises.[101] In addition, he has argued that once offenders are organized into gangs, social psychology would predict that their motivation to commit crimes would increase. Group members often identify with the group and act so as to display loyalty to its aims. Their mutual interactions are likely to reinforce commitment to shared norms and values. When the group is a criminal gang, group identity and group norms will likely encourage offending.[102] In sum, the danger created by the formation of a conspiracy arguably transcends the harm of the planned offense.

97. Pinkerton v. United States, 328 U.S. 640, 643 (1946).
98. State v. Verive, 627 P.2d 721, 733 (Ariz. Ct. App. 1981) (conspiracy versus attempt).
99. Callanan v. United States, 364 U.S. 587, 593–94 (1961).
100. *See* Ianelli v. United States, 420 U.S. 770 (1975).
101. Neal Katyal, *Conspiracy Theory* 112 YALE L.J. 1307 (2003).
102. *Id.* at 1315, 1346–55.

VIII. Conspiracy: Act and Intent

Most American jurisdictions today condition conspiracy liability by statute on two objective elements: (1) agreement that a crime will be committed by one or more parties, and (2) an overt act in furtherance of the planned crime by any party to the agreement. As the overt act need not be performed by the defendant, it is arguably a circumstance element. The overt act need not be substantial enough to meet the standard for attempt liability. For example, if the intended crime is the intimidation of a witness, the substantial step required for attempt might involve going to the location where the offender expects to find the witness. The act of looking up the victim's address might suffice for an overt act, but not a substantial step. Similarly, the acquisition of matches might suffice for an overt act toward arson, but would not suffice for a substantial step. Note that a conspirator need neither perform nor agree to perform an overt act to be liable for conspiracy.

A second issue is whether the actus reus includes as a circumstance element that another person must also agree to the commission of the same crime. Traditionally, conspiracy did indeed require an agreement among two or more offenders.[103] Without such plurality, it seems the conspiracy does not increase the danger of the planned crime, or any other crime, as the conspirator has no collaborators. Nevertheless, the Model Penal Code proposed conspiracy liability based on a unilateral agreement. In other words, an offender could become liable by agreeing with an undercover law enforcement agent that the agent would commit a crime.[104] This reform flowed from the Model Penal Code's primary aims of identifying dangerous individuals for incapacitative and rehabilitative treatment, and maximizing deterrence by conditioning liability on subjective expectations rather than actual circumstances or results. The Model Penal Code was less concerned with the dangers of criminal organizations, and more concerned with each individual's willingness to offend. To the drafters, conspiracy was just another inchoate offense, punishable insofar as revealing a willingness to complete the offense. A substantial minority of jurisdictions follow the Model Penal Code in imposing liability for unilateral conspiracies.[105]

The most important actus reus issue in conspiracy overlaps with the mental element. This is agreement, which requires mental assent as well as its overt

---

103. *See, e.g.*, Commonwealth v. Hunt, 45 Mass. 111 (1842).
104. Model Penal Code § 5.03(1) (1962).
105. *E.g.*, Ohio Rev. Code Ann. § 2923.01(A)(2) (2015).

expression. Where statutes define the mental element of conspiracy, they require either "intent" or "purpose" that a crime be committed, or promoted, or facilitated. Some statutes leave the mental element undefined, simply requiring that the defendant "agree" or "conspire." In any case, "agreement" and "conspiracy," like "attempt," are taken to imply intent. Thus, intent that an offense be completed is not only the mental element of liability, it is also a sine qua non of the act element. What else is required for an agreement? Presumably, (1) the act of communicating that intent to another, and (2) the circumstance that another has such an intent and has communicated it to the accused. "Agreement" also implies (3) knowledge of this circumstance, although the requirement of this additional mental state is rarely spelled out by courts.

When convincing evidence of verbal agreement is available, all of the required acts, circumstances, and mental states are proven. But because such evidence is often unobtainable, the intertwined issues of agreement and intent that a crime be committed are frequently litigated. Courts have therefore permitted prosecutors to prove agreement through patterns of activity serving the same criminal purpose. In the Arkansas case of *State v. Griffin*, the defendant was convicted of conspiracy to commit an assault when he assaulted an officer investigating a road accident, a crowd of onlookers joined in assaulting the officer and his partner, and the defendant persisted in his attack.[106] There was *no* evidence of advance agreement, but pursuit of a common goal in one another's presence was deemed tacit agreement.[107] Yet it might be doubted that the pursuit of the same end inevitably implies agreement to anyone else's act.

It may seem that the provision of aid to one who is known to be committing a crime implies agreement to his or her commission of the crime and intent that it be committed. Yet this is not necessarily so, where the aid is compensated, the compensation is not contingent on the success of the crime, and the aid is of a kind also provided to others who use it for noncriminal ends. In the federal case of *United States v. Falcone*, a supplier of sugar, yeast, and cans to an illegal distillery was absolved of conspiracy to manufacture liquor.[108] On the other hand, in *Direct Sales Co. v. United States*, a drug wholesaler was convicted of conspiracy to distribute narcotics illegally for selling large quantities of narcotics to a doctor who was manifestly selling them to addicts rather than prescribing them for medical need.[109] Both decisions seem sensible but it is hard to state a principle that reconciles them. Is it that the drug wholesaler

106. Griffin v. State, 455 S.W.2d 882 (Ark. 1970).
107. *See id.* at 885–86.
108. 311 U.S. 205 (1940).
109. 319 U.S. 703 (1943).

was dealing in regulated goods? Yet it arguably complied with those regulations by selling them to a doctor. Why should it be held responsible for the doctor's violation of a regulation?

In the influential decision of *People v. Lauria*,[110] a California court set out to reconcile *Falcone* and *Direct Sales*. Lauria operated a telephone answering service used by several prostitutes to arrange meetings with clients.[111] The court held that the supplier of goods and services used in crime is a conspirator only if he both knows of their illegal use and intends to further that use. The court reasoned that intent to further the illegal use of goods and services can be proven indirectly when (1) the supplier receives a share of the proceeds of crime or charges a premium for sales to criminals, (2) there is no legitimate use for the goods or services sold, or (3) sales for use in crime comprise the bulk of the supplier's business, which would not otherwise be viable. Finding none of these circumstances present, the court upheld the dismissal of charges against the answering service.

The court struggled to account for the result in *Direct Sales*, in which the volume of drug sales to a single doctor was high enough to prove the wholesaler's knowledge of the doctor's illegal aims, but not high enough to comprise the bulk of the wholesaler's business. The court could have made more of two factors. First, the obviousness of the doctor's illegal aims meant not only that the wholesaler was aware of them, but that the doctor was aware of the wholesaler's knowledge, supplying the mutual awareness required for agreement. Second, although the scale of the transaction was not great enough for the wholesaler to depend on the sale for its own profitability, it was great enough that the doctor's ability to pay for the drugs depended on his selling them illegally. This arguably gave the wholesaler a stake in the doctor's crime. Instead of offering these arguments, the *Lauria* court suggested that where the purchaser's intended crime was sufficiently grave or dangerous such as a felony—mere knowledge of the purchaser's intent should suffice for proof of agreement.

Two actus reus issues that arise in attempt liability—impossibility and abandonment—are seldom seen in conspiracy.

Assuming the aim of punishing inchoate offenses is to incapacitate the dangerous, the argument for leaving attempters of the impossible unpunished is that there was never any danger or need for intervention. This argument is less compelling in the context of conspiracy if conspiracies dangerously facilitate offenses beyond those planned. Perhaps for this reason, courts have almost

110. 59 Cal. Rptr. 628 (Cal. Ct. App. 1967).
111. *Id.* at 630.

uniformly rejected impossibility arguments against conspiracy charges. Of course, if the conspiracy is entirely organized by law enforcement agents, a preventive rationale for punishment is elusive. A few successful impossibility claims have raised this problem.[112] On the other hand, if conspiracy requires agreement to commit a crime, conspiracy to commit a noncriminal act, like an attempt to commit such an act, is not a crime. Finally, federal courts have held that the conspiracy is not terminated by the defeat of its object by law enforcement if some conspirators continue to pursue that object.[113]

The prevailing view has been that abandonment is a defense to a charge of conspiracy, only if (1) an overt act is required, and (2) the defendant withdraws his agreement before the overt act is committed. Once the overt act is committed, the crime is complete. The Model Penal Code permits a defense of abandonment, but only if the defendant effectively thwarts the conspiracy's aims, while showing a "complete and voluntary renunciation."[114]

Withdrawal may limit the temporal duration of the conspiracy even if it does not eliminate liability. Thus, if the defendant clearly communicates his withdrawal to all of his confederates, after an overt act has been committed, he remains liable for the conspiracy, but it is over as far as he is concerned. This may be significant for two reasons. First, the conspiracy's extension in time has certain procedural consequences. Thus, the out-of-court statements in furtherance of the conspiracy of the defendant's co-conspirators are admissible against him, but only if those statements coincided with his participation. Next, a defendant can be tried for conspiracy any place where an act in furtherance of his conspiracy takes place. Finally, the statute of limitations only begins to run on a defendant's conspiracy charge once his participation in the conspiracy has concluded. Shortening one defendant's participation in the conspiracy may therefore afford procedural advantages to that defendant.

Yet the temporal extent of the defendant's participation in the conspiracy is important for a second, more important reason. A conspirator may be liable as a co-conspirator for crimes committed in furtherance of a conspiracy as long as he remains a part of it. The extent of his co-conspirator liability depends on other questions regarding the scope of the conspiracy, such as who he has agreed with. We will reconsider these questions of scope below, in discussing co-conspirator liability as one form of participation in crime.

---

112. *E.g.*, Woo Wai v. United States, 223 F. 412 (9th Cir. 1915); WAYNE R. LAFAVE, CRIMINAL LAW 685, 687 (2010).

113. United States v. Recio, 537 U.S. 270 (2003).

114. MODEL PENAL CODE § 5.03(6) (1962).

IX. Complicity

We now turn from inchoate offenses to doctrines of accessorial liability for the offenses of others. The oldest and most important form of accessorial liability is complicity. We will also discuss perpetration by means and co-conspirator liability, and briefly mention vicarious liability for the acts of agents, including liability of corporations.

Matthew Hale's *History of Pleas of the Crown* distinguished four roles for offenders.[115] Perpetrators of offenses were "principals in the first degree." Those "present aiding and abetting" criminal conduct were "principals in the second degree." Persons who "procure, counsel, command or abet" another to commit a crime were "accessories before the fact," while those aiding and abetting the offender to escape liability for a completed crime were "accessories after the fact." According to Hale, the first three categories—principals in both first and second degree and accessories before the fact—were treated identically in all cases. In other words, those who aided and abetted the commission of the crime (rather than the prevention of its punishment) were fully liable for every kind of offense. Unless the statute defining the offense provided otherwise, accessories after the fact were fully liable for high treason, innocent of mere trespasses and misdemeanors, and liable for felonies and petty treasons, but subject to benefit of clergy. An accused accessory had a right not be tried before the principal he or she was alleged to have abetted, and could not be convicted if that alleged principal was acquitted.[116] A principal of the second degree could be tried (and convicted) before a principal of the first degree, however.[117]

According to Hale, the conduct required for liability as a principal of the second degree was conjunctive: it involved both aiding *and* "abetting," that is, encouraging. The conduct required for an accessory before the fact was encouraging. Aid only gave rise to accessorial liability if provided while "knowing and consenting to the design."[118] Yet an abettor had to actively promote the crime rather than merely consent to it: "words that sound in bare permission make not an accessary."[119] Thus the conduct required for accessorial liability—"abetting," "counseling," or "commanding"—implied the purpose of promoting the crime. Arguably one who combined verbal consent to a crime with active assistance manifested a similar purpose to promote the crime.

---

115. 1 MATTHEW HALE, HISTORIA PLACITORUM CORONAE 612–22 (1736).
116. *Id.* at 623–24.
117. WAYNE R. LAFAVE, CRIMINAL LAW 706 (2010).
118. 1 MATTHEW HALE, HISTORIA PLACITORUM CORONAE 615–16 (1736).
119. *Id.*

By the middle of the nineteenth century, English legislation had reclassified accessories before the fact as principals, and so eliminated procedural distinctions between principals and accessories. Eventually, all American jurisdictions adopted this reform. Most refer to aiders or abettors in the commission of the crime as "accomplices," although some codes still use the traditional terminology.[120] Those who subsequently aid the offenders in escaping liability for a crime are at most guilty of a different offense.

Some states adopted the Model Penal Code's basic approach to parties to crime. The Code makes individuals liable for offenses committed by conduct for which they are "legally accountable." This includes the proscribed conduct of innocent actors they culpably cause, and the offenses of others in which they are complicit.[121] The Code makes one an "accomplice" in another's offense if "with the purpose of promoting or facilitating" its commission, he "solicits" or "aids" the other to commit it.[122] States generally condition accomplice liability on aiding or encouraging the commission of an offense, but some statutes and cases require both aid and encouragement.

Accomplice liability presupposes that offenders cannot be accountable for the voluntary acts of another by causing them. Instead they become accountable for acts of others by joining and supporting them. Thus, the conduct and mental states required for complicity in a crime are very similar to those required for liability for conspiracy to commit that crime. The difference is that the accomplice's liability depends on the perpetrator actually completing the crime, whereas the conspirator's liability depends on his fellow conspirator agreeing to commit the crime, and one of them committing a minor act toward execution of the agreement.

X. Accomplice Conduct

Because the accomplice need not cause the success of the crime, the accomplice's conduct can be superfluous. Suppose Paula Principal intentionally kills Victor Victim with a gun Alice Accomplice provided for that purpose. Although Alice's act may have been necessary to Victor's death, Paula was a voluntary actor arguably breaking the chain of causation. Nevertheless, Alice is guilty as her accomplice. Now suppose Paula uses a different gun, already in her possession. Although Alice's act was causally superfluous, she is still complicit because

---

120. Wayne R. LaFave, Criminal Law 706 (2010).
121. Model Penal Code § 2.06(2)(a) (1962).
122. *Id.* § 2.06(3).

she provided aid. Next, assume Alice successfully urges Paula to shoot Victor. Although Paula is a voluntary actor, arguably barring Alice's causal responsibility, Alice is complicit because she encouraged the offense. Finally, assume Alice is 1 of 10 members of a crowd, all urging Paula on as she carries out her prior plan to shoot Victor. Even if we are sure Alice's encouragement made no causal difference, she is complicit in the offense she encouraged.

Although aid and encouragement need not cause the success or completion of the crime, they must nevertheless meet certain criteria of efficacy to satisfy the act requirement of complicity. Thus, encouragement must be communicated to a perpetrator before the completion of the offense. Expressing approval to a bystander or congratulating the offender after the fact are not sufficient. What about aid? Hale's discussion suggested that the communication of consent to the perpetrator was essential for both principals in the second degree and accessories before the fact. Hale treated spatiotemporal presence as essential, but was untroubled about what action was necessary to constitute aid. The collapse of the distinction between principals in the second degree and accessories before the fact combined with the emergent conception of action as remote causation to render the concept of aid problematic. Aid would of course have to precede the completion of the crime, and it would have to be done with an intention to promote the success of the crime. But could it be unknown to the perpetrator?

Consider another hypothetical: Suppose Alice accompanies Paula to a convenience store and agrees to stand watch outside while Paula robs the cashier. Clearly Alice is Paula's accomplice, even if she just stands outside and takes no further action, because her agreement encourages Paula. Indeed, she would be complicit even if she broke her promise and left her post. But now suppose that while passing by, Alice sees her friend Paula don a ski mask, pull out a gun, and enter the store. Unknown to Paula, Alice decides to stands watch outside the store. A policeman approaches the store and Alice diverts him by saying she just saw a purse-snatcher flee around the corner. Is Alice complicit in the robbery even though Paula knew nothing of her aid? If so, how tangible must the aid be? Finally suppose that, unbeknownst to Paula, Alice stands by to divert police or other witnesses, but no one comes. Is this aid, or is it merely an unrealized intention to aid?

Two famous cases illustrate these difficulties.

The case of "the Gallup 14" arose from a labor dispute in a New Mexico mining town.[123] After a protracted strike, the mining company moved to evict miners from their homes on company land. After these evictions led to arrests

123. State v. Ochoa, 72 P.2d 609 (N.M. 1937).

of miners, a meeting was held at which a protest was planned for the next day, and Juan Ochoa and Manuel Avitia were designated as spokespersons. At the planned protest the next day, some members of the crowd attempted to free one of the arrestees, shooting broke out, and the county sheriff was killed instantly by two nearly simultaneous shots, the first through his heart and the second through his head. The two killers were shot and killed. Nevertheless, dozens of other members of the crowd were charged with first degree murder. Eventually, Ochoa and Avitia were convicted as accomplices to second degree murder, and the convictions were upheld on appeal. The New Mexico Supreme Court conceded that there was no evidence that Ochoa and Avitia had known of or agreed to any prior plan to kill the sheriff. Moreover the court did not require that an accomplice communicate approval to a perpetrator, so long as he shared his intent and provided aid. The court's theory was that after the killers began shooting at the sheriff, Ochoa and Avitia had aided them by assaulting a deputy, thereby preventing him from coming to the sheriff's defense. The difficulty with the court's theory was that although it was unclear whether the assault on the deputy had begun before or after the shooting, the evidence suggested that the sheriff had been killed instantly as soon as the shooting began. If so, Ochoa and Avitia could not have had the intent to aid a murder before the shooting began, and no longer had the opportunity to aid a murder after the shooting began. Perhaps for this reason, they were soon pardoned, on condition they leave the state![124]

In the late nineteenth-century Alabama case of *State v. Tally*,[125] the four Skelton brothers pursued one Ross from Scottsboro to Stevenson and killed him there for seducing their sister. The Skeltons were also siblings of the defendant's wife. The defendant, Judge Tally, went to the telegraph office in Scottsboro to see if anyone would send a telegram to the victim. Ross's relative did indeed send a telegram of warning to be delivered to him at Stevenson, whereupon Tally telegraphed the telegraph operator at Stevenson, saying: "Do not let the party warned get away. . . . Say nothing." When Ross arrived in Stevenson and alighted from his coach he was attacked immediately by the Skeltons and killed. The telegraph operator did not deliver the warning to the victim, but had little time to do so, and may or may not have been dissuaded from doing so by Tally's telegram. Nevertheless Tally was convicted as an accomplice to murder.

The court reasoned that Tally could only be convicted if, knowing the Skeltons' intent to kill, he intended to aid them in so doing, and either encouraged them by promising to aid them, or actually aided them by "contributing"

124. *See* LEAH WORTHAM, THE GALLUP 14 (2000).
125. 102 Ala. 25 (1894).

to Ross's death. Nevertheless, the court insisted, a contributory act need not have caused or been necessary to the death. Tally's act was sufficient aid if it "deprived [the deceased] of a single chance of life . . . though it cannot be known or shown that the dead man . . . would have availed himself of that chance."[126] The court concluded that Tally had not encouraged the Skeltons by communicating his intentions to them, and that his keeping watch at the telegraph office provided the Skeltons with no aid. To deprive the victim of a chance required that Tally affect events in Stevenson. Yet the court concluded that Tally did so, reasoning that the Stevenson telegraph operator could have intercepted the defendant in the middle of the road, might have done so had Tally not influenced him, and this might have saved his life, even though he was surrounded by four assassins. Upon these suppositions, the court found that Tally had succeeded in depriving the victim of a "chance." Yet it is not clear why standing by to prevent warning did not also deprive the victim of a chance. A better explanation of the decision is that Tally aided the Skeltons by depriving Ross of his kinsman's aid rather than by reducing Ross's probability of survival, or increasing the Skeltons' probability of success.

Yet even if we are sure that aid need not cause success, we are still left with a puzzle about how consequential conduct must be to count as aid. Suppose that Tally's telegram not only had no impact on the killing, but also had no impact on the warning. Thus, suppose the telegraph operator in Stevenson delivered the warning to the victim as soon as he alighted from the coach (but the victim was killed anyway). If Tally failed in preventing aid from reaching the victim, does that mean that Tally merely attempted to aid the killers, but did not succeed? A further question is what legal consequences should follow from such a failed attempt to aid. In most American jurisdictions, a failed attempt to participate does not make one complicit in a completed or attempted crime.

By contrast, the Model Penal Code—placing its usual priority on culpability over conduct and consequences—imposes inchoate liability for merely attempting to participate in a crime. Recall that the Code imposes solicitation liability for requests to commit an offense that fail in either of two ways: because they are not heeded or because they are never received (solicitation liability is always for failure, because if solicitation succeeds, the soliciting actor is an accomplice in the resulting offense). The Code similarly imposes liability for efforts to aid an offense that fail in two ways.

First, suppose the defendant succeeds in committing conduct expected to aid an offense, but the offense is never attempted (Tally prevents Ross from

126. *Id.* at 69.

being warned, but the Skeltons decided to hunt rabbits rather than pursue Ross). The Code treats as an attempt "conduct designed to aid another to commit a crime that would establish his complicity . . . if the crime were committed by such other person . . . although the crime is not committed or attempted by such other person."[127] About a quarter of American jurisdictions have adopted this doctrine that unrequited aid is an attempt.

Second, suppose the offense is completed, but the defendant fails in providing aid (the telegraph operator at Scottsboro never sends Tally's message, but the Skeltons kill Ross). The Code treats as an accomplice in an offense one who "with the purpose of promoting or facilitating the offense . . . aids or agrees *or attempts to aid* such other person in planning or committing it."[128] A few jurisdictions have explicitly adopted this rule equating failed and successful aid. Yet this rule merely moves the line-drawing problem back from criteria for causation or criteria for aid to criteria for attempt. Courts still must decide how consequential conduct must be to count as an attempt to aid.

In keeping with its subjectivism, the Model Penal Code does exculpate assistance or encouragement where the defendant intentionally renders it ineffective. Thus, an actor is not complicit where "he terminates his complicity prior to the commission of the offense and (i) wholly deprives it of effectiveness . . . or (ii) gives timely warning to. . . authorities or otherwise makes proper to prevent . . . the offense."[129] In a New Hampshire case applying this standard, a high school student was found complicit in the theft of an exam when he agreed to stand watch, but instead went home.[130] The court reasoned that although he did not provide aid, he became an accomplice by agreeing to do so, and thereby encouraging the theft. Silently breaking his agreement to aid did not deprive it of its encouraging effect.[131]

XI. Accomplice Culpability

Because the accomplice participates in the perpetrator's crime, it seems that his or her culpability should be the same. Thus, the *Ochoa* court observed that the "aider and abettor . . . must share the intent or purpose of the principal."[132] Yet the accomplice cannot always have the same mental state as the principal, for

---

127. MODEL PENAL CODE § 5.01(3) (1962).
128. *Id.* § 2.06(3).
129. *Id.* § 2.06(6)(c).
130. State v. Formella, 960 A.2d 722 (N.H. 2008).
131. *Id.* at 726.
132. State v. Ochoa, 72 P.2d 609, 615 (1937).

two reasons. First, his conduct is different: rather than fulfilling the act element of the offense, the accomplice aids or encourages. Second, unlike the principal, the accomplice needs to be conscious of the intentions of another actor, the principal. Thus, the Alabama Supreme Court offered the following compound test for Judge Tally's culpability: "did Judge Tally . . . knowing the intention of the Skeltons to take the life of Ross, . . . do any act intended to further their design and aid them in the taking of his life."[133] Thus the court required that Tally acted with both knowledge of, and purpose to further, the principals' aims; and with purpose to aid them. A similar position was taken by Judge Learned Hand in *United States v. Peoni*, denying that Peoni's sale of counterfeit currency made him complicit in the later possession of that currency by a downstream purchaser. Complicity required that the aider "participate" in the offense "as something he wishes to bring about, that he seek by his actions to make it succeed."[134]

Not all courts have required purpose with respect to both the principal's aims and the facilitative effect of conduct in achieving those aims. Some have required knowledge with respect to both. Thus, in *Backun v. United States*, the court upheld the conviction of A as an accomplice in the interstate transportation of stolen goods, where he sold the stolen goods to B, knowing they would be resold out of state.[135] The court reasoned that even the seller of lawful goods would be complicit in a crime, if he knew the goods would be used in committing it. Knowing aid should suffice for accomplice liability:

> Guilt as an accessory does not depend on "having a stake in the . . . crime" but on aiding . . . the perpetrators. . . . The seller may not ignore the purpose for which the purpose is made if he is advised of that purpose, or wash his hands of the aid he has given the perpetrator of a felony . . . . In any such case, not only does the act of the seller assist in the commission of the felony, but his will assents to its commission, since he could refuse to give the assistance by refusing to make the sale.[136]

One difficulty with this approach is that it imposes liability on an informant who collaborates with an offender in order to gather evidence against him. A Colorado decision denied Wilson's complicity in Pierce's burglary where Wilson boosted him in a window and then summoned a police officer to arrest him. The court reasoned that Wilson lacked the intent to permanently deprive the owner of property, which is required for theft. Accordingly, Wilson did not

---

133. State v. Tally, 102 Ala. 25, 54 (1894).
134. 100 F.2d 401, 402 (2d Cir. 1938).
135. 112 F.2d 635 (4th Cir. 1940).
136. *Id.* at 637.

share in the intent required for burglary (here, the intent to commit theft).[137] The California Supreme Court took a similar position in *People v. Beeman*, where the defendant argued he had collaborated with burglars so that he could later recover the goods for the victim.[138] The court reasoned that

> When the definition of the offense includes the intent to do some act or achieve some consequence beyond the actus reus of the crime . . . the aider and abettor must share the specific intent of the perpetrator. . . . [A]n aider and abettor will "share" the perpetrator's specific intent when he or she knows the full extent of the perpetrator's criminal purpose and gives aid or encouragement with the intent or purpose of facilitating the perpetrator's commission of the crime.[139]

The *Wilson* and *Beeman* decisions suggest that the culpability required for complicity depends on the mental element of the principal's offense. Thus we have two potential criteria of culpability: intent to aid (or encourage), and the mental element of the offense. The Model Penal Code combines these two ideas by requiring that the accomplice act with "the purpose of promoting or facilitating the commission of the offense,"[140] but also providing that "when causing a . . . result is an element of an offense, an accomplice in the conduct causing such result is an accomplice in the commission of that offense, if he acts with the kind of culpability . . . with respect to that result that is sufficient for the commission of that offense."[141]

How does this scheme apply? Because the crime of theft requires purpose with respect to a result element, permanently depriving an owner of property, it seems clear that an accomplice in theft must have purpose with respect to this result, as well as a purpose of promoting or facilitating the offense. But what about a crime such as negligent homicide, requiring only negligence with respect to a result? Can one act with the purpose of promoting or facilitating negligent homicide, without having purpose with respect to the death of the victim? How can one intend to aid a crime that does not require intent?

Courts applying the Model Penal Code's definition of complicity have disagreed on this problem. In *State v. Etzweiler*, the New Hampshire Supreme Court found that a defendant who loaned his car to a manifestly drunk driver could not be complicit in the driver's negligent homicide unless he intended the driver to cause death.[142] Indeed, the court reasoned that even if Etzweiler

---

137. Wilson v. People, 87 P.2d 5, 6 (Colo. 1939).
138. 35 Cal. 3d 547 (1984).
139. *Id.* at 560.
140. Model Penal Code § 2.06(3)(a) (1962).
141. *Id.* § 2.06(4).
142. 480 A.2d 870 (N.H. 1984).

had intended the drunk driver to cause death, it is impossible to aid someone to achieve an aim unintentionally.[143]

The opposite result was reached in the Connecticut case of *State v. Foster*.[144] Foster and Cannon confronted Middleton and accused him of assaulting Foster's girlfriend. Foster gave Cannon a knife and asked him to detain Middleton, while Foster went to get the girlfriend so that she could identify Middleton. Cannon and Middleton fought, and Cannon stabbed Middleton, unintentionally killing him. The defendant was found complicit in negligent homicide, because he provided the knife intending that Cannon stab Middleton if he resisted detention, and he was negligent of the risk that Middleton would be killed.[145] Thus he intentionally aided the conduct, while having the kind of culpability with respect to the result required for negligent homicide.

Which of these two decisions is more faithful to the Model Penal Code? The Model Penal Code Commentary reveals that the term "commission of the offense" as used in Section 2.06 refers only to the conduct element of the offense.[146] Recall that in the Code, complicity is defined as one way that a person can be "legally accountable for the *conduct* of another."[147] Thus the *Foster* decision is consistent with the intended meaning of Section 2.06, requiring purpose to promote or facilitate with respect to conduct elements, but not result elements.

XII. Perpetration by Means and Discrepant Liability

Accomplice liability traditionally depended on the liability of the principal, who had to be convicted first. If the person committing the proscribed conduct lacked culpability, there was no crime to be an accomplice in. In the 1891 Missouri case of *State v. Hayes*, the defendant solicited Hill to burglarize a store.[148] Hill went along with the plan in order to implicate Hayes. Yet Hayes successfully argued that because Hill lacked the intent to steal, there was no burglary for Hayes to be complicit in: no liability for Hill, no complicity for Hayes.[149] Of course this argument would not preclude Hayes's liability for solicitation.

---

143. *Id.* at 874–75.
144. 522 A.2d 277 (Conn. 1987).
145. *See id.* at 286.
146. MODEL PENAL CODE COMMENTARIES, pt. 1, §2.06, at 210 (1985).
147. *Id.* § 2.06(2).
148. 16 S.W. 514 (Mo. 1891).
149. *See id.* at 515.

What if Hayes had induced Hill to enter a building and remove goods by telling Hill the property belonged to Hayes? Again, Hill would not be liable because he would lack the culpable mental states required for the offense. Hayes would not be complicit in Hill's burglary, but instead would be liable as the perpetrator. Recall that the Model Penal Code makes one person accountable for the proscribed conduct of another in two ways: as an accomplice in culpable conduct, and as a cause of innocent conduct. In causing innocent commission of proscribed conduct, Hayes would be a perpetrator by means. In *Muni v. United States*, the defendant engaged in fraudulent transactions, predictably causing bank employees to unwittingly communicate false information across state lines.[150] Muni was deemed to have caused this conduct, and held liable as the principal.[151]

What if one aids or encourages a perpetrator who acts with a culpable mental state, but is excused from responsibility? Is this complicity, or perpetration by means? It might be perpetration by means if A causes B's offense, for example by compelling it at gunpoint. But suppose B is insane and feels compelled to kill as a result of a command hallucination. B tells A of his plans, and A encourages him. Psychiatrists agree that B exercised no choice and was impervious to external influence. As A did not cause B's conduct, she cannot be a perpetrator by means. Yet in most jurisdictions she can be an accomplice to an excused offense. For example, the New York Penal Law provides that it is no defense to accomplice liability that the perpetrator "is not guilty of the offense . . . owing to criminal irresponsibility."[152] In fact, this provision adds that the perpetrator's lack of a required culpable mental state is no bar to complicity, thereby treating perpetration by means as a variant of complicity. Almost 20 states have "innocent agent" statutory provisions similar to the Model Penal Code's,[153] although some of these—like New York's—include causing innocent conduct within complicity.

It has long been accepted that an accomplice can be guilty of a lesser crime than a principal, as a result of a less culpable mental state.[154] But if—as in New York—an accomplice can be guilty even though the perpetrator is innocent, it should also be possible for the accomplice to be guilty of a different, and more serious crime than is the perpetrator. Indeed, the Delaware Supreme Court applied a provision like New York's to hold an accomplice liable for first

150. Muni v. United States, 668 F.2d 87 (2d Cir. 1981).

151. *Id.* at 89.

152. N.Y. PENAL LAW § 20.05 (2015).

153. John F. Decker, *The Mental State for Accomplice Liability in American Criminal Law*, 60 S.C. L. REV. 237, 255 (2008).

154. Salisbury's Case, 1 Plowden 100 (1553) (accomplice in murder guilty of manslaughter because lacked malice).

degree murder, while the killer's liability was reduced to manslaughter as a result of his partial excuse of extreme emotional disturbance.[155] A California court reached a similar decision when a killer's liability was mitigated by an unreasonable belief in the need for self-defense, but his accomplice's was not.[156] In these cases, discrepant liability was based on the accomplice's greater responsibility. Courts have *not* generally held accomplices liable for graver offenses than perpetrators based on a more culpable mental state. Suppose a loan shark orders his henchman to injure a defaulting debtor, but in assaulting the debtor, the henchman carefully avoids injury. It may seem that the loan shark should be liable as an accomplice to assault with intent to injure, but he will not be, because no such crime was committed.

XIII. Co-Conspirator and Accomplice Liability for Secondary Crimes

Suppose A solicits B to burglarize a store. B agrees and performs as promised. Both are guilty of conspiracy by virtue of their agreement. Both are guilty of burglary—B as perpetrator and A as an accomplice. But is A also guilty of B's burglary by virtue of their conspiracy to commit burglary?

Does it make a difference to A's liability for burglary as either an accomplice or co-conspirator, if B hires C to commit the burglary instead of committing it himself?

Suppose B is the burglar and while leaving with the loot, he is resisted by a security guard. B punches him and escapes, thereby committing robbery. Is A guilty of this robbery as well, by virtue of either his complicity in the burglary, or his conspiracy to commit burglary?

Finally suppose that while returning from the burglary, B sees an elderly pedestrian on a deserted street and takes the opportunity to rob this victim. Is A also liable for this second robbery, as an accomplice or a co-conspirator?

Federal law makes A guilty of B's burglary, not only as an accomplice, but also as a co-conspirator. In the leading case, Daniel Pinkerton was held liable for his brother's crimes in furtherance of their agreement to evade income tax liability. Writing for the U.S. Supreme Court, Justice Douglas reasoned that just as the overt act in furtherance of a conspiracy by any of its parties was attributable to all, so completed offenses committed in furtherance of the conspiracy should also be attributed to all. The Court recognized exceptions for

155. Pendry v. State, 367 A.2d 627 (Del. 1976).
156. People v. McCoy, 24 P.3d 1210 (Cal. 2001).

crimes that "did not fall within the scope of the unlawful project, or . . . could not reasonably be foreseen as a . . . natural consequence of the unlawful agreement."[157] This effectively makes each conspirator liable for crimes he negligently encourages by joining the conspiracy. Under this rule A is arguably guilty as a co-conspirator, not only in B's burglary, but also in B's robbery of the security guard, if it seems foreseeable that such a guard might be present. A is not liable for the robbery of the pedestrian under this test.

Whether A is liable for C's burglary is a more difficult question. The burglary is clearly in furtherance of the goal of the conspiracy, but arguably C is not a party to A's conspiracy with B, because A and C have not agreed with each other. Yet, courts applying the *Pinkerton* rule have treated the membership of the conspiracy as subject to the same foreseeability standard as the offenses committed in furtherance of it. If A should foresee the necessity to the goals of the conspiracy of recruiting someone to perform a certain task, A is deemed a co-conspirator of that unidentified but foreseeably necessary agent. In *Kotteakos v. United States*, participants in fraudulent loans with the same company were not deemed co-conspirators in one another's crimes, because the Court did not see the success of any one of these transactions as depending on the success of another.[158] In *Blumenthal v. United States*, however, the Court found a single conspiracy among distributors of contraband, because each could have foreseen the necessity of others populating all the "links" in the chain of distribution.[159] On this reasoning, A is a co-conspirator of C because he knew that the conspiracy's object required a burglar, and he need not have known who the burglar would be.

Justice Rutledge's dissent in *Pinkerton* treated co-conspirator liability as a novel conflation of the offense of conspiracy with accomplice liability for a completed offense.[160] Yet Justice Douglas's majority opinion cited earlier federal decisions that when "parties were associated together for . . . [an] illegal purpose . . . any act done . . . to accomplish that purpose was the act of all,"[161] Douglas also recalled a Justice Holmes opinion, likening a conspiracy to restrain trade to a partnership, in which each is liable for the act of all.[162] The principle that collaborators are responsible for crimes in furtherance of a common plan has a long pedigree. The 1885 Illinois case of *Hamilton v. People* held that as three defendants "were all co-conspirators in a dangerous criminal

---

157. Pinkerton v. United States, 328 U.S. 640, 647–48 (1946).
158. 328 U.S. 750 (1946).
159. 332 U.S. 539 (1947).
160. 328 U.S. 640, 649 (1946) (Rutledge, J., dissenting).
161. *Id.* at 647 (citing Johnson v. United States, 62 F.2d 32, 34 (9th Cir. 1932)).
162. *Id.* (citing United States v. Kissel, 218 U.S. 601, 608 (1910)).

enterprise . . . whatever was done by one, in contemplation of law was done by all, and all are therefore equally responsible."[163] The 1837 North Carolina decision of *State v. Haney* found that "where a privity and community of design has been established, the act of any one of those who have combined together for the same illegal purpose, done in furtherance of the unlawful design, is . . . the act of all."[164] Recall that sixteenth-century English cases held all parties to a planned act of violence liable for death caused as a result.[165] Commenting on such a case, sixteenth-century jurist Edmund Plowden reasoned that

> he who commands an unlawful Thing to be done shall be judged Accessary to all that follows from that same Thing, but not from any other distinct Thing. As if I command a Man to rob such a one . . . and the other defends himself and a Combat ensues . . . and the Person attempted to be robbed is killed, I am Accessary to this Murder. . . . So if I command one to beat another and he beats him so that he dies thereof, I shall be Accessary to this Murder, for it is a Consequence of my Command, . . . which naturally tended to endanger the Life of the other.[166]

Subsequent commentators agreed that solicitors were responsible for the probable effects of their proposals, down to Blackstone who concluded that "he who commands or counsels another to commit an unlawful act is accessary to all that ensues."[167] Early American cases imposing murder liability on co-felons for killings in furtherance of and foreseeably resulting from the attempted felony were applications of this principle.[168]

Consistent with its rejection of felony murder liability, the Model Penal Code rejected co-conspirator liability. Thus, under the Model Penal Code, A is not liable as a co-conspirator for any of B's crimes. By virtue of soliciting B's offense, A is an accomplice in that offense when it is completed. Yet he cannot be liable for either of B's robberies because he is not complicit in them. Under the Model Penal Code, A does not become C's accomplice by soliciting B, although he might become C's accomplice by providing aid to B that also helps C commit A's intended crime.

---

163. 113 Ill. 34, 38 (1885).
164. 19 N.C. 390, 395 (1837).
165. *See* R. v. Saunders, 75 Eng. Rep. 706 (Q.B. 1576); Mansell & Herbert's Case, 73 Eng. Rep. 279 (K.B. 1555); Salisbury's Case, 1 Plowden 100 (1553); Lord Dacre's Case, 72 Eng. Rep. 458 (K.B. 1535).
166. 2 Plowden 476 (1578).
167. 4 William Blackstone, Commentaries on the Laws of England 37 (1769).
168. Francis Sayre, *Criminal Responsibility for the Acts of Another*, 43 Harv. L. Rev. 689, 703–06 (1930).

A few states have explicitly adopted co-conspirator liability by statute. Among the dozen most populous states, Texas provides that "all conspirators are guilty of . . . [any] felony . . . committed in furtherance of the unlawful purpose and . . . that should have been anticipated as a result of the carrying out of the conspiracy."[169] New Jersey holds each person "legally accountable for the conduct of another person . . . when he is engaged in a conspiracy with such other person."[170] Additional states have adopted co-conspirator liability by common law decision. California jurors are instructed that each "conspirator is vicariously liable for the unintended acts by coconspirators if such acts are in furtherance of the object of the conspiracy, or are the reasonable and natural consequence of the object of the conspiracy."[171] Pennsylvania courts have held a conspirator to be "chargeable with the acts of his co-conspirator."[172]

Other states have doctrines similar in effect to co-conspirator liability. Illinois has a functionally equivalent provision that "any acts in the furtherance" of a "common criminal design or agreement" are "considered to be the acts of all parties to the common design or agreement. . . ."[173] Does this provision rest liability for secondary crimes on conspiracy or complicity? It is not entirely clear. The provision codifies the 1974 decision in *People v. Kessler*, which imposed attempted murder liability on an accomplice to burglary, because he shared a "common design" with the shooter; but which cited the co-conspirator rule of *Hamilton v. People* as authority.[174] North Carolina has a similar common law rule rooted in the "privity and community of design" formula of *Haney*. Current law imposes liability for crimes committed in pursuit of or as a natural and probable consequence of a "common purpose"[175] to commit a crime. Michigan case law makes all accomplices liable for secondary crimes that are "natural and probable" consequences of the "common enterprise."[176] California cases simply impose liability for all crimes that are "natural and probable" consequences of any crime in which the defendant is complicit.[177] Thus, about half of American jurisdictions impose liability for foreseeable secondary crimes. Some condition such liability on complicity, some on conspiracy, and some on an older "common design" doctrine. In addition, we have seen that many jurisdictions have special doctrines of accomplice liability extending felony murder

---

169. Texas Penal Code § 7.02(b) (2015).
170. N.J. Stat. Ann. § 2C: 2-6 (2015).
171. Cal. Crim. Jury Instr. 6.11(2015),(approved in People v. Hardy, 825 P.2d 781 (Cal. 1992)).
172. Commonwealth v. Glover, 582 A.2d 1111, 1114 (Pa. Super. Ct. 1990).
173. 720 Ill. Comp. Stat. 5/5-2 (2015).
174. 315 N.E.2d 29, 32–33 (Ill. 1974).
175. State v. Barnes, 481 S.E.2d 44, 70 (N.C. 1997) (citing State v. Haney, 19 N.C. 390, 395 (1837)).
176. People v. Robinson, 715 N.W.2d 44, 49–50 (Mich. 2006).
177. People v. Culuko, 92 Cal. Rptr. 2d 789, 802 (Cal. Ct. App. 2000).

liability for killings by co-felons foreseeable as a consequence of participation in certain felonies.

Why should a conspirator or an accomplice be liable for crimes he does not intend to aid or encourage, merely because they are foreseeable? Professor Neal Katyal defends the *Pinkerton* rule on grounds of utility rather than desert.[178] He argues that co-conspirator liability usefully deters gang membership, and facilitates investigation and prosecution of organized crime. By making each gang member potentially liable for the acts of all, co-conspirator liability greatly enhances the penalty for conspiracy, and the leverage prosecutors can use to pressure members into implicating their leaders. Katyal argues that this leverage sows mistrust, disrupting group solidarity and organizational discipline, rendering gangs less efficient in pursuing their criminal ends.[179]

Notwithstanding these considerations, about half of American jurisdictions lack doctrines imposing liability on conspirators or accomplices for unintended but foreseeable crimes. These jurisdictions impute liability for the conduct of others only on the basis of complicity, not conspiracy. Moreover, they impute to accomplices only those crimes they intentionally aid or encourage. By this standard, A would not be liable for either of B's robberies. His encouraging B to commit a burglary would not necessarily make him liable for C doing so, under this test.

XIV. Vicarious and Corporate Liability

Two remaining forms of participatory liability are used in the regulation of businesses: vicarious and corporate liability. Both operate on principles of agency derived from civil law, holding a principal liable for the conduct of an agent. Both cut somewhat against the trend of increasing subjectivization of liability, as they often require little or no culpability. Yet because neither form of liability typically triggers sentences of incarceration, they are marginal examples of criminal liability. Critics of these forms of liability often propose that they be reclassified as civil so as to maintain the integrity of the criminal law's requirements of act and culpability.

Vicarious liability holds an employer or property owner liable for the criminal act of an agent, without any conduct on the part of the person punished. It is not a general doctrine of criminal law, but applies only where it is included within the definition of a particular offense. It is often applied to owners of motor vehicles

178. Neal Katyal, *Conspiracy Theory*, 112 YALE L.J. 1307 (2003).
179. *Id.* at 1372–75.

for parking violations, regardless of the identity of the driver; to proprietors of bars that sell liquor to minors; and to owners of businesses subject to commercial or safety regulations. It is frequently applied to activities that are licensed, often with notice to the licensee of certain legal duties. The penalties are usually confined to fines. The penal sanction of a fine often functions as a milder substitute for the noncriminal sanction of license revocation or suspension. Liability of an employer may depend on proof of the circumstance that the employee was acting in the course of his employment. Liability of a proprietor may depend on proof that the perpetrator was using the property with permission.

Vicarious liability is often also strict liability, imposed on a superior even if he directed a subordinate to follow the law. Such strict liability is widely accepted in tort, as a means of internalizing the social costs of enterprises, but does not seem justified by the deterrent and retributive functions of criminal punishment. As we have seen, the Supreme Court has treated severity of punishment as evidence of legislative intent to require proof of culpability, but has stopped short of holding that due process conditions severe punishment on culpability. Some of the key Supreme Court cases on strict liability have involved vicarious liability. In *United States v. Dotterweich*, the Court limited misdemeanor liability for interstate distribution of mislabeled or contaminated food or drugs to executives bearing a "responsible relation" to the offense.[180] In *United States v. Park* the Court confined that status to those with authority over the conduct and the power to prevent it through the exercise of reasonable care.[181] The Court reasoned that passive violation of this duty of reasonable care "imports some measure of blameworthiness"[182] and a "measure of culpability."[183]

Corporate liability is one form of vicarious liability that may be generally applicable to all offenses. Corporate liability is necessarily vicarious, because corporations cannot act or experience culpable mental states except through agents. In many cases—including *Dotterweich* and *Park*—where corporate officers are charged with vicarious criminal liability, corporations are also charged. Nevertheless, corporate liability is a general doctrine of criminal law, not confined to particular offense definitions. In the 1909 case of *New York Central & Hudson River Railroad Co. v. United States*, the Supreme Court held that it did not violate the due process rights of corporate shareholders to impute "the act of [an] agent, while exercising the authority delegated to him . . . to his employer and impos[e] . . . penalties on the corporation for

180. 320 U.S. 277, 285 (1943).
181. 421 U.S. 658 (1975).
182. *Id.* at 673.
183. *Id.* at 674.

which he is acting."[184] Today, a corporation can potentially face liability for any offense culpably committed by its agents on its behalf, including homicide offenses.[185]

The key question in corporate criminal law concerns the scope of corporate responsibility for the acts of employees. Just as top executives seek to exculpate themselves on the grounds that offending subordinates acted without their knowledge and even contrary to their directives, corporations argue that offenders acting without the authorization of a high-ranking corporate officer acted without corporate authority.

Courts divide on the question of whether corporate liability depends on authorization of the offense by an organizational leader, or whether the apparent authority of the corporate employee implicates the corporation. Thus, in finding a car dealership liable for theft, a Minnesota court reasoned that "[i]f a corporation is to be criminally liable, . . . the crime must not be a personal aberration of an employee acting on his own; the criminal activity must . . . reflect corporate policy. . . ."[186] On the other hand, a federal court concluded that "a corporation may be held criminally responsible for antitrust violations committed by its employees if they were acting within the scope of their authority, or apparent authority, and for the benefit of the corporation, even if . . . such acts were against corporate policy or express instructions. . . ."[187]

Some scholars argue that the apparent authority of corporate employees suffices to implicate the corporation in regulatory offenses subject to vicarious or strict liability, but that offenses requiring culpability are attributable to the corporation only if committed with the actual authority of corporate officers, acting with culpability.[188] Consistent with this approach, the Model Penal Code limits corporate liability to (1) noncriminal violations, (2) liability based on omission to perform a legal duty imposed on the corporation (so that no one else could be liable), or (3) offenses authorized or recklessly tolerated by the board of directors or a "high managerial agent."[189] Other scholars have proposed that corporations should be liable for offenses predictably encouraged by their corporate culture or "ethos," even if not authorized at high levels,[190] but this is not prevailing law.

As corporations cannot suffer death or incarceration, corporate criminal sanctions are limited to fines or other material deprivations. To be sure, a court can

---

184. 212 U.S. 481, 494 (1909).
185. Commonwealth v. McIlwain School Bus Lines, 423 A.2d 413 (Pa. Super. Ct. 1980).
186. State v. Christy Pontiac-GMC, Inc., 354 N.W.2d 17, 19–20 (Minn. 1984).
187. United States v. Basic Constr. Co., 711 F.2d 570, 573 (4th Cir. 1983).
188. WAYNE R. LAFAVE, CRIMINAL LAW § 13.5, at 740 (2010).
189. MODEL PENAL CODE § 2.07(1) (1962).
190. Pamela Bucy, *Corporate Ethos: A Standard for Imposing Corporate Liability*, 75 MINN. L. REV. 1095, 1127–33 (1991).

metaphorically confine a corporation by suspending or supervising its operations, or even execute it by liquidating it, but these are still essentially burdens on property.[191] Accordingly, criminal sanctions against corporations do not pose the same problems of legitimacy as do vicarious and strict liability for natural persons. Indeed, it is not obvious why such sanctions—which primarily affect the property interests of unconvicted shareholders—should be considered criminal at all.

XV. Conclusion

This chapter has examined doctrines of two kinds that extend liability for criminal offenses. One extends liability to actors who plan and initiate those offenses, by defining inchoate crimes corresponding to them. These include crimes of attempt, solicitation and conspiracy. The other kind of doctrines extends liability for offenses to those who support their commission by aiding, encouraging, agreeing to, or permitting these offenses. These include complicity in crimes, liability for perpetrating crimes by means of innocent agents, liability as a co-conspirator or an accomplice in secondary crimes arising out of a common plan, and vicarious liability of individual and corporate employers.

A common feature of most of these doctrines is that actors liable under them must have at least as much culpability as is required for the commission of the offense, but do not fulfill the conduct element of the offense.

Most of these doctrines are relatively modern, emerging in the nineteenth and twentieth centuries. For some of these doctrines—notably attempt—the conduct required has diminished over time. The rise and expansion of these doctrines illustrates the general movement of American criminal law toward more subjective standards of liability. This subjectivization of criteria of liability played an important role in the development of more proactive and investigatory law enforcement institutions. Imposing liability for inchoate crimes incentivizes law enforcement to intervene and arrest before a crime takes place, and to identify and incapacitate potential criminals by offering criminal employment opportunities. Imposing accessorial liability better enables law enforcement to recruit informants. The subjectivization of criteria of liability also reflects the replacement of a trespassory model of offending as manifest violence with a more utilitarian model of offending as culpable imposition of risk.

---

191. *See* Albert Alschular, *Two Ways to Think about the Punishment of Corporations*, 46 AM. CRIM. L. REV. 453 (2009); Gerald Lynch, *The Role of Criminal Law in Policing Corporate Misconduct*, 60 L. & CONT. PROB. 23 (1997); Symposium: A National Conference on Sentencing of the Corporation, 71 B.U. L. REV. 189 (1991).

NINE

Justification and Excuse

I. Introduction

In this final chapter, we turn our attention from offenses to defenses. Defenses are claims that the defendant should not be found guilty and punished even though he or she committed an offense. The defendant ordinarily bears the burden of producing evidence to justify a jury instruction on a defense (unless the prosecution's case has already supplied it). Constitutional due process permits legislatures and courts to place the burden of persuasion for such defenses on the defendant as well, but legislatures or courts sometimes choose to place the burden of persuasion on the prosecutor on particular defenses.

In analyzing particular offense types we have discussed some defenses that apply only against specific offenses. Thus, provocation and extreme emotional disturbance mitigate intentional murder; an affirmative defense sometimes precludes felony murder liability for non-culpable co-felons; abandonment can preclude liability for incomplete attempts. In this chapter, however, we consider defenses that apply generally across a broad range of offenses. Our discussion will focus on general defenses of two kinds: justifications and excuses.

Justifications deny that the defendant's conduct and thoughts, although satisfying the offense definition, were legally wrong. Justifications thereby deny that the defendant's commission of the offense was prohibited. In this sense, legal rules establishing justifications address the public and modify the criminal law's directives about how they should behave. Justifications generally point to some public interest superseding the interest the offense harms or endangers. Thus justifications negate the reasons that ordinarily justify criminalizing the offense. Justifications include *law enforcement, defense* against aggression, and the *necessity* to avert danger from a cause other than human action.

Excuses deny that the defendant's legally wrongful commission of the offense merits punishment. Excuses generally deny the defendant's responsibility for his or her wrongdoing, on the basis of circumstances interfering with capacity to choose. In this sense, excuses negate the reasons ordinarily justifying the punishment of criminal wrongdoing. They address courts rather than the public and affect their application of the criminal law's proscriptions, while leaving those proscriptions unchanged. Excuses include *duress*—coercion to commit the crime—and *insanity* that causes the crime. In some jurisdictions necessity is treated as an excuse rather than a justification. We have seen that sometimes reasonable *mistake of law* (for example based on a misleading official statement) is available as an excuse.

In sum, a justification applies normative principles of criminalization directly to the criminal's act. An excuse applies normative principles of punishment directly to the criminal. For this reason, defenses bring these fundamental principles of criminal law into sharper focus.

Yet, as we have observed throughout this book, principles of criminalization and punishment are contested in American law. Utilitarian and retributivist approaches to these fundamental questions coexist, sometimes making the law of justification and excuse uncertain and discretionary. Moreover, because criminalization and punishment assign normative worth to acts and actors, the exercise of discretion to justify or excuse can be politically contentious. When justifications selectively authorize force, they can seem to exalt some assailants or debase some victims. Whether a defender must endure violence before defending herself, or can treat the victim's unwanted presence as a threat; whether the defender can protect possessions, habitation, or freedom of movement as well as his person; whether and when an officer can use deadly force to compel obedience—all these judgments distribute status. Excuses absolve only a few offenses as compelled, although all offenders might reasonably claim their crimes were determined by social conditions, upbringing, or genetic endowments over which they had no control. Excuses extend compassion on a necessarily selective basis, requiring normative judgments as to which pressures justify a loss of control. Perhaps it is not surprising, then, that some very controversial criminal cases posing issues of race and gender equality have focused on defenses.

II. Distinguishing and Comparing Justification and Excuse

Why distinguish justifications and excuse? After all, both lead to the same result: acquittal. Yet in our everyday moral discourse we distinguish between justifying conduct as right and excusing it as blameless.

Moreover, the concept of justification would seem to inhere in the concept of criminal law. That criminal law forbids and punishes unauthorized violence necessitates that it recognize exceptions for the coercive force the law's agents must deploy to resist offenses and arrest and punish offenders. If criminal law presupposes a state, it will likely authorize the state's use of force to conscript soldiers, fight enemies, and maintain civil order. Thus it is difficult to conceive of a system of criminal law that would not carve out exceptions to prohibitions for authorized official conduct. The idea of excusing blameless wrongdoing certainly has a great deal of moral traction, but it does not inhere in the concept of criminal law in the same way that justification does. To be sure, excusing blameless wrongdoing is consistent with a conception of punishment as expressing blame. Yet a system of criminal law could locate all judgments of blameworthiness in the offense definition, rather than carving out an exceptional category of blameless offenses.

The concept of justification is ancient. Thus, the Athenian court system provided a separate forum for the trial of those homicides that the killer claimed to have been lawful.[1] Medieval English law identified a narrow category of justified homicides, precluding liability for execution of death sentences and for the killing of an outlaw or a manifest felon who resisted capture.[2]

The category of excuse emerged more gradually. Defensive and accidental killings were felonious homicides, but were routinely pardoned by the Crown. These circumstances were not yet called excuses, but the concept of excuse was incipient in this practice of pardoning based on categories of exculpatory circumstances.[3] Matthew Hale introduced the idea of excuse, which excluded certain classes of persons from criminal liability on grounds of incapacity to exercise volition. Incapacitating conditions included immaturity, permanent and temporarily insanity, idiocy, involuntary intoxication, ignorance or mistake of fact, and various forms of compulsion including duress, marital compulsion, self-defense, and self-preservation (i.e., private necessity).[4] Hale distinguished public necessity and law enforcement authority from these as justifications of the act rather than excuses of the actor, and included within law enforcement the prevention of some crimes of violence.[5] Michael Foster justified deadly force to prevent all of the gravest felonies, and so justified self-defense against murder as an exercise of law enforcement, while excusing self-defense against lesser assaults.[6] Blackstone adopted Hale's conceptual scheme,[7] and classified

---

1. Douglas M. MacDowell, Athenian Homicide Law 70 (1963); Eugene Milhizer, *Justification and Excuse*, 78 St. John's L. Rev. 725, 749 (2004).
2. 2 Frederick Pollock & Frederic William Maitland, The History of English Law before the Time of Edward I 478 (1968).
3. *Id.* at 479.
4. 1 Matthew Hale, The History of Pleas of the Crown 14–51 (1736).
5. *Id.* at 52–53.
6. Michael Foster, Crown Law 273 (1762).
7. 4 William Blackstone, Commentaries on the Laws and Customs of England 20–30 (1765–1769).

homicides as felonious, justified, or excused.[8] Like Hale, and in keeping with the medieval law of homicide, Blackstone continued to treat most instances of self-defense as excused, reserving justification for conduct motivated by a public purpose. Like Foster, however, he included self-defense against murder as a justified exercise of law enforcement. In the late nineteenth century Stephen applied utilitarian ideas to the concept of justification, thereby redefining selfishly motivated offenses as justified as long as the private gain outweighed the harm done. Accordingly, self-defense and private necessity were redefined as justifications.[9]

Today, theorists point to four considerations in distinguishing justification from excuse: (1) the distinction between criminalization of conduct and punishment of persons, (2) the requirements of legality, (3) the allocation of the burden of proof, and (4) the implications for liability of third parties.

(1) *Prohibition and Punishment.* Justifications and excuses acquit offenders for two quite different reasons. As we have seen, a defense of justification is a claim that, though the actor fulfilled the definition of a criminal offense, she *did no wrong.* Although an offense, her act was not legally prohibited. Recall that criminal law has *two* distinctive functions: to forbid conduct, and to punish perpetrators. A justification exempts conduct from prohibition as well as exempting the actor from punishment. By contrast, an excuse denies a particular actor's responsibility for conduct that is concededly wrongful, that is, forbidden by law. Thus an excuse exempts an actor from punishment but does not exempt the act from prohibition. The act is legally wrong, even though the actor is not punishable.

(2) *Legality.* Defenses of justification supplement statutory offenses to complete the criminal law's definition of our legal duties. If legal actors know of the availability of defenses of justification, they can make responsible choices, exercise their rights, and conform their behavior to the law. In other words, the criteria of justification are "conduct rules" for actors subject to the criminal law, as well as "decision rules" for persons charged with administering the law.[10] For this reason, criteria of justification should be public and prospective. Even if enacted through common law judicial reasoning, justifications should not be eliminated retroactively by judicial decision. Yet it is hard to define criteria of justification very precisely, because they often depend upon discretionary factual judgments involving estimates of risk. Accordingly, criteria of justification

8. *Id.* at 179–87.

9. THE CRIMINAL CODE OF CANADA (1893) art. 12, p. 13; arts. 45, 46, p. 29.

10. Meir Dan-Cohen, *Decision Rules and Conduct Rules: On Acoustic Separation in Criminal Law*, 97 HARV. L. REV. 625 (1984); Mitchell Berman, *Justification and Excuse, Law and Morality*, 53 DUKE L.J. 1 (2003).

are often defined by standards of reasonableness. This creates a risk that judicial narrowing of justificatory criteria will undermine the prospectivity of the criminal law's conduct rules.

Excuses, by contrast, are premised on the actor's incapacity to make a responsible choice under the circumstances. Thus, the availability of excuses need not and should not enter into the decision-making of actors. Criteria of excuse are only decision rules for courts or juries, not conduct rules for actors. Because criteria of excuse are not intended to guide the actions of those to whom they are applied, there is less need to insure their specificity, publicity, and prospectivity. Accordingly, discretionary standards are less problematic as criteria of excuse than as criteria of justification.

(3) *Burden of proof.* Although due process does not require the prosecution to bear the burden of proof beyond a reasonable doubt on defenses, most jurisdictions nevertheless place such a burden on the prosecution to disprove justifications. Why is this? Perhaps because proving the absence of justification is a necessary part of proving that the defendant violated a criminal prohibition. In a liberal state, citizens should not have to account for their values and attitudes until shown to have violated law. In addition, this allocation of the burden of proof benefits law enforcement officers, who are the main beneficiaries of justification defenses. Placing the burden on the prosecution to disprove justification reassures officers that they will not likely face prosecution for their uses of force.

(4) *Third parties.* Because justifications approve and permit conduct, it follows that third parties may justifiably assist, and may not interfere with, justified conduct. By contrast, excuses exonerate persons as blameless for wrongful conduct. It follows that third parties may not assist, and may interfere with, excused conduct. One who assists the excused but wrongful commission of an offense could be liable for the offense as an accomplice, unless she also has an excuse. Excuses are personal.

The distinction between justification and excuse is often difficult to apply in practice. One reason is that our leading theories of criminalization and punishment, retributivism and utilitarianism, may disagree about what conduct is justified and what conduct is excused. Thus defenses that seem like justifications from a retributive point of view may seem like excuses from a utilitarian point of view, and vice versa.

When should a utilitarian grant a defense of justification? As noted, justification is a doctrine of criminalization. From a utilitarian viewpoint, conduct is antisocial insofar as its reasonably expected consequences for the social welfare are worse than those of alternative courses of conduct. That conduct is wrong in this sense is not a sufficient reason to prohibit it, because compensatory damages can often also discourage harmful conduct. Yet the expected net harmfulness of conduct is a necessary condition for its prohibition. Thus, the utilitarian will justify offenses that, under the circumstances, are *necessary to prevent a greater evil.* Because utilitarianism demands conduct aiming at maximizing the general good, utilitarians will be skeptical of claims that self-defense is always justified. The self-defender will have a *duty to retreat,* if possible, rather than kill her assailant. Similarly, she may not justifiably kill in defense of any interest less weighty than life itself—her use of force must be *proportionate* to the interest defended. Although the utilitarian self-defender can clearly take one life to save several, she may not take several lives in defense of one. Nor is it clear that she is justified in killing an assailant to avoid great bodily harm or a risk of death.

These doubts that defensive force *is justified* do not preclude *excusing* defensive force. Utilitarians might approve excusing wrongful conduct that is hard to deter because of (1) the high cost to the actor of abstaining from the conduct, or (2) the actor's incapacity to act in his own best interest. The first category might include disproportionate defense of self or loved ones, disproportionate duress, and disproportionate necessity, where the offender harms an interest to protect his own or a loved one's lesser interest. On the other hand, there are utilitarian arguments against excusing "undeterrable" offenders. The public might not be very attentive to the details of criminal law and might be deterred as much by the punishment of an undeterrable as by that of a deterrable offender.

Because retributivism justifies punishment on the basis of moral desert, it conditions criminalization on moral wrongdoing. Retributivists often base their conception of wrongdoing on Kantian moral philosophy. In this tradition, moral agency and moral responsibility depend on each actor having a broad sphere of freedom. The Kantian rejects any idea that individuals are morally constrained to always choose the one option that maximizes good consequences. Instead they must be permitted to act within a sphere of freedom so long as they respect the equal freedom of others. Accordingly, the retributivist approach to punishment is often aligned with a rights-focused approach to criminalization. Actors are free to exercise their rights and need not consider the social welfare in doing so. On the other hand, they are not permitted to pursue the public welfare at the expense of others' rights. Thus interpreted, retributivism justifies more frequent use of defensive force than utilitarianism would permit, because it does not condition justified defense on proportionality of harm, or the impossibility of retreat. Yet such retributivism rejects justification by reason of lesser evils, as this sacrifices the rights of others to the common welfare.

Rather than excusing offenders who cannot be deterred from wrongdoing, retributivists would excuse those who cannot fairly be blamed for their wrongdoing. In practice, these may turn out to be many of the same people the utilitarian would excuse as undeterrable on grounds of fear or incapacity. Retributivists may excuse those who do harm under pressure of "necessity," if the exigency is a significant and imminent threat to self or an intimate. Because this defense is an excuse rather than a justification, and the rationale is fear rather than social welfare, it may not matter if the interest threatened outweighs the interest the offender harms. On the other hand, the retributivist may condition necessity and duress not only on an incapacitating fear, but also on circumstances morally justifying that loss of capacity. Thus, the retributivist may conclude that the offender does not deserve to be excused if he selfishly imposes on another a greater harm than he himself is threatened with.

Defenses are often conditioned on reasonable-person standards. Yet these standards may have a very different meaning and purpose depending on whether one adopts a utilitarian or a retributivist approach to justifying prohibition and punishment.

When a utilitarian asks whether an offense was justified, she may be interested in whether the offense did achieve the best result; or whether it seemed to the offender likely to do so; or whether it would have seemed likely to, to an average person with the defendant's knowledge; or to a person in defendant's situation who had made the socially optimal investment in information. To the utilitarian considering whether an offense was justified, the reasonable person may be the optimally informed social welfare maximizer. When a utilitarian considers whether an offense should be excused, however, she is no longer asking whether it was the best choice. Now she wants to know whether it was a deterrable choice under the circumstances facing the defendant. In determining this she may compare the defendant to a quite different hypothetical person in the same circumstances: the person of typical responsiveness to deterrent sanctions, or of sufficient responsiveness to make deterrent sanctions cost-effective.

A retributivist might be disinclined to condition justification defenses on reasonableness. Justification means acting within one's rights, not calculating consequences. However, a reasonable person standard can become more relevant when the retributivist considers excuses. A retributivist might treat punishment as deserved for acts that manifest disrespect for others. Ordinarily, the commission of an unjustified offense manifests such an antisocial attitude. An excuse, however, precludes this inference from a bad act to a bad character, by pointing to circumstances external to character that explain the conduct. Thus, the retributivist may ask whether a "reasonable person" could have acted as defendant did, facing the same circumstances. The "reasonable person" here means the person of good character.

Despite the conceptual differences between justification and excuse, defenses can resist classification for several reasons. Thus, retributivist analysis might justify some offenses (such as disproportionate or cheaply avoidable defensive force) that utilitarian analysis might consider merely excusable, in whole or in part. Similarly, utilitarian analysis might treat some offenses as justifiable (such as those necessary to prevent a greater harm to the offender or an intimate, whether threatened by a human actor or by circumstances) that retributivist analysis might consider merely excusable. Moreover, although the use of a "reasonable person" standard generally connotes a defense of excuse for retributivists, it may indicate either a justification or an excuse for utilitarians. Finally, decision-makers that establish a defense may be moved by both utilitarian and retributivist reasons, for example when they condition a defense on both good consequences and incapacitating fears. They may compromise disagreement about whether conduct should be justified or prohibited by excusing it, or by shifting the burden of proof. Indeed, they may simply reject the distinction between justification and excuse.

III. Law Enforcement (and Other Exercises of Public Authority)

In Anglo-American law, the authority to enforce law was originally the only basis of justification for otherwise criminal conduct. Seventeenth- and eighteenth-century common law rules permitted arrest on a warrant issued by justices of the peace, on evidence that a crime was committed and that the suspect probably committed it.[11] Officers could also arrest without a warrant for felonies and breaches of the peace committed in their presence. In addition, upon discovery of a felony or a dangerous wounding, officers could arrest on "probable suspicion."[12]

Incident to the power of arrest, officers had powers to attack the person and to invade property. If necessary in order to execute a lawful arrest for a felony or a dangerous wounding, an officer could break into private property and even kill.[13] A possible rationale for using deadly force in such cases was that felonies were capital crimes, so that guilty felons had no incentive to yield

---

11. 4 William Blackstone, Commentaries on the Laws and Customs of England 287 (1765–1769).
12. *Id.* at 289.
13. *Id.*; 1 Matthew Hale, History of Pleas of the Crown 489 (1736).

peacefully. Moreover, killing of fleeing felons imposed no greater penalty than was due. Possible counterarguments were that some felonies were clergyable and many felons were pardoned, that suspected felons might be innocent, and that killing felons without trial deprived them of due process. Hale held that if the suspected felony had not been committed, or if the homicidal officer had no probable cause to suspect an individual, the officer would be liable at least for manslaughter. An officer authorized by a warrant would not be liable. An officer could justify the arrest on probable cause of a suspected felon who later proved to be innocent, but Hale was not certain the officer could justify killing the reasonably suspected innocent to prevent his flight.[14]

An officer could use deadly force to overcome resistance to arrest even for a misdemeanor or in a civil case. The officer was not obliged to retreat in order to avoid bloodshed.[15] "This is founded in reason and publick utility," Michael Foster explained, because "few men would quietly submit to arrest if in every case of resistance, the party impowered to arrest was obliged to desist."[16] It was otherwise if a misdemeanant or civil defendant merely fled, without offering any resistance. If the arresting officer used deadly force and caused death, under these circumstances, it was murder.[17]

In addition to killing to effect the arrest of a felon, an officer could use deadly force to execute a sentence, to overcome resistance to a sentence, and to prevent escape or riot.[18] An officer was also justified in killing to prevent any "forcible and atrocious" crime such as murder, robbery, burglary, arson, or rape—a narrow category of some of the oldest and gravest felonies.[19]

Private persons could also escape liability for enforcing law. Hale referred to this defense as an excuse: "The necessity of the preservation of the peace of the kingdom by the apprehending notorious malefactors excuseth some acts from being felony. . . . If a thief resist, and will not suffer himself to be taken . . . if he be kild by the pursuants, it is no felony."[20] Hale added that private persons could be summoned to assist officials in the suppression of a riot and would not be punishable for acts of violence committed in doing so.[21] Because such killings were not felonious there was neither punishment nor forfeiture of goods, and no need for a pardon. In this sense, such killings were justified.

---

14. *Id.*
15. *Id.* at 481.
16. Sir Michael Foster, Crown Law 270–71 (1762).
17. *Id.* at 271.
18. *Id.* at 180–81.
19. 4 William Blackstone, Commentaries on the Laws and Customs of England 180–81 (1765–1769).
20. 1 Matthew Hale, History of Pleas of the Crown 53 (1736).
21. *Id.*

According to Blackstone, a private person witnessing a felony was obliged to arrest the culprit, and could break into private property or kill in order to effect such an arrest. A private person was also justified in arresting a suspected felon on probable suspicion, although not to break into private property or to kill.[22] In addition, private persons were empowered to kill to prevent the "forcible and atrocious" crimes enumerated above.[23] Blackstone explained this limitation as follows:

> [W]here a crime, in itself capital, is endeavored to be committed by force, it is lawful to repel that force with the death of the party attempting. But we must not carry this doctrine to the same visionary length that Mr. Locke does; who holds, "that all manner of force without right upon man's person, puts him in a state of war with the aggressor; and of consequence, that being in such a state of war, he may lawfully kill him that puts him under this unnatural constraint." However just this conclusion may be in a state of uncivilized nature, yet the law of England, like that of every other well-regulated community, is too tender of the public peace, too careful of the lives of the subjects, to adopt so contentious a system; nor will suffer any crime to be *prevented* by death, unless the same, if committed, would also be *punished* by death.[24]

Thus the power to prevent murder and other capital felonies was a creature of law. It was a delegation of governmental authority to preserve the public peace, not a natural right of individuals to defend their own liberty.[25] As Hale put it, in the "case of a felony attempted, as of a felony committed, every man is thus far an officer, that at least his killing of the attempter in case of necessity puts him in the condition of se defendendo. . . ."[26] For Hale, however, the right to kill depended on its necessity to prevent the crime.[27] If lesser force would suffice, killing was not justified. This implied an obligation to retreat, if possible, to avoid crimes against the person. It did not require flight from a dwelling to save oneself in the face of burglary, because—although this would prevent death—it would not prevent the felony.

How did this justifying power to enforce law differ from the excusing privilege of self-defense? The difference was that citizens were merely excused for using deadly force against threatened violence that would not necessarily

22. 4 WILLIAM BLACKSTONE, COMMENTARIES ON THE LAWS AND CUSTOMS OF ENGLAND 289–90 (1765–1769).
23. *Id.* at 180–81.
24. *Id.* at 181–82.
25. SIR MICHAEL FOSTER, CROWN LAW 273–77 (1762).
26. 1 MATTHEW HALE, HISTORY OF PLEAS OF THE CROWN 485 (1736).
27. *Id.*

amount to murder or other capital crime. Excusable self-defense was "that whereby a man may protect himself from an assault, or the like, in the course of a sudden brawl or quarrel, by killing him who assaults him."[28] In short, homicide excused by self-defense was committed to prevent manslaughter. Unlike the power—indeed the duty—to prevent an atrocious felony, which was an exercise of legal authority, the privilege of self-defense was a natural right of self-preservation and was subject to legal limitations in the interest of preserving the public peace.[29] This way of distinguishing between justification and excuse had the paradoxical implication that the killer of a burglar or a highway robber was uncontroversially justified; whereas one who killed to save his own life would not be justified unless he could prove that the attacker was attempting murder rather than some lesser attack on the person.

Blackstone's framework for justifying law enforcement was absorbed into American law. Writing at the end of the nineteenth century, Clark and Marshall declared that officers could kill if necessary to apprehend a felon or prevent an escape;[30] and that both officers and citizens could kill if necessary to prevent a felony.[31] Although legal authority to arrest could justify force of various kinds, unlawfulness of the arrest would bar these justifications. Rollin Perkins wrote in 1940 that

> One who undertakes to make an arrest without lawful authority, or . . . in an unlawful manner, is guilty of an assault if the other is ordered to submit to the asserted authority, is guilty of battery if he lays hands on the other for this unlawful purpose, and is guilty of false imprisonment if the other is actually detained or is detained for an unreasonable length of time without proper disposition. . . . If an officer shoots at an arrestee when he is not privileged to do so, he is guilty of an aggravated assault. And if death results from an arrest, . . . which was not authorized at all, or from the use of deadly force which was not privileged under the circumstances . . . the arrester is guilty of manslaughter or . . . murder.[32]

Perkins added that the victim of an unlawful arrest was privileged to use reasonable force in resistance.[33]

---

28. 4 William Blackstone, Commentaries on the Laws and Customs of England 184 (1765–1769).
29. *Id.*
30. William Lawrence Clark & William Lawrence Marshall, A Treatise on the Law of Crimes 179–80 (1900).
31. *Id.* at 182–83.
32. Rollin Perkins, *The Law of Arrest*, 25 Iowa L. Rev. 201, 263–64 (1940).
33. *Id.*

Today, most jurisdictions permit arrest without a warrant on probable cause to believe a felony has been committed, for a misdemeanor committed in the presence of an officer, or on a warrant.[34] An officer may defend himself against the arrestee, and has no obligation to retreat. In most jurisdictions, officers may use the nondeadly force they reasonably believe necessary to effect arrest. The general constitutional standard for use of force in effecting an arrest is provided in the 1989 case of *Graham v. Connor*, in which officers injured a helpless (and innocent) man passed out from diabetes.[35] The court held that the right to make an arrest "necessarily carries with it the right to use some degree of physical coercion or threat thereof to effect it." That force must be "reasonable" however, to meet the Fourth Amendment standard of a reasonable seizure. Reasonable force is judged "objectively" from the perspective of a hypothetical reasonable officer, who should consider (1) the severity of the crime, (2) the threat to safety posed by the suspect, and (3) the suspect's resistance or flight. At the same time, "the calculus of reasonableness must embody allowance for the fact that police officers are often forced to make split second judgments—in circumstances that are tense, uncertain, and rapidly evolving—about the amount of force that is necessary in a particular situation."[36]

Controversy over police use of force has focused especially on police killings. Today, most jurisdictions have abandoned the common law rule permitting police to kill a fleeing suspected felon, as few felonies remain capital offenses. This drastic reduction in the scope of capital liability was both a goal and an achievement of utilitarian advocacy. From this utilitarian perspective, if deterring a particular felony does not warrant killing an offender, it cannot warrant killing to prevent the escape of a suspected offender. Killing is disproportionate to the societal interest in effecting arrest of all but the most dangerous felons.

This utilitarian critique of the common law fleeing-felon rule is reflected in the Model Penal Code's alternative approach. Model Penal Code Section 3.07(2)(b) restricts deadly force in effecting arrest to the following situations:

(i) the arrest is for a felony; and
(ii) the person effecting arrest is . . . a peace officer or is assisting a person. . . he believes to be . . . a peace officer; and
(iii) the actor believes that the force employed creates no substantial risk of injury to innocent persons; and

34. WAYNE LAFAVE, CRIMINAL LAW 591 (2000).
35. Graham v. Connor, 490 U.S. 386 (1989).
36. *Id.* at 396–97.

(iv) the actor believes that:
(1) the crime ... involved ... the use or threatened use of deadly force; or
(2) there is a substantial risk that the person to be arrested will cause death or serious bodily harm if his apprehension is delayed.[37]

This Model Penal Code standard was incorporated into Fourth Amendment law in 1985 in the case of *Tennessee v. Garner*,[38] which held that an officer is constitutionally permitted to use deadly force only insofar as necessary to arrest a suspect in a crime that posed danger of "serious physical harm" or where the suspect's continued liberty otherwise poses such a danger. In this case an officer fatally shot a fleeing burglary suspect that he correctly perceived to be an unarmed juvenile, in order to prevent his jumping a fence and getting away. The case concerned the civil liability of the officer and other agents and agencies of the state for violating the victim's civil rights, rather than the officer's criminal liability for homicide. In reversing the dismissal of the civil rights suit, the Supreme Court held unconstitutional as applied a provision of the state criminal code authorizing the use of any force necessary to effect the arrest, and a departmental policy allowing the use of deadly force if necessary to arrest a felon. The Court's reasoning was frankly utilitarian, identifying "the balancing of competing interests" as the basis of Fourth Amendment reasoning. The Court concluded that

> notwithstanding probable cause to seize a suspect, an officer may not always do so by killing him. The intrusiveness of a seizure by means of deadly force is unmatched. The suspect's fundamental interest in his own life need not be elaborated upon. The use of deadly force also frustrates the interest of the individual, and of society, in judicial determination of guilt and punishment. . . . The use of deadly force to prevent the escape of all felony suspects, whatever the circumstances, is constitutionally unreasonable. It is not better that all felony suspects die than that they escape. Where the suspect poses no immediate threat to the officer and no threat to others, the harm resulting from failing to apprehend him does not justify the use of deadly force to do so. . . . A police officer may not seize an unarmed, nondangerous suspect by shooting him dead. The Tennessee statute is unconstitutional insofar as it authorizes the use of deadly force against such fleeing suspects.[39]

---

37. MODEL PENAL CODE § 3.07(2)(b)(1962).
38. Tennessee v. Garner, 471 U.S. 1 (1985).
39. *Id.* at 10–11.

The Court noted that about half the states had restricted the use of deadly force by statute to arrests of persons suspected of violent felonies or otherwise posing a threat of violence. In addition, many urban police departments had adopted regulations restricting police use of deadly force in this way.[40]

The subsequent case of *Scott v. Harris*[41] slightly modified the cost-benefit calculus prescribed by *Tennessee v. Garner.* This decision upheld the granting of summary judgment to the defendant in a civil rights suit against an officer who rammed the plaintiff's vehicle with his squad car during a high speed chase, causing severe injuries. The plaintiff had fled from an officer attempting to flag him down for speeding. The Court held the attack obviously reasonable, because of the danger to the public posed by plaintiff's driving revealed by a video of the chase, and held that police could place a lower value on the life of a suspect who created danger to the public than on the lives of law-abiding citizens. The decision has been criticized on the ground that a diverse jury was the proper judge of reasonableness, and might have placed a higher value on the life of the suspect, empathized with his fear of police, and seen the high speed pursuit as unnecessarily creating the danger used to justify deadly force.[42]

As of this writing, most states have adopted statutory justifications for law enforcement use of deadly force consistent with the Model Penal Code and *Garner.* Among populous states, this includes Georgia, Illinois, New Jersey, New York, North Carolina, Pennsylvania, Texas, and Virginia.[43] Yet a number of states retain the common law fleeing-felon rule, including California and Florida.[44]

What is the legal effect of a state fleeing-felon rule after *Garner*? Such a rule can acquit officers of state homicide charges, but leave the state vulnerable to federal civil rights suits. Federal law also criminalizes the deprivation of Fourth Amendment rights by officers, but conditions liability on willful deprivation.[45] Thus a systematic state policy of advising police that they can legally use deadly force to apprehend non-dangerous fleeing felons may effectively insulate police from liability.

---

40. *Id.* at 16–18.
41. Scott v. Harris, 550 U.S. 372 (2007).
42. Dan M. Kahan, David A. Hoffman & Donald Braman, *Whose Eyes Are You Going to Believe:* Scott v. Harris *and the Perils of Cognitive Illiberalism*, 122 HARV. L. REV. 837 (2009).
43. O.G.C.A. §16-3-21 (2001); ILLINOIS PENAL CODE; § 7-5(A) (2012); NEW JERSEY PENAL CODE 2C:3-7(B)(2) (1981); NEW YORK PENAL LAW § 35.30(1) (2004) ; NORTH CAROLINA PENAL CODE § 15A-401 (2011); 18 PA. C. S. § 508(A)(2007); TEX. PENAL CODE § 9.51 (C) (1997); VA. PRAC. JURY INSTRUCTION § 62:4 (2014).
44. CALIFORNIA PENAL CODE § 196 (1872); FLORIDA PENAL CODE § 776.05(2) (1997).
45. 18 U.S.C. § 242 (1968).

Even when justification rules conform to *Garner*, they may do little to control police behavior. There are few criminal prosecutions of police for homicide, because of indulgent exercises of prosecutorial discretion. The *Garner* test is also less protective of life than it may seem, because it focuses attention primarily on the decision to use deadly force rather than on how it is used. Thus, once the conditions for deadly force have been met, Garner imposes little obligation on police to preserve the life of a defendant. This problem is illustrated by the police killing of Amadou Diallo in the Bronx in 1999. Four plainclothed officers confronted Diallo, an African immigrant, because on driving by him at night, they thought he resembled a rape suspect. When he fled to his apartment building, they pursued, demanding that he stop and show his hands. When instead he pulled a wallet from his pocket, one officer shouted "gun!" and the four officers fired 41 shots at Diallo. Because of pretrial publicity, the case was transferred from the Bronx to Albany. At trial, the officers offered a justification defense under a statute based on the Model Penal Code, and were acquitted of all charges.[46] It seems that once juries find a justification for firing a gun, however thin (here based on two seemingly unreasonable misperceptions), they assume police are authorized to keep shooting until the victim is dead.

The scale of police violence has not been recognized until recently, because governments have avoided quantifying it. A compilation by the *Washington Post* projected that in 2015, police would commit a little fewer than 1,000 fatal shootings nationwide.[47] There are approximately 1.2 million law enforcement officers in the United States,[48] for a gun homicide commission rate of about 80 per 100,000.

At the same time, risks facing police from suspects are lower than commonly supposed. According to a national police memorial fund, in 2015, the number of fatal shootings of police was 42,[49] for a gun homicide victimization rate of 3.5 per 100,000. This means that police are 20 times more likely to fatally shoot a member of the public than to be fatally shot by a member of the public. Moreover, police do not face more risk of homicide than other members of the public. According to the Centers for Disease Control, for 2013, the number of fatal shootings overall was 11,208 for a population of 317 million.[50] Thus, the

---

46. Jane Fritsch, *The Diallo Verdict*, N.Y. TIMES, Feb. 26, 2000.
47. Kimberly Kindy, *Fatal Police Shootings in 2015 Approaching 400*, WASH. POST, May 30, 2015.
48. BJS, CENSUS OF STATE AND LOCAL LAW ENFORCEMENT OFFICERS, 2008 (July 2011) NCJ 233982; BJS FEDERAL LAW ENFORCEMENT OFFICERS, 2008 (June 2012), NCJ238250.
49. NATIONAL LAW ENFORCEMENT OFFICERS MEMORIAL FUND, PRELIMINARY 2015 LAW ENFORCEMENT OFFICERS FATALITIES REPORT (12/29/2015).
50. CENTERS FOR DISEASE CONTROL, 2013 MORTALITY MULTIPLE CAUSE MICRO-DATA FILES, TABLE 10; U.S. CENSUS BUREAU, MONTHLY POPULATION ESTIMATES FOR THE UNITED STATES, JANUARY 1, 2010 TO DECEMBER 1, 2014 (2015).

gun homicide victimization rate for police, 3.5 per 100,000, is very similar to the gun homicide victimization rate for the entire population, 3.6 per 100,000. Considering that police forces are overwhelmingly comprised of young adult males, who face a homicide victimization rate considerably higher than that of the general population,[51] it seems that police officers face a lower risk of homicide victimization than the general public.

The enforcement of law justifies force not only to arrest offenders after the fact, but also to prevent offenses before they occur. We will consider defense against attacks on the person in the next section. However, both officers and private persons are sometimes justified in using force to prevent property crimes. Recall that the common law justified deadly force to prevent "atrocious" crimes, including burglary, robbery, and arson. The Model Penal Code allows the use of deadly force to protect property in limited circumstances. The threatened property crime must be (1) an effort to dispossess the victim of his home or (2) a felony; and either (a) the crime must involve the use or threat of deadly force or (b) the victim must not be able to safely use lesser force to resist the crime.[52] This provision does not permit the victim of a theft to use deadly force merely because no lesser force would be effective. Thus it does not permit a defendant to shoot to prevent a thief from stealing a car.

The trend has been to limit the use of deadly force to the protection of life and habitation. Yet the interest in habitation functions primarily to absolve the defender of any obligation to save himself by retreating from his home. It is not clear that it justifies deadly force independent of the defender's interest in physical safety and in autonomy. In the California case of *People v. Ceballos*, the defendant set up a trap gun in his garage after an attempted break-in there. The burglar returned and was shot by the trap gun while trying to break in. Ceballos's conviction for assault with a deadly weapon was upheld, despite California Penal Code Section 197, justifying homicide "[w]hen resisting any attempt to murder any person, or to commit a felony, or to do some great bodily injury upon any person; or . . . [w]hen committed in defense of habitation, property, or person, against one who manifestly intends or endeavors, by violence or surprise, to commit a felony."[53] The court read into this section Blackstone's restriction of justifiable homicide to the prevention of "forcible and atrocious" crimes, and concluded that burglary met this standard

---

51. ALEXIA COOPER & ERICA L. SMITH, BUREAU OF JUSTICE STATISTICS, HOMICIDE TRENDS FOR THE UNITED STATES, 1980–2008 NCJ 236018 (2011).
52. MODEL PENAL CODE § 3.06(3)(d)(1962).
53. People v. Ceballos, 12 Cal. 3d 470 (1974).

only when it actually endangered life, by virtue of the presence of a victim. Thus Ceballos could use deadly force to defend his premises were he present, because he would also be defending himself. Yet his right of self-defense was not simply a right to preserve his own life. A previous case made clear that he could remain present to defend his property even if he expected a burglary.[54] He could use deadly force to defend not only his person, but his presence on his property.

In addition to authorizing law enforcement, the common law permitted the use of force in exercising other forms of governing authority, including the private authority of household governance. According to Blackstone, excusable homicide included unintentional killing in using lawful force:

> So where a parent is moderately correcting his child, a master his servant or scholar, or an officer punishing a criminal, and happens to occasion his death, it is only misadventure; for the act of correction was lawful: but if he exceeds the bounds of moderation, either in the manner, the instrument, or the quantity of punishment, and death ensues, it is manslaughter at least, and in some cases . . . murder; for the act of immoderate correction is unlawful.[55]

The Model Penal Code authorizes the use of force in the exercise of various forms of custodial authority. Parents, guardians and teachers of minors, and guardians of incompetent adults may use force involving no degradation or danger of injury, if they perceive it necessary to ensure the welfare of the victim or others in their care.[56] Correctional officers and the crew of ships and airplanes are granted broader powers to use force to maintain order and safety, including deadly force under some circumstances.[57]

IV. Defensive Force

As noted above, the common law justified homicide committed to prevent certain "forcible and atrocious" felonies, but at best only excused homicide

---

54. Nakashima v. Takase, 8 Cal. App. 2d 35 (1935).
55. 4 William Blackstone, Commentaries on the Laws and Customs of England 182–83 (1765–1769).
56. Model Penal Code § 3.08(1), § 3.08(2), § 3.08(3) (1962).
57. *Id.* § 3.08(5), § 3.08(6).

to resist other attacks on the person. The distinction is well illustrated by a fourteenth-century case in which

> It was presented that a man killed another in his own house se defendendo. It was asked whether the deceased came to have robbed him; for in such a case a man may kill another though it be not in self defense. . . . And the twelve said not. Wherefore they were charged to tell the way how . . . it happened, whereby he should obtain the king's pardon.[58]

At this early point, the defender was not even justified in defending against murder or rape.[59] In the seventeenth century, Coke and Hale limited justified killing to the contexts of robbery and burglary and murder on the king's highway.[60]

The tradition of justifying deadly force to repel burglary and robbery, but not murder, may seem puzzling, but it can be explained in two ways. First, defense against an assault may be described more simply as a fight. Recall that the common law viewed death resulting from mutual combat as manslaughter. If the deceased started the affray, the defendant was still guilty of manslaughter if the deceased desisted or retreated before being killed. If the defendant struck first, he might be excused if he had desisted or retreated, because then he would be killing to prevent manslaughter. Thus a claim of self-defense always looked like an exculpatory interpretation of what had been a mutual breach of the king's peace. Evidence of a robbery or burglary, by contrast, convincingly shifted all the blame for the breach of peace onto the deceased. Second, one who killed to prevent murder might have been able to prevent the crime by flight. Thus there was always uncertainty whether deadly force was truly necessary to prevent murder. By contrast, a victim of burglary or a robbery could not thwart the crime by fleeing while leaving his property undefended. Thus, a claim that one killed to prevent burglary or robbery was more credible than a claim that one killed to prevent murder.

Only with Foster and Blackstone did the category of justifiable homicide to prevent a felony expand to encompass defense against murder itself. Foster was the first writer to present self-defense as sometimes justified: "there are Cases in which a Man may without retreating oppose Force to Force, even to Death. This I call justifiable self-defense."[61] This association of justification with

---

58. F. Coron. 305 (3 Ed. III.).
59. Joseph Beale, *Retreat from a Murderous Assault*, 16 HARV. L. REV. 567, 572 (1903).
60. *Id.*; EDWARD COKE, THE THIRD PART OF THE INSTITUTES OF THE LAWS OF ENGLAND 47 (1644).
61. SIR MICHAEL FOSTER, CROWN LAW 273 (1762).

a right to stand one's ground was understandable, as justified resistance to a property crime and justified force in arrest required no retreat. Yet these justified uses of force required no retreat because they could not achieve their defensive purpose of maintaining possession of property or an arrestee if the defender instead retreated. Thus no writer had previously argued that justification was incompatible with a duty to retreat. Nor had previous writers seen any reason that the victim of an assault was justified in killing when he could save himself by retreating. Foster, however, justified defense against murder, even when the killer could have avoided death by retreating instead. Thus one could justifiably "repel Force with Force in Defence of his Person, Habitation, or Property, against one who manifestly intendeth and endeavoureth with Violence or Surprize to commit a known Felony upon either. In these Cases he is not obliged to retreat . . . and if . . . He happeneth to Kill, such Killing is justifiable."[62] Foster explained the privilege of killing to resist an attempted murder as both a natural right and a legal duty.[63]

To justify self-defense against a murderous attack, the defender would have to prove (1) that the assailant had intended to kill, or possibly to inflict a life-threatening wound; and (2) that the defender had not provoked the attack or assented to mutual combat. If the combat was mutual, the defender would be neither justified nor excused, but would be guilty of manslaughter. However, even if the defender had initially provoked an attack or joined in mutual combat, if he then withdrew or otherwise demonstrated his desistance, he regained a limited privilege of self-defense. If the other party persisted in combat and attempted to kill the defender, that assailant would be attempting voluntary manslaughter. Although the defender would not be justified in killing under these circumstances, he would be excused. This excuse of self-defense depended on the imminence of the danger to life, and the necessity of killing to avert it. Thus, the excuse of self-defense against manslaughter was unavailable if the defender could have retreated and failed to.[64] The excuse was likewise unavailable if the defender, having forfeited the privilege of self-defense by provoking or agreeing to combat, failed to regain that privilege by desisting.

Although Blackstone agreed with Foster that excused self-defense against manslaughter was conditioned on inability to safely retreat, he did not address Foster's claim that the defender faced with attempted murder had no duty to

62. *Id.*

63. *Id.* at 274.

64. 4 William Blackstone, Commentaries on the Laws and Customs of England 184 (1765–1769).

retreat if possible. For Blackstone, deadly force was justified by the imperatives of enforcing law, not the natural liberty of individuals.

The division between justifiable and excusable defense meant that the defender was—literally—on safer ground resisting burglary or robbery in his own home than resisting an assault on his person. Matthew Hale wrote that "[r]egularly it is necessary that the person that kills another in his own defense, fly as far he may to avoid the violence of the assault before he turn upon his assailant," yet "[i]f a thief assault a true man either abroad or in his house to rob or kill him, the true man is not obliged to give back" (retreat), "but may kill him and it is no felony."[65] He offered resistance to burglary as his paradigmatic case for justified homicide, "for his house is his castle of defense,"[66] while restricting justifiable self-defense against murder to those attacked on a royal highway.[67] Foster and Blackstone only later extended the category of justifiable homicide to the resistance of murder anyplace.

Thus, the English common law bequeathed Americans a confusingly bifurcated scheme of self-defense—an excuse, identified with private interest, and limited by requirements of imminence, necessity, and proportionality; and a justification, identified with public authority, without such limits. It was unclear whether this justification applied to defense against murder, and whether, if so, the defender was obliged to retreat.

During the nineteenth century, utilitarian reformers redefined the public interest as the balance of private interests, and so redefined self-defense as justified only insofar as necessary and proportionate. Yet the antebellum American South had a culture that condoned dueling.[68] After the Civil War many American courts embraced a more Lockean view of self-defense as vindicating individual liberty, rather than the public welfare. Thus conceived, justified self-defense did not depend on the unavailability of retreat.

Foster's position was supported by Edward Hyde East's 1803 treatise.[69] The mid-century American authors Joel Prentiss Bishop and Francis Wharton repeated Foster's formula as well.[70] After the Civil War, many state courts adopted this position. In the 1876 decision in *Erwin v. State* the Ohio Supreme Court asked "Does the law hold a man who is violently and feloniously assaulted

---

65. 1 MATTHEW HALE, HISTORY OF PLEAS OF THE CROWN 481 (1736).

66. *Id.* at 487.

67. *Id.* at 494; *see also* EDWARD COKE, THE THIRD PART OF THE INSTITUTES OF THE LAWS OF ENGLAND 5b (1644).

68. BERTRAM WYATT-BROWN, SOUTHERN HONOR 167 (1932); KENNETH GREENBERG, MASTERS AND STATESMEN: THE POLITICAL CULTURE OF AMERICAN SLAVERY (1985).

69. 1 EDWARD HYDE EAST, TREATISE OF PLEAS OF THE CROWN 271–72 (1803).

70. 2 JOEL PRENTISS BISHOP, COMMENTARIES ON THE CRIMINAL LAW §§ 633–634 (1865); 2 FRANCIS WHARTON, TREATISE ON CRIMINAL LAW 85 § 1019 (1874).

responsible for having brought such necessity upon himself, on the sole ground that he failed to fly from his assailant when he might have safely done so?" No, answered the court, "a true man, who is without fault, is not obliged to fly from an assailant, who, by violence or surprise, maliciously seeks to take his life or do him enormous bodily harm."[71] Here the court borrowed Hale's language, but without its limitation to a victim resisting a robbery or violent burglary.

Some courts identified the right to stand one's ground with a specifically American ethos of martial honor. In its influential 1877 decision of *Runyan v. State*, the Indiana Supreme Court concluded that

> the tendency of the American mind seems to be very strongly against the enforcement of any rule which requires a person to flee when assailed, to avoid chastisement or even to save human life. . . . The weight of modern authority, . . . establishes the doctrine, that, when a person, being without fault and in a place where he has a right to be . . . he may, without retreating, repel force by force, and if . . . his assailant is killed, he is justifiable.[72]

A Minnesota court characterized the common law's duty to retreat as an anachronism, ill-adapted to a frontier society with widespread use of guns.[73] Several courts insisted that resisting rather than retreating was a natural right of liberty.[74] In 1917, in an opinion written by Justice Holmes, the U.S. Supreme Court rejected a duty to retreat, and instead considered the availability of safe retreat one factor in weighing the necessity of killing. The Civil War veteran Holmes later explained that he considered the impulse to stand and fight to be human nature.[75]

A majority of state courts addressing the issue between the Civil War and World War I permitted defenders to stand their ground.[76] The remainder conditioned deadly force on the impossibility of safe retreat, or on the defender being in his or her own home, facing an adversary who was not a co-occupant.[77] The conflict between these positions was not always apparent, because of their

---

71. Erwin v. State, 29 Ohio St. 186, 200 (1876).
72. Runyan v. State, 57 Ind. 80, 84 (1877).
73. State v. Gardner, 104 N.W. 971 (1905).
74. State v. Bartlett, 71 S.W. 148 (Mo. 1902); State v. Meyer, 164 Pac. 926 (Wash. 1917); Miller v. State, 119 N.W. 850 (Wis. 1909).
75. Brown v. United States, 257 Fed. Rep. 343 (1917); Richard Maxwell Brown, No Duty to Retreat: Violence and Values in American History and Society 1–30 (1991).
76. Joseph Beale, *Retreat from a Murderous Assault*, 16 Harv. L. Rev. 567, 576 (1903); Richard Maxwell Brown, No Duty to Retreat: Violence and Values in American History and Society 1–30 (1991).
77. Joseph Beale, *Homicide in Self-Defense*, 3 Colum. L. Rev. 526, 540–41 (1903).

contingency on debatable factual judgments. Thus, the duty of retreating was conditioned upon the safety of doing so, while the right to stand one's ground was conditioned on not having initiated or agreed to combat. A given jurisdiction might adopt no rule on the question of right, and simply require that the force used be necessary under the circumstances, leaving the jury to decide whether the availability of retreat rendered any particular killing unnecessary. With that important caveat, it seems fair to conclude that the right to stand one's ground was the prevailing rule in the United States before promulgation of the Model Penal Code.

The operation of such a rule is illustrated by a 1964 Colorado case, *People v. Lavoie*.[78] The defendant was driving home from work late at night when his vehicle was deliberately hit from behind and driven through an intersection by a car containing four drunk young men. The defendant stopped, got out, and displayed a gun. The four young men exited their vehicle and approached the defendant, saying "we will make you eat that gun" and making other threats to beat him. The defendant shot and killed the assailant farthest forward. At his trial for murder, the judge gave a directed verdict of acquittal The Colorado Supreme Court endorsed this result, emphasizing that the assailants were interfering with LaVoie's right to proceed home unmolested. As a consequence, LaVoie was under no obligation to flee, or avoid confrontation. He was under no duty to bear the risk that they would kill or injure him. His right to kill the first assailant implied his right to kill all four if all continued to advance. The decision embodies the principle that right need never yield to wrong, rather than the aim of minimizing loss of life.

Some scholars have attributed America's rising homicide rates after the Civil War to then-prevalent stand-your-ground rules.[79] More likely the experience of civil war encouraged violent disputing, and the social norms tolerating such conflict were also reflected in legal rules. Perhaps the economic and political uncertainties attending rapid westward expansion also encouraged private violence.

One early twentieth century summary of self-defense law concluded that defensive force was permitted insofar as four conditions were met: (1) The defender reasonably believed it necessary to prevent a battery inflicting unlawful injury or violation of a right; (2) The battery was imminent or continuing at the time of the defense; (3) The force used was proportionate to the injury or wrong; so that deadly force was generally permitted only to prevent death,

78. People v. LaVoie, 395 P. 2d 1001 (1964).

79. Richard Maxwell Brown, No Duty to Retreat: Violence and Values in American History and Society 20–30 (1991).

grievous bodily harm, the use of deadly force, or the success of a crime involving a threat of deadly force; and (4) The defender was without fault in provoking the attack or assenting to mutual combat; or, having wrongly initiated hostilities, withdrew, or clearly and credibly communicated an intention to do so. In some states, the requirement of retreat, if possible, even for those who did not initiate hostilities, was a fifth requirement.[80]

Notice that under this scheme of rules, where deadly force is not justified, a resulting homicide may still be mitigated to manslaughter. This could happen under the following five scenarios: (1) A battery has been committed and has ceased by the time deadly force is used; (2) A battery is committed that does not threaten sufficiently serious injury to warrant deadly force in defense; (3) The defendant agreed to mutual combat; (4) The defendant initiated combat with ordinary force and his or her antagonist unjustifiably responded with deadly force; (5) In the minority of states requiring retreat, the defendant could have safely retreated.

The Model Penal Code proposed two important changes in this scheme. First, it imposed a duty of retreat if the defender knew that safe retreat was possible. The defender was not obliged to retreat from the home, however, even if the assailant was a cohabitant. The defender was not obliged to retreat from his or her workplace, unless attacked by a coworker.[81]

Second, the Code abandoned the requirement that subjective belief in the necessity of force and the imminence of attack be objectively reasonable.[82] It nevertheless punished uses of force motivated by unreasonable fears, in a novel way. If the belief in the imminence of attack or necessity of force was reckless or negligent, the defendant would be convicted of inflicting any resulting injury recklessly or negligently:

> When the actor believes that the use of force . . . is necessary for any of the purposes that would establish a justification . . . but the actor is reckless or negligent in having such belief or in . . . failing to acquire any knowledge . . . which is material to the justifiability of his use of force, . . . justification is unavailable . . . for any offense for which recklessness or negligence, as the case may be, suffices to establish culpability.[83]

Consider Harold, who killed a stranger approaching him rapidly in a dark alley while pulling a shiny object from his pocket (that turned out to be a cell phone).

---

80. Joseph Beale, *Homicide in Self-Defense*, 3 COLUM. L. REV. 526, 526–45 (1903).
81. MODEL PENAL CODE § 3.04(2)(b)ii (1962).
82. *Id.* § 3.04(1).
83. *Id.* § 3.09(2).

He explains to police that because he was in a "bad neighborhood," he thought the stranger might have been a robber and the object might have been a gun or a knife, and he did not want to take the risk of waiting to find out. Harry is arguably guilty of reckless manslaughter under the Code. He perceives a substantial risk that he is killing unnecessarily, but undervalues the safety of a stranger because of a prejudicial view of the population of an entire neighborhood. Now consider Irving, who kills in similar circumstances, but who feels certain the cell phone is a gun and that a robbery has commenced. Irving would arguably be liable for negligent homicide. He unreasonably failed to perceive the substantial chance that his victim was harmless.

This doctrine, often referred to as "imperfect self-defense," contrasts with the traditional rule barring self-defense altogether when the defendant's expectations are cognitively unreasonable, or his cost-benefit analysis is normatively unreasonable. It achieves an effect similar to the traditional rules imposing manslaughter liability on defenders who initiated combat, or overreacted to provocation, but it applies in different fact scenarios.

The Model Penal Code bars the use of deadly force in self-defense by anyone who attacked first, with the purpose of inflicting death or significant injury—but does not bar otherwise justifiable deadly force by one who initiated combat with nondeadly force. Nor does the Code impose manslaughter liability for such killings in defense against partially provoked attacks. They are fully justified, leaving the killer liable only for his assault with nondeadly force.

As a result of the Model Penal Code's influence, a number of states adopted a duty to retreat,[84] but more recently stand-your-ground laws have become more popular than ever. Of the dozen most populous states, California, Florida, Georgia, Michigan, North Carolina, Pennsylvania, Texas, and Virginia currently have statutory provisions or standard jury instructions permitting a defender in any place where he has a right to be to use deadly force in response to an unprovoked attack on life, with no obligation to retreat.[85] Only New York and New Jersey explicitly require retreat outside the home,[86] while Ohio and Illinois do not resolve the issue.[87]

This retreat from the duty to retreat resulted from the surprising convergence of two movements with quite different concerns: gun rights advocates

---

84. Note, *Justification: The Impact of the Model Penal Code on Statutory Reform*, 75 COLUM. L. REV. 914, 937–38 (1975).
85. CAL. CRIM. JURY INSTRUCTION 505 (2012); FLA. STAT. § 776.012 (2)(2014); GA. CODE. ANN. § 16-3-23.1 (2006); MICH. COMP. LAWS § 780.972 (2015); N.C. GEN. STAT. § 14-51.3 (2011); 18 PA. CONS. STAT. ANN § 505(b)(2.3) (2011); TEX. PENAL CODE ANN. § 9.31(e) (2015); VA. PATTERN JURY INSTRUCTIONS § 62:1, § 62:6 (2014).
86. N.Y. PENAL LAW § 35.15(2)(a) (2004); N.J. STAT. ANN. § 2C:3-4(B)(2)(b) (2015).
87. 720 ILL. COMP. STAT. 5/7-1 (2004); OHIO REV. CODE. ANN. § 291.09(b) (2015).

and feminists. Gun rights advocates have generally opposed a duty to retreat and a requirement of proportional force, because these effectively condition the right of private citizens to use deadly force on the application of discretionary standards calling for situational judgment. Feminists have criticized the restrictive application of self-defense law to battered women who kill their abusers. From their perspective, self-defense law is too rule-bound, giving insufficient weight to the circumstantial and psychological pressures facing victims of prolonged domestic abuse. Such victims may have little practical opportunity to leave an abusive relationship because of economic dependence, social isolation, parental responsibility, or the risk of violent retaliation.[88] They may have little confidence that law enforcement authorities will adequately protect them and their children if they report abuse. Finally, prolonged abuse is demoralizing. Psychological research suggested that prolonged domestic abuse could cause "battered women's syndrome," a condition of "learned helplessness" that could prevent victims from perceiving or pursuing opportunities to escape.[89] Based on these considerations, feminist scholars and advocates suggested three reforms of self-defense law.

First, they advocated the elimination of a duty to retreat, at least as applied to battered women killing their abusers. Their concern was that defense attorneys representing such women found themselves in a dilemma. They could bolster the credibility of their clients' claim to have feared imminent violence by introducing evidence of a history of such violence. Yet this evidence would also show that their clients had reason to expect violence before it became imminent. This would suggest that their clients had ample opportunity to avoid deadly force by leaving the relationship. Most defensive killings of abusive partners took place in the home, where defenders ordinarily have no duty to retreat. Thus controversy focused on the Model Penal Code's exception to this exemption for killings of cohabitants. The Florida Supreme Court struck down such an exception, only to have its decision rendered irrelevant by legislative passage of a stand-your-ground law.[90]

Second, they critiqued the requirement of imminence. A number of highly publicized cases involved "non-confrontational" killings of abusers while they slept.[91] Defendants in such cases argued that prior abuse warranted an

---

88. Martha Mahoney, *Legal Images of Battered Women: Redefining the Issue of Separation*, 90 MICH. L. REV. 1 (1991); Alafair Burke, *Rational Actors, Self-Defense and Distress*, 81 N.C. L. REV. 211 (2002).
89. LENORE WALKER, THE BATTERED WOMAN (1979).
90. Weiand v. State, 732 So. 2d 1044 (Fla. 1999).
91. *See, e.g.*, State v. Norman, 378 S.E. 2d 8 (N.C. 1988) (denying an instruction on self-defense). One of the most famous of these cases, the trial of Francine Hughes for setting fire to her sleeping husband, ended in an acquittal on grounds of temporary insanity.

expectation of violence before it was imminent, and that the practical and psychological difficulties of escaping such relationships made defensive force necessary to forestall that violence, while the difficulty and danger of defending oneself during an attack made a nonconfrontational killing necessary. If credited, such arguments implied that deadly defensive force could be necessary even though an attack was not imminent. It would follow that self-defense could be conditioned on necessity alone, without an independent requirement of imminence.[92] One study showed that imminence is most often invoked to bar self-defense instructions in confrontational killings, where the defendant is being faulted for failing to retreat in jurisdictions where retreat is not required.[93]

Third, they critiqued the reasonable person standard generally used for assessing necessity as gender-biased. Pointing to the research on "battered women's syndrome," advocates argued that a terrorized victim of abuse should not have to prove that an average person would have felt mortal fear under the same circumstances. Because most violence takes place between men, a generic reasonable person standard for self-defense may well be identified with the behavior of a man, who may be expected to respond to an unarmed assault with his fists. They proposed that the reasonableness of using deadly force against an abuser should depend on the reasonableness of the defender's own perception of danger. In the Washington case of *State v. Wanrow*, the court viewed such a standard of reasonable perception as necessary to take into account the likely inability of a small, disabled woman to protect herself and others from a large intoxicated man without using deadly force.[94] In *State v. Leidholm*, the North Dakota Supreme Court applied a similar standard, requiring consideration of the defendant's past experiences and psychological characteristics. It followed that the jury should consider evidence of battered women's syndrome in assessing the reasonableness of the defendant's use of deadly force against her alleged abuser.[95]

The use of such testimony to show the reasonableness of self-defense poses a number of difficulties. First, courts have been reluctant to allow experts to testify that a defendant suffers from battered women's syndrome, as this would require the expert to supplant the jury by concluding that the defender had in fact been beaten. Thus most courts allow the expert to testify only to the general characteristics of victims of prolonged abuse. In jurisdictions permitting a defender to stand her ground—now a majority—the defendant has no need

---

92. Alafair Burke, *Rational Actors, Self-Defense, and Duress: Making Sense, Not Syndromes, Out of the Battered Woman*, 81 N.C. L. REV. 211 (2002).

93. Victoria Nourse, *Self-Defense and Subjectivity*, 68 U. CHI. L. REV. 1235 (2001).

94. State v. Wanrow, 88 Wash. 2d 221 (1977).

95. State v. Leidholm, 334 N.W. 2d 811 (N.D. 1983).

of battered women's syndrome to justify her failure to retreat. In jurisdictions requiring imminence of the threat—also a majority—battered women's syndrome presumably cannot justify a preemptive killing. Yet defense attorneys are eager to employ such testimony because it bolsters the credibility of the defender's claim that she expected death because she had suffered protracted abuse. Absent testimony about learned helplessness, jurors might mistakenly assume that no one would remain in such a relationship. Battered women's syndrome testimony explains how the defender could have been subjected to life-threatening abuse without leaving. Finally, expert description of the harmful psychological effects of abuse also engages the sympathy of jurors.

The controversial trial of Bernhard Goetz for the shooting of four youths affords us a somewhat different perspective on an individualized standard of reasonableness. Goetz, who was white, was formerly the victim of a robbery and beating. He frequently rode the subways at all hours, armed with a gun. In fact, he had twice previously warded off robberies by brandishing it. Nevertheless, when four black youths approached him in a subway car and asked him for money, he shot three of them and missed the fourth. He then shot the fourth successfully, leaving him paralyzed. Goetz made statements to police that he had decided to fire the last shot because he saw that the victim was unharmed, and—somewhat inconsistently—that if he had not run out of bullets he would have continued shooting until all four victims were dead. He was charged by a grand jury with attempted murder. A lower court quashed the charge on grounds that the grand jury wrongly applied an objective reasonable person standard. The court ruled that they should have asked whether it was reasonable for Goetz to see the shootings as necessary to prevent grievous injury, taking into account his past experiences and their psychological effects. The New York Court of Appeals reinstated the charges, holding that New York's standard required comparing Goetz's actions and beliefs to those of a reasonable person in the same situation, with the knowledge Goetz had.[96] At trial, Goetz could argue that prior experience gave him reason to fear that he was being robbed and would be beaten. However, he was precluded from arguing that his previous mugging had left him too traumatized to restrain himself.

By the time of Goetz's trial, extensive pretrial publicity had made Goetz into a hero to many New Yorkers who shared his anger about crime. At trial, Goetz's defense attorney focused cross-examinations and argument on the criminal records of the complainants. Goetz's defense opened with evidence of his prior robbery and beating. He offered psychological testimony that a self-defender,

---

96. People v. Goetz, 68 N.Y. 2d 96 (1986).

once mobilized by fear to start shooting, might continue shooting unreflectively. This testimony was effective in persuading jurors that there was reasonable doubt that Goetz was aware he was no longer in danger when he fired the paralyzing shot. The jury acquitted him of all serious charges, a verdict some observers saw as an expression of racism.[97]

The result raises the normative question whether we want juries to credit defenders' subjective fears, which may be distorted by prejudice or hostility. It is easy to be in favor of empathy, but self-defense is a zero-sum game, in which more empathy for one combatant means less empathy for the other.

On the other hand, Goetz's jury empathized with him, not because they were required to by an individualized standard of reasonableness, but in spite of the fact that they were told not to. Perhaps some members of the jury of 10 whites and 2 blacks[98] already identified with him, and needed no special encouragement from judicial instructions or expert testimony to do so. So if jurors are going to empathize selectively with some defendants while applying a reasonable person standard, perhaps it somewhat evens the scales to apply an individualized standard of reasonable necessity to everyone, allowing defense attorneys to use expert testimony to try to elicit empathy for less advantaged defendants.

V. Necessity

The defense of necessity was recognized in trespass before it was invoked in criminal cases. In the sixteenth-century case of *Reniger v. Fagossa*, a captain was justified in jettisoning cargo on the ground that "in every law there are some things which when they happen a man may break the words of the law, and yet not break the law itself; . . . that is, where the words of them are broken to avoid greater inconveniences, or through necessity, or by compulsion, or involuntary ignorance."[99]

Hale presented necessity along with duress as a form of compulsion by the will of another. The difference was that necessity was compulsion by a legal authority, and so provided justification or "privilege."[100] He offered, as examples of necessity justifying the use of force, a warrant imposing a duty to arrest a resisting fugitive, or an order from a justice of the peace or sheriff to assist in suppressing a riot.[101]

97. Douglas O. Linder, *The Trial of Bernhard Goetz* (2011), *available at* law2.umkc.edu/faculty/projects/ftrials/goetz/goetzjury.html; George Fletcher, A Crime of Self-Defense: Bernhard Goetz and the Law on Trial 170–98 (1988).

98. Otto Friedrich, "*Not Guilty*," Time Mag., June 29, 1987.

99. 75 Eng. Rep. 1 (K.B. 1550).

100. 1 Matthew Hale, History of Pleas of the Crown 52 (1736).

101. *Id.* at 53.

Hale rejected the position of Hugo Grotius and Samuel Pufendorf that a starving man might excuse theft on grounds of necessity. Hale saw this claim as reliant on the subversive argument that an emergency suspended law and substituted a law of nature, abolishing property and returning all goods to common possession. For Hale, no private necessity could outweigh the security provided to all by a rule of law. Necessity was not an exception to the authority of law, permitting each to decide for his self. Instead, it was an expression of that authority, a power to violate private rights limited to persons legally bound to do so.[102] Where government was effectual, necessity was not its own law. Where government ceased to be effectual, however, its commands might no longer bind. Thus, an imprisoned felon could be excused for escaping a burning prison.[103] In wartime, civilians could be excused of treason for saving themselves by obeying the commands of an occupying army.[104] A ship at sea was its own polity, its commander expected to legislate according to public necessity.

Blackstone's discussion tracked Hale's, but subtly recast it. For Hale, it seemed that all conduct was governed by a rule or master, and was permissible only insofar as properly obedient to law. Blackstone, by contrast, treated conduct as willed. Because a criminal offense required a vicious will, any constraint upon the defendant's will was presumptively exculpatory. Although Blackstone's positions on cases agreed with Hale's, he classified necessity not as the exercise of public duty, but as a "deficiency of will," negating mens rea.[105]

Early American cases on the subject reflected these two conceptions of necessity—as a claim of obedience to proper authority, and as a claim that the defendant lacked a criminal purpose. They arose most often at sea, where life-threatening emergencies were common, and the power of law distant. In an 1810 decision on circuit, Justice Henry Livingston permitted the defendants to argue that they were innocent of shipping goods to an embargoed port in the West Indies because a storm had made it unsafe to sail toward any American port. Livingston argued that consideration of this claim was required by the principle "found in a every code of laws divine or human... and ingrafted into the common law of the country from which our jurisprudence is borrowed . . . that the concurrence of the will in what is done, where it has a choice, is the only thing that renders a human action culpable."[106] He concluded that common law precedents showed that "the necessity which leaves no alternative but

102. *Id.* at 54.
103. *Id.* at 611.
104. *Id.* at 49, 54–58.
105. 4 William Blackstone, Commentaries on the Laws and Customs of England 32 (1765–1769).
106. The William Gray, 29 F. Cas. 1300, 1302 (1810).

the violation of law to preserve life" could "excuse" even treason and murder.[107] In the 1834 case of *United States v. Ashton,* crewmembers were charged with mutiny on the high seas when they defied orders by returning their leaky vessel to port. Justice Story held that the prosecution was obliged to prove beyond a reasonable doubt that the orders disobeyed by the crew were reasonable.[108] The 1846 Massachusetts case of *Commonwealth v. Blodgett* concerned the Dorr Rebellion in Rhode Island. Soldiers in service to the Rhode Island government pursued insurgents into Massachusetts, arrested them there, and attempted to return them to Rhode Island. They were charged under a statute, aimed against rendition of fugitive slaves, which forbade kidnapping persons to transport them out-of-state. The trial court refused to instruct the jury that these soldiers were immunized by military orders, but allowed them to argue that the kidnapping was necessary to defend Rhode Island against insurrection. The jury nevertheless convicted. Judge Shaw of the Massachusetts Supreme Judicial Court approved these instructions and upheld the conviction.[109]

The famous 1842 case of *United States v. Holmes* tested Justice Livingston's claim that necessity could excuse even murder. An American ship carrying immigrants hit an iceberg and sank with half its passengers. The captain, one passenger, and seven sailors escaped in a small "jolly boat." The remaining 32 passengers and 9 crewmembers set forth in a leaky longboat, riding mere inches above the water. The first mate, Francis Rhodes, asked the captain to take some of the passengers aboard his lifeboat, saying it would otherwise be necessary to draw lots and throw some passengers overboard to keep the boat afloat. The captain reportedly responded, "I know what you'll have to do. Don't speak of that now, let it be the last resort." Then he rowed away. Later, with the boat taking on water during a storm, Rhodes ordered the crew to "go to work," and to spare women and children and not to part any married couples. They threw 14 men overboard, and two women who refused to be parted from their brother. Only one sailor, Alexander Holmes was apprehended. A grand jury charged him with manslaughter.

The prosecution argued that because there was time to decide how best to meet the exigency, the defendant could not claim that he lacked culpability or was deprived of choice. Instead, he was constrained to argue that his choice was justified. Accordingly, the remainder of the argument was notable for its focus on the process of decision more than the fatal result:

> The prisoner['s] defense is that the homicide was necessary to self-preservation. First, then, we ask: Was ... the danger instant,

---

107. *Id.*
108. United States v. Ashton, 24 F. Cas. 873 (1834).
109. Commonwealth v. Blodgett, 53 Mass. 56 (1846).

> overwhelming, leaving no choice of means, no moment for deliberation? For, unless the danger were of this sort, the prisoner, . . . has no right, without notice or consultation, or lot, to sacrifice the lives of 16 fellow beings . . . Admitting, . . . [however] that death was certain, and that the safety of some persons was to be promoted by an early sacrifice of the others, what law, we ask, gives a crew, in such a case, to be the arbiters of life and death, settling, for themselves, both the time and the extent of the necessity? No. We protest against giving to seamen the power thus . . . , for their own safety, to throw overboard, whenever they may like, whomsoever they may choose. If the mate and seamen believed that the ultimate safety of a portion was to be advanced by the sacrifice of another portion, it was the clear duty of that officer, and of the seamen, to give full notice to all on board. Common settlement would, then, have fixed the principle of sacrifice, and, the mode of selection involving all. . . . Thus far, the argument admits that, at sea, sailor and passenger stand upon the same base, and in equal relations. But, we take [a] third, stronger ground. The seaman, we hold, is bound, beyond the passenger, to encounter the perils of the sea. To the last extremity, to death itself, must he protect the passenger. It is his duty. It is on account of these risks that he is paid.[110]

Thus, the decision to jettison human beings was objectionable because of who was chosen, and why and how. The sacrifice of an individual could perhaps be justified if necessary to the public interest, as determined by democratic decision, and if properly authorized. Individuals, especially those charged with the governance of the boat for the safety of all, could not sacrifice others for their own private interest.

The defense attorneys responded by reviewing the desperation and danger confronting the castaways. They then argued that the drawing of lots was customary when castaways were rationing a dwindling supply of food, not in deciding who would board a lifeboat while a ship was sinking. The situation confronting the castaways was more like the latter than the former. Thus, there was no time for the casting of lots; the principle of selection chosen by the mate, saving the women and their mates, was more humane (and presumably would have been acceptable in determining who could board the boat in the first place). Finally, they argued that Holmes was either under the orders of his commanding officer, or in a state of nature where he was free to save himself.

---

110. United States v. Holmes, 26 F. Cas. 360, 363 (C.C.E.D.Pa.1842).

In instructing the jury, Justice Baldwin conceded that necessity could, like self-defense, justify the sacrifice of life.

> Where . . . a case does arise, embraced by . . . [the] "law of necessity," the penal laws pass over such case in silence; for law is made to meet but the ordinary exigencies of life. But the case does not become "a case of necessity," unless all ordinary means of self preservation have been exhausted. The peril must be instant, overwhelming, leaving no alternative but to lose our own life, or to take the life of another person. An illustration of this principle occurs in the ordinary case of self-defense against lawless violence, aiming at the destruction of life, or designing to inflict grievous injury to the person; and within this range may fall the taking of life under other circumstances where the act is indispensably requisite to self-existence. For example, suppose that two persons who owe no duty to one another that is not mutual, should, by accident, not attributable to either, be placed in a situation where both cannot survive. Neither is bound to save the other's life by sacrificing his own, nor would either commit a crime in saving his own life in a struggle for the only means of safety.[111]

On the other hand, the sailor's office of conveying the passenger safely precluded him from sacrificing the passenger to save himself.

> The passenger, not being bound either to labour or to incur the risk of life, cannot be bound to sacrifice his existence to preserve the sailor's. The captain, indeed, and a sufficient number of seamen to navigate the boat, must be preserved; for, except these abide in the ship, all will perish. But if there be more seamen than are necessary to manage the boat, the supernumerary sailors have no right, for their safety, to sacrifice the passengers. The sailors and passengers, in fact, cannot be regarded as in equal positions. The sailor . . . is bound to set a greater value on the life of others than on his own. And while we admit that sailor and sailor may lawfully struggle with each other for the plank which can save but one, we think that, if the passenger is on the plank, even "the law of necessity" justifies not the sailor who takes it from him.[112]

---

111. *Id.* at 366.
112. *Id.* at 367.

Moreover, if a selection had to be made, the proper method was to draw lots rather than to stand in judgment over one's peers. Here, Baldwin noted *and approved* as fair and pious this grisly custom of the sea:

> There is, however, one condition of extremity for which all writers have prescribed the same rule. When the ship is in no danger of sinking, but all sustenance is exhausted, and a sacrifice of one person is necessary to appease the hunger of others, the selection is by lot. This mode is resorted to as the fairest mode, and, in some sort, as an appeal to God, for selection of the victim.[113]

The jury convicted, and Baldwin sentenced Holmes to six months incarceration and a $20 fine.

The maritime custom of cannibalism by lot, although approved by Baldwin, was condemned by an English court in the famous case of *R. v. Dudley and Stephens*. Legal historian Brian Simpson has documented how this practice became increasingly familiar to the public in the nineteenth century, as commercial shipping and emigration proliferated, along with legal regulation, record-keeping, and journalism. Like industrial accidents of other kinds, maritime disasters were frequent and came increasingly to the attention of officials and courts. Reformers advocated for improved maritime safety. The reading public regarded survivors of these episodes with sympathy and even admiration, and consumed their harrowing adventures with ghoulish degustation.[114] Simpson documents about two-dozen known incidents of cannibalism involving English shipping during the nineteenth century.[115]

Dudley captained a yacht, bound for delivery to Australia, with a crew consisting of Stephens, Brooks, and Parker, an adolescent. The vessel came apart and sank in the South Atlantic, and the four sailors clambered into a small boat, with no water and little food. Parker became very ill from drinking a quantity of seawater and weakened more rapidly than the others. After about two weeks, Dudley mentioned the possibility of sacrificing one to save the rest, and mentioned drawing lots. In the ensuing days, Dudley repeated his proposal, made clear that he had Parker in mind, both because he was near death, and because—unlike Dudley and Stephens—he had no dependents. Dudley eventually received Stephens's assent. It does not appear that Brooks or Parker agreed to this plan. On the nineteenth or twentieth day. Dudley cut Parker's

---

113. *Id.*
114. *See, generally*, A.W. BRIAN SIMPSON, CANNIBALISM AND THE COMMON LAW (1984).
115. *Id.* at 95–146.

throat, while Stephens held his feet, and all three men drank the blood and ate the body. On the twenty-fourth day, they spotted a sail, rowed into its path, and were rescued. The survivors believed the killing of Parker saved their lives.[116]

The British Home Office was determined to use the case to put a stop to this practice. The judge assigned to the case, Baron Huddleston, succeeded in inducing the grand jury to charge murder, by instructing them that there was no authority supporting a defense of necessity in English law.[117] This was not entirely true. The Benthamite English Criminal Law Commissioners had included a defense of necessity in their 1843 digest of English criminal law.[118] Similarly, James F. Stephen's Homicide Law Amendment Bill of 1874 had proposed such a defense.[119] At the trial, Huddleston prevented the defendants from offering a defense of necessity, but then persuaded the jury that they could enable the defendants to present their legal argument to a higher court through the unusual expedient of a special verdict. Rather than convicting or acquitting the defendants, the jury agreed to a narration of the facts, authored by Huddleston. The resulting special verdict provided that "there was no drawing of lots," that Brooks had "dissented" from the killing, and

> That if the men had not fed upon the body of the boy they would probably not have survived to be so picked up and rescued. . . . That the boy, being in a much weaker condition, was likely to have died before them. That at the time of the act in question . . . there appeared to the prisoners every probability that unless they then fed or very soon fed upon the boy or one of themselves they would die of starvation. That there was no appreciable chance of saving life except by killing some one for the others to eat. That assuming any necessity to kill anybody there was no greater necessity for killing the boy than any of the other three men.[120]

A panel of five judges ruled the jury's findings sufficient to prove both defendants guilty of murder. Judge Coleridge's opinion for the court tracked much of the reasoning in Judge Huddleston's grand jury instruction. He invoked Hale's conclusion that private necessity could not justify a criminal offense. Only a public interest in the prevention of crime could justify the use of force. Thus, "Lord Hale regarded the private necessity which . . . alone justified, the taking

---

116. *Id.* at 55–72.
117. *Id.* at 199–204.
118. English Commissioners on Criminal Law, 4th Report, Art. 39 (1839); English Commissioners on Criminal Law, 7th Report (1843).
119. A.W. Brian Simpson, Cannibalism and the Common Law 235 (1984).
120. R. v. Dudley & Stephens, 14 Q.B.D. 273, 275 (1884).

the life of another for the safeguard of one's own to be. . . 'self-defence.'"[121] Coleridge concluded that the "American [case] . . . in which it was decided, correctly indeed, that sailors had no right to throw passengers overboard to save themselves, but on the somewhat strange ground that the proper mode of determining who was to be sacrificed was to vote upon the subject by ballot, can hardly . . . be an authority satisfactory to a court in this country."[122] Coleridge likewise dismissed the views of Francis Bacon that a starving man could justifiably steal food, and that one drowning man could thrust another from a plank. Coleridge obliquely acknowledged that Stephen had endorsed a general defense of necessity, but said that Stephen had privately assured him that the defense would not apply in this case.[123] In rejecting these authorities, and ignoring the English Criminal Law Commissioners, Coleridge seemingly rejected the utilitarian principle that doing harm to avoid greater harm is justified.

Next Judge Coleridge argued against excusing the killing out of compassion for the defendants' suffering or in recognition that the pressures they faced might have been difficult to resist.

> . . . It must not be supposed that in refusing to admit temptation to be an excuse for crime it is forgotten how terrible the temptation was; how awful the suffering . . . We are often compelled to set up standards we cannot reach ourselves and to lay down rules we could not ourselves satisfy.[124]

But why was it necessary to thus violate the Golden Rule, and hold the defendants to a standard the judges could not fairly expect them to meet? Coleridge's answer was that it was necessary to do so, to avoid the dangerous consequence of encouraging crime.

> the absolute divorce of law from morality would be of fatal consequence; and such divorce would follow if the temptation to murder in this case were to be held by law an absolute defence of it. . . . It is not needful to point out the awful danger of admitting [this] principle. . . . It is plain that the principle leaves to him who is to profit by it to determine the necessity which will justify him in deliberately taking another's life to save his

121. *Id.* at 282.
122. *Id.* at 285.
123. *Id.* at 285–86.
124. *Id.* at 288.

> own. . . . [S]uch a principle once admitted may be the legal cloak for unbridled passion and atrocious crime.[125]

In this way, Coleridge acknowledged that the prisoners were being used as a means to the social welfare, by being made an example of. As George Fletcher has observed, this concern for social consequences seemed at odds with Judge Coleridge's rejection of a defense of lesser evils:

> The rejection of excusing conditions and the concern for the social impact of the judgment both express a utilitarian philosophy of criminal justice. If Lord Coleridge could embrace utilitarian thinking on these points, one wonders why he recoiled from the prospect of justifying the killing on the grounds of lesser evils. . . . The outcome of the case is Kantian at the level of justification and utilitarian at the level of excuses—the worst possible combination for Dudley and Stephens.[126]

Because Dudley and Stephens were neither justified in achieving the lesser evil, nor excused by their desperation, they were convicted of murder—but in the end served only six months.

Although *R. v. Dudley and Stephens* rejected necessity as a defense to homicide, and cast doubt upon its validity as a defense to any crime in England,[127] contemporaneous American authorities generally approved a necessity defense. Bishop's 1892 treatise held that "every law of man . . . has in it the implied exception . . . that obedience shall not be required when it is impossible . . . [a]nd always an act done from compulsion or necessity is not a crime."[128] He added that the "necessity, to excuse, must be urgent, and without fault or carelessness of him who pleads it," whereas "the greater the crime, the greater must be the necessity to excuse it."[129] In their 1900 treatise, Clark and Marshall endorsed Stephen's formulation of the defense and cited the *Ashton, Gray*, and *Holmes* cases, as well as ones justifying the violation of minor police

---

125. *Id.* at 287–88.

126. George Fletcher, Rethinking Criminal Law 824–26 (1978).

127. Subsequently English courts were generally resistant to the defense. Southwark London Borough Council v. Williams, 2 AER 1975 (1971). On the other hand, in the famous case of *Re A (Conjoined Twins)* (2000) 2 WLR 480, an English court permitted surgeons to separate conjoined twins, causing the death of one so that the other could live a life of normal length and function, whereas otherwise both would have died within months. One judge, Lord Brooks, justified this expected homicide on grounds of necessity.

128. Joel Prentiss Bishop, New Commentaries on Criminal Law 206 (1892).

129. *Id.* at 211.

ordinances on grounds of safety or convenience.[130] An 1899 Missouri case justified a police officer's participation in criminal gambling to gather evidence of crime.[131] A 1920 Washington case justified speeding by emergency vehicles.[132] A 1929 California case speculated that a prisoner facing life-threatening conditions could justify escape, but did not find such conditions.[133]

Finally, in the troubling case of *State v. Wootton*, defendants were permitted to justify very serious crimes on grounds of necessity. The case arose out of a strike at a copper mine in Bisbee, Arizona, organized by the radical Industrial Workers of the World (IWW). Shortly after World War I broke out, the mining company circulated rumors that the "Wobblies" were in league with the Germans, and planned to organize an insurrection or blow up the mines. They induced the sheriff to deputize two vigilante groups, largely composed of company employees. At dawn, some 2,000 armed men rounded up over a thousand striking miners and forced them onto a train, which proceeded under armed guard to New Mexico, and stranded them there without shelter. During the roundup, one worker fatally shot a "deputy" and was in turn shot to death.

Some 200 of the vigilantes were charged with kidnapping, and one, H.E. Wootton, was brought to trial. Wootton's attorney argued that the deputies were justified by the reasonable fears that the Wobblies were conspiring to commit violence and overthrow government. He offered to prove that the IWW was an anarchist conspiracy to overthrow capitalism by force, and that its members intended to commit riot, murder, and mass destruction in Bisbee in a treasonous effort to impede the war effort. Because the county lacked the troops to control an insurrection, had unsuccessfully sought military assistance from the state and federal governments, and lacked sufficient cells to confine all the suspected conspirators, it became necessary for the county to deport them.[134]

Quoting Wharton, Judge Patten held that "Necessity is a defense when it is shown that the act charged was done to avoid an evil both serious and irreparable; that there was no other adequate means of escape; and that the remedy was not disproportionate to the evil."[135] Patten proceeded to reason that the right to invade the rights of others, to save one's own dependents from harm, was a

---

130. William Lawrence Clark & William Lawrence Marshall, A Treatise on the Law of Crimes 190–94 §82 (1900); Commonwealth v. Brooks, 99 Mass. 434 (1868); State v. Wray, 72 N.C. 253 (1875); Commonwealth v. Knox, 6 Mass. 76 (1809).

131. State v. Torphy, 78 Mo. App. 206 (1899).

132. State v. Gorham, 110 Wash. 330 (1920).

133. People v. Whipple, 100 Cal. App. 261 (1929).

134. Comment, *The Law of Necessity as Applied in the Bisbee Deportation Case*, 3 Ariz. L. Rev. 264 (1963); Note, *Necessity as a Defense*, 21 Colum. L. Rev. 71 (1921); George Soule, *The Law of Necessity in Bisbee*, 113 The Nation 21–23 (1921).

135. Comment, *The Law of Necessity as Applied in the Bisbee Deportation Case*, 3 Ariz. L. Rev. 264, 265 (1963).

natural right that could neither be extinguished by statute nor confined to public officials.[136] He cited cases permitting the destruction of property to prevent a fire from spreading, and Wharton's claim that this principle would permit even the destruction of a house with its inhabitants inside to prevent the destruction of a city. Patten ruled that the deportations were not authorized by martial law, as none had been declared; nor were they lawful arrests because they were not previously warranted or subsequently approved by a court.[137] However, he also invoked the precedent of *Commonwealth v. Blodgett* in support of a jury instruction that kidnapping could be justified by the need to suppress an insurrection.[138] As Judge Patten conceived the defense, it was a natural right on the part of individuals to carry out the functions of government, including the protection of their own rights and interests. Such a natural right was necessary because the availability of effective government institutions was highly contingent. The judge concluded that the necessity of the vigilantes' actions was a question of fact for the jury, and so instructed them. The jury quickly voted to acquit,[139] and charges against the other 200 vigilantes were dropped.

The authors of the Model Penal Code conceived necessity quite differently: as a default rule serving the announced purposes of the Code to "safeguard conduct that is without fault from condemnation" while "forbid[ding] and prevent[ing] conduct that unjustifiably . . . inflicts or threatens substantial harm to individual or public interests."[140] The Code treated necessity as a justification rather than an excuse, and conditioned it on a sober calculation of net welfare. Conduct was justified if it was the lesser evil, regardless of whose interests were protected, and regardless of the actor's motives or affect. Indeed, the Code treated necessity not as a rare and controversial defense, but as the paradigmatic defense of justification, more fundamental than public authority or self-defense. Section 3.02 of the Code was titled "Justification Generally: Choice of Evils," and provided:

> (1) Conduct that the actor believes to be necessary to avoid a harm . . . to himself or to another is justifiable, provided that:
>
> (a) the harm . . . sought to be avoided . . . is greater than that sought to be prevented by the law defining the offense charged; and
>
> (b) . . . the . . . law defining the offense provides [no] exceptions or defenses dealing with the specific situation. . . ; and
>
> (c) a legislative purpose to exclude the justification. . . does not otherwise plainly appear.

---

136. *Id.* at 267.
137. *Id.* at 269–71.
138. *Id.* at 274.
139. *Id.* at 275.
140. Model Penal Code § 1.02 (1)(a), (c)(1962).

Section 3.02 also contained what we might call an "imperfect necessity" provision, making the actor liable for a crime of recklessly or negligently causing or risking harm if he was reckless or negligent in creating the risk he sought to avoid by committing the offense.[141]

The Model Penal Code has been criticized for restricting necessity to a defense of justification, rather than excusing actors who caused net harm out of fear or desperation. George Fletcher noted that courts repeatedly denied an instruction on necessity to prisoners who escaped prison in order to avoid threats of murder and sexual assault, and invariably concluded that the speculative social cost of eroding prison discipline outweighed the welfare of the prisoner. Thus, in *State v. Green*, the Missouri Supreme Court refused an instruction on necessity where the defendant escaped to avoid a threatened gang rape a few hours hence. Although the defendant had complained to guards about previous rapes and been instructed to submit, fight, or escape, the court reasoned that the defendant had time to report the threat, which was not sufficiently imminent to justify escape.[142] In *People v. Richards*, a case with similar facts, a California court refused a necessity instruction on the ground that the harm of escape to the public outweighed the harm of sexual assault to the defendant.[143] Fletcher argued that a test focusing on the pressures overbearing the prisoner's will would avoid submerging the concrete interests of an individual beneath the abstract interests of "society."[144]

Fletcher praised the 1974 California decision in *People v. Lovercamp*, which invoked Hale's principle that a prisoner could be excused for escaping a fire, criticized *Green* and *Richards*, and granted an instruction on necessity as an excuse for escape to defendants who had fled a threatened sexual assault. The California court conditioned such an instruction on five circumstances: (1) an imminent, specific threat of death, sexual attack, or grave injury; (2) no time for a complaint to the authorities or a history of futile complaints; (3) no opportunity to petition courts; (4) no use of force in the escape; and (5) the prisoner immediately reporting to authorities upon attaining a position of safety.[145]

Yet it may be argued that the objectionable reasoning in *Green* and *Richards* was not the weighing of the prisoner's interests against the public's interests. Perhaps the mistake was in undervaluing the prisoner's interests in safety, bodily integrity, sexual autonomy, dignity, and civil rights; and in equating the

---

141. *Id.* § 3.02.
142. State v. Green, 470 S.W. 2d 565 (1972); GEORGE FLETCHER, RETHINKING CRIMINAL LAW 827 (1978).
143. People v. Richards, 75 Cal. Rptr. 597 (1969); GEORGE FLETCHER, RETHINKING CRIMINAL LAW 828 (1978).
144. *Id.* at 827–29.
145. People v. Lovercamp, 118 Cal. Rptr. 110 (1974).

public's interest in prison discipline with the prevention of escape but not the prevention of rape or murder. Thus, there is no inherent reason that a prisoner cynically exposed to sexual violence by negligent authorities could not be justified in escaping. In the Illinois case of *People v. Unger*, a prisoner escaped after reporting sexual assaults and receiving death threats as a consequence. He was awarded a necessity instruction under a statutory provision based on the Model Penal Code, providing that "conduct which would otherwise be an offense is justifiable if the accused was without blame in occasioning . . . the situation and reasonably believed such conduct was necessary to avoid a public or private injury greater than the injury which might reasonably result from his conduct." The prosecution argued that this defense should have been unavailable, as it would have been under *Lovercamp*, because the defendant did not immediately turn himself in. The court responded that under the statute—which does not require that the danger prevented be temporally imminent or physically present—Unger could justify remaining at large as well as escaping, if he could show that turning himself in immediately would have subjected him to the same danger.[146]

Today, almost all American jurisdictions have a defense of necessity. Of the dozen most populous states, only Michigan and Georgia lack such a defense, and they treat some cases as instances of duress that would be treated as necessity elsewhere. Necessity is currently codified and classified as a justification in Texas, New York, Illinois, Pennsylvania, and New Jersey.[147] It is recognized in jury instructions in California and Florida,[148] and in case law in Ohio, North Carolina, and Virginia.[149] Florida, Ohio, and Virginia classify the defense as a justification, whereas North Carolina calls it an excuse, and California jury instructions do not address the question (although the *Lovercamp* court called it an excuse). In most jurisdictions, necessity requires (1) a reasonable belief that (2) the offense will avoid a more harmful consequence that is (3) imminent, (4) not avoidable by lawful means, and (5) not culpably caused by the defendant.

How culpable must the defendant have been in creating the danger to lose the defense under criterion #5? The Model Penal Code resolves the latter problem with its "imperfect necessity" doctrine, making the defendant liable for the harm he causes, with whatever culpable mental state he had toward the

146. People v Unger, 362 N.E. 2d 319 (1977).

147. Tex. Penal Code § 9.22 (1994); NY Penal Law § 35.05 (1968); 720 ILCS 5/7-13 (1962); 18 Pa.C.S. § 503 (1973); N.J. Stat. § 2C:3-2 (1979).

148. 2-3400 Cal. Crim. Jury Instruction 3403; 3.6(k) DURESS OR NECESSITY (2014).

149. State v. Prince, 71 Ohio App. 3d 694, 699 (1991); Dayton v. Gigandet, 83 Ohio App. 3d 886 (1992); Columbus v. Spingola, 144 Ohio App. 3d 76 (2001); State v. Gainey, 84 N.C. App. 107

harm he thereby avoided. Disqualifying the defense completely at one level of culpability creates troubling moral discontinuities. Suppose we disqualify a defendant who recklessly creates the danger he avoids. Although he created one danger recklessly, we hold him fully liable for causing another harm intentionally. On the other hand, if he caused the danger negligently, he would not be liable for causing the harm at all, despite his moral fault.

Another troubling aspect of criterion #5 is that because the harm avoided may be harm to one's self, it can be risked culpably without being risked criminally. Thus, suppose that J, despondent over H's infidelity, jumps from a cruise ship to commit suicide. H grabs a small life preserver and jumps in to save J. Unfortunately the life preserver is not buoyant enough to support both. J has a change of heart, wresting the life preserver from H, who drowns. As J created the danger to self intentionally, J may be denied a necessity defense even though the self-endangerment was not criminal. In his famous essay "The Case of the Speluncean Explorers," Lon Fuller posed the similar question of whether and why we should punish reckless adventurers who survive by resort to cannibalism, while provoking fatal efforts to rescue them.[150]

A minority of jurisdictions impose a sixth condition on a successful necessity defense: they require that the judgment that the harm averted outweighs the harm of the criminal offense has not been foreclosed by legislative deliberation. For example, the New York Penal Law provides that "[t]he necessity and justifiability of such conduct may not rest upon considerations pertaining only to the advisability of the statute."[151] This is an issue most likely to arise in cases of civil disobedience, where defendants openly violate a law for the purpose of challenging its justice in court, both to publicize their views and to win an authoritative judgment that the law is unjust.

In the 1980 Vermont case of *State v. Warshow*, protestors were convicted of trespass when they formed a picket line to block workers from entering and operating a nuclear power plant. They offered to show that the operation of the plant posed a substantial and imminent danger. The Vermont Supreme Court upheld the denial of an instruction on the proposed defense on grounds that harm was not sufficiently probable, substantial, or imminent.[152] A dissent argued that these were questions of fact properly left to the jury.[153]

(1987); Long v. Commonwealth, 478 S.E. 2d 324 (Va. Ct. App. 1996); Buckley v. City of Falls Church, 371 S.E. 2d 827 (Va. Ct. App. 1998).

150. Lon Fuller, *The Case of the Speluncean Explorers*, 62 HARV. L. REV. 616 (1949).

151. N.Y. PENAL LAW § 35.05 (1968); *see also* State v. Thomas, 103 N.C. App. 264 (1991); Long v. Commonwealth, 478 S.E. 2d 324 (Va. Ct. App. 1996).

152. State v. Warshow, 410 A. 2d 1000 (1980) (Barney, C.J.).

153. *Id.* at 1005 (Billings, J.).

A concurrence reasoned that permitting the defense would subvert democracy by "allowing a jury to redetermine questions of policy already decided by the legislative branches of the federal and state governments."[154] One might respond that the right of a jury trial in criminal cases is guaranteed to enable the jury to protect political dissent by providing a popular check on prosecutors, including by nullifying the law. Because the jury decides only the case before it, its endorsement of civil disobedience arguably does not subvert democracy by thwarting legislatures any more than prosecutorial discretion does. Instead, justifying civil disobedience on grounds of necessity arguably informs democracy by providing a forum for the reasoned expression of popular disaffection. However we do well to remember that in American history, the power of local juries to resist national policy has been mobilized on behalf of not only the Underground Railroad, but also the Ku Klux Klan.

VI. Duress

The defense of duress is closely related to that of necessity. The actor is absolved of guilt for conduct compelled by threats rather than natural dangers. The two defenses were often grouped together in older treatises, and sometimes treated as interchangeable. A defense of duress is in some ways easier to accept than a defense of necessity, because it does not preclude vindication of a victim. It concedes that the victim has been wronged, but points the finger of blame at someone else.

Hale viewed both necessity and duress as jurisdictional claims that the accused should not be liable for violating a criminal prohibition because he was subject to a different law. Yet where necessity conferred official authority to violate criminal prohibitions in service to the public interest, duress subjected the agent unwillingly to an unlawful authority. The paradigmatic cases of duress were unwilling participation in riots and supplying occupying enemy troops. Thus where necessity identified the accused with law, or subjected him to natural law, duress excused disloyalty to the law. Indeed, some English authorities took the view that treason was the only crime excused by duress.[155]

An 1838 English decision disapproved duress,[156] and Stephen agreed that it "ought in no case whatever be admitted as an excuse for crime,"[157] as doing

---

154. *Id.* at 1003 (Hill, J.).
155. Walter Harrison Hitchler, *Duress as a Defense in Criminal Cases*, 4 VA. L. REV. 519, 525 (1917).
156. R. v. Taylor, 8 C & P 616 (1838).
157. JAMES FITZJAMES STEPHEN, A HISTORY OF THE CRIMINAL LAW OF ENGLAND 108 (1883).

so would undermine the criminal law's deterrent force. Yet although Stephen denied that duress could excuse perpetrators, he conceded that English law made duress available to excuse an accomplice "compelled to . . . [aid or abet] by threats on the part of the offenders instantly to . . . do him grievous bodily harm. . . ."[158]

Cases permitting the defense were rare in nineteenth-century America.[159] In an early American treason prosecution, the defendant was taken prisoner by the British during the Revolution and then served in the British army. The judge instructed the jury that "nothing will excuse the act of joining an enemy but the fear of immediate death" and its continuation throughout the defendant's service. Nevertheless, the jury acquitted.[160] An 1846 Illinois decision held that a threat of death could excuse complicity in robbery, and hence of a resulting felony murder, but only if the threat continued throughout the assistance.[161] Wharton suggested that duress could excuse one "compelled to do wrong by threats on the part of the offenders instantly to kill him, or to do him grievous bodily harm, if he refuses,"[162] while Bishop viewed duress as included within the excuse of necessity, which he saw as required by natural law. Clark and Marshall endorsed Stephen's narrow excuse for aiders and abettors.[163] At the end of the nineteenth century, several American decisions suggested that duress would excuse offenders faced with an imminent and unavoidable threat to their lives. A Mississippi court wrote "[w]e can conceive of cases in which an act . . . may be committed . . . under such circumstances of coercion as to free him from criminality. The impelling danger, however, must be present, imminent and impending, and not to be avoided."[164] In an influential 1893 opinion, an Alabama court observed that "at common law no man could excuse himself, under the plea of necessity or compulsion, for taking the life of an innocent person," but expressed doubt that the threat of future punishment could deter an actor faced with an immediate threat of death. Thus, the court denied the defendant an instruction on the narrower grounds that the threat was not immediate when issued, and that the defendant had an opportunity to escape his confederates before arriving at the murder scene.[165]

---

158. James Fitzjames Stephen, A Digest of the Criminal Law, Art. 31 (1877).

159. 2 James Fitzjames Stephen, A History of the Criminal Law of England. 106 (1883); Walter Harrison Hitchler, *Duress as a Defense in Criminal Cases,* 4 Va. L. Rev. 519, 519–20 (1917).

160. Respublica v. McCarty, 2 Dallas 86 (1781).

161. Baxter v. People, 8 Ill. 368, 384–85 (1846).

162. 1 Francis Wharton, Treatise on Criminal Law § 9 (1874).

163. William Lawrence Clark & William Lawrence Marshall, A Treatise on the Law of Crimes 195 (1900).

164. Bain v. State, 67 Miss. 557 (1890).

165. Arp v. State, 97 Ala. 5, 12–13 (1893); *accord,* People v. Repke, 103 Mich. 459 (1895).

An early scholarly examination of duress was Walter Hitchler's 1917 article "Duress as a Defense to Crime." Hitchler viewed the common law's hostility to this defense as irrational. From a deterrent standpoint, he thought "duress should excuse whenever the motive to crime . . . is such as would necessarily countervail the fear of any penalty which it is just and expedient that the law should threaten."[166] Note that Hitchler's argument was not that the execution of a gangster's demands under threat of death is socially optimal as the lesser of two evils. Instead, he argued that inflicting proportionate punishment on the coerced collaborator could have no deterrent effect and so was socially suboptimal. Increasing temporally remote punishment to the point that it could outweigh the effect of imminent violence would presumably have other social costs, such as eroding respect for law and inviting corruption and nullification. In short, Hitchler offered a utilitarian argument for duress as an excuse rather than as a justification.[167] Hitchler applied this principal of deterrent proportionality to argue that duress should be available as a defense to all crimes, where the threat was sufficiently grave and imminent. He added that even if duress was unavailable for murder, it should be available for manslaughter, and for accomplices in felonies whose confederates kill, and who therefore face liability for felony murder.[168] He concluded that duress should be a defense to all crimes with the possible exception of capital murder, and that the required threat should vary with the severity of the crime and of the punishment proportionate to that severity.[169]

Although not following Hitchler in every respect, the Model Penal Code provision reflected his general approach, conditioning duress on a threat to use unlawful force against anyone that a person of reasonable firmness in the defendant's situation would have been unable to resist.[170] This standard allowed the jury to consider situational factors such as the relative strength and past interactions of the parties, and the availability of weapons, but not differences in maturity, courage, or independence.[171] The Code made the defense unavailable to a defendant who recklessly placed himself in danger of duress, and unavailable for a crime of negligence if he negligently placed himself in danger. The Code put the burden on the prosecution to disprove duress.

---

166. Walter Harrison Hitchler, *Duress as a Defense in Criminal Cases,* 4 VA. L. REV. 519, 521–22 (1917).
167. A similar analysis was followed by the British criminal law authority Glanville Williams. GLANVILLE WILLIAMS, CRIMINAL LAW: THE GENERAL PART § 246 (1961).
168. Walter Harrison Hitchler, *Duress as a Defense in Criminal Cases,* 4 VA. L. REV. 519, 528–29 (1917).
169. *Id.* at 532–35.
170. MODEL PENAL CODE § 2.09 (1962).
171. MODEL PENAL CODE COMMENTARIES, PART I, Sect. 2.09, at 372–377 (1985).

Today, a significant minority of jurisdictions define duress along the lines proposed by the Model Penal Code. Among the dozen largest states, Texas, New York, Pennsylvania, and New Jersey apply duress to all crimes; condition the defense on a threat of unlawful force that a person of reasonable firmness would be unable to resist; and bar the defense for those who recklessly place themselves in danger of duress.[172] Most other states require a threat of imminent great bodily harm to excuse any offense,[173] and many states bar the defense for at least some forms of homicide.[174] This exclusion is usually limited to intentional murder. In most jurisdictions one who is coerced to participate in a felony can offer duress as a defense to a felony murder committed by one of the other felons.[175] Duress is not typically classified as a justification. Typically the defendant is responsible to prove it by a preponderance of evidence,[176] but in a minority of jurisdictions the prosecution bears the burden to disprove it.[177]

Jurisdictions requiring an imminent threat may apply that requirement very differently. In the Texas case of *State v. Anguish*, the defendant was charged with robbing a bank and several related crimes. He offered to show that his troubles started after he accused an FBI agent of conspiring to commit murder. The defendant recounted that since that time he had suffered repeated burglaries, threatening phone calls, an attempted kidnapping, and arson. He claimed that he had robbed the bank four days after being ordered to do so by two men who lay in wait for him in his car, put a gun to his head, and threatened to kill his wife and daughter. He believed their motive was to discredit him so that his accusations of the FBI agent would not be believed. He claimed to have reported previous harassment to law enforcement authorities to no avail, and so doubted that he could protect his family by reporting these new threats. A Texas Court of Appeals denied the relevance of this testimony to a defense of duress on the ground that neither the defendant's family nor the bank were

---

172. N.Y. Penal Law § 40.00 (1968); Tex. Penal Code § 8.05 (1994) (however Texas requires a threat of imminent great bodily harm to excuse a felony); 18 Pa.C.S. § 309 (1973); N.J. Stat. § 2C:2-9 (1979).

173. 720 ILCS. 5/7-11 (2010); State v. Prince, 71 Oh. App. 3d 694, 699; People v. Merhige, 212 Mich. 601, 610–11 (1920); Sam v. Commonwealth, 411 S.E. 2d 832 (Va. Ct. App. 1991); State v. Cheek, 351 N.C. 48, 61–62, 520 S.E.2d 545, 553 (1999); Fla. Std. Jury Instr. (Crim.) 3.6(k) (2014); Cal. Criminal Jury Instruction 3402 (2008) (immediate threat to life).

174. California Penal Code § 26 (2008); State v. Grinnell, 678 N.E.2d 231 (Ohio Ct. App. 1996); O.C.G.A. § 16-3-26 (1968) ; State v. Gay, 334 N.C. 467, 490 (1993).

175. Wayne LaFave, Criminal Law 519, 522 (2010); State v. Hunter, 740 P. 2d 559 (1987); People v. Sims, 374 Ill. App. 3d 231 (2007); McMillan v. State, 181 Md. App. 298 (2008); People v. Mehrige, 212 Mich. 601 (1920).

176. Texas, §2.04, §8.05 (1994); NY Penal Law 25.00, 40.00 (1965); Takacs v. Engle, 768 F.2d 122 (6th Cir. Ohio 1985); State v. Cheek, 351 N.C. 48 (1999); N.J.S.A. 2C:2-9 (1979).

177. Fla. Std. Jury Instr. (Crim.) 3.6(k) Duress or Necessity (2014); Cal. Crim. Jury Instruction 3402 (2008).

physically present at the time the alleged threats were made, so that such threats could not be carried out immediately. Moreover, the fact the defendant allowed several days to elapse before robbing the bank indicated that he did not expect the threatened killing to occur imminently. The court rejected the defendant's argument that his belief that contacting the authorities was futile made the danger sufficiently unavoidable to count as imminent.[178]

By contrast, in *United States v. Contento-Pachon*, the U.S. Court of Appeals for the Ninth Circuit allowed a duress defense to a Colombian taxi driver who traveled to the United States with 129 balloons of cocaine in his stomach. Contento-Pachon reported that he was first approached by one of his fares with an offer to carry drugs into the United States for a drug gang. When he refused, the gang threatened to kill his wife and child if he did not carry the cocaine. He testified that he did not seek help from the police because he believed the Colombian police were under the control of the drug traffickers. After repeated threats, he agreed to carry the cocaine. He was told that he would be watched throughout the trip and that if he deviated from the gang's instructions, his family, who remained behind in Colombia, would be killed. Contento-Pachon therefore failed to contact authorities during a stopover in Panama, and when he landed in Los Angeles. He was denied a duress defense at trial, on the ground that the threatened injury was not spatially and temporally immediate, and that he could have avoided his crime by contacting the police. The Ninth Circuit concluded that the defendant had reason to fear that the threats against his family would be carried out quickly in Colombia if he ceased collaborating en route to the United States. The court also viewed Contento-Pachon's allegation that the Colombian police were corrupt as a triable issue of fact. Finally, they saw the possibility that the entire family could have escaped beyond the reach of the gang's retaliation as being a question of fact for the jury.[179]

Thus, in contrast to the Texas court, the Ninth Circuit was willing to see a threat against family members at a remote time and place as being imminent, if the defendant was helpless to prevent it. It seems likely that the Ninth Circuit would have viewed the imminence and inescapability of the threats against Anguish's family as a factual question. By contrast, it seems likely that the Texas Court of Appeals would have viewed the threats against Contento-Pachon as insufficiently immediate to warrant a jury instruction.

We saw that the requirement of imminence has been criticized in the context of self-defense, as barring consideration of the pervasive threat of violence implicit in abusive domestic relationships. In the case of *In re Romero*,

---

178. Anguish v. State, 991 S.W. 2d 883 (1999).
179. United States v. Contento-Pachon, 723 F. 2d 691 (1984).

a California court allowed evidence of battered women's syndrome to support claims that abuse victims who participated in their partners' crimes perceived imminent threats to life where such threats were not explicit and continuous.[180] In the Kansas case of *State v. Crawford*, the defendant drew on self-defense cases involving battered women in an unsuccessful effort to evade a statutory requirement of imminence. Crawford went on a robbery and kidnapping spree in response to a cocaine dealer's pressure to repay a substantial debt. Crawford claimed to fear that the dealer would harm a child of his living in another city, and that Crawford's addiction to cocaine and dependence on the dealer for his supply rendered him helpless to resist the dealer's pressure. The court found the evidence of a threat to Crawford's child insubstantial, and viewed evidence of his drug dependence as undermining his claims that the robberies were motivated by the fear of violence.[181]

In contrast to these other jurisdictions, the Model Penal Code does not require an imminent threat of violence. It merely requires a threat of violence that would overcome the resistance of a person of reasonable firmness in the circumstances facing the defendant. Under this standard, Anguish and Contento-Pachon could have argued that an average person in similar circumstances—for example, faced with corrupt or unresponsive law enforcement—would have found threats by gangs to kill their families difficult to resist. Rather than barring the defense for severe crimes, the Code factors the severity of the crime into a normative judgment of the reasonableness of succumbing to the threat. Presumably the person of reasonable firmness would not kill to avoid a slap. At the same time, the reasonable firmness standard bars consideration of the unusual psychological incapacity of a defendant to resist pressure. Such incapacity could only be considered under the excuse of mental disease or defect (or infancy, if the offender were a juvenile). Such a reasonable firmness standard would preclude Crawford's claim that addiction rendered him particularly vulnerable to pressure from his supplier, but also Romero's claim that battered women's syndrome reduced her capacity to resist her abusive partner's demands.

Crawford was also denied a duress defense for a second reason. Like the Model Penal Code, the Kansas code bars the defense for one who recklessly places himself in a situation where coercion to commit a crime is probable. The Kansas Supreme Court viewed Crawford's dependence on and debt to a dangerous criminal as the predictable product of his own criminal activity.[182] What

---

180. *In re* Romero, 13 Cal. Rptr. 2d 332 (1992).
181. State v. Crawford, 253 Kan. 629 (1993).
182. *Id.*

counts as recklessly placing oneself in danger of duress? In *Williams v. State* a Maryland court denied a duress defense on this basis to a defendant charged as an accomplice in an armed robbery. Williams had previously delivered drugs for a dealer to pay off a debt to the dealer's brother. Convinced that Williams knew the location of the dealer's "stash," three men abducted Williams and threatened to kill him unless he led them there. Williams chose a house at random and accompanied his abductors as they threatened the homeowner and searched the house. The Maryland court invoked the Model Penal Code provision and reasoned that by working for a drug dealer, Williams had recklessly created a risk that he would be targeted as a robbery victim.[183] Yet it seems odd to punish someone for assuming a risk that he will become a *victim* of crime. On like reasoning, a victim of domestic abuse might be blamed for risking duress by entering or remaining within an abusive relationship—particularly if the crime charged is complicity in the abuse of other household members. In sum, even though the Model Penal Code provision on duress lacks a requirement of imminence, it may offer little help to victims pressured into crime by abusive partners. Both the Model Penal Code's reasonable firmness standard and its exclusion of defendants who recklessly risk duress may preclude abuse victims from excusing themselves.

Excluding duress for those who recklessly place themselves in danger of duress is troubling because it lengthens the time frame of the crime just enough to include inculpatory choices that reduce the defendant's later autonomy, but not enough to include exculpatory circumstances—such as poverty, exposure to risks of violence, deficient law enforcement and educational opportunity, abuse or neglect during childhood—that might have reduced the autonomy of those imprudent choices.[184] *The Wire*, a deeply researched television drama about drug gangs in Baltimore, illustrates how these factors combine to force vulnerable young people into criminal gangs.[185] Richard Delgado has argued that such factors should make duress available in such circumstances.[186]

A common feature of both the Model Penal Code's reasonable firmness standard and the imminent-great-bodily-harm standard is that they set proportionality limits on the defense. Yet these proportionality standards seem somewhat different in function. The reasonable firmness standard focuses on the competing pressures on the accused of a threat of unlawful force and the

183. Williams v. State, 646 A. 2d 1101 (Md. App. 1994).

184. Mark Kelman, *Interpretive Construction in the Substantive Criminal Law*, 33 STAN. L. REV. 591, 593–94, 643–44 (1981).

185. THE WIRE (HBO 2002–2008).

186. Richard Delgado, *"Rotten Social Background": Should the Criminal Law Recognize a Defense of Severe Emotional Deprivation?*, 3 LAW & INEQUALITY 9 (1985).

deterrent threat of punishment. It is designed to excuse the defendant when the unlawful force threatened by an assailant is disproportionate to the *punishment* imposed for the crime, because such punishment would be ineffectual as a deterrent. By contrast, the imminent-great-bodily-harm standard appears to balance the severity of the threatened harm against the severity of the crime ordered, excluding threats of less-than-deadly force on the one hand, and excluding the crimes of intentional and attempted killing on the other. It thereby avoids excusing the intentional infliction of harm more severe than that threatened.

If the crime the actor committed must be less than the crime he was threatened with, the excuse of duress appears to collapse into necessity, and the defendant's conduct seems morally justified. Indeed, some scholars have argued that duress should be assimilated with necessity and treated as a justification.[187] The main difficulties with this proposal are the collateral implications of justifying compliance with duress for the conduct of others. If robbing or raping a victim on threat of death is justified, then presumably it would be wrong—indeed criminal—for the victim to forcibly resist. Moreover, an uninvolved observer who was not personally threatened would be justified in helping the defendant overcome the victim's resistance. Yet it seems clear that a bystander who did so should be liable as an accomplice.

If duress is an excuse rather than a justification, its exculpatory effect should depend only on the unfairness or inefficacy of punishing the actor's conduct, not on the net harmfulness of the conduct.[188] There are at least four kinds of reasons to excuse coerced wrongful conduct. First, there is the utilitarian reasoning employed by Hitchler and the Model Penal Code: threatened harm should excuse offending when it precludes deterring the offense at any reasonable cost. Second, there is a retributivist variant of this deterministic argument: coercion should excuse insofar as it deprives the offender of free choice, and so absolves the offender of blame. Third, Joshua Dressler has offered a less deterministic version of this retributivist argument. According to Dressler, coerced crime is voluntarily chosen in the sense that the offender has physical control of his movements, is conscious, and is capable of practical reason. What excuses the offender's choice is that (1) his options are wrongly constrained by a threatened crime, and (2) the threatened wrong is so great that society considers it unfair to expect him to endure it for the benefit of another. Because of the

187. Peter Westen & James Mangiafico, *The Criminal Defense of Duress: A Justification Not an Excuse—and Why It Matters*, 6 BUFF. CRIM. L. REV. 833 (2003); Thomas Weigend, *Kill or Be Killed: Another Look at* Erdemovic, 10 J. INT. CRIM. JUST. 1219 (2012).

188. Joshua Dressler, *Exegesis of the Law of Duress: Justifying the Excuse and Searching for Its Proper Limits* 62 SO. CAL. L. REV. 1331, 1350–53 (1989).

wrongness and the scale of the harm he is threatened with, the offender lacks a "fair" opportunity to avoid the crime.[189] According to Dressler, this test will sometimes allow an actor to impose more wrongful harm on another than he is threatened with, but when it will do so depends on the intuitive judgment of factfinders.[190] A troubling feature of this test is the scope it thereby gives factfinders to discriminate by exercising differential sympathy. Finally, a somewhat more jurisdictional account of excusing coerced crime is that the criminal law cannot fairly punish an offender whose options were wrongly constrained by crime that the law failed to adequately protect him from.

All four of these rationales might excuse very grave crimes, including murder. Can this ever be acceptable?

Consider the harrowing case of Drazen Erdemovic, tried before the International Criminal Tribunal for Yugoslavia.[191] Erdemovic was a Croat married to a Serb in Bosnia-Herzegovina. In an effort to survive the Bosnian civil war he served in armies of all three ethnic groups. He was beaten and driven out of a Croat enclave for helping Serbian refugees escape. He later joined a reconnaissance unit of the Serbian militia, but was demoted for saving a Bosnian prisoner from execution. He witnessed a commanding officer named Pelemis order the execution of a soldier who disobeyed an order. In July 1995, Erdemovic's unit was deployed to a farm in Pilica, and was told that truckloads of Bosnian civilians were going to be brought from Srebenica to be executed. Erdemovic protested, and was told by the commander on the scene that if he did not wish to participate he could line up with the victims to be shot. He proceeded to shoot and kill over 70 civilians. Later in the day, Pelemis arrived and ordered Erdemovic and others to proceed to the village hall where another 500 Bosnians were being held, and to execute them. Erdemovic refused, and was joined in that refusal by three others. He was not threatened at the time; however, the next day, one of the other soldiers who had participated in the executions at Pilica shot Erdemovic in the stomach and chest. Erdemovic survived and proceeded to turn himself in to the International Criminal Tribunal for Yugoslavia and confess.[192]

An appellate panel considered whether duress could be available as a defense to to crimes against humanity or war crimes that included the killing of noncombatants.[193] By a vote of 3-2, the court concluded that duress

189. *Id.* at 1356–67.

190. *Id.* at 1365–75.

191. An excellent account of the difficult issues in this case is Luis Chiesa, *Duress, Demanding Heroism and Proportionality*, 41 VAND. J. TRANS. L. 741 (2008).

192. TRIAL TESTIMONY OF DRAZEN ERDEMOVIC, NOV. 19TH AND 20TH, 1996, pp. 178–204, 221–36, 258–309.

193. *Prosecutor v. Erdemovic*, IT-96-22-A, Judgment on Appeal, P 10 (Oct 7, 1997).

was unavailable. They reasoned that although many international authorities recognized duress as a defense to international crime, there was little international law authority on the question of whether this defense could excuse intentional killing. A plurality opinion reasoned that the validity of the duress defense did not entail its applicability to intentional killing, because domestic legal systems divided on this question. Although civil law systems generally permitted duress to excuse any crime less grave than the harm threatened, common law systems generally precluded duress from excusing murder. Given this dissensus, the plurality turned to policy considerations. They emphasized that war crimes and crimes against humanity are particularly heinous and are often gross in scale, while the soldiers committing them are often pressured to commit them by orders backed by deadly force. To allow duress to excuse soldiers would perversely incentivize commanders to threaten them and thereby immunize them from liability. This would undercut international criminal law's deterrent threat. By applying the common law rule, the plurality hoped to "give notice . . . that those who kill innocent persons will not be able to take advantage of duress as a defence and thus get away with impunity."[194]

Two dissenters responded that because most legal systems in the world are civilian systems rather than common law systems, the prevailing rule conditions duress on the harm threatened being greater than the harm caused. They argued that the gravity of international crimes will usually exceed the harm threatened, but that this does not justify courts in ignoring such threats in assessing the blameworthiness of defendants. Instead, they argued, the gravity of international crimes are considerations of proportionality, properly weighed on a case-by-case basis, and balanced against the gravity of the threat. Thus offenders threatened with death, who provided nonessential aid to a killing, could be excused for saving their own lives by participating in grave crimes without actually causing any harm. More controversially, defendants such as Erdemovic who actually killed, should be allowed to offer proof that their acts made no causal difference because others would have inevitably taken their places. It would be noble for such defendants to sacrifice their own lives for a principle, the dissenters concluded, but the law cannot demand nobility.[195] The dissenters did not argue that such killings are justified, but that they are excusable, because the actor has no meaningful choice, and the harm he causes is not disproportionate to the threat.

In a surprising response, the plurality conceded the proportionality of the harm to the threat, but then rejected proportionality as an improperly

194. *Id.* Joint Separate Opinion Judge McDonald and Judge Vohrah at 42.
195. *Id.* Opinion of Judge Stephen; Opinion of Judge Cassesse.

utilitarian measure of wrongdoing. Yet it declined to substitute a Kantian morality of fairness that might dictate compassion for the sailor at sea on a plank, or the refugee caught in the crossfire of civil war. Instead, the plurality insisted on loyalty to the authority of a distant law: "The approach we take does not involve a balancing of harms for and against killing but . . . is based upon a recognition that international humanitarian law should guide the conduct of combatants and their commanders."[196] By that logic, duress is inculpatory and should be unavailable even for minor infractions.[197] That logic is challenged by the jurisdictional argument that a system of criminal law cannot fairly demand loyalty without also providing credible protection.

Let us now shift from the gravity of the crime committed to the gravity of the threat imposed. How grave must the threat be to excuse the offense? Must it be a threat of death, as in California; grievous bodily harm as in many states; or unlawful force as required by the Model Penal Code? But surely there are some nonviolent threats that might be more compelling than a threat of unlawful force—for example, to expose an embarrassing secret, to destroy a cherished memento or an irreplaceable artwork, or to cause someone to be deported, convicted of a crime, or to lose a needed job or custody of a child. Why should not a threat that would suffice for extortion liability, if it induced payment of funds, also suffice for duress if it induced an otherwise unwilling participant to join in a crime?

One problem is that offenders who regularly collaborate in crime routinely and knowingly give each other leverage to blackmail one another. Yet this objection can be met by barring the defense for defendants who recklessly placed themselves in danger of duress. A deeper difficulty is that without the requirement of unlawful force, a reasonable firmness standard may be too inclusive. Humans are naturally sociable and hierarchical, and tend to follow the directions of leaders and authority figures, whether the setting is an army, a corporation, a family, a gang, or fraternity.

Stanley Milgram demonstrated this pliability in a famous series of psychology experiments, in which experimental subjects were told they were administering a learning test to subjects they could not see. As they were given wrong answers by the hapless (but fortunately fictional) "learners,", they were pressured by psychologists to administer what they thought were increasingly severe and painful electric shocks to these supposed subjects. The psychologists

196. *Id.* Joint Separate Opinion Judge McDonald and Judge Vohrah at 42.

197. It has been noted that arguments against excusing murder on grounds of duress often undermine the defense of duress altogether. Leo Katz, Bad Acts and Guilty Minds, 69 (1987); Joshua Dressler, *Exegesis of the Law of Duress: Justifying the Excuse and Searching for Its Proper Limits* 62 So. Cal. L. Rev. 1331, 1332 (1989).

made no threats, but simply repeated that the experiment required that the testers continue. About two-thirds of subjects raised the shocks to the highest level, past the point where learners cried out, protested, and ultimately fell silent.[198]

These results suggest that military commanders ordering the commission of war crimes—and gang leaders ordering crimes of violence—will not ordinarily have to threaten their subordinates with death to win compliance. They need only threaten disapproval. If by a "person of reasonable firmness" we mean a person of average firmness, such a standard could arguably exculpate most accomplices. The requirement of a threat of unlawful force or a threat of great bodily harm ensures that some harm more tangible and severe than authoritative displeasure must be threatened.

But maybe pressure from authorities *should* exculpate. After all, the same responsiveness to authority that induced Milgram's subjects to shock their fictitious victims, and that induced some of Erdemovic's colleagues to kill remorselessly, also causes us to obey most laws most of the time. We saw in our first and third chapters that criminal law depends for its deterrent efficacy far more on voluntary compliance than on threats. Why should compliant individuals be blamed if they find themselves governed by tyrants, commanded by war criminals, or protected by gangsters? On the other hand, if responsiveness to social authority is a pervasive trait, perhaps it is a mistake to conceptualize crime as a problem of insubordination or deviance. Perhaps crime is better conceived as a matter of disloyalty, resulting from the failure to transfer obedience to the law from other social groups. If so, perhaps the law's failure to protect an offender from violence should excuse his or her obedience to a rival authority.

VII. Insanity

The insanity defense is an excuse, based on incapacity, available in almost all American jurisdictions. It is usefully compared to infancy, another incapacity that can preclude punishment. Under the common law, children under 7 were categorically exempt from criminal liability, and children under 14 were rebuttably presumed exempt. Offenders exculpated by either insanity or infancy are generally subject to the jurisdiction of another legal system, focused on the offender's welfare, but nevertheless deploying incapacitation and rehabilitation to control crime. In the case of insanity, this is the mental health system. In the case of minors this is juvenile justice, a branch of the child welfare system.

---

198. STANLEY MILGRAM, OBEDIENCE TO AUTHORITY (1974).

Exculpation on grounds of insanity is common in most legal systems, but not universal. Roman law exempted the insane from responsibility,[199] but Anglo-Saxon law—more a system of compensation than of public punishment—did not.[200] Pardons were granted in the thirteenth century on the basis of madness, but not as a matter of right.[201] An early sixteenth-century report shows a defendant acquitted of felony because of an unsound mind.[202]

Common law treatises distinguished "lunacy" from "idiocy," but considered both exculpatory. Coke explained the exemption of the insane from liability by analogizing their actions to those of brute animals.[203] Hale reasoned that humans are properly subject to law insofar as they have the faculties of understanding and free will, "and because the liberty or choice of the will presupposeth an act of the understanding to know the thing or action chosen by the will, it follows that, where there is a total defect of the understanding, there is no free act of the will. . . ."[204] Hale divided exculpating incapacities into natural, civil, and accidental. Infancy was a natural incapacity; coercion, public necessity, and unlawful force imposed civil incapacities, whereas "dementia," accident, and ignorance were accidental incapacities. Dementia excused those "totally deprived of the use of reason . . . and in effect in the condition of brutes" at the time of their crime.[205] While observing that "doubtless most persons . . . are under partial insanity when they commit" felonies, Hale suggested excusing anyone who acted with less understanding then a 14-year-old child.[206] Hawkins's 1716 treatise explained that "in respect of their want of reason . . . those who are under a natural disability of distinguishing between good and evil, as infants under the age of discretion, ideots and lunaticks, are not punishable by any criminal prosecution whatsoever."[207]

The influence of this treatise literature was clear in two high profile eighteenth-century cases involving peers. In the 1723 trial of one Arnold for

---

199. OLIVIA F. ROBINSON, THE CRIMINAL LAW OF ANCIENT ROME 16 (1995).

200. Homer Crotty, *History of Insanity as a Defence to Crime in English Criminal Law*, 12 CAL. L. REV. 105, 110 (1924).

201. 2 FREDERICK POLLOCK & FREDERIC WILLIAM MAITLAND, THE HISTORY OF ENGLISH LAW BEFORE THE TIME OF EDWARD I 480 (1968).

202. NIGEL WALKER, CRIME AND INSANITY IN ENGLAND 27 (1968).

203. Joel Eigen, *An Inducement to Morbid Minds: Politics and Madness in the Victorian Courtroom*, *in* MODERN HISTORIES OF CRIME AND PUNISHMENT 70 (Markus Dirk Dubber & Lindsay Farmer eds., 2007).

204. 1 MATTHEW HALE, THE HISTORY OF PLEAS OF THE CROWN 15 (1736).

205. *Id.* at 31–32.

206. *Id.* at 30.

207. 1 WILLIAM HAWKINS, PLEAS OF THE CROWN 1 (1716).

shooting Lord Onslow, Justice Tracy seemed to draw on it in instructing the jury that a defendant exempt on grounds of madness

> must be a man that is totally deprived of his understanding and memory, and doth not know what he is doing; no more than an infant, than a brute, or wild beast, such a one is never the object of punishment. Therefore I must leave it to your consideration, whether the condition this man was in . . . doth shew a man, who knew what he was doing, and was able to distinguish whether he was doing good or evil, and understood what he did. . . .[208]

Here we see both the familiar analogy of the insane defendant to a child or a wild beast; and a view of insanity as an inability to tell right from wrong. In the notorious 1760 trial of Lord Ferrers for killing his steward, the prosecutor drew on Hale's view that partial insanity was not enough to excuse, and on Hawkins's conception of insanity as moral cognition. The prosecutor argued to the jury that they could not acquit unless the defendant entirely lacked any "faculty to distinguish the nature of actions" and "to discern the differences between good and evil."[209] Blackstone's brief treatment of insanity largely tracked Hale: total idiocy or insanity was excused, whereas the intermittently insane were excused only for acts committed during an episode of madness. Blackstone added that offenders excused on grounds of insanity should be confined.[210]

A broader conception of insanity was successfully advanced in the 1800 treason trial of James Hadfield for an attempted assassination of King George III—whose own recovery from madness had inspired greater public sympathy for the insane.[211] Hadfield explained that his motive was to precipitate the second coming of Christ by making himself a victim of state execution. Because the crime was carefully planned, with an expectation of being resisted or punished, it bespoke awareness of the act, its circumstances, and its criminality. Accordingly, an insanity defense seemed precluded. Nevertheless, Hadfield's attorney Thomas Erskine argued that delusion was the distinctive signature of insanity, and that Hadfield was so firmly in the grip of his religious delusion he could not avoid his crime to save his life. The trial judge endorsed this defense and the jury acquitted. During the trial, Parliament hastened to pass the "Criminal Lunatics Act" of 1800, requiring, for the first time, the confinement of

208. Arnold's Case, 16 How. St. Tr. 695 (1724).
209. NIGEL WALKER, CRIME AND INSANITY IN ENGLAND 62 (1968).
210. 4 WILLIAM BLACKSTONE, COMMENTARIES ON THE LAWS AND CUSTOMS OF ENGLAND 25 (1765–1769).
211. Hadfield's Case, 27 How. St. Tr. 1281 (1800).

those acquitted on grounds of insanity, subject to the discretion of the Crown.[212] This was the beginning of the now-familiar institution of compulsory commitment of those acquitted on grounds of insanity.

The social context of the insanity defense changed markedly during the nineteenth century in both England and America. The medical profession rose in stature as doctors gained greater insight into the mechanisms of disease. By the middle decades of the nineteenth century, public mental hospitals began to proliferate in the United States. Like prisons, these new custodial institutions were seen as enlightened mechanisms of social improvement.[213] The spread of these institutions created administrative opportunities for doctors, and produced a cadre of confident experts on mental health.

The first serious scholarly treatment of criminal insanity in either society was an 1838 treatise by Maine physician Isaac Ray.[214] Ray criticized English law as the product of a system in which defendants were not represented by counsel, and emphasized the need for medical testimony—preferably from impartial, court-appointed experts. Drawing on the ideas of pioneering French physician and phrenologist Philippe Pinel, Ray characterized insanity as a mental disease, with physiological causes. He rejected both the "right and wrong" test advanced by Hawkins and the emphasis on delusion advanced in the *Hadfield* case. He criticized the exclusive focus on intellectual deficiency in English law, and—again drawing on the ideas of Pinel—argued that insanity included purely affective derangement, "mania without delirium." He argued that legal definitions of insanity should take account of evidence that criminal acts were often "irresistibly impelled" despite full understanding of their nature. He proposed that crime should be excused whenever medical evidence indicated it was the product of a mental disease.[215]

The 1843 jury charge by Justice Shaw of Massachusetts in *Rogers v. Commonwealth* combined Ray's irresistible impulse test with Erskine's emphasis on delusion. Judge Shaw offered a divine decree as the paradigm of a delusion producing a crime by commanding the will rather than distorting reason. He concluded that an offender should be excused if his criminal "act was the result of the disease and not of a mind capable of choosing; in short, that it was the result of uncontrollable impulse, and not of a person acted upon by motives, and governed by the will."[216]

---

212. 39, 40 GEORGE III C. 94 (1800).
213. DAVID ROTHMAN, THE DISCOVERY OF THE ASYLUM (2002).
214. ISAAC RAY, A TREATISE ON THE MEDICAL JURISPRUDENCE OF INSANITY (1838).
215. Winfred Overholser, *Pioneers in Criminology: Isaac Ray*, 45 J. CRIM. L. & CRIMINOLOGY 249, 254–56 (1954).
216. Rogers v. Commonwealth, 48 Mass. 500, 503 (1843).

The famous trial of Daniel M'Naghten took place in England in the same year. The defendant fatally shot a minor government official, mistakenly believing him to be the prime minister, Robert Peel. He believed that Peel's party was persecuting him. The case was seen as an opportunity to reform the law. M'Naghten was defended by prominent barrister Alexander Cockburn, who quoted Isaac Ray liberally, and offered several medical experts who argued that M'Naghten's delusions of persecution had deprived him of self-control. The prosecution offered no medical testimony in rebuttal, Chief Justice Tindal reminded the jury that, if acquitted, M'Naghten would be confined for public safety, and the jury acquitted.

Although the trial was a victory for reformers, its aftermath was a defeat. Queen Victoria, who had been the target of an assassination attempt, expressed her concern to the prime minister. The House of Lords summoned a dozen trial judges to answer a tendentious series of questions challenging the exculpatory significance of delusions and the competence of medical experts to testify about events they had not witnessed, and asking how juries should be instructed. Chief Justice Tindal answered for the judges, that juries should be told that "to establish a defence on the ground of insanity, it must be clearly proved that, at the time of the committing of the act, the party accused was labouring under such a defect of reason, from disease of the mind, as not to know the nature and quality of the act he was doing; or, if he did know it, that he did not know he was doing what was wrong."[217] This standard adopted the disease conception of insanity, effectively requiring expert medical testimony, but it also confined insanity to a cognitive deficiency, requiring delusions about the act itself, a deluded belief in justifying circumstances, or some other inability to discern that the act was wrong.

In the United States, these two positions competed for the next century. New Hampshire, in 1869, adopted Ray's position in its simplest form, instructing juries to acquit whenever the crime was "the off-spring or product of a mental disease."[218] The more common approach was to add together the irresistible impulse test from *Rogers* with the cognitive test of *M'Naghten*. Thus in the 1863 case of *Hopps v. People*, the Illinois Supreme Court held that the defense acquitted anyone "affected with insanity ... [when] such affection was the efficient cause of the act ... [b]ut this ... insanity must ... create an uncontrollable impulse to do the act charged, by overriding the reason and judgment and obliterating the sense of right and wrong as to the particular act done. . . ."[219] An

217. M'Naghten's Case, 4 St. Tr. N.S. 847 (House of Lords 1843).
218. State v. Pike, 49 N.H. 399, 402 (1870).
219. Hopps v. People, 31 Ill. 385 (1863).

influential 1886 decision of the Alabama Supreme Court held that the defendant would be acquitted if a mental disease had *either* precluded him from knowing his act was wrong *or* had produced the act and deprived him of free agency and the power to avoid the act.[220] Yet many jurisdictions embraced the *M'Naghten* standard alone. In the infamous trial of Charles Guiteau for the assassination of President Garfield, the court refused a requested instruction that he should be acquitted if, knowing his act was wrong, he was powerless to resist committing it.[221] On the other hand, the court offered Shaw's example of a divine decree as the sort of delusion that could preclude awareness of the wrongness of conduct.[222] At the turn of that century, roughly half of the states that had formulated standards for insanity had adopted the *M'Naghten* rules alone, while the other half excused offenders on the basis of either inability to recognize the wrongness of the offense or inability to resist it.[223]

The *M'Naghten* rules continued to be attacked by reformers as medically uninformed.[224] Yet scholars also criticized them as legally primitive. In 1917, Edwin Keedy proposed that mental diseases should exculpate if, and only if, they negated the mental element of the offense.[225] He thereby denied that insanity was an excuse, negating the defendant's responsibility for a criminal offense. Instead, it was simply evidence rebutting the prosecution's proof of the mental element, and thereby denying that any criminal offense had been committed.

In 1954, the U.S. Court of Appeals for the District of Columbia in *Durham v. United States* broke with both of the prevailing tests by adopting the New Hampshire rule excusing crimes that were simply a product of mental disease. This rule gave experts free rein to describe the defendant's symptoms and their effect on the crime, without having to pretend belief in an archaic vocabulary of discrete mental faculties.[226] On the other hand, the *Durham* Product Rule was criticized on three grounds.

---

220. Parsons v. State, 81 Ala. 577 (1886).
221. United States v. Charles Guiteau, 10 F. 161 (D. Ct. D.C. 1882); Homer Crotty, *History of Insanity as a Defence to Crime in English Criminal Law*, 12 CAL. L. REV. 105, 121 (1924).
222. Guiteau's Case, 10 F. 161, 170 (1882).
223. WILLIAM LAWRENCE CLARK & WILLIAM LAWRENCE MARSHALL, A TREATISE ON THE LAW OF CRIMES 232–38 (1900).
224. SHELDON GLUECK, MENTAL DISORDER AND THE CRIMINAL LAW 169–170 (1927); Benjamin Cardozo, *What Medicine Can Do for Law*, *in* LAW AND LITERATURE AND OTHER ESSAYS 70, 108 (1931); William O. Douglas, *The Durham Rule: A Meeting Ground for Lawyers and Psychologists*, 41 IOWA L. REV. 485 (1956).
225. Edwin Keedy, *Insanity and Criminal Responsibility* 7 J. CRIM. L. & CRIMINOLOGY 484, 486 (1917).
226. Durham v. United States, 214 F. 2d 862 (1954).

First, by allowing experts to testify directly on the causal impact of insanity, the test invited experts to testify about events they did not witness, thereby invading the jury's function. Trials would become contests between experts offering conflicting accounts of what occurred, substituting their judgments of the defendant's credibility for the jury's. Trials often pit psychotherapists (testifying for the defense) against administrators of public asylums (testifying for the prosecution). The former are habituated to eliciting patient reports of their own symptoms in a nonjudgmental setting. The latter are accustomed to inmates misbehaving and giving deluded or dishonest accounts. Thus experts may be no better positioned to judge credibility than jurors.

Second, the rule attenuated the jury's traditional function as a normative judge of the defendant's blameworthiness. It was argued that the pertinent question was whether the mental disease excused the crime, not merely whether it caused the crime.

Third, it was objected that without some specification of the functions impaired by mental disease, the concept was empty. The term had no set meaning outside of a legal context. It seemed to cover any psychiatric diagnosis, but diagnostic categories were organized more by behavioral dispositions and functional deficits than by physiological causes. Thus, offering a diagnosis as a causal explanation of behavior had a certain circular quality. Moreover, diagnostic decisions were often driven by practical exigencies—the authorization of drug prescriptions, insurance payments, hospitalizations, legal guardianships, and so forth.[227] In practice, expert witnesses and juries often equate mental disease with psychosis—a diagnostic category covering any condition involving delusions. Yet because psychoses typically involve volitional and affective as well as cognitive impairments, the fact that conduct is caused by a psychosis does not mean it is caused by delusion.

The D.C. Court of Appeals reacted to these criticisms by defining mental disease functionally. In the 1962 case of *McDonald v. United States*, the court required juries to be instructed that a mental disease or defect "includes any abnormal condition of mind that substantially affects mental or emotional processes or behavioral controls."[228] In this way, they returned to a standard of either cognitive or volitional impairment similar to tests combining a *M'Naghten* standard with an irresistible impulse standard. At that point, such tests were used in a substantial minority of jurisdictions, with a majority of jurisdictions using a pure *M'Naghten* test.[229]

---

227. Abraham Goldstein, *Insanity*, 2 ENC. CRIME & JUSTICE 736–40 (1983); HERBERT FINGARETTE, THE MEANING OF CRIMINAL INSANITY 19–52 (1972).
228. McDonald v. United States, 312 F. 2d 847 (D.C. Cir. 1962).
229. ABRAHAM GOLDSTEIN, THE INSANITY DEFENSE 45, 67 (1968).

In drafting the Model Penal Code provision on insanity, the American Law Institute drew language from both *M'Naghten* and *McDonald*: "A person is not responsible for criminal conduct if, at the time of such conduct as a result of mental disease or defect he lacks substantial capacity either to appreciate the criminality of his conduct or to conform his conduct to the requirements of law."[230] This test is often described as having two "prongs." "Appreciating the criminality of his conduct" is a cognitive prong, corresponding to the *M'Naghten* formula's knowledge of the wrongness of conduct. The term "appreciate" was supposed to add an affective element—the term referenced the ability to empathize with others and understand how one's actions affected them. It was assumed that this term obviated the *M'Naghten* language of understanding the "nature and consequences" of one's acts. The phrase "conform his conduct" was a volitional prong, corresponding to the *Rogers* irresistible impulse test.

Herbert Wechsler had unsuccessfully proposed a variant of the ultimate Model Penal Code rule that required that, as a result of mental disease or defect, the defendant so substantially lacked cognitive or volitional capacity that he could not justly be held responsible.[231] This test would have allowed the jury to consider whether, in light of environmental circumstances facing the defendant, even partial impairment rendered him blameless; or whether, in light of the heinousness of his crime, even substantial impairment failed to exculpate him. This variant was rejected as too subjective, allowing the jury to exculpate on the basis of considerations of social justice rather than psychological capacity, and also permitting prejudice to work for or against particular defendants. The Model Penal Code formula was adopted in the District of Columbia[232] and in about two-thirds of the states.

The ascendancy of the Model Penal Code's formulation of the irresistible impulse test was short-lived, however. John Hinckley's acquittal on grounds of insanity for his attempted assassination of President Reagan in the District of Columbia led Congress to repudiate the Model Penal Code standard and legislate a *M'Naghten* standard. A number of states followed suit, sometimes by simply eliminating the phrase "or to conform his conduct to the requirements of law." In short, they eliminated the volitional prong of the Model Penal Code test. Some states even narrowed the *M'Naghten* formula. Where *M'Naghten* required that the excused defendant suffer from a defect of reason precluding either (1) knowledge that his act was wrong, or (2) knowledge of the nature

230. MODEL PENAL CODE § 4.01(1)(1962). The Code did not define "mental disease or defect" other than to exclude an "abnormality manifested only by repeated criminal or other antisocial conduct." § 4.01(2).

231. MODEL PENAL CODE TENTATIVE DRAFT NO. 4 § 4.01 (1955).

232. United States v Brawner, 471 F.2d 969 (1972).

and consequences of his actions, many states conditioned the defense only on a deficiency of the first kind—moral cognition. In eliminating the volitional prong, a number of states added provisions allowing the jury to find the defendant "guilty but mentally ill" if he acted with a volitional rather than a cognitive impairment, or simply if he suffered from a mental disease but was not cognitively impaired.

In surveying insanity law in its 2006 decision in *Clark v. Arizona*, the Supreme Court found that 14 states still employed the Model Penal Code formula and 3 employed a more traditionally phrased irresistible impulse test. Another 17 employed a traditional *M'Naghten* formula. Ten states had a modified *M'Naghten* rule conditioning the defense only on impairment of moral cognition. One state conditioned the defense only on inability to understand the nature and consequences of action, and one jurisdiction has a simple product rule. Four jurisdictions had eliminated the insanity defense altogether.[233] At this writing, only eight states place the burden to disprove insanity on the state. About 20 states have adopted a guilty but mentally ill option, including three of the four states that have abolished the insanity defense.

Does elimination of the volitional prong make a difference? At the time the Model Penal Code was proposed, Professor Abraham Goldstein wrote an influential book arguing that there was little difference in process or results between jurisdictions employing the *M'Naghten* rules and those employing an irresistible impulse test.[234] Because cognition and volition were not separate functions, psychiatric testimony addressed both, and an impairment of one function was usually accompanied by impairment of the other. Expert witnesses were not restrained by trial courts from offering evidence of volitional impairments in *M'Naghten*-rule states. Expert witnesses in both kinds of jurisdictions equated mental diseases with psychoses, because that was typically the test of insanity in the more familiar context of civil commitment. A requirement of psychosis meant that some cognitive impairment was effectively required in "irresistible impulse" jurisdictions. Nor did the language of "irresistible impulse" preclude excusing long-planned crimes as insane. Finally, Goldstein argued, the community's normative standards of responsibility would inevitably limit the insanity defense, regardless of how instructions were phrased.[235] Professor Alan Stone has argued that replacing an irresistible impulse test with a *M'Naghten* test would have made no difference in the Hinckley case itself, as all the defense witnesses agreed that Hinckley had a cognitive impairment, and none of the

---

233. Clark v. Arizona, 548 U.S. 735, 749–52 (2006).
234. Abraham Goldstein, The Insanity Defense (1968).
235. *Id.* at 45–96.

prosecution witnesses did. Because the jury credited the defense witnesses, it is likely they would have acquitted under a *M'Naghten* test.[236]

On the other hand, there are cases where it seems that the test of insanity could make a difference. Some schizophrenic offenders experience command hallucinations, voices ordering them to commit offenses. To be sure, these hallucinations represent an impairment of cognitive function, but the cognitive error may be an incident of the antisocial conduct rather than its cause. Thus a delusion may operate more as a bizarre self-interpretation of the offense, rather than as a motive for it. A test focusing on moral cognition can draw the jury into a moral evaluation of a psychotic defendant's deluded understanding of his or her own motivations. Consider the disparate outcomes of two trials conducted under a standard requiring inability to distinguish right from wrong. In *People v. Serravo*, a Colorado jury acquitted a man who claimed that he stabbed his wife in response to a divine command that he punish her for not supporting his business plans to build a sports complex (even though he concealed his perpetration of the attack). The trial court instructed the jury that the defendant was incapable of distinguishing right from wrong if, because of a mental disease, he believed his offense was morally right. The Colorado Supreme Court determined that such instructions should require that the defendant believed his offense conformed to moral standards prevailing in society, but that this standard would excuse a crime such as this, committed in the belief it was commanded by God.[237]

By contrast, Andrea Yates was convicted under a similar standard in Texas, when she drowned her five children in the bathtub to fulfill a command by Satan, who threatened to torment them. A prosecution expert explained that the fact that the defendant attributed her command hallucination to a devil rather than God showed that she knew the conduct was wrong.[238] Granted that the greater harm Yates inflicted may explain why she was convicted while Serravo was not, but both trials invited jurors to evaluate the religious content of the defendants' deluded interpretations of their own psychotic symptoms. Yet it is hard to believe that schizophrenics have any greater power to resist commands because they attribute them to evil rather than benign spirits. Determining blameworthiness on the basis of such self-diagnosis seems at best unhelpful, and at worst a threat to religious freedom.

---

236. ALAN STONE, LAW PSYCHIATRY AND MORALITY 79–92 (1985).
237. People v. Serravo, 823 P. 2d 128 (Colo. 1992).
238. Deborah Denno, *Who Is Andrea Yates: A Short Story about Insanity*, 10 DUKE J. GENDER L. & POLICY 1 (1999).

Finally, some defendants do seem to have irresistible impulses, without delusions of any kind. Andrew Goldstein unsuccessfully sought hospitalization after several unprovoked attacks on others. Eventually, he pushed a woman under a subway train for no reason at all. In confessing, he said, "You feel like something is entering you, like you're being inhabited. . . . I wasn't thinking about anything about pushing. When it happens, I don't think, it just goes whoosh, whoosh, push. . . ." When asked if he knew it was wrong, he said "Yeah definitely, I would never do something like that."[239] Goldstein was convicted under New York's *M'Naghten* standard.[240]

In *Clark v. Arizona*, the U.S. Supreme Court considered modified *M'Naghten* rules that—like those applied to Serravo and Yates—focused only on moral cognition. Clark, a 17-year-old paranoid schizophrenic, shot a police officer, who he claimed he mistook for an extraterrestrial. The prosecution successfully argued that Clark knew his offense was wrong. Clark also sought to argue that his belief the officer was an extraterrestrial precluded his fulfillment of the mental element of aggravated murder (the knowing killing of a person who was a police officer). The trial court applied Arizona case law precluding the consideration of evidence of mental disease or cognitive incapacity to disprove the mental element of the offense. Clark appealed to the Supreme Court, arguing that due process required an excuse for cognitive incapacity caused by a mental disease; and that due process required consideration of any evidence negating an offense element, including expert testimony about mental health. The Court responded that insanity standards varied too widely to conclude that a particular definition of insanity was required by due process. Indeed, due process permitted the withholding of an insanity defense altogether. The Court added that ignorance of the nature and consequence of conduct would interfere with capacity to evaluate it, so that deficient factual cognition of the kind Clark alleged at trial entailed deficient moral cognition anyway. In addition, the Court held that due process allowed Arizona to confine the use of evidence of cognitive incapacity to harbor culpable mental states to the insanity defense. Arizona could reverse the burden of proof on this issue because of the limited reliability of psychiatric opinions.[241] The decision suggested that due process required either an insanity defense, or an opportunity to use evidence of mental incapacity to negate mental elements, but not both.

---

239. Michael Winerip, *Oddity and Normality Vie in Killer's Confession*, N.Y. TIMES, Oct. 18, 1999, at A25.

240. The conviction was overturned on other grounds, but he then pled to voluntary manslaughter.

241. Clark v. Arizona, 548 U.S. 735 (2006).

The narrowing of the insanity defense after *Hinckley* prompted some reformers to suggest that a verdict of "guilty but mentally ill" could fill the void. Such a verdict could satisfy the denunciation and victim vindication aspects of retribution. If accompanied by compulsory mental hospitalization and treatment, such a verdict could also achieve incapacitation and rehabilitation. The model for this reform was the English disposition of offenders successfully pleading criminal insanity from the 1880s up to the 1960s. No acquittal on grounds of insanity was available during this period—the insanity defense served only to achieve confinement and treatment in a hospital rather than imprisonment. In the United States, an acquittal on grounds of insanity generally establishes a presumption of dangerousness and authorizes the state to confine the defendant until she ceases to be dangerous, or ceases to be ill, even if the duration of that confinement exceeds the sentence that might have been imposed for the crime. Due process permits states to place the burden on the inmate to demonstrate sanity or non-dangerousness. The confinement of defendants not guilty by reason of insanity can last for decades.[242]

A verdict of guilty but mentally ill often leads to a quite different disposition. It can lead to hospitalization and treatment until the convict ceases to be insane, at which point he serves the remainder of his sentence in prison. Yet often it leads to confinement in a prison, for convenience, with an expectation of treatment there. Budget cuts and disciplinary policies often prevent "guilty but mentally ill" convicts from receiving any treatment at all.

A third disposition of insane offenders is far more common than either acquittal on grounds of insanity or verdicts of guilty but mentally ill. Defendants who are so cognitively impaired that they are incapable of understanding their trials or assisting in their defense are found incompetent to stand trial. They are generally hospitalized for observation and perhaps treatment to facilitate their attaining competence. They may not be held without reason,[243] but are sometimes held for periods as long as the likely sentence for the offense. Despite the very demanding standard of purely cognitive impairment for incompetence to stand trial, defendants are perhaps 100 times more likely to be found incompetent than to be found not guilty by reason of insanity.

It is apparent to any observer of the criminal justice system that many offenders have led very difficult lives, full of poverty and abuse, and that many offenders suffer from psychological disabilities. Yet successful insanity pleas

242. Addington v. Texas, 441 U.S. 418, 494 (1979).

243. Jackson v. Indiana, 406 U.S. 715 (1972); Robert Miller, *Hospitalization of Criminal Defendants for Evaluation of Competence to Stand Trial or for Restoration of Competence: Clinical and Legal Issues*, 21 BEHAV. SCI. & L. 369 (2003).

are vanishingly rare. According to one study, the annual number of acquittals on grounds of insanity nationwide late in the twentieth century was around 1,200,[244] compared to nationwide arrests of around 15 million. The likely explanations are that (1) few cases go to trial; (2) the most obviously insane defendants are found incompetent; (3) expert witnesses are expensive; (4) because the consequence of a successful insanity defense is lengthy confinement, it is only worthwhile for very serious crimes of violence; and (5) juries are reluctant to acquit even very disturbed offenders who seem dangerously violent.

The practical irrelevance of the insanity defense raises the obvious question as to why it persistently attracts so much popular and scholarly attention. Perhaps we can answer this question by posing another one. Why does insanity excuse at all? Insanity seems unique among the defenses. All the other defenses point to some external circumstance to explain the defendant's conduct as justified or excused. Necessity requires a threat to a public interest. Law enforcement requires official authorization and a lawbreaker. Self-defense, duress, and the partial defense of provocation require aggressive wrongdoers. Reasonable mistake of law requires an official misstatement. Such external circumstances appear to exculpate by breaking the inference we would otherwise draw from a bad act to a bad character.[245] Yet the insanity defense points to no external circumstance, and instead seems to offer up the defendant's character itself as an excuse.

This poses a dilemma. If we are responsible for our characters, it seems insanity should not excuse; but if our characters are the product of unchosen genetic endowments and environmental circumstances, it seems that no one should be blamed. The solution to this dilemma is the "empty" concept of mental disease, a term calling for medical testimony, and yet not truly a medical concept; a metaphor of infection, suggesting an external cause of behavior, but not identifying one.

What then is the function of the insanity defense? A plausible answer, suggested by Professor Alan Stone, is that the insanity defense is ultimately apologetic:

> why not abolish the insanity defense? Who is standing in the way? My answer is the law itself.... The contradiction between ... [the] experience of being without choice and the moral intuition of free will is one of the inescapable contradictions of human existence. That contradiction

---

244. Carman Cirincione & Charles Jacobs, *Identifying Insanity Acquittals: Is It Any Easier?*, 23 L. & Hum. Behav. 487 (1999).

245. George Fletcher, Rethinking Criminal Law 799–802 (1978).

> is expressed and denied by the insanity defense. The insanity defense is the exception that "proves" the rule of law. . . . [I]t demonstrates that all other criminals had free will—the ability to choose between good and evil—but that they chose evil and deserve to be punished.[246]

It seems then that the purpose of the insanity defense—which acquits very few—is to mark all other defendants as responsible for their characters, and to thereby insulate us all from blame, not only for crime itself, but for the soil of suffering in which it grows.

246. ALAN STONE, *The Insanity Defense on Trial*, 33 HARV. L. SCH. BULL. 21 (1982).

Conclusion

AMERICAN CRIMINAL LAW is sometimes portrayed as a clash between two doctrinal systems: a common law scheme articulated by Blackstone and other treatises, and the Model Penal Code. It has also been portrayed in narrative terms as a historical movement from manifest to subjective criminality. Finally, its study is often prefaced with a comparison of retributivist and utilitarian approaches to punishment.

This book has shown the connections among these three familiar frames. American criminal law has not been directly influenced by retributivist moral philosophers until fairly recently. However, American criminal law is retributive in function because retribution—mobilizing collective blame to vindicate victims—is an essential function of a rule-of-law state and is critical to the authority of law. Common law theorists understood this. Their ideas were concerned less with punishment as a moral practice than with prohibition and enforcement as political practices. They saw punishment as the vindication of victims and the vindication of a sovereign monopoly on violence. Their concerns with the regulation of violence and the assertion of the rule of law help explain the common law's focus on physical force and on actual results.

American criminal law has also been shaped by the rise of a utilitarian reform movement, aimed at reconceptualizing the rule of law as a scheme for maximizing public welfare by protecting private interests from risk of harm. These utilitarian ideas are also better conceived as political ideas about the modern liberal state than as moral ideas. They were developed over a century and a half of legislative reform in England and America and culminated in the Model Penal Code, which influenced legislation, but did not entirely displace the legacy of common law rules, and the ideas about state authority that underwrote them.

Thus, a theme of this book has been the emergence of a utilitarian discourse of culpable choice from an earlier discourse of governing authority. The vestiges of that earlier discourse reveal criminal law's essential function, which is not to maximize utility, but to bind citizens to the rule of law by guaranteeing a status of civic dignity in return for fidelity to the authority of law. The fundamentally political character of criminal law as a guarantor of civic status also makes it a potentially powerful weapon of subordination. As a result, criminal law is inevitably an arena of political contestation.

Not all legal systems include criminal law. Societies with less centralized authority often contest status continuously, and manage conflict through a combination of compensation and revenge. Criminal law is the law of state prohibition and punishment. It vindicates victims by mobilizing the public to join in judgments of blame, and thereby includes them in a community defined by civic dignity.

The English criminal justice system emerged with the English state. It conceptualized crime as violent trespass against royal authority. The American system of criminal justice also spread with the penetration of state authority. The history of American criminal law is also the history of contestation over status, particularly along lines of race.

Criminal offenses are state prohibitions of conduct. A rule-of-law state forbids and punishes conduct—expressed choice—rather than status. In the English common law, such conduct consisted of manifest trespasses against the royal peace. In the American system, it is limited to conduct that is not constitutionally protected, and is ideally conduct that disrespects the civic dignity of others. A rule-of-law state proscribes forbidden conduct impersonally, specifically, publicly, prospectively, and legislatively.

In modern American criminal law, culpability is conceived in utilitarian terms as an expectation of harm. This utilitarian conception emerged out of an earlier structure in which culpability was manifest in trespasses against royal authority, absent certain excuses—including accident and mistake—that defeated an inference of disloyalty. This utilitarian conception of culpability was promoted by Bentham and Stephen in England, and ultimately incorporated into America's Model Penal Code by Wechsler.

The regulation of violence is an essential function of criminal law. Homicide has therefore been the paradigmatic crime of injury in Anglo-American law. It was the arena within which a new utilitarian conception of offending as causation plus expected harm emerged. The concept of injury transformed from trespass to causation. More specifically, homicide transformed from killing to causing. The culpability of homicide moved from malice to expected death.

Consensual exchange of property and consensual family formation are critical institutions of a liberal society. Accordingly theft and rape are paradigmatic crimes against consent. The emergent utilitarian model of criminal law therefore involved the transformation of theft from a crime of trespassory taking to a crime of violation of consent by fraud and coercion as well as force. The law of sexual assault has traversed a similar path from a manifestly criminal trespass to a violation of autonomy, by a broader range of means, although the transformation occurred later and remains in important respects incomplete.

In the emergent utilitarian conception of law, criminal liability depends more on culpability than conduct. Accordingly, liability can be attributed on the basis of sufficiently culpable participation in the form of aid, encouragement, or agreement, and sufficiently culpable anticipation in the form of incomplete attempt and conspiracy.

Finally, the defenses of justification and excuse have also endured a transformation. Justifications were originally conceptualized as official duties to enforce law, and were later extended to authority to define and pursue the public interest. Eventually, utilitarianism redefined the public interest as the net public welfare and justified self-regarding offending that maximized the net public welfare. Excuses were originally conceptualized as statuses of subjection that excused disloyalty to sovereign authority. The emergent utilitarian model redefined them as circumstances interfering with choice.

The story of American criminal law has been the story of the emergence of a modern conception of criminal offending defined by culpable choice. Yet understanding contemporary criminal law requires that we also remember the model of offending as trespass against sovereign authority out of which it emerged. The enduring function of criminal law as the cement of civic loyalty is what makes a modern liberal society of choice and consent possible. Yet because criminal law expresses blame and distributes status it also remains an arena for the expression of some of our most illiberal impulses.

Index

CPSIA information can be obtained
at www.ICGtesting.com
Printed in the USA
BVHW042045150821
614245BV00003B/44

9 780195 321203